OXFORD HISTORY OF
THE CHRISTIAN CHURCH

Edited by

HENRY AND OWEN CHADWICK

THE POPES
AND
EUROPEAN REVOLUTION

OWEN CHADWICK

CLARENDON PRESS · OXFORD
1981

Oxford University Press, Walton Street, Oxford OX2 6DP

OXFORD LONDON GLASGOW
NEW YORK TORONTO MELBOURNE WELLINGTON
KUALA LUMPUR SINGAPORE JAKARTA HONG KONG TOKYO
DELHI BOMBAY CALCUTTA MADRAS KARACHI
NAIROBI DAR ES SALAAM CAPE TOWN

*Published in the United States
by Oxford University Press, New York*

British Library Cataloguing in Publication Data

Chadwick, Owen
  The Popes and European revolution. –
  (Oxford history of the Christian Church).
  1. Papacy – History – 1566–1799
  2. Papacy – History – 1799–1870
  3. Europe – Politics and government – 18th century
  4. Europe – Politics and government – 19th century
  I. Title   II. Series
  262'.13'09033   BX1361   80–40673

ISBN 0–19–826919–6

*Printed in Great Britain by
Western Printing Services Ltd., Bristol*

PREFACE

THIS book tries to describe the difference made to the papacy by the European Revolution of 1789 to 1815; or, in other words, what Catholicism was like before the deluge and what is was like after, what the continuity and what the differences.

Those who read the book will see that the point of view is sufficiently unusual in that it is not particularly French. English historians have normally seen the process through the eyes of the nearest Church to the English; and that has the merit, not only that the French was then the most numerous and prosperous Catholic Church in Christendom, but that France caused the revolution which overwhelmed the *ancien régime* not only in France itself but in all Europe. I have consciously avoided this point of view; not because I believe that there is little now to say on that matter (I believe the contrary) but because a volume on the vital French part in the process is already under preparation for this same series, by our expert in French Catholicism, Professor John McManners of Oxford.

I have consciously taken a viewpoint further south and further east; to try to see how it felt in Rome, or Naples, or Venice, or Innsbruck, or Freiburg im Breisgau, or Madrid, or Cadiz.

A part of the book started as the Prideaux lectures at the university of Exeter; another and overlapping part, as the Paddock lectures at the General Seminary in New York. To the trustees of those hospitable foundations I owe thanks.

In the Vatican archives I was helped by Monsignor Hermann Hoberg and Monsignor Charles Burns. At the archives of the Society of Jesus in Rome I received much kindness from Father Lamalle. The librarians at the Vatican library and the library of the Gregorian university, as well as the never-failing friends at the library of Cambridge university and the Bodleian library at Oxford, produced not only rare books but good advice.

In particular Lord Acton collected a mass of literature in order himself to write a book about this very theme. The book never got itself written; for Acton was not a writer of books but a man who sometimes hoped that he would be. He died nearly eighty years ago. But I could not have done this work without his frequent assistance.

Professor McManners, Dr T. C. W. Blanning and Mrs H. Chadwick helped me with various points of the text.

The Leverhulme Trust through the British Academy generously endowed travel in Italy.

CONTENTS

PART II. REFORM AND REVOLUTION

ABBREVIATIONS

A.H.P.	*Archivum Historiae Pontificiae* (Rome, 1963–).
A.H.S.I.	*Archivum Historicum Societatis Jesu* (Rome, 1932–).
A.S.V.	*Archivio Segreto Vaticano.*
C.I.C.	*Codicis Iuris Canonici Fontes* (Rome, 1923–39).
D.B.I.	*Dizionario biografico degli italiani* (Rome, 1960–).
D.D.C.	*Dictionnaire de droit canonique* (Paris, 1924–).
D.H.E.E.	*Diccionario de historia eclesiástica de España* (Madrid, 1972–5).
D.H.G.E.	*Dictionnaire d'histoire et de géographie ecclésiastiques* (Paris, 1922–).
D.I.P.	*Dizionario degli istituti di perfezione* (Rome, 1974–).
D.S.	*Dictionnaire de spiritualité, ascétique et mystique* (Paris, 1923–).
D.T.C.	*Dictionnaire de théologie catholique* (Paris, 1930–72).
H.J.	*Historisches Jahrbuch der Görres-Gesellschaft* (Munich, 1880–).
L.T.K.	*Lexikon für Theologie und Kirche*, ed. M. Buchberger, 2nd edn. (Freiburg im Breisgau, 1957–68).
Realenc.	*Realencyclopädie für protestantische Theologie und Kirche* (Herzog–Hauck), 3rd edn. (Leipzig, 1896–1913).
R.H.E.	*Revue d'histoire ecclésiastique* (Louvain, 1900–).
R.S.C.I.	*Rivista di storia della Chiesa in Italia* (Rome, 1947–).
R.S.I.	*Rivista storica italiana* (Naples, then Turin, 1884–).
R. stor. Risorg.	*Rassegna storica del Risorgimento* (Rome, 1914–).
T.R.E.	*Theologische Realencyklopädie* (Berlin, 1976–).
Z.K.G.	*Zeitschrift für Kirchengeschichte* (Gotha–Stuttgart, 1909–).

Note on references in the footnotes

To find the full reference for one of the footnotes to the text, see the page-numbers after the name of the author in the index, which will give in bold type the appropriate page of the Bibliography.

PART I

The Church of the Old Regime

I

THE RELIGION OF THE PEOPLE

THE people of Catholic Europe were in majority poor and illiterate. Though in France and Catholic Germany elementary education made progress, in southern Italy and rural Spain and Portugal, even in the eighteenth century, many of those who could read and write were clergymen, even if only in minor orders. In such conditions priests were intellectual as well as moral leaders, seminaries were chief places of education. In remote parts priests still stumbled over the Latin of the mass, ignorant of its meaning, or fumbled over ceremonies because the rubrics could not be followed. But the Counter-Reformation educated the clergy. An illiterate priest was a scandal, even to his people. The priest might be mocked for worldliness, or resented for vice. But he was outwardly regarded. Even if Italians mocked behind his back, or boys shouted as he passed in the street, the people liked to greet him by stooping to kiss his hand.

The nearness of magical powers

The difficulty of the whole Church lay in the widening gap between the mental habits of educated and illiterate. In southern Italy fauns hid in the woods, and an occasional clergyman of the deep country reminded his bishop more of a satyr than of a priest. Bishops were educated men and sharply distinguished between rites of the Church and superstitious affections of their people. They would not concede that in illiterate, passionate, and earthy society credulity was a gate towards creed.

The rites of the Church were at times entangled with folk-lore about fertility. The strangest arts of magic might be observed in remote southern-Italian villages in moments of childbirth. And remedies which less eminent priests used to cure superstition were almost as strange.

A southern-German priest, Hermenegild Adam, wrote a book of devotion entitled: *An Easy and Sure Way to Heaven*, which by 1771 had ten editions. If magic is suspected, Adam recommends that a priest bless the place, and then it be sprinkled with 'Ignatius-water' or 'Three Kings' water' (that is, water blessed at St. Ignatius' Day or Epiphany) or St. John's wine—or 'what is still more powerful, a mixture of all three'. Then should be read the first verses of St. John's gospel. If a cow is bewitched, Adam recommends that it be given blest bread or salt, and fumigated daily with the smoke of blest sulphur or palm branches or herbs. Evidence shows that this kind of treatment was especially frequent in cattle-disease. The book of ritual for the diocese of Bamberg (1773) contains a formula of blessing 'Against disease in animals': 'we beg thy mercy that these animals which are so sick may be healed in thy name and by the power of thy blessing. Let all the power of the devil be driven from them. Be thou, Lord, the stay of their life and their healing.'[1]

The diocese of Bamberg and Würzburg approved a ritual against flood and fire 'which are thought to be beyond human control'. The priest in surplice and white stole should bear the holy sacrament in procession with the people, headed by a man ringing a bell, place it on a table covered in white cloths and with two lighted candles, and then sing or read to the four points of the compass the beginnings of all the four gospels.

Into the twentieth century the Roman pontifical made provision for the blessing of bells. Church bells were rung as a precaution against storms. This was a popular belief which went back to pre-Christian times. Even the leaders of the German Reformation had not succeeded in extinguishing it from the Lutheran churches.

Bells when hung were consecrated for this purpose by the bishop. After certain psalms and prayers the bishop blessed salt and water, mixed them, washed the bell with the mixture (hence the common name 'baptism of bells'), and anointed them with the holy oil consecrated to anoint the sick. Under the bell he lit incense, and the deacon sang from St. Luke's gospel. The bell was given the name of a saint, so that bells (the fancy ran) were like voices of saints summoning the people to church. The washing and naming produced such a likeness of baptism that in Catalonia, even into the eighteenth century, a man and a woman stood as godparents when the bell was blessed.

Observation began to suggest that lightning was attracted to church towers when ringers pulled bells throughout a storm. Benjamin Franklin made in 1752 his first lightning conductor, and seventeen years later the first German conductor was erected on a church tower in Protestant Hamburg. Before the end of the century conductors began to appear on church towers in Catholic parts of Germany. The middle class started to try to stop the people ringing bells. The easiest way was to turn the bell-ringing from a continuous chime throughout the storm to a warning ring beforehand and a ring of thanksgiving afterwards, like the 1939 sirens

---

[1] Goy, 172–4.

before and after an air-raid. The people were not quickly content with the changes, and a witness spoke of little old mothers miserable at silence during storm. Bell-ringers extended the warning into the storm to keep the old protection.

Some towns were slower than villages to accept the new ways. The payments to bell-ringers at Ochsenfurt, for special ringing in storms, still appeared in the accounts at the end of the eighteenth century. But this is not true of big towns. In 1735 the Archbishop of Bologna felt it needful to take precaution against popular superstition about bells, by explaining that the word *baptism* of bells was only a nickname, that storms were not made to cease by the motion of air caused by bells swinging (otherwise cannon would be more efficacious) but that when the bells rang people prayed and prayer was what was important. But in the same breath that he warned against superstition, he protested about the growing indifference of parishes to the blessing of new bells. He made a public offer to bless bells and for two years afterwards no one sent him an invitation.[2]

The expertise of Swiss clock-makers and bell-makers was encouraged by this faith. When a Swiss village built a new church it demanded an excellent peal of bells and would seek large money to hire a capable founder. Only a few founders had their factory. The founder came to the village, and built by the church a furnace and foundry, while the entire community followed his effort with anxious interest because it concerned their future safety.

Countrymen in Spain still wanted to ring church bells to get good weather for harvest, still suspected irrigation because only rain water was good for wheat, still hid in their cottages at time of eclipse and kept their cattle within the byre, still begged their priests to lead litanies through the fields in time of drought—and their needs were met sufficiently often to confirm the opinion that the remedies were effective. Many crucifixes placed in the fields were not intended at first to remind the worker to lift up his heart, but to remind God that he was not forgotten and should bestow a fertile crop. The Benedictine Father Feijóo, who dedicated himself to the curing of superstition, went to the little chapel of St. Louis at Cangas de Tineo to see the famous miracle, the covering of the doors and walls of the hermitage, the vestments of the priest, and the vessels of the altar, with tiny white flowers. Feijóo saw that they were laid by insects. The people saw these eggs elsewhere—but in the hermitage were sure that they were flowers.[3]

[2] Lambertini, *Raccolta*, 3.99–103; cf. Goy, 189.
[3] Feiióo, *Cartas eruditas y curiosas* (Madrid, 1781), Carta xxx, 297 ff.

Conservatism during the eighteenth century is shown by the slow way in which demonic powers began to be discounted. As late as 1766 few houses in the district of Straubing in southern Germany had not a specially blest paper nailed upon their doors as a protection against the entry of demons. The householder must have valued the paper, because he could only acquire it on payment of about a pound of butter.[4] In a world where faith was strong, and the art of many physicians ignorant or contemptible or fraudulent, a man was as likely to find cure from disease with a saint as with a doctor, in many remote districts (where doctors did not exist) far more likely.

A Bavarian priest named Johann Joseph Gassner led a faith-healing mission to the people. He said that illness was the victory of the devil and that most diseases could not be cured by doctors but must be exorcised. His results were wonderful enough to win him the support of the Bishop of Regensburg, Count Fugger, who invited him to be his private chaplain. In December 1774 more than 2,700 people surrounded Gassner in Ellwangen hoping for cures. In the next year Regensburg became a magnet for pilgrims from all southern Germany. No one doubted that people were healed, and the movement expired only with Gassner's death four years later. Yet Rome suspected. Bavaria and Austria refused entry. Catholic governments disliked what they saw.

Occasionally parish priests needed to be firm amid their people's excitement. At Gerace in Calabria (1777) a crowd seized a woman in convulsions and dragged her to church to have the demon exorcised. They demanded that the priest come to exorcise. But this was the eighteenth century, and the priest refused to come. And when the woman and the demon had been roughly handled, the convulsions suddenly ceased and the poor creature ran away.[5]

That priest may have refused to come because the Church discouraged exorcism. The old Roman book of ritual provided a form of exorcism. But a decree of the Inquisition (25 June 1710) proclaimed 'grave disorders' from so many exorcisms, and for the future forbade priests to exorcise unless approved by authority and using the Roman ritual and no other. Bishops confessed that cases of possession might demand exorcism, but they were rare, and presumption against the use of the rite grew as the century passed. The Archbishop of Ferrara (1781) insisted that his permission was necessary, and where it was given, the exorcism must be in daylight, in public, amid no crowds, with at least one or two other clergymen and two or three respectable witnesses, all if possible related to the

---

[4] Soldan–Heppe, 2.308.   [5] Swinburne, *Travels in the Two Sicilies*, 2.231.

possessed. A famous confessor who was very familiar with cases of possession, and with demands for exorcism, laid it down that though demonic possession occurred, and no one denied the wisdom of the Church in providing a rite of exorcism, nearly all cases of possession are due to psychological states and are imaginary, especially when they occur in women.[6]

But though we can mark some little signs of slow change, we still find confessors needing to argue in their monthly meeting whether a woman sins if she collects herbs on the day of St. John the Baptist, or whether another woman sins if to escape disease she marks herself with Scriptural texts or with incantation-rhymes, or whether a man sins if he avoids sitting down to dinner when the company numbers thirteen. Confessors agreed that these persons sinned mortally and yet might be excused on a plea of invincible ignorance.

Witchcraft

The symbol of this changing mood within a popular faith was decline in the killing of witches.

The number of witches executed for their craft climbed during the seventeenth century. For old half-demented women that was the most perilous age of European history. The regions where the danger from human ignorance and barbarity survived longest into the eighteenth century were mountainous lands—Alpine countries, Highlands of Scotland, Carpathians, Spain.

This was not a belief only of the illiterate. The Protestant, Christian Thomasius, who was born at Leipzig in 1655, and became a beneficent reformer to save witches from destruction, believed unquestioningly in witchcraft until he reached the age of nearly forty. He believed not just in spells but in pacts and fornications with the devil, and in witches flying through the air. In September 1694 his faculty sent him to take part in the trial of a witch and for the first time he looked with a lawyer's eye at the documents of a case. He voted for severity and was vexed that his colleagues disagreed and released her under supervision. This experience made him angry with himself, that he was so uncritical about a tradition, and seven years later he was in full cry against every sort of witch-trial.

Lawyers were the instrument of change; not because (for the most part) they disbelieved witches but because in all their departments of justice they looked at the nature of evidence with newly critical eyes. They be-

[6] Diocesan Synod of Ferrara (1781), appendix 16; Liguori, *Theol. Moral.* 5.549.

came ever more suspicious of rumour or gossip and scandal, ever more demanding in their desire for proof. By 1700 the number of executions was sinking rapidly, not because courts questioned that the crime existed or that it deserved the penalty of death, but because they raised their hitherto low standards of proof. And since, in the nature of the alleged crime, no proof (to satisfy modern courts) could exist except confession by a culprit, the diminishing number of cases depended solely upon confessions extracted by torture. Lawyers were slower to doubt the necessity or rightness of torturing suspects. But they began to wonder; and this combination of higher legal standards with the use of torture gave to the cases after 1730 a peculiar horror.

The Protestant world, which pursued witches as zealously as Catholics, was quicker to accept the doubt. As early as 1721 the Prussian law code called witchcraft fantasy, though there was a last trial in Prussia seven years later. The last English witch to be tried (1712) was Jane Wenham of Hertfordshire, though she was not the last witch to be rabbled by the mob. Ten years later came the last execution of a Scottish witch.

Some Catholic countries were almost as quick to alter their legal practices. The French government found it hard to quench the persecuting zeal of local administrations but on the whole succeeded.

Epileptic fits gave all spectators the evidence that a body was possessed by an evil spirit. Possession by demons was part of orthodoxy. The decline of belief in witches marched hand in hand with a decline of belief in demons. But both processes can only be glimpsed, not tracked.

Some observers noticed the thin or peculiar nature of the evidence. In Spain the Benedictine Feijóo talked of the inadequacy of the legal process. The takers of evidence were stupid, accusers were illiterate, witnesses were illiterate, prosecutors expected to convict, torture was used, the confessed defendants began to believe that they were real witches and that the strange horrors suggested to them had happened, and then confessed to the acts of which they were charged; often with minds unbalanced by excess of fear.

In Austria and Bavaria and the mountain cantons of Switzerland this scepticism was slow to develop. As late as 1739 Austria issued a curious article ordering death for the devilish crime of witchcraft, and for all who at night eat meals and dance with the devil under the gallows, or make storms and thunder and hail and plagues of vermin; but in this condemnation, says the order, are not to be included mathematicians, astronomers, or astrologers.[7]

[7] Soldan–Heppe, 2.329.

The scandalous case, because it won most publicity and caused later improvement, was the trial (1749) of the sub-prior of the nunnery at Unterzell in the prince-bishopric of Würzburg, Maria Renata Singerin. She had a reserved personality which made her friendless in the convent where she lived for fifty years. A dying nun told the provost that her disease came from the spells of Maria Renata who worked devilry against the sisters. When exorcists came to drive out of mentally sick sisters the demons that possessed their bodies, these demons pointed to Maria Renata. When Maria Renata was challenged, she said that it could not be true because sorcerers and witches do not exist. Thus she proved herself heretic as well as suspect witch. They ransacked her cell and found pots of oil, roots, and herbs, which they took to be instruments of magic, and a yellow dress which they took to be the robe for the witches' dance. The prince-bishop ordered her to be imprisoned, two Jesuit fathers and two lawyers investigated her (whether with or without torture we do not know but may guess) and brought her to confession. She said that she was a witch since childhood, as a nun made a pact with the devil, and often attended witches' sabbaths, and cursed God and St. Mary, and fornicated with the devil, and had conversations with a cat that talked, and bewitched six sisters, and made two fathers of near-by monasteries into lunatics, and blasphemed with the Host, even by pinpricks at a witches' sabbath. The faculties of divinity and medicine in the university of Würzburg both declared such devilry to be possible.

On the morning of 21 June 1749 she was beheaded and then her body burnt (by this date burning alive had almost ceased as a penalty). Spectators said that they saw a vulture at the moment of death and thought it a devil in disguise. At the cremation her gallows-chaplain Father Georg Gaar delivered a sermon to the multitude, praising the wise severity of laws against these crimes, and speculating that this might be God's warning against the men of our time who do not believe in witches, or magic, or the devil, or God. Father Gaar plainly thought himself, and told the people, that they only needed to read the evidence from Unterzell to be persuaded of the justice of the sentence and the truth about witchcraft.

This event, and the sermon when it was printed, started a public debate within Catholicism. An Italian Girolamo Tartarotti, who studied in Rome and Venice and was dedicated to showing witchcraft as imaginary, supposed that his battle was almost won. Then he was astonished to read the sermon of Father Gaar. He printed an Italian version of Gaar's sermon with ferocious notes. The ensuing controversy marked an important stage in the dying of the old world, partly because it showed how some instructed theologians still leapt to defend Father Gaar, and partly because it proved the matter to be no longer of truth or dogma but of free debate on which Catholics might take different sides. Tartarotti was among the first to observe the social evidence, and point out how odd was the circumstance that witches always appear in the countryside and never in towns, and especially in countryside where land was poor and where people had neither entertainment nor sufficient employment.

Another Italian, Beccaria, in the Austrian domain of Lombardy, published his treatise *On Crime and Punishment* in 1764. This treatise of penal reform did as much as a book could do to make torture disreputable in legal systems. Once torture was dropped, no evidence could find a witch guilty.

The last execution of a witch on German soil happened in 1775; in Spain 1781; in Switzerland (with Protestant judges) 1782; and finally in Poland 1793. These were not the last deaths if lynching is added, and Mexico after 1860 witnessed a revival of judicial executions.

The last Swiss execution, which happened at Glarus, had Protestant judges. But in general simple Catholics retained these beliefs longer than simple Protestants. This was partly because a very conservative tradition of theology carried the old axioms into the nineteenth century; and partly because old liturgies contained rites of exorcism and blessing which were familiar and which the people found efficacious and did not wish to do without. Perhaps it owed much to the quicker spread of elementary education in Protestant lands because they were more prosperous and because the ideals of education ran deep within the Protestant consciousness.

As soon as governments stopped killing, witches declined; when governments stopped torturing, witches declined faster, so fast that the change in ideas is revolutionary. Bavaria of the eighteenth century was one of the most conservative countries, if by conservative we mean that many educated men continued to believe in the power of witches. On this very subject even the Munich Academy of Sciences conducted an acrimonious debate during the 1760s, when the assailants of witchcraft derived their best material from Italians like Tartarotti or Muratori. Yet by 1809 an old Bavarian who had been tortured on a charge of magic and acquitted, and then lived on a pension to compensate him, was a prodigy. People looked upon him as a survival from a vanished age. Yet his story was doubted by a later historian, who suspected that the old man pretended to be accused of sorcery in order to increase interest and therefore alms.[8]

[8] S. Riezler, *Geschichte der Hexenprozesse in Bayern* (Stuttgart, 1896), 314 n.

But if traditional divines believed, a traditional people believed more uncritically. Yet something changed in popular ideas. In the earlier eighteenth century parish priests still advised their people on the best ways to protect themselves against spells (faithful practice of church duties; use of the sign of the cross; devotion to the Blessed Virgin and the saints; carrying of a blessed waxen Agnus Dei). These instructions vanished from many books before the coming of revolution, and where they survived they became private care by word of mouth.

virtus

The people, especially of rural Italy and Spain, revered the man whom they saw to be filled with God. The *saint* was near the heart of peasant religion.

To win the lottery might mean physical comfort or release from destitution. How to predict the winning numbers? A doorkeeper in Rome met the tramp Benedict-Joseph Labre, later a saint by a people's acclamation and then canonized. The doorkeeper said afterwards, 'Because of the high opinion I formed of his sanctity, I thought I might ask him for the number that would win the lottery.'

This was the idea of *virtus*. The people accepted the old idea, stemming from the earlier days of western Europe, of the *virtue* in a good man, that is, power to save, which as power of spirit could command the physical.

A curious conversation among peasants is recorded from Monte Lupone near Ancona. One thought the best way to know the winning number was to walk up the Aracoeli steps in Rome saying 'Hail Mary' and 'De Profundis'; another, to make the novena of prayer to executed criminals, walking at night along the exact route which they took to their deaths, and in the church of the Beheading of St. John the Baptist, where they were buried, the penitent dead would whisper the right numbers; some said, 'St. Alexis—sleep under your house stairs as Alexis used to sleep and then go out at midnight and an owl hooting or a donkey braying or a dog barking might give you the right number'; others said, 'St. Pantaleone—wake up at midnight shouting his name and leave pen and ink on the table for him to write down numbers.'[9]

This power over the physical applied to natural disasters. When Vesuvius erupted in August 1779, flames rose high from the mountain; but when Alfonso Liguori looked out of the window of his monastery at

[9] De la Gorce, *Labre*, 174–5, 178. Alexis of Edessa (5th cent.) became an important figure in western folk-lore; Pantaleone (*c.* 300) became a patron (among other things) of physicians.

Pagani, and made the sign of the cross, the flames 'disappeared into the crater' and left nothing but smoke—an *educated* witness believed the saint to have worked a marvel. The people thought sin to cause physical disaster, and holiness to gain physical salvation. 'How can we expect to have rain if these sins go on?', said the bishop to the mayor of Arienzo in a drought, when he heard how soldiers, billeted in the town, behaved disgracefully. Severe flooding at Padua was suspected of being due to the playing of comedies in the theatres on holy days.[10]

This belief was a strong force against incoming ideas of tolerance. An atheistic book dishonoured society, might injure society. Some educated Italians believed that the famine of Naples in 1764 was caused by the laxity of government in allowing the import of books by heretical or atheistic Frenchmen like the encyclopedists. During the famine—which contemporaries felt as a landmark in the history of Naples—a pathetic procession of 8,000 or more women, wearing crowns of thorns and crosses, went to the archbishop to beg him to expose the relics of St. Januarius.[11]

Therefore natural calamities, as of old, were met by public and national acts of religion. When Vesuvius erupted in 1794, the cardinal archbishop and his clergy, followed by a barefoot procession of penitents wearing sackcloth and halters round their necks, walked in procession to Magdalene bridge in Naples, and there turned the statue of St. Januarius face towards mountain, and cried for mercy. On the evening of 14 January 1703 an earthquake so shook Rome that the bell on the Pope's table rang without being touched. The Pope (Clement XI) held a consistory and urged the cardinals to works of penance, went to St. John Lateran and proclaimed an indulgence, cancelled the plays and fancy dress balls of the carnival. When a further and worse shock, severe enough to make cracks in St. Peter's, was felt on 2 February, he enforced the laws of modesty in women's dress and Sunday observance and of fasting. Soldiers paraded in churches with rosaries, processions walked barefoot over wet roads with sackcloth, chains on arm, crosses on shoulders, ashes on head. But (for this was also the eighteenth century), Pope Clement ordered the scientists to examine whether they might find ways of predicting earthquakes. A century and a quarter later the *Te Deum* then ordered to give thanks for escape was still sung annually,[12] and the litany still included a petition against earthquakes then introduced.

[10] Berthe, 2.248, 472; Chiericato, *Decisiones Miscellaneae*, 347.

[11] Berthe, 2.193; Acton, *The Bourbons of Naples*, 111.

[12] Pastor, xxxiii.492–5; N. Wiseman, 220; descriptions of the earthquakes in Lucantonio Chracas, *Racconto istorico de' terremoti sentiti in Roma, 1703* (Rome, 1704).

This strong popular conviction carried with it the axiom that natural disasters follow sin. And this axiom complicated the task of governments when they wished to help in disaster. The labourers on the states of the abbey of Callavena in the diocese of Verona represented to the Pope (1696) that they work very hard in the fields, they have had bad harvests for several years, and wonder whether it is the result of an excommunication unwittingly incurred. The Pope ordered the Bishop of Verona or his vicar that if the men fast three days and go to confession and communion and give alms and pay their debts, they are to be absolved from all censure, and to be blessed, and all their lands blessed, and they shall be given a plenary indulgence. The advisers of the government of Venice, in whose territory the abbey lay, were disturbed. The infertility of the earth, and the incidence of famine, fall upon just as well as unjust. They foresaw alarming consequences for government if peasants attributed hardship to ecclesiastical censure incurred unwittingly, and told their government that this was a novel doctrine in religion. Though they were understandably perturbed, the doctrine had deep roots in peasant life and was far from being novelty.[13]

The worst of these natural disasters, and that which caused the European religious argument, was the Lisbon earthquake of 1 November (All Saints Day) 1755. It was only ten minutes in length, but a series of after-quakes, a tidal wave, and fire, completed the destruction of part of the city, with the loss of several thousand lives. Parish priests of the city behaved with heroism, putting up crosses outside their ruined churches, living by them in huts or tents, preaching open-air sermons exhorting the people to repent, collecting statistics of the dead and injured, and organizing relief; and it should not lessen admiration for this heroism to remember that the parish priests and most of their people believed this to be the only effective insurance against further shocks. One of the best of Spanish physicists, who enquired into the incidence of the seismic waves, nevertheless believed that the quake was stayed by the intercession of the Blessed Virgin. All the city knew how a girl of fifteen was dug out of the ruins of her home after being trapped for nine days, still clutching a little statue of St. Anthony of Padua, who had been born in Lisbon and was patron of Portugal. All the city knew how St. Anthony's most famous statue, in the church next to the cathedral, was found undamaged though nearly everything else in the church was a heap of burnt rubble. Amid the debris of the Franciscan church where died twenty friars and some hundreds of others who took refuge, the one unharmed object was an

[13] Cecchetti, 1.46–7.

image of our Lord of the Poor. With the king's approval the Patriarch of Lisbon organized two long penitential processions, and at the king's request St. Francis Borgia (died 1572) was appointed special protector of the realm against future earthquakes.

Again, government disliked some of what they saw. They disliked the inference that Lisbon must be as wicked as Babylon to deserve so terrible a fate. They disliked too much time dedicated to prayer when men should clear boulders and mend drains. Above all at a time when government must persuade men to stay and revive ordinary life, they disliked hell-fire sermons which raised an already emotional temperature and so increased desire to flee from wrath to come. The politician who later became the Marquis of Pombal laid the foundation of his future dictatorship of Portugal by practical measures after the earthquake, and no one hated emotional preachers so bitterly as Pombal.[14]

The *virtue* of a good man passed into objects associated with his body or presence. If 'a saint' passed by, the people of rural Italy or Spain would lie in wait with scissors to snip a corner from his old cloak, if possible without him noticing. When he died they would ransack his house to find crucifix, or threads of his cassock, or holy pictures. If the saint lay in state before his funeral, mothers lifted their babies into the coffin to touch the corpse, or brought rosaries or scapulars or medals to be blest by the contact. A woman in dangerous labour clasped a crutch which a saint had used. A man who broke a leg while falling down a mountain used as painkiller a picture of the Madonna which a saint had given. At St. Nicholas in Bari (1777), which was one of the three great magnets of Italian pilgrimage outside Rome, the priest continued to let down a silver bucket into the hole under the altar, where bones floated, and give the water as a cure for sore eyes and disordered stomachs. The champion matador of Seville wore an amulet round his neck, probably with a print of the Carmel Mary inside; and also paid for a large number of candles to burn in the chapel of St. Joseph, next to the amphitheatre, during all the time of the bullfight. When the Saviour's handkerchief, which wiped the sweat from his brow, was held aloft at Oviedo cathedral, some 9,000 peasants lifted, as high as they could, baskets full of cakes and bread, and so believed that their food was made healthy.

On occasion this desire for physical contact became frenzied. Each year in the feast at Messina a procession of floats passed, and the time came when

[14] For the religious argument in Portugal and Europe, see T. D. Kendrick, *The Lisbon Earthquake* (1956).

the girl who played the part of the Madonna climbed down from her float. Experience taught the town that at this moment she needed protection from over-reverent hands grasping at her for 'relics', snatching bits of garment, pulling at her hair. They had to give her a massed escort to ensure her safety.[15]

One of the most curious signs of this deep popular sense of spirit in the physical was the practice whereby householders, in large Italian towns, put crosses low down on the outside walls of their houses in the street. European cities provided little in public sanitation, and men stopped to urinate without much thought of privacy. Householders disliked their house being fouled and knew that they could deter passers-by who would refrain from being irreverent to a cross. Authority resented this attempt to use or misuse the cross.

Bishops reminded their people of the rule that no cross nor crucifix should be inscribed on a floor because it was irreverent that it should be trodden by feet or get muddy or foul; how much more should the rule apply to this habit in big towns. In Bologna three successive archbishops issued strong warnings against the practice and demanded that all such crosses should be removed; but the continual repetition shows that householders found the custom a protection; and in a bizarre way it bore witness to a widespread reverence or affection for the cross among the common people. Another place felt to be unfitting for a crucifix was an inn-sign, which Italian bishops were known to force innkeepers to remove.[16]

In the city society was devout; that is, the upper classes were prominent in cults and brotherhoods; in Naples they thought little of reason, were pessimistic about the world because it was wicked, and lived with a strong sense of sin, at times in a most terrifying sense of pressure from the depravity of the human heart. This genuine devotion was compatible with (probably) the highest number of prostitutes in any European city, steady and not particularly private consorting with mistresses, and willingness by professional men to fake documents in support of legal claims. Yet the genuineness is proved not only by the innumerable little signs of fervour and penitence and self-sacrifice, but by the social prestige of the powerful evangelists; Alfonso Liguori, as a missioner in Naples, was fashionable with society as well as the idol of the poor; and he was not a man to diminish by one iota his demands for the sake of popularity or influence. A French traveller thought that a quarter of the population of Naples never went to

---

[15] Swinburne, *Travels*, 1.299; Doblado, 158; Townsend, 2.21; Berthe, 2.312, 378; Tuzet, 379.

[16] Lambertini, *Raccolta*, 4.76 ff.; cf. Sabina Diocesan Synod (1736), 19.

mass. That in so large a city—third largest in all Europe—a sizeable fraction never went to church except at family occasions or Easter is very probable. But this French traveller was the most superficial observer ever to record his Italian impressions in two volumes,[17] and the Italian evidence does not suggest so large a fraction, which in any case no one could count.

The Jews

When strongly integrated communities had another small community living within their gates, with different and strange customs, it is hard to know whether the motive for maintaining separation is purely religious even when it is confidently stated by contemporaries to be religious. But whatever the mixture of motive, the religious difference between Jew and Christian was one important part of the social difference. Treatment of Jews which posterity found abhorrent and oppressive had in part a religious motive, the purity of faith and society before God. Here intolerance had the same root as intolerance against Protestants or atheists; the suspicion, for example, of the common man in Naples that the city could never prosper if books, wicked by their error, were sold in the shops.

The Jews had a bad time in the seventeenth century. The age of the Counter-Reformation and wars of religion was not liberal in its ideas. When Protestants suffered in Catholic lands and Catholics in Protestant lands, Jews could not expect happiness. And in the East, where most Jews lived, the clash of Catholic Pole and Ukrainian Orthodox threw them down between the warring parties and easily led to pogrom and massacre. Many fled into the relatively tolerant Turkish empire, but also into Germany, Vienna, Venice, Hamburg, Amsterdam, Rome. By 1660 the size of Jewish communities in western Europe was increased by numerous refugees from Cossacks. They were not allowed by law into Spain or Portugal.

Catholicism was part of Polish nationality. Therefore Poles were intolerant of anyone non-Catholic, Protestant, Greek Orthodox, or Jew. But the Jews had a status confirmed by regulations of government. And they were very numerous, certainly too many to expel, and were necessary to the economy. About half the Jews of Europe outside Russia lived in Poland, some 750,000 people. Nearly one Pole in ten was a Jew. They kept inns, sold spirits and beer, and traded. A considerable part of Polish anti-semitism was as much by competition in trade as by difference of religion.

[17] Dupaty, 2.162.

The Jew in Poland had to circumvent rules if he wished to travel, found certain posts or professions banned, and was liable to high taxation and capital levy. If he passed a church or a Jesuit college, he was watched to see whether he fulfilled his duty to drop coins in a box to maintain the building or the students. But the worst thing in Poland, worse than anywhere else in Europe, were sudden outbreaks of mob violence and judicial murder.

Polish common people believed in ritual murder; that is that Jews needed the blood of Christian babies to prepare for the Passover. An apostate Jew in 1710, Jan Serafinovitch, who was son-in-law to the rabbi of Vilna and had a record of mad fits, gave evidence in court that Christian blood was needed not only for the Passover meal, but for the eggs given to the newly married, and for anointing the eyes of the dying. He described how a rabbi collected the blood, first by pricking the baby's finger, then by stabbing its back, then rolling it in a barrel with protruding nails, and finally nailing it to a cross.

Catholic leaders in Poland seldom believed these lies or hallucinations. But bishops are found taking part in the prosecutions. And popular superstition was shown by repeated cases brought to court. A child born out of wedlock, and exposed by a mother seeking to preserve her name, could easily be palmed off as murdered by Jews. Because Poland had no strong central government, the fate of Jews varied from region to region. They kept the inns over most of Poland and Lithuania, in Minsk and Brest-Litovsk a numerous Jewish community flourished, Catholic authorities rarely made the expected efforts to compel them to Christian sermons. But in other places they were at the mercy of mobs, and then of evidence extracted under torture. The fate of rare Christians who became Jews was brutal. The authorities needed a ghetto and its walls as much or more to protect a Jewish community from Christians as to protect Christians from Jews. A series of fearful trials for ritual murder, with torture, swept the country in the fifteen years after 1747. That church officials did not do all that they should was shown by the repeated efforts of Jewish leaders to get instructions out of Rome. From the Dominican general they won an order to his Polish friars to restrain the people in their sermons from persecuting Jews or believing slander. From the Carmelite superior they won an instruction to his houses that the stories of ritual murder were legend and that the friars ought to fight the superstitions of the mob. After a trial for ritual murder in Volhynia the Jews sent an emissary to ask protection from Pope Benedict XIV. The Pope was dying. The case was referred to Cardinal Gangan lli (later Pope Clement

XIV), who asked for documents on ritual trials and finally produced a report full of charity and good sense, one of the most humane documents to come out of Rome during the eighteenth century. In January 1760 he recommended Pope Clement XIII to condemn the slander. The nuncio in Warsaw was instructed that the Pope would do everything possible against false accusations over blood. The nuncio was tardy to publish, but at last (1763) the King of Poland confirmed the Pope's orders.

This was the worst area of Europe for cases of persecution. From Silesia to the Urals public order was more insecure than in all the rest of Europe. And much the largest Jewish population lived in eastern towns. In Italy they were safer.

In Padua Jews from Poland studied medicine. They were listed at the university with the designation *Hebraeus Polonus*. Though they had to pay a special fee for 'protection' and were supposed to lodge in the city ghetto they were among the few Jews of that age to benefit from a normal education at a university. Their families at home were often anxious lest these non-religious courses were unfitting in a Jewish student, but their communities needed them as physicians and clubbed to pay their fees and travelling expenses.

Padua was in the republic of Venice, one of the most tolerant states of Europe in the eighteenth century. The port of Leghorn in Tuscany was the other great centre of Italian Jewry, where they lived freely without special clothes and could be represented in the city council. In Venice and Leghorn they took an important part in the trade with the Levant which made the prosperity of both towns, and although like most Jews in Europe the majority were traders, a few owned merchant ships. Occasionally the memory of a Shylock burst forth in mob demonstration as when officers of Venice took down a vast picture of ritual murder which Jew-baiters erected at the Rialto. In Genoa the city made an agreement with the Jewish community (1752) whereby Jews could live outside the ghetto and wear black and not go to sermons. In Italy as a whole the social relation of Jew and Christian was the most civilized in Europe until Prussian Protestants led by Lessing started to be liberal if not admiring.

An attempt by the government of the two Sicilies to (re-)introduce Jews into Sicily and Naples failed. In 1740 King Charles of Bourbon published an edict, which allowed them to reside and did not oblige them to wear distinctive dress or to live in a ghetto. Several Jewish traders arrived in Naples and Barletta and Lecce. The crowds had a violent opinion against these newcomers. Father Pepe denounced in Naples, popular preachers excited congregations, merchants were split in their opinion. By 1741 the Jews of Naples had to have a special quarter because they were not safe elsewhere. A few months later there was fierce argument over the need to oblige them to wear distinctive dress. Shop windows were broken, passers-by rabbled. When Messina was struck by plague in 1743, the government had lost. The people were stronger than their king. Three years later he repealed the edict. By then it had long been a dead letter and repeal was formality.

The Papal State felt a duty to preserve its sacredness as Christian and Catholic. But like other states its authorities knew that the existence of Jewish communities diminished the taxes on its own citizens. In Ferrara and Ancona lived sizeable Jewish communities (328 Jewish families in Ferrara in 1703) who must wear yellow badges except on journeys but were hardly molested and owned shops outside the ghetto.

The ghetto in Rome by the Tiber had a high wall with several gates. By the main gate hung the pessimistic inscription, Isaiah 65: 2: 'All the day long have I stretched forth my hands to a gainsaying people.' Outside was a guardpost. Jews were not allowed to own land or house, and therefore must rent houses in the ghetto from Christian landlords. The city government fixed the level of rent that might be charged. That Jews prospered was shown by increasing numbers (1699, about 10,000; 1732, more than 12,000). But they were liable to specially high taxes for the privilege of residence. They had a few bankers. But a majority of canonists now agreed that usury was as illicit for Jews as for Christians. Most of the Roman Jews were engaged in small trades, with a proportion of jewellers and goldsmiths, or dealers in cloth from the Levant. They must wear yellow (badge on hat for men, bandeau for women); and when the yellow grew more orange and then more red, so that at last it could almost be mistaken for a cardinal's hat, government ordered nothing but yellow. They traded outside the ghetto walls but must sleep inside.

In the Counter-Reformation Pope Gregory XIII laid upon them the duty of hearing sermons. Every sabbath afternoon a 'representative' congregation of some 500 men and women, separated by sex, paraded to listen to a sermon, if possible by a preacher who understood their languages or even who was Jew by race and Christian by religion. Most of the ghetto avoided sermons by paying a small fee. Rich hired poor to attend as their proxies. Eye-witnesses reported that this parade had a formal air. External reverence was maintained. If a member of the congregation fell asleep, or was shocked at what the preacher said and publicly stopped his ears, he was poked by a beadle's staff. Rome preferred these occasions to take place in a hall rather than a church.

Outside the ghetto stood a 'house of catechumens', where Jews were prepared for baptism. This house always had residents, and a steady stream of converts was baptized. A visitor of 1724 reckoned the number of baptisms that year at about 5,000. Doubtless a number of these conversions were change of heart. But a voluntary convert received 100 *scudi*, which payment drew destitute Jews to Rome. Pregnant Jewish girls might seek the house of catechumens to hide their shame; young Christian men, falling in love with a Jewish girl, need only tell the authorities that she was considering baptism, and could get her out to the house of catechumens or a convent; and if a Jewish baby were baptized by a Christian midwife because its life was in danger, and then it lived, it was legally Catholic and must be educated as Catholic. Pope Benedict XIV had to decree (1747) that a Jewish child must not be baptized if its parents were unwilling. He also had to take precautions against Jews who wished to desert their wives and therefore sought baptism.

Clement XIV befriended the Jews of Poland when he was a cardinal and kept the policy of government from being rigid. His successor Pius VI immediately (20 April 1775) codified the old Jewish laws of the Papal States and in theory drove back the Jews into the ghetto, prevented their riding in a coach in the city, insisted that they always wear the yellow patch, declared it illegal to hold conversations with Christians in the streets. Like much legislation in the Papal States, the law must be understood to signify hope and theory more than exact practice. Eleven years later, moved by the new toleration in the Austrian empire, the Jews of Rome asked for relief, and were given a commission to review their plight. The commission met, and took evidence. It saw no need to hurry. Nothing was done before soldiers of the revolution marched into the city.

As late as 1781 an excellent bishop, Cardinal Mattei of Ferrara, prescribed rules for Jews in his diocese (Synod of Ferrara, June 1781). No clergyman or layman may eat, drink, play, stay the night, sing, go to a funeral with Jews. No one may take employment in a Jewish household, especially as maid or wetnurse. Everyone must be out of the Jewish quarter by midnight. No one is to summon a Jewish doctor to attend him at his house. Notaries are not to give Jews honourable titles in legal documents. Jews must wear the yellow marks on hats, and during the last three days of Holy Week must stay indoors. If a Christian procession approach, they must disappear. They are not to go near the porches of churches, and their street-cries must be silent near churches. Their shopkeepers are not to sell books about the Catholic religion, or sacred images. Nuns and girls' schools are not to buy their wares. Nevertheless, wrote the cardinal, they 'are to be embraced with Christian charity' and are not to be treated with abuse insult or mockery.

So upright a prelate could not see how the conditions which he decreed (in conformity with general law) rendered his exhortation to charity vain. This is curious. The Ferrara minutes nevertheless show how relatively free were the Jews, crying their wares through the streets, selling anything in the shops provided the goods were not specially Christian, using Catholic lawyers for legal documents, and rich enough to employ servants.

The saints

Holiness was power—over health, food, crops, babies, death. Holiness was God's way of judging the people. The saints therefore had power to influence God by their intercessions, as the priests said, to work miracles as many of the people thought. Therefore the high points in much religious life of the people were saints' days. Even taverns and cabarets displayed portraits of saints.

A saint might become revered, and heal the infirm, so that afterwards the day of his death became an unofficial festival of that town; and if the cult passed beyond his town, he became more than a local power, and men might beg the bishop to establish his day of death as a feast for the diocese, and kings might ask the Pope to make his day a feast for a kingdom. And as one holy man rose in repute among the people, by natural course he took the place of some earlier holy man, once revered but now becoming a memory in history or a survival in the ritual of the Church. Spanish insurance companies, rivals in insuring vessels at sea, each had a patron saint. Their saint was no mere title of a company. The patronage might mean protection.

Here are two examples of cults changing during the eighteenth century.

St. Anthony of Padua was believed to be the protector against fire and diseases of cows or pigs. His day was not a holiday of obligation, that is, by law of Church and State men might freely work. But in Italy of the seventeenth century most villagers did not like to work on St. Anthony's day, lest their cottage burn down or cow die, or lest their neighbours blame them for like disasters. By the middle of the eighteenth century this refusal to work was much less common. This is an example of the way in which popular cult varied; not because the people turned less to saints, but because they altered their idea of what a saint demanded from them by way of reverence, or because they found new or different saints to invoke.

No one should exaggerate such signs of fading. St. Anthony was still the patron of lovers and marriage, mountaineers and glass workers, shipwrights and donkeys. Still he was the saint to help in the recovery of lost property. He was thought to have taken part in the capture of Oran by the Spanish fleet (1732), and a picture from the middle of the century shows him in admiral's uniform freeing Alicante from the corsairs of Algeria. In Padua itself his relics lay, his day a tumultuous feast. As late as 1800 the government of Naples got leave from Rome to make his day a feast of obligation.

A second example was St. Christopher. He was patron of travellers; because travelling was perilous, and (it was said) whoever looked upon him was saved from the danger of an unprepared death. To attract or help their people, therefore, Italian parish priests of the seventeenth century often hung a giant painting of St. Christopher over the porch of the church where any passer-by must look. By the middle of the eighteenth century, though Christopher was still patron of travellers, no such custom existed; to the relief of educated Catholics afraid of superstition. But large pictures of St. Christopher could still be seen in the twentieth century, painted on the west front of an occasional church in Italy.

The historian's lot was not easy. Newer historical studies were more discerning about the nature of saints' lives and the date of documents. In Tuscany of the 1740s a group of learned critics started demolishing the legends of local saints and doubted the authority of famous relics. In a city like Florence this caused no trouble, because countrymen hardly knew or cared what professors wrote in the city and continued to revere the Madonna's girdle in the cathedral at Prato or the tunic without seam. But academic demolitions were bound in time to upset the countryside, and deepen the gulf between the religion of the people and the intelligence of the educated.

For example, in the valley of Trent in southern Tyrol a people's saint was St. Adalpreto. Girolamo Tartarotti, whom we have already met assailing witch-trials, set about proving, not that St. Adalpreto did not exist, but that evidence about him was worthless or erroneous, and that so far from being a martyr he was schismatic and perhaps died discreditably.

This proof had not the least effect upon the people of the Trentino, except to persuade them that Tartarotti was a heretic. When he died (16 May 1761) Rovereto decided to put into St. Mark's church a monument with an effigy of so famous a citizen. The vicar-general of the diocese banned the monument, and then laid upon the church an interdict which he maintained though the Empress Maria Theresa from Vienna threatened to confiscate his property. To this day that monument to Tartarotti stands not in St. Mark's church but in the town hall of Rovereto. The argument over St. Adalpreto continued into the nineteenth century. The cult of that saint is dead. Probably but not certainly Tartarotti's work of demolition was one cause of the death.[18]

Occasionally the people found a new saint.

Benedict-Joseph Labre (1748–83) was a French boy who formed a fierce spirituality of atonement by suffering, partly from reading sermons of a stern near-Jansenist preacher. He tried to be a Trappist and then a Carthusian; but when he was rejected by different houses of these demanding orders, because they feared for his reason, he became a wandering pilgrim to the shrines of Europe, begging his way, kneeling long hours before pictures or statues—to the House of Nazareth at Loreto (which was to become his favourite retreat after Rome), the cave of the Archangel Michael on Monte Gargano, the shrine of St. Nicholas at Bari, Moulins, Our Lady of Montserrat, Saragossa, Burgos, St. James of Compostella, Besançon, Einsiedeln, Rome—shrine to shrine, rosary at belt, cross in hand, breviary in knapsack. In 1777 he settled in Rome, a tramp in rags, body covered with lice, begging at the gate of the French ambassador for scraps the morning after a banquet, prostrate before a crucifix or the reserved sacrament, sleeping in an archway of the Colosseum, so that he was known as the beggar of the Colosseum, silently present wherever a church held the Forty Hours devotion, so that some knew him as the beggar of the Forty Hours; living off orange peel or apple cores from garbage bins, or occasional charity, or scraps amid the cobbles after a street market; serving irregularly in hospital, or reading books of devotion at the Minerva library; receiving communion so rarely that a priest or two suspected him of Jansenist heresy. When his legs swelled, he was taken into a hostel for the destitute.

His death turned the city upside down. A contemporary who passed through the emotion of those days compared it to an earthquake in a people's soul. It was Holy Week. They took the body into the church of the Madonna dei Monti. Children cried, 'The saint is dead', sick came to find healing and were not disappointed, and on Easter Sunday crowds so packed the church that priests could celebrate neither mass nor evening office. Corsican mercenaries, fetched from a neighbouring barracks, could not control the crowds which wanted to snatch relics from the bier. Their violence could not stop people snipping off half the beard and tearing out the hair and cutting little pieces of cloth from the shroud. The church at last was cleared by the troops, and shut for four days. Not everyone was

[18] *D.B.I.* s.v. 'Adalpreto'; Venturi, *Sett.rif.* 1.382–3.

pleased. The French ambassador Cardinal de Bernis reported to his government that the sight edified some and scandalized others.[19] But de Bernis was not the kind of cardinal who could understand that Labre was anything but a lice-ridden tramp.

Another example of popular feeling to discern a new saint was found in Don Gaetano, a monk of Palermo. He lived a penitential life, and shortly before he died told his confessor that at the consecration of the sacrament he was always embraced by the incarnate Lord. He died gently as he knelt before the Host. The confessor told the congregation about this holy soul, and said that men found in him evidence of power to work miracles. The people begged the bishop to lay out the corpse to public view. Soon a crowd of infirm, lame, blind, queued to be in contact with the corpse. One was healed, a youth with a twisted leg who never before walked without crutches. Sick babies were passed over the heads of the crowd to the guardian of the bier who lifted them down to touch the saint. From all about came cries ,'Thank you, thank you, Don Gaetano.' Hands tore away the garments, twice they needed to clothe the body anew. This discovery of a saint was watched by a stiff German Protestant who was both incredulous and moved at what he saw.[20]

All visitors to southern Italy and Sicily were astonished by the feasts of the Church. St. Rosalia, at Palermo, lasted five days; St. Agatha at Catania, four; Corpus Christi at Syracuse, a week. No normal work; far into the night meetings in the street; milling crowds, where dukes or higher clergy lent a cheerful hand with beggars and labourers; a mixture of pre-Christian Saturnalia with Christian veneration for the holy; ardent work for the decorations, chariots for processions, triumphal arches, floats; women buying new clothes, scarlet bunting everywhere; fantasies (by candles and glass) of artificial light in churches; salvos of cannon; trumpeters, pages, halberdiers; parades with tambourines, escorted by urchins whistling through their teeth; northern visitors, if they regretted the expense and doubted the friendly tumult, found the experience noble and not tasteless. Patrick Brydone though a Scot was proud of being a John Bull, suspected southern emotionalism, and was a rationalist with a streak of irreverence. He felt a sudden movement of the heart when confronted by St. Rosalia. He said that he had never seen anything which so affected him, and was not surprised that she won the allegiance of Sicilians. When he joined the feast in the streets, he confessed to a feeling of ecstasy; and thought that if this was the effect of superstition, he wished the British

[19] Giuntella, 139; De la Gorce, 207, 200.
[20] Tuzet, 409–11; the witness, Bartels.

were a little more superstitious. For a moment he wondered whether the triumphs of philosophy were insipid.[21]

This was the true, and primitive, experience of sainthood. By comparison the formal canonization of saints had less spontaneity. For a man to be a saint of the Catholic Church, he needed a posthumous group of people determined that he be entitled saint, with money or power. Politics, kindness, loyalty might enter the process and verdict.

Nevertheless the saints made during the eighteenth century, in number twenty-nine, reflected popular sentiment.

Of the twenty-nine, all but two were monks and nuns. The other two were a great archbishop (Turibio of Peru) and a university professor who however was not made saint because of what he taught from his chair. One of the twenty-nine had been married, for Jane-Frances de Chantal (sainted 1767) was a widow with four children. But afterwards she founded a religious order. This predominance of monks and nuns was a sign of the special links which bound the religious orders to Rome, and a sign how a member of an order was more easily brought to official notice because the order had continuing organization, a corporate memory, and the money to take a cause through the requisite courts. Five of the new saints were founders of religious orders (Piarists, Somaschi, Lazarists, Servite nuns, and Camillans). But although the high percentage of religious derived from the administrative structure of the Church, they also showed the people's opinion. Monks and nuns were too many to be respected because they were monks or nuns. But ordinary people could hardly imagine a saint who failed to live the sort of life, or practise the hours of prayer, only possible to monks and nuns.

Twenty-two of the new saints were male, and seven were female. The presence of the women showed how the people had no expectation that a saint should be a priest (still less a bishop, for only two of the twenty-nine were bishops). Several of the new male saints were not ordained, but lay brothers. St. Felix of Cantalice, who died in 1587 and was canonized by Pope Clement XI in 1712, was just such a people's saint—once a cowherd's boy till he was trampled by bullocks and then a Capuchin lay brother from the far south of Italy, who could not read and was given the duty of begging for the friar's livelihood through the streets of Rome and whom the common people of Rome came to love, and at his shrine found healing after he was gone. Such a saint was not only a religious ideal, but a manifestation that ordinary people mattered.

Out of the twenty-nine new saints, ten others besides Felix of Cantalice

[21] Brydone, 2.221-2.

were members of branches of the Franciscan order. Educated opinion sometimes despised modern Franciscans. But the ideal of the little man of Assisi lived strong among the people's devotion. No other order could compare—among the twenty-nine were three Dominicans, three Jesuits, one Carmelite.

This popular aspect was partly seen when a state's patron was made a saint. Among the twenty-nine three patrons of states or peoples were canonized, Turibio for Peru (1726), Stanislaus Kostka who was regarded as a second patron of Poland (1726), and Johann Nepomuk (1729) whom the Czechs revered as their patron. All these had other claims, Turibio because he was one of the two out of the twenty-nine who served as missionary in the Americas, Kostka because he was a mystical visionary, and Nepomuk because he was the patron saint of bridges, and after his canonization his statue often appeared on bridges as an aid to stability against floods or bad engineers.

The mystical visionary (seven out of the twenty-nine) was not popular in the same way, unless his or (more often) her shrine became a place of healing (as at Cortona with St. Marguerite, canonized 1728). These were the saints of tranquillity and remote cells. They were too contemplative, too withdrawn, and too rarefied to make impact upon the people. But their causes were promoted by religious orders, and their writings valued as reading for modern monks and nuns. John of the Cross, with his pure allusive poetry, was an intellectual saint (canonized 1726) and could never be a magnet for the people. The devil's advocate argued that he showed no evidence of *heroic* virtue; but of all the canonizations of the eighteenth century, his received most approval from posterity.

John of the Cross was one of five Spaniards out of the twenty-nine. The administrative structure of the Church was reflected by the majority of Italian saints (sixteen) among the twenty-nine, though two of the Italians were more venerated in Austria than in Italy. Three were French, three Poles, one Czech, one German. Only eight of the twenty-nine were not Italian nor Spanish. In the previous century, when Spain was dominant in Italy, more Spanish than Italians were made saints. Catholic governments used to press more vigorously for their subjects as possible saints. During the eighteenth century they still asked from time to time, but ceased to mind excessively if they failed. They were still ferocious if the Pope wanted to make a saint out of someone whom they disliked. France thundered so loud against the plan to canonize Bellarmine that he failed to become a saint until 1930.

If the mystical tradition was as eminent as ever among the new saints, the tradition of care for the sick was more in evidence. Only one saint of those canonized during the seventeenth century had much to do with hospitals. Five of the new saints of the eighteenth century were specially concerned with nursing, and two of them were the two most celebrated founders of nursing orders, Vincent de Paul (died 1660, canonized 1737), and Camillus de Lellis (died 1614, canonized 1746) whose nursing order has been seen as a predecessor of the Red Cross. Catholic Christianity maintained the mystical and contemplative inheritance but took a step further towards the recognition that doing good to the needy is an equal mark of holiness.

St. Mary was a central figure in the piety of the later Counter-Reformation. To her were dedicated 214 of the churches of Naples, all with various sub-titles; and the next most numerous patron of churches was St. Peter with only fifteen. At the beginning of the eighteenth century the city of Naples had eleven miracle-working Madonnas.[22] In 1708 Pope Clement XI ordered all Catholics to celebrate the feast of the Immaculate Conception, but did not narrowly define what was meant. A Servite father, Cesario Shguanin (died 1764) asked Rome to define the doctrine of the Assumption of St. Mary. Pope Clement XIII referred it to the Inquisition, who put the petition among their minutes.

The historians had scruples about all such proposals. Muratori wrote a passage of his essay *On a Well-Ordered Devotion* criticizing the exaggerations of the cults of his day. Under Benedict XIV men discussed whether the word *assumption* did not encourage the belief that a pious opinion was a dogma of faith, and whether it would not be better to revive old names like *falling asleep* or *passing over*.

In a direct reply to Muratori's doubt, Alfonso Liguori wrote a book *The Glories of Mary* (1750) which has a claim to be one of the most influential books to come out of the eighteenth century. We may call her mediatrix, advocate, guardian, salvation. It is the divine will that she is associated with her Son in the work of redeeming mankind. She is all-powerful with the heart of God and all merciful with his children. 'A true servant of Mary cannot perish.'

In the country towns of Spain it was the habit to awaken labourers with a hand bell, tinkled through the streets an hour before dawn, since most labourers lived in a town as much as 6 or 8 miles from the fields which they cultivated. But religion made this civic alarum beautiful. It was called the Dawn Rosary. The bell-ringer was chosen for his voice, and knocking at each door he would melodiously sing a couplet inviting the inhabitants

[22] Statistics of dedications: de Maio, 149.

to leave their beds and join him in a procession in honour of the Mother of God.[23]

Feast days

Hard life though he might lead, up early, late to bed for small reward, the working man had many holidays because the calendar brought frequent holy days on which no one might work.

I

Feast Days at Bamberg[24]					
	1589	1609	1642	1769		1789
Whole	36	47	44	35	then reduction	18
Half	14	6	10	12		nil

In addition to the feasts of the Church and saints' days, most communities kept special days—for good crops, against bad weather, in case of epidemic. It was no more than the holidays of some modern workmen with five weeks in addition to bank holidays. To farming communities it felt excess of leisure when much was to do in the fields. Tarragona in Spain (1727) had ninety-one days of obligatory holiday during the year, the people could not work crops from bad land, could not pay their taxes, and therefore disregarded the rule.[25]

Economic pressure drove the 'beneficiaries' to want fewer holidays. Religious motives pressed for fewer saints' days. The leaders of the Church were continuously uneasy, not about devotion to saints which was part of Catholic faith, but excess of saint-worship found among backward communities. Conversely they worried about the inability of peasants to earn their living. In cases of 'necessity' people could get leave to work in the fields on feast days after mass and in some Italian dioceses this leave was not hard to get, though the labourer did well to get a certificate which he could show to passing policemen or indignant neighbours. No one was allowed to carry merchandise, or thresh grain, or use loaded wagons; no muleteer could work. A particular difficulty lay in mills. Defendants, accused of milling on Sundays, said that they were not working, the only thing working was wind or water, but courts were unimpressed with this type of argument. The system of licensing still operated in Italy of the mid-century.[26]

---

[23] Doblado, 210–11.   [24] Goy, 54 n. 4.
[25] *Collectio Lacensis* (1870), 1.785. Benedict XIII allowed the bishop to reduce the number of feasts by seventeen in view of the people's predicament.
[26] Lambertini, *Raccolta*, 3.269 ff.

When the learned Prospero Lambertini, afterwards Pope Benedict XIV, wrote his work on the canonization of saints, he argued for fewer saints' days because so many could not be celebrated aright and because they made it hard for the poor to earn bread. In his earlier career as an archbishop he made this opinion known. The moment therefore that he became Pope in 1740, he received numerous requests to act—from King Charles of Naples, the Bishop of Bamberg who gave evidence from Germany that Protestants were less poor because they could work on days when Catholics must be idle, the Archbishop of Trani in south Italy who wrote that once mass was over these days of 'religion' were days of idleness and drunkenness which issued in gambling and blasphemy and bloody brawls.[27] From Modena the historian Muratori conducted a campaign to press the Pope to act.

Benedict XIV asked the opinion of some forty cardinals, bishops, theologians, canonists. Was reduction needed for the people's sake? Should the bishop of each diocese, or should the Pope decide for the whole Church? Should feasts be divided so that work after mass was allowed on the days of many saints? Should some saints' days be moved to Sunday? The result of this enquiry showed that most saints' days meant inebriation and debauchery, but that people were attached to their familiar days of holiday, might not wish to offend a saint by neglect, and would not easily accept abolitions. Almost alone among the Pope's advisers, Muratori wanted to abolish days which provoked popular superstition. The bishops hardly thought that even a Pope could act against a people's wishes. While Muratori wanted to destroy days for which common people cared passionately, bishops recommended the Pope to make possible the abolition of days for which people cared little. Others, like Archbishop Vidal of Messina, wished to change nothing. And some of both sides raised the most interesting of all the questions: whether this revived demand for more working days did not show a new desire, at least in some working men, to gain a higher standard of living? Archbishop Davanzati of Trani was sure that most people would be glad and grateful for fewer feasts.

Strong opposition to reduction came from the townsmen of northern Italy. Places and people who had not enough work could see no reason to reduce holidays. Here working men wanted to lessen hours of labour, not extend. Cardinal Quirini, who was to make himself the leading proponent of no change, was bishop of just such a city, Brescia. Pozzobonelli of Milan was his ally. In such cities men were often half employed.

[27] Venturi, *Sett.rif.* 1.136–8 and ff.

Devotion to the saint, it is clear, was not the only reason for wanting to keep the saint's day.

Benedict XIV began to issue leave for bishops to apply to Rome for a lessening of feast days in their diocese, and during the next years advantage was taken by twenty-two Spanish bishops, as well as bishops from the Papal States, Tuscany, Naples, Poland, Lombardy. Archbishop Borgia of Fermo reduced his weekday feasts from thirty-five to sixteen. His decision was not popular. Most of his people took no notice. Devout men pressed bishops to keep their favourite saint.

Three years before his death the historian Muratori of Modena published (1747) at Venice pseudonymously (under the name Lamindus Pritanius) the noblest of his books about religion, 'on an ordered practice of devotion', *Della regolata divozione de' Cristiani*. Chapter 21 of this essay, which many Catholic reformers began to treat as a handbook, declared that feasts were far too numerous and appealed to the dissertation of Pope Benedict XIV. Muratori thought that conservative bishops could not have studied the question.

It is an astounding thing that charity, which one might imagine to be a special quality in bishops, has not lifted its voice high enough to make them listen to the supplications of at least half the human race, which is stopped by feasts from getting food for themselves and their families. The glory of saints cannot suffer in the least whether we pay them more devotion or less, while the poor cannot do without bread. Can anyone suppose that saints, filled with charity, can take pleasure in seeing poor people deprived of necessities so that they can receive honour? . . . An ill-regulated piety (from people in easy circumstances who will not suffer in consequence) demands a new feast of obligation and so imposes a new burden on the poor. . . . Is not this excess of feasts the reason why our country has the most beggars and mendicants? . . . Finally, this plethora of feasts, far from ministering to the devotion of working men, usually leads them towards damnation, because most of them spend the day in bars and illicit gambling and spending the week's wages while wife and children starve. . . . If they go to church, it is only because they have nothing else to do. . . . Honourable men who want to work spend half the day bored.

The book was full of this concern for the working man.

Muratori's pseudonym was penetrated, and a war of pamphlets arose. Cardinal Quirini, who on a journey happened to come across the argument raging over the decision of Archbishop Borgia of Fermo, led the field against Muratori, going so far as to claim that doctrine was in question and that no feasts should be abolished or made days when anyone could work. The argument grew so hot that Muratori for a time was at risk of condemnation. He became passionate on the question, even accusing the bishops of Naples and the Papal States of not reducing feasts because they made a tidy income by issuing licences to work, and denouncing their police for scouring the countryside to spot an illicit worker and levy a fine for their own pockets. When he collected other essays on the question, he could not persuade publishers at Trent, Venice, or Modena to take the risk. When he tried to issue an appeal to the bishops of Italy he could find no one who dared to print.

Two decades later we find evidence that discontent among the people outran any endeavour to meet their needs by altering the calendar. Parish priests in southern Germany started to take independent and unauthorized decisions because their people disregarded the calendar. German bishops wanted to change dates because they were afraid of being attacked as 'Protestant' if they abolished saints' days. Bamberg (1770) abolished eighteen feasts by transferring them to the previous Sunday, and left eighteen feasts as well as Sundays. Under the same papal brief Cologne drastically restricted the number of feasts. Venice failed to reduce feasts till seventeen years later; when the Senate won the Pope's approval, cited the example of other Catholic powers, abolished twenty feast days and ordered all shops to remain open, and all farm labourers to work, on the ex-feast days.[28]

To remove eighteen days of holiday from working men could not be achieved in the twentieth century without machine guns or double pay. Preachers were enlisted and pamphlets circulated to prove that the Church had this power, printers were compelled to print new calendars. Common people rumoured that work on one of the abolished days would be visited with divine punishments, crops sown on that day would perish, sick cattle were the result of men working and so offending a saint; the Pope is a heretic, we are turning into Lutherans, it's the fault of our parsons and we won't go to confession; even in the nineteenth century some countrymen still refused to work on feasts which the Church abolished during the eighteenth century. In Auerbach in the Upper Palatinate, when the pastor announced the new orders (1770) the congregation stood up and shouted, crying 'Drive him from the pulpit, the seven sacraments are abolished,' and thumped out to hold protest meetings in the bars. The pastor of Schnaittach feared for his life. In 1786 peasant unrest forced the Elector of Bavaria to restore ceremonies on feast days and rescind the decree which ordered work on the abolished feast days. Tipsy undergraduates at Bamberg made a demonstration (1770) on Whit Tuesday because it used to be

[28] Bamberg: Goy, 56–7; Cologne: Klersch, 3.191; Venice: Cecchetti, 1.102–6.

a holiday and now was not. Police officers who were ordered to make people work on an ex-feast sometimes kept quiet at home or went out into the country so as to see nothing.

Archbishop Trautson provoked riot in Vienna when he tried to reduce feast days. Twenty years later feast days in Vienna were reduced without anything worse than a grumble.

Benedict XIV's act caused him to be suspect. In parts of Catholic Germany ran the saying 'The Pope's become a Lutheran.' Even in 1768 Joseph Baretti described to the ignorant English how this Pope 'once offered all the Italian princes an utter abolition of all holidays, Sundays excepted, which offer procured him the appellation of *papa protestante*, the Protestant Pope.'[29]

Processions

Amid the drama of the streets on high days of the Church, processions were an invariable centrepiece.

We have the order of procession at the celebration in Cologne of the canonization by Pope Benedict XIII (31 December 1726) of the Jesuits Aloysius Gonzaga and Stanislaus Kostka. At the church porch was a picture, 28 feet high, of the two new saints kneeling before the Holy Trinity. Towards this came in solemn order: (1) two genii, (2) three flags, (3) a choir of secondary-school boys, (4) drummers and trumpeters, (5) the triumphal car bearing St. Stanislaus, (6) a silver statue of the Mother of God with angels, (7) a group of women, (8) a silver statue of St. Ursula patron of Cologne, (9) nuns carrying lighted candles, (10) a statue of St. Joseph with angels, (11) a youth club making music, (12) a silver statue of St. Gerold with angels, (13) 600 members of a brotherhood, (14) drummers and trumpeters on horseback, (15) the triumphal car of St. Aloysius drawn by six dapple-grey horses of the archbishop's ceremonial carriage, (16) students with torches, (17) the Jesuit fathers, (18) the choir, (19) genii with flowers and incense, its canopy carried by students of the law faculty.[30]

In this way the procession was a tremendous popular event, spectacle, devotion, theatre, good work. If it was reverent, this was the reverence of whole-heartedness and *naïveté*, not the restraint of awe. The Corpus Christi procession at Barcelona about 1770 began with an eagle dancing before the holy sacrament, then two giants who danced and leapt, then a mule, then an ox, then a dragon which formerly was escorted by little

[29] Goy, 70, 75; Arneth, *Maria Theresia*, 4.56 ff.; Baretti, *An Account*, 132.
[30] Klersch, 3.185.

devils, then a lion and flag followed by other animals, then twenty-four kings in 'histórić costume'—apostles—angels with musical instruments.

Thus the procession gathered to itself all sorts of fun, or theatricality, or bright ideas, which a popular sense of drama might suggest. The customs from various Spanish churches were collected by a Jesuit critic. Christ was represented by the president of the 'Guild of the Cross'. On Palm Sunday he came riding into the town on a she-ass, escorted by twelve elders dressed as apostles, in coats of different colours down to their heels. The townsfolk brought their blankets and coverlets to spread them in the way and in the churchyard boys climbed olives and mulberries to cut branches. On Monday three crosses were set up by the altar rails. On Tuesday, the scene of St. Peter's denial was played in church, with a girl dressed as kitchen maid singing 'You too were with Jesus in Galilee', and a bald old Peter thundering out in harsh and angry tones, 'I know not what you are talking about', until from behind the organ in the gallery a piercing voice crowed like a cock three times; and the bald Peter retired into a 'shed' prepared under the gallery and sat there weeping and blowing his nose. Early (4 a.m.) on Good Friday the preacher showed the Christ with a 'Behold the Man' and loud commotion from the congregation, and when Pilate gave sentence the town notary informed the prisoner. At 3 p.m. Joseph of Arimathea and Nicodemus and St. John the Evangelist appeared with towels and hammers and pincers and ladders, with an image of our Lady in the midst, worked by wires. On Easter Sunday at 5 a.m. was 'the Sermon of pleasantries'—when the preacher was expected to change the atmosphere by telling a string of funny stories and behaving like a buffoon in the pulpit. It was a popular relief, and attracted a vast congregation.

Not all these customs happened in a single town. Our informant collected them from various towns in Spain.[31]

The old hooded processions of flagellants were less common. But in Italy and Spain and Portugal and south Germany they might still be seen, and as late as 1719 Trier witnessed a procession of more than a thousand flagellants, bearing chains on their body, carrying skulls, and wearing crowns of thorns.

The scourging devotion fell into a measure of disrepute during the later Middle Ages, being condemned by a Pope and falling under more than a suspicion of being associated with heresy. But in monasteries and nunneries, the discipline was enshrined in the rules; a self-scourging, for example on Fridays, during the time it took to say a *Miserere*, after a devotional reading

[31] Isla, 2.494 ff., 537.

on the Passion, to remind of the Crucifixion, chasten the body, and make satisfaction for sin. Jesuit devotion was in one of its aspects an encouraging of laymen to make use of experiences found edifying in monasteries, and they were willing to encourage such self-scourging, under conditions and in a devotional context. Therefore the practice had a revival during the Counter-Reformation, and the classical statement of its value was written by a German Jesuit, James Gretser, to defend a procession at Augsburg which Protestants criticized. The defence showed that public processions began to repel. Private monastic edification was one thing, blood visible in the streets was another. The French Parlement banned public use after a case at Bourges in 1601, and henceforth public processions of flagellants were less common in France than anywhere else in Catholic Europe.

The main cause of the persistence of public processions was the dramatic representation of Holy Week. On Good Friday, or (more often) Maundy Thursday the village would make its representation of the Passion, during which the Lord's scourging was acted—more than acted—by a group of flagellants. In most areas of Catholic Europe, the procession of flagellants was confined, by the eighteenth century, to the ceremonies of Holy Week; unless at some special mission to a parish in southern Italy or Spain.

In Spain Maundy Thursday was the high day of discipline. The 'disciplinant' wore a full skirt streaked with red ochre, a starched upright triangular cap 1¼ yards in height, a hood that covered face and head and ended in a point below the chin, white shoes with black heels and toes. The procession moved down the street between balconies with decorated carpets whence women admired. The sources show that many bystanders still watched without any sense of repugnance, and some watched with edification. In the cathedral at Girgenti in Sicily a French traveller saw 200 middle-class citizens striking shoulders with whips of cord and changing hands when the arm grew tired. Another Frenchman walked by the church at Licata and heard a curious din. The French consul tried to discourage him going in, but he insisted. In a dim light he could see the nave full of people flogging themselves, and heard moans and sighs and convulsions. Suddenly a priest called 'Enough', a little bell rang, silence fell.[32]

That the consul tried to dissuade him from entering is a sign how not everyone expected to find the occasion edifying. European taste was changing. By 1700, it is clear, some spectators were so far from being edified by what they saw that they found the occasion irresistibly comic. French bystanders mocked. Urchins of the streets in Rome began to mock. A visitor to Rome saw a great procession of 500 flagellants in 1707,

[32] Tuzet, 384.

marching from San Marcello to St. Peter's by torchlight, escorted by Capuchins with lumps of sugar and cakes to strengthen the weak. He observed that the passers-by cried mockery—speculating on protective covering underneath the shoulder cloth, shouting 'leathern doublet' or 'corset' or 'breastplate.'

In fact, spectators slowly ceased to believe that the rite was wholly real. Its function as public ceremony started to replace its function as act of devotion. Nearly twenty years before, a spectator in Madrid reported that gallants took part in the procession because it was a social occasion but no one really hurt himself, it was more like ritual dance. A brotherhood of flagellants often hired extras to make the ceremony more impressive, and these extras improved neither the reality nor the morality of the rite. The public practice became suspect as show. A Dominican saw a ferocious missioner at Civita Vecchia using a chain scourge repeatedly on his body and could not at first understand how the man could endure—until he perceived that though the noise of flogging terrified the flesh was un-scarred.[33]

A few perceptive men already perceived another objection. Experience began to tell them of a mysterious connection between flagellation and sex. An amused Spanish observer noticed how prolific in engagements to marriage was the rite of Maundy Thursday.[34] And the medical science of the north began to be possessed of enough case histories to give pause to people who argued about the practice. In 1700 the French abbé Jacques Boileau, brother of the poet, published the first big Catholic assault against it and, though vaguely and unconvincingly, could use medical evidence.

But this evidence was the property of few. Catcalls did more than doctors to discourage the devotion. Nevertheless, even the people were shocked by certain forms which formerly they welcomed or endured. At the Holy Week procession of flagellants in Civita Vecchia early in the century appeared two men called Hieronymos, St. Jeromes, naked but for loincloths, who fearfully beat their whole body with instruments of metal and glass. They tried to appear in the following year but were stopped by police. Distaste grew. A diocesan synod at Naples (1726) condemned 'the barbarous custom' of St. Jeromes, a procession of naked men flogging themselves to blood. The missioner at Civita Vecchia tried to make all the clergy of the town join his flagellant procession. All refused except the Franciscans, and the incumbent, because he had the traditional honour of carrying the crucifix—but even he refused to go barefoot or wear a crown of thorns.

[33] Förstemann, 211 ff.; Labat, *Voyages*, 7, 16 ff. [34] Isla, 1.109-11.

In Spain government discouraged all public rites of flagellation. As a devotion in monasteries or in congregations it continued frequently, especially at private meetings for flagellant brotherhoods. A description has survived of such corporate devotional flagellation in a crypt at Cadiz, almost at the end of the eighteenth century; and of another in the Oratorian church at Barcelona (1786), this last from an English tourist who was not edified.[35]

Taste moved against the dramatic. State governments and a few bishops of Germany moved against Christmas cribs as childish, or elaborate holy sepulchres in churches on Easter Eve, or statues girt with clothes. It was expensive for country churches to undress saints, because some statues were only carved in bare parts and undressing meant destruction and new figures.

Social ideas moved against the beggar and therefore the mendicant friar. An odd by-product of this swing of opinion was the end of an old Christmas custom. As a form of seeking alms, poor men in southern Germany went round the houses at Epiphany singing carols, and rotating on the end of a stick a big star made of gold paper. Authority made no exception of its dislike of this form of begging. Carol singers of the nineteenth century were a bourgeois revival of poor men's begging in the older world. Other old customs can be seen dying. In 1700 south-German Catholics decorated doorposts at Epiphany with three crosses and sometimes with the letters CMB, initials of the three wise men. By 1795 the custom was only found in clergy-houses or convents.[36] Such change was not due specially to 'enlightenment'. In all ages the customs dear to families changed, cults died, new cults were born. The taste even of the common people now expected more plainness of ornament.

Educated Catholics could hardly bear to see the toy donkey drawn up the church on Palm Sunday, cherished by their grandfathers and now, like the crib, but worse than the crib, seen as childish. Town by town and then village by village the living tableaux representing the Passion were changed into processions which carried pictures of the scenes of the Passion, popular art instead of popular 'play-acting'. They found pictures more prayerful than theatrical scenes. But one motive was cost. Pictures were cheaper to produce and carry. They needed neither costumes nor scenery. Pictures might not be great art but were likely to be more artistic than scenery which a village could afford to build. The costumes of such

---

[35] Labat, *Voyages*, 7.26; Pignatelli, *Synodus Diocesana* (1726); Townsend, 1.122–3, cf. 2.435–6.
[36] Goy, 31–2.

processions, at least in villages, had not been specially preserved in a 'theatrical box' but were lent by villagers for the occasion. Some educated men wanted even to get rid of pictures, and thought it best of all if the procession carried nothing but a simple cross.

At Herzogenaurach in Franconia the pastor instituted about 1680 a procession on Good Friday. A century later a Protestant critic wrote a scornful description of this event, and said that we have no need to visit Hottentots to see barbaric customs. About 1 p.m. a cavalcade of 600 people started out. Nearly 2,000 spectators watched ten groups pass by, the history of salvation from the fall of Adam to the Cross, each group with a scene of the Old Testament and a New Testament counterpart. They dared to include Jonah singing out of the mouth of a whale, and flagellants, and blue-cowled moaning penitents bearing crosses round the scourging scene. The Protestant onlooker inferred that the actors were of the lower classes but was specially disturbed to see the Countess of Bayreuth among the spectators. This Protestant article shocked the bishop of the diocese, Erthal of Würzburg, and the pastor of Herzogenaurach was summoned to a court of enquiry. He defended himself that he tried to stop the use of church vestments by actors, and the flagellants, and the cross-bearers. The superior of the near-by Ursuline convert told the court to take no notice of such an anti-Catholic attack, and said that many Protestants came over to be edified by the spectacle. The diocesan authorities would have liked to ban the procession but feared or respected the opinions of the village. They ordered it changed into a cortège of penitents carrying pictures of the passion with an open-air sermon. The police were warned to intervene if necessary. It was not necessary. The villagers celebrated their new duty without disturbance.[37]

This distaste for the dramatic, or sense that it was irreverent, made a difference to popular processions before the end of the century. The Council of Castile (1780) banned giants from processions and ordered that no one dance. Six years later the Bishop of Barcelona suppressed the centurions who watched over the sacrament on holy Thursday and Good Friday, because 'they execute absurd drills which interfere with the prayers of those who come'.[38] Such restrictions may be found in that age throughout Catholic Europe. Processions continued to be social events of entire communities, retained parts of their drama or their colour or even their clothing. But Catholic taste grew more sensitive, or more austere, or more bourgeois. It moved away from an older freedom of popular devotion because that freedom did not edify. They began to dislike

[37] Goy, 36–9.   [38] Sarrailh, 656.

flagellants, and moaning penitents, and 'soldiers' who gambled too gleefully, or 'Jewish' mockers who jeered too noisily at the foot of the cross. They wanted minds to be lifted to prayer; and for a time did not easily see what the village of Oberammergau in high Bavaria taught a more modern intellectual world, that theatre can lift to prayer.

A procession of the Blessed Sacrament through the streets, whether on a feast day or to the sick, did not stop traffic in a city as formerly. The busy street went on bustling—waggons moved on, coaches drove by, horsemen failed to dismount, passers-by, instead of kneeling for a time on both knees in the street, made quick genuflection and went their way. Italian bishops issued proclamations that vehicles should stop and riders dismount and men kneel properly till all the procession had passed.

In Spain, especially in Andalusia, the custom of reverence lasted longer. As the sacrament passed, anyone who failed to kneel in the street and beat his breast gently was looked upon as a probable heretic. A noisy party would be silent if it heard the tinkling in the street outside and kneel till the tinkling died. If the tinkling was heard inside a theatre, the actors stopped, the audience knelt. A Spanish exile who heard the postman's evening bell in London wanted instinctively to kneel.[39]

Brotherhoods

In every Catholic town could be found clubs, part religious part secular, known as brotherhoods, confraternities, or sodalities. They were not only male. People united in a common object, for almsgiving or prayer or Sunday-school teaching or insurance. They reached back into the Middle Ages but differed from the old medieval guild where the members belonged to the same profession and made a (usually middle-class) trade union. They might arise because a group of like-minded people formed a particular reverence for a new devotion, like prayers for the gift of a holy death, or for the release of souls suffering in purgatory. Often they were called by a saint's name, St. Andrew's, St. Anthony's, St. Mary's the commonest. They could arise in consequence of crisis in the state, like war or siege or plague. Brotherhoods existed to encourage the use of the rosary, or devotion to a particular saint, or agreement to make an annual pilgrimage, or to print good books, or to pay the cost of a funeral or a physician or a hospital bed. The Brotherhood of the Cross in Cologne was dedicated to the conversion of Protestants and Jews. In services members of brotherhoods usually wore a uniform, sometimes a penitential pilgrim's robe

[39] Doblado, 14.

with pointed hat. In size they varied from several hundred to a handful. Some had a fixed number like twenty, and elected a new member only when one died. They might apply to a magnate, bishop or archbishop or cardinal, to be their 'protector'. Where the brotherhood had an aspect of social insurance, even Protestants applied for membership but were rejected if known.

Some brotherhoods had their pious duty in the consolation of prisoners condemned to death. At Civita Vecchia, for example, the Brotherhood of Death walked in procession in front of the victim, singing *Miserere* sadly. Round the victim walked several religious with large drawings of scenes from the Passion which they held in front of his eyes. At the square the brotherhood lined up from one side to the other and no one else but guards and religious and other convicts were admitted. While the victim stood on the scaffold, the brotherhood knelt in the square saying aloud the Lord's Prayer and the Hail Mary. Meanwhile Capuchins who were chaplains to the parade of convicts preached sermons 'to bring them to hate their crimes and to lead a life which would not force justice to make an end of them like the end of this their comrade'.[40]

Brotherhoods rose and fell in numbers and popularity according to time and fashion and need. Old brotherhoods of the Counter-Reformation vanished and left hardly a trace, new brotherhoods were formed for new needs all through the eighteenth century. Cologne had four brotherhoods for the care of domestic servants who easily became destitute or turned into prostitutes.

All through the eighteenth century the motives of social care and insurance were more and more evident in the begetting and practice of brotherhoods. In city states like those of the Rhineland government sought to control them as part of its system of welfare.

Some brotherhoods were poor. But members left money or property, many brotherhoods exacted entrance fees, some fined their members for cursing or brawling, by the eighteenth century a few brotherhoods had enough capital even to lend to their municipality.

The confraternity processions still to be seen during Holy Week in Malaga or Seville, with each bearing a platform or float for an ornate statue of the Madonna or saint in a scriptural scene, were then to be found in many more towns and on other days, with special costumes marking social events of the year.

A brotherhood had a social life as well as a religious duty, and evoked a loyalty which adhered as much or more to the club as to the devotion. To

[40] Labat, *Voyages,* 7.19.

a parish priest a brotherhood could be a nuisance because it was an independent kingdom which overlapped with his jurisdiction. Brotherhoods
were specially important as escorts at funerals. They therefore might claim
the right to tell the parish priest what to do, who was to carry the corpse,
which route the procession should take. . . . The conflicts between parish
priests and brotherhoods were neither so frequent nor so fierce as the
disputes between rival brotherhoods, but the natural constitutional
antagonism could not but generate heat.

Brotherhoods competed to show rich ornaments in their procession, or
the most disciplined parade, or for precedence. Through the church or the
saint this loyalty was linked to faith. As a social act it could produce odd
consequences, like fighting in the streets. Bishops tried to order the
ceremonial of processions down to the last detail, but brotherhoods were
very insistent on their rights and, if they thought that they were being put
upon, a solemnity might be disturbed by hissing or blows. At Policastro
in south Italy the rivals destroyed the solemnity of Corpus Christi by using
their banners, and even the statue of St. Nicolas,[41] as weapons. The
altercation was not trivial. It commanded religious as well as social
loyalties. It could be compared to the violence of otherwise good Protestants who broke up Methodist religious meetings of the same age.

When Benedict Labre was buried in Rome on Maundy Thursday, his
body was escorted to the grave by the Brotherhood of Madonna dei
Monti, all armed with knives and ready to resist efforts by two rival
brotherhoods to snatch the corpse or relics of the saint. Nothing untoward
occurred, and the cortège passed into church with reverence.[42]

Most citizens of Rome practised their religion solely by means of a
brotherhood. Their brotherhood was attached to a church, and therefore
gave them a loyalty to a parish and its priests. But membership of the
brotherhood, not membership of the parish, was what mattered. The
brotherhood in Rome might, but did not always, consist of members of
the same trade; mingled well-off with poor; had very little religious
instruction—these were not educating bodies—but went through Latin
psalms as part of the brotherhood ritual. The better side of a brotherhood
was, first, its mingling of classes, and second, its charitable works, sub-
scribing to decorate the chapel, visiting sick, caring for prisoners, decent
funerals for members.

Throughout Catholicism brotherhoods continued to flourish almost all
the century. They played a public role in dramas of the Passion, in processions, and in saints' cults, and lost function where the tremendous

---

[41] De Rosa, *Vescovi*, 172–3.   [42] Giuntella, 139–40.

scenes of the street were pruned or destroyed. They were prominent on pilgrimage, and lost function as pilgrimage was restricted. They were powerful corporations of laymen whom authority eyed with doubt. As bishops increased control over their dioceses, they limited the independence of brotherhoods. But their function at funerals remained; a procession of brothers in their cloaks, with coats of arms and burning torches, following a member to the grave, was impressive enough to be a strong motive for enrolling as member of a brotherhood. The insignia might be placed on a member's coffin at his burial.

Meetings of brotherhoods were accused by certain reformers of becoming rivals to church services. Permission to found a new brotherhood was sometimes given only on condition that no one was thereby drawn away from church. Like any enclosed group they were criticized for being cliques, or persons pretending to holiness while they only kept rules and ritual. Preachers kept reminding them that insignia get nobody through the gates of heaven. Though their members were married, they had a whiff of the monastery or nunnery, and shared a little in the declining reputation of monks during the last decades of the century. But for the most part they were seen as a natural way of life inseparable from Catholic faith.

Here was an ancient fountain of charitable endowment. It still garnered gifts and bequests. Some of the endowment was well used, some was not used for utility by intention of the donors, and some was misused by the corrupting passage of years. As benevolent despots started to provide better welfare in their states, they looked at the property of brotherhoods with interest and envy.

Pilgrimage

Near in idea to the cult of the saint was the practice of pilgrimage.

That God blessed a particular place, as a source of grace or healing, was ancient in Christianity and before. The medieval pilgrimage continued into the eighteenth century. Men travelled fewer miles than in the Middle Ages, but that was not because they disbelieved in going long distances but because they had newer and as powerful sources of special grace nearer home. Simple people had experience of healing, and spring, picture, statue, altar was a new source of grace. The number of places to which men went on pilgrimage always grew. That sometimes diminished the resort to older and more famous sanctuaries. But so far as we can discern pilgrims were just as numerous.

Authorities of Church and State agreed in preferring the shorter pilgrimage. They hardly minded about solitary wanderers or small groups. But when whole villages uprooted themselves for days in the year to visit some distant sanctuary, they perturbed those responsible for order, bishops and policemen and even prime ministers; overnight camping, food in transit, security, morality, sanitation. Hungarians made traditional pilgrimage to St. Ursula at Cologne—until the middle of the eighteenth century, when the stream of Hungarian travellers so troubled the states that the Austrian government refused to issue passports. Fifteen thousand Venetians a year visited Assisi to pray near St. Francis, until the Venetian government, concerned at the loss of currency, refused (1771) to issue passports.[43]

Except on rare and exceptional occasion, pilgrims travelled ever smaller distances. One consequence was the declining use for pilgrim hostels. On the famous old route over the mountains and along northern Spain to St. James at Compostella, stood the most historic line of hostels in Europe. These hostels were now too well endowed for modern needs. The house on the Pyrenees had 9,000 *pesos* of annual revenue because formerly it must welcome a flood of pilgrims as they passed. But now no flood passed. An abundant income served a few travellers, a few tramps, a few wandering friars. The French King from 1671 forbade Frenchmen to make the pilgrimage without royal licence and the leave of the diocesan bishop. The correct inference is not that pilgrimage declined but that Compostella ceased to be so powerful a magnet to the faithful.

Late in the century an English tourist called at the pilgrim hostel in Oviedo on the Compostella road. He found the older inhabitants still able to remember how in former times 'all young men of spirit' from Italy and France (the locals exaggerated) would make the journey to Compostella before their marriage. And 'even now', observed the Englishman, 'it is not uncommon to see straggling some few old men, and many companies of young ones. . . . We saw twelve fine made fellows, who came from Navarre, singing the rosary.' But at Oviedo they told him how 'the rage for pilgrimage is much abated'.[44]

Nevertheless, Compostella continued to attract, because it attracted some pilgrims at least who went there for motives less than the highest. A record has survived from a Picard peasant who went there during the reign of Louis XV because he was in debt after military service and wished to escape his creditors. He and his companions were beaten along the roads, stole grapes from vineyards, cuddled maids at inns, lived off public charity, avoided towns where they might have to pay, disturbed sermons in

[43] Pastor, xxxviii.466.   [44] Townsend, 2.17.

Spanish churches by loud laughter; and yet were moved by the Burgos crucifixion: 'You felt the blood running down before your eyes.' At Compostella they listed the relics and from the stalls bought 'hats, shells, metal badges and the rest of the nonsense', and yet revered the relics which they saw.[45]

Therefore the wardens of hostels, or the police, demanded evidence not so much of identification as of good Christian status. A pilgrim might be asked for certificates that he had confessed and received communion, so that he would qualify to receive alms. Near the Holy House of Loreto a woman who kept a hostel for pilgrims gave a rough-looking pilgrim a mattress in her cellar. He had a French accent which caused her to suspect him of being 'a French heretic' (that is, a Jansenist). When she knew that he was saying his prayers at the shrine, she rummaged in his wallet to make sure that he had the two certificates of confession and communion.[46]

By the middle of the century, bishops and many parish priests in south Germany started to discourage pilgrimages which took more than a day. Parish priests had an economic motive as well as a moral, for pilgrimages to distant sanctuaries took the money of the faithful out of the parish. Ministers of agriculture or economic affairs, landowners and squires, had similar motive, for they lost labour for several days. Nearly everyone responsible preferred to divert pilgrims to sanctuaries which lay within half a day's journey so that villagers returned inside the day and had no need to camp overnight. This was less easy to do by policemen than by encouragement of a new or lesser cult. If pilgrims tried to cross frontiers, they could be refused entry. But, for men to be persuaded away from a distant sanctuary, they must believe in a near-by sanctuary as an equal source of grace. Wise south-German bishops started to encourage local cults to diminish the magnetism of distant cults. The people could still go; but under the various discouragements, they would go by stealth, or in smaller groups, or without a priest.

The magnets of pilgrimage constantly increased without encouragement from bishops. Two religious of Steingaden set up a statue of the scourged Christ, which in 1738 was given to Wies. There miracles happened, a little chapel was erected, pilgrims came. Seven years later Abbot Hyacinth of Steingaden needed to build a big church.

In a snowstorm in the Black Forest a traveller was lost. After his rescue he erected a cross in the snow, soon a public chapel, and then the resort of pilgrims.

[45] G. Manier, *Pèlerinage d'un paysan picard*, ed. B. d'Houët (Montdidier 1890).
[46] De la Gorce, 162–3, 170–1.

All through the century the great sites attracted many. Einsiedeln was host to about 100,000 pilgrims a year. In May 1761 it gave communion to 40,000, in May 1763 to 43,000, but some of these were parishioners. Mariazell in Styria was like Einsiedeln or Altötting as a goal of German and Austrian pilgrims. To run the parish, which without pilgrims had only 700 or 800 people, who were foresters or miners or shepherds, needed (1785) an incumbent and eighteen curates; and in summer and autumn, when the crowded pilgrimages came, they borrowed twenty or more monks from the near-by Benedictine house of St. Lambert to hear confessions and help with services. In the year 1725 it had 188,000 pilgrims, in 1757 373,000. Nearly all pilgrims came from within the frontiers, Bohemian, Moravian, Hungarian. Maria Taferl, second biggest centre for pilgrims in Austria proper, had 71,000 in 1702; 186,000 in 1751; 360,000 in 1760. At smaller sanctuaries: Mariastein (Tyrol) over 20,000 yearly; little Eldern near Ottobeuren, 24,600 communicants in May 1763.[47]

In southern Spain the memory of a Muslim world made the life of a woman more restricted than in the rest of Europe. No woman might respectably go out of her own house on visits unless to a church or sanctuary or pilgrimage. To some women pilgrimage to a near-by shrine was the only escape into a wider world. They wore dresses and veils, and went on foot even if they were rich enough to own a carriage. But these distances were always small.[48]

During the last two decades of the century the criticism of enlightened Catholic bourgeois became ever more vocal. God is a Spirit who may be found everywhere; to think of a single object as uniquely blessed is materialism; pilgrimage disturbs society and agriculture, brings danger to morals and health; the best destination of a pilgrim is the altar of his parish church. These critics had small chance against the popular conviction of a picture or fountain which (so peasants had experience) brought special blessing.

Austria banned overnight pilgrimage 1772, confiscated endowments to help pilgrims 1773, banned all pilgrimages unaccompanied by the parish priest 1784.

The critics could point to numerous risks attached to pilgrimage; and certain customs gave them ammunition. Over decades a popular and crowded event could develop habits which were less than edifying. At Cloppenburg on Maundy Thursday, the people had the custom of walking in solemn pilgrimage to a chapel of St. Mary, where they kept vigil all

---

[47] Schreiber, 59–61, 84; Wolf, 136–7; Wodka, 272–3.
[48] Labat, *Voyages*, I.394–5 (in Cadiz).

night in memory of the disciples who prayed or failed to pray in the garden of Gethsemane. A godly custom; to which over the years was appended the less godly custom that on the way home in the morning they picked up stones to batter down or damage the doors of houses where lived Jews. The clergy locked the chapel, the people took the key by force. The Jews appealed to the crown, which banned the pilgrimage. For several years more the people took no notice of the ban.

Critics could have no immediate success against such convictions.

Occasionally authority was frustrated because the spot turned out to be more important than the picture or statue. This was obvious when the goal of pilgrims was a healing spring. Normally it was a statue or picture, and when bishops moved the object into a parish church the people, not without a sense of loss, turned their devotions to the new site. But this did not always happen. At Lindenberg in the Upper Black Forest a shrine on top of a hill was destroyed by authority, a new parish church built with the stones in the valley, and the holy picture of the Blessed Virgin solemnly transferred. The peasants took no notice. They went on pilgrimage to the top of the hill and said prayers among the ruins. When they were asked they said that the place brought God's mercies, not the picture. The clergy could not persuade them to abandon the opinion. They kept asking for the chapel on the hill to be rebuilt.

By Ottobeuren the Bavarian commissioner broke down the shrine of St. Mary in Eldern, and moved the holy picture into Ottobeuren where it rests to this day. But the people of Eldern kept seeing a vision, of the commissioner's restless soul, condemned to go backwards and forwards in a cart of flame along the old route of the pilgrims which passed the cemetery. Even in the second quarter of the twentieth century men claimed to have seen the commissioner's ghost. And after a time the men of Eldern built a little new chapel on the place of the old. The spot did not lose its *virtus* when St. Mary's image left.[49]

In German areas of mixed religion pilgrimage took a new aspect, that of political demonstration, and brought resentment and on occasion brickbats in Protestant streets through which it passed. The rival demonstrations of modern Northern Ireland are successors to this polemical use of pilgrimage. But a few Protestants took part in Catholic pilgrimage. Protestants also needed grace or healing and resembled a modern Protestant traveller to Lourdes.

A new church or monastery was not easy to build. Plenty of evidence survives of worry over half-built seminaries, cathedral façades in need of

[49] Schreiber, 65, 69, 83.

repair, leaking churches. Far the easiest places to build or repair were resorts of pilgrims. A steady income from the offerings of the travellers enabled new monasteries or new chapels and new shrines to be undertaken without too much worry about expense. Sometimes the clergy reached an arrangement that the builders should over a period of years receive all or part of the pilgrims' offerings until costs were paid—not everyone liked the idea of pilgrims thinking they gave their mite to a monastery when they gave to a firm of builders.[50]

Indulgences

With the pilgrimage was bound the indulgence. Part of the devout gain of visiting some authorized and historic sanctuary was the resulting indulgence. All Franciscan and Capuchin churches possessed the right of the Portiuncula indulgence, asked for by St. Francis of Assisi for the day when the Portiuncula church was reconsecrated. Ordinary people had vague ideas of the nature of an indulgence. They associated it with re-mission of time in purgatory for their dead relatives or themselves. How important it still was at the end of the century was proved when the new Bavarian government of Würzburg tried (1809) to limit days of indul-gences to two in the year, and received a protest from the church authori-ties that the measure would compel vast crowds to come together to confession and communion and therefore the discipline of confession would collapse. And how easy it was to misunderstand is shown by numerous sermons that warn the congregations, who came for an indulgence, that their indulgence is no substitute for penitence of heart.

Luther's assault upon the most famous of indulgences ended the worst abuses of the practice. No one tried to defend the penny-catching methods of late-medieval hawkers. The Council of Trent insisted upon the power of the Catholic Church to offer an indulgence and declared it a devotion 'very helpful' to Christians ('maxime salutarem'). The divines of the Counter-Reformation tried to declare more precisely what was permissible. Bellarmine (*de indulgentiis*) defined the indulgence as an act of judicial forgiveness accompanied by a 'payment', or gift in compensation, from the treasures of the Church. He stood by those old doctrines which Protestants repudiated, that this treasure was the overflowing merits of Christ, the Blessed Virgin, and the saints; that the Pope had sovereign

---

[50] Cf. the dispute at the shrine of Monte della Guardia outside Bologna, where was one of the pictures of the Madonna believed to be painted by St. Luke. Lambertini, *Raccolta*, 4.121 ff.

power in giving; that the indulgence once given was unconditionally valid in the eyes of God, and saved a soul from a possible punishment which sin deserved. He left undecided whether this validity lay in God's justice—a reward of merit—or in God's overflowing mercy.

The Jansenists of the seventeenth century, with a deep sense of sin and of God's tremendous acts of forgiveness, had little use for the indulgence, which to them looked small. And in the faith of their Italian or German successors of the eighteenth century the indulgence had no part. But Italian and German Jansenists were all educated. In the devotion of the common people, the indulgence continued in an undiminished if not extended popularity. Every pilgrimage ended in an indulgence, every resort of pilgrims wanted the privilege of indulgence, every jubilee (a special form of pilgrimage) carried unusual gifts of indulgence; and apart from pilgrimage, an indulgence was attached to special forms of prayer, before a crucifix or a picture, with a rosary; and each brotherhood needed or liked to be allowed an indulgence connected with its own rites or forms of worship. Brotherhoods printed 'a calendar of indulgences' which listed indulgences and the circumstances in which they were available to the members.

In 1669 Rome sought to limit abuses by invalidating all indulgences which claimed to release from more than 1,000 years in purgatory; and simultaneously founded a Roman Congregation 'for indulgences and holy relics', which survived till 1904. This Congregation tried further to diminish popular abuses. Jansenist reformers of the eighteenth century sought to abolish the indulgence so far as it claimed to be other than the remission of penalties imposed by the Church upon the sinner. Their endeavours had very small success, and the people continued to expect an indulgence as one of the rewards of pilgrimage or of a particular practice of devotion.

Inside the church

Sanctuary

Every consecrated parish church was a sanctuary for suspects running from the police. A man accused of crime, or pursued by creditors as a bankrupt, could flee to the altar, whence he could not be removed; and if constables seized him they and those who ordered them to use force were at once excommunicated.

This was the old law of Christendom, rooted in centuries of history and memories of barbaric times. It arose from two different feelings within society. One was fear of injustice. The common people could not be confident enough about the just working of tribunals to trust their fate to judges. This feeling had not died in the eighteenth century. The tribunals of the age of the Enlightenment acted with more efficiency and impartiality than tribunals in the age of Chivalry. But in 1700 they still burnt witches and Beccaria published only in 1774 the great treatise that helped to end torture. Powerful men had henchmen in the mountains of Calabria or the Abruzzi and still could wreak their will like feudal barons. Ordinary people accepted sanctuaries in part because they still saw that poor people could be oppressed and might only be protected by havens of refuge.

The second feeling shows the nature of popular faith. The people had a sense of repulsion at sacrilege round the altar, rough hands tearing a human being away to death, in the very place where the priest sacrificed and where souls waited for the most solemn moments of their lives. In Italy or Spain of the eighteenth century this religious need of sanctuary was still as strong as the social need about justice for the oppressed. For example, a man who took refuge in a sanctuary could not waive his right to freedom from arrest. It was not he who was protected but the altar, and all that went with the altar. The right of sanctuary was more to do with the holiness of the place than with the need of the refugee. If a man was in sanctuary and decided to face trial, he could not ask the police to come in and arrest. He must walk out into the square.

The altar reached out to all the church building—choir and nave, porch and sacristy. If a refugee climbed on the roof, or touched the outside wall or the doors even if they were locked, he had sanctuary. Monasteries had it with their precincts, vineyard and baths and threshing-floor and stables. Consecrated cemeteries had it—whether a bell-tower had it was doubted by lawyers—hospitals or orphanages or seminaries which the bishop erected, the site of a church if the foundation stone was laid though the church was not built, the houses of canons (which must not be rented to laymen); the eucharist when it was borne through the streets under a *baldachino* between lighted candles, on its way to a sick-bed; the palaces of cardinals (if outside the city of Rome) and the houses of parish priests and that part of the bishop's palace in which he lived with his family—all had sanctuary.

So vast an extension of the rights of sanctuary was not compatible with public order. In the age of the Reformation Protestant states either abolished sanctuary or limited it so drastically that it became an unimportant survival. The same pressure came upon the states of the Counter-

Reformation. Violent criminals could not be allowed such escape if the least confidence in public order were to survive. The French king early acted to abolish sanctuary like the Protestants. Some other Catholic powers followed the example in Germany, Bishop Gottfried of Bamberg (1618) the first. Still other Catholic powers pressed the Pope for change.

In 1591 therefore Pope Gregory XIV issued the bull *Inter alia* which remained the fundamental law of sanctuary for Catholic states and caused revolution in the manner of its working.

The Pope withdrew all right of sanctuary from highwaymen, ravagers of fields, homicides who kill or mutilators who maim in holy places (churches and cemeteries), and traitors against their sovereign. If any of these persons took refuge in a church, the court could apply to the bishop that they be taken out. When the bishop received an application he must bring the accused out of sanctuary into his episcopal prison, there try him with the ordinary process of evidence to see if he had reasonable grounds for thinking him guilty, and if he found strong probability hand him over to the police for trial in the State's court.

This bull transformed the law and practice of sanctuary. By exempting classes of persons from any right to sanctuary, it allowed the possibility that rough hands would indeed tear away a body from the altar, and with the approval of the Church. It partially satisfied the governments of Catholic states in their obsession with treachery and their justified concern with public order. And it created for the lawyers, and therefore for the relations between church court and secular court, a series of doubts and quarrels.

Who was a highwayman? Anyone who robbed once on a road, or must he be (so to speak) a professional? Suppose that a man standing within the church porch fires a gun and kills a man standing in the road outside sanctuary—has he killed *in church*? Or suppose a man stands in the road outside sanctuary and shoots a man in the church porch—has he killed *in church*? Is a homicide only the man who kills, or is he also the man who paid to kill? What is a mutilator? Must he knock out an eye or cut off a tongue, or is it enough if he breaks several teeth or spills a lot of blood? If a boy runs away from boarding-school and takes refuge, is he to be sent back to the schoolmaster? If a man takes refuge in a canon's house and the canon's life is in danger, can the man be moved? If he occupies a hospital ward and starts to disrupt services to the sick, can he be moved? All these cases, and more like them, concerned crimes which occurred and which afforded argument between bishops and lawyers of government and sometimes led to small-town conflicts between Church and State. The

Church insisted on the absolute rule, that in doubt only the bishop or his representative can decide whether a suspected criminal has the right of sanctuary and whether police have the right to arrest even in the holy place.

These never-ending local battles caused several Popes to give anxious consideration to the law. The first Pope of the eighteenth century, Clement XI, held an agonizing series of consistories to debate the issue, without result. Catholic governments in quest of order started little by little to disregard the rules; and even when they nominally accepted the rules, local sergeants had small patience if a murderer sat almost unprotected within their grasp. In 1701–2 the republic of Venice reserved the right to fetch suspected murderers out of church, and would not allow sanctuary for deserters from the army or for men banished.[51] Nor were the fights always broils of remote municipalities. Five years after a Spanish Concordat with Rome (1737) limited the right of sanctuary throughout Spain, a murderer fled into the Capuchin friary at Pamplona and was fetched out by force. The bishop's protest went higher until he excommunicated the royal council in Navarre, government expelled the bishop's officer, and it came to pitched battle between troops and bishop's men.[52] Even the city of Rome preserved so many sanctuaries that (it was said) policemen had to carry round a street map when chasing a criminal.[53]

Against this pressure from Catholic governments, a priest of Rome published defence on penal grounds. He put sanctuary into the context of reform of crime and punishment in that age. It was part of the humanizing of the penal system, the chief instrument which protected a ruthless society from the too frequent infliction of capital punishment. The right to punish does not derive from revenge but must intend to reform, it is inseparable in moral law from compassion. At the lowest level the execution of a man may start a vendetta and society will be the healthier if sanctuary prevents the supreme penalty from being inflicted. Sanctuaries, however they are at times misused, tend to a chance of reformation. And if this is the duty and interest of the State, how much more is it the duty of the Church? Would a mother chase away a starving child, or fail to protect it from a wild animal? How much more barbarous would bishops be if they chase out of church men who have come to them seeking refuge and comfort?[54]

---

[51] Cecchetti, 1.93.   [52] Gams, 3.2.339, 371.   [53] De Brosses, 2.198.
[54] Lorenzo Mascambrone, *Degli asili de' cristiani* (Rome, 1731), a powerful and late defence, dedicated to Pope Clement XII and designed to encourage him to stand firm against pressure from the Catholic powers or his own advisers.

But whatever the defence, and whatever the reluctance of Popes to depart from the 'uninterrupted' traditions of the Church, they must step by step concede. For if they refused a little, governments might take all. Therefore Popes gradually conceded until over the decades they conceded nearly all.

Popes removed the right of sanctuary from anyone whose act resulted in death or serious injury (except by accident or self-defence), forgers of papal letters, police officers who wrongly drag men out of sanctuary, men who pose as police officers to rob houses, bank clerks who embezzle funds, makers or knowing passers of forged or debased coins;[55] *all* homicides (except by accident or self-defence, not only those who kill with weapons in churches, and not only laymen—Clement XII, *In supremo*, 1735, applied only to Papal States but afterwards applied by his successor on the widest front, adding that to kill 'with weapons' including killing with sticks or stones). Benedict XIV considered the many cases where a criminal did not kill a man outright but gave him a mortal wound from which he died in the next few days or weeks. The criminal ran to church and had sanctuary because he had not killed before his victim died. Benedict decreed that a doctor should examine the victim and if he certified that the wound could be fatal, the culprit lost his right of sanctuary. Benedict's agreements with different Catholic governments, the Concordats, always carried concessions about the right of sanctuary. He declared (1752) that anyone who killed in duel was a homicide in this sense of having no right of sanctuary.[56]

In the later nineteenth century Holyrood Palace at Edinburgh, the last surviving sanctuary in Protestant Britain, housed a few miserable bankrupts; a survival from a past age, unimportant in law or national life. The Catholic law of sanctuary had not reached so far, even when the revolution came. But that was the direction in which it moved, all through the second half of the eighteenth century. Once it was established that any suspected homicide could be dragged from the altar with the approval of the Church, the old law lost its religious importance, or became more a duty of the Church to maintain old privilege than an act of faith or a protection of the people against oppression.

Meanwhile the right of sanctuary disturbed the interior of churches.

A refugee, once inside the sanctuary, had rights. They might try to stop him getting into the sanctuary but once they failed they could not cheat to bring him out to arrest. In Civita Vecchia (1710) assassins beat a merchant and left him dying on his doorstep, knocking on the door

[55] Benedict XIII, *Ex quo* (1725): *Bull. Rom.* (Turin), 22.198 ff.
[56] *Officii nostri* (1759) *Detestabilis* (1752).

before running away. The police not only put extra men at the city gates, but sent guards to ring the various sanctuaries.[57] Once the suspect was inside church, he was there unless he was proved to be a member of one of the categories which had no sanctuary.

Inside the church no guards were allowed. This clause was very often broken, a continual series of protests and enactments tried to keep out guards. But officers had too easy a method of keeping watch, for no one could easily distinguish a constable in plain clothes from an ordinary worshipper. If the guards could not guard, still less could they chain or handcuff. If a refugee escaped from the galleys wearing chains, no one need take off the chains when he reached church; though probably a friend from outside brought a file or a member of the congregation took pity. Guards could surround the church so long as they allowed everyone access. But they could not prevent kindred or friends of the refugee bringing food and clothing, for that would be to face him with a choice between dying of hunger or trying to leave the church, and so frustrate the purpose of sanctuary. If the accused had neither friends nor kindred nor money, and was destitute, the clergy of the church had the duty of feeding him and paying for the food out of the charitable funds of the church.

Nevertheless the pictures we have of men in sanctuary are of little groups squalid but not too uncomfortable. In southern Italy the worst part of sanctuary was the filth which they brought into church. This was not usually by the absence of sanitation, for the law said that refugees must be allowed to go outside to relieve themselves within thirty paces of the church wall. This may not have made the surroundings of the church sweet to passers-by but little Mediterranean towns of the eighteenth century were not grieved by streets that were not sweet. They were more grieved about dirt in church. In southern Italy refugees lit wood fires, so that walls were black and congregations coughed their way through the service. They brought in cooking pots and camping stools, and were not past setting up house with prostitutes and mistresses. In Naples one group of forgers set up their printing machine in church. Near Naples sixteen refugees together occupied a monastic chapel of such dimensions that monks could hardly get inside to say their offices.[58]

Church authorities were entitled to make refugees work for their keep, for example by sweeping the church floor. Authority saw that idleness begot sin. But if the refugees were tough—and if they arrived carrying

---

[57] Labat, *Voyages*, 6.95.
[58] De Rosa, *Vescovi*, 130, 134; De Maio, 130–1; P. A. Ricci, *Synopsis Decreta et Resolutiones Sacrae Congregationis Immunitatis* (Praeneste, 1708), 200.

weapons no one easily took them away—they were not easy to set to work with happiness, unless they were that proportion of men who were innocent and true refugees from the threat of injustice or oppression.

A long list of cases and condemnations showed how police tried to circumvent these rules. A police corporal in plain clothes went to a refugee and suggested that they eat together and sent him out to the fountain to get water, where constables waited. At Ancona (1699) a disguised policeman pretended to be one of the refugees and persuaded a Jew to escape with him by saying that no police were in the neighbourhood, and officers in plain clothes were waiting outside.[59] Where the bishop succeeded in getting a captured man restored, the reinstallation in sanctuary was supposed to be a matter of due solemnity which the people must see, for they were presumed to be scandalized by breach of sanctuary. The habit of coaxing refugees out of sanctuary by craft was well established despite repeated protests.

But as the century wore on, and murderers left, the sullied huddles of refugees in churches became more passive and hopeless and older. Most of them were bankrupts. Perhaps they were also on an average more educated, for they sometimes took piles of books to read in church until authority realized that nothing in the rules of sanctuary stopped it confiscating books to pay off debts. But the books might not be taken, nor any other property even of debtors, until the bishop allowed a certain time in which they might pay their creditors—usually two months. He was also entitled to confiscate their accounts. The rule of two months was used to make time of grace—and afterwards churches could expel the debtor from sanctuary and throw him to the mercy of creditors. Therefore the debtors' sanctuaries of the decaying system of Italy or Spain did not resemble the debtor's prison of the British with its permanent residents.

Because sanctuary first concerned the holiness of the altar, and only second the saving of a man, no refugee need be a Catholic. (This however was strongly challenged by those seeking to limit the right of sanctuary.[60]) Jews and heretics were entitled to seek sanctuary, provided that the heretic was not fleeing on account of his heresy. But Benedict XIV (1751), otherwise so humane a Pope, revived an ancient law against Jews who became Christians and then returned to be Jews. The age of Enlightenment, growing always more tolerant, was apt in fits to become less tolerant.

Here are cases which show the spread of popular ideas on the subject.

---

[59] Ferraris, 4.382.
[60] 'Pompeo Neri' (for the authorship see Venturi *Sett.rif.* 2.107), *Discorso sopra l'asilo ecclesiastico* (1763), 110.

1. On 24 June 1705 a student of philosophy named Christen aged twenty, at the Raven Inn in Lucerne between 3 and 4 a.m., stabbed a girl five times in the breast. He ran to the Franciscan church but they refused to let him inside. Then he ran to the Jesuit church, which was quickly surrounded by fifty men with guns. Negotiations with the bishop's commissar and the papal nuncio took a little over a fortnight, while the Jesuits did what they could to save his life, and then Christen was executed.[61]

The case shows magistrates very determined to get their man; Catholic enough to go through the forms to be observed; one religious order determined not to be entangled with so unpopular a matter, and another religious order convinced that, whatever the unpopularity and the guilt, it was the duty of good Christian men to hope that more blood might not be shed and therefore that they should help the young man to run away; and above all the bishop's court, reaching a conclusion patently wrong according to law—for stabbing a girl in the middle of the night was not in the least treacherous and this homicide was unquestionably a man with right to sanctuary as the law stood at that moment. Why did the bishop's court reach a verdict so glaringly out of keeping with the law? Because its members had no desire to see so gross a murderer escape, and because they shrank from open conflict on weak ground with the government of the canton of Lucerne.

2. How important it still was is shown by the *simultaneous churches*, that is, churches which since the settlement of the wars of religion were churches shared between Protestants and Catholics. Since Protestants rejected sanctuaries, had these churches the right of sanctuary? Catholics felt no doubt that they had. In November 1743 the Faculty of Law at the great Protestant university at Halle in Germany was asked to decide whether in towns of mixed religion government must observe the Catholic right of sanctuary. The faculty decided that it must.[62]

But the question showed controversy growing. The powerful Protestant cantons of Zurich and Berne began to threaten that they would act highhandedly if any more cases of sanctuary occurred in shared churches. They started to do so; with the result that Catholic pastors or abbots, with the approval of their cantons, helped the refugee to escape before Protestant police could arrive. In 1752-3 this became a warm argument throughout the Swiss confederation.

[61] Bindschedler, 282-3.
[62] J. H. Böhmer, *Consultationum et decisionum juris*, 3 vols. (Halle, 1733-54), III, 1, no.65, pp. 295 ff.; Gröll, 80.

3. At the annual fair at Bernegg a thief was arrested. The police took him towards the town hall, along a path across the cemetery. The Catholic priest looked out of his vicarage, saw what was happening, and shouted that the ground was sanctuary. When he got no reply, he came out and started to argue with the official, whose squad was already three or four paces outside the cemetery. While argument raged the thief slipped his captors, back into the cemetery; when they went after him the parish priest protected him and pushed him into St. Sebastian's chapel which was not shared but solely Catholic. A mob started to batter down St. Sebastian's chapel, the Protestant pastor in the shared church next door had to stop his baptism. The local governor came and said that as it was 'a little theft' the crime would not be capital, so the parish priest agreed for the sake of peace. Final peace was reached only two years later when the parish priest apologized to the governor for excess of zeal, and government compensated St. Sebastian's for damage wrought by the mob.

By now both sides would cheerfully have been rid of sanctuary in Switzerland. Catholics maintained it partly because they needed to show that they were not Protestants and partly from genuine loyalty to the laws of their Church. Trivial crimes did not matter, big crimes were excepted. Cases still occurred in the Swiss cantons, which did not reach final agreement till 1785.

Reduction in number of sanctuaries became common as a stage towards abolition. In old cities many little churches huddled together near the centre, a sanctuary stood round every corner. As exceptions grew, city governments began to ask whether they might declare one or two important churches to be sanctuaries, and withdraw the right from all other churches. Genoa asked for this privilege, explaining the inconvenience when streets were narrow and sanctuaries every few hundred yards, and pointing out the rising number of crimes. In its petition the city said, 'we want to join due reverence for the Church with law and order.' They asked that the archbishop be empowered to nominate one or more churches at the centre and one in each suburb, and then that the police might freely extract a refugee from any other church to transfer him to a nominated church. Pope Clement XIV (brief of 11 June 1773) accepted the plan, and added that if a man fled from one of the nominated sanctuaries to any other sanctuary he might at once be handed to the police if the magistrate (out of reverence to the Church) would promise to diminish his penalty by one 'grade'.[63] In Spain, where the government pressed harder, the same Pope (1772) reduced sanctuaries to a maximum

[63] *Bull.Cont.* 4.581.

of two in each 'city or place', which often meant one church for each diocese. The bishop designated certain churches, but it was a condition that extraction of accused from other churches must happen without irreverence, that clergymen might not be extracted without the bishop's leave, and that police might extract accused laymen only in the presence of the bishop's deputy or the parish priest.[64]

Another stage, halfway to abolition, was the ending of the bishop's prison. According to law, if an accused took refuge and his case (if proved) granted him no sanctuary, he must be moved to the bishop's prison while the bishop examined the evidence, and only if the bishop was satisfied was he handed over to the police. Magistrates hated this part of the law. They regarded bishop's prisons as insecure, and they were right. They resented the long delay, and the longer chance of escape. No part of existing law was attacked more steadily. But bishops also disliked bishops' prisons, and some bishops preferred that if they had a prison it should be insecure.

Flanders, seeing the French to the south of them behaving like Protestants over sanctuary, developed a custom (supported by their more radical canonists) whereby magistrates could take criminals out of churches with only a courteous message to the bishop and with no obligation to send the bishop all the papers.

But other Catholic countries felt something irreverent in this way. Reverence for the altar still meant that the decision must be made by church authority and not by magistrate. They found an ingenious compromise. One cell in the state prison could be designated the bishop's prison. If an accused man were extracted from church with the bishop's leave, he could be put straight into the town gaol with the proviso that he go to a particular cell while the bishop considered his papers. This system was established, with most care about detail, in the Palatinate, where government got two decisions from Rome to approve.[65] But it happened more informally in other lands, until it was common. The happy form of words saved everyone trouble. Some bishops were freely willing to let the magistrate conduct the enquiry on their behalf, to determine whether the case was reserved.

A late Swiss case shows how the law at last became nothing but ritual to preserve reverence for the holy place. In 1795 the police of Rapperswil hunted a band of robbers and chased a man, suspected of being their chief,

---

[64] *Bull.Cont.* 4.488.

[65] *Inter graviores*, 30 Sept. 1758 (Clement XIII) *Bull.Cont.* 1.43; *Alias*, 21 Jan. 1774 (Clement XIV) *Bull.Cont.* 4.688. Benedict XIV gave an indult to Milan to act in this way, 1757. Clement XIII (18 June 1768) extended the Milan rule to Switzerland.

into the Capuchin monastery. They followed and arrested. The Capuchins protested to the papal nuncio. The nuncio demanded that the accused be sent back from prison to the Capuchins. The magistrate said that though he respected sanctuary he could not do what the nuncio wanted because the friars felt a religious duty to help the criminal to escape. So agreement was reached. The accused was taken back to the Capuchins and in front of their door had his chains removed. Then he was ceremoniously pronounced a case which could not claim sanctuary, sanctuary was refused, and he was led out again to his chains.[66]

This story of the Capuchin friars pointed to another feature of a declining system of sanctuary. Clergymen and blood were bad fellows in the Catholic mind. We have just seen the Pope telling the city of Genoa that they could have some refugees from churches if they agreed to lessen the penalty by one 'grade'. Pope Clement XIII (1760) gave the Duke of Bavaria for three years the right that deserters from the army should have no right of sanctuary, on condition that they be not put to death. The forgiveness of a criminal was still seen as a Christlike act of grace. Catholic theory on occasion did not shrink from trying to apply to the State the gospel story about the woman taken in adultery. Where the Pope had power of government, as in the Papal States, he might put the doctrine into practice with sudden acts of absolution or amnesty. Pope Paul V (1612) gave the Brotherhood of St. Mary of the Purification in Spoleto the privilege, on the day of the beheading of St. John the Baptist each year, of pardoning one man, accused on a capital charge, provided that he was not yet in prison and was not guilty of the worst crimes, homicide, heresy, treason, forging money, sacrilege. The court of the brotherhood asked (1770) if they might extend the pardon to anyone already in gaol, and got what they wanted. At Sinigaglia the Brotherhood of Death, who had the special work of praying with criminals on their way to the scaffold and of burying corpses of the executed or corpses thrown ashore by the sea, received (1772) the privilege of releasing one criminal who was condemned to a sentence of life imprisonment.[67]

Secular Catholic governments did not indulge in these sudden acts of grace, unconnected with political amnesty or a change of monarch. But the mood affected attitudes during those last decades when sanctuary was legal shelter. As the criminal, or refugee, was compassed about by closer entanglements of police or magistrate or law, monks or parish priests sometimes saw their Christian duty to assist in helping an escape. When sanctuary was secure, the refugee needed no such help. But now sanctuary

[66] Bindschedler, 394.   [67] *Bull.Cont.* 4.253 and 429.

was insecure. An abbot found in his abbey church, or a parish priest found by his altar, a refugee waiting miserably and desperately for the few days or hours which it would take the magistrate to bully bishop or nuncio into allowing arrest. Some abbots and priests asked no question about guilt. They showed a postern door, or provided money, or a horse, or a guide across the frontier by night. Driven into a corner by hue and cry, they were known to refuse to give evidence, or to prevent a corpse in their churchyard from being exhumed, or to stop policemen from looking into the register of burials.

This feeling among clergy was in part the religious respect for human life and the duty of compassion. But they could plead, or sometimes tried to plead, a duty in law; namely, that a priest who shared in the shedding of blood became by old canon law *irregular* and could no longer act as priest without dispensation from Rome. An Austrian cleric (1787) refused to tell the police the whereabouts of a criminal because, he said, 'that is incompatible with the character of a priest'.[68] Priests who heard confessions were recognized, by law of State as well as Church, to be debarred from repeating what they learnt in confession, and therefore could not give that evidence in any lawcourt. This law had no application to what a priest heard outside the confessional, where he was expected to do his duty as a citizen, like any other man. But a man who hears of a grave crime in private and knows it is his religious duty not to pass it on, would be a hard or complex character if the attitude failed to spill over into a general compassion for guilty men or women who came to him for help.

As governments modernized their legal systems they could not tolerate the attitude. A prisoner at Linz (1783) set fire to the gaol and in the confusion escaped to the Capuchin monastery. The Capuchins helped him on his way. The police asked the father guardian, 'Which way?' The father guardian refused to say. They appealed to the Bishop of Passau. The bishop backed the father guardian, for otherwise he might become *irregular*. Government had no patience with these pleas. They gave the father guardian four weeks to get leave from his ordinary to give evidence or they would close the Capuchin monastery. The father guardian gave his evidence.[69]

Four years later the Holy Roman Emperor Joseph II incorporated in his new code of law for Austrian lands the declaration that all subjects, *of whatever character*, must give evidence in criminal cases. (It was rescinded by his successor, but from 1803 was again part of Austrian law.) At the

[68] Gröll, 114–15.   [69] Gröll, 111–14.

same time a new criminal order gave police the right to search all buildings, and did not exclude sanctuaries.

It hardly needs saying that of all the cases which reached Rome from all lands, the cases over sanctuary were among the most numerous and most troublesome. In the Curia was a special Congregation on Immunity, for the purpose of deciding these disputes. Its records are packed with staccato judgements which do not hide human tragedies beneath their legal language.

Giuseppe Mule, corporal, and the other constables of the Duke of Monteleone's squad ask for absolution. From the church of St. Nicolas outside the bishop's village they took Giuseppe Cavallo by force and when he ran away outside the church shot him dead with two arquebuses.
Absolution granted, on condition that they promise not to do it again, and perform the customary act of penance in front of the cathedral doors.[70]

Before the end of the century most Catholics were as glad as Protestants to see the end of sanctuary. It reappeared, as a formal right, in a few Concordats of the nineteenth century. But no one wanted its old form, with legal strife, local bitterness, and accusations that vile men were helped to slip from justice. The revolution swept away its last traces. That Catholics could not care was shown when the Revolution in turn was swept away, and they revived much which it destroyed—but not sanctuary.

Instead, they diminished the number of offences which carried the penalty of execution.

The crib

Within the church were places of special reverence, altar with relics, sacred picture or statue, and the reserved sacrament in a tabernacle. But the centuries created two seasonal objects of special cult: sepulchre and crib. The sepulchre on Easter Eve grew to be an elaborate construction, and frequent focus of prayer. As late as 1752 the Holy Roman Emperor took his eleven-year-old son to pay devotional visits to sepulchres in eighteen different churches within a single week.[71]

With the sepulchre was linked the Forty Hours devotion, 3 p.m. Friday to 7 a.m. Sunday, watching at Christ's grave. This started early in the sixteenth century, from the sufferings of the Pope at the sack of Rome, to be a form of prayer in which the faithful took part in times of crisis; and from moments of crisis it became normal, at least in the Rhineland and

[70] *A.S.V.*, Sacr. Congreg. de Immunitate, Litterae (1725), xiii, fo.214.
[71] Padover, 15.

some other Catholic areas. In Cologne of 1700 the cathedral, ten collegiate churches, two abbeys, nineteen parish churches, and ninety-two chapels or places of worship regularly practised the Forty Hours devotion.[72]

The crib, with the stable of Bethlehem and shepherds and wise men, descended from the sacred medieval drama. Its origin lay in a puppet form of the theatre.

The theory that St. Francis of Assisi invented the crib at Greccio has long been demolished. Greccio was but one stage in the growth of dramatic devotion at the nativity. Evidence that Franciscans encouraged the crib is hard to find. Some Franciscan churches are known to have possessed early cribs, but hardly more than churches of the Augustinians. And yet, without much evidence, everyone feels that the childlike devotion of the crib was fitting to a Franciscan spirit. The earliest genuine crib in the modern sense, of which we have knowledge, was made by Gaetano da Thiene (died 1547) who founded the order of Theatines. One Christmas in the church of Santa Maria Maggiore, he had a vision in which the Madonna let him hold the new-born babe in his arms. So he manufactured a crib for himself, and perhaps kept it in his cell, for it is not said to have been placed in church. In front of it he used to weep and sigh and pray and give addresses. The evidence relates only that he had a child in a manger, not whether the child was surrounded with other figures.

Here we have the authentic devotion of a private individual before a manufactured crib. It was associated with no particular school, no characteristic theology. It was the art of the Counter-Reformation and congruous with the devotion of the Counter-Reformation. It grew so easily out of the old drama and the old art, and the Counter-Reformation gave it only that fervour which it imparted to every devotion that it touched.

Not only Jesuits, but every religious order, encouraged the crib. Oratorians introduced it to Marseilles. It is found in Dominican churches, Augustinian, Capuchin. The diarist John Evelyn went to Rome at Christmas 1644, and loosely attributed the scenes to 'friars'.

On Christmas eve . . . I went from church to church the whole night in admiration at the multitude of scenes and pageantry which the friars had with much industry and craft set out, to catch the devout women and superstitious sort of people, who never parted without dropping some money into a vessel set on purpose; but especially observable was the puppetry in the church of the Minerva, representing the nativity.

[72] Klersch, 3.174–7.

The word *puppetry* suggests the dressed dolls or waxworks which were common in older cribs, and sometimes more offensive to sensitive taste than the carved or porcelain figures which eventually rose to dominance.

At Altötting in 1601 was the first crib with moving figures of which we have certain knowledge. The idea was not new. It began in a succession of scenes placed one after the other, a graphic history, such as the six scenes of St. Michael's at Munich in 1607, with a nativity, adoration of the shepherds, circumcision, adoration of the kings, murder of the innocents, and flight into Egypt. Mechanical ingenuity—the influence of clockmakers with elaborate clock-dramas, perhaps even the influence of marionettes and puppet-shows—began to devise means of uniting the successive scenes into a single moving tableau. Sometimes the beauty of the clock was united to the beauty of the mechanical crib. In autumn 1616 the Archbishop of Cologne sent the procurator of the Jesuit mission in China a gift for the emperor in Peking; a clock with a mechanism which operated at 12.00 to bring moving figures out above the clock face. The shepherds came, then the wise men who made their obeisance almost in Chinese fashion, ox and ass lowered their heads, manger, Joseph rocked the cradle, and a concealed musical-box gave out gentle baby-sounds.[73]

Such a crib was an expensive rarity. As the custom took hold of popular reverence—and this was in south Germany, Austria, and Italy—it was popular art. The figures must be crude to be cheap. By 1600 the crib was still confined for the most part to churches, and was not yet of the home. But wealthy noblemen of the sixteenth century placed it in their chapels, from their chapels it passed to another room, and so from homes of the rich it passed downwards towards homes of the poor. The custom of Christmas cribs in rich houses flowered during the seventeenth century. But it never became universal in houses or churches. And its geographical distribution was curious. From south Germany it was taken, not without criticism, into a few Lutheran churches of the seventeenth century. But in Catholic France, except Provence where Italian example prevailed, it was rare. In Italian houses gifts of chestnuts, apples, and tomatoes were often brought to the crib. The Piazza Navona in Rome has long been famous for the sale of little crib figures for the home.

The most celebrated of all cribs is the exhibition of the Infant at the Franciscan church of Aracoeli at the head of the stairs up the Capitol in Rome. The little statue was certainly revered by the third quarter of the sixteenth century. A Spanish friar of 1581 declared that the statue was carved at Jerusalem from wood on the Mount of Olives, baptized in the

[73] *A.H.S.I.* 9 (1940), 110.

river Jordan, and then brought to Aracoeli. By it was a statue of the
Emperor Augustus, to whom the Sibyl pointed out the star of the wise
men. The child was brought in solemn procession to the crib at mattins of
Christmas, and taken away in solemn procession on the evening of Epiphany. The people came to believe in its miraculous powers, and later it
was given a carriage and servants to visit the sick. The wood from the
Mount of Olives was believed to have been turned into the colour of flesh
by a miracle. Before the crib was erected a wooden platform on which
boys or girls made little speeches and blew toy trumpets. At the Epiphany
procession it came to be the custom that the child blessed the city from the
top of the long stairway.

In Italy, especially southern Italy, the crib was popular throughout the
eighteenth century. In south-German churches it continued, though less
frequently and with less complex machinery. Though in houses it was
mostly of the middle class, it was an important variety of popular
devotion. In 1744 the Jesuit church at Münster first installed a crib, twelve
years earlier the Jesuits at Vienna, but it may have been their second crib.
The close connection of government and culture between Naples and
Spain brought it into the churches of Spain and Portugal, especially
Portugal.

On occasion even educated men drew their knowledge of the Bible
from the crib or from art and not from reading the text. Bernini was
astonished when Poussin did not paint the Magi as kings in *The Adoration
of the Magi*, because he insisted that artists should follow the text of the
gospel where (Bernini was sure) the wise men were said to be kings.[74]

Defenders of the crib needed to refute critics: not so commonly
Protestants with their religious condemnation of statues as Catholics who
objected to the devotion as childish, an affair of toys. No question but that
representations of the crib, because cheap and crude, verged on bad taste;
that some cribs in noble houses were ostentatious contraptions which
elicited more praise of the mechanic than marvel for the works of God;
that some of the objections, valid against forms of drama, were valid
against forms of crib; and that even when the crib was of art and simplicity, the devotion never suited the senses of all worshippers, however
devoted to the Christmas feast. Even devout men complained that it was
not serious religion.

The criticisms became more vocal among Catholics as the seventeenth
century passed into the eighteenth, and as the fervour of the Counter-
Reformation gave way to the refinements of the Enlightenment. Pastors

[74] Wittkower, 110.

wanted cribs made simpler, so that human admiration might give way to prayer. For as the artists were allowed their chance, they built round the crib a range of figures, trumpeters and hawkers, and houses opposite with balconies. The more numerous the scenes, the more like a theatre, the more diverted the attention. In 1782 Salzburg, in 1789 Regensburg limited the representations to the centre pieces of the nativity. The Lutheran churches of Germany which accepted the crib during the seventeenth century were nearly all rid of it by 1700. Before the end of the eighteenth century, especially in Mainz and Austria, some authorities banned cribs as out of keeping with the spirit of the times. In 1782 the Austrian government forbade them in churches, but the decree was not universally observed and was withdrawn in 1804. In 1803 the administrator of the bishopric of Würzburg declared that cribs were now abolished in churches and were only kept for the sake of children.

Mrs Thrale (Hester Piozzi) travelled in Italy during 1786 and expressed a characteristic view of the rational but romantic stranger in Naples.[75]

There is a work of art peculiar to this city, and attempted in no other [she was wrong], on which surprising sums of money are lavished by many of the inhabitants, who connect or associate to this amusement ideas of piety and devotion. . . . In many houses a room, in some a whole suite of apartments [is she exaggerating?] in others the terrace upon the housetops, is dedicated to this very uncommon show. The figures are about six inches high and dressed with the most exact propriety.

She complained that the scenes were so various that the nativity, though central, was obscured,

so that sometimes I scarcely saw it at all; while a general and excellent landscape, with figures of men at work, women dressing dinner, a long road in real gravel, with rocks, hills, rivers, cattle, camels, everything that can be imagined, fill the other rooms, so happily disposed, too, for the most part, the light introduced so artfully, the perspective kept so surprisingly.—one wonders and cries out it is certainly but a baby house at best; yet. . . .

The owners altered and improved them each year; some gave for them the equivalent of £1,500 or £2,000; and according to Mrs Thrale some families, rather than omit them, would fall into ruin. She found a house where the three wise men wore anachronistic 'Mohammedan' clothes. When she mentioned it to the proprietor he said that he would alter it next year 'if there was nothing heretical in the objection'.

[75] Mrs Piozzi, *Observations in a Journey through Italy* (1789), 2.42–3. Beautiful examples of the kind of crib which she saw may now be seen in the Museo di San Martino at Naples.

The romantic movement of the nineteenth century revived the crib. Several churches which abolished their cribs between 1780 and 1800 recovered them between 1820 and 1840. But there came to be a difference. When German Protestants at last accepted the crib, they imagined it to be part of children's Christmas, and linked it with Christmas tree and toys. But in Catholic origin, and still during the eighteenth century, the crib was not a toy for children. It was of the altar, not of the children's corner; attracted not toymakers but famous designers; was of universal devotion like the medieval drama, not of children's art like the doll's house. The more Christmas became the children's feast, the more childlike the crib. In Protestant parts of Germany churches ceased to receive it, but it came into homes, and the little figures shone by the Christmas tree instead of the altar.

Christmas trees were almost unknown in Catholic churches. By the end of the eighteenth century they penetrated from the Protestant homes into a few Lutheran churches of Germany. Catholics looked down on the innovation.

The Sacred Heart

Among mystical writers the use of the heart of Jesus as a symbol of affection in the God-Man is found as early as the later Middle Ages, and was extended by the devotional theologians of the Counter-Reformation. These devotions, practised in the cloister, were the food of pious meditation, and the exercise of minds which needed mental image to aid their prayers. The more feminine of the gentle guides to spirituality, like St. Francis de Sales, used the thought of the Lord's heart as a way to elicit pure affection in nuns whose souls they directed. It stood for the sweetness and kindness of the divine love. The Oratorian Father Eudes (1601–80) ordered for his French nuns special exercises of devotion to the heart of Jesus and the heart of Mary, and marked a stage in the cult because he instituted (1646) a liturgy for the Feast of the Heart of Jesus, which was celebrated not only within his convents but at the cathedral of Autun, and later in dioceses where the bishop approved. Rome (1669) was asked for approval and refused.

The devotion was still of nuns, some clergy only, brotherhoods organized by favourable priests. They contemplated a wounded heart, from which flowed a stream of grace. At the age of twenty-nine Marguerite-Marie Alacoque entered the convent of the Visitation at Paray-le-Monial and two years later, on St. John's Day 1673, while praying before the

Sacrament, began to see a vision, of rest upon the breast and of gifts from the heart. Her symbolism was of flames and of brightness, and accompanied by the sight of a crown of thorns. Soon the Lord in her vision began to ask that a public liturgy be established. At first her convent was divided, but after a few years made a chapel of the Sacred Heart.

Three years before Marguerite-Marie died in 1690, Rome was asked for a mass, an office, and a feast day. It refused. Then the exiled Queen of England, Marie d'Este, wife of James II, who learnt to pray with a Jesuit friend of Marguerite-Marie, asked the Pope to allow the Visitation nuns their feast. In 1697, perhaps more for the sake of the queen than for the sake of the nuns, the Sacred Congregation of Rites approved the use of a mass for the Feast of the Sacred Heart, but no mass proper to the cult. In 1704 the Roman censor placed the most important book, advocating the cult, on the Index of prohibited books: the work by a Jesuit father, Jean Croiset, *Devotion to the Heart of Our Saviour* (published first in 1691).

A bowdlerized version of Croiset's book was translated into Italian (Venice, 1731) and Spanish (1734). The cult began to make headway in Italy, but among convents. Yet its widespread growth could not but impinge on popular beliefs. At a plague in Marseilles the people associated the staying of the epidemic with devotions in honour of the Sacred Heart, and now (1720 onwards) the cult began to spread among townsmen of Provence.

Rome was again asked to approve; this time petitions came from Spain and Poland as well as Provence and the Visitation nuns. But, argued Cardinal Prospero Lambertini, the cult supposes the heart to be the seat of feeling, a doubtful opinion which casts a question upon this mode of devotion. Rome (1729) refused its assent. But when Queen Marie of France, who was Polish, asked the Pope for the feast, Benedict XIV (formerly that same Cardinal Lambertini) sent her models of the Sacred Heart made of gold and silk, but still refused the application.

From Provence the cult spread into Italy. Paul Danco was one of sixteen children of minor nobility from Piedmont. He joined the Venetian army to be a crusader, but left after a few years, was confirmed at the age of twenty-five in 1719, and was clothed by his bishop in a simple black habit of no religious order. He was associated with Capuchins, and the order of Passionists which he founded had strong similarities to reformed Franciscans. His first name for his order was *The Poor of Jesus*. He saw a vision of the Virgin in a black tunic with the emblem of a white heart with cross above, and within the heart the words JESU PASSIO with three nails. No evidence shows a direct link between the Passionists' heart upon the robe and the development of the cult of the Sacred Heart during those years, but it is hard to think that no connection existed.

The Passionists obtained a provisional rescript from Benedict XIV in 1741. The Rule appeared in 1746. Clement XIV gave them full recognition in 1769. Their centres at first lay in Tuscany and the Papal States near the Tuscan border.

By the third quarter of the eighteenth century brotherhoods existed, in honour of the Sacred Heart, at Rome and Venice and in Tuscany. When Rezzonico became Pope as Clement XIII in 1758, he was known to have founded such confraternities in the north. The Polish bishops applied again for a feast. In 1765 the Pope granted a feast of the Sacred Heart. Not all the Catholic Church was yet clear in its mind. Though the Spanish early received the cult from France, they associated it with the Jesuits, and when they expelled the Jesuits from Spain they carefully erased from their churches all emblems of the cult.[76]

The parish service

So many priests, on so many endowments to say mass for the souls, meant many altars in churches and many masses. These masses were not supposed to be said simultaneously but to overlap in time. In the parish church of St. Columba at Cologne the high altar had a series of masses including a chief mass or 'high mass' at 9 a.m. (Sundays 9.30 a.m.) but about twenty other masses at side-altars. On Sundays one of the masses had a sermon not at high mass, but at early sung mass, so that the sermon, which lasted one hour, was preached from 7.30 a.m. to 8.30 a.m. At 1 p.m. on Sundays they catechized children, at 3 p.m. daily they had vespers and compline but this was not a people's service. In St. Columba's at Cologne, and over most of Catholic Europe, no communion was given to the congregation at the time of communion in the mass. Communion was almost always given apart from the mass, usually after the end of the service. This arrangement aimed to keep the people in church until the end of the mass, labourers who lived afar or domestic servants or nursing mothers being unwilling or unable to remain for a distribution of the sacrament which to a big congregation might take half an hour. Cardinal Quirini of Brescia wrote pastoral letters (1742) to revive the practice of communion at the proper time of communion. Argument ensued, and Pope Benedict XIV allowed both practices.

The custom whereby men sat on one side of the church and women on

[76] Pastor, xxxvii.406.

the other, which was maintained in most places for most of the seventeenth century, faded during the eighteenth century at least in cities and areas not remote. Some Italian and Spanish communities had allowed women into church only if they were veiled, but this also faded. Many bishops and parish priests sought to preserve both customs, but especially the separate seating.

The atmosphere of a people's mass was not silent. Men and women moved about, freely, in and out, simple worshippers ejaculated, groaned, rocked to and fro, beat the breast, or prayed their private prayers aloud, sometimes too loud. To the horror of intellectuals who cared about an atmosphere of devotion, bags were passed to collect money. Beggars were not supposed to be inside the church, their place was the porch or the steps outside. In Vienna beadles patrolled the churches, parts of Germany and Belgium almost managed to maintain this discipline. But keeping out beggars was far from easy, and kindly worshippers disliked rejecting them in a sacred place; so they might harass penitents who queued for a turn in the confessional, or communicants who moved towards the altar; and their importunate laments added to the noise and the distractions of prayer. Dogs followed masters or mistresses into church and made messes and noises, though the poor at the porch were supposed to keep them out. Boys were inclined to be noisy, lovers inclined to use their eyes, babies were discouraged but still came. In one Italian diocese parents who brought babies under two years old into church were excommunicated. In many towns and villages young men showed pertinacious reluctance in preferring not to enter church but to hear mass crowded in the porch. This was especially common in country villages.

To go to confession as often as once a month was thought by the eighteenth century to be abnormally frequent. The evidence, not from statistics but from eye-witnesses of queues, suggests that women went to confession more frequently than men.

Spitting in church was not uncommon. In Padua diocese they provided that a spittoon should be placed on the steps of the altar, and cleaned eight times in the day. This was partly caused by chewing tobacco, which some people took to masticate and others as snuff. Authority continued to be against all forms of tobacco in church but succeeded in preventing it only as smoke. Even celebrating priests could be observed to take snuff, and were not thought irreverent by the people, only by priests who cared for clean linen.

In a crowded city church a man of property needed to beware. Dr Burney, when he visited Italy to study its church music, suffered too often from pickpockets in church. He was a foreigner and easier prey. Yet Italian confessors at a monthly meeting needed to argue whether a thief who stole a handbag from a worshipper who was rapt in prayer committed only the sin of theft or also the sin of sacrilege.[77]

Where the choir gave no musical rendering, the people joined in singing the Nicene creed. This and the Lord's Prayer were the only parts of the liturgy where in a majority of churches people joined with priests. (At catechism children were taught to recite in Latin the Apostles' Creed, Our Father, and Hail Mary). Muratori provided a vernacular Italian translation of all the mass, not because he expected mass in the vernacular (though he hoped for readings of Scripture in the vernacular) but as a way of enabling the people to become a congregation.[78] Other such aids to worship existed, but no evidence suggests that they were common until south German Catholics made them common towards the end of the century.

Besides the clergy, the verger (or sacristan, or sexton, or caretaker) was an important officer. He was usually responsible for keeping the registers of baptisms, marriages, or deaths, and the inventory of vessels and vestments. In various churches he was elected by the parishioners, though canon law ordered the priest to choose. His election was celebrated with the ringing of church bells, and for loss of church property he might be fined. He knew the people, sometimes better than the priests, and could therefore be useful to a city council and in his function as registrar give information about statistics. Exceptional vergers might be found—the verger at the sanctuary of the Madonna of the Oak in southern Holland was a member of the Franciscan third order who won such name for his way of life that others wanted to join, and he founded a little order called The Penitent Little Brothers of St. Francis. The bishop moved the community to another sanctuary where they made a contract with the rector (1723) to maintain their verger's house and look after the garden, serve at mass and train boys to serve, provide bread for the sacrament, and generally keep the church in good order; while joining in the hours of prayer and often receiving the sacrament. Finally they started to keep a school because Catholics found schooling hard in Protestant Holland.[79]

A country priest still had to think what to do about the old rule that no one could bring weapons into church. In Italy and Spain the rule was

[77] Chiericato, Dec.Misc. 20; cf. 25, 36–7, 97–8.
[78] The translation, with explanations, makes the entire central section of his Della regolata divozione (1747).
[79] D.I.P. s.v. 'Brouwer, Daniel de'.

disregarded because sword and dagger were part of costume and in certain regions insignia of rank. But countrymen, if they travelled far to church, took with them guns and brought them into the nave because it felt as natural as bringing in a hat. Bishops minded little about swords and daggers because they accepted the fashion of the age but did all they could to be rid of firearms. They might seek to persuade the parish priest to find somewhere, if necessary in the ground-floor room of his vicarage or his veranda, where artillery could be put during time of service.

The squire in a country parish often had his rights in church, a special seat or pew, his coat of arms and/or motto, a window from his private apartment looking into the altar. In north Italy these private windows were often found. Authority disliked them. A rich man who built a church was known to include his window in the plan, and then won a form of founder's privilege by his generosity. But if more than one family of squires lived in the parish this caused faction. The Bishop of Mantua, in trouble with two noblemen over the privilege of a window, referred his trouble (1726) to Rome and was ordered not to allow the window.[80] Southern noblemen also tried to get thrones in the choir, for it needed a series of decisions to keep them where they belonged. But if outside the choir, the seat might lawfully be 'elevated' and nothing could stop peasants making genuflections in that direction. Some noblemen wanted the throne to be grand like a bishop's so that they sat under a canopy, and this dignity also had to be banned.

The Sunday school

Parents were liable to punishment if they failed to bring a newborn child to baptism within a few days. (A just comparison is with states of the twentieth century which exact penalties from parents who fail to register a new birth within a few days or weeks.) They must choose a *Christian* name, that is a name in the calendar of saints; not a name like Diana. Authority discussed whether to allow, but finally consented, when a squire of historic family wanted to revive an old family-name not in the calendar.

After mass the boys and girls of a parish went to church to be instructed in 'Christian doctrine' or 'catechism' as the exercise was indifferently known. Early in the century two or three boys used to run through the streets of an Italian city ringing handbells to remind families, but the custom faded or lapsed. Attendance was regarded as compulsory for any

[80] *Thesaurus Resolutionum*, 3.316.

boy or girl aged between seven and fifteen inclusive. The parish priest was ordered to keep a register of those who ought to attend, and to mark them off when they came. He was permitted to keep them after the age of fifteen if they wished or he thought it needful; but the commonest attendants over the age of fifteen were parents who felt themselves as ignorant as their children or who refused to let small boys or girls come alone.

That attendance was not universal is easily proved by the anxieties and arguments on modes of persuading parents to do their duty. Priests were exhorted to exhort parents 'constantly' from the pulpit. Confessors were told to ask parents in the confessional whether they always sent their children to catechism. Schoolmasters were ordered to keep their lists of children who ought to be present.

In the early part of the century, at least in some towns, boys and girls met at a chapel, formed two processions divided by sex, and marched to Sunday school, greeted at the church porch by the parish priest. This custom also lapsed or faded. The clergy used lay assistants to teach and tried to keep the classes to small numbers, if possible not more than ten. In certain towns parishes reached an agreement whereby boys went to a Sunday school at one central church, girls to another. But this arrangement displeased bishops and others who cared about the parish system. Canon lawyers were known to lay it down that every parish priest was bound to teach *his* children, and that the law was not obeyed by central Sunday schools at separate churches.

An adult who was not mentally deficient and who did not live in remote country, and yet could not say the Creed, the Lord's Prayer, and the Ten Commandments was regarded as guilty of grave sin. Most adults allowed priests small occasion to know whether they could say the Ten Commandments. But sometimes they were asked in the confessional and then could not dodge, and might be sent away to learn the words. A town priest who in his confessional invariably asked all persons, whatever their education or social class, whether they knew the Ten Commandments was regarded by experts as rash and imprudent.[81]

What catechism should be used was not quite agreed, and became slowly more controversial. Germany and Austria normally used a form of the famous catechism written by St. Peter Canisius in the Counter-Reformation. The official catechism approved by Rome, especially from 1726, was that written by Cardinal Robert Bellarmine, also in the Counter-

---

[81] Chiericato, *Dec.Misc.* 4–5; *Decisioni di casi de coscienza*, 1.234; 3.284–5; Diocesan Synod of Ferrara (1781), 25 ff. and appendix, 16–23; Lambertini, *Raccolta*, 1.86 ff.

Reformation. But the French, divided into Jesuits versus Jansenists, used various catechisms. And since the catechisms of the Counter-Reformation looked dated, and Italian priests yearned for someting simpler, more pastoral, more devotional, and sometimes more Biblical, French catechisms began to be used in Italian churches. By the sixties of the eighteenth century the parish question 'Which catechism?' was an issue in high ecclesiastical politics.

The rite of confirmation was supposed to be administered every year in the see town and at time of visitation in the country. It was held in the morning early, candidates and bishop fasting, males sitting separate from females, godparents present if possible. Children must be not less than seven years old, and were expected to be between seven and twelve, and must know the Lord's Prayer, Apostles' Creed, Ten Commandments, Hail Mary, sign of the cross, and the act of contrition—they might know more because they were expected to go to catechism on Sundays. In outlying parts like the Maremma, where bishops were seldom seen, parents were even allowed to bring babies to confirmation. Since visitations happened less often than the rules expected, they were crowded when they happened, and were noisy irreverent tumultuous affairs. In the country many children could grow into adults without receiving the sacrament.

If an adult was confirmed he must first go to confession. This was not a rule for the children everywhere, but was usually treated like a rule. When the candidate was confirmed, his godparent (in many places) laid his hand on his shoulder as the rite was performed. The candidate must carry a certificate from his parish priest, and a clean white bandage which was tied round his head after the anointing, and which he was not supposed to remove for four hours so that the chrism could dry. Authority took trouble to see that children came with brushed hair and not barefoot in tattered clothes. They also took precautions against ostentatious clothes. The candidate was allowed to change his legal name at confirmation. The change was recorded in the parish priest's confirmation register.[82]

Despite all these provisions, confirmation was not usually a profound moment in the lives of boys or girls or their families. The first communion was much more ceremonious, more moving, and an important feast within the family.

One Spanish boy's Sunday in Seville towards the end of the eighteenth century ran thus: before breakfast he went to the Oratorian chapel for confession and communion. He arrived at 6 a.m. in summer and 7 a.m.

[82] Roman Council of 1725, xxvi.4 (Mansi, xxxiv.1895); Diocesan Synod of Ferrara (1781), 59 ff.; Fliche and Martin xix.1 (3rd edn), 75.

in winter. The church was full, with queues at some ten confessional boxes, and he needed to wait half an hour in his queue, kneeling uncomfortably. Immediately after confession he went to a priest in a stole to receive communion, given every five minutes to any persons who had finished confession, without any liturgy. Then he heard a mass celebrated at one of the side-altars, thence home to breakfast. The morning he spent with other boys, or even at books, after dinner he played the violin for the Oratorians' orchestra in the gallery of the church, where music was excellent, and therefore he listened during the afternoon to an hour's sermon. This musical part of Sunday, unlike the early morning, gave the boy much pleasure. Then he went out for a walk with other boys whom he met at church.[83]

German hymns

The common people hardly found the centre of devotion in the rite of communion. Mass was a spectacle, which baroque taste made ever more dramatic and colourful; and, for prayer, they accompanied the rite with personal devotions, private prayer book (if they could read), rosary, lighting of candles, devotion to picture or statue or crib. In Catholic parts of Germany flourished the most congregational of these side-devotions at mass, the German hymn.

The later Middle Ages knew German hymns as well as Latin, and macaronic verse, hymns of mixed language. From this source Protestants, searching for congregational ways of devotion, adapted their most fruitful innovation in Christian worship. The Lutheran hymnody which stamped Protestant Germany and was both beloved and an evident aid to worship, could not but attract pastors in Catholic Germany. The Counter-Reformation was a time when the German Catholic hymn flowered. The first diocesan hymnbook was approved in 1756 for the diocese of Bamberg. The hymns were intended (like early Protestant hymns) for private devotion in the home; and for processions, pilgrimages, special services, devotions of brotherhoods; but also, at least in some places, accompanying mass at its beginning or before and after sermon. German village churches, which could not provide singers for high mass, started to use hymns as music for mass without choir. In atmosphere, however, hymns were no integral part of mass. They were songs of special devotion which when they came into church did not quite acquire the Protestant status of integration into the liturgy, but still were a form of private devotion.

Because their origin was popular, they were not chosen for good taste.

[83] *The Life of Blanco White*, 1.24 ff.

They were private lyrics, emotional, stark, individual, even at times comic. The best English parallel in tone would be a more fey group of Christmas carols. Here is an example (1657) from one of the few true poets among the authors:

> O Love, who formedst me to wear
> The image of thy Godhead here;
> Who soughtest me with tender care
> Through all my wanderings wild and drear:
> O Love, I give myself to thee,
> Thine ever, only thine to be.[84]

Here is a later example which gave most offence to Catholic critics of taste:

> Hail Jesus
> In whom I trust
> Christ Jesus
> Sweet Jesus
> I salute Thee with my heart
> Sweet Jesus.[85]

In this way the hymn, still bearing its stamp of personal and individual prayer, was not adapted to mass or integrated into mass. It remained like the rosary, though more congregational than the rosary, personal prayer during or outside mass.

Catholics in areas of mixed religion well knew the Protestant use of hymns. That knowledge led to diverse attitudes. Educated Catholics often wanted to make their hymnody congregational, adapt it more fully to mass, and be prepared to use the best of Protestant words and tunes. Villagers, faced with a proposal, or an order, that they should sing German hymns or even new hymns, could be suspicious: 'They want to turn us into Lutherans.' In towns the change was easier. When a Cologne choir started German hymns (1730) a lady in the congregation appealed to the Jesuit superior, then the mayor, and finally the archbishop. The choir said that their innovation stopped the incoming of Lutheran hymns, and got their way.[86]

During the last three decades of the eighteenth century the German

---

[84] *Liebe, die du mich zum Bilde*, by Johann Scheffler; translated by Catherine Winkworth. Scheffler however was a convert from Lutheranism and the hymn may have been written, though not published, during his Lutheran days. Its mysticism certainly owed something to his Protestant past, where he was much influenced by Boehme.

[85] Goy, 249, from the Würzburg hymnbook of 1793.

[86] Klersch, 3.186–7.

Catholic Enlightenment made a serious effort to reform hymnbooks. They purged archaisms, lessened the mystical, drove out the fey, increased moral teaching, tried to make hymns congregational. In these same decades Protestant reformers attempted precisely the same with Protestant hymnbooks, that effort which the Protestant nineteenth century later ridiculed as prosy, rationalistic, Christianity and water. As Catholic reformers found it not easy to see the virtues in simplicity or emotionalisms they sometimes fell into equal traps of style and taste. Here is the same verse in two editions, divided only by twenty-three years:

1777: O God, I trust
     What Thy Church teaches,
     Written or unwritten;
     For Thou hast said it.

1800: O God, I trust
     What Christ teaches,
     He came and said, there will be
     light,
     So was the world enlightened.

The second author was a priest working in the Protestant city of Nuremberg and ready to use Protestant phrases or hymns.[87] The 1777 version was much the more successful in Catholic dioceses. Some new hymnbooks stank more of the study than of the people's mind.

This series of new books met various fates. In many parishes they were quietly and successfully introduced. Wise bishops were careful not to force new hymnbooks upon parishes which did not want them, but allowed their use if parishes wished. Unwise efforts to enforce new hymnbooks could—as in Protestant churches during that age—be met by murmuring, catcalls, or rebellious counter-singing. In Mainz (1787) a new hymnbook, which contained no Protestant hymns, was numbered and arranged in columns like a Protestant hymnbook. In a few towns, especially Rüdesheim, the resulting battle between pastor and people led to violence and the arrival of police.

This *émeute* at Mainz made other bishops prudent. The enlightened Bishop Fechenbach of Würzburg was asked (1802) whether they might use hymns of Protestant origin. He replied: 'On both sides old prejudice has not yet faded. A book which printed Catholic and Protestant hymns indiscriminately would very easily offend; would divide people from priest, make them indifferent to worship, and on the whole cause more evil than good.'[88] Such a remark, and indeed the entire history of these attempts to reform Catholic hymnody, proves more conclusively than any other evidence the depth of affection which hymns of the Counter-Reformation had already won among the Catholic population of Germany.

[87] Goy, 254–5.   [88] Goy, 263, 270.

Nevertheless, the attempt to reform was not vain. These hymnbooks offended a later romantic Germany. But they took a long stride in turning the hymn from private aspiration into part of public liturgy; and thereby were important in making the mass more congregational and so more plainly central to a people's devotion.

Bible-reading

A difference between northern Catholic Europe and southern lay in the reading of the Bible in translation instead of Latin. Literate Frenchmen and Germans and Poles could easily buy French or German or Polish translations. Literate Italians, Spaniards, and Portuguese could not. Some translations were banned because they were Protestant, some because they were Jansenist. The bull *Unigenitus* of 1713 condemned the proposition 'the reading of the Bible is for everyone' and the proposition 'Sunday should be kept holy by reading good books especially the Bible— it is damnable to want to stop a Christian from such reading' (propositions 80 and 82). But in the north laymen with enough money could easily buy translations and use them for devotions. This is not to say that the practice was yet widespread. Very few seminarists possessed a copy even of the Latin Bible. The university press at Ingolstadt possessed no Hebrew letters though it was 300 years old. The number of hours devoted to Biblical study by ordinands declined before the needs of other subjects (in the Augsburg diocese: 1609, three hours a week; 1691, two hours; 1713, one hour).

Since the Counter-Reformation the Roman Catholic Church as a whole had no conscious wish to discourage the study of the Scriptures by persons capable of study. But persons capable of study could (and on the whole should) use the Latin.

The difference between north and south arose partly because popular education was more advanced in the north; and partly because in Spain, Portugal, and central and southern Italy censorship was more effective. But the chief cause was the indirect influence of Martin Luther. If German Catholics were not given a German translation by a Catholic, some of them would find another. Pious Catholic laymen wanted to understand the Bible, and the Church refused to deny them that chance.

Those who disliked Bible-reading—except by Latinists in the Vulgate version—saw an illiterate people and had no wish to place in their hands a book which they could not understand. They inherited a tradition from the Counter-Reformation which refused to appeal against Church to

Bible, and was content to accept the Scriptures so far as the Church presented them to the faithful people, and stood in line of the terrifying 1559 Index which prohibited the printing or ownership of all vernacular translations without leave of the Inquisition. Pope Pius IV (1564) amended this rule, so that permission could be granted by bishop or Inquisition on the advice of the priest of a would-be reader. Clement VIII (1596) made the bishop's leave depend on Pope or Inquisition; and this was till 1757 the law of the Church. Northern Catholic Europe paid small attention to this law.

Early in the eighteenth century an Italian traveller crossed the Alps into the Tyrol and, going to mass, was astonished and gladdened to hear the priest first sing the Latin epistle and gospel from the altar, and then come forward to the chancel steps and read the same epistle and gospel in a German translation. The traveller wished that Italian churches could follow the same custom.[89] All the century this habit spread in France and Germany. And in the fifties it began to spread southward. In a meeting of clergy held in 1755 the Bishop of Campagna in south Italy told them that all the evils of the church came from too little attention to the Bible, and recommended them to buy a New Testament, and especially to study the Epistles of St. Paul with the Commentary of the Frenchman Natalis Alexander. But the bishop had leanings towards Jansenism. The leading Jansenist in Rome, Giovanni Bottari, wrote a paper, never yet printed, in favour of the reading of Scripture in the vernacular.[90]

Since law badly observed was likely to be bad law, Pope Benedict XIV considered change. Perhaps the decree was not due to him (for in his last two years he was so gouty as to be hardly capable of work) but to men whom he chose for their liberal outlook. On 13 June 1757, the Holy Office allowed translations of the Bible to be printed and owned if they were approved by Rome or furnished with Catholic notes. Henceforth, anyone was free to buy or use a Bible in his own language provided the version was approved by authority.

Southward spread of the use of Bible in translation was slow, because the approval of authority was not easy to get. Under Pope Clement XIV a Turin translation of 1769 was freely sold in the Rome bookshops. Antonio Martini undertook a translation of the whole Bible into Italian— New Testament 1769–71, Old Testament 1776–81. The Italian version was printed in parallel columns with the Latin. He justified his work by

[89] It was Muratori; cf. *Della regolata divozione* (1748), 195; for the date, Zlabinger, 133 n.
[90] De Rosa, *Vescovi*, 73; Jemolo, *Giansenismo*, 253; Giuntella, 166 n.3.

appealing to the 1757 decree. Rome never gave this Italian translation its formal blessing. But Pope Pius VI (17 March 1778) sent Martini a letter in language remarkable in the light of past history:

You believe that Christian people are much to be encouraged to read the Bible. It is an excellent opinion. The Holy Scriptures are like springs of water that bring life to the soul, and their use ought to drive away errors widespread in this corrupt age, and show the way of truth and righteousness.

Some people said that this letter of the Pope was heretical, and should be censored by the Inquisition. But the Pope did not object when Tuscany made Martini (1781) Archbishop of Florence.

The first Catholic translation into Portuguese began to appear in the year of this letter of Pius VI; the first Spanish translation by a Catholic not until twelve years later. On 26 December 1789 the Spanish Inquisition suppressed the decree of the Index which banned the reading of the Bible. It allowed vernacular translations if approved by the See of Rome and published by Catholic authors with commentaries from the fathers or approved doctors. If these conditions were not fulfilled, the ban remained. But in the last decade of the eighteenth century Spanish churchmen paid less heed to the rules of the Inquisition.

That Bibles could be bought does not prove that men read Bibles. Even the New Testament alone was bulky in its two languages and if a man wanted a pocket Bible he must still go to one of the Protestant translations. It took another century and more before a Pope (1893) recommended the faithful to read the Bible with more attention and freedom, and in consequence the Naples edition of Martini's *St. Matthew* was brought out at a cost of 25 cents. But the publishing record shows how the habit grew. By 1800 there were seventy-one different vernacular translations.

Those who taught priests in seminaries began before the end of the century to show their pupils how they should foster the reading of the Bible among their parishioners; but only in some seminaries, and among men of open mind like Johann Michael Sailer, for many priests continued to think the private reading of the Bible useless if not harmful. Even Sailer wanted only the New Testament to be placed in the hands of the people and thought the Old Testament too abstruse to be safe for popular reading. Among superstitious and illiterate Protestants the Bible was used like an amulet, to be put in the cradle of a new baby or laid upon the head of the sick. Such practices were hardly found in Catholic countries, even though Biblical mottoes were used as charms, and when the Catholic priest of south Germany wanted to ward off damage from a storm, he

might still come before the people and recite the first verses of the four
gospels to the four points of the compass.[91]

Church ornament

Art and architecture follow their laws, and the traditions of the schools.
But they must speak to the mood of their generation, or lead their
generation towards new ideas so far as such fresh inspiration is consistent
with the wishes of clients who control commissions and employment.
Therefore the art of an age, so far as it appeared in churches, made a rough
guide not only to the aesthetic mood for the artist, but to the religious
expectations of his employers.

Through all the middle years of the seventeenth century Gianlorenzo
Bernini (1598–1680) ruled the architecture and statuary in papal Rome.
To this day, despite ancient excavation and high modern flats, the Rome
which gives the city its enchantment is the Rome of Bernini and of his
successors in the first half of the eighteenth century. Roman art moved
away from the austerity of the Counter-Reformation. The Council of
Trent wanted reality, a bleeding Christ, ugly and lacerated. The fathers
wished to strip the truth of its idealized beauty, and its acceptance in the
world of the Renaissance, and show it naked and shocking. The ending of
the wars of religion brought a mellower mood. The artists did not turn
their backs upon truth. In the age of high baroque, as in any age of art, we
find much that is insincere or is conventional. But the best men realized
that artistic truth sought to portray not just reality seen by the naked eye,
but the emotion which it evoked. They tried to bring an immediacy of act
and feeling into the mind of the beholder.

Therefore they must portray movement. Bernini and his contemporaries
subtly developed the use to this end of colour and garments. Flowing
drapery upon statues was used to bring life to the figures, colour direct or
indirect was used to heighten contrasts and elicit feeling. Though they
sought to portray emotional moments, their work was not emotional in
the way of excess or sentimentality. This art was one of the strongest in
the Christian centuries. The emotion which they sought to show was
intelligent; an uplifting of the worshipping mind towards mysteries
beyond the objects which the eye could see; to group or frame statues or
church ornaments so that they pointed towards a reality not themselves.
The bodies of statues grew more slender, the folds of their garments more

[91] *L.T.K.* s.v. 'Bibelübersetzungen', and literature there; *Realenc.* s.v. 'Bibelverbot';
Darlow-Moule, 2.801 ff.; *Cambridge History of the Bible*, 3.358 ff.

abundant and tumultuous, the saints more agonized or more exalted, the touch of guardian angels more delicate and kindly, the flight of cherubim and seraphim more restless. Bernini used light in a more direct way; no longer a tranquil background of colours but a sudden illumination, a vision of the moment. When he applied (1645-52) this technique to a chapel like the Cornaro chapel in the church of St. Mary of the Victory, the 'effects' reached their climax—above the altar St. Theresa entranced in her ecstasy, half-conscious but clothed in a robe of such turbulence as to make her experience felt as alive, and touched by the gentlest of boy angels with his arrow: and rays of light shining down upon her from the magnificent gilded canopy of the altarpiece, while aloft in the vault the heavens open, angels push clouds to left and right, and through the space of light falls the blessing of the spirit-dove as though inspiring from on high the ecstasy below by the altar.

Bernini has been said to be the first artist who sought to unite in a whole the painting, the sculpture, and the structure of the building.[92] Between 1656 and 1667 he built the greatest of his works, the piazza of St. Peter's. He designed a square to embrace 100,000 or more pilgrims before the steps of the basilica, to receive a Pope's blessing; surrounded by colonnades to protect processions or pilgrims from heat and rain, but not so high as to prevent a blessing Pope from being seen by all the crowd; incorporating the old entry to the papal palace and the royal staircase. He himself imagined the arms of the colonnades to be like the arms of Mother Church reaching out to embrace her children. At first he meant to enclose the whole piazza with the colonnade. But his patron Pope Alexander VII died, and the last arm of the colonnade was never built. No church was ever given a more beautiful forecourt than the piazza of St. Peter's. Those with memories claimed that it was more beautiful still before the improvers of the twentieth century pulled down the buildings of the Borgo to make a wide road to the Tiber, for in former days men had the gay surprise of coming out into the piazza from an overcrowded cluster of little streets and houses.

One mark of high baroque was the fresco in the domes of churches. Rome and Italy began early in the seventeenth century but the habit became common only during the later seventeenth century. The biggest of all such frescoes were those painted by Father Pozzo in St. Ignazio (1691-4) and by Gaulli in the Gesù (1672-82); both Jesuit churches. These frescoes showed a momentous component in the baroque sense of movement. The artists began to avoid, or at least to seem to avoid, pattern or regularity.

[92] Wittkower, 105-6.

Cherubim were sprinkled over the vaults as if haphazardly, angels flew in no formation, individual freedom was used to bring excitement into the ornaments of the church, the eye can find no centre and nowhere to rest, each casual figure is seen for itself and yet as part of a whole which is not just the vault on which it is painted but the whole church interior. This individuality had extraordinary consequences in the rococo churches of Catholic Germany.

The course of the Counter-Reformation opened south Germany to a strong influence of Spanish and Italian culture. Before 1700 Spanish influence disappeared. But the Italian grew stronger than ever before. Until after 1700 all the leading builders of churches in Bavaria and Austria were Italians. As German architects developed their own schools of baroque and rococo, they leaned upon Italian models, though the best of them quickly transformed the style into a unique and independent mode which became one of the wonders of church architecture. In secular building French models became the fashion; in religious building Italian, especially Roman, models remained dominant.

In south-German lands the people's religious interests entered. The time when princes or prince-bishops built noble churches was passing. The only cathedral to be made new in these decades was Salzburg, though baroque modes of restoration were introduced, not without incongruity, into cathedrals like Passau, Freising, and Würzburg. Prince-bishops won more fame by building palaces.

But in the parishes, religious houses, and pilgrimage churches, a wave of church restoration swept over Bavaria and Austria (it was less marked in the Catholic Rhineland, less marked in city parish churches than in the countryside).

2

Bavaria, Franconia, Suabia	Churches built	Foreign architects	German architects
1650–1700 'the lean years'	35	20	15
1700–37	99	11	88
1739–80	131	15	116

According to one estimate of Italian building during the whole eighteenth century, some 2,000 churches, oratories, and palaces were built in the single Italian province of Treviso.[93]

How money was provided for these labours is still not clear to history.

[93] N. Powell, 151; Wittkower, 240.

It is certain that the Catholic south preserved less of the medieval inheritance, in church interiors and exteriors, than the Protestant north; for the Reformation appropriated endowments to other uses, while the Counter-Reformation sought to preserve old endowments intact. The existence of these endowments made possible the wave of church building and restoration which was in some part, though probably not a large part, caused by the destructions of the Thirty Years War, and economic depression in the decades which followed.

Several churches were beautifully restored as pilgrimage churches. These were characteristic of the devotion of the people. They were not parish churches; often lay distant in the woods; had money from the offerings of the numerous pilgrims; provided exceptional and tremendous services for special days or occasions, pulpit occupied by a passionate mission-preacher. Sometimes like Einsiedeln in Switzerland they lay under the protection or patronage of an abbey, and the abbot used his endowments and his knowledge of architects to help the people and the peoples' money to a rich restoration or construction.

The way in which these south-German churches were restored throws light upon the worshipping ideals of the generation.

The church interior must be a unity. It was no longer a place where a congregation could stand passive in the nave while behind a screen priests and choir conducted prayers. There was no separation, no division from the choir, no long chancel which kept the high altar away from the people. This was partly because they wanted the church to show the community of all Christian people; partly because the dramatic, theatrical effect of what went on in popular liturgies made the church floor feel almost like a stage set for divine drama; and partly because the missionary revivalist preacher must be able to feel the people about him and his voice must reach to the furthest corner. All the late baroque and rococo churches have a large dominant space in the centre, with side-chapels between the pillars but with nothing to distract attention from the openness of the centre and its all-embracing quality as focus. The pulpit was given amazing new ornamentation. To emphasize the importance of preaching the word, the way up to the pulpit was often concealed by a door in the pillar or a stair hidden from the congregation so that the preacher appeared without warning. As he stood in the pulpit, he was surrounded with ornaments round the woodwork, and above his head the sounding-board, sometimes in two or three tiers of cherubim. At Irsee monastery the pulpit of 1725 was made in the shape of a ship, with St. Michael as its figure head, and the preacher spoke from the bows, while above the sounding-board the sails were set; the staircase was hidden behind the pillar in such a way as to make the pulpit float in space. Likewise the high altars were magnificent with ornaments or statues (usually with halos), and like the preacher in his pulpit were felt not to be remote. In the Austrian pilgrimage church of Mariazell a silver Christ looked as if he floated in the air above the altar.[94]

In many rococo churches ornaments could emphasize the office of preaching by seeming to give weight to the pulpit. But another kind of rococo pulpit is unique in Christian history: the pulpit so light in seeming construction that it floats, near the angels and saints. The marvellous example of these airy pulpits was made by an unknown woodworker for the little country church of St. Johann in Oppolding, (south Germany), so delicate and fanciful in its scrolls and curves, cherubs and flowering roses, with the divine but quite domestic dove lighting from above the mind of the preacher. The utility of the rostrum, in elevating a speaker so that he and his audience could see and hear, almost disappeared before the desire to show the preacher as lifted by his office towards God. Such light and airy pulpits were imitated, though less simply, in certain churches of Latin America, the church of Popayán in Colombia, or at Jujuy in the Argentine.[95] At Popayán the pulpit was made to look like a chalice, its sounding-board the chalice lid with masks and urns, and the preacher looked to be sustained by little pilasters which rested upon the heads of cherubs. The stair to the pulpit at Jujuy has angels ascending and descending in Jacob's dream, and above the preacher's head a winged angel summoned the congregation with a blast upon his trumpet.

This rejection of remoteness sometimes tamed reality. The crucifix stood upon the altar, or hung from the rood. But in the late baroque it looked at home, horror vanished, the cross was taken up into glory. The aristocratic tranquillity of a pre-revolutionary world was reflected in the mellow colour of church interiors.

Into this wide central space under its dome shone light. The awe of rococo churches was achieved by their use of light. In making a home for worship, builders may decide, like the builders of Chartres cathedral, that they need darkness to set the little rays of light which are all that is given to a fallen world. On this view the sense of awe and devotion cannot be helped by too much openness, by excess of illumination, by glare; but rather by shafts of light coming down upon the worshipper in his privacy. Bernini and the baroque masters had not quite abandoned this doctrine. They still used subtle contrasts of darkness with light, to provide a general

[94] N. Powell, 36.   [95] Brantz, pl.21; Kubler-Soria, pl.92b, 93b.

indirect light which made the church less shadowy than a Gothic church but still fostered a sense of mystery.

Late-baroque and rococo artists wanted light, almost dazzling light. It was the age of the last of the great Venetian painters, Tiepolo, whose genius lay in the use of this transparent light. They still used contrasts to set off the light, especially at the altar which with all its ornaments was usually kept dark and therefore prominent amid the diffusion of light. But he who enters a rococo church can be overwhelmed by brightness, white walls, white light from the windows, filling the open space under the dome. Sometimes they concealed the windows to give mystery to the incoming light. But this light was intended to suggest glory, the wonder of heaven, the vision of the divine. Silver rays pointed down at the altar, shiny surfaces glinted, there was occasional use of tricks, like mirrors in the roof to pick up reflexions. On a sunny day this brightness could startle the worshipper as he entered.

A large central space, and whiteness, and lightness, could be hard, or cold, or glaring. No dark corner remained, and if they left the church so bare they would banish mystery. From this danger they protected themselves by the most extraordinary use of colour and shapes known in the Christian centuries.

Stucco made this possible. Fine and easy to work, it could model reliefs freely, of every shape and size. Though architects used it in Roman times, Gothic builders of the Middle Ages discarded it, and when Raphael started again to fashion ornaments in stucco, he made conscious revival. In baroque art came its full flowering. Bernini and Borromini were masters of the craft: as may be seen in Borromini's decoration of the church of St. John Lateran. The need created Italian schools called *plasticatori* or modellers in stucco. The medium was so light and easy that it afforded infinite variety in ornamenting walls. The decorator in stucco could create on the walls of his church every flower in the encyclopedia, every animal known to the zoologists.

This use of stucco reached its zenith in the rococo churches of south-German Catholicism. They needed shapes, lines, figures, excitement, to contrast with the austere whiteness and prevent it becoming harsh. By multitudinous colour and shape they brought back the sense of mystery which light alone would banish. Pillars and capitals, pulpit and altar, walls and ceilings, were covered in grapes or foliage, lozenges or escutcheons, crowns and mitres, inlay of jewels, fawns and flying creatures, angels garlanded with roses. The material allowed a large object to be supported on very little; and therefore they could deepen the sensation of airiness by making objects look as though they flew without support—angels by a pillar, cherubim peering down at an altar. In Rohr (Austria) the Blessed Virgin flies through the air at the east end, sustained only by an iron prop hidden in a cloud and by a near-by angel. The rococo artists gave the worshippers a sense of the nearness of heaven by seeming to set at nought the laws of gravity.[96]

They followed the Italian school, in not leaving any focal point at which the eye could rest. Ornaments were scattered with what looked like abandon. No strict pattern must be apparent. Gaiety and exuberance were friends of charming disorder. In a magnificent building like the abbey of Ottobeuren, the richest rococo church in Germany (1737 onwards) the white marble space could still be so dominant as to have the feeling of austerity. In a pilgrimage church like the Wieskirche, built far out in the woods by a local abbot and the piety of peasants between 1746 and 1757, blood-red pillars set off such a host of other patterns and colours that the church was later christened 'the dance floor of God.'

These Catholic rococo churches introduced the worshipper to the symbols of Paradise. They were far from the south-Italian missioner lashing with his scourge in the pulpit. For all their exuberance and vitality, they were tranquil. The vileness of the world was put out of sight. The blood-red pillars of Wieskirche were symbolic, for it was the pilgrimage church of Christ's scourging. But the blood-red colour lost its ferocity, as though the cruelty of whips was forgotten before the redemption to which they led. Angels smile, cherubs are childlike in affection, the Blessed Mary shows her loving nature upon her countenance.

In Spain and Portugal bright sunlight made this dazzling use of rococo impracticable. Spanish rococo workers, though influenced by Bernini and Borromini, drew as much from France as from Italy. The art was more aristocratic; less popular in its feeling. The Spanish contribution was the development of the high altar. Ever since Bernini erected a *baldachino* canopy over the altar of St. Peter's in Rome, the *baldachino* became always commoner and in later baroque churches it was almost a rule. The Spanish built up the high altar further, with twisted columns and a mass of gilt and extraordinary shapes. In the Transparente chapel at Toledo cathedral (1721–32) Narciso Tomé[97] played a charming rococo game with the beholder, seeming to rest the heavy and fantastically ornamental super-structure above the altar upon the light figures of two angels kneeling reverently at each side of the altar. Above the altar is an intricate disorder of archangels and clouds, cherubim and divine rays, swooping and

[96] N. Powell, 84   [97] Kubler–Soria, 159 and pl.14b.

mingling; and the eye goes to an alabaster Last Supper, and then to a vision of the Virgin, and still higher to the virtues, and then into the Biblical scenes painted in the frescoes on the vault. Tomé's meaning could not be mistaken. He sought to show the Lord's Supper as the way to the open gates of heaven far above; and all the company of heaven comes down to rejoice in the sacrament of the altar.

Though later Catholic writers condemned these rococo altars, part altar and part reredos, as luxurious clutter hiding the simplicity of an altar, suitable for museums or art galleries but not churches, they remain an achievement of Christian architecture. The high altar in San Martin Pinario at Santiago de Compostella (1733), the novitiate altar at St. Luis in Seville (1730), were but two outstanding representatives of a type to be found in many places in Spain and Portugal and Latin America. They were art for the people's heart as well as for the connoisseur's sensibility.

Music

The Counter-Reformation, puritanical in its attitude to art, demanded simplicity in music. This attitude was canonized. Church music must follow the simplicity of plainsong. Palestrina, who was in charge of the papal chapel during the later Counter-Reformation, showed how this simplicity could be made beautiful and not monotonous by the colouring of its tone and its purity. For Palestrina's successors this form of church music was the received tradition. Anyone who introduced variety or modern harmonies must overcome the feeling that he departed from the authentic custom of the Catholic Church, and was usually accused of introducing secularity where it was unfitting.

Throughout the seventeenth and eighteenth centuries Catholic music made inroads upon this tradition dominated by Palestrina. But it remained at the base of Catholic church music. An English visitor to Flanders in 1772, Dr Burney, noticed how the singing of the people, at their work or in the streets, carried the hint of the plain chant, because this was the music on which they were nourished at church. In south Germany and Austria many choirs would only allow this type of music at the penitential seasons of Advent and Lent. In Italy visitors commented on the musical taste of peasants. The reason was believed to be, that they heard so much plainsong performed, however ill, that they had a yardstick by which to judge more elaborate musical performances. 'It seems', wrote that excellent judge Dr Burney as he studied the music of Vienna, 'as if the national music of a country was good or bad, in proportion to that of its church services,

which may account for the taste of the common people of Italy.' Town
churches provided the equivalent of free concerts, some of high quality,
two or three times a week (depending on the incidence of saints' days). At
Bologna (24 August 1770) an itinerant band stopped under the window of
Burney's lodging to greet the visitor with a serenade. 'Twas the best I had
heard here. However the music of the churches here, which the common
people hear every day, is a good school for them and enables them all to
sing with taste and expression of the right sort.' Elsewhere he heard a
couple of peasants who said to each other in the middle of a mass, 'This
music is execrable' and decided to leave. Dr Burney approved their
discrimination. At one of the Naples churches where choir schools took
turns to sing, members of the congregation hastily left when they discovered that on that day it was the turn of an ill-favoured school.[98]

   For Palestrina's followers lived in a world of musical revolution, the
flowering of European music which led to Bach and Handel and Haydn.
Until 1600 church music was the guide to music outside church. After
1600 church music looked conservative while music outside church was
free to experiment; and therefore music played at concerts or operas
affected taste and so changed the atmosphere of music at mass and other
services of the church. All through the seventeenth century, though more
quickly during its second half, the new methods and variety began to
appear in church—anthems, motets, Passion narratives, *Magnificat*, *Te
Deum*, even the mass. Choirs were moved away from the altar into
galleries or organ lofts.

   Composers wrote for two or four (on a few grand occasions even
twelve) choirs, carrying the idea of antiphonal singing to its limit and
producing sounds which might be rich and luxuriant but could also be
over-complex manoeuvres. The oratorio, introduced by St. Philip Neri
in the sixteenth century, and really a concert of music using sacred words
and performed in church, grew ever more common and popular, until
after 1700 it became one of the frequent uses of any Italian city church
with a famous choir.

   Conservatives, and sometimes men who were not conservative but
cared about religious worship, fought a losing battle against these innovations. They disliked the use of churches as concert halls; offered a
burlesque derivation of the word oratorio—'oratorio a non orando' ('a
performance of prayerful music is so-called because no one prays');
declared that the new music was profane or theatrical, or operatic, or even
sensual; used the many bombastic efforts by second-rate composers to

   [98] Burney, *Journal*, 92 and 165; Scholes, *The Great Dr. Burney*, 1.163.

show how empty and ridiculous was the novelty; and persuaded Popes and synods to stop the trend by authority. As early as 1643[99] Pope Urban VIII condemned a state of affairs when the mass was for music instead of music for the mass. A succession of decrees condemned the singing of words in church that were not the words of the liturgy or the Bible—and still the composers found lovely emotional moments in the lives of the saints, which they used increasingly. A Roman Congregation (1665) tried to ban solos in church, a provincial council at Avignon (1725) tried to ban the singing of carols in church at Christmas, Pope Benedict XIV (1742) even recalled the Catholic Church to the rules of the Council of Trent.

The people—especially the people of Italy—were too strong for authority. They wanted to hear in church the kind of music that they learnt to love, their ears were no longer attuned to the strictness and austerity of a Palestrina. And the composers no longer wrote music exclusively for performance in church. Even the lesser men, and beginners, might be in the predicament that they could not make a living in church alone. Young Haydn kept himself from starving in Vienna by playing first violin at the 8 o'clock mass in the chapel of the Brothers of Mercy; then going to a nobleman's chapel at 10 o'clock to play the organ; then hurrying to sing in the cathedral choir at 11—and on weekdays he gave piano lessons and tried to sell sonatas. Not the church fees but one of the sonatas enabled him to buy a decent suit of clothes. In Italy money began to be in opera. Bernardo Pasquini who was organist at Santa Maria Maggiore in Rome till his death in 1710 was also pianist at the Capranica theatre. When the composer wrote both for opera and for church, he might divide himself and have two different styles. Or he might, like Pergolesi (1710–36) at Naples freely allow an operatic style into church and plan solos and melodies and runs and repeats. Even if he were not whole-hearted like Pergolesi, he would be a rare composer who did not allow the need of one group of clients to affect the need of another group of clients. And by the second quarter of the eighteenth century opera brought him more reward than mass.

Good judges of that age blamed this trend for a decline in Italian church music. Opera hired lovely voices, churches hired what was left. Even the music of the Sistine chapel was criticized because its choir, never paid to excess, could no longer attract the best singers. Church choirs improved themselves on special occasions—the patron saint's day, the greater festivals—by hiring virtuosi as soloists. Sometimes a church was very lucky. The violinist Tartini fled from Padua because authority dis-

[99] For the legal provisions, Pons, Droit ecclésiastique et musique sacrée, vol.3.

approved his marriage, and took shelter in a monastery at Assisi; and then visitors started to swell the congregation of the monks' chapel when they heard such otherworldly sweet sounds which came so mysteriously from behind a curtain. When he returned to Padua the church was lucky to keep him against every sort of offer from all over Europe, because his wife was delicate and preferred Padua. But churches could not easily keep such star performers, especially if they were singers. We have another Italian instance in a nun of Milan who being a nun was not open to the musical market. At the convent of St. Mary Magdalene (1770) she sang with a voice of such rare sweetness that men travelled to hear her sing solo motets.[100] The Counter-Reformation would have had qualms allowing a nun thus to sing solo before visitors; though this nun was hardly before the visitors, because she was kept invisible to her audience.

In Palestrina's day the members of the choir must be ecclesiastics. Women were forbidden and boys' voices less commonly used. The Sistine choir had thirty-two voices (eight soprano, eight alto, eight tenor, eight bass) and its musical college kept understudies so that the number was never less than thirty-two. But this was large for a choir. St. Stephen's cathedral at Vienna in the middle of the eighteenth century had only six boys and nine men, though with ten members of a strong orchestra in addition to the organist and the sub-cantor (instruments were banished during Lent).[101] St. Anthony at Padua, a famous pilgrimage church, had sixteen voices, but accompanied by four organs, eight violins, four violas, four violoncellos, four double basses, and four wind instruments. One of the string players was for a time the most famous violinist in Europe, Giuseppe Tartini (died 1770), himself an eminent composer. Two choirs of four voices each was not uncommon for a lesser Italian church. Always the choirmaster could be seen beating time, usually from the organ loft.

Because women were not permitted, and boys not always up to their task, *castrati* became indispensable to Italian music. The full quality and range of their voices, the ability of the experienced male singer to en-compass complex vocal effects, became necessary to Italian opera during the seventeenth century and unquestionably contributed to the ecstasies with which it was received by the connoisseurs of Europe. During the eighteenth century *castrati* singers like Farinelli won the highest reputation and wealth. To castrate small boys was illegal, and the operation did not ensure that the adult *castrati* would be able to sing with purity. The story went that the *castrati* suffered an accident in childhood. But Italy was so peopled with musical *castrati* that no one believed the legend. The choir

[100] Burney, *Journal*, 54.   [101] Hughes, *Haydn*, 11.

of St. Anthony at Padua, sixteen strong, had eight *castrati*. Florence cathedral had a choir of eight, of whom three were *castrati*. When Venice fell to the Revolution in 1797 the choir of St. Mark's still had twelve *castrati* in a choir of twenty-four persons. Saint Onofrio, a choir school with ninety boys at Naples, had among them sixteen *castrati* who needed to sleep in a specially warm dormitory. When enquirers asked where such illegal operations were performed, every city denied knowledge and guessed at its neighbour. Dr Burney, who pursued their investigation, found reliable evidence that some of the Naples boys came from Lecce[102] in Apulia. This was probable, for the South was desperately poor, and parents who allowed their boy to be made a eunuch could probably ensure him afterwards a comfortable existence in material terms, and the chance of fame and fortune.

The moral theologians weighed the moral doubt and were not agreed. Those who reproved the practice argued thus; the Church condemned a literal interpretation of the text 'those who make themselves eunuchs for the sake of the kingdom of heaven', and what is immoral if done for the sake of the soul, must be more immoral if done for the sake of stipend and career; further, that preservation of a beautiful voice is not so important to a man as to justify such interference with nature; further, the existence of *castrati* makes church services sound theatrical. To the contrary, those who allowed the practice (provided that the boy was willing and there was no danger to life), argued thus: (1) the divine praises are sung in church more purely, and must therefore draw men's souls towards God, (2) the preservation of a good voice is far from trivial if its possessor escapes poverty and wins comfort and distinction—the operation is no different from any other surgical operation which helps a man to enjoy life, and (3) because the Church commonly uses *castrati* in choir and what the Church tolerates widely cannot be immoral. Even St. Alfonso Liguori, though he preferred the strict opinion, would not wholly condemn when sensible men held the contrary. When Pope Benedict XIV was preparing a papal bull on music, he came under pressure to include a total condemnation. He was against *castrati*, but refused to put a ban into his bill. He understood the limits of power in his office.[103]

Some 'traders' even invested money—adopted orphan children, had them castrated, educated them, and in return received part of their pay while minors.

[102] Burney, *Journal*, 163; confirmed by the research of Häbock.
[103] Liguori, *Theologia Moralis*, lib.iv, no.374, with authorities there cited; Benedict XIV, *de synodo dioecesana*, xi.7.1, col.1283.

The most famous of all *castrati*, and most successful because he became favourite of a King of Spain and a kind of prime minister, was Farinelli, whose real name was Carlo Broschi, and who was born (1705) at Andria near Bari, and probably castrated in Naples at the age of nine or ten. His father was no poor man, but a prosperous musician. A count of other famous Italian *castrati* does not make the South their common home. Some of the best —B.Ferri from Perugia, F. A. Pistocchi from Palermo, P. F. Tosi from Bologna—were like Farinelli sons of musicians, Tosi the son of the cathedral organist. Several of the most celebrated were natives of Bologna or Lombardy where musical opportunity was plentiful. But Caffarelli was the son of a poor workman of Bitonto and sang so beautifully in a church choir that a musician who heard him persuaded his father to send him to a surgeon at Norcia and then paid for his education and training under N. Porpora at Naples. Porpora was the first of all international singing masters.

An extraordinary change in moral sensitivity or taste passed over Europe in the sixty years after 1770. Dr Burney, a most humane man, showed no sense of repugnance. Sixty years later a *castrato* could not safely sing before an English audience, and when Mendelssohn heard one of the last of the famous *castrati* he was filled with a sense of loathing. But the change was partly of fashion in music. The *castrati* of 1820 lived into a world where the orchestra had risen in importance compared with the solo voice. The bell-like purity of the male soloist fitted the Italian tradition of the earlier eighteenth century, where instruments were always subordinate to voices. The fashion of opera was now different, Mozart wrote a big part for a *castrato* in the opera *Idomeneo* (1781). When he came to *Die Entführung aus dem Serail* (1782) where the principal male singer is a eunuch from the Turkish harem, he gave him a deep bass voice.

Italy was the home of European music and the fount of Catholic music. The Pope and other heads of the little states encouraged court music, like the numerous little German courts of the Empire. But in Italy this was not music only for the aristocrat, not only for the middle class. Church music was part of the way of life for the people. In Florence clubs of artisans rose early each Sunday morning, dressed in white, and under the name of *laudisti* (singers of praise) moved from church to church, singing a psalm outside the portals. Dr Burney attended at Figline, 20 miles from Florence, the feast of the patron saint, and found himself among 20,000 people. After mass, where he found the music 'pretty', he attended the 'games', an acting of the story of David and Goliath, for which costumes were borrowed from theatres for miles round, and 1,500 peasants divided into two armies to play Philistines and Israelites, and marched to old instruments like cymbal and systrum, and carried out a sham battle which they had rehearsed for three months; and when David cut off Goliath's head a stream of blood poured out and many spectators shrieked with horror; and in the evening Dr Burney went to church again and heard the story of David and Goliath sung as an oratorio, until the feast ended with fireworks. Wherever he went in Italian churches he stood among crowds to listen, and realized that these crowds were habitual when three times a fine cambric handkerchief was picked from his pocket during services, the last time though the pocket was carefully buttoned.[104]

Italians dominated south-German music until well into the eighteenth century. Between 1729 and 1757 another Italian, the younger Scarlatti, controlled the music of the Spanish court. The first eminent Austrian musician at the imperial court, Johann Joseph Fux (died 1741) was a composer in the austere tradition of Palestrina. In Germany, France, and the Netherlands, and to some extent in Spain and Portugal, church music was more bourgeois in its appeal, and therefore under less temptation to introduce excitements and flourishes derived from Italian opera. Dr Burney was not impressed with the music of the Catholic Netherlands, decided that Antwerp violinists were mere scrapers and the high mass there, for all its elaborate ceremony and gorgeous vestments, a model of dreariness. In parts of Austria and Tyrol, and in Bohemia, the people's music was celebrated. Burney met a group of 'gypsies' near Ips in Austria on pilgrimage to a hill shrine of the Virgin, and heard them singing plainsong chants in unison as they walked. On Sunday morning in Vienna he was delayed by a chanting procession 2 to 3 miles long. In a Bohemian village he found a schoolmaster who had four clavichords in his room to teach the children, and was told that the farm labourers, after learning music at school, liked to sing in the parish choir as their recreation. The village schoolmaster was almost always the choirmaster. At the little walled town of Hainburg in Austria the schoolmaster taught seventy children, paying two assistants from his salary, conducted the choir, was sacristan, guarded the church registers, kept the church clock in repair, and rang the church bells as a protection against thunderstorms. His church had a fine organ, accompanied by two violins. On feast days he introduced 'cello, double bass, horns, trumpets, and drums.'[105]

The village choir of Spain was not unlike the church band in Protestant England. In one village[106] the singers included three parish clerks, a bass

---

[104] Burney, *Journal*, 103, 174–5.   [105] Hughes, *Haydn*, 6–7.   [106] Isla, 2.72–4.

who was the parish carter, a boy treble who had been castrated to qualify him for a more famous choir; they sang in a low balustraded gallery over the west door, to the accompaniment of pipes. The psalms were sung to plainchant.

Musical masses divided into two types: *Missa brevis* ('short mass') and *Missa solemnis* ('solemn mass'). This division corresponded in the musical sphere to the liturgical distinction between low mass and high mass. But it became the more necessary for musical reasons. As musicians poured their art into liturgy, mass became intolerably long for normal days or occasions, so that full musical mass or *Missa solemnis* could only be performed on one or two special feasts of the year. The *Missa brevis* became mass for ordinary days, and usually contained only *Kyrie Eleison* and the *Gloria* set to music, though in south Germany it might mean a short and plain version of all the musical portions of the mass. Some of the solemn masses were so long that they could hardly make part of a liturgy. Johann Sebastian Bach, though a Protestant, hoped that the longest of his masses might be used in Catholic liturgy. If that had happened, the sacrament would have been lost in a tremendous musical experience. No Catholic church is known to have used it in the liturgy.

In the Lutheran north musical genius began to change the conditions of Catholic music and worship. Bach and Handel, writing for Protestant churches, learnt from the flourishing tradition of Catholic music. But they were not restricted by decrees of popes and synods, or by the feeling among heirs of the Counter-Reformation that musical innovation was somehow unCatholic or by the wishes of an Italian working population for music which they could enjoy. They had freedom to develop a tradition to its height. The flowering of Protestant church music during the first half of the eighteenth century brought to bear upon Munich and Vienna a new kind of influence. Slowly the Italian dominance of Catholic church music faded in northern lands before new names and a different art, Haydn, later Beethoven and Schubert.

Compared with the tradition of Palestrina or even Fux, this new church music was more 'secular' in spirit. For most of these composers church music was the lesser part of their composition. Within a mass by Haydn might be found solos which, if removed from a church, were suitable in concert hall or on stage. The more worldly Mozart, obliged to set masses by employment at the court of the Archbishop of Salzburg, put a melody for the *Kyrie* into a C major mass of 1779, and eleven years later used the same melody as a beautiful aria of the soprano Fiordiligi in the comic opera *Così fan tutte*. His setting of the *Agnus Dei* in the same mass reappeared seven years later in one of the songs in *Figaro*.[107]

The Palestrina tradition at last was broken. The distinction between two kinds of music, one suitable in church and the other outside church, was blurred. The old guide-lines were gone. The new Austrian composers were as free as Bach or Handel to experiment. And part of their experiment was to recapture the old structure of counterpoint for other uses.

The world of Catholic music was broadened. The new composers, though at times so 'secular' in the feeling of their music, were often deeply Catholic individuals. Haydn made a miserable marriage and was unfaithful to his wife. But he would not begin the day's composition without kneeling in prayer to God and the Blessed Virgin, and if inspiration failed was sure that his sins had forfeited the grace of God. He started his manuscripts with the words 'In God's name' and ended them with 'God be praised'. If in the midst of a composition he stuck, he would walk up and down telling his rosary until a new idea came. Yet even Haydn underestimated his church music by the side of his worldly music. When he was told that his *Stabat Mater* was successful in Paris, he said absurdly, 'The Parisians have heard nothing yet; if they could only hear my operetta *L'isola disabitata* . . .' He produced eighty operas in fifteen years and would have been astounded to find posterity hardly knowing that he wrote opera.

The religious world of Haydn and Mozart had this characteristic of the Catholic eighteenth century, that it was a world of happy religion. Haydn's *Creation* (1796–8) corresponded in the Catholic sphere to Addison's *The Spacious Firmament* in the Protestant sphere. Though the Protestant wrote a brief lyric and the Catholic a masterpiece; all God's world rejoiced in its Maker. 'I was never so devout as when I was at work on *The Creation*,' Haydn said. 'I fell on my knees every day and begged God to give me strength to finish.' At one of the last Viennese performances, part of which he was well enough to attend (1808), the audience started to applaud the C major *And there was light*; and the old man lifted trembling hands and could be heard saying 'Not from me—it's all from above.' It was cheerful religion. Sometimes Haydn's masses were attacked as too gay for religious music; and when he heard the criticism he said that his heart leapt for joy at the thought of God and he could not help his music doing the same. In such writing, words like *Lord have mercy* were sung to music which in losing all the quality of lament seemed to lose most of the quality of penitence. The *Benedictus qui venit* in the so-called Mariazell mass of 1782 is a beautiful melody, but Haydn lifted it straight from an aria in one of his

[107] Wienandt, 217; Blom, *Mozart*, 171; *Musical Times*, 5.68 and 108.

operas.[108] Like rococo architects, these were not men of an otherworldly religion, or (if they were) the other world was close to this world and penetrated all its being. This was not just the mood of musicians. Mozart's first employer, the Archbishop of Salzburg, demanded jubilant and even dashing services at high festivals.

Mozart was an Austrian Catholic, but was never at ease with the human race, resented the Archbishop of Salzburg, and in the last years of his short life (1756–91) was attracted to the freemasonry which Popes condemned. He only wrote three works of church music after he left the archbishop's service. But despite the restlessness and sometimes misery of his personal lot, his musical genius lay in all that was blithe and bright and gay. The works most Catholic in feeling were the series of 'short masses' which made a form of chamber music for churches. Mozart's church music touched heights, not because he was profoundly religious, but because he possessed genius for purity of sound, so that it was religious neither because it was majestic, nor because it was mystical, but because it rang with humanity in a mood of exhilaration. The publican is not very penitent, the burning bush does not affright, the thunder of Mount Sinai is muted, awe is so confident that sometimes it approaches irreverence, but never did the Lord's friends so happily and so chastely enjoy the wedding feast at Cana. It is an epitome of one strand in the religion of the eighteenth century.

When Mozart was hired by a stranger to write a *Requiem* he was already dying, probably of uraemia, and imported into the work a new feverish quality. He failed to finish, and we can never know how much was his and how much was due to the composer who afterwards completed. Certainly the harmony and happiness of music had not deserted him in these last months; and though into it came nobility and solemnity and searching of the heart, its tone was unlike that of a requiem which the Church expected. The hope of immortality was closer to the hopes of mortality than Catholic faith taught. But the prayer for the dead from this *Requiem* (*Let light perpetual shine*) was sung at Haydn's funeral.

Conclusion

Decades before Catholic Europe was conscious of an Enlightenment, the habits of popular religion were affected. The mingling of magic with the religion of the common man was as evident as in the Middle Ages. This mingling was fostered by materialistic moments in the cult of saints, by

[108] Hughes, *Haydn*, 17, 58, 100 ff., 125 ff., 193.

certain forms of faith-healing, by the use of holy objects like relics or Biblical texts in the manner of charms, by the more superstitious goals of pilgrimage and the crudities of a mental haze about indulgences.

Witches were less persecuted; Jews less uncomfortable, but still they were not comfortable and were not allowed at all into Spain or Portugal or southern Italy; good Catholics were soon to ward off storms with lightning conductors as well as bells, in places instead of bells; pious Catholics were to seek scientific means of predicting earthquakes, in parts of Italy medicine advanced as fast as anywhere in Europe; saints were beloved, but historians criticized their lives and documents, and governors who wanted workmen to work attacked the number of their days with success; sanctuaries were sacred through the century, but in the end sanctity was all that was left of their former power, until Catholic countries hardly differed from Protestant; public opinion moved against the beggar and therefore the mendicant, but haphazardly, and much more in towns than in the countryside; educated opinion grew ever more confident in assailing the *childish* (as they supposed) in cults, dramas, processions, cribs; and used the power of local governments to expel whatever was not (as they supposed) adult and edifying.

The congregation became, almost imperceptibly but still surely, weightier in the structure of worship; in the constant endeavour of parish priests to stop brotherhoods from being rivals to parish churches, in sporadic efforts to make the people understand by the use of readings in the vernacular; or in the rare encouragement of Bible-reading by laymen; or in the various attempts to revive the receiving of communion at its 'proper' place in the liturgy, or in Germany by the use of hymns which, though hardly ever taken from Protestant hymnbooks, were nevertheless sung in the vernacular and almost integrated into the liturgy; or in the 'popularizing' of some forms of church music.

These slow changes were hardly visible even to informed contemporaries. But they made a turning-point towards the later history of the Church. None of them was due at first impetus to what a later age agreed to call Enlightenment.

2

THE CLERGY

Numbers of clergy

THE number of clergy was great. Southern Italy without Sicily had in 1740 between 4,000,000 and 5,000,000 people, 50,000 secular priests, and 31,000 monks or friars or regular canons. The average, if the religious orders are omitted, was one priest to less than 100 people. (If the monasteries were included, and the erroneous assumption made that all monks were priests, it would have been one priest to about sixty people.) A population of 30,000 might be served by 400 priests, not including monks. In 1762 the diocese of St. Agatha of the Goths, with 30,000 people, had thirteen monasteries all claiming some form of exemption from the bishop; a cathedral and another large collegiate church, a total of sixty-six priests, each claiming more moderate forms of exemption. And although the parishes looked to be over-staffed—Airola had eighty priests and 6,000 people—many of the priests were chaplains living on an endowment to say mass, and had no pastoral duties. For Imola in the north we have the 1797 census of people and the 1765 list of clergy—more than thirty years apart but they give a comparison. The diocese had 128 parishes with 94,000 people—that is, an average parish had 736 parishioners. To serve these 128 parishes were between 200 and 250 clergy—that is, in modern anachronistic terms, each parish of 736 parishioners had both a vicar and a curate. But no one must think that the 250 parish priests were all the clergymen in the diocese. The total number of clergy in 1765 was 979 priests—and if we deduct our 250 parish clergy that leaves 729 non-parochial clergy. Of course we must count the bishop and his staff; and the cathedral chapter, and another collegiate chapter at Lugo, so that altogether the diocese had fifty-two canons; but when we have subtracted everyone we can think of, and remember that hardly anyone retired (so some were ill or senile), we are still left with more than 600 clergymen not canons, not serving parishes, and not on the bishop's staff; nearly three times the number of clergy engaged in the parishes.[1]

These were the numbers of secular clergy. In addition the diocese

---

[1] Berthe 2.50; Leflon, *Pie VII*, 1.205.

contained 246 monks or friars in twenty-five houses. So that, if we assume (a very erroneous assumption) that all monks and friars were in minor orders or higher, we should have in Imola diocese one clergyman to every seventy-five parishioners.

The Venice census of 1766–7 showed that the state, on rough calculations, had not less than one priest or cleric or monk or nun to every 133 laymen.

The diocese of Capaccio in 1734 had one cleric (including clerks in minor orders) to hardly more than fifty people—that is, the clergy numbered about 2 per cent of the population.

Naturally large numbers in a diocese reflected larger numbers in certain parishes. Mayorga in Spain had 500 families, seven parishes, twenty-four priests, a Franciscan friary with seventeen friars, a Dominican friary with four; and a second well-endowed Dominican house.

The diocese of Pamplona in northern Spain had 923 parishes. In 1801 these parishes were looked after by 850 priests, nearly always one priest to each parish; but a few priests looked after two or even three parishes, in an odd case a priest looked after four parishes, and in another case one priest looked after five parishes.[2]

Where two or more parishes were held in plurality, either because priests were few or because endowments were short, priests met the rule that they might celebrate only one mass in a day, except on Christmas Day when they might celebrate three times. During this epoch men accepted that where two parishes were too far apart for a single mass the priest might lawfully celebrate twice provided no assistant was available. This rule was not a mere matter of form. A bishop banned a priest from celebrating twice because he said that other priests were available; and when the parish priest appealed to Rome, the bishop won.[3] These cases were very rare, and in remote hills parish priests disregarded the old rule.

The larger number of clergy lived in towns. The countryside might be understaffed. But if villages were not too remote, small hamlets had their parish church and priest. When the earthquake of 1703 devastated the hill country near Spoleto in central Italy, a commission to enquire and assist went out from Rome and reported on casualties and destruction of churches. Table 3 shows most of the villages in the county of Cascia:

[2] Cecchetti, 1.164–5, 215–16; Sarrailh, 646; *Hispania Sacra*, 26 (1973), 365.
[3] Benedict XIV, *de synodo*, vi.8.3, col. 997.

3

	Survivors	Dead	Churches destroyed	Priests
Meltignano	261	121	3	1 died
Colle di S. Stefano	75	22	1	1 died
S. Trinità Castello	38	3	1	1 died
Civita Castello	28	13	1	1 survived
Trevi	59	20	1	1 survived
Collemarino	44	20	1	1 survived
Manigi	73	15	1	1 survived
Castel S. Giovanni	107	17	3	1 survived
Fogliano	323	17	3	
Col Forcella	77	none	2	1 survived

In the Cascia district a population of under 6,000 had thirty-seven
curates alive or (three) dead, which makes one curate to just over 154
people. That was not unreasonable compared with the towns. But the
enquiry showed how two hamlets each with forty-one souls had their own
churches and own curates; and one village of 120 inhabitants had three
churches, though still only one curate. The report had a pathetic line:

Villa Reganelli   Survivors 37; dead 27; church fallen; curate fled.[4]

Spanish country parishes had rather more people to each priest. The
Spanish census of 1787 showed 15,000 priests caring for 17,000 parishes.
In Estremadura ten years later each parish priest had about 1,000 par-
ishioners.[5]

A bishop's report from the little south-Italian diocese of Ugento at about
the same period shows that the parish of Salve, with 1,346 souls, had
fourteen churches or chapels; that of Miggiano, with 370 souls, had eight
churches or chapels.[6]

The number of clergy still rose, though slowly, during the last decades of
the century. But this did not apply to mountain areas. Roads were bad or
did not exist, villages were at or below the level of subsistence and could
not maintain a church, in places a priest could not, or could hardly, live.
Mountainous areas show a decline in the number of clergy so marked that
it must be due to emigration in search of a livelihood. The very remote

[4] Chracas, *Racconto istorico de' terremoti* (Rome, 1704), 171, printing the commission of
enquiry.
[5] Sarrailh, 646–7; A. R. M. Carr, *Spain*, 47 n.
[6] S. Palese, 'Per la storia religiosa della diocesi di Ugento agli inizi del Settecento' in *Studi
di storia pugliese in onore di Giuseppe Chiarelli*, 4 (1976), 326.

vicariate of Castelnuovo, in the mountainous country north of Lucca, had in 1684 one secular priest for every thirty-five people, and in 1755 one priest to every eighty-three people.[7] This fall had not only economic cause, or the economic reasons were affected by politics. During the wars of the first half of the century many columns of troops passed that way. Many remote villages had no priest except a traveller, or sometimes a priest only in summer when the roads were passable. In the Tuscan hills was a village of twenty-three families who said goodbye to their priest in the autumn and had neither service nor sacrament until they greeted him again in the spring.

Italian peasants often had no money to give. If a priest lived in a village, they did not give him money, but chickens, or fish, or cakes, or pastry, or even bits of linen cloth. The *offerings* in money were almost nil. The country priest must live either on the endowment of a benefice, or be paid by a monastery; and neither of these was frequent in the country. In the hills of Calabria or central-southern Italy villagers might not see a priest for weeks at a time, unless a monastery was near, or a travelling missionary passed, or a bishop sent out an itinerant confessor to celebrate sacraments.

But in town, endowment was plentiful, and accounted for the numbers of town clergy; the endowment of a chantry priest, to say mass for the dead soul. A well-to-do person made provision by will for regular liturgies to be celebrated for the peace of his soul. A majority of non-monastic priests were supported by these private endowments. Some of them also had parish responsibility. But many had no pastoral care; and some regarded it as a useful stipend early in the day, to be followed by respectable leisure or by secular work and wages.

He who examines little Italian towns, about 1750 or 1760, realizes what an extraordinary difference was made between northern Europe and southern Europe by the transfer of endowments. Reformation and Counter-Reformation reformed the Church. But the north suppressed monasteries and chapters and chantries and transferred their money. The south religiously preserved the endowments. And by the eighteenth century the result was a different world of social life. The life of an Italian country-town had an *ecclesiastical* atmosphere—cassocks everywhere, processions in streets, bells frequent, crowds at services, priests not highly respected for their priesthood (too numerous for that) but only for other, and more personal, reasons. No child could escape the stamp of liturgical experience. It was part of the social order; at times it was the social order; at times it was too much of a social order.

[7] *R.S.C.I.* xxix (1975), 405.

The second big difference between north Europe and south lay in the absence or presence of monasteries. Radical north abolished monks and let clergy marry. Conservative south did neither. Monks, like clergy, were too numerous to be respected universally. But in Spain and Italy the ideals of monasticism remained magnetic. This affected parish life of the eighteenth century. Not many of the best clergymen went into parishes. The prestige of the monastic spirit—a prestige so different from its notoriety in England early in the reign of King Henry VIII—was a sign of ideals triumphant in the Counter-Reformation. In addition, a clergyman who must be celibate whether or not he was a monk, naturally and for reasons of family life looked towards a community instead of an isolated post. The posts which beckoned good men, if they felt no vocation to be monks, were canonries, not parishes; especially not country parishes— and most of the people lived in country parishes.

The Cardinal Protector of Ireland asked a physician from Dublin whether there were too many priests; and received the answer that there were not too many, but too many who should never have been ordained.[8] If the governors of states worried about the quantity of clergy, the governors of the Church worried about their quality. In the middle of the century Pope Benedict XIV uttered a sad cry: 'How many dioceses have no seminary! How many seminaries have not sufficient staff of teachers! How many young men have to be sent home from the course at just the time when they most need pastoral care! How few are the dioceses which only ordain men who have been trained in seminaries!'[9]

Ordination was the bishop's worst problem. Clergy were many, good clergy for parishes were fewer. How to distinguish the young man with a vocation? How to refuse an ordinand backed by powerful patrons? How to know whether letters of recommendation from a parish priest were written under threat from a dagger? How to reject a good man because the number of priests had reached the limit which government permitted in that district? How to check that the candidate who came to the examination was the ordinand and not a hired passer of examinations? Except for the vow of celibacy, a young man found advantage in ordination— tax exemptions, a stipend low but higher than he could otherwise command, certain legal privileges. The number of ordained men rose slowly and relentlessly. In the little southern diocese of Capaccio the number of clerics of all sorts rose sharply during the century before 1734; and even the number of priests increased steadily.[10] By Italian averages

---

[8] Fenning (1975), 421.   [9] *De synodo* xi.2.6, col. 1251, shortened.
[10] De Rosa, *Vescovi*, 105 and 127.

that diocese had no excess of clergy even at the later date, one to every 500 people (excluding monks who were clerics), and of priests hardly more than one per 1,000.

Everyone admitted that priests were too many. Sometimes government tried to set limits. From 1770 the government of Naples prohibited ordinations where one priest already served 100 people, or from any family where two brothers or uncles of the candidate were already priests, or from any family which could not provide all the other brothers with an inheritance equal to the amount which the ordinand must put down before his ordination. Such a rule was clumsy, for it excluded excellent future priests as well as dim wits, and was easily evaded. When the government of Tuscany passed a law to limit ordinations in monasteries, the abbot quietly transferred the ordinand-monk for a time to another house of his order[11] where he could be ordained. Bishops sometimes set limits by demanding that their ordinands possess a small private income, like 40 *scudi* a year.[12] But this was not far from simony.

In some dioceses appeared the extraordinary phenomenon of vacant parishes. Candidates were many, good candidates few. An occasional ruthless bishop refused to lower his standard, or raised the qualifications needed before he would ordain, or renounced ungodly compromise with a patron. This fitted the policy of reform canonized by the Council of Trent. Results seldom fulfilled a bishop's hopes. Bishop Zuccari of Capaccio followed this plan and by 1789 had many parishes vacant and looked after by acting curates of a lower standard than he might otherwise prefer; which was not at all in accordance with the reforms of Trent.[13] Bishops who raised the standard of examination before they would accept candidates for ordination, became extremely unpopular, not only with the clergy, and were likely to be accused of being rigid, or illegal, or innovating.

Private Masses

The mass-priest was not a burden to himself though he and his colleagues composed a clerical proletariat. But the number of endowed masses could burden a parish or a religious order. Bequests for masses for the departed grew with will after will, until priests could hardly say enough and far too many priests were needed, too many for the good of either Church or society. This was an enigma which only the State, in the end only revolu-

---

[11] De Potter, *Ricci*, 2.10.
[12] e.g. Sabina Diocesan Synod (1736), 54; but many other such provisions.
[13] De Rosa, *Vescovi*, 147–8.

tion, could solve. Sensible bishops tried to reduce the load. They sought to amalgamate trust funds and thereby to reduce the numbers of masses that needed to be said. Rome was always keenly conscious of its duty to maintain the intention of donors in old endowments and at first rejected schemes of this sort. Early in the eighteenth century Pope after Pope allowed the heads of religious orders to reduce the burden of ancient masses upon the members of their orders, at discretion. Then Pope Benedict XIII allowed the same discretion to all bishops who were present at the Roman Council of 1725. His successor Clement XII gave a direct power to the Archbishop of Bologna to lessen the number of masses as he thought fit. Everyone felt discomfort at these proceedings while they confessed them to be necessary. They might offend the sacred intentions of those who left money, and it was not quite certain that they might not affect the lot of souls in purgatory for whom the masses were offered. The Archbishop of Bologna said that of the permission given him by the Pope he made only a very sparing use.[14]

The secretary of the Venetian Council of State wrote (1764) a memorandum on private masses,[15] explaining that the decline from a single parochial mass to numerous masses at side-altars was a corruption of the Middle Ages; that the continually growing number of endowments for private masses hurt the State, that there were more masses to be celebrated than priests to celebrate, and so money was sent illegally abroad to satisfy the trust; that the Dominican friary of St. John and St. Paul (1743) failed to say 16,400 masses which it was endowed to say, and the Cistercians of Our Lady of Orto failed to say 14,300 masses during the following year.

A little country church, or rather its priest, suffered under this burden. The dominance of the high altar was diminished because parishioners came in at any morning time on a Sunday and heard mass in small groups at one of the side-altars. Where mass-endowment was plentiful, and the priest had no assistant in deep country, he could do hardly anything else with his time but celebrate sacraments and say his breviary if—no small if —he was faithful to the trust deeds and to the rules of the Church about priests.

Exemption

One advantage of the clergy, which encouraged the number of ordinations, was exempt or charitable status. According to old laws, still in force in

---

[14] Benedict XIV, *de synodo*, v. 10, cols. 964–6.
[15] Cecchetti, 1.96 ff.; numbers of endowed masses in certain parishes of diocese of Ugento (Apulia) by Palese, in *Studi di storia pugliese in onore di Giuseppe Chiarelli* 4 (1976), 327.

Catholic states with whatever modifications, the clergyman (not only priest or bishop but cleric in minor orders) was part of charity and therefore exempt from taxation. In the Papal States, where the law remained largely unmodified, this exemption applied to a priest's private inheritance as well as his stipend. In a 1695 case from the area of Monte Cassino in the kingdom of Naples Rome reiterated that a cleric could not be tried in the civil court but only in the church court. Benedict XIV abolished the privilege of exemption from secular courts for clergymen in *minor orders* who murdered.[16] The exiguous nature of the concession shows extraordinary continuity in the old claims. The clergy were (in legal theory, only in small part in practice) exempt from death duties, tax on their produce, contributions in war or plague or famine. They were under no obligation like the laity to billet soldiers in cases of necessity. All these exemptions could only be overcome by appeal to Rome. The question therefore of contribution by church endowments to the exchequer was not only a chief issue in the politics of every Catholic state, and a running sore between State authorities and bishops or abbots, but a staple of negotiations and bargains between Rome and Catholic cabinets.

Fashion

In towns the mass-priest, duty done, often dressed as a layman, in wig and gay coat. Authority disliked these customs.

But though the town priest might not wear a cassock, and might wear a wig, he was usually known to be a priest. The first signs of a remarkable change in clerical dress appeared during the earlier decades of the eighteenth century.

The clergy, it was agreed, must wear distinctive dress except at home. And it was expected that this dress was a black cassock. Four centuries before, when laymen turned to short coats, the clergy were not permitted to follow. But cassocks were very inconvenient in remote country, mountains and floods and storms and muddy paths, and already remote country priests only wore them when they were about to officiate or when they thought that authority might be looking or when otherwise their people might think them hardly a priest. Some bishops were reduced to insisting that country priests wore cassocks at least during the liturgy. Before the end of the seventeenth century attempts began to get this inconvenience recognized, so that men might wear shorter clothes even if the bishop saw. The province of Milan, which looked back to St Charles

[16] Ferraris, 2.611.

Borromeo as its reformer and had for many years a Spanish government, was strict about the cassock. In 1693 the clergy of Como, who ministered in rugged impassable country, tried to abolish the rule that priests in very poor parishes must wear cassocks on all public occasions. They failed.

By the twenties of the eighteenth century urban clergy in some north-Italian towns made their own customs. They started to appear in the streets in coats or jerkins—and, specially strange to conservatives, not black but coloured, without any long cloak above to conceal its shortness. They could still be discerned to be priests because at the top of the jerkin was the linen band which was not what most laymen wore and was already known by the people as a 'clerical collar.'

This innovation grew rapidly; so rapidly that innovators shocked the Archbishop of Bologna by appearing thus in the cathedral on a patronal festival and joining a solemn procession through the streets.[17] Nevertheless the archbishop made no attempt to force his priests to conform to old rules. He only tried to insist that whatever the length of clothes they should be black, that priests wore the round clerical hat or 'crown', and that the cut of the clothes should be the cut of the cassock—yet it might be short if on a journey, and even in the city if the man was out on private purposes and provided that it was modest and not ornamented and had a black cloak over. He was (just) willing to tolerate during winter storms, at least in remote parts of the city and in the country, a coloured overmantle because mud and dust are not friendly to black. All this was enforced with a fine of 10 *scudi*, of which 6 *scudi* were to go to charity and 4 to the police.

The 'clerical collar', however accidentally it appeared, was already regarded as a symbol of the calling. Laymen were thought improper if they wore this collar. It was fastened either with a button in the middle at the front, or with a ribbon tied round the neck.

Authority liked priests (unless they were Capuchin friars or certain other religious orders) to be clean-shaven. Every Pope from 1523 to 1700 grew a beard, no Pope after 1700, and the change of fashion was reflected among clergy.

A curious argument was the wig.

Clergymen ought, it was agreed, to be distinguishable by their dress, as were Jews, butchers, lawyers, and several other callings. The Church was never reconciled to clergy who appeared on public occasions as laymen. But clergy were also men and parted their hair or bought styles of shoes as their lay friends wore or bought. Towards the end of the seventeenth century laymen, if not peasants, began almost universally to wear artificial

[17] Lambertini, *Raccolta*, 4.30 ff.; Ferraris, 2.585.

hair. If a clergyman wore artificial hair, was he only following the harmless custom of his age and refusing to distinguish himself too glaringly from his fellow-men, or was he flaunting one of the pomps and vanities of this wicked world, irreconcilable with his cloth?

The controversy in the Roman Catholic Church was not more vehement than the controversy over long hair among Dutch Protestants during the 1640s. But at times it was very vehement. Perhaps because of the accident that King Louis XIII went bald and needed a wig, France became the centre of the wig trade and the arbiter of fashion. By the second quarter of the eighteenth century a wig—full-bottom or bob-wig or tie-wig or bag-wig—was a necessary costume for anyone who held an official post and wished to be treated seriously; from kings and their ministers and judges, down to vergers and bailiffs and beadles. A gentleman who wished to avoid the charge of singularity and not to be too conspicuous, would not think of going out in his own hair. The chief though partial exception was Prussia, where the martial tradition held against the fashion, since no man could fight a war in a full-bottomed wig.

Clergymen also were officials and had solemn duties and needed to be taken seriously, and some were gentlemen who naturally followed the mode of their class, and some lost their hair and preferred to look like other people. Archbishop Tillotson of Canterbury (died 1694) appeared in a big curly wig, and through all the eighteenth century the wig became as necessary to the uniform of Anglican bishops as to that of English judges and barristers. Lutheran superintendents in Germany wore equally elaborate wigs, the largest in pictures being worn by Hermann Barckhaus superintendent of the church of Hanover.

That Anglican and Lutheran dignitaries should so readily have taken to the wig, in such a way that it became a symbol of office, was a sign how naturally Catholic priests or bishops would begin to wear wigs. An additional reason was a widespread medical belief that wigs, specially in a cold church in winter, protected from colds and catarrh and bronchitis and even toothache.

Authority disliked wigs. Bishops allowed that bald heads might need wigs, and after a time were prepared to accept medical certificates that a wig was good for a priest's health. Among monks the custom hardly caught except for these two reasons. A few French Augustinians distressed observers by appearing in wigs, the French Oratorians had to pass a solemn veto (1684). But in Italy and Spain the custom hardly touched monastic orders.

The fundamental ban was an ancient rule of the Church that no priest might celebrate the liturgy with his head covered; and in the most solemn parts of the liturgy this applied to skull-caps, birettas, or even mitres. Birettas could be doffed easily, wigs could not. Two or three canonists of repute held that a priest might celebrate mass in a wig if it was so like his own hair that the congregation could not tell the difference. But this was not the opinion of most. The main efforts of authority were directed towards preventing priests from officiating in wigs in church, and from wearing elaborate full-bottoms. Unless bishops felt exceptionally strong on the point they were satisfied with the hard task of coming anywhere near these two objectives. If they went further, they tried to allow priests to wear wigs only with a licence, on account of baldness or doctor's orders. But they hardly succeeded in these measures before the age, in the third quarter of the eighteenth century, when wigs began to fade from general use. Many priests of many dioceses could appear in wigs provided that the wigs were small and provided that the occasion was not a sacrament.

A French pamphleteer who was fanatical against clergymen in wigs, asked the Pope to publish a bull banning the habit universally. When Pope Clement XI forbade wigs (4 May 1701 and 7 December 1706) he refrained from applying it to all the Church and restricted its effect to Rome. In China, for example, to celebrate the liturgy with head un-covered was felt by the Chinese to be irreverent, and Rome had no objection when Christian priests conformed.

Pressure continued. In 1725 Pope Benedict XIII held his Roman provincial council; and as he was a Dominican with monastic objection to wigs, and was a very austere man, and had an aversion to wigs because they hid the tonsure, the council banned wigs not merely in church but everywhere. This council, being provincial, did not oblige dioceses outside the Roman province, not even the dioceses in the northern Papal States. Archbishop Lambertini of Bologna explained his rules of licensing to his clergy, complained that often they were not observed, and confessed publicly that under doctor's orders he himself wore a small white-haired wig in winter as a protection against coughs and colds, but that he always removed it at the first breath of spring.[18] He said comically that if he made the rules too stiff he would suffer a procession of clergy to his palace, escorted by their barbers.

Cardinals were not subject to the decisions of a provincial council. Portraits show cardinals in enormous full-bottoms. How ingrained or how natural the habit is seen by a Pope's travail in stopping his own cardinals.

[18] Lambertini, *Raccolta*, 5.71-2.

Benedict XIII strenuously tried to make the cardinals set an example, but with three he failed. He sent Cardinal Alberoni out of a procession when he saw him wearing a wig.[19] When Lambertini himself became Pope, methods of persuasion were gentler.

In 1726 an enterprising publisher at Augsburg printed a lovely book (*Roma Sancta*) of engraved portraits of all the cardinals under Pope Benedict XIII, with later additions of cardinals till 1740 in another edition. These show the state of hair, not quite reliably because, as priests often pleaded, hair can look like a wig and a wig like hair. The book shows that hardly an Italian wore a wig, perhaps two or three who may have been bald, and they only a small wig. Apart from the three cardinals at the curia, Alberoni, Giudice (both of whom caught customs of the Spanish court), and Alessandro Albani, the great wigs were worn by cardinals not in Rome, especially eminent French and German bishops, a de Rohan, a Schrattenbach, a Schönborn, a de Bissy. This may be a sign, and not the only sign, that Italian clergy were less inclined to a hierarchy of class than their northern fellows. It may also be a sign of that stricter control from the centre which Roman Congregations were able to maintain in the southern churches.

The Revolution ended wigs. But already they were long falling out of use. The first contemptuous use of *bigwig* in the English language is recorded in 1792. For the last quarter of the century bishops hardly needed to bother themselves or their priests. The Emperor Joseph II abolished wigs for court wear after 1780. By reason of the rule that no one should celebrate the liturgy with covered head, they never acquired in the Roman Catholic Church the quasi-liturgical status which they won in the Church of England, so that it became improper if an Anglican bishop went to church in his own hair in the same way that an English judge could not appear in court in his own hair or the Speaker of the House of Commons preside in his own hair.

A fashion which the nineteenth century was to look upon with horror was the taking of snuff in church. When tobacco first invaded Europe, it met all the resistance likely for such an innovation, and in the second half of the seventeenth century two Popes decreed excommunication against anyone guilty of the habit within St. Peter's. The question whether to take snuff was a breach of the fast and therefore not to be taken before mass was also discussed, and many good men held for the stricter view. Various

[19] Pastor, xxxiv.159; Giuntella, 154; for wigs generally, J. B. Thiers, *Histoire des perruques* (Paris, 1690, hostile to their use); C. F. Nicholai, *Über den Gebrauch der falschen Haare* (1801); Lambertini, *Raccolta*, 5, notificazione 8.

bishops wanted to condemn it in their diocesan synods. But by the second quarter of the eighteenth century the habit was so common, priests cheerfully and freely took snuff in church, and no one minded. When still zealous bishops drafted vetoes into their decrees, the secretary of the Congregation of the Council at Rome tried to persuade them to omit the offending clause since it could only stir needless controversy. Pope Benedict XIII, who was the most severe Pope of the century, and more inclined by nature and training to strengthen than to weaken bans on innovation, examined the question, decided that snuff had nothing uncleanly, and rescinded the rules which forbade it in St. Peter's.[20] A cassock stained with grains of snuff was not a rare sight among the clergy.

These changes of fashion did not affect the old bans on priests going to the theatre, or dicing, or hunting. Men argued that the prohibited hunt was only that of large animals like boar and bear, and that the hunting of fox or hare was not forbidden to clerics. This seemed to most opinion lax. No one minded a clergyman going out with a gun to shoot partridge for recreation three or four times a year. Bishops varied, and a few freely gave licences to priests to go shooting, but these bishops did not escape criticism.[21] Everyone distinguished fishing from hunting, for fishing was quiet and contemplative, and apostles were fishermen. Moralists were willing to sanction hunting to rid the land of pests that devoured crops. In deep country the battle against hunting parsons was not quite lost, but was not won. Whether the ban on dice included a ban on draughts and chess was argued, for some said that chess was a game of skill and others a game of chance, but authority was satisfied if the game were not played in public and not for money, or for trivial sums of money by way of recreation.

The ban against theatres did not stop priests going to comedy at Rome. Priests were not allowed to enter taverns or restaurants except on long journeys. This rule was so inconvenient that Roman restaurants had a separate unmarked door leading to a private room where priests could buy their meal and lunch or dine without entering the public room. This device was characteristic of the Church of the *ancien régime*. Old rules must be accepted because they were old rules, and no one thought it right to rescind them, and everyone wanted to maintain the authority of law. But when the old rule was silly, they found unostentatious ways to go round and do with cheerful nonchalance what the letter of the law disapproved.

Another sign in the decline of that austere spirit which in Protestanism

---

[20] Benedict XIV, *de synodo*, xi. 13.3, cols. 1297 and 1308.
[21] Ferraris, 2.656.

was known as puritan but which was the direct inheritance of the Counter-Reformation was a new openness of priests about certain social habits. Might a priest dance? In the Bible Aaron's sister, and King David, were recorded in a dance; the movement could hardly be of its nature sinful, no one suggested that laymen sinned if they danced, what was not sin for a layman could not be sin for a priest, dance was only a pleasant way of taking exercise rhythmically—so it was argued by north-Italian priests who shared the pleasures of their parishioners, especially at the time of carnival when any man might enjoy honourable amusement. This was contrary to all the tradition of the Church. Bishops argued in reply that it was nonsense to say that what was not sin for a layman was not sin for a priest; a priest sinned if he were a surgeon, barrister, merchant, or huntsman; a man consecrated to the sanctuary was called to avoid certain acts of general society; no exception could be made for the carnival, which even for laymen was often an occasion of sin.

At the carnival of 1737 country priests in Bologna diocese joined in dancing. The diocesan authorities were horrified. They found that they had insufficient proof against some of the clergymen—which suggests that parishioners refused to testify and therefore felt no objection if their priest joined in the dance—but others, against whom they had proof, whether because the priest confessed or parishioners gave evidence, were summoned to the see-city and disciplined. Nevertheless the archbishop felt it necessary to issue a strenuous warning in preparation for the carnival of the following year.[22]

The argument had importance in a Church where priests must be celibate.

Celibacy

A parish priest could hardly do his work unless he had a housekeeper. No one minded if the woman in his clergy house was his mother or aunt or grandmother—even his niece or the wife of his brother, whether the brother were alive or dead. No one minded if he had a married couple, so that the woman was married to his servant. This provision, especially the last, accounted for the comfort of many priests. But many others still needed someone to cook or clean, and this necessity was recognized and accepted both by the people and by bishops. Authority had a realistic view of the probabilities. They talked about the long dark evenings of winter when a country priest could not go out, and sat long hours by the fire with the only person who could solace his loneliness, his housekeeper; the

[22] Lambertini, *Raccolta*, 4.92 ff.

picture ran so deep into popular consciousness that a common old nickname for the priest's concubine was *focaria*, the woman at the fireside. In
the eighteenth-century bishops still sought to enforce conditions—that the
woman must be of good reputation, that no scandal be caused in the parish,
that if no kinswoman were also living in the house the woman must be
over a certain age (sixty according to a few rigid canonists, fifty in certain
dioceses, forty in others). These rules were hard to enforce. The Archbishop of Bologna (where the rule was the moderate forty years) announced to his clergy in July 1738 that it was being broken extensively,
and that 'intolerable abuses' existed all over the diocese. Not even the
highest were quite exempt from interference, because during the first two
decades of the century Pope Clement XI tried to get a powerful bishop to
put away his housekeeper.[23] Bishops sometimes called for an annual
statement of residents in clergy houses and issued licences to housekeepers
or female servants on due assurance that proper conditions were fulfilled,
and on the receipt of a testimonial to the woman's character. Clergy
occasionally argued that a servant was so ugly that she need not fall under
the rule of age. Authority replied that this was to exaggerate the importance of a well-formed body. They replied that experience showed
how any woman not mentally deficient nor permanently ill could find a
husband.

Pope Clement XI, by a decree of 1 February 1703, forbade all clergy to
teach music to women.

In the eighteenth century bishops were able, like the Archbishop of
Bologna, to issue circular letters about so delicate a subject as the state of
celibacy in their diocese, and even print them so that they could be bought
in bookshops. Once the nineteenth century entered its second half any
bishop who issued such a circular would be a fool, because a city or
provincial or national press would reprint that circular and the bishop
would publish shame on his church. In 1740 bishops need not think so
cautiously. They saw what they conceived as evil, and cared nothing
whether the world knew, for they expected that the world could only
join with them in condemning the evil when it knew. They continued to
expect assent, from nearly all their people, to ancient disciplines of the
Church.

Large numbers of future priests were in effect destined to the calling by
their parents when they were boys. For a long time no one knew whether
adolescents, who received minor orders while they were in training at a

---

[23] Clement XI, *Epistolae et Brevia*, 2.463; Lambertini, *Raccolta*, 4.172 ff.; Denzler, 2.272 ff.;
Ferraris, 2.639.

seminary, were bound for ever to the celibate life. This habit of minor orders, and expectation that such a boy would go forward to priesthood whether or not he were capable of living a single life, was an important part of the trouble which authority found in seeing that the restraints demanded by the Counter-Reformation were observed. In 1745, as part of his general policy of bringing practical sense into the administration, Pope Benedict XIV lightened the burden a little by ordering that if a boy was ordained deacon before the age of sixteen he must decide at his seventeenth birthday whether he would accept the celibate life or not. That so sensible a Pope should still feel it necessary to force a boy to choose at the age of seventeen is a sign of the feeling in the Church about the priestly life as unmarried. The decree could hardly do much by way of relief. The boy, though already a deacon, was free to decide not to go forward to the priestly life; and if he so decided he was restored to the status of a layman.

From parts of Germany early in the eighteenth century news of clerical concubines came to Rome with sufficient scandal to make the Pope act. Clement XI sent a letter to Archbishop Lothar Franz Schönborn of Mainz, who was also Bishop of Bamberg, to record his regret at hearing of parish priests living in clergy houses with women as though they were wives, and requiring him to see in future that no priest who lived with a concubine should take charge of a parish.[24] The Pope therefore did not feel able to ask the archbishop to see that no priests lived with women as concubines, only to see that no parish priests lived with women.

South Germany and the Rhineland were the areas where the question became most anxious because Catholics lived side by side with Protestants who argued that no church order could justify celibacy of priests. German bishops held to the general rules of the Church with a measure of success until, as we shall see, the last quarter of the century.

The Counter-Reformation largely established the rule of celibacy for priests. A bishop's power to suspend or fine was formidable, popular opinion stood behind authority, though working-class opinion minded marriage far more than it minded priests' women. The Counter-Reformation had not quite succeeded, nor could its heirs. In remote dioceses the old discipline was more respected in the spirit than in the letter. The Assistant Bishop of Oviedo in northern Spain told an English visitor that so long as his curates did not have children in their vicarage, he did not enquire too closely into their women.[25]

---

[24] Clement XI, *Epistolae et Brevia*, 2.2375.
[25] Townsend, 2.150.

The training of the clergy

The Council of Trent required a seminary in each diocese. This order was impossible for tiny dioceses. Trent allowed that where a diocese was too small to make a seminary it might join with one or more dioceses in a provincial seminary.

Dioceses were very slow to provide seminaries. Trent ordered dioceses to have seminaries, but compelled no ordinand to attend. Therefore bishops had no absolute need of a seminary, and often had neither men nor money to make a college. They were given power to levy tax on their clergy for this purpose. But a bishop who knew his priorities preferred not to tax his clergy. And if a bishop looked round at his brothers' seminaries in 1700 he would have seen a few eminent and excellent, and many miserable, exiguous, and rotten. Many of these had only a handful of alumni (twelve, six) and such inadequate buildings that young men must be sent home for half the course. Bishops feared to start seminaries which they saw no clear way to make worthy.

A seminary was a diocesan seminary, not a bishop's seminary; that is, it had four trustees (often called *deputies*), two from the chapter and two from the city clergy, in each case the bishop choosing one and the chapter or the city clergy electing the other. These four trustees could not be dismissed at the bishop's nod but must render to the bishop an annual financial statement. The trustees shared in appointing the head of the seminary. But the bishop was dominant, often the only voice to count. On buildings, books, confessors, statutes, money he was held bound to consult, but not held bound to follow, the advice of the trustees. Because he could consent or refuse to ordain he could control curriculum and standards; while if the seminary was not to be starved the bishop's *mensa* needed to give money. Seminaries were often spoken of as the bishop's, treated as the bishop's, treated by the bishop as his, even though it was not under his absolute rule. In effect the Council of Trent had made the bishop responsible. If the bishop failed to pay what was due from his *mensa*, or tried to convert the house to other use, or otherwise was found to 'destroy' the seminary, the trustees must act. This was not easy for trustees.

Where a religious order ran a college—Jesuits most often, but also Sulpicians, Lazarist fathers of St. Vincent de Paul, Bartholomites—they found men for teachers and money for stipends. Some of these colleges educated ordinands because they educated all comers. In a country like Poland, where places of higher education were few, seminaries of religious orders were important to the education of the country. Bishops in Poland were not short of colleges. But when a religious order conducted the seminary, it was exempt from the bishop's control and thereby might not obey the rules laid down by Trent and might refuse to do what the bishop wanted. A Polish bishop of 1730 could count at least nineteen seminaries in the country. Of these nineteen one or two were hardly more than boys' boarding-schools, several had but a handful of ordinands, and all but two were controlled by religious orders, eight by the congregation of St. Vincent de Paul (sign of French influence in Poland), five by Jesuits, and four by Bartholomites. If a bishop wanted a good seminary he might need to invite an order of priests to direct. If he invited he partly lost control of ordinands in his diocese. But he could be forced.

Cardinal Francesco Barberini (the younger), who in the Roman Curia was chairman of the Congregation of Bishops and Regulars and therefore had the widest acquaintance among priests, confessed his anxiety about finding a suitable rector for his seminary. Obscure bishops were dis-couraged and wondered what they could do if a man like Barberini sought in vain for a good head. Therefore they looked for a religious order. But nearly all their advisers, theorists of the seminary, sought to dissuade them from this plan.

In France religious orders (Sulpician, Lazarists of Vincent de Paul, Jesuits) directed nearly all the good seminaries and deprived bishops of control. Some Italians regarded the example of France, which in later history-books appeared as progress, not as a model but as a warning. It might do for a populous city with a cardinal as its archbishop who had weight at Rome to control the religious orders. A humble bishop of a tiny diocese had no voice or hardly more than a whisper at Rome. A Jesuit or Bartholomite rector of his seminary would listen to his general or superior and pay small heed to the bishop.

The example of the Vigevano seminary in north Italy frightened Italian bishops (1714). A college founded early in the Counter-Reforma-tion was given to a religious order and went bad. The bishop stepped in and was warned off, not his business. The bishop carried the fight to Rome, which Solomon-like ruled that the bishop could intervene but the order could choose its teaching staff. The fight continued, unsatisfactorily. One bishop and adviser of bishops held up the Vigevano case as sufficient proof that bishops should not entrust their seminary to a religious order.[26]

But the orders had the best teachers. They attracted able priests, could draw professors from all over the Catholic Church, and could provide the leisure without which no man may learn. A lot of bishops had no choice.

[26] Cecconi, 186, 190–1.

The bishop of a miserable little see might not be able to control his religious orders. But if he refused to invite them to his seminary he probably condemned its pupils to suffer under incompetent lecturers and might be faced with closing the seminary.

Pope Innocent XIII (1721–4) gave bishops jurisdiction in seminaries run by religious orders.[27] This hardly worked.

Italy was the western country where dioceses were most numerous, and therefore where bishops of little sees had sorest difficulty to make good colleges. When the country was poor, they were slowest, Sardinia had only three seminaries before 1700 but none of them flourished till the eighteenth century. One of the new Sardinian seminaries founded in the eighteenth century (Iglesias 1763) must instantly close doors and not re-open for nearly thirty years. By contrast every Sicilian diocese contained a seminary except the Lipari islands which, however tiny, opened a seminary in 1784; and three of the colleges (Palermo, Monreale, Girgenti) had excellent reputations. Seminaries founded in Italy: Trent to 1600, 128; 1600–1700, seventy; 1700–1800, forty.

The name seminary covered manifold institutions. At Muro in the kingdom of Naples the word was used to describe a little-boys' school, supposed to teach elementary Latin, if not writing, to future ordinands. At Turin the word was used to describe a famous college of the university, which flourished for most of the eighteenth century.

This variety was partly explained by a conscious distinction between *lesser seminary* and *greater seminary*. The lesser seminary was a school for teaching grammar to the ignorant boy whose parents sent him to train for orders. The greater seminary was a college for training future clergymen. But in most dioceses this distinction did not exist. Seminaries accepted boys of twelve years and saw them through to ordination.

Even in small dioceses these seminaries might be large. Some included not only postulants to fill the large number of clerical posts, but young men whom their parents wished to be ordained but who themselves had no such desire and used the classes as a way to higher education and a lay profession. The parents of the Italian upper class often educated their children by a tutor privately. Bourgeois parents sometimes used the seminary. Italian families with several children liked to send one of the sons into the priesthood, one of the daughters into a nunnery. In parts of Italy this desire had the status of convention.

Therefore the seminarists were many. In 1761 Girgenti in Sicily had 18,000 inhabitants and a seminary with 360 students. Such numbers, in

[27] *Seminaria*, 193.

conditions of cheap living and austere food, generated teenage troubles. The Archbishop of Trani, who directed a large college, told a visitor that 'though under his immediate inspection, the collegians were above his hand; and often, when he thought the whole seminary buried in silence, wrapped up in studious contemplation, or deep in theological lucubrations, he has been surprised, on entering the quadrangle, to find all ring again gigs and tarantellas.' The visitor found it easy to believe the archbishop as he listened to the din under his windows. In 1756 the seminarists at Nola barracked sermons, made themselves unpopular as a disgrace to the town, and threatened violence to would-be reformers.[28] Such events were not often reported. The effects of the seminary upon the young included discipline, familiarity (good and bad) with divine things, a narrowness, and a measure of education.

Pope Benedict XIII Orsini, who was an emotional Dominican, wished passionately to make the ideals of the Counter-Reformation a reality everywhere in the Church. In 1725 he held his Roman provincial council to this end, and accompanied its provisions with separate briefs to put the resolutions into effect. The bishops of Italy were exhorted to carry out the decree of the Council of Trent and improve seminaries where they existed and make new where they had none. Into the Curia he put a new Congregation of cardinals, the Congregation of Seminaries, to stir the bishops, help their plans, settle disputes. The Pope's personal stimulus was weighty, his new Congregation was born dead. Practically no trace survives of effective action by this Congregation. But as a direct consequence of the Pope's briefs, several new seminaries were created in Italy and Spain, while most bishops took a critical look at the sad little cluster of rooms and teenagers which they dignified by the name of college.

Bishops said that they had no money. Benedict XIII's brief *Creditae nobis*[29] (1725) told them how to tax their clergy. Taxing clergy was not comfortable for bishops. They could do it only with the consent of the trustees and experience showed that it led to lawsuits, forced policemen to chase clerical defaulters who omitted to pay, and poisoned the air between bishops and clergy. The tax had to be well based legally if it was to survive. The Archbishop of Trani (1763) tried to tax his clergy for the seminary which he had moved into better buildings, and the tax was claimed to be invalid because he ordered the clergy to elect a particular trustee for the seminary, instead of allowing them to elect freely.[30]

St. Charles Borromeo of Milan had not been afraid to levy 10 per cent

---

[28] Swinburne, 1.278; Berthe, 1.540–3, 562.   [29] *Bull. Rom.* xxii. 174 ff.
[30] Cecconi, 194.

on his clergy, but even he was challenged. Pope Pius V (1567) ruled that not more than 5 per cent should henceforth be exacted from clergy's income. The diocese of Alatri had no seminary until 1689 because 100 years before the bishop tried to tax the clergy at 6 per cent and the clergy appealed and won. Pope Benedict XIII was still kinder—3 per cent normal, up to 5 per cent in cases of necessity. But, said one bishop, 'if the diocese is very poor, to lay a tax would be quite contrary to prudence, and indeed an act of inhumanity.'[31] Wise bishops preferred to found or improve seminaries by suppressing a decayed monastery and taking the endowment and the buildings, or dissolving old brotherhoods, now with few members, and using their funds. At Assisi, for example, the seminary (1772) had money for scarcely ten pupils who lived in a tiny house with a poor teacher. On 11 April 1772 Pope Clement XIV gave a faculty to the Bishop of Assisi to suppress five or six brotherhoods and apply their endowments to the seminary.[32]

But this could be done only if the monastery or brotherhood, with the endowments which the bishop wanted to seize, could not defend its rights. In 1724 the Archbishop of Cologne, who had no seminary and was under heavy pressure from Rome, found a college of priests which (so the Cologne nuncio claimed) failed to study, were idle, did no good, and 'offered occasion to scandal'. The archbishop may have thought it simple to abolish so useless a community and take their money for a new seminary. It was not simple. The college of priests differed sharply from the nuncio in their judgement of themselves, and finally Rome upheld their right to remain.[33]

To reduce costs, living was of the simplest, food was at times attacked as inedible, buildings unsuitable. A bishop provided clothes for poor students, and even a pension to parents who depended on the wages of the son who now disappeared into the seminary. But if the ordinand were rich he received no grant. If parents said that they were poor and could not pay, the bishop tested their means. Upper-class parents disliked it if their sons joined a college where food was squalid and the manners of other young men were the habits of peasants. At Padua for a time seminarists of noble birth were educated in a separate building.[34]

Despite all these difficulties seminaries were more improved during the eighteenth century than in the two previous centuries. They were found

---

[31] Cecconi, 200.   [32] *Bull. Cont.* 4.416.
[33] Clement XI, *Epistolae et Brevia*, 1.225; 2.440; cf. 2.707–9; *Thesaurus Resolutionum*, 3.50, 57–8, 232.
[34] Serena, *Barbarigo*, 308.

endowments, more learned staff, more books for the library; were given new buildings by moving into the bishop's palace, or by building fine new buildings, sometimes important architecturally (Brindisi), or by purchasing a disused palace or by acquiring a suppressed monastery, or after 1773 by occupying empty Jesuit colleges (Orvieto, Viterbo, Ancona, Fano, etc., mostly but not exclusively within the Papal States).

Boys of twelve years old entered because their parents wished. If the parents could not afford to pay, the bishop's *mensa* or the seminary funds paid all or part of their keep. To this payment only ordinands were entitled. If the seminary accepted other boys, they paid normal fees. To get a free education for their children, parents therefore had an interest in saying that they aimed to be priests.

To stop parents or boys pretending, for the sake of free education, bishops usually exacted from parents or other sponsors a pledge that they would pay back *all* the boy's expenses if he failed to complete the course to the priesthood.

This necessary proviso produced agony in the minds of some of the best boys. A boy of twelve might be truly in earnest, with the generous heart of a boy of twelve. As he grew, and gathered knowledge of the world, and saw the holiness demanded of a priest—as he felt sexual powers developing and saw ahead the life of celibacy—he began to doubt, and yet knew that if he withdrew from the seminary he cast intolerable burden on poor parents to pay back fees. A bishop left a description of the agony thus: 'he does not fail to recommend himself to the Lord—fervently and frequently renews prayer for light, asks the advice of spiritual directors—and gets into such a state of agitation that finally he casts himself at the bishop's feet.' In such a case, advised this humble prelate, 'a bishop will use mercy more than justice.'[35]

Since priests' offices and masses had employment and endowment, no diocese lacked candidates for the priesthood. The difficulty was distinguishing those with from those without vocation. The mass-priest had a useful endowment for an obligation which was met by half an hour at the altar before breakfast and thereafter was free to do what he liked—seminarists who aimed at this pleasant future were hard to distinguish beneath their cassocks from future priests who would spend themselves for their parishioners. And bishops were subjected to pressure from powerful parents or patrons to relax the tests for their children or clients; or from kind clergymen who found an educated man in dire poverty and knew that they could relieve his plight if they certified him as fit for holy orders.

[35] Cecconi, 94.

The seminary was a gate which could be used to deter the excess of ordinations. Even a Pope once talked about the trouble in keeping out 'the superfluous and useless crowd of priests'.[36] Several Italian dioceses of the early eighteenth century insisted that no man might be ordained unless he spent a defined period in a seminary. The Roman provincial council of 1725 ordered all ordinands to spend at least six months before ordination in a seminary, or if no seminary existed then in common life at the bishop's palace. The rule applied only to the dioceses round Rome. Since so many dioceses still had no seminary or a bad seminary, Pope Benedict XIV suggested that ordinands be gathered every Sunday to a named church where they would be instructed in the sacraments and preaching and on the need for a life according to a rule; or that ordinands should be attached to parishes as helpers in the Sunday school and companions of the priest when he carried the sacrament to the sick or the viaticum to the dying, and be allowed or compelled to join the regular meetings of the clergy to discuss cases of conscience.

Men who worked on the staff of seminaries thought that a priest who had received his training in a seminary was likely to be not only a more competent priest, but a holier man.[37]

The young men were expected to wear a cassock all the time, even in the streets; in Rome (by 1766) it was a mauve cassock with red buttons. But lawgivers admitted exceptions silently by ordering that this rule be observed 'especially' in the city and at any church act. The reason for the red buttons was 'a modest pomp appropriate to young men destined for the royal priesthood'. They must be of legitimate birth (dispensation available), of families resident in the diocese and of a suitable height and appearance. Apart from the early grammar (Latin) and later philosophy (elementary) and theology (advanced) they were specially taught chanting, because discords caused laughter in musical people, and 'calculation' because a village priest was the only person there to know when the calendar ordered a feast and therefore a holiday.[38] But apart from these basic studies, which included more or less of the Bible (and the Catholic eighteenth century began to be conscious that its priests knew the Bible less intimately than was right), some higher seminaries provided excellent courses in Hebrew and Greek, in various branches of natural science, and in history.

The seminary at Padua was founded soon after the Council of Trent and for a century and a quarter was a sorry little institution. During the third

---

[36] 'superfluam atque inutilem', Benedict XIV, *de synodo*, xi.2.10, col. 1252–3.
[37] Giovanni di Giovanni, *passim*.   [38] Cecconi, 124–6, 142.

quarter of the seventeenth century the Bishop of Padua, Gregorio Barbarigo, who came of a wealthy Venetian family, took steps to create a munificent endowment for his seminary. During the thirty-two years of his episcopate he was reckoned to have spent 80,000 *scudi* on the seminary alone. The Padua seminary became one of the eminent places of learning in Europe, at a time when Italian scholars and scientists led the world. This was the age when Austria and Poland threw back the Turks from Vienna, and for a few years it looked as though Venetian fleets and armies might destroy the Turkish empire. When Athens fell to the Venetian army the Bishop of Padua rejoiced with his students. He even asked the Pope if he might be made Patriarch of Constantinople, and hoped to celebrate in St. Sophia the reunion of the Greek and Latin churches. Therefore he was determined that his seminary should produce Greek scholars. The fame of the classical education in the seminary crossed the Alps. The seminary's printing press (1684 onwards) became one of the leading publishers of classical texts, and published the first book in Albanian. Moreover Barbarigo wanted his students to understand the new developing sciences. The seminary of Padua possessed an observatory a century before the university of Padua acquired an observatory. They studied Galileo and Isaac Newton as well as the older astronomers. Mathematicians at the Padua seminary were counted among the leading followers of Galileo. Not without argument and conflict, they at last got leave to print at their press the first edition of the complete works of Galileo (1740–50).

The scientific interest of a seminary was not unique to Padua. A few seminaries were among the best places of education in Europe. The Jesuit Girolamo Saccheri (died 1733) who was a brilliant mathematician, a forerunner of non-Euclidian geometry, received his education from the historic seminary at Milan. Even travellers in Sicily were surprised at the learning and 'enlightenment' of lecturers. The seminary at Girgenti was ruled by an enlightened bishop and respected far and wide. A visitor of 1778 noticed a thesis pasted up on a board, to be maintained in the schools there: 'that the Copernican system is impious, absurd, and contradictory to Holy Writ; from which it is evident, that the earth stands still, and the sun moves round it, like the sails of a windmill round the pivot.' Two Lutheran visitors, who came only a few months apart and were both graduates of Göttingen, and as serious northern Protestants were inclined to be scandalized at features of Mediterranean society, took contradictory views of this seminary. One thought that the lecturers tried to force the young into mental machines and crammed their heads with theological nonsense. The other recorded how the library was admirable and the teaching so excellent that he wanted all monasteries to send their novices to be educated at Girgenti. He observed also how young men who had no intention of taking holy orders could follow the lectures and receive a good education. But this same observer discovered in Girgenti a group of Franciscan tertiaries who taught that the earth does not move, and was shocked.[39]

In Spain seminaries were so central to culture and higher education that government began to press for reform. The same pressure is found in Sicily, Portugal, France, Austria, but the Spanish reformed universities first and therefore drove fresh air into the stuffy lecture-rooms in Spanish seminaries. In the diocese of Barbastro Francisco Ferrer founded a religious order (1718) called the *Religious Society of Evangelical Worker Priests* for the purpose of training seminarists. Here the discipline was as strict as any in Italy, for it applied to young ordinands all the severity of a rigid monastic rule. This was the invariable danger of applying the ideals of the Counter-Reformation out of time to seminaries. They risked making the seminary into a monastery and its boys into budding monks.

Government had different ideas. They wanted wider studies, astronomy, natural sciences, agriculture. Critical of religious orders, they wished to eliminate monks from teaching future parish priests, and to put every seminary under its bishop. In the thirty years after 1759 the Spanish bishops created ten seminaries. Many of these got empty Jesuit colleges. The expulsion of the Jesuits from Spain (1767) enabled government to plan a drastic reorganization of seminaries by a royal decree of 14 August 1768, *The erection of seminaries in cities and large towns after the plan of the Council of Trent*. Henceforth the staff must always reside, no monks could teach, the new curriculum must follow no limited 'school', government retained the right to inspect, the pupils need not be present every day in the cathedral. This decree opened Spanish seminaries to new and disturbing ideas. The volumes of the French naturalist Buffon were banned by the Spanish censors and circulated only in secret. Yet towards the end of the century they were standard reading among the seminaries of the Basque country.[40]

In Austria and Germany late in the century governments started to attempt remedy for the inadequacy of training for orders. The direction of reform was always to diminish the numbers of miserable little seminaries, have larger institutions, therefore staff them with more learned professors,

[39] Unfavourable, Bartels; favourable, Münter; cf. Tuzet, 335–6, 526.
[40] Sarrailh, 459.

if possible associate their courses with university courses, and lengthen the time of training necessary before ordination. Most plans for reform made ordinands do less dogmatic theology and study of the schoolmen, more study of the Bible and the Fathers and Church history and 'pastoral theology', a phrase which first appeared during the later eighteenth century. It could hardly be denied though at the time it was denied that old syllabuses, hallowed because they were designed in the Counter-Reformation, made a narrow mental zareba for an ordinand in the age when Voltaire was already an old man and Edward Gibbon published his first volume of the *Decline and Fall*.

The most remarkable of these plans was developed (1772–7) for the hereditary Austrian dominions of the Empress Maria Theresa, by the Benedictine Stephan Rautenstrauch. He created a new faculty of *pastoral theology* at Vienna, a course of five years. This was the time when the name (but not of course the reality) of pastoral theology first became common in the Church. Textbooks must be written for the new course, and it was specially provided that these textbooks should be in German and not Latin. During the five years the ordinand was to receive instruction in all the pastoral duties of a priest, as teacher, leader of worship, and director of souls.

For a time these attempted reforms of seminaries had less success than they deserved. The reason was plain; bishops usually disliked what governments proposed. However ministers of education changed syllabuses to get modern clergymen, the fact was that ordinands must be accepted by bishops; and bishops usually preferred a small inadequate seminary of their own to a larger institution in which they had no authority. The chief enemy of Rautenstrauch's plan at Vienna was the archbishop.

Maria Theresa's successor and son Joseph II carried out a high-handed and theoretically admirable reform by abolishing all the small seminaries in the Austrian Empire and concentrating men in larger colleges known as the general seminaries. This was the least lasting innovation of Joseph II's numerous reforms of the Austrian Church. Bishops disliked general seminaries so vehemently that the Emperor's successor must reverse the plan.

Nevertheless, as the number of seminaries rose through the century, so (on the whole) rose the quality. In cities of Germany—for example, Trier, 1773—the quality of staff and candidates was high enough to identify the seminary's curriculum with that of the university. In Freiburg im Breisgau the general seminary was part of the university system. The Trier seminary was a direct consequence of the fall of the Jesuits. Ex-Jesuit buildings were empty, ex-Jesuit professors available. The rulers of Bonn and Münster founded universities, new seminaries were created not only in Trier but in Münster (1776), Paderborn (1777), and Hildesheim (1780). The breaking of Jesuit control of many colleges forced revision of the curriculum, for the Jesuit pattern of studies was accused of being ultra-conservative and of being out of touch with modern needs.

Such science as that of Trier or Padua was far from typical. Many seminaries were content if they imparted to their students Latin, good manners, elementary Christian doctrine, elementary moral theology, how to say mass, and how to chant. That was no small task when so many students came from homes without books and with peasant manners. Even in Bologna, chief city of the Papal States after Rome, the seminary was much nearer to this modest level than to the seminary at Padua. The Bologna seminary was founded soon after the Council of Trent but had such inadequate buildings that for a century and a half the seminarists must be sent home for a period in the middle of their course, between learning Latin and learning theology. By 1736 it was still unfinished and had no library that mattered, but it could hold forty students without sending them home and was able to draw, at least a little, on help from the theologians and canonists at the university.[41]

Archbishop Capecelatro of Taranto laid down rules (1789) for his seminary which were unusual in their openness, characteristic of the man, but oddly fitted the mood of those last decades of the century. The students are not to engage in useless disputations, shall avoid curious disputes of theology like predestination or original sin, and the sophisms of school-men. The aim of the institute is not to produce pedants or fanatics or even theologians, but honest and useful citizens. The way to 'avoid hell and obtain heaven' consists not in going to church very often or frequent prayers or fasts or pilgrimages, things which are of very little use and often hurtful to our neighbours; but in practising charity. In the seminary the students were taught agriculture to enable future country priests to teach peasants.[42] Archbishop Capecelatro was in all respects an unusual man, and a more unusual archbishop.

Bishops were known to insist on retreat, even of a week or ten days, perhaps at a monastery, as a time of prayer before ordination. In south Italy the newly ordained priest invited family and friends to a dinner on the evening of his first mass, despite the frowns of bishops who regarded the occasion as unedifying. We have however the memory of awe at a

---

[41] Lambertini, *Raccolta*, 3.211 ff.   [42] Croce, *Uomini*, 2.173.

first mass from a Spanish priest. Accustomed from the cradle to kiss the hand of every priest; never seeing the host without veneration among those who handled, the clouds of incense and the jewels of the monstrance, the new priest sensed what he later called 'the overpowering feeling of a God dwelling among men,' and described how he approached the altar as 'the sole worker of the greatest of miracles'.[43]

It mattered where the new priest went to serve. Almost no care was taken over his choice of parish. He was left to fend for himself—find a patron, compete for a benefice, get work as a mass-priest, be taken on as an assistant. This worried those who cared for their seminarists, but they could do little in the way of remedy. Experience showed that a promising scholar, bound by the rules to serve in the diocese which paid for his training, lost all desire for scholarship if he were sent to a remote hill town where neither books nor educated conversation could be found.

He must however have a 'title', a curacy or altar or canonry or university post where he would serve. No bishop could ordain a man who had no future work agreed. This was a universal regulation, and an important safeguard. But the security was less than it appeared. In the large number of endowed posts it was not difficult for unscrupulous candidates to find someone who would agree to give them 'cover' which was legally a title to be ordained. Abuses are reported infrequently. But in a little cathedral near Naples, shortly before 1700, was a canonry known as 'the ordination canonry', because it provided a title for orders and had no other function. A man wanting holy orders got himself ordained by a lax bishop to this canonry and then resigned the canonry and left the diocese. Once while the see of León in Spain was vacant, and no bishop could watch, certain 'fictitious' chaplaincies were founded with the sole object of supplying titles for ordination.[44]

Bishops still concerned themselves occasionally with the ancient rule of the Church that no illegitimate could become a priest. The rule was always more a way of discouraging fornication than of keeping innocent children out of a vocation, and dispensations were easy, from the bishop for minor orders or from Rome for a benefice. The Council of Trent, still remembering the hereditary parishes of the earlier Middle Ages, decreed that if a son of a priest was ordained he might not serve in the same parish or chapter or chapel as his father; and the rule was occasionally brought into force even during the eighteenth century.

[43] Doblado, 123.   [44] De Maio, 45; *Thesaurus Resolutionum*, 3.227.

Examination before appointment to a parish

The seminary produced a number of men who were called licentiates; and the university produced a number of more highly qualified men who were bachelors or doctors of divinity. For any post that had no charge of people's souls bishops did much as they liked; that is, for priests within monasteries or friaries, assistant chaplains, and above all the massing priests whose function was to celebrate the sacrament but had no responsibility for anyone's souls. These ordinations, where much depended on the judgement or whim of the individual bishop, were places where unworthy ministers easily slipped through into holy orders. But since such a man had no parochial responsibility, or only as an assistant or locum in case of illness or absence or vacancy, bishops seldom perturbed themselves unduly about the lack of test. They had a strong interest in a seminary, and sometimes a good knowledge of its students. With that they were mostly content. They perforce left the testing of monks and friars to their orders.

But where a priest was to be appointed to the charge of a parish, the Council of Trent decreed a more rigorous test; and over this test, known as the *concursus*, argument continued.

In the zeal of the Counter-Reformation, the Council of Trent made some rules so ideal that they failed to take account of practical difficulty. They ordered a seminary in every diocese, and 200 years later the Roman Catholic Church still struggled to obey the decree despite the heap of evidence that if a little diocese made a seminary it was sure to be bad. So with the *concursus*. The Council was ahead of its time in decreeing a strict examination before entry upon a parish. But the passage of years showed that the system of examination needed to be regulated if it were not to produce worse evils than those which it aimed to cure. Bishops discovered that they could not do what they were supposed to do without grave ills. Therefore they played about with the system and by 1700 it began to approach anarchy.

When a parish was vacant by death or resignation, the bishop must nominate a day for a *concursus*, that is, a public examination of candidates for the vacant benefice. He must do this within ten days of learning of the vacancy (later defined by two different Popes as not less than five days nor more than twenty days). The bishop, or the patron if not the bishop, may invite candidates to stand for election; but anyone may suggest suitable men, and anyone may apply; the candidates do not need to be of the diocese in which the parish is sited. At the *concursus* the candidates shall be examined by the bishop or his vicar-general and at least three examiners who shall be qualified in theology or canon law ('or otherwise suitable') and who shall take an oath to do their work with integrity. They are not to accept fees for examining. At the end of the examination the examiners inform the bishop which candidates are worthy and the bishop shall nominate from the worthy whomsoever he thinks best.

This system was widespread in the Roman Catholic Church, in outline; with the important exceptions, that if the patron was a layman or lay-woman, the candidate need not compete in the *concursus* but must never-theless be tested by the examiners; and if the Pope was patron, or had a right to appoint by reservation, the bishop should hold the *concursus* in the usual way but leave the final choice to Rome. In addition, if the benefice had no or very little income, so that no candidates came forward, the bishop need not (because he could not) hold a *concursus*. And finally, if the parish was divided into quarrelling factions, and the bishop saw that competition between candidates would exacerbate, he might at his discre-tion refrain from public *concursus* and arrange that the examination be private.

In interpreting these provisions, Pope Pius V (1567) made one addition which proved the source of strife. He thought that justice demanded a right of appeal from the bishop's choice. A failed candidate might appeal— from bishop to archbishop, or to a neighbouring bishop as delegate from Rome, or to Rome. What happened if after all the examiners were suspected of corrupt practice, or the bishop of eccentricity in judgement? These appeals had the merit that while they were being heard the man selected by the bishop continued to act in his new parish. They had the demerit that they caused endless friction. Failed candidates frequently accused the bishop of being unreasonable in his choice, or the examiners of holding an unfair examination. A doctor of divinity could not accept that a bishop did right if he preferred a candidate with no degree. Many of the examinations were organized inefficiently, so that a candidate might easily say that he was asked hard questions while his rival faced simple questions. Some dioceses tested by written papers and answers, others by oral methods. And failed candidates, who had little to lose, engaged in light-hearted appeals, forcing the successful candidate to desert his parish for a distant hearing, exhaust his purse, and leave his parishioners to someone whom he hardly knew. Failed candidates who had a low opinion of the successful candidate could not understand the choice; and if they were already in his diocese might henceforth feel sour towards their bishop. Some wise churchmen held that every single appeal damaged the Church, and that at all costs appeals must be made rare. Lambertini, who was successively Bishop of Ancona (1727–31) and Archbishop of Bologna (1731–40) was proud that he narrowly restricted appeals in both dioceses.[45]

Certain dioceses took the easiest method of averting appeals. Their examiners were supposed to test knowledge and character. Since no objective test could be applied to comparisons of character, they restricted the examination to knowledge; for men could not complain if examiners declared that their papers gained fewer marks. This was hardly in accordance with the mind of the Catholic Church, which when choosing parish priests put goodness above brains.

Lambertini was secretary of the Congregation of the Council which had the duty of interpreting and enforcing the decrees of the Council of Trent. In 1720 this Congregation made decisions which were issued in the following year and attempted to bring uniformity into the modes of examination—always written, same questions to all candidates, no candidates allowed out until the examination was ended, all papers to be written in the candidate's own hand and signed, papers to be done in Latin except the specimen sermon which should be in the language used in the parish; above all, no appeal, against either examiners or bishop, shall lie unless it is lodged within ten days, and then it can only be made on the basis of the documents already lodged with the *concursus*—*curriculum vitae*, testimonials, examination papers, reports of examiners. No one could at this stage introduce new evidence except very important evidence about character.

In 1721 these provisions were encouraged but optional. Twenty-one years later, when Lambertini was Pope, he turned them into a decree and added an important provision against trivial appeals (the constitution *Cum illud*, 14 December 1742). Since some appeals lay when the bishop refused to choose the obvious applicant because he had private information about the man which was not known to the examiners or other candidates, the bishop might write a private letter to the appeal judge setting forth his information and the appeal judge must keep this letter secret. If the bishop had reasons to distrust the discretion or even the character of the appeal judge, he might send his evidence to the Cardinal of the Congregation in Rome. If the appeal judge held with the bishop, no further appeal was possible. If the appeal judge held against the bishop, then the bishop's successful candidate had the right of appeal to still a third judge; and then the verdict was final.

This last provision was very discouraging to failed candidates. The menace of incessant and vexatious appeals was stayed.

[45] Benedict XIV, *Bullarium*, 2.14.

Certain other cases extended the rules, even though dioceses still differed widely in their practice. A case was put forward from the abbey of Subiaco (1741), where it was questioned whether the bishop was limited to accepting the candidate whom his examiners put forward as best; and Rome ruled that the bishop was free to choose whomsoever he thought from all the candidates whom the examiners certified to be worthy. In Taranto the archbishop repelled from the *concursus*, and refused to allow the candidature of, a priest whom he believed to be notorious for keeping a concubine. The candidate denied that he kept a concubine and challenged the validity of the *concursus*. Rome upheld the archbishop's freedom. In Capua the archbishop repelled from the *concursus* a candidate suspected of stabbing one of the parishioners and burying his corpse in the parish, so that various men were out to kill him before he even became their parish priest. The aggrieved candidate sued the archbishop at Rome and lost.[46]

The examiners must test knowledge and character. How they tested character varied according to bishop, examiners, testimonials, and *curriculum vitae*. The usual formula included morals, gravity, prudence, reputation, love of the Church. These tests were not capable of analysis and therefore escape the historian. Tests of knowledge were clear. They were bound to examine the candidate in his knowledge of Christian doctrine, of cases of conscience (because they were choosing the confessor of perhaps 1,000 people) and of ability to expound the gospel. No one who wanted to be the new rector of the parish was exempt from this test. A professor of divinity at a university, who wanted to enter parish life, must face the competition equally with the newly fledged ordinand.

The questions at various examinations have survived. Here are the questions set (1722) for the parish of St. Nazario in the diocese of Albenga near Genoa:[47]

1. What texts of the Bible prove the right of excommunication?
2. Can excommunicated persons hold social intercourse with each other?
3. What might a man do if he kills a cleric in self-defence, and is declared excommunicate?
4. Can Catholic soldiers killed in a war with the Turks be classed as martyrs?
5. [A very long and elaborate question on the lawfulness of a contract over changing money].

The questions show what the examiners thought important to test. They wanted their priests to be sure of those special texts of the Bible

---

[46] Cases, *D.D.C.* 3.1481–2; *Thesaurus Resolutionum* 9.134 ff.
[47] *Thesaurus Resolutionum*, 2.358.

which would aid their preaching and instruction. But they were not specially concerned with any knowledge of Christian doctrine. What concerned them was the moral doubt, manslaughter, excommunication for sin, usury, and commercial integrity. They meant, first, to examine future confessors and (very secondary) future preachers. They selected two candidates as worthy, one learned with a doctor's degree. The bishop chose the less learned because he rated him the better pastor.

Here are the questions from another competition:

1. What is the meaning of the words of the Council of Trent *de justificatione*, 'if anyone says that men are righteous without the righteousness of Christ by whose merits we are justified, or by their righteousness itself formally, let him be anathema'?
2. Can a parish priest who sins with a penitent hear the confession of the penitent? If he does, is it valid?
3. Can a confessor, who is unable to absolve a penitent, nevertheless tell him *I absolve thee* after first telling him his intention not to absolve? [The circumstances derived from the need not to cause scandal among a waiting queue of penitents, or in a family.][48]

Again the examiners plainly tested a confessor rather than a preacher. They expected accurate knowledge, not only of the doctrine of justification at the Council of Trent, but of papal decrees on moral theology.

Spanish dioceses had the habit of setting a thesis which the candidate must argue, and this could be very difficult: one example—'whether the justification of sinners is the greatest marvel wrought by God'. They were also in the habit of setting a gospel text for a short specimen sermon.

The Spanish method of *concursus* for a theological or legal canonry (only insisted on for these canonries after 1725) was more severe than the Italian but not necessarily fairer. Candidates were divided into threes. The senior of the three, in presence of dean and chapter, drove a silver knife into the pages of a book of theology at three places—sometimes the Bible, usually Peter Lombard's *Sentences*. Each candidate must then defend a thesis on one of the subjects thus chosen by chance. He was given only twenty-four hours to prepare his thesis, and was not allowed to bring notes. Most candidates took only three or four hours sleep. He defended his thesis before the chapter from a special pulpit in the cathedral. The public could attend but usually left their seats empty; for he must lecture in Latin for one hour from memory. Then the other two candidates assailed the thesis, each for half an hour. The use of Spanish was permissible by way of explanation.

[48] *Thesaurus Resolutionum*, 1.315, Ugento diocese.

After this trial the candidates must each preach, from memory, a sermon lasting one hour, subject likewise chosen by lot. One candidate related how his efforts to memorize were vain, he could not sleep, in the vestry beforehand his knees shook, but once he got going extempore in his lecture he lost his alarm and knew what he wanted to say. For the sermon he prepared only a skeleton. This was effective. But he did not win the canonry for a reason which may have been less rare in Spain than in Italy: 'As the decision of the chapter had been taken before the trial, and no one except the successful candidate had any idea of getting the canon's stall, I was satisfied with the usual compliment, of being made honorary theological examiner of the diocese.'[49]

Congregations need not listen to a bad preacher, and hardly knew if he was shaky on the doctrine of justification. But they wanted advice in situations, most of which were trivial, sordid, and monotonous, but occasionally when the happiness of an entire family or the safety of a man in vendetta was at stake—and more frequently when someone's hope of eternity stood in question. Bishops were inclined to lament the quality of candidates at a competition from this point of view, and examiners on occasion reduced their standards below the level which they thought tolerable so that the bishop might be able to fill the parish. Poor parishes attracted fewer candidates, and less qualified. In such cases examiners were known who gave candidates previous warning of the questions which would be asked. They might set questions that demanded answers which required little thought because they could be answered parrot-fashion. In a Neapolitan diocese where the system of oral examination continued, one poor old priest was caught answering questions from a crib hidden in the lining of his hat. In another Italian diocese (1738) the vicar-general noticed that all the answers by one approved candidate were verbally the same as those of another competitor, and ordered a new *concursus*. A candidate in Seville, not previously known for eloquence, preached at short notice a superlative sermon which gratified all the hearers, but one recognized it as a lately published Spanish translation of the great French preacher Bourdaloue. Under such conditions even testimonials might be suspect. In south Italy bishops feared that a fee had passed if they could not otherwise account for a testimonial. Unscrupulous secretaries in Naples could make a living by fabricating testimonials for priests who wanted to impress a *concursus*.[50]

To the rule that poorer parishes attracted less good candidates, there

[49] *The Life of Blanco White*, 1.79–85.
[50] ibid. 1.103–4; Berthe, 2.118, 122; *Thesaurus Resolutionum*, 9.17.

were exceptions. Many clergy liked to be in or near a big town, whether because they preferred educated men in their congregation, or the stipend was higher, or they aimed at a canonry and would be more easily known, or because they liked the amenities of a city. But some equally good men sought what were known in Spain as 'meagre cures'; whether because their health was delicate and they needed work not too strenuous, or because they wanted for family reasons to be near their kin, or because for reasons of the heart they wished to work near the place where they were born, or because their uncles and great-uncles held that living for generations and they wished to follow the way of their family. 'Being fond of field sports and freedom,' we are told of one country priest in Andalusia who was more of a gentleman than his visitors expected, and who would normally have been found in a canonry or dignity, 'he preferred the wild spot where he had been born, to a more splendid station in a Spanish cathedral.'[51]

Many parishes, in areas of the Church a majority of parishes, were in lay or monastic patronage. The patron was entitled to advertise and invite candidates. He rarely invited. Most patrons or monasteries chose a man and sent his name to the bishop. The bishop could only test him, not with a competition but with his examiners; and if the examiners found the single candidate 'worthy', the bishop must allow him to succeed.

This was the area where money was most likely to change hands quietly. Unscrupulous lords were not above making the best of their inherited right. We find questions directed to confessors such as this: I have been an incumbent for three years. I now find that my family or friends paid money to get me chosen. Am I bound to resign?[52] If simony was discovered it instantly invalidated the choice.

Doubts about simony could be delicate. The church of St. Christina in the diocese of Cesena had so miserable an income that no one was likely to want it and the bishop did not advertise a competition because he was sure of no candidates. Instead he tried to tax the parishioners to make a better stipend. The parishioners had no wish to be taxed and were very disturbed. So they found a curate in Ancona with some money of his own, who said that he was willing to endow the parish if he were appointed the incumbent, without a *concursus* but not without an examination.

This proposal gave trouble to everyone's conscience. No question, it was simony; the man was buying the parish; but, despite the simony, best for the parish. The candidate had only made as a condition that he undergo no competition, and the bishop was already sure of no competitors. After

[51] Doblado, 180.   [52] *Decisioni* (Bologna), 2.121.

a heated discussion the plan was accepted under conditions. If the simony invalidated the choice, the Pope's dispensing powers must make it good.[53]

This case touched the ill-endowed parishes on which no man might live. In the poor diocese of Campagna[54] during the eighteenth century the parishes were so ill endowed that the bishop would never hold a *concursus*. He managed with curates-in-charge, or even a deacon, or help from a monastery. For a normal parish, competition was brisk and the answers of leading candidates were by modern standards learned. In the parish wanted by no one but a failed clergyman the standard was different. The Bishop of León reported that for such parishes no one came forward but 'wretched sons of the province' with a little Latin and a memorized textbook of moral divinity which they forgot soon after they were appointed. He wanted the right to re-examine clergymen whenever he thought fit. Rome foresaw endless trouble if it conceded this right. He might only re-examine a priest if he had evidence for a suspicion that he could not do his work.[55]

In this way the *concursus* of the Council of Trent, once purged of its worst features by Prospero Lambertini, was an instrument for maintaining a standard, not among the clergy but among the parish clergy. It forced the bishop to enquire into the previous lives of future incumbents; forced the clergy to pay attention to their studies; made it hard for the already immoral to escape the net; and meant that previous record, whether in pastoral care or teaching, was taken into account in making appointments. It was less haphazard in its selecting process than the nomination by patron practised by the Church of England in that age.

Moreover it protected the bishop. The lay patron demanded that his man get the post. The bishop could not stop it—provided that the patron's candidate passed the examiners. The bishop found it extremely hard to resist patrons, but at least he had a measure of backing. He was protected also from the enthusiasms of the people. This was particularly important when the virtues of the person whom they wanted were not the virtues appropriate to a clergyman. A Spanish priest named Gonzalez Velasco came to a competition with a reference which said that he was very respectable. But from other sources the bishop heard that his virtue lay in courage as a guerrilla leader in the mountains and that he was suspected of murder and going to bullfights and womanizing. In such cases the *concursus* enabled the bishop to postpone, further enquire, or reject out of hand.

In their use of the *concursus* not all countries conformed to the practice of Rome and Italy. In Spain the size of dioceses and difficulty of travel

[53] *Thesaurus Resolutionum*, 2.318–20 (1723).   [54] Cestaro, 37.
[55] *Thesaurus Resolutionum*, 3.245.

made bishops hold large competitions not at each vacancy but every few years—in Toledo, one of the largest dioceses, in 1801, 1807, 1811, 1814, 1816, but the years from 1808 to 1814 were years of war. At such a *concursus* the number of candidates was large; to 1801 for example, held in the archbishop's palace at Toledo, came 176 candidates, of whom all but twenty-nine were from the diocese of Toledo and fifty-eight were graduates and 28 per cent had not yet received priest's orders.[56] These large public competitions were regarded as a model everywhere in Spain except the Basque provinces. In the republic of Venice, and the Austrian province of Lombardy, bishops had the habit of holding a competition several times a year for several vacant parishes. These exceptions show that bishops met continual difficulty in organizing a *concursus* because they must arrange for notice, examiners, candidates, travel, and if several vacancies occurred in quick succession the burden began to be intolerable. Hence the gradual development of systems like the Spanish, which had the demerit of allowing some parishes to suffer an interregnum of up to three or four years.

Under the system of patronage, as in the Church of England and in those parts of the Roman Catholic Church where lay patrons were strong, a priest might be offered a living; that is, it could come to him as a vocation and unexpectedly. Despite all the merits of the *concursus* system in ensuring the general standard of parochial clergy, no priest could be offered a parish. He must be an applicant. Against his neighbour he must be a conscious competitor for a post which he chose to want. This was sure to diminish the sense of 'vocation' outside religious orders, where it remained in all its force since the vow of obedience bound a man to go where he was sent.

Beneath the ordered system of examination can be detected the misery of the failures. Too many applicants, too many ill-educated priests, men longing for a benefice where they could find independence, or get a house where they could care for an old mother or a sick sister, an ecclesiastical underworld of hopeless men wistful for a benefice, failing again and again, and trying by fair means or foul to win the coveted prize. These yearnings came out in the questions which such priests asked when they went to make confession—'Is it wrong to pay someone money so that he shall not be a rival candidate for a parish?'—'Is it wrong to pay someone money so that he will get me access to the bishop?'—'Is it wrong to accept a job on the bishop's staff without any pay so that I shall have a claim on him later?' —'Is it wrong, when the electors to a parish look like electing someone whose incumbency will be a disaster to the church, to pay electors not to

[56] *Hispania Sacra* 27 (1974), 240 ff.

vote?'—the miserable scruples were probably not very common, but they were common enough for practised confessors to need advice from their textbooks on how to give counsel.[57] This was the debased side of the number of priests, the excess of candidates, the clerical proletariat.

Confessors were forced to answer more innocent questions from candidates: 'I was a candidate at a *concursus* for the office of confessor and answered the questions right by sheer luck, and was appointed. Yet I am utterly ignorant of moral theology—may I with a good conscience hear confessions?'[58]

Ordination of coloured priests

A few diocesan synods passed regulations that no one of Jewish family could be ordained. Rome refused to uphold these decisions, but not quite steadily. In Portugal, where Jews were excluded from the country, the government wanted a law that persons of Jewish family could not be ordained and Popes Sixtus V (1588) and Clement VIII (1600) conceded the law. In the Indies continued pressure that the Church ought not to ordain negroes or coloured or half-castes. In 1683 Rome ruled that colour was nothing to do with qualifications for holy orders. Shortly afterwards the Archbishop of Lisbon refused to ordain a man because he was coloured, and pleaded the decision of earlier synods. Rome ruled against him and declared such decisions null.[59] It was ready to accept a Mexican resolution that children of parents where one was Indian and the other African should only be accepted for ordination with care. This resolution was not to do with colour, but concerned children neither of whose parents was Christian.

Confession

By its fourth canon the Roman provincial council (1725) defined the duties of the parish priest: to instruct his people in the faith and to minister the sacrament; visit the sick and help the dying; pray daily for his people; set an example by manner of life in the way to salvation; preach every Sunday a sermon which shall be short and easy to follow; declare sins to avoid and virtues to seek; on Sunday afternoons teach catechism to the children between seven and fourteen years; and encourage the children's parents.

The definition failed to mention the most weighty of the duties, that of sitting in the confessional.

---

[57] e.g. Liguori, *Theol. Moral.* 4.441 ff.   [58] *Decisioni* (Bologna), 3.268–71.
[59] Benedict XIV, *de synodo,* xii. 1.2–4, cols. 1315–16.

Not every priest could hear confession, except in cases of extreme emergency. The parish priest could hear the confessions of his parishioners and needed no licence. Other priests needed a licence from the bishop.

This work was seasonal. A pious person might make confession once a month, for such an interval counted as frequency. But the people made their confessions in crowds, either at a special event like a parish mission, or at Easter when they could not be Catholics unless they fulfilled the duty and therefore would suffer disadvantage in State as well as Church. Hence a parish priest was confronted in Holy Week with the need to sit hour after hour in the confessional, because in most parishes virtually the whole population came to his box; so that authority had to decree that if confronted by a queue he could not skimp by hearing the barest declaration and then giving absolution, he must hear each individual in full and in detail, for he was the doctor of that soul. A few dioceses allowed him to get help from the priest of a neighbouring parish. But this was not frequent and was perhaps irregular. The question was discussed whether a priest could cut short a long-winded confession, and some advisers said that at times it must be necessary. But most opinion held this dangerous. A too deliberate penitent went on and on because he or she suffered from over-scrupulousness. To choke off the flow usually made scruples worse.

Despite its infrequency, the sacrament was a weighty part of religious life. Ordinary folk believed in mortal sin, for which no man might be forgiven without confession. They did not need to be specially fervent or conscientious to arrive at the confessional. They might merely have stolen a cow and could not think what to do.

The Catholic eighteenth century was still engaged in a prolonged endeavour to raise the standard of its priests. Everyone must confess, few confessors knew what to say or whether to absolve. Therefore the age saw the publication of numerous guides to confessors. The authors of the books were forbidden by the seal of secrecy to use actual cases in the way a lawyer could cite cases in his handbook. They must hide under feigned places and conventional names and altered circumstances. But since they guided real men, hearing real problems which agonized souls, they were bound to reflect reality; and therefore, as through a dark mirror, we see reflected in these handbooks the moral concerns which tormented consciences in that age.

Through the moral textbooks can be discerned the poor man and still more poor woman coming in a rough world to want a puzzle explained or a family trouble unravelled, a conscience quieting, a doubt satisfying, a self-justification for a crime to be projected on to another's shoulders, an insurance against the wrath of God, a burden of guilt to be washed away. I stole but I was starving and desperate—is stealing in despair sin? I took the goods of my master but he grossly underpays and exploits me—is it wrong to help myself? I needed heat and cut wood in the copse that belongs to all the village but the village said that no one was to cut—was I only disobedient or did I also steal? I longed to have a relic of the saint in my cottage and when no one was watching I cut off a bit, it was for the glory of God and health of my family, yet something felt not right? I am an officer in the army and drew pay for several soldiers who do not exist—am I bound to pay back the money? I am a soldier in the army and this war is evil—is it wicked to desert? I am an officer in the army and am ordered to shoot hostages—what is my duty? I am a lawyer and am sure now that my client is guilty—can I go on defending? Am I bound to obey my husband when he orders me to cook and sweep the house though this would be extraordinary in our social class? Am I bound to follow my husband when he moves from one town to another because he has changed his job? I killed a husband in self-defence when he attacked me because he found me lying with his wife—was it only self-defence or was it worse? Can it be my duty as a son to marry the girl whom my father has arranged though I cannot bear the sight of her? Neither my fiancée nor I wants to have children—is it right for us to marry? The question of Montagu and Capulet could still be dimly heard—is it right for us to marry when we do not love each other but the marriage will end vendetta between our families? May I reject my husband's advances because we cannot feed all the children we have already? Is it wrong for me to imagine intercourse with another woman so that I can have successful intercourse with my wife? . . . For the first time confessors were being asked about (clumsy and crude) methods of birth control.

So the questions ran on and on and on; now reflecting eternal predicaments of human beings and now the special conditions of a people's life and customs and belief in the old regimes of Europe; some of them easy to answer, some depending on circumstances, some posing the insoluble.

Sex was a staple. Everyone was agreed that it was wrong to take a pill to prevent the conception of a baby; for conception brought into the light a new child destined to eternity, than which no act of humanity could be nobler or more God-given. But over abortion penitents and confessors and moral theologians who advised confessors were continually anxious and often disagreed. What if a baby starts, and will bring shame and scandal, or will endanger mother's life, whether because she is incapable of bearing children with safety or because her relatives will kill her when they know? Many good doctors thought that nothing was wrong if an abortion was procured before the embryo was 'animate'—most put this at forty days, a few put it at eighty days—some reputable moralists allowed abortion, given certain conditions, at any stage up to eighty days of pregnancy. These conditions were concerned with the health of the mother. To take a drug to procure an abortion was sin because it was murder. Under Pope Innocent XI (1679) the Inquisition condemned the doctrine that to kill an embryo is not murder and that it should be done if thereby the mother's life would be saved. To take a drug to save the mother's life—even though the drug might have the effect of procuring an abortion—could well be legitimate.

But what if birth endangers mother's life? Above all, what is to be done when mother or physician must choose between saving mother's life and saving baby's life? Mother already possesses life for eternity; baby, unless it comes out and is baptized, none. Therefore mother may have as much an obligation to risk her life for her baby's life as a grown man has a duty to risk his life to try to rescue a drowning child. Stiff men would not allow it right for a mother to take a drug to abort, even if her death was morally certain if she did not abort, when the choice lay between the death of a mother and the death of a baby. For the mother was faced with a moral choice between murder and likely but not absolutely certain death through illness; and she ought not to doubt which she should choose. Other moralists hold this doctrine to be over rigid. Probably, however, professors of ethics had not the least effect on what happened at the bedside and doctors or midwives did what sense or ignorance or compassion dictated. The Church had more mercy than its doctrine. If abortion was homicide, a mother who took a drug to procure abortion was liable to excommunication as a murderer. Why did a Pope not excommunicate? 'Because perhaps he understood the weakness of women. They are driven by terrible fear of what will happen and then take the drugs; and if they are not revolted by such a crime, they will take very little notice of excommunication.'[60]

Sex was one of the two commonest subjects, among uneducated penitents the commonest. It included the delicate manoeuvrings between engaged couples, for an engagement was a binding pledge not easily broken, as weighty as marriage and in certain areas celebrated with more splendour.

One moral strain among well-to-do young men in courts and cities was the duel. In 1592 Pope Clement VIII condemned all duelling. But a man

[60] Liguori, *Theol. Moral*, 2.215.

who refused to fight was thought a coward, would lose his friends, might easily lose his place at court and his office and salary. Thirty years after Clement's bull duelling was the commonest and deadliest exercise among the courtiers of Catholic France. The French government was more successful than any other government in stamping it out. But in Germany, and at times all over Europe, it continued through the eighteenth century. The case came up sufficiently often for confessors to be concerned. Given that it is wrong to fight a duel, is it wrong to pretend to fight a duel so as to preserve one's honour? If an army officer would be cashiered if he refused to fight, what is his duty? One loop-hole was self-defence—if a man is going to kill you, and then offers to concede you weapons to defend yourself, duelling is not a duel but self-defence. Pope Benedict XIV (*Detestabilem*, 10 November 1752) tried to strip the act of every shadow of excuse.

Confessors were instructed that any trade or profession which continuously put life in peril was unlawful for a Christian man. A tight-rope walker at a carnival, balancing on a wire far above a carpet of swords pointed upwards, and afterwards coming to confession, was told that he ought to stop. Despite the tolerance of bull-fights in Spain, matadors fell under this disapproval. 'It is certainly illicit for anyone to engage in a profession which continuously endangers life and limb.'[61]

In the middle of the eighteenth century many people who could write brought along to confession a little paper on which they prepared themselves and so were able to give more ordered account of what troubled their consciences. This relatively new habit eased a confessor's work while it might lengthen his time. But his patience was more apt to be taxed by illiterate men or women who came to confession and were incoherent, knew that they ought to say something but could not begin to express what it was they wanted to say. Then—while a long queue might wait—a priest slowly and painfully extracted by questioning what it was that the inarticulate meant. The 'seal' made anything said in confession, however criminal, absolutely secret, so that the people had confidence in the sacrament. The little papers of the educated caused an argument, whether they fell under the seal; and it was soon determined that (however good men should respect the confidence of other people's private affairs) these papers did not come under the seal of secrecy, which applied only to what was said in actual confession.

The confessional was a gentler world than the pulpit. In the sermon the preacher lashed general sin, the immorality of a class or a city. In the box

[61] *Decisioni* (Bologna), 2.19–20; but not all moralists agreed with this verdict.

the pastor tried to understand, was willing to make excuses or at least to hear excuses without repugnance. About the middle of the century Italian women not of the upper class adopted topless dresses so that their breasts were exposed. A famous preacher noted with interest that his own attitude was entirely different in pulpit and in confessional. In sermons he whipped the women with words, *lascivious, vile, immoral.* He thought their behaviour all those things. But when he found it in the confessional he realized that fashions are odd, that the power of a common custom is infectious, that though he must reproach the woman in his box he could not think it to be for her so heavy a sin.[62]

This was the underlying reason why handbooks for confessors, when read by a Protestant north or by austere Jansenists among Catholics, shocked by 'laxity'. The tradition became a proverb in the order which Liguori founded, 'lion in the pulpit, lamb in the confessional.'

A Pope of the Counter-Reformation decreed that when a doctor attended a patient, he should not begin to treat until he warned the man that he ought to make his confession; that he should not go to treat him more than three times unless the confessor certified in writing that the patient had confessed; and even that doctors, before they were qualified, should swear to observe this rule, and should not be licensed by bishops until they were known to have taken this oath.

This was one of those rigidities of the Counter-Reformation which the Catholic eighteenth century quietly put aside. Everyone agreed that it was absurd to apply it to cases like gout. Even so, it was unworkable; doctors would not tolerate such a breach of their sense of moral obligation; Spain formally abrogated the rule; in France it was a dead letter; in Naples it was still partly observed, but only for 'dangerous' illnesses; the difficulty of deciding when an illness is dangerous caused more argument, and neither doctor nor priest had the least desire to tell some patients that they were in danger. Pope Benedict XIV, who greatly helped the Church by disposing of inherited nonsense, really settled the issue. It would be excellent if all men and women were brought up to the knowledge of a need for penitence and confession on their sick-beds. Then fewer would die in peril of damnation. But if a patient is 'obstinate' and refuses to confess, the doctor is not therefore to be held to desert him, because this would be a failure in charity, and the law of charity takes precedence of all rules.

As part of this discipline, priests encouraged to confession parishioners who faced unknown danger—a woman of delicate health who was near

[62] Liguori, *Theol. Moral.* 1.343.

her first labour, or who by earlier experience had difficult hours in labour; a traveller setting out on a distant voyage; a criminal condemned to the scaffold; a soldier starting for the wars.

With a celibate clergy, too many priests, and crowds in the confessional, the disease of solicitation in the confessional, either by penitent or by confessor, was anxious enough to take up plenty of argument by lawyers and advice by professors. If a priest in the confessional solicited, the penitent was bound under solemn duty to report what happened to authority, which in this case meant the Inquisition. As the Inquisition grew less important and less active during the century, the trial or imprisonment of poor sacrilegious priests became its chief duty during the last decades of its life. The confessional was the only place where a priest was bound to meet a young woman or boy without witnesses and with no one to over-hear what was said; and sudden or overwhelming temptation could afflict a man who heard a woman explaining her frailty and how easily she consented. The rule that the penitent must denounce was extra-ordinarily difficult to operate because wicked or obsessed women, or women suffering from hallucination, could denounce an innocent priest. The land was misty and unpleasant, and had borderlands where no one quite knew what was right or wrong—as when a priest said 'If I were a layman I would like to marry you'; or another priest said 'Don't forget me for I love you in my heart', which was capable of a purely spiritual meaning; or another priest said 'I don't want to hear your confession; it would affect me, for I can't help being in love with you', which could not carry a purely spiritual meaning, and yet might be said under stress and with good intention to avoid sacrilege.[63] Against these sudden emotions the confessional box gave a measure of protection. But such cases were a reason why bishops felt it absolutely necessary to retain rigid control of the number of persons licensed as confessors. They could not stop any parish priest from being confessor to all his parishioners, for that duty was inherent in his office. But they could and did control by licence any non-beneficed priest and sought to ensure his stable character and his training.

Bishops knew the miserable training which many of their priests possessed for this work, how difficult in practice, how much wisdom and knowledge needed, how few with the right equipment. In parishes where nearly all the people came, clumsy confessors could not only hurt a pious soul by imprudence, they created scandal. Marriage was the worst. What was he to do when he found that a marriage, contracted by one party in good faith, was in fact null because he discovered the other party to be

[63] Liguori, *Theol. Moral.* 4.514–15.

married before? The moral theologians of the eighteenth century regarded this case as the most testing which could fall on a confessor,
because any course he adopted, any advice he gave, had the gravest
possible objections. What is he to do if the night before the wedding he
discovers from one party that there is fatal impediment to a valid wedding
and yet the wedding cannot be stopped without scandal and unhappiness?

Those who tried to train confessors knew that not very educated men
were about to attempt to help suffering men and women in some of the
most delicate and insoluble problems known to human existence, and were
realistic that neither wisdom nor psychological subtlety are qualities
readily found. They therefore tried to create an extensive system of rules
which could be learnt and applied not only in normal situations but in
abnormal. This body of knowledge became so long, as it tried to meet
every sort of crisis, that unacademic priests shrank from trying to acquire
what they needed. The shortage of confessors arose partly because parish
priests could not get enough assistant priests to qualify as confessors. The
young men felt not only that the work was painful but that the effort
needed to master its practice might be too difficult. When was a sin a
reserved case, where absolution might not be given without reference to a
higher authority, bishop or even Pope? Under what circumstances was a
normally mortal sin only venial? The tradition of questioning penitents
demanded delicacy and courage and a wide knowledge of the world and
men and other men's occupations. If a physician came to confession, for
example, it might be necessary to ask him whether he was properly
qualified or was practising as a quack and pretending to be qualified, and
whether he gave false certificates of ill health, as for example in cases
where his patients wanted to be exempted from rules of fasting and to buy
meat at fasting seasons, and whether he sufficiently warned patients, in the
case of dangerous illness, or illness that might become dangerous, that they
ought to ask for a confessor. If a chemist came to confession he might need
to be asked whether he gave drugs illegally, as for the purpose of procuring
abortion. Confronted with a crowd of rustic penitents, the priest was
likely to find a man who failed to mention glaring sin because he had no
idea that it was sin, like lying with a neighbouring girl under a hedge; and
another man who failed to mention glaring sin because he was compelled
to go to confession and had no intention of mentioning what embarrassed
him or even what he thought the priest to disapprove. Therefore the
training of confessors in that age expected them to ask question after
question, probing the likely temptations—tailors measuring women's
busts for a new dress, priests saying mass inside a quarter of an hour,

publicans serving drinks over the bar when the customer had evidently taken too much already, nearly all males of any age swearing, which peasants regarded not as sin but as articulacy—a whole age of social life neglected by historians. On the one hand confessors were trained to expect and require a *complete* confession, for all was not right with God if something was held back from him in the sacrament. Therefore they were not assumed to behave, as their later successors behaved, as if all was well unless the penitent said that it was not well. They went into hair-raising detail of questioning, for example, with boys over masturbation. But the best educators of confessors distinguished sharply between men and women. They tried to stop their cruder priests from this sort of probing with women and girls. If they probed they must do it with generality. When they wanted to know whether a woman had refused her husband his conjugal rights, they were to ask the vaguer question, 'Have you been obedient in all things to your husband?' They were aware of the danger of suggesting sin to women. With boys they evidently thought this hardly possible.

Three kinds of confessor needed warning in the handbooks. One was the man who learnt a lot of moral theology by rote and then applied it stupidly in his confessional—as when he asked penitents, 'Is your sin mortal or venial?' for they would have no idea. The second kind was the over-rigid. To refuse absolution for a time was one thing and might be necessary. To make its future bestowal conditional on some intolerable penance was another. To postpone the absolution of a thief until he restored was or might be good. To postpone the absolution of a boy who confessed rudeness to his parents until he went home and kissed his mother's feet was bad because the act was unnatural, might be too hard to perform, and so the cause of further sin.[64]

The third was subtler and less ignorant. A small number of people, more often in towns than the country, and much more often women than men, were very rewarding to a confessor. They were truly prayerful, received gifts of contemplation, showed signs of holiness, and on occasion were given mystical experience which gave every sign of being authentic. These privileged souls needed help and direction in a way which the farm labourer did not. At first sight their direction demanded a confessor of far higher quality, a man of such prayerful experience that he would know from reality what penitents described. Therefore a type of confessor existed who regarded this as his work and left peasants to the assistant priests, crude advice for crude sin. Alfonso Liguori, a man dedicated to

[64] Liguori, *Theol Moral.* 4.280 ff.

mission to the poor, wrote an excellent treatise on the ways in which a
confessor should seek to guide contemplative souls. But he loathed the
type of confessor, of whom he saw plenty, who spent time with the
privileged and waved away the queue, saying he had no time left: 'Go to
someone else.' He knew also, as all wise priests knew from experience,
that a young confessor would sometimes meet illiterate rustics who knew
more about God, and Christ, and the Church, than many sophisticated
members of the upper class.

Pope Benedict XIII (1725) allocated two of the canonries in each
cathedral to train priests—that is, not ordinands, but already ordained
priests, especially confessors.[65] A theologian (Bible or doctrine) should be
chosen for one canonry, a moral theologian and experienced confessor
chosen for the other. This second was usually known as the penitentiary.
His duty consisted not only in hearing many confessions, but in helping
to educate confessors further in their moral duty.

The bishop summoned all confessors (which included all parish priests)
to a monthly meeting, usually in the cathedral. Some dioceses even held
it weekly. The weekly meeting quickly found that attendance sagged, and
after a time bishops needed to exhort their men to get anything like a full
monthly meeting.[66]

This meeting took various forms. By a standard type the clergy met
first for a little food and then went to the church (or if convenient, a church
hall, occasionally to the bishop's palace) from which others were excluded.
The president sat at a table with an hour-glass, reference books, and a
secretary who kept the roll of those present. The president started by
reading decrees of synods which concerned the clergy; then proposed a
moral case, of which notice was given at the last meeting; summoned at
least two men to discuss it, choosing by lot or in turn; after which the
president determined what was right or called upon an expert. Then they
might move to a moment of the liturgy, and talk about the rite, or even
practise what should be done. Finally they ended the hour with silent
prayer, collect or litany, and an announcement of the next meeting. Since
the meeting lasted an hour, not more than one case could be discussed.

Various collections of cases debated were afterwards printed. These
cases varied from the very ordinary and everyday to the exceptional or
hardly imaginable. But they showed the moral decisions which specially
troubled people and confessors.

An area of moral difficulty which took as many pages as sex in the hand-

[65] *Bull. Rom.* xxii. 182.
[66] Benedict XIV. *Institutiones Ecclesiasticae* (1750), xxxii, 209 ff.; cf. Ferraris. 2.1175.

books, and as frequent debates in the bishop's monthly meetings, was commerce. Part of the trouble was the inability of confessors to fathom the machinery of market or bank, the temptation peculiar to trader or money-lender. Usually he started his life as a confessor with the single principle, *usury is wrong*. Sometimes he ended his life knowing no more and still clinging fast to an ancient verity. But if he was confessor in a north-Italian city, or a sea-port, or Vienna, or Munich, or Cologne, he had to learn fast.

Easier cases were little to do with usury, shares, or interest. 'Bonomio cultivated in his vineyard vines brought from Tuscany. From their grapes came wine so perfect that experts think it Tuscan wine. Can he sell it if he is asked for Tuscan wine, and at a Tuscan price?' (No.) 'Is it immoral for dealers at an auction to make a ring to keep prices down (or up)?' (Yes.) 'Can merchants who have a monopoly agree on a minimum price?' (No.) 'Is a government behaving morally if it makes a monopoly for the good of the state?' (Yes.) 'Can a painter who perfectly imitates the work of an Old Master sell the painting as an Old Master?' (No.) 'At the fair in Mantua Luca and Lucillo each bought 100 sacks of corn to sell in Venice. The bargee put Lucillo's 100 sacks underneath Luca's 100. Near Ferrara Lucillo was offered money for his corn, and not to disturb the loading sold Luca's. Further down the river the barge was holed and the remaining corn flooded and ruined. Who lost money?' (Disagreement.) 'Can you rent a house to people knowing it will be used as a brothel?' (No.) 'And what do you do if you rent a house and afterwards discover that it is used as a brothel?' (You must turn them out whatever the loss.) 'Is it wrong to try to turn other metals into gold, that is, is it wrong to practise alchemy?' (No if not for gain [!], if no pact with the devil, if it does not waste time, and if the alchemist can afford the outlay.)[67]

All these were overshadowed by rates of interest.

A *Mons Pietatis* was a lending bank. That is, the Church approved them, even designed and governed them, as ways of helping poor or oppressed—for example a starving pauper or a Christian heavily in debt to a Jewish money-lender. These *Montes* were once criticized as *usury*. But they were long approved, formally by the Lateran Council in the age of the Renaissance.

Montes were of different types. In the 'ideal' form they collected money from the rich, charged their expenses, and lent the rest to poor people at no rate of interest and if necessary with a favourable time for repayment.

In a slightly less 'ideal' form, the *Mons Pietatis* undertook the same duty,

[67] *Decisioni* (Bologna), 4.14; Chiericato, *Dec. Misc.* 15; Chiericato, *Erotemata*, ch.22.

but to make its operations more extensive, charged borrowers with sums to cover the expense of office and secretaries. Then it lent money at low rates of interest, below the level of the market.

A third type of *Mons* took a long step nearer to the modern bank. It could not raise money from charity, or anything like enough money. So it borrowed in the market, paid depositors interest at 5 per cent and recouped interest and office expenses from the borrowers. Therefore it was bound to charge borrowers a rate of interest more than 5 per cent.

A fourth and final type was the *Mons Pietatis* set up by the State. Government might borrow its money, or compel its people to lend it money, paying them 4 or 5 per cent.

But all this is *usury*? And usury is immoral and illegal in Catholic states?

In the world of high banking which they did not well understand, confessors struggled with questions from sophisticated penitents.

The *Mons* at Padua was founded in 1491 and by 1680 had a capital of more than 125,000 ducats. It charged 5 per cent to borrowers. Since the yield on the 5 per cent was more than needed to pay expenses, the city used the profit for hospitals or schools.

Not everything was right. A man who borrowed £100 (*solidi*) must pay 100 *bagatini* a month (12 *bagatini* to the £, therefore £5 a year = 5 per cent). But the *bagatinus* was a metaphysical coin, it bought nothing, you could not find specimens. Therefore if a poor man borrowed £7, since the interest was less than £1 and no coins existed less than £1, the borrower had to pay £1 to get his £7; so that under the apparent rule of 5 per cent the small borrower, that is the truly poor man whom the *Mons* aimed in moral theory to serve, paid a rate of interest at more than 14 per cent. This extra money, which was thought to add up in all to hundreds of thousands of ducats, was suspected of going into the pockets of the bankers, who need only account for interest at 5 per cent. Moreover the bankers, rightly suspecting that poor men would not easily pay back the capital, exacted a further sum, above the (alleged) 5 per cent, by way of 'security' —this money went to charity, the hospitals or schools.

The moralists attempted to lay down rules in this difficult area of life; especially, though without much hope, to maintain the doctrine, first, that the object of a bank is to help poor and not rich, and secondly, that the only ultimate justification for rates of interest is to pay expenses. And around these principles they met the temptations which troubled bankers —to delay paying out, to ask for a tip before agreeing the loan, to hand to a borrower clipped or debased coins hard to spend, and to cheat at the disposal of a security where a borrower failed to repay, by selling the security to themselves under a fictitious name at less than the market price. If the departments concerned with public accounts found these abuses hard to cure, the authority of the Church found them still harder.[68]

Country priests met usury but in simpler forms. I borrowed £100 from a Venetian merchant and agreed to pay it back at harvest in the form of flour at the then market value—is that usury? A farmer borrowed £100 from me to buy horses, and I lent him the money on condition he works my farm at a fair wage—usury? I am owed 1,000 ducats but because I cannot get them Antonio gave me 800 ducats in return for the right to the debt—usury? Can I borrow 1,000 ducats from Peter if I lend him my house to live free until I pay back the money?

No man can be under a moral duty to starve. If a poor man had to have money, and could not get money except at an exorbitant rate, the borrower did not sin, only the lender for his extortion. And borrowing in certain crises of life, especially over dowries, marriage contracts, widowhood, feudal vassalage, was recognized as lawful and established use.

Is it lawful for Jews to be usurers? Since society needs credit, and lending is only possible at interest, and interest is not lawful among Christian men, can a non-Christian lend at usury? The moralists answered No, emphatically.

These doubts of the confessional were reflected in high and public argument among dignitaries. Between 1740 and 1743 such a controversy grew fierce at Verona between the bishop and his chapter, and in the chapter between two parties of canons, on the right to lend at interest. The citizens followed the strife eagerly. In 1744 Scipione Maffei, a layman and a historian, published a learned treatise *On the Use of Money* (*Dell'impiego del danaro*) in which the attitude is weighty.

Times are changed, argued Maffei. You must understand old rules in the light of the circumstances in which they were issued. You cannot apply the norms of the Biblical world or the medieval world without considering. Usury was condemned because it was a way by which rich oppressed poor. But since the discovery of America it is a way to increase prosperity which helps the poor. It is not the poor nowadays who need to borrow, but the rich. Money is alive, it can create. If money-lending oppresses the poor it is still abominable. But often it helps. It is the road to prosperity. And, for example, in Venice nunneries are forbidden by law to buy property. They must have endowments to live, what can they buy? If they cannot invest money, they are reduced to buying statues, pictures, tapestries. Usury is the only way to a steady income.

[68] The Padua *Mons Pietatis* in Chiericato, *Dec. Misc.* 110 ff.

Leading theologians condemned Maffei's thesis, and one of them asked whether he had become a Calvinist. All usury is wrong; any doctrine that it is ever right is heresy. Dominicans preached against him, Venice banned the book and prohibited public discussion of the question, Verona ordered him out of the city.

The argument went up to Rome. Benedict XIV, who was a friend of Maffei and thought him wrong, refused to approve, and just, but only just, refrained from outright condemnation (*Vix pervenit*, 1 November 1745). Benedict said that all usury was hateful, preachers must continue to preach against; but he left a little door open to revise the technical old scholars' formula which defined what is usury. Maffei was deeply hurt. He asked if he could republish in Rome, and got Benedict's leave provided he printed the encyclical as a preface.

The leading rigorist theologian of all Italy was the Dominican Daniel Concina. In 1746 Concina printed a violent book at Naples, *The Doctrine of the Church of Rome on Usury* (*Esposizione del dogma che la chiesa romana propone a credersi intorno l'usura*). He loathed the upper-class tone of Maffei's book. Concina filled his pages with hatred of luxury, stock markets, speculation, gambling in shares or projects.

In his parish, away from these lofty debates, the priest heard many more confessions of poor than of rich. He was far more likely to see the torments created by borrowing at interest, far more likely to regard bankers as wicked, far more likely to follow a Pope who proclaimed the easy rule, 'All usury is immoral.' But, despite the simplicity of public attitudes among Church leaders, the confessor still faced very awkward questions in his box, from quite lowly traders or farmers.[69]

Every Catholic must make his confession once a year. Outsiders were inclined to think the confessional the source of priestly influence. It brought a man into intimate relations with families who might be important in the world. The prime minister in Naples, Tanucci, was obsessed with the power which, he fancied, confessors must be exercising over the royal family, especially its women, and over magistrates.

This diagnosis among some contemporaries is very uncertain, and in any case escapes the historian. The priest's authority was more likely to weigh heavily upon the poor. The poor man must go to confession at Easter or suffer civil disadvantage; there he might be asked, 'Did you steal'? If he lied and said that he had not, he feared that spiritual powers would make his life unlucky during the coming year. If he said truly that he had, he

---

[69] Apart from Noonan and Nelson, see Venturi, *Sett.rif.* 1.118 ff.; and *D.B.I.* s.v. 'Ballerini'.

might have to restore what he had taken, because if he refused to promise he might be refused absolution—and so suffer disadvantage.

The archives of Pamplona afford a glimpse into the practice of Easter duties in the diocese. In the age of the Counter-Reformation, in fulfilment of reforms proposed by the Council of Trent, a diocesan synod of Pamplona (1590) decreed that in the period of Easter (Palm Sunday to Low Sunday) everyone must confess and receive communion; and anyone who failed should be liable to the greater excommunication and a fine of four *reales*. In the later eighteenth century the clergy of each parish still kept lists of their parishioners as a register that these two duties were fulfilled; if they failed to keep such a list they were liable to a fine. Bishop Murillo y Velarde (1725–8) added to this duty a prior examination in Christian doctrine for all the people—that was, in effect, the need for the priest to include in his certificate an assurance that the persons on the list could say the creed, Lord's Prayer, Hail Mary, the Ten Commandments, the duties of a churchman, the seven sacraments, the works of mercy, and an act of contrition—all in the vernacular. Forms of the certificate have survived: 'I, the undersigned, parish priest of Legaria, certify: all the persons of this village eligible for confession and communion have been examined in Christian doctrine and have fulfilled their Easter duties in the year 1801.' Nearly all the parishes in the diocese of which returns for 1801 are extant certify that all the parishioners fulfilled the obligation. An innkeeper was in trouble for failure to conform, a lunatic who had sane intervals, a young man vanished when ordered to do his duty, one man was suspected of playing off two parishes against each other, one was said to have joined a band of smugglers, they experienced special difficulty with the mountaineers of Santander and the iron-workers of Biscay. But the archive proves how normal and accepted the practice, how regular the priests in working the register and issuing tickets of confession and communion, how natural to the parishioners.[70]

In a city priests found it less easy to know whether all their parishioners kept their duties. Prospero Lambertini said that 'in well-regulated dioceses' the priests kept lists, thereby showing that not all dioceses had his approval. In Bologna diocese during the 1730s the penalty for failure to make confession and receive communion at Easter was the ordinary procedure by way of interdict, that is, exclusion from church, loss of burial by the church, and placarding of the name on the main door of the church. But in 1735 so many citizens of the town failed to make their Easter duties that the archbishop made a special public pronouncement,

[70] *Hispania Sacra*, 26 (1973), 362 ff.

urging defaulters to make their communions on 8 September, which is the day of the Nativity of the Blessed Virgin, or on 18 September, which was the day of procession to the cathedral. The records show that urban life was predictably much less favourable to the rule because in a city men and women could pass unnoticed.

Even so, they might meet circumstances when they would be asked to show their tickets. And the difference between town and country should not be exaggerated. In the Padua diocese (1744–53) the number of those who failed to make confession at Easter was 0·09 per cent in the country, 0·43 per cent in the city; that is, the defaulters in the city were nearly five times as numerous as those in the countryside. But even in the city they numbered less than one in 200 people. At Modena at nearly the same period they rose to 2 per cent. At Piacenza (1744) fifty-three persons who failed to do their Easter duties were reported to the civil power and ordered to do them within fifteen days or lose 'the sovereign's grace'.[71]

The argument over the Bologna postponement of 1735 shows how the rules, for all their social power, were starting to weaken. Defaulters pleaded advice from their confessors. They disclosed their state; the confessor recommended that in that state they should abstain from their annual communion; they had no wish to be guilty of sacrilege by nevertheless receiving their communion. The archbishop hoped that the postponement gave them all time to bring their lives into order. But the argument shows how the first faint doubts, on the rightness of receiving communion solely for reasons of compulsion or social pressure, began to enter the minds of townsmen.

The confession ticket had name, Christian name, number of children in family. At communion a priest, usually a junior, collected the tickets. Sometimes the tickets were distributed during communion, given to the head of the family and collected by the priest when he visited the home to bless.

The authority of the priest rested upon a wider area of popular belief than the rules of the confessional.

That the unworthiness of the priest hindered not the effect of the sacrament was a truth admitted, not without regret or difficulty, within the Catholic Church. Priests varied in their morals and the respect which they won from the people. They were too many to win much respect merely because they were priests. And yet some of the things which they did had *virtus*—were God's, and embodied God's power. Therefore the

[71] Fliche and Martin (Italian edn.) xix.1.76.

priest had social and religious power as source of some of the weightiest acts known to mankind—sacrifice of the mass, absolution from mortal sin, influence upon man's fate in the next world but even in this world, minister of holy and happy death.

Mothers took their babies to be sprinkled with holy water at time of mass. The formula of the priest at the altar, *Lamb of God*, was made into a waxen ornament or amulet, though Rome discouraged and sought to control the manufacture. Lucerne peasants believed that at ordination priests had the choice between keeping off unseasonable weather, or hindering the loss of souls who are dying, or recovering stolen goods.[72] If the house caught fire countrymen had no extinguishers, they sent for the priest who was to walk rapidly round the fire with his monstrance, for when fire reached great heights men could hear roaring and believed that this was the noise of demons bellowing. The priest was the only useful protection against witches, thieves, or devils.

Part of his power lay in his knowledge of books. This feeling among the people was not just a respect for learning or literacy. Those who understood books had mysterious knowledge which might be needed in dealing with magical influences.

This expectation that he was a vehicle of supernatural power enabled him to perform in that society acts which were impossible to his successors. But his life was not thereby made comfortable. If weather was bad, or drought destructive, or cattle-plague prolonged, and the people disliked their priest, they might start to suspect that he was in part responsible for their disasters. He must be precise in the way in which he carried out ritual acts, for the slightest departure from what his people knew might lead them to fear that what he did was invalid from want of a right form. Some countrymen held it unlucky to meet a priest on the road, and would evade, especially if two or more priests walked together, or wore cassocks. They expected him to be celibate and would not feel that a married priest could do what they needed for their welfare. But just as they sat very lightly to any idea that they themselves needed to marry, and probably by a majority (in the country) lived together without marriage, they were much less fussy about the priest's private life so long as he was not married. They still shared the old belief that the children of priests would be unlucky in their lives.

Because the exercise of the priests' right to refuse absolution could easily carry civic danger and might carry eternal damnation, bishops and

[72] Bächtold-Stäubli, vii.310.

penitentiaries are found advising priests what to do in tense predicaments. I have refused Easter communion to a man who says that he will come and threaten to murder me if I persist: am I justified in yielding? Readers of Manzoni's great novel *The Affianced* (*I promessi sposi*) will remember the predicament of this type which lies at the heart of the book's plot. And just occasionally we meet agony in the confessor that for some penitents, recidivists, the sacrament is poison. A man raped a girl and comes to the confessional so that he feels free to rape again.

Therefore this sense of 'holiness' entered also, or especially, the confessional. Though men were compelled to go to confession, they did not thereby repudiate or resent this duty. On the contrary, if someone tried to take away their favourite confessor, or deprived them of sufficient chance to make confession, the protest of countrymen could reach the level of violence. When Castelluccia in Calabria was destroyed by the terrible earthquake of 5 February 1783, it was the *municipality* which besought the bishop to send confessors, they had 2,000 people and only two priests, without more confessors the souls of the people would perish, and they were helped only by a missioner from neighbouring Franciscans.[73]

In 1722 the Bishop of Capaccio went into the territory of the abbot of St. Mary of the Angels, who claimed to be outside his diocese, and summoned all the confessors to be examined. Only two obeyed. The bishop deprived all the disobedient of the faculty to hear confessions, and posted the edict on the church doors. This caused tumult. A mob armed with guns and sticks assembled in the square outside the bishop's palace, assaulted his officers and servants, and besieged him for an hour until he pacified them. Then he escaped to a neighbouring town whence he launched an interdict on the makers of the tumult. The people of that country could not have made it plainer that their confessors meant more to them than the bishop.[74]

The confessor in his box was the nearest thing known in the eighteenth century to the psychiatrist in his clinic. Not that wisdom could always be predicted of either adviser. It was as if everyone, once a year, whatever his state of soul, was forced to consult the psychiatrist and was lucky if he found one competent to diagnose. But whatever the advice, sane or foolish, the sacrament ended with an objective moment, a putting aside of the past by absolution, a new start.

[73] De Rosa, *Vescovi*, 147–8.   [74] *Thesaurus Resolutionum*, 2.379.

Residence of priests

A priest might for reasons of health or old age or plurality of parishes not reside in his parish. Bishops tried to control this by insisting on a licence from themselves or their vicars. Bishops behaved less sternly than their predecessors of the high Counter-Reformation, who had been known to order their police to throw into prison any parish priest whom they found outside his parish. On the whole the licensing system worked. For celibate priests country parishes could be lonely. Therefore if the country parish lay within reach of the town the priest was tempted to combine his residence in the country with town life. A parish priest near Foligno slept in the parish and celebrated mass and then spent the rest of that day in Foligno: was that 'residing'? Rome ruled that it was not.[75] Other priests did the opposite, spent their days in the parish and slept the night in town, was that 'residing'?—and again Rome ruled that it was not.

Repair of churches

Whether parishes kept their churches in repair varied according to the prosperity of a region, the existence of an endowment, and the size of the bishop's fund known as the *mensa*. No diocese ever reached a time when a fair number of its churches and vicarages were not in need of repair.

The law varied from country to country. No provisions existed like those in the Church of England where the owner of the great tithe must repair the choir and the people must tax themselves to repair the nave unless an endowment for repair existed. In the Roman Catholic Church the parish priest was responsible to pay out of the endowment of the benefice the money necessary to keep both church and priest's house in repair; furniture for both came under the same rule. This rule dated far back to the time when the income of a benefice was supposed to be divided into three, one part for the priest's stipend, a second for repairs, and a third for charities. In some parishes funds were still divided according to an agreed formula, and most parishes had old charitable endowments separate from the endowment for the priests' stipend. But by lapse of time these financial provisions became untidy. An endowment, once sufficient to pay priest and repair buildings, might now be inadequate even to support the priest.

In northern Italy (Lombardy and Venezia) endowments or gifts for the repair of churches were sometimes administered by 'officers of the fabric'

---

[75] Lambertini, *Raccolta*, 1.185 ff.

(*fabbricieri*), in effect churchwardens, whose accounts could be inspected by the bishop. In southern Italy the survivals of feudal society made patrons more often responsible; but where patrons did not maintain, funds existed known as *luoghi pii laicali*, which were monies assembled by bequest, or gift, or old endowment, and which were administered partly by clergy and partly by laymen.

The rule that the priest was responsible for the upkeep of both church and house from his endowment, could only lead to the ruin of parish churches and houses. Bishops tried to ensure that from the revenue of every parish a proportion was set aside for repairs. This was not achieved in most parishes.

Impoverished congregations with a ruined church usually thought that they need only apply to the bishop and that it was his duty to mend or rebuild. Bishops constantly used part of their *mensa* for repairs, more usually to reconstruct ruined churches than to pay for minor works. But they were not obliged. If the parish had no endowment to repair, and the bishop was satisfied that the parish priest could spare nothing from the endowment from his own stipend (which was itself an opening for argument between a priest and his bishop) then the bishop was entitled to lay the duty on the patron of the parish—squire, monastery, chapter, etc.—and give him a fixed time by which he must repair; if he failed to repair he lost the right of patronage.

For example, an earthquake destroyed parts of the city of Ragusa (Dubrovnik), including the church of St. Mary of Umbla. The patron of the church was the cathedral chapter, which told the congregation that they must pay to rebuild the destroyed church. The people refused and said that it was the duty of the patron. The case went to Rome which ruled in favour of the congregation. The chapter must pay for rebuilding within six months or lose its rights of patronage.[76]

But many parishes had no patron in this sense and were in the free gift of the bishop. Then the congregation was bound to tax itself for the repair of church and priest's house; and the duty to pay tax fell upon all property-owners or tenants in the parish including those owners of property who had land but did not live in the parish. These taxings, especially as they were to be distributed between owners and tenants, easily became a source of litigation.

If all this failed—no parish endowment, no patron, no parish tax—then the parish was entitled to apply to alienate the endowments which it

[76] Lambertini, *Raccolta*, 5, notificazione 12; Peckius; Reclusi; Sabina Diocesan Synod (1736), 62.

possessed for charitable purposes. And if it had no such endowments, then the only resource was to declare the church irreparable and sell the site and make the people go to worship in the next parish. All the century little ruined country churches were disappearing, the stone used where possible for another sacred building.

Probably no better system was possible. It sank to its worst if a parish priest served in a parish for many years and refused to spend a penny on either church or house and then died, leaving his successor to inherit not only the endowment of the parish but a huge debt. The only resource would be for the new priest to sue his predecessor's family for money which he ought to have allocated for dilapidations. It would not be a promising start to a parish ministry, and reduced the number and quality of candidates for the parish. The bishop's official for one part of the diocese, known as the vicar-forain and in function like an English rural dean, had the duty of supervising the parishes so that they could not run into such a calamity. Yet the calamity occurred.

The receptive church

In Italy, especially in southern Italy, was a form of parish known as the *receptiva* church. This was a college of priests (sometimes also of laymen) all of local origin who administered the property, divided the income from tithes and fees, and elected one of their number to be parish priest. As self-perpetuating bodies conscious of class, they co-opted the younger sons of rich families, and lived in an enclosed world cut off from the people and causing anxiety to bishops by their independence, secular tone, and failure to care. It was not a collegiate church because only one of the priests was the parish pastor. The bishop had the safeguard that he could ratify the admission of the priest to office. The parish priest when elected had the power in the parish but only one vote in the choice of other priests to share in the corporation and to divide the income. The *receptiva* church could be *fixed* or *unfixed*; that is, with a fixed number of priests to share the income however the income rose or fell, or varying numbers of priests according to the income. The corporations were also known as *patrimonials* because the members must be of local origin. The Bishop of Capaccio (1726) forced all the priests of two *receptive* churches at Montisani to wear cassocks and birettas and cottas in church, but totally failed in an attempt to make them all help the parish priest in daily mass and in teaching children.

In a few dioceses all parishes were *receptiva*. This made the bishop almost powerless in some of his important duties. In all the mainland part of the kingdom of the Two Sicilies nearly one-third of all parishes were *receptiva*. The function was essentially parasitic on the church, or at best municipal; a clergy always co-opting other clergy who might have no function except to draw pay and no qualification except to be of a local family.

Historians have wondered whether the existence of so many *receptiva* churches in south Italy contributed to the poor quality of parochial life in parts of that country. Such a guess awaits more evidence.

Patronage and election

The country priest was normally in the grip of his patron or squire. In parts of Italy the patron was so often ecclesiastical or distant that this was a little less important. In south Germany country priests were regarded by squires as their private chaplains if not servants. In certain rare parishes the people had an immemorial right to elect their priest, and in Catholic cantons of Switzerland many parishes had this right of election. The canton of Uri was in the habit of electing all its officers annually and made no exception for the priest; and when the parish priest of Altdorf protested they dismissed him from the parish.[77] Venice was unique, in that all the parishes of the city had the right to elect their priest.

Bishops looked on popular election of a priest with repugnance. Experience led them to think it not compatible with their system of competition which ensured the moral and minimum intellectual standard of the new priest. In theory the electing congregation was in a position no different from a lay patron, whose candidate must be acceptable to the bishop. But just as bishops found it hard to resist lay patrons who had bite, they found it equally hard to resist a majority of electors. And yet they knew how a city election gave a chance to every sort of improper influence, for it must happen unsupervised. Kindred could try to bribe or use lower means of persuading electors, patrons and lords could bring pressure on tenants.

Bad roads were connected with a superstition that on occasion made the work of country priests awkward. When public roads were impassable, attendance at mass and Sunday school fell. Fewer people came to church in winter. Sometimes the road was impassable from mud or landslide while travellers could pass if they left the road for the field. Therefore a country priest, carrying his sacrament to the sick, or escorting a corpse from its home to the churchyard, wished to use field footpaths. But

[77] Schwegler, 245.

Italian peasants held it for certain law that if a corpse with cross aloft went down a private path, that path was henceforth and for ever a right of way for the public. Consequently landlords and squires and farmers were known to refuse the priest all access to their fields even though the road was impassable and only over private land could a dying man be brought his sacrament or a dead man be brought to his grave. The refusal was very shocking to clergy, and bishops did what they could when they heard.[78] Their only resource was to persuade everyone that these ideas about rights of way were false.

In the difficulty of communication the outlook of the clergy seldom reached far beyond their parish or at least their diocese. The monsignori of the Curia were notorious for their belief that Rome was the centre of the world and that nothing outside Rome mattered. But this illusion was not confined to priests, being shared by nearly every citizen of Rome. The same kind of parochialism was equally evident in Naples or Venice or Seville. 'They think', wrote Monsignor Consalvi bitterly of the Roman clergy, 'that their world is all the world and that everyone thinks and sees things as they do.'[79]

A priest's books

A parish priest was supposed to possess a working private library. He could not borrow books. If he lived in a historic city like Brescia or Padua he could read in superlative libraries; but no country priest had such access. That an occasional priest collected an excellent library was shown when authority was forced to rule that the income of a benefice, surplus to the priest's stipend, could not all be spent on books for the vicarage. Diocesan officers sometimes laid down a list of the books which, they thought, all priests should own. Such a list from north Italy made an expensive little library: the gospels (no mention of a whole Bible), Lives of the Saints, six devotional writers including the works of St. Francis de Sales, five books on rubrics and the liturgy and the conduct of priests, a commentary on the Psalms 'to help devotion when saying the daily office', the Roman catechism, and three authors on moral divinity and the duty of the confessor.[80] The collection includes no history of the Church (except in the biographies of saints), and only Christian doctrine so far as *applied* in

---

[78] Lambertini, *Raccolta*, 5.1 ff.
[79] Consalvi to Litta 16 January 1796; in P. Wittichen, 'Briefe Consalvi's aus den Jahren 1795–96 und 1798' in *Quellen und Forschungen aus Ital. Archiven und Bibliotheken*, vii (1904), 154.
[80] Chiericato, *Dec. Misc.* 49.

prayer or worship or moral guidance. The books he was thought to need were of worship and ethics.

That a majority of priests, even in the diocese which recommended this list, possessed even half these books is not probable.

Clergy and secular work

Everyone agreed that teaching in school or college or university was work fit for priests and it made no difference what subjects they taught. As undergraduates they might not *read* natural sciences or medicine, because the business of a priest was theology. But nothing stopped them *studying* science at home, and nothing prevented them becoming professors and *teaching* physics or medicine. Several leading scientists were priests.

Everyone agreed that the State might lawfully call upon priests or bishops to serve its needs. No one protested that Alberoni was prime minister of Spain or Richelieu and Mazarin and Dubois and Fleury prime ministers of France, or that cardinal-legates governed provinces of the Papal States. Most cabinets in Catholic states included one or more bishops. The only people to suggest that bishops and abbots ought not to be secular rulers in Germany were politicians, not all Protestant, who could see no other way out of a current political difficulty but by turning a bishopric into a secular state.

Everyone agreed that clerics might not engage in trade. They might not be merchants, bankers, or shopkeepers. Popes however needed to go on repeating the ancient ban, which cannot have been easy to enforce. It was agreed that the veto could not apply to a priest who would otherwise starve. Lawyers also needed to insist repeatedly that business contracts were not invalid because one party was a priest.

Everyone agreed that if a beneficed priest had a smallholding attached to his benefice he might lawfully cultivate the land for his maintenance and that of his household. Manual labour, if good for monks, must also be good for priests. He could sell his corn, or loaves from his corn, or grapes, or wine from his grapes, or calves from his cattle, or pigs fed from his acorns—provided all this was not designed to trade for profit but to maintain himself and his household.

Over some professions came argument.

Might a priest practise as a doctor? Instinctively authority answered no. The Archbishop of Bologna once lumped physicians with merchants and traders as though the work was so obviously unsuitable that no one could think the opposite. This was ancient custom within the Church. But by the second decade of the eighteenth century argument began whether the custom was always sensible.

In the mission field priests with knowledge of European medicine were the only physicians within thousands of miles. They could not help using their knowledge. And missioners saw how medical mission brought home the nature of the Christian message more naturally, and yet more dramatically, than any other form of mission. Certain religious orders consciously combined mission with medical care. Popes (Clement X, Clement XII) recognized and sanctioned this special work in mission overseas.

Those with special experience felt rare congruity between the work of the priest and the work of healing bodies. A French royal physician, who was a Benedictine monk, published a book to prove that nothing is so suitable to the priest as the practice of medicine and to review the numerous doctors who were priests or monks. This thesis caused smiles and a little ridicule. A canon of Camerino in the Marches of Italy made up pills from hyacinth, juleps, and cochineal, and was ordered to desist. The cause went to Rome, which refused to make him stop.[81]

By the second quarter of the century even Italian bishops complained about priests who practised as doctors. The bishops sounded as shocked as if a priest gave up priestly work to become a soldier. But when they came to argue the question, they found that a simple negative was in accord with neither good sense nor Christian charity.

Suppose that a man becomes an expert physician and then decides that he has a vocation to priesthood and is ordained. He goes to a parish and takes the sacrament to a sick-room, and finds a patient in a bad way and too poor to summon a doctor, or too ill for a doctor to arrive in time, or too remote from a town where a doctor could be found. Is the priest to be stopped from acting as physician as well as priest? It was soon agreed that (provided that the priest was truly qualified as a doctor and provided that no general practitioner was available) a priest-doctor must do all he could for a patient.

Suppose that a priest becomes interested in medicine and qualifies as a doctor while he is a priest. They thought it far from certain that this was a way in which any priest ought to spend time. But suppose that it happened. Such a man within a community of priests might reasonably be consulted by his companions on disease and its remedies; and if by the community, it was hard to see why in emergency he might not be consulted by others outside the community.

[81] F. Aignan, *Le Prêtre médecin . . . avec un traité du café et du thé de France, selon le système d'Hippocrate* (Paris, 1696); Ferraris, 2.627 (case of 1693.)

Pope Benedict XIV started to introduce sense into this diversity of opinion and custom. A priest might practise as a doctor but only with the bishop's licence. This licence should only be given for one of two reasons —either that the town had no doctor or not enough doctors, or that the priest was impoverished and needed to earn his living. If the second of these was the reason, the licence should be given only until such time as he received a benefice on which he might live.

The licence should be given only on three conditions: first, that the priest was a truly qualified doctor; second, that he did not operate on patients as a surgeon; and third, that he required no fees for his services. Since this last condition was not compatible with the licence to a priest to practise if only thus could he earn his living, nothing was to stop the priest-doctor accepting gifts from patients who wished to show gratitude.

The ban on operating was very ancient, and rested on a medieval decretal of Pope Innocent III. The reason for the ban was fear that the priest would unwittingly kill. The chances of a patient who needed the knife were less happy than they were to become a century or more later. Therefore into the system of licensing was built the proviso that the priest-doctor should not operate as surgeon. Pope Benedict XIV could imagine circumstances where a patient's life could only be saved (if saved at all) by using a knife and would not quite say that a priest would never use a knife. But the idea was so repellent that he made the concession with reluctance.

To men who disliked these new practices, St. Luke was a help. Objectors argued that he stopped being a physician when he became an evangelist. Advocates of change contended that he was physician and evangelist simultaneously, and could find nothing in the New Testament to the contrary.

The Secretariat of Briefs at Rome sent out many licences to priests to practise as physicians, and always added a clause: 'without charging fees, with love of God towards all men, and on condition that there are not enough doctors.'[82]

Unlike physicians lawyers had often been priests. The canon law of the Church was entangled with the civil law of the State. Ecclesiastical courts were tribunals where priests naturally practised law as advocates or judges; on occasions which were usually uncomfortable, practice in ecclesiastical courts became entangled with practice in secular courts. No one objected if a priest-lawyer acted in a secular court, even in front of a lay judge, if the case touched the Church or the needs of the poor. The public had an instinct that the practice of civil law was unfitting to a priest. But those

[82] Benedict XIV, *de synodo* xiii. 10. cols. 1413–17; Ferraris, 2.627–8.

who understood law best saw how impossible it was to separate canon law from civil law. Authority therefore had small objection to clergy practising as lawyers, provided that they were truly qualified lawyers. It was agreed that in criminal cases it was wholly unfit that a priest should be prosecutor, he could act only on behalf of the defence. Nothing stopped him charging fees—but only so long as he held no benefice on which he might live. And it was generally assumed that he would only appear in a secular court— unless the case concerned himself or the Church—if he acted as poor man's lawyer.

Missions

Because the best clergy were not in country parishes, and because the monastic ideal was still magnetic, and because remote parishes were too poor to house a resident priest, the centre of popular religious life did not always lie in the mass. Neither Reformation nor Counter-Reformation succeeded in such a revolution from the habits of the Middle Ages. Northern countries usually found their centre in morning prayer with sermons. Southern countries found their centre in devotions outside mass or accompanying mass—benediction, processions, pilgrimage, various cults. Because every priest was expected to say mass, and priests were too many, churches were filled with side-altars, several little masses proceeding in quick succession if not simultaneously. The parish masses were cele- brated with a numerous congregation, but we do not always find them at the heart of the people's faith. The moments that stirred men's souls were the abnormal.

The heirs of the Counter-Reformation sometimes astound by likeness of behaviour to that found in the heirs of the Reformation. In those years John Wesley and George Whitefield preached tremendous sermons of evangelism to Yorkshire weavers or Cornish miners. The people of England, as distinct from the middle classes of England, began to find the focus of their Protestant faith in the abnormal instead of the normal; the quality of utterance, the emotional moment, the directness of appre- hension. In the same way the people of Italy found their focus in the emotional moment, mission, meditation on the passion, procession to a place or picture, excitement of a special course of sermons by a famous itinerant.

Missions began in the country because country parishes had less pastoral care and some had none and missions were one form of itinerant ministry. The most interesting mission work was preached among mountains and marshes. But theorists of mission believed in missions also for towns, since townsmen, as one of them said, have hearts quite as hard as countrymen's hearts;[83] and theorists also agreed that in towns missions were easier, because numbers create excitement, the more coals heaped together the more incandescent the flame. In towns they needed careful organization beforehand—not to conflict with other arrangements like Lenten courses, not to cause resentment against religious orders with houses in the town by sending a missioner from a religious order outside.

Popular missioners were found in several orders. In Cartagena in Spain the Capuchin Father Diego (1786-7) preached a mission in the great square to 10,000 people daily, many queuing from dawn for front places though he did not begin till 6.00 in the evening. When the magistrates banned queuing till 2 p.m. the result was broken heads and they perforce rescinded the order. Father Diego was learned, eloquent, and modest, denied that he worked miracles as the people said, and needed a police guard to prevent them ripping away his clothes. One of the leading missioners in southern Italy during the middle years of the century was a Scolopist, Domenico Pirrotti (to be declared in 1934 a saint); and this was strange, for the Scolopists were a teaching order. He was expelled from Naples and went on with his work in the northern Papal States, a warm promoter of the cult of the Heart of Jesus. In Naples the Dominican Father Gregorio Rocco was the famous evangelist of the city, fat, always carrying a crucifix, frightening taverns and brothels, diminishing gambling, founding charities, stopping brawls, making street lights out of shrines on street corners, preaching in a mixture of threats and jests, popularizing the Christmas crib; a leader of the city slums, deciding petty law suits, clownish in manner and rude in energy, at once beloved and feared.[84]

In 1742 at the request of Cardinal Spinelli, Archbishop of Naples, Alfonso Liguori undertook a long series of missions in the suburbs of Naples. He preached two or three times a day, and spent long hours in the confessional; wore an old patched cassock and rode everywhere on a donkey; taught the people to use the rosary and visit the Blessed Sacrament. In later Redemptorist missions the spirits were moved more hotly. In some churches the atmosphere could be almost unbearable. The missioner preached with a standing portrait of the Madonna by his side, lashed himself with a scourge in the pulpit, solemnly cursed with bell and candle impenitent sinners among his hearers, the blasphemers and men of

[83] Segneri, *Parocco istruito*, ch.26, in *Opere*, vol. xxv (Florence, 1832), 97.
[84] Townsend 3.147; *L.T.K.* s.v. 'Pirrotti'; Acton (1956), 82-4; Swinburne, *Travels*, 3.107-8; Croce, *Uomini*, 2.118-20.

vendetta. He used popular hymns with modern tunes. Some south-Italian missioners called on the people to show penance for their loose tongues by licking the dusty floor of the church. This last humiliation had bitter critics among the clergy. Parish priests criticized violent missions as causing terror among their people. When Liguori heard the criticism, he exclaimed, 'My God, what do we do it for?'[85]

The effects of a mission were dramatic. Men handed over pistols and daggers, women threw away low-cut dresses, young men offered themselves as ordinands or monks. After a mission by fourteen Redemptorists at Sarno, the taverns were deserted for ten years. Occasionally a rite that marked a mission persisted into the long future. In the mission at Nola in 1757 the church bell was rung on Thursday evening in thanksgiving for the eucharist. Forty years later, in an Italy infested by looming revolution, the Nola bell still sounded out every Thursday evening. Even in the Naples of the nineties they still pointed out people who had been converted in Liguori's mission forty years before.[86]

'From such missions', wrote the Jesuit who was their scathing critic, 'the devil draws innumerable sacrileges, and renews his hold upon miserable sinners, who go from their howlings without any inward penitence of soul.'[87] This was not the experience of the popular missioner.

The missioner would arrive at a town with solemnity. A Maltese missioner to Civita Vecchia (about 1710) came in a carriage with a young assistant as catechist. Outside the town they got out of the carriage, took off their shoes and cloaks, and put on big collars made of black leather. With a great bell in their hands they came forward to the town gate where they were ceremoniously received by the Brotherhood of White Penitents, which in procession two by two escorted them to the church where the parish priest waited to conduct them to the altar for private prayer. The missioner went up into the pulpit and read his letter of authority from the Pope and announced when he would preach at night. Then he was taken to his lodgings in the Dominican house. His carriage meanwhile went to the back door of the Dominicans and deposited a chest with a crucifix, made in several pieces so that it could be put together; another chest with scourges of various types; and a third chest of medals and rosaries, together with the shoes and personal luggage of the missioners.

[85] Berthe 1.401–2; 2.30–1, 56, 110, 333, 367, 544. One of Pannini's drawings shows the floor-licking; of which there is an example as late as 1823 in Förstemann, 220, and about 1880 in P. Jullian, *D'Annunzio* (Eng. trans. 1972), 8. For its use as a private devotion by preachers, cf. F. Lagrange, *Vie de Mgr Dupanloup* (3rd edn. 1883) 1.407–8.
[86] Croce, *Uomini*, 2.122–3.   [87] Isla, 1.59.

In the church the catechist prepared a platform about 8 or 9 feet square just by the pulpit, covered in a Turkey carpet. When the bell rang for the mission sermon the church was quickly full. The missioner preached from his platform a long but good sermon (on 'that you receive not the grace of God in vain') which made women weep and cry for mercy. At the end the doors of the church were shut, and the catechist and sacristan distributed scourges to anyone who wished; and all the lights were put out, and the missioner exhorted them to this type of penitence, and set an example, and cried encouragement to the people to chastise the enemy of God. This went on about a quarter of an hour. Then they relit the candles and everyone went out of church in silence, while the catechist and sacristan collected the scourges.

The next morning the chief citizens of the town paid calls of courtesy on the missioner, who returned them during the following days, always in bare feet, wearing the leathern collar, and carrying a bell. He preached once in the Dominican church but was crowded out and moved to an open-air pulpit in the square, where they built him a platform, and provided two or three great marquees from the harbour. The penitential exercises took place behind closed doors in the Dominican church, or later, when the Dominicans showed disapproval, in the Franciscan; but the mission included five public processions of flagellants through the city, the missioners bringing up the rear. At the end of the last of these processions he preached a long sermon in the square and announced the indulgences attached to his mission. He used his last day in paying or receiving visits of courtesy. Then the Brotherhood of Blue Penitents escorted him to the town gate, all knelt to receive his blessing as he entered his carriage, and so he and his catechist went out of the life of the town.[88]

The Dominican prior sighed with relief when he went, and probably was not the only citizen of the town to be glad of a return to normal occupations. No town could remain unchanged by so exalted, dramatic, popular, ceremonious, emotional, and violent an incursion into its heart.

Because bishops could not give pastors to remote villages, they often encouraged travelling missioners. A group of missioners went to a village or group of villages, and preached for several days, a week, even two weeks. In the earlier eighteenth century the Oratorians were the leading village missioners of southern Italy, the Jesuits in the north. But the way was open for a religious order dedicated to giving missions in villages. In 1732 Alfonso Liguori founded the Redemptorists for this purpose. The

[88] Labat, *Voyages,* vii. 16 ff.

order received papal approval in 1750 and became the chief instrument of village evangelism in Italy before the revolution. The first Redemptorist mission in the Papal States was given as late as 1773 at a village near Veroli. Huge crowds assembled from all the surrounding district.

The missioners usually returned to the village after a few weeks or months for after-care.

Leonard of Port-Maurice (1676–1751), child of a Ligurian sea-captain, was sent to Rome to be educated by a rich uncle. He became a Franciscan and then an itinerant missioner in Corsica and central Italy. During the second quarter of the eighteenth century he was the celebrated parish missioner of Italy. From the bridge of a ship in Civita Vecchia harbour he preached a course to the convicts in the galleys; his mission at Gaeta stopped the carnival, to the vexation of officers in the garrison; he had power among the students of the university of Pisa.

Pope Benedict XIV revered him and brought him to Rome to prepare for the jubilee of 1750 and preach to the crowds which assembled. At a mission of preparation on 13 July 1749, late afternoon, a cortège walked from the convent of Ara Coeli to the Piazza Navona. Two friars carried a cross, then two more with skulls and four with bones, then the banner of the Holy Name, then Leonard with the Franciscan missionaries. In the Piazza Navona stood a crowd, with people at all the windows and on the roofs, reckoned on the last day of the mission at 100,000, silent; the fountains stopped, selling at the market stalls forbidden. At the windows of the palace watched the Pope with cardinals and members of the nobility. Leonard wore a heavy chain on his neck and a crown of thorns on his head. From a wide platform Leonard's voice could be heard throughout the square crying 'Penitence . . . Hell . . . give back what you stole . . .' When he snatched up his scourge and began to strike himself, the crowd cried 'Mercy Mercy!' In the evening all the bells of Rome rang long peals.[89]

Leonard of Port-Maurice extended a devotion which in the end became near universal: the stations of the cross. These originated during the fifteenth century, in attempts by western artists or leaders of monastic prayer to reproduce artificially the stations or points of meditation, which they found as pilgrims in Jerusalem. The word *station* in this sense is first found in an English writer of the fifteenth century. The Franciscans who guarded the Holy Sepulchre in Jerusalem and guided visitors took their groups of pilgrims to say prayers at various points along the Via Dolorosa which Jesus took between Pilate's house and Calvary. Originally the tour

[89] Giuntella, 171.

started at Calvary and went eastwards towards Pilate's house. From early in the sixteenth century the pilgrims started the other way, and followed the path of Christ. The number of stations varied from time to time, and the stopping-places at Jerusalem were not at first the same as the stopping-places reproduced for devotional purposes in western convents. Western writers who commended the use of the reproductions ended by influencing practice on the Via Dolorosa in Jerusalem. The stations as the modern Church knows them derive directly from western reproductions of the sixteenth century, indirectly from Franciscan guides of medieval pilgrims in the holy city.

Leonard of Port-Maurice, Franciscan by formation, began in the late 1720s to extend the devotion; first through Pope Clement XII (1731) to all the houses of friars minor. The Pope's brief reserved the stations, now fourteen in number, to friars minor, and granted the same indulgences to the devotion as would be gained by a visit to the Via Dolorosa in Jerusalem. Leonard was not satisfied. He wanted to be able to erect stations without applying to Franciscan superiors. In 1741 Benedict XIV allowed the right to every parish priest with the leave of his ordinary. Henceforth stations of the cross were possible in every parish church—except where a convent of friars minor existed. This last restriction, which perpetuated the old Franciscan guardianship of the Holy Places, was not removed till 1871.

Leonard fixed the number of stations at fourteen. The congregation walked from point to point in church, symbolically treading the road from Pilate's house to Calvary, and at each carving or picture was led to make devotions. He made the cult the centre of his mission to the people. In the course of his journeys he erected 572 sets of stations, and by his friendship with Popes Clement XII and Benedict XIV was able to commend the devotion to all the churches.

On 27 December 1749 Leonard caused the most famous of all stations to be erected, those in the Colosseum. The ruins of the Colosseum were long venerated as the place where early Christians died as martyrs to the beasts or the sword. By the fifteenth century the still-ruined amphitheatre was used for passion plays during Holy Week, and the use helped to protect the remains from further demolition as a stone-quarry. In the age of the Counter-Reformation these performances were stopped, and for several decades the building quietly dilapidated, its tunnels the dormitory of tramps or fornication. In 1675 a Theatine got the Pope's leave to enclose the amphitheatre as a place of prayer upon the passion.

The earthquake of 1703 damaged the ruins by bringing down a mass of masonry from the second floor. In the forties the tunnels of the labyrinth became so notorious for their crimes and immoralities that the governor of Rome (1744) threatened severe penalties. Five years later Leonard of Port-Maurice created stations of the cross round the amphitheatre. Every Friday henceforth, until the Italian occupation of 1870 (and in 1919 it was revived) a procession made the stations in the Colosseum. Eye-witnesses thought that Rome never saw a more solemn office than on 19 September 1756 when Pope Benedict XIV consecrated the Colosseum as a church.

Leonard of Port-Maurice was made blessed 1796, saint 1867, patron of popular mission 1923. Even in early years, even in the Colosseum, the stations did not always attract crowds. They were a special devotion. An 1809 engraving shows a Capuchin friar preaching one of the stations in the Colosseum. Amid unkempt ruins stands a wooden pulpit before a picture of Veronica wiping the sweat; the pulpit has a tall crucifix at the side, and on the steps sits a penitent with a face masked in a pointed hood; the congregation numbers only nineteen—two children, seven men, and ten women, of whom only two among the women look not to be poor; the preacher is in earnest, the attraction of his hearers rapt.[90]

At first the cult was common only in Italy. Alfonso Liguori adopted it from Leonard of Port-Maurice and made it a work of his Redemptorist order; and with them it passed the Alps into Austria. In France the devotion was already known during the eighteenth century, but won the parishes only during the second quarter of the nineteenth century. It reached England still later.

The Sermon

Reformation and Counter-Reformation made the sermon more important throughout the Roman Catholic Church. It was not so momentous to Catholic congregations as to Protestant, unless it was a revivalist missioner's sermon to a mass of poor people. At least, writers who considered the printed Catholic sermon in Germany as less powerful than the Protestant printed sermon, attributed something to the circumstance that in Protestant Germany the sermon, in Catholic Germany the altar, was central to the way of worship. Because in Protestant Germany the larger transfer of old endowments enabled education to make more rapid advances, the Protestant preacher in town addressed a more sophisticated audience. Until 1704 and beyond the sermons at the French court were

---

[90] Pinelli's engraving at the Museo Francescano in Rome; reproduced in *D.I.P.* 2.241-2; Justi, *Winckelmann*, 1.689-90; Pastor, xxxv. 171, 325; H. Thurston, *The Stations of the Cross* (1906); *D.S.* 2.2575 ff.; A. Wallenstein, *Franciscan Studies*, 12 (1952), 47-70.

some of the most enduring utterances in all Christendom. But in Italy, even urban Italy, bishops needed to persuade priests that a 'homely talk' was not the same as a sermon.[91]

Everyone knew that the sermon was not the influential utterance of the priest, and this diminished its importance in the priest's eyes. Even Pope Benedict XIV held what was said in the confessional to be weightier than any sermon.[92] For in the pulpit the priest spoke to the general, in the box he spoke to a soul in particular and known circumstances. This conviction weakened the endeavour which ordinary priests put into the sermon. It was not the centre of their ministry.

They were protected from the moral consequences of this by the people. Though the priest might imagine that he did more good by a 'homely chat' than by a carefully prepared and formal sermon, the people loved to hear oratory. The lamentable taste of some sermon rhetoric about 1700 is intelligible only on the realization that this was what congregations wanted. Priests had no need whatever to exhort people to go to hear sermons. It was a people's recreation. A patriarch of Venice once complained that from all over Italy famous preachers came to his diocese for a fee 'like that of opera-singers'.[93]

History does not easily penetrate the power of the spoken word in the context when it was spoken. To read oratory of any kind, a hundred years after it was delivered, is to invite misunderstanding, for its force depends on matching the mood and circumstances of the hearers, a mood now lost. Therefore, most speakers, most sermons, sound ridiculous if read aloud a century later, unless like Pericles' speeches or Donne's sermons they have that indefinable quality of permanence whereby circumstances of delivery and mood of the moment cease to matter.

Catholic preaching of the eighteenth century has no high reputation. Bossuet and Bourdaloue both died in 1704, and in the same year Massillon was pushed out of the French royal pulpit on suspicion of excessive severity if not Jansenism. Massillon lived on till 1742, and the decline was more in celebrity than in power of preaching. But this school of grand French preachers had no successors because their orotundity and ornament were no longer attuned to the matter-of-fact ideas of speakers and hearers in the age of the Enlightenment. The fashion of speech changed, and with it declined the supreme *literary* sermon. The utterances of Bossuet or Massillon contributed to literature and art as well as morality. But now all the treatises on how to preach, without exception, required simplicity.

[91] Lambertini, *Raccolta*, 1.103 ff.   [92] Benedict XIV, *Bullarium*, 7.327–8.
[93] *La visita pastorale di Pyrker*, lxx.

Alfonso Liguori, in his instructions on preaching, was the head of the school of simplicity, demanding short sentences, easy words, concrete ideas, so that a common people might understand. Liguori repeated this cry again and again, almost to tedium. But he was far from alone. Everyone else who wrote instructions to preachers cried the same message. The people (they said) did not need rhetoric and men-pleasing but a crucified Lord. The sermon was not intended to please sophisticated ears but to make everyone, that is the people, uncomfortable. The story was told of the compliment by King Louis XIV to Massillon: 'In my chapel I've heard a lot of excellent preachers who made me pleased with their sermons. But every time I hear you I'm very displeased with myself.' The age was fond of this kind of anecdote. Louis XIV once asked Boileau why an unknown preacher drew such crowds; and Boileau answered, 'Sir, people always run after what's new. Here's somebody preaching the gospel'.[94]

The mood was curiously out of keeping with the general temper of late baroque. In art and architecture, music and liturgy, the age welcomed elaboration provided it was gay. In the spoken word it moved towards plainness of speech. The Catholic sermon of the eighteenth century was 'worse'—that is, worse to the reader of a later age—than sermons of the late seventeenth century because men now distrusted 'good sermons'. They suspected that beautiful words captivated ears and left hearts cold. The people needed direct, gospel truths; vocabulary short; moral duties inculcated.

The sermon of the eighteenth century acquired its dubious reputation partly because more sermons were printed and therefore the chance of printing folly was greater; as the ferocious Jesuit critic of Spanish preachers in that age wrote, 'Though parish priests and monks preach as bad as possible, yet friars preach worse, because there are more among them who preach bad.'[95] But the reputation of sermons also suffered because the best of all books on preaching were written with the aim of making them better.

In fact, the importance of the sermon rose among Catholics of the eighteenth century. If it did not rise in reputation (for men lamented that sermons were bad and grew worse) there was a rising demand that a sermon should not be bad, because it was part of the liturgy. The priest did not lose the role of a cultic figure, a man of altar and sacrifice. But he was expected also to know how to teach by sermons. His burden grew heavier, while he rose in stature. Good bishops were more urgent about the education of men whom they might ordain.

[94] A. Bayle, *Massillon* (Paris, 1867), 108; Dargan, 2.248.   [95] Isla, 1.19.

To print volumes of sermons was not expensive. They found a ready market. The sermon might well be of an hour in length, in Catholic churches half an hour became gradually as common. The hour-glass was not an article of furniture in a pulpit. Insistence on the sermon meant that many town preachers had to make utterances for which they were ill equipped by training and which, if they were good pastors in their parishes, and sat frequently in the confessional, they had no time to prepare. Therefore books of sermons, one for each Sunday of the year, were plentiful and much used. Such collections were published by men without high qualifications for their task. When the spoken word was printed and lost its 'personality', it could read absurdly. Here as one example was a sermon, printed in 1701 by a south-German Benedictine Placidus Urtlauff in his collection for the use of other preachers:

23rd Sunday after Pentecost: Matthew 9, 34.
(1) Archimedes did a wonderful work. (2) Application to humanity. (3) Every man is mortal. (4) Whether you can make glass that will bend and not break. (5) A man who thinks himself pure glass. (6) Remarkable anecdote. (7) A thousand years are but as yesterday in God's sight. (8) Man is dust and ashes. (9) Why man was made from the earth and not from gold. (10) Why Adam, but not Lucifer, obtained mercy after he sinned, and why Christ never said to the risen from the dead what he said to the healed, that they ought to go and sin no more.[96]

Confessing that we cannot easily judge the quality of a sermon from a printed utterance, at a time when mood is lost, and from a different social context, we nevertheless infer from this and from numerous other such sermons that preachers talked nonsense to their people as well as sense. Even if the sermon was short—and south-German Catholics had a proverb, 'Countrymen love short sermons and long sausages'—certain collections designed to meet the demand for brevity hardly breed more confidence in the mind of the later reader.

But some collections proved their success by the continued demand for their printing. The most important collection was published from the sermons of a Jesuit of Trier, Franz Hunolt (died 1746, sermons published in Cologne in six volumes 1740–68). The title of Hunolt's collection typified the age: *Christian Moral Teaching on the Truths of the Gospel*. It had a bloated style and some too childish stories, but was so full of good doctrine and plain sense that it went on being republished far into the nineteenth century.

[96] Kehrein, 1.91,112.

Liguori's men in south Italy met the variety of Italian dialects. Germans had an odd form of this difficulty. Their people understood German, few were fluent in Latin. But to speak German was faintly disreputable from the past. It reminded them of Luther and the German Bible, and his cry for a language understood by the people. Therefore the German Catholic continued curiously to mix Latin with his German, in a manner liable to make his sermon most difficult for a non-Latinist to follow. This habit was common in the early years of the century, and thereafter declined as German became accepted as a language. But congregations liked to hear a preacher who understood words beyond their own understanding. In Spain congregations who knew neither Greek nor Hebrew complained if their preacher could not quote his Bible in the original languages.

Beneath the variety of quality—and doubtless sermons were no more varied than university lectures which ranged from deplorable to distinguished—the handbooks show a trend. The doctrinal *body* of many sermons was not profound, for profundity was incompatible with simplicity. They could become too simple in more than one way. On the one hand they might leave truth unmentioned, and enforce rosaries, reverence for pictures or statues, indulgences, or the merits of saints; and if they so enforced they were heard by the people but discontented members of city congregations. Or they might leave truth largely unmentioned and enforce moral precepts, against pride, or vendettas, or fornication. In his pastoral letter of 1762, Cardinal Trautson of Vienna complained that preachers nowadays do not preach the word of God,[97] and had these part-silences on truth in mind. The difficulty was, that in deserting the old manner of using Scripture—for preachers of the seventeenth century could sometimes be accused of playing word-games with the text—they did not easily keep the text of the Bible in the centre of the sermon. A notorious German sermon, preached with the aim of urging labourers to vaccination, was printed and then got into handbooks as a warning how not to use the Scriptures: St. Joseph cared for his baby's health. If vaccination were then known he would certainly have had the child vaccinated. So must we do. . . .[98]

An observer recorded the start of a sermon by a Franciscan in the Carmelite church at Tivoli near Rome (1709). The record was graphic:

The preacher went into the pulpit looking glum, as if he was in a bad temper with the world. He sat down, took out his handkerchief, slowly wiped his face nose and ears, blew his nose two or three times carefully looking into his hand-

---

[97] Gastgeber, 45.   [98] Goy, 95.

kerchief, took snuff, got up, looked all round the congregation as though he was trying to see someone, put his hood down, knelt, said a Hail Mary, stood up again, sneezed vastly two or three times, blew his nose again, looked at his hand-kerchief carefully, made a little sign of the cross with his right thumb on his fore-head, mouth and breast, and in a tremendous voice, as though he was calling a fire-alarm, cried 'Out of this holy place, all you irreligious people who doubt the virtue or the miracles of the very holy scapular of the Holy Virgin.'

The observer, who was the Dominican Labat, went out at once, fearing as he said that a very poor sermon was bound to follow such a start.[99] The preacher used no public ascription to begin, other than his Hail Mary which was more in the nature of his private prayer.

No book did more to shatter the more absurd uses of Biblical texts than the skit of 1760 by the Spanish Jesuit Isla, under the title *Father Gerundio*. This was an enchanting novel about the training of Gerundio as a preacher and his subsequent sermons. It was written in a style that made it a classic of Spanish literature. Thereafter no Spaniard could ever preach sermons that were 'baroque' in the sense of playing word-games with the text of the Bible. ('Silence you should call *taciturnities of the lips*: to praise, to *panegyrize*; sight, *visual attingence of objects . . . To exist* is vulgar, *existential nature* is a great thing', i. 470.) Many were shocked that a priest and a Jesuit should use humour and ridicule as a way of reforming the most solemn of utterances, the Inquisition banned the book six years later, and until 1900 the Index kept it upon the list of prohibited books. But *Father Gerundio* marked the end of baroque preaching as symbolically as *Don Quixote* marked the end of the Crusades. No other book could compare in showing how the common sense of the eighteenth century devastated the quaintness and the conceits of its forefathers.

Bigger minds wondered whether the ejection of rhetoric from sermons was so wise.

As a young man Fénelon wrote a book on the use of eloquence in preaching. He did not print. After his death the book was published (1717) posthumously as *Dialogues sur l'éloquence*. Perhaps because the book was written when he was young, and therefore was a product of the seventeenth century, he was not in the least afraid of eloquence. The book makes one of the noblest treatments ever penned upon the vocation of a Christian preacher. It was the work of a humane and highly educated priest speaking to a world of educated Frenchmen, and its atmosphere has almost nothing in common with the mood of Liguori's instructions to south-Italian mission preachers. Though it is wrong for a sermon to have pleasing as its

[99] Labat, *Voyages*, 3.398–9.

aim, the aim of a sermon is to move and pleasing is part of persuasion. You not only have to tell an audience that something happened, you must make them feel that it happened, and you must not therefore neglect the art of speaking provided that this art is kept subordinate to the end and never becomes the object of the sermon.

This controversy—whether the best sermons were plain men speaking to plain men, whether the cultivation of expert speaking was a proper use of nature's gifts or a betrayal of a gospel simplicity, was much argued during the middle years of the eighteenth century. A majority held for the austere view; to use art was 'Ciceronian', non-Christian. But the better instructors agreed that no man ever has time to prepare a sermon. Therefore, if the sermon is to be useful, it must be founded in a general preparation, of wide reading or close study.

In the cities where hearers were educated a preacher might become famous and popular. 'The experience of our times' wrote Fénelon ruefully[100] 'shows that a speaker can speak strongly of morality without turning his back upon a fortune.' Young men aimed to become good preachers as a young musician aimed to become a famous composer; and we find occasional traces of rivalry among city pulpits, in the ability to draw and hold and edify the crowds. Fénelon even gave the curious advice that men should not go to hear a preacher who made them lose their appetite for other preachers. 'On the contrary, I am looking for a man who gives me such an appetite and esteem for the Word of God that I may be the more disposed to listen to it everywhere else'.

Many good men preferred to preach without notes, and memorized the words of their sermon. Spanish congregations would not allow preachers to use notes. But congregations noticed when the effort to remember was painful, and commented on the staring eyes and furrowed brows. The leading advisers preferred their preachers to memorize the structure, and to let the words come. A memorizer became 'imprisoned' in his own language. Some preachers were still so energetic in the pulpit that they ended sweating and breathless and could do nothing for the rest of the day. Fénelon thought it unnatural. 'If you don't gesticulate in private life, don't gesticulate in a pulpit.' It could also be as boring as a monotonous voice. But Fénelon admitted that the sight of a numerous audience could move a speaker beyond his wont.

In churches or cathedrals with poor acoustics, the preacher could acceptably *chant* his sermon to make it heard.

The predicament of the preacher at the courts of the eighteenth century,

[100] *Dialogues*, I.

or in the little country parish with a squire present, was sufficiently delicate to produce warnings in the handbooks against praise of the mighty or rich from the pulpit. In 1787 a south-German preacher put the Blessed Virgin into the genealogy of the eminent family of the prince. Such isolated instances were quoted as warnings.

Towards the end of the century the growing flight to the towns caused preachers to worry about the discontent among their agricultural people. Peasants felt their lower stations contrasted with townsmen, and we find the first sermons in Christian history which discourage fantasies about city lights and city culture. One south-German handbook for preachers[101] printed a model sermon to countrymen: you are busier than men in cities but this is a blessing. When does sin come most easily, in work or idleness? Countrymen are fitter than townsmen, have better disciplined children, villages have no theatres nor brothels nor corrupt societies, villagers say their prayers more regularly, work in the fields is a school of wisdom. But, recommended this handbook, let the preacher beware of setting forth his theme so that countrymen despise townsmen, or suppose that God will not be found everywhere.

In the age of Enlightenment the gap grew between educated preachers and rustic hearers. This became painful over country superstitions. St. Leonard was the saint who protected cattle from disease. In villages of south Germany the country folk therefore celebrated St. Leonard's day. If the preacher encouraged his people's devotions he blessed materialistic superstition and might find himself saying from a pulpit things which he could not believe. If he discouraged their devotion, he probably lost influence and trampled on popular instincts of reverence whereby a people confessed its dependence and looked towards the power of God. At least, advised the handbook after confessing this perplexity, the preacher will never talk more about the temporal than the eternal, or more about agriculture than Christ.

The cathedral chapter

In nearly every diocese lay a collegiate church with canons as well as the cathedral church with canons. Big dioceses might have several such colleges of canons. The collegiate canons were less important than the cathedral canons, for the chapter of the cathedral had a special place in the constitution as the historic council of the bishop. On rare occasions a collegiate chapter competed with a cathedral chapter and claimed itself to

[101] J. M. Sailer, *Vorlesungen*, in *Werke*, xvii. 13.

be a cathedral, so that the diocese of Pistoia had to become the diocese of Pistoia and Prato with cathedrals at both towns. Because of its responsibilities the cathedral chapter worked under slightly different rules of conduct from the canons of a collegiate church. Among other differences, the minimum age for a cathedral canon was twenty-two or twenty-three, for a collegiate canon it was fourteen. If the canon had cure of souls it was twenty-three.

In this way the canons in a diocese were important not only by historic position but by numbers and endowments.

Canons were chosen by a mixture of local rules which were supposed to be an agreement between the bishop and the chapter, but sometimes the bishop dominated and sometimes the chapter excluded the bishop from any part in the choice. Much depended on local custom, local statutes, historic rights, ancient exemptions, and historic claims. Nowhere was history so powerful as in the relation between bishops and chapters, and history bred an extraordinary diversity of practice.

Within two months of accepting a canon's stall the new canon must make the profession of faith before the bishop and before the chapter. Theoretically this distinguished him from the parish clergy. But most diocesan statutes insisted on the same profession of faith from the beneficed clergy. The canon must do it by law of the Catholic Church, the incumbent only by ruling of the diocese.

Elaborate statutes, reinforced in the Counter-Reformation, decreed the rules of residence. A canon must reside at his cathedral for nine months in the year, which must included Advent, Lent, and the great festivals, and which must not mean that all the canons went on holiday simultaneously. Until 1737 canons could do what they liked and go where they wanted during their three months' holiday, and needed to ask no permission of chapter or bishop. The appearance of so many holidaying canons led to questions; for Rome ruled that they could be absent only within the diocese, and if they went out of the diocese they needed the bishop's permission. The new rule was very difficult to enforce.

The object of all these strict rules of residence was the regular worship of God in choir. The canon must attend, and be marked or pricked into his place by a marker (two markers, to check each other). Part of his pay came from the prebend and part from 'distributions' (as they were called) for daily attendance, and these he lost if the marker could not prick him on the daily list. The cathedral stood there to glorify God, the work of a canon was worship. This sense of obligation to worship was strong in the eighteenth century; so strong that the most sensible Pope of the century,

Benedict XIV, least liable of all men to vehemence or excess of zeal, used very strong language to canons who thought they did their work by attending in choir and listening to a trained choir singing the office to a beautiful setting. The canons, he said, must sing. They had no need to sing harmony or complex music. But sing they must. Silence while others sang failed to fulfil the worshipping duty of the canon.[102] Benedict confessed that this demand was unenforceable. He laid it upon their consciences. Therefore in duty bound they must know how to chant Gregorians (so Rome, 1735).

Pope Benedict XIII at the Roman synod of 1725 declared a preference in choosing canons (other things being equal) for candidates who could sing Gregorian chant. Six out of the twelve canons of a Camerino chapter (1725) even voted against allowing a colleague to retire on pension because they wanted not to count the twenty-eight years during which he was so tone deaf that he had the music sung by deputy.[103]

These rules of residence were known and often kept. But they were liable to so many exceptions that the services of cathedrals were hard to maintain with unvarying dignity. Here were many of the ablest priests of the Church, with leisure to spare. Bishops and Popes and governments looked to canons for help. These nine months of residence, which sounded strict on paper, could become much shorter if the canon was absent for 'reasons of evident utility to Church or State'. If a Pope summoned a canon to a particular work the canon must go in obedience. Since canons were expected to be more learned than parish priests, they could without much difficulty get leave to study, even an absence at a university for a few years at a time. They could get leave for a holy purpose, like the desire to go on pilgrimage. Cathedrals were often engaged—this was the experience going far back into the Middle Ages—in lawsuits or at least argument over property, and a canon who pursued a case through the courts for the cathedral's benefit might need to be long absent. Political conditions of the eighteenth century showed an old rule as no mere survival, that tyranny, or the violent enmity of a people, could justify a canon's absence from his cathedral. Reasons of health, or something so general as 'Christian charity', could justify absence. In all such cases the canon was expected to get a bishop's licence not to be in choir.

The Church suffered a little sense of contradiction over canons. Their first and only duty was the divine praises. But the fact was, they were too useful to be in choir all the time. The eighteenth century wanted the

---

[102] *De synodo*, xiii, 9, 11, col. 1404; cf. Ferraris, 2.178.
[103] *Thesaurus Resolutionum* 3.236.

Church to be effective and needed their aid. If the bishop wished two canons to serve on his staff, their service was counted as residence in the cathedral though they were absent.

If they were away for any of these good reasons, they were not held bound to provide a substitute.

The Council of Trent allotted one canonry in each cathedral to a theologian who should instruct the clergy. This provision was not well observed. In 1725, by the bull *Pastoralis officii*, Pope Benedict XIII summoned bishops to remember to appoint a canon-theologian and subjected the choice of such a canon to the examination in the *concursus*, like any parish priest—for till then a canon was not tested by *concursus* before entering upon his canonry. After it was established that the canon-theologian should be chosen by *concursus*, advertisements appeared which quite resembled modern notices of vacancy.

For example: in 1736 the canon-theologian of Bologna cathedral became Bishop of Assisi. Accordingly the archbishop issued a public notice that the *concursus* would be held on a date just over a fortnight later (not long for applicants who might be afar); laying down the conditions, that the man must be a doctor of divinity and hold a post in a university of repute; that his duty was to expound Holy Scripture; the questions and answers must be written.[104]

That the notice should declare the field of study to be Holy Scripture was not idle. Tradition expected the canon-theologian to teach the Bible and Christian doctrine. But many bishops believed that this was not the field which they urgently needed. The most anxious duty of their parish priests was to sit in the confessional. What the clergy most needed was instruction in moral divinity and cases of conscience. Bishops thought that clergy more easily gained a knowledge of the Bible and of doctrine from forms of worship and listening to sermons. Questions were raised whether this canonry, as well as the canonry for the penitentiary, might lawfully be used for a moralist. They soon agreed that cases of conscience were so closely entangled with doctrine and Bible that the canon-theologian might lawfully be a moralist. Church lawyers then asked whether they might not be eligible for the theological canonry, but though bishops needed good lawyers, and sometimes got them into the canonry, a knowledge of church law without a knowledge of divinity was not regarded as fulfilling the aim of the canonry.

Therefore two of the cathedral canonries were allotted to theologians, one Biblical/doctrinal, one moral; whose work was instruction of the

[104] Lambertini, *Raccolta*, 3.198 ff.

parish clergy. The theologian's main duty was to give, or arrange for, forty lectures a year in the cathedral, which clergy (not monks) were bound to attend. The penitentiary's main duty was to hear confessions; and when he sat in the confessional he was counted as one of those who worshipped in choir. But he also, in many dioceses, guided the monthly or weekly meeting of clergy to discuss cases of conscience, which all confessors must attend and other priests were encouraged to attend.

For bishops of impoverished dioceses with meagre cathedrals, the search for any canon capable of being a theologian could be unending. The Archbishop of Conza (1775) in southern Italy enquired everywhere and could find no candidates who were both worthy and willing to come. The climate was unhealthy, the place disagreeable, the prebend small, the clergy ignorant. Qualified theologians had more interesting openings.[105]

The repair of cathedrals was not usually hard. Unless they were a pilgrim resort like St. Peter's at Rome, they had small resource in the offerings of visitors. Part of the endowment was allocated annually to the fabric fund, and in the cheapness of labour went far. Even a destruction beyond the normal corruption of time, as by earthquake, seldom dismayed chapters for more than a few years. Pope Benedict XIII was sufficiently concerned to issue a constitution ordering half the first year's income of any benefice (not a benefice reserved to the Pope) to be sent to the fabric fund of the cathedral. Like all new arrangements for taxing the clergy this was largely a dead letter outside the Papal States, and this only at times when (as at Ferrara in 1781) bishop or chapter felt the need of the money.

Cathedrals were not well heated. In winter the choir was a refrigerator. Old canons might not survive if compelled to praise God in choir throughout the winter. The old rules disliked any weakening of rigour. They continued to forbid hats or blankets in choir. But respecting the needs of old age, authority began to bend the rules. In conditions of northern climate or high country, it became possible for canons during the three cold months of the year, to sing divine praises in sacristy instead of choir (weekdays only). And mattins, the dawn office, most trying of all to old bones, could after 1722–3 be 'anticipated', that is, sung the evening before and not at dawn.[106]

An English visitor stayed in a canon's house in Sicily during 1778, and admired the plates off which he ate, and reported that the house was furnished like the mansion of a decayed country gentleman, with heavy

---

[105] Cestaro, 31 n.18.
[106] Benedict XIV, *de synodo* xiii.9.13, col. 1406; cf. *Thesaurus Resolutionum* 2.334.

chairs and tables, and pieces of tarnished gilding on the walls, remnants of ancient finery.[107] A canon of Girgenti cathedral had a respectable coach for driving in the city—for the island's roads were seldom suitable for coaches.

In French and many Spanish cathedrals the dean had rights in chapter as chairman of the meeting and other special rights in cathedral varying according to statute. In Germany deans had the custom of conducting visitations of parish churches. In Italy the chairman was usually the senior canon. Sometimes he was called the archdeacon. No member of the chapter was allowed the title *Very Reverend*.

Not all canonries were open to all clergymen.

In Germany the old exclusion of the Holy Roman Empire still operated. In German tradition canonries were usually reserved for noble families. The statutes of the chapter at Cologne required that canons be subdeacons, that they have studied two years at a university, and that they be of princely origin. This was not true of all German chapters, for some had canonries open to 'plebeians'.

Germany was a law to itself because the structure of chapters was built into the historic constitution of the Holy Roman Empire. In Germany the canons elected the bishop without interference from clergy or laity. But since the bishoprics were part of the base of Catholic secular power in Germany, and by generations of tradition were occupied by allies or kinsmen of the princely families of Catholic Germany, the chapters needed to be a tight band of aristocrats to ensure the continuity of this political force. Moreover in the old constitution of the Empire was recognized the right of canons to make conditions to a candidate for the see, so that they could refuse to elect him until he agreed. These conditions were called capitulations and resembled the demands made upon the future Holy Roman Emperor before the electors would elect. Though rooted in German practice and acceptable to German Catholic opinion they began to be offensive in the wider Church as the principles of the Counter-Reformation were applied. Other countries so organized the appointment of bishops that the same chances of electoral sharp practice seldom applied. On the whole canons demanded conditions recognized by bishops for the good of the Church. But among the conditions were inevitably safeguards for the maximum independence of the chapter from the bishop.

At the end of the seventeenth century the chapter of Würzburg came before the public eye. Canons and bishop-designate made a pact before the election of 1675. The bishop was elected and then failed to keep all the pact

[107] Swinburne, 3.365.

because he doubted its legality. After he died his successor but one, Godfrey of Guttenberg, made a pact (1684) with the chapter and after his election appealed to Rome to get himself absolved from the duty to observe the undertaking or oath. The case dragged on until 1695, when Pope Innocent XII (*Ecclesiae Catholicae*) condemned all capitulations before the election of bishops or abbots. Germany quietly refused to accept this change in its habits. Canonists taught that Innocent XII had not condemned capitulation, but only bad capitulation; he had stopped agreements for private gain, not agreements for the good of the Church. The chapter of the see of Passau in Austria (1713–14) tried to circumvent the ban on capitulations before election by making the pact and then making it subject to confirmation by the Holy See—thus making the pact after the election while Innocent only condemned pacts before the election. Popes Clement XI, Benedict XIII (1727), and Benedict XIV (1754) confirmed and extended the bull of Innocent XII; and these reiterations at once weakened the force of capitulations and showed how the potent and very conservative German canons were not quickly deterred from ancient abuse which they refused to allow to be abuse.

A curious survival remained from the Middle Ages at a collegiate church of St. John at Haugis in the diocese of Würzburg. The future canons must undergo a rite of initiation which included stripping to the waist and running the gauntlet between two rows of canons who beat them with rods. Since new canons were senior persons and sometimes bishops of other dioceses, the rite felt childish even if now ritual. In 1740 the Bishop of Würzburg banned it as unedifying. The custom no doubt arose from the medieval idea that novices must be treated roughly to discourage unsuitable postulants before they became monks. But whatever the origin, the chapter felt aggrieved at the bishop's order. They said that an ancient and immemorial custom of their chapter ought not thus to be ended. They appealed to Rome. Rome decided that the bishop had sense.[108]

The chapter met to administer the property of the cathedral. Everyone present had one vote, no one could vote by proxy or letter (a few cathedrals had a contrary custom). Its consent, for example, was necessary if the bishop wanted (he usually wanted) to put his seminary into buildings belonging to the cathedral. They had the right to be consulted by the bishop over the ceremony of high days, and on the summoning of a diocesan synod and on the decrees of a diocesan synod—though the bishop need not follow their advice. When a bishop moved or died or retired or

---

[108] Benedict XIV, *de synodo*, xi.3.3–7, cols. 1261–3.

was captured by enemies the chapter became the bishop for nearly all important purposes. During an interregnum it made decisions binding on the whole diocese, until the next bishop confirmed or annulled. Temporarily it inherited all the bishop's jurisdiction, and must within eight days of his death choose a canon as 'vicar-capitular' who should act as bishop. It did not inherit non-diocesan functions of the bishop—as for example the Bishop of Padua could confer higher degrees at the university but his chapter in interregnum could not.[109]

This acting power could be very weighty. When French invaders drove Spanish bishops out of their sees in the Napoleonic wars, cathedral chapters saved several dioceses from anarchy.

The bishops of the Counter-Reformation thought that they would more easily reform the Church if bishops established their right to visit cathedrals or collegiate churches and amend what was wrong. Most Italian cathedrals admitted this right. The chapter of Genoa claimed to be exempt from its bishop and failed (1722). The chapter of Verona claimed to be exempt from its bishop because it was immediately under the patriarch of Aquileia, and partly won. If a cathedral had in the distant past obtained exemption from the bishop, the bishop could visit only if he associated with him two canons of the cathedral. But whereas bishops achieved much with Italian chapters, outside Italy the constitutional conflict was fought harder. The chapters of the German see-states, where most canonries fell to members of aristocratic families, were too powerful for their bishops to be effective in 'reform'. The conflict was hardest and commonest in Spain. For historic reasons, going back to the fight against the Moors, many Spanish chapters achieved the widest exemptions from interference by their bishop. Catholic historians were not always sorry. They observed that Cologne would now be a Protestant town if the chapter had not resisted its bishop in the Reformation.

The natural conflict of constitution between a bishop charged with ruling the whole diocese and the powerful corporation with separate interests and established rights led so inevitably to cases and sometimes lawsuits, that a Jesuit thought it worth while to write an admirable handbook *On the Best Way of Keeping the Peace between Bishop and Cathedral Chapter* (A. G. Andreucci, Rome, 1737).

The axiom that chapters are always more in need of reform than bishops did not go unquestioned.

[109] Ferraris, 2.348.

Retirement and pension

No one was expected to retire. Everyone expected and was expected to serve in see or parish until death.

This was not different from the expectations in the world which surrounded the Church. But it was particularly hard for the Church. Other men had wives or families or children to care for them in old age, monks had their communities, bishops and priests, unless they had kindred (and of course many had) could rely only on housekeepers and servants. Illness or weakness in old age was a constant source of trouble for the church administration. A parish priest in a remote and hard country parish needed lighter work if he and the parish were to survive. To move him was just as difficult as to move the contemporary clergyman in the Church of England with his parson's freehold.

A bishop could get leave from the Pope to resign, and if he achieved this leave he might be allowed to take a pension from the revenues of the see. A canon in a cathedral was the church officer who came nearest to a satisfactory pension, for if he had served for forty years he was exempt from attendance at the cathedral and from all other duties of his canonry, even, after a decision of 1716, from the duty to reside, while he kept the entire stipend: if the chapter was short of priests he could stand in to help, and indeed must stand in to help if summoned by a bishop in case of need. This retirement of a canon was called *jubilation*, was the only satisfactory mode of pension in all the Church, and had the merit of being retirement on full pay. But the condition of forty years' service limited the number of canons who so retired; and some cathedrals would not recognize years of service in a parish as among the forty years and some doubted whether periods when the canon was on leave of absence, as for study or for the needs of the Church, ought to count towards his jubilation. But mostly cathedral chapters were kind to their canons in jubilation. Siena even elected a canon who had retired seven years before, as its dean.[110]

A commoner method was used to provide pension, not on full pay, by appointing a coadjutor. This was well known with bishops who grew too old or ill for their work. The coadjutor did the work for the ill man and though he had not the office and only a proportion of the stipend he had the right of succession when the bishop died. The coadjutor therefore remained as resource. But the burden of old clergy unable to work lay heavy upon the Church.

If a parish priest resigned—whether for ill health or any other reason—

[110] *Thesaurus Resolutionum*, 3.287 (1726); cf. Benedict XIV, *de synodo*, iii.4.6, col. 876.

he might try to resign in favour of a particular successor; that is, he offered to resign but only if a certain person was appointed to his place. In corrupt times and corrupt places this was a way of securing a pension, for into the agreement could be built a secret clause that the new incumbent should pay part of the stipend to the old. This secret agreement was guilty of the crime of selling an office in return for money and all authorities tried to make it impossible.

Other critics wanted to be rid not only of the secret clause but of the whole practice. Many complaints about it reached Rome. They said that it got men into parishes without making them pass the test of the *concursus*; that it led therefore to unworthy appointments; that it could make parishes hereditary because so many of these priests resigned in favour of their nephews or other kindred.

Wise opinion refused to abolish the practice. Pope Clement XI assembled a commission to consider whether it should be banned, and the commission was unanimous that it should continue. Authorities who did not wish to see it abolished had a simple and overriding reason. Too many clergy were old and incapable. If one of them offers to resign it is much better to accept the resignation than to say that he cannot—provided at least that he is not selling the living. Even if he appoints his nephew the parish will get a younger man. And these family connections are not always bad. An uncle wishing his nephew to succeed takes pains about the nephew's character and learning. So authority preferred to allow such resignations, and only tried to insist that the candidate pass the *concursus* examiners (though not the *concursus*) and that he be not less than twenty years old instead of the usual twenty-four years which was the minimum age for holding a parish.

The bishop

In Germany chapters elected bishops. That was not so free as it seemed, for most canonries were confined to noble families, and the actual election was often a foregone conclusion by reason of subtle political links between Bavaria or Austria and the chapter. The Pope needed to confirm but very rarely tried to refuse.[111]

In most other states the Head of State appointed under a Concordat. In France the King nominated all French bishops under the Concordat of 1516. The Pope needed to confirm but made no attempt to refuse.

The medieval privilege known as *Monarchia Sicula* gave the ruler of

---

[111] But at the founding of the new see of Fulda (1752) a new and interesting mode of election was agreed.

Sicily the right to choose all the bishops of Sicily. Pope Clement XI made a courageous assault upon other provisions of the *Monarchia Sicula* but did not question the way in which the king nominated bishops. When Sicily was united under one Bourbon ruler with Naples, the Bourbon kings tried to extend this right to their mainland dioceses, for under a Concordat of 1529 they had only the right to nominate twenty-four bishops of the mainland.

A proportion of the bishops in Sicily, Naples, Sardinia, Portugal, Spain were chosen by the sovereigns of those lands. The proportion grew steadily all the century. Far fewer bishops were chosen by the Pope, or elected freely by chapters, just before the Revolution than three-quarters of a century before.

All this royal nomination had no bad effect upon the Catholic Church. Governments must be seen to choose good men and had an interest in nominating men acceptable in their dioceses. When the Pope hesitated to accept, as over several sees in southern Italy, he hesitated because he suspected the candidate of being Jansenist or opposed to papal power, not because he feared an otherwise unworthy bishop.

All bishops had common duties: to confirm children, consecrate holy oil, care for the people especially the clergy, test and ordain clergy for parishes, visit the parishes from time to time, hold a diocesan synod (the Council of Trent expected every year), guard truth and avert heresy or unbelief, report to Rome with regularity, and from time to time pay a visit to Rome. The bishop's name was mentioned in the prayers at every eucharist in his diocese, wherever he went to church he sat on a throne with a *baldachino* above his head and he could concede to a holy place an indulgence of up to 100 days. He was expected by Trent to try to found a seminary if none existed. He had a fund at his disposal known as the *mensa*, which received the income from endowments or property and offerings, and from which he must live, and pay the expense of secretaries or Curia, and finance good works in the diocese. The *mensa* claimed a contribution, of which more anon, from each of the diocesan clergy.

Within this framework the common name concealed an extraordinary variety of function. The Bishop of St. Agatha of the Goths had 30,000 people, the Archbishop of Naples had hundreds of thousands. One bishop of a poor south-Italian diocese travelled over country with almost no communications and suffered at least six different accidents on the roads, none of them with worse than a dislocated wrist, but in one smash he only just escaped death. By contrast Bishop de Melo of Algarve in Portugal from 1787, after a short spell in his diocese, became confessor to the queen and enjoyed a scholarly and literary life at court; and when this function ended, did not go back to any diocese but moved into the palace of the Inquisition at Rossio where he devoted his time and money to building up and organizing a magnificent private library.[112] And some bishops presided over so small a diocese that they hardly had enough to do if they resided.

They varied from millionaire to poor man. The poorest bishops in south Italy had 'palaces' with broken windows and leaking roofs, in one case at least with a front door rotten with age or worm. At the coronation of the Emperor Joseph II in Frankfurt the Archbishop of Mainz had fourteen resplendent carriages in his retinue. When the two Spanish cardinals arrived in Rome for the conclave of 1769 their lavishness in spending money caused astonishment and mockery among the citizens.[113]

Whether he were rich or poor, his people regarded him (if they regarded him with respect) as a leader, usually their chief. This regard took all shapes. When the Spanish rose against French conquerors they frequently turned to bishops to organize military resistance. When the water supply at Tarragona needed repair, it was the bishop who saw that the pipes were mended. Spanish bishops drained marshes, built textile mills, founded hospitals, improved local methods of agriculture, made a model farm or built a paper factory. They were expected to protect the poor against depredations of local squires or oppressive acts of distant government. During the famine of 1763–4 Bishop Liguori of St. Agatha in the kingdom of Naples distributed a store of vegetables which he had collected in expectation of this emergency; and when the supply was exhausted, sold his carriage and bishop's ring, and was only stopped by the chapter from selling the cathedral silver. A bishop's *mensa* was never enough for the welfare of his diocese. Some bishops spent so much time begging by letter that a south-Italian forger once made large sums out of fabricating appeals for money from a bishop.[114]

Where the bishop had his see, was a city, whatever the size of town. Men argued whether a bishopless town could ever be a city, and Popes Benedict XIII and Benedict XIV ruled that it could.

The rite of confirmation was supposed to be administered every year in the see-city. Bishops with remote or mountainous dioceses sometimes felt their inability to confirm so acutely that they asked Rome to allow parish priests to confirm, though with holy oil which the bishop blessed. Rome steadily maintained the bishop to be the normal minister of confirmation and refused most of these requests. But not all failed. In 1733 the Bishop of

[112] Berthe, 2.73; Almeida, 3.484.   [113] Padover, 23; Sarrailh, 128, 633 ff.
[114] Berthe, 1.558.

Concepción in Chile applied to Pope Clement XII. He said that many of the islands of Chile were 300 leagues from his see-city; that the journey was risky by land because of tribes and more risky by water because of reefs; that only one bishop ever penetrated the region; that for many years no one had been confirmed. He therefore begged the Pope to allow priests, soon to set out, the faculty of confirming. Popes occasionally accepted these pleas of necessity. Pope Clement XI and Pope Benedict XIV both renewed an ancient privilege of the Franciscan superior in Jerusalem to confirm though he was only a priest. In the Americas vast distances made necessity more evident. But Rome was not easy to move. When in 1751 Pope Benedict XIV allowed the Archbishop of Lima and the Bishop of Quito to sanction confirmation by their priests, he limited the right to a period of ten years.[115]

To deny that in necessity it could be done, was impossible partly from old precedent, and partly from the practice among Catholics of the Greek rites, who followed the custom of the Greek Orthodox Church and used the priest as the normal minister of confirmation. Catholic theologians, not contemptible in number or weight but a minority, denied that such a practice could make a valid confirmation. By the middle of the eighteenth century the possibility of exception was admitted.

The many little parishes of an ancient city caused a special problem about confirmation. Occasionally a bishop felt that to give so many addresses placed an intolerable burden upon himself and, since the subject must always be the meaning of the rite in simple language, led to excess of repetition. The Archbishop of Bologna, when confirming in his fifty-four city parishes between the late autumn of 1732 and the spring of 1733, printed and distributed his address to the parish priests, asking them to use and expand it for their people. Since the archbishop was a very learned man who found difficulty in coming down to the people's level, the priests must have found it hard to appropriate the address for themselves and still harder to explain or expand it to their people.[116]

Among a bishop's chief expenses was hospitality. He was liable to be criticized if he failed to keep open house. If he wrote many books he might be assailed for spending in study time which should be given to people. He was criticized if he grew too infirm to work. But resigning a see was not easy. It could be achieved only by leave of the Pope.

Canonists had a mnemonic in verse to remind them of the six reasons which justified a bishop's resignation: crime, illness, ignorance, his people's

---

[115] Benedict XIV, *de synodo* xiii.15, col. 1485; cf. vii. 7–8, cols. 1039 ff.
[116] Lambertini, *Raccolta*, 1.46 ff.

wickedness, grave scandal, irregularity of his life. But of these six reasons illness accounted for almost all of the many applications. And illness often failed to win the leave.

If he was given leave to resign because of infirmity, he was granted a reasonable pension from the *mensa* of the see. But few bishops could gain this leave though infirmities were many. The idea of a marriage with the see still lived. And, more urgently, churches and Popes were more afraid of a vacancy than of a sick bishop. They foresaw squabbles with the government over the succession, or pressure from local magnates, or the probability of a bad choice, or unedifying applicants, or a long interregnum while difficulties were settled. If they had a good man they preferred to keep him even when he grew too old to work.

For old and ill bishops the use of coadjutors was rarer in Italy than else-where. Germany was in the habit of using suffragan bishops with titles from the vanished sees of the east, *in partibus infidelium*. France apart from the see of Lyons hardly used suffragans of this sort. Rome insisted that a sufficient stipend (about 300 ducats in the middle eighteenth century) be allotted to the suffragan bishop. But the stipend had its snag because in the moment that a diocesan bishop died his suffragan's responsibility ended, and the stipend was needed both for any new suffragan whom the dio-cesan bishop might wish, and to prevent the old suffragan from falling into poverty or bringing discredit to the order of bishops.

In default of retirement, bishops applied to be translated to a lighter see; for a few sees were still sinecures, or had a tiny diocese with no heavy burden. These translations on ground of health were allowed more often than retirement. They raised no difficulty of pension, nor of burdening a bishop's *mensa* with the cost of keeping a retired bishop in such a way that his poverty would not bring discredit to the order of bishops. More-over translations were accepted in several countries, by reason not of health but of preferment. Poland habitually moved bishops from minor sees to major, and almost everywhere it was recognized. The idea of a marriage between bishop and see continued to push against retirement or translation. Spain, which freely accepted translations, nevertheless seemed to observe them with a prick of guilt; for in 1656 the Spanish king forbade his ministers to ask the Pope for a translation from small see to big unless the bishop had already served eight or ten years. This was the sort of rule which Rome would have liked to enforce; that a translation was for the Church and not for private (or State) advantage, and that no bishop should be translated unless he occupied the first see sufficiently long to serve its people. It remained mere aspiration. Governments controlled the choice of bishops more often than Rome, and moved them around much as they wished, and easily won the assent of authority.

Translation needed the Pope's leave. In theory (and in practice only in the Papal States) the Pope could translate a bishop without the bishop's leave. No man could be made a bishop against his will. Once a bishop, he must go where he was sent. This was the theory. It seldom worked.

In the archives are heart-rending appeals from old and ill bishops longing to resign or at least to be transferred to a less onerous diocese. However insistent and sad they rarely got what they wanted. Many sick bishops soldiered on miserably, married to a church for which they could no longer care.

The ideal of the Catholic Church was the relation between Church and State which existed in the Papal States. Not that the Pope ought to be Head of State except in those lands which Emperors and history gave his predecessors. But in spiritual matters bishops should be able to lay down laws which were right for their people and then see that the laws were enforced. No one suggested that a bishop ought to interfere in the closing time of shops on weekdays. But the closing time on Sundays and feast days concerned him intimately because sabbath rest was a divine law. Yet most governments if not all could hardly concede these claims if they wished to remain governments. They were willing to accept suggestions from bishops but not decrees.

To look at towns in the Papal States is to watch the system working, and to some extent see a model of what was aimed at when State officers served without question, or almost without question, the wishes of Church authorities.

Bologna for example was the most important and historic city within the Papal States after Rome, with a strong civic tradition and a medieval university famous for law and medicine which still attracted students from all over Europe.

Should barbers shave and dress hair on Sunday mornings or evenings? They had established the right, not without reluctance on the part of the bishop, who made sure that they opened only till the cathedral bells started ringing for mass or in the evenings after 10 p.m., and provided that cards were not played on their premises. It was difficult to enforce. The barbers' lads complained that they could not get to mass and catechism, some barbers stayed open all day. The rule had to be reasserted. In 1735 the bishop said that for a second offence he would prohibit a barber from working on Sundays and for a third offence expel him from the diocese. So the prohibitions were repeated, slowly weakening as the years passed;

for although the penalty sounded severe, it was nothing to the draconian punishments threatened for these same offences in the high age of the Counter-Reformation.

By the bishop's decree, then, he could stop a man from working on a feast day—as an individual, not as one of a class. And he could expel a man from his diocese, not from the state, and hope he found employment in another diocese within the same sovereign state.

Food shops established the right 'in case of necessity' to open on Sundays. Their apprentices also complained that they could not get to mass or catechism. The bishop likewise made them shut at the sound of the cathedral bells and not reopen before the afternoon, and sent to every shop, to be displayed, a timetable of the hours throughout the year when the bells began to ring.

The frontiers of Church and State continually crossed. The university of Bologna, famous for medicine, needed bodies to dissect. Everyone agreed that it could have the bodies of executed criminals. But too few criminals were killed to satisfy the maw of the anatomy school. Every few years came a quarrel between medical faculty and clergy. In 1727 the anatomists tried to take without leave a body after a sudden death, and the parish priest resisted. The vicar-general secured the widow's consent, celebrated requiem mass, and handed over the body. Another case forced the archbishop to rule (1737) that the anatomists must apply to himself or his vicar-general, who would try to get the kindred to agree, celebrate requiem and release the body.[117]

The burden upon the bishop and his Curia was heavy. Apart from all his spiritual duties, he was constantly issuing licences for all sorts of dispensations—it might be the wearing of a wig, or a priest needing a housekeeper, or a couple wishing to marry within the prohibited degrees of affinity; he had to see that midwives before they practised at birth understood and passed a test in the mode of baptizing babies; was connected with public health because he could dispense from public rules of fasting; published jubilees or other instructions that came from Rome; commended special devotions and regulated places of pilgrimage; was not specially concerned with hospitals so far as they were the work of monks and nuns but often concerned himself with the provision of chaplains and almoners. Above all he was responsible for the administration of the *mensa*.

The *mensa* needed a load of paper which some bishops grudged and others were incompetent to carry. Occasional reformers wanted to abolish the system and hand over endowments to lay accountants who

[117] Lambertini, *Raccolta*, 3.17 ff.; 263.

would maintain the value of the endowment, distribute the income equitably, relieve the bishop of a burden, and stop a spendthrift bishop from impoverishing his successor and his see, or too old a bishop from letting the *mensa* slip from his shaky hands into the grasp of chaplains or valets. Bishops preferred to keep control of their *mensa*. It was the power of doing good. Even in a small diocese in south Italy the *mensa* was four times the stipend of a judge, in a large diocese ten times. This was not much in view of the administrative system which the money must support. None of the Italian dioceses except Rome had incomes rivalling the great French or German or Spanish sees, Mainz, or Strasbourg, or Cambrai, or Seville, or Toledo.

Sardinian bishops tried to supplement their incomes by exacting fees ('taxes') at ordination or institution, even at confirmation and the rite of admitting a nun. This practice when known was abhorrent to Catholic tradition. Pope Clement XIV tried to stop it with a bull of 1769. The Pope allowed the bishop or his chancellor fees at issuing licences to work on feast days, or to preach in Advent or Lent; at examining account books; at enquiring into relics or indulgences, or privileged altars; at issuing a faculty to collect alms; at putting parish registers into the bishop's archive, and enquiring into the registers—and a small number of other occasions.

The bishop had a vicar-general, his deputy for the whole diocese, and three or four vicars-forain, his deputies and advisers in each part of the diocese. With his leave the vicar-general could exercise the entire jurisdiction. The vicar-forain had wider powers than an Anglican archdeacon. He could license the priest's housekeeper, send an agent instantly at a priest's death to check the inventory in the vicarage, rebuke the clergy if they appeared without cassocks; ensure that churches and vicarages were kept in repair and seminary-tax paid; collect evidence in cases of crime or discipline; in certain cases lock up men (not clergymen) in the bishop's gaol; and allow clergy leave to be non-resident for up to four days.[118]

A clergyman need not hesitate to become a candidate for a see. At the 1761 vacancy of the see of St. Agatha of the Goths in the kingdom of Naples, a well-endowed see, some sixty candidates presented themselves by various routes, not all the candidates being suitable. Moral theologians of that age discussed the question 'whether a man may rightly want to be a bishop', and on the whole concluded with the Epistle to Timothy that he might. Priests were not ashamed to go to their own bishop and ask him for a letter recommending them as suitable for a see. But Popes or patrons

---

[118] Excellent account of the duties of vicars-forain in the Papal States early in the century in Sabina Diocesan Synod of 1736 (appendix, 197 ff.).

were known to prefer a priest who had not applied partly because he had not applied.

The bishop normally wore purple (at least on formal occasions) unless he were a monk, when he might continue to wear his religious habit. He was addressed by the old Roman title of *Illustrissimo*, but in the eighteenth century more commonly by the modern *Excellency*, which some bishops disliked as too pompous. His arrival in his diocese or enthronement was a ceremonial occasion, with fireworks and the discharge of cannon.

Residence of bishops

The ideals of the Counter-Reformation still lived for the episcopal office. If men discussed what a bishop should do at a time of crisis, they frequently asked themselves how St. Charles Borromeo of Milan would act. Even in the eighteenth century, full of mellow dioceses like Barchester, the grim heroic Borromeo was still the model of a Catholic bishop. If plague or earthquake struck, the bishop was expected to be there and in the lead. A bishop was allowed to leave his see if the attack was directed against him personally, by tyrant, mob, Turk, Calvinist. But if attack fell upon his people and only upon him as one of his people he must stay. In 1720 plague devastated Marseilles. The bishop stayed (and won wide fame) and received a letter of praise from Pope Clement XI.[119]

In theory the bishop was more at risk in plague than the parish priest. Contagion was regarded with horror. The priest could leave his sacrament upon a cloth for the patient to take, and use a pencil to anoint with last rite—for it was agreed that everyone was bound to take whatever precautions were ordered by the doctor. To baptize by pouring on water brought no contagion. But the bishop must confirm, and confirmation meant the laying on of hands, and theologians would not allow the waving of hands near the confirmed. But this was all a riddle of the lecture-room. Bishops did not confirm with such regularity that they would be likely to confirm in a contagious disease. The parish priest must hear the confessions of the sick. That did not mean contagion but meant listening near by, in foul air, perhaps for a few minutes. It was asked whether in infected bedrooms a priest might come in and bestow absolution without waiting to hear the confession and hurry away; and it was agreed that this would not do. Priests and bishop were doctors of the soul, and must stay to hear the symptoms before they could rightly give the remedy.

The bishop then must be in his see. Courtier bishops hung around Versailles. In Spain and France and Germany bishops might be bishops of

[119] Clement XI; *Epistolae et Brevia*, 2757.

more than one see. The Elector and Archbishop of Cologne in 1731 was also Bishop of Münster, Osnabrück, Hildesheim, and Paderborn; and though German bishops seldom ministered (that is not quite the right verb) to five dioceses, they occupied two or three sees not infrequently. The Saxon prince Clement Wenceslaus was Bishop of Freising and Regensburg at the age of twenty-two, Coadjutor-Bishop of Augsburg at the age of twenty-four, Archbishop-Elector of Trier (1768) at the age of twenty-eight.

The German chapter must elect (no one quite knew whether this was law or immemorial custom) one of its own canons as bishop. Therefore princely houses must secure canonries, preferably canonries in more than one chapter, for their younger male children in order that they might later be qualified for election as head of a sovereign state; and this was best done while the young sons were minors.

From 1500 to 1803 421 German bishoprics (not counting bishoprics swallowed by the Protestants) needed a new election. Subtraction for sees held in plurality leaves 347 new bishops. Of these bishops thirty-eight were of the families of electoral princes of the holy Roman Empire, forty-two imperial counts, 123 imperial knights, 129 local noblemen, ten members of the bourgeois, and five foreigners.[120]

Historic families rested their strength upon these customs. In 1730 the two Wittelsbach families between them had two archbishoprics (Cologne and Mainz) and nine bishoprics. The Schönborn family, ennobled in 1701, occupied during the century twelve bishoprics, including three arch-bishoprics. It had a little peril, as the fate of the Wittelsbach showed. To nurture sons as celibate priests was not the surest way to perpetuate the dynasty.

The costs were high, and German chapters gained. When Archduke Maximilian Franz was elected to Münster (1780) the Austrians gave each of their supporter canons 8,000 *Thaler*, each prelate 10,000, the dean 12,000 with some 'presents'.

In the nose of the Counter-Reformation everything about this system stank. But it maintained the power of the Catholic Church in Germany. It was accepted as extraordinary but justified. It was the way to maintain Catholic power against that majority of Germans who were Protestants, and therefore to be tolerated as of service to the Church. Occasionally a Pope expressed his disapproval. Pope Clement XII wrote a discouraging letter about German pluralities in June 1731, but he refused to print, and it lay unknown until his successor as pope published. The accumulation of

[120] Statistics in Feine, *Besetzung*, 67.

bishoprics needed papal consent which was seldom refused; for refusal was a political act, it meant (for example) backing Bavaria against Austria.

In the Counter-Reformation Pope Sixtus V (1585) strengthened much older exhortations and rules and required bishops to visit Rome to make a report on their diocese and profess submission to St. Peter: the practice known as the visit *ad limina*. Benedict XIV (1740) renewed it and made it more precise. The practice was not well observed in Italy and worse observed beyond the mountains. It was ruled that Italian bishops should come once in three years, other bishops of western Europe once in four, others at longer intervals. These journeys required a long period of absence from the diocese, and Benedict XIV sought to limit the time away, four months if Italian, seven months if beyond seas or mountains. Bishops in the Papal States obeyed, others obeyed when and if it was convenient; and for distant German or Spanish bishops it was convenient only if they wanted something out of Rome. Bishops, however, often wanted something out of Rome and to that extent maintained the practice as a rule with many exceptions.

In connection with the visit *ad limina* the bishop brought a report on the state of his diocese. These reports make valuable matter, still largely unused, for historians. But they were not inseparable from personal attendance at Rome. Bishops reported to Rome without travelling.

Even in Italy wars and destitution affected bishops' residence. A test case is the number of bishops living at any one moment in Naples.

At the end of 1731 twenty-four bishops, ten years later about thirty bishops, twenty years after that twenty-one bishops, lived in Naples;[121] usually bishops from the remote places of Calabria or Basilicata, often on the plea that Naples was the nearest town where they could get proper treatment for their health, but leaving in their dioceses laxity and anarchy.

Since the kingdom of Naples had 130 sees, to have thirty non-resident was not so high a proportion. The motives for their absences illuminate the nature and difficulty of the bishop's task during these years. While rigorously enforcing the residence of bishops, the Council of Trent allowed them the grace of being absent from the diocese for three months in the year, and this freedom accounted for some of the prelates observed in the salons of Naples, Paris, or Madrid.

The austere Friar-Pope Benedict XIII held a Council at Rome in 1725 which much concerned itself (tit. xvii) with the residence of pastors. Neither its resolution nor the rebukes of the Pope had much effect in

[121] *R.S.C.I.* xxix (1975), 463.

Naples. In 1741 Benedict XIV's secretary of state told the papal nuncio in Naples that he heard of thirty bishops in Naples. The nuncio reported that some went home when he urged them, and left nineteen. Of these nineteen three could not return to their dioceses (one of these was Palermo) because government expelled them for a quarrel over jurisdiction; two could not return because they were hated in the diocese and were unsafe (such hatred usually came from the barons, not the people—one of these two returned seven months later with an armed escort); one had to be in Naples for family reasons; two were in Naples because the Congregation of Rites gave them charge of the process to make Carlo Carafa a saint;[122] four failed to reside because it was not the custom in those sees to reside, evidently because their sees were near to sinecures; two were only passing through Naples; and almost all the others had pleas of ill health, in two cases incurable.

Four years later (1745) anonymous letters accused the Archbishop of Taranto of misappropriating the rich *mensa* of his see to live in luxury in Naples. Rome asked the nuncio in Naples, who took the side of the archbishop. He was defending the rights of the Church in a vital lawsuit, and so far had been away for one year. He was in debt and had pawned two chalices, but he was fighting for what his predecessor fought—and had leave from Rome. The Curia was not satisfied by this excuse. Benedict XIV was the first Pope to put the pastoral need of residence in a diocese above the need to preserve the temporal power of a see.

A year later (3 September 1746) Benedict XIV issued an encyclical on the duty of residence—*Ad universae Christianae reipublicae statum*—which mentioned the kingdom of Naples as the place where the rules were least observed. The bull allowed the sequestration of a quarter of the income of a bishop absent without leave. The nuncio in Naples used this fine as a threat, but he did not think the mode of proceeding happy, and in one case had scruples of conscience. An enquiry of 1756 showed that the Bishop of Marsico Nuovo had been away for seven years out of eleven years of his episcopate. He was mulcted of a quarter of his income. But the nuncio had to allow that the bishop had been threatened with murder by the landowners over feudal rights, that he was heavily in debt through various lawsuits over jurisdiction, and that from a distance he provided preachers and paid for furniture and increased the staff at the seminary and gave alms to people in distress. All this effort hardly diminished the

---

[122] Carlo Carafa (1561–1633), of the great clan of Neapolitan noblemen, founded the *Pii operarii*, a community of priests (without vows) dedicated to missions and teaching. The process did not succeed further than the title *Venerable*.

number of bishops in Naples, which continued above twenty to the end of the century.

In conditions of health, no pension, remoteness, bad roads, no roads, insecurity, conflicts with landowners, the number was irreducible. More than 100 bishops were resident in their sees and working in their dioceses. A note of the nuncio in 1761 showed that of the twenty-two bishops then in Naples only two could really be said to neglect their duty.

Visitations

The Council of Trent ordered the bishop to visit his parishes every year. These visits were not so regular as the Council hoped. The bishop might be infirm, roads impassable, parishes too impoverished to support a visit. The bishop travelled with a suite of chaplains and secretaries too numerous for a poor parish to entertain, and if a bishop intended to visit such parishes he needed to pay the expenses of his retinue and not burden his hosts with the need to lay large tables or cook menus worthy of the day.

The Council of Trent decreed that the visitor must come with a 'modest suite' (understood later to be not more than ten men with seven horses) and to receive no fees—the suite might be fed frugally but decently. The Archbishop of Otranto who visited Frascati in June 1703, took a preacher, a confessor, a theologian, a canon-lawyer, a 'chancellor' to keep the records, a secretary, a master of ceremonies, two chaplains, one to be his assistant and the other to look after the alms, an accountant to examine the local savings bank, a 'precursor' to collect the dues, and four servants to wash up and cook—fifteen men besides the bishop. In Tuscany during the third quarter of the century the dinner might cost the parish priest and the parish 100 *scudi*, and few rural parishes could meet the charge.[123]

Nevertheless, a bishop who did not visit felt not very guilty, but still guilty.

The model bishop of the Counter-Reformation was St. Charles Borromeo of Milan. Into the eighteenth century manuals of pastoralia continued to appeal to Borromeo's example. They remembered how he tramped to villages where no bishop had ever penetrated, over mountain paths where horses could not go, to visit parishes and reform churches and people. In the ideals of the Counter-Reformation the bishop ceased to be the courtier and civil servant, resided ever in his diocese, and drove or rode or walked at regular intervals, so that no church and no priest was un-

---

[123] Maria d'Aste, 24; De Potter, 2.158; Crispini, *Trattato, passim*; a handbook many times reprinted and the normal handbook for visitations.

known to his watchful eye. The pastoral staff was conceived in the text-books as more than symbol, a walking-stick needed to climb mountains or plumb marshes to seek out the people.

The bishop arrived; was greeted by the bells and a procession; met the children to be confirmed; summoned the clergy; invited complaints; made orders on priests' concubines, or ruined buildings, or superstition, or confessions heard without licence, violations of ecclesiastical immunity, theft of church property, diversion of bequests from the intention of testators, and the other innumerable disorders which affected church and people in a rough and backward and illiterate country. His vicar-general or chaplain or secretary made a record of what happened, for by the eight-eenth century bishops realized that they could help their successors by leaving notes upon each parish. From time to time he sent a report to the Congregation of the Council in Rome. The diocesan archives often perished or were mutilated. Reports to Rome survived. Till very recent times the archives were hardly used, and make an important source of new historical evidence about rustic society and the religious practice or superstition of the people.

Until 1725 bishops had no model for their reports to Rome. That year the Roman council required a questionnaire to be drafted. This form was written and published by Prospero Lambertini, then secretary of the Congregation of the Council. It asked bishops to inform Rome of the following: the geography of the diocese, population; privileges of the bishop; state of the chapter and number of canons, and whether the canons included a theologian and a penitentiary; the condition and number of parish churches, whether they are properly furnished and have endow-ment for repair; the number of monasteries and nunneries, and whether they are exempt from the bishop; state of the seminary if any, its courses and discipline and endowment; number of hospitals and brotherhoods with incomes; state of the Mounts of Piety, that is the savings banks; residence and absence of bishop, whether and how often he visits the diocese, whether he ordains and confirms or uses another bishop; whether and how often he holds a diocesan synod; whether the bishop preaches, or if hindered arranges for others to preach; whether he has a treasury for fines which he levies and whether these go to charity; whether the canons maintain the worship of the cathedral and have statutes which they observe; whether parish priests reside, and keep marriage and baptismal registers, and preach on Sundays and feast days, and catechize children; whether clergy wear clerical dress, and regularly attend meetings to discuss cases of conscience; whether there are cases of scandal among the clergy or monks; whether nuns observe enclosure and how their dowries are paid; whether the list of masses to be celebrated is posted up in sacristies; whether the bishop visits hospitals and sees their accounts; what is the moral and religious condition of the people. The bishop might add any other information which he thought it good for Rome to know.[124]

So formidable a demand could not be answered without a lot of enquiry. Bishops were not very regular in sending these reports. Nor were members of the Congregation in Rome always prompt to read the mass of information which they were sent, for complaints came that bishops had no answer to urgent requests for advice.

To fulfil his heavy tasks a bishop needed a lavish *mensa* to pay a staff of secretaries. He had a vicar-general, his deputy for all the diocese. Out in the country he had a small number of vicars-forain, who acted like an English archdeacon or rural dean in keeping the bishop informed about one area of parishes, supervising the conduct of the clergy and state of the buildings. He was entitled to use two canons of the cathedral who thereby were exempted from cathedral duties without losing cathedral pay; and by constitution he must use two canons of the cathedral (not necessarily the same two) to advise him about the conduct of the seminary. But he depended heavily on various people who would work without reward. His examiners, for example, were debarred from receiving any fee for examining. With such a staff the bishop of a less rich diocese found it hard to get the information which the letter to Rome required, as least so regularly as Rome wanted, or said that it wanted.

These reports have the defect, known in medieval visitations, of throwing light upon the newsworthy. To judge the Italian or Spanish Church only from visitation papers is like writing a history of modern times only from law reports. A parish priest who practised sorcery or revelled in obscenity was pilloried in the reports. A priest who did his duty and comforted his people seldom won honourable mention from this type of document.

A visitation was not popular. It disturbed the hard-won peaceable compromises of traditional classes. Barons, who liked to control churches on their fief, feared the bishop as an invader. Heads of monasteries suspected him of wanting to tread upon their exemption from his control. Remote villages, accustomed perhaps to a pastor with his concubine, had no wish that he or they should be disturbed. Peasants engaged in a strike against tithes might threaten violence if a bishop came near them. The

---

[124] Printed in Migne, *Theologiae Cursus completae*, xxv. 1595.

business of getting information was hard. To invite complaints was to encourage informers. Early in the century we find informers reporting 'witches' because they found feathers in the bedroom and pins in the mattress.[125] To prevent the worst ills of this system the bishop in Italy usually appointed four or five 'investigators' to bring him knowledge of the clergy's discipline, habits, morals, and dress. Unaccustomed parishes saw the coming of the bishop to be like the arrival of a chief constable. Priests were not eager to be treated as though they were policemen instead of shepherds of a flock or (more likely) instead of poorly endowed conductors of services. The clergy were of the people and were content to remain of the people. Reforming bishops wanted them to be different from the people, and realized that unless they felt different from the people they could not raise themselves, let alone their parishioners, from the incivility of a barbarous countryside. Hence the reforming drive necessarily demanded separation between priest and people, different standards, clerical dress, regularity of conduct. Residing among countrymen with whom drunkenness and fornication were not sins, and probably born of a family where drunkenness and fornication were not sins, the priest had a better chance of living sober and celibate if his bishop could elevate him upon a pedestal. To this end he must be obliged always to wear different clothes, and to follow a simple rule of life.

Visitations needed energy. If a bishop grew old and lived long, he could not visit. Even when he had energy, there might be areas where it was imprudent to visit—whether by reason of hostility in the local lord or danger of demonstration from the people. In certain dioceses excellent and energetic bishops failed to visit for decades. They put more faith in missioners, and were reluctant to disturb public order by visiting. An admirable bishop, Anzani of Campagna, came to visit Pietrafesa in May 1762 and, now an old part-paralysed man, pathetically begged his clergy to treat him as a father, to love him and not fear him, and not to hate the idea of *visitation* because of 'ridiculous' prejudice among the common people, but to realize that if he ordered a reform it was for their good and that they ought not to eye as an enemy someone who wanted only to make things better.[126]

That the visitation declined cannot surprise. A priest of Pavia (1791) wrote a formidable little book against the burden it placed on parishes,

---

[125] Maria d'Aste, 604–5. For the effect of a tithe strike on a visitation of 1775 in south Italy, see Cestaro, 29–30.
[126] De Rosa, *Vescovi*, 83–4.

the 'very rare' benefits which issued from it, and the humiliation of clergymen which ensued.[127]

That visitations were important is attested by reports from new bishops who succeeded an old predecessor and blamed the state of the diocese upon his long illness and inability to visit. And sometimes these exercises were far from unpopular. In the diocese of Capaccio near Paestum (1771) a gang of bandits, headed by several priests accused of murder, terrorized the mountains and were rumoured to plan an ambush upon the visiting bishop to steal the church plate and the bishop's property. As the bishop approached these hills of danger, peasants came with sticks or guns and made a people's guard to see that the visitor was not molested.[128] Frequently the people welcomed a visiting bishop as a protector against predators, especially the landowner. But they dare not trust his power too far, for the bishop went away while the landowner stayed.

Psychologically and historically the north of Italy was far sundered from the south. It lay open to the trade and the ideas of Germany and France. Lombardy, the most prosperous land in all Italy, was from 1713 part of the Austrian Empire. But the differences lay mostly among the attitudes of the educated. The poor of Lombardy or Venetia behaved much like the poor of Naples.

The bishop of Padua, Cardinal Rezzonico (who in 1758 was to become Pope Clement XIII) visited his diocese, and the record of his visitations is published.[129] The town was rich, the university eminent, palaces famous, cathedral restored by the bishop. But the riches belonged to few, the palaces were surrounded by hovels, beggars besieged the door of the bishop's palace.

The priests were good, if up country rough. The visitations show no trace of any struggle against unbelief, only of a desperate fight against ignorance, crowds of illiterate with none fit to teach. The bishop reproached certain parishes or areas with 'pagan' customs or superstition, the terrible public wailing at funeral processions in the mountains to the east of Brenta, magic in the marshes to the south of Padua, the supernatural *virtus* in water or olive oil blest by the priest, the belief in witches' power, the opening of a window at the moment of death that the soul may fly beyond these walls. In such country places, even round Padua in

---

[127] Paolo Minucci, *Del diritto della procurazione pretesa dai vescovi nelle loro visite* (Pavia, 1791).

[128] De Rosa, *Vescovi*, 143.

[129] C. Bellinati, *Attività pastorale del cardinale Carlo Rezzonico* (Padua, 1969); cf. *R.S.C.I.* (1971), 603 ff.

the high days of the enlightened republic of Venice, the rustic priest was
the centre of *civilization*, though it would be overstating to call him the
centre of *culture*.

Diocesan synods

The second instrument of reform designed by the Counter-Reformation
was the diocesan synod. The not realistic Council of Trent liked it to meet
every year. That was never possible.

The bishop summoned all the clergy (not monks) to one of the towns of
the diocese, usually the cathedral. Clergy were obliged to attend and could
be admonished or even (in theory) fined if they failed. Canons need not
attend except that the chapter must send a representative. The bishop's
chancellor kept the minutes. They were to sit in their canonicals according
to most precise rules of precedence, clergy of the same order by the date
of ordination. The bishop presented an agenda previously drafted and at
times previously circulated. This agenda was discussed, and resolutions
taken.

The frontispiece of the decrees of the diocesan synod of Sabina (1736),
held in Magliano cathedral not far from Rome, shows the scene. In front
of the altar, on which the candles are not lit, sits the bishop in mitre and
vestments, flanked on either side by a priest in biretta. At each side of the
choir-stalls sit five priests in birettas, and opposite the bishop, on benches
constructed across the aisle of the choir, three tiered rows of priests in
birettas. All look clean, even marshalled.

The resolutions tried to reform what was amiss in the diocese. For
example: the diocesan synod of Policastro in southern Italy (1784) ordered
no one to pay idolatrous worship to the statues of saints, or any reverence
to statues or relics not approved by authority; demanded that religious
festivals be kept as holidays and by attendance at mass, and not by drunkenness or fornication; condemned irreverent behaviour in church, especially
trading; ordered no one to enter church with a pack of hounds, or wearing
armour of any kind except a sword; tried to get back church property
which was alienated; condemned magical remedies for illness; fiercely
attacked public drunkenness; tried to persuade people that it was better to
sleep on the floor than to share a bed; and disciplined the behaviour of
clergy—dress, carrying weapons, residence, behaviour at wedding feasts.

These diocesan synods were important in the life of that area. Their
decisions were collected, and often published, and then became part of the
body of precedents on which church lawyers worked. The provincial

synods of the diocese of Benevento, for example, were published in a single splendid folio volume of 1724,[130] a volume the more splendid because in that year the Archbishop of Benevento was also the Pope (Benedict XIII).

Nevertheless, through the eighteenth century, the desire to hold diocesan synods weakened. Like visitations, they were held because the Council of Trent, which reformed the Church, said that they should be held. But now the Council of Trent was further away, and its provisions were not always adapted to a new age. Whether they were lax or whether they were sensible, bishops felt freer not to observe the letter of the law precisely.

The diocese of Barcelona illustrates what happened. Between the Council of Trent and 1638, bishops of Barcelona held diocesan synods with a good measure of regularity. Then political troubles prevented them until they began again in the 1660s. But henceforth they were confined to (about) one synod for each tenure of the bishopric. They held synods in 1699, 1715, 1721, 1725, 1735, 1751, 1755. In 1767 the bishop intended to hold a synod but withdrew the plan. The next such synod was held in 1890.

Between 1690 and 1804 the seven successive bishops of Alessano near Otranto in the heel of Italy visited their diocese nearly every year, except the bishop of 1780–90 who managed only two visitations in ten years. Only one of the seven held a synod, and he only once (1748).[131]

This growing infrequency had causes which are not far to seek. Nearly everyone disliked diocesan synods.

The lawyers in Rome supported because their vocation was to maintain the system of reform settled by the Council of Trent. In theory they approved and were content to keep track of what was decided and to build up their body of precedents. But often they disliked the way in which diocesan synods behaved.

This feeling was partly due to discomfort felt at the centre when the circumference does not behave as it prefers. Diocesan synods had local interests, and eccentric characters among the members, and strong-minded reforming bishops presiding. They were liable to be carried away by zeal. They would pass a resolution deciding for their diocese a thorny problem about which theologians of all the Catholic Church argued for centuries without reaching a decision—like, whether curates must reside in their

---

[130] *Synodicon Beneventanensis Ecclesiae* (Rome, 1724).
[131] S. Palese, 'Sinodi diocesani e visite pastorale della diocesi di Alessano e Ugento dal Concilio di Trento al Concordato del 1818' in *Archivio storico pugliese*, xxvii (1974), 453–500.

benefices by the law of God or only the orders of the Church[132] (Archbishop Lambertini of Bologna said, 'It is better to reside than to argue why
one must reside') or whether incumbents were *owners* or only *stewards* of
their stipends? They would rush into the condemnation of all rates of
interest though Rome, with its experience of cases coming from the
international Church, knew that in a web of banking simple sweeping
damnation was not in accord with prudence. They might suddenly
encourage parishioners, accustomed for centuries to receiving the sacrament once in a year, to a daily communion. The Diocesan Synod of Malta
excommunicated priests who secretly carried weapons; the Diocesan
Synod of Larino suspended from mass for one day priests who failed to
attend the regular meeting to discuss moral cases. Such decisions Rome
thought foolish or not in accordance with the true law of the Church.
Diocesan synods had a habit of legislating to prevent—that is, they would
suddenly declare that no one in the diocese should read the Bible in the
vernacular though no one in that diocese was ever tempted to read the
Bible in the vernacular.

Rome tried to correct what it thought to go astray, by decisions of the
Congregation of the Council, the congregation charged with enforcing
and executing and interpreting the reforming decisions of the Council of
Trent. It tried to stop legislation which it regarded as unnecessary or over-
zealous or provoking. It sought to persuade bishops not to legislate about
matters which were not issues in their diocese. Though Rome had no
objection to synods, and as interpreter of the Council of Trent was bound to
encourage or sanction them, it had a more reliable instrument for dealing
with diocesan problems in the Congregation of the Council, to which
bishops or clergy could appeal directly.

For some of the same reasons governments were suspicious of diocesan
synods. But they had an even stronger interest in not allowing zeal to run.
A diocesan synod which legislated thoughtlessly crossed beyond the hazy
frontiers which divided the spheres of Church and State. Just as governments were afraid of papal bulls which affected the law of the land or
public policy in a state, so they were afraid of diocesan synods and could
much more easily control their acts. No Catholic government in Europe
would allow decisions of a synod to be published, or to be law, without its
consent.

The government of Naples usually insisted on redrafting. The bishop
sent the resolution of his synod to the government which gave the bishop
its comments, and so published as they stood, or refused to publish, or

[132] *Raccolta*, 1.185.

published an amended form. These emendations made the text clearer, or suppressed passages, or even redrafted so as to alter the sense of the decision. Lawyers of the State aimed to make sure that the resolutions, so far as they affected either clergy or laity, were in accordance with the law of the land.

Two amended resolutions from the Synod of Policastro in 1784.[133]

Resolution	*Text as amended*
In processions laymen must keep separate from clergy and women from men. . . .	To prevent disorder in processions we strongly urge organizers to see that laymen keep separate from clergy and women from men. . . .
The Council of Trent decreed that the Lord Christ gave Peter and his successors the right to proclaim indulgences and that their use is salutary. . . .	The Council of Trent decreed that the Lord Christ gave the Church the right to proclaim indulgences and that their use is salutary. . . .

Lawyers were specially concerned when bishops used their traditional power to penalize with fine or excommunication, because punishment affected the civil rights of their citizens.

Bishops of high principle disliked this treatment and preferred not to risk the appearance that State controlled Church. The inherent conflict helps to explain the disobedience (to the Council of Trent) of excellent reforming bishops who never or hardly ever called their clergy to synod.

The anxieties of the State about liberty of the subject were reflected in the anxieties of common people. Past experience of the resolutions of diocesan synods had not bred confidence in the people that they were likely to have more freedom after their synod met. Bishop Anzani of Campagna in south Italy told Rome (1762) that his people had a horror at the very word *synod* and excused himself for failing to assemble by predicting that riot would follow.[134]

In synod the bishop was dominant. He and his advisers drafted the resolutions, presented them, controlled discussion. The clergy were not entitled to air complaints in open synod, but only by means of a representative who could present a gravamen in writing. The bishop of Sinigaglia in the Marches was heckled at a diocesan synod by two priests who were vexed at the burdens being imposed, and shouted at him, 'You are supposed to preach like us and you don't.' The bishop tried to compel them to public penance, but Rome commuted the punishment to private penance.[135] A synod was no place of free speech. If clergy thought the

[133] De Rosa, *Vescovi*, 183 ff.   [134] De Rosa, *Vescovi*, 86.
[135] Ferraris, 2.840, (case of 1692).

bishop to ill-treat them by rigour or unfairness or prejudice, they could achieve more by appealing directly to Rome. And the bishop had so much power outside the synod that the assembly could hardly partake, and was not intended to partake, of the nature of a democracy. Country clergy arrived at the synod expecting rather to be ordered than to order.

Many dioceses had the custom that when the bishop read the resolutions at the end of synod the clergy signified assent by crying 'Placet.' From this 'Placet' a few bold lawyers argued that the assent of a majority of the clergy was necessary if decrees of the synod were to have force. But this was entirely unacceptable to most lawyers, and bishops steadily acted without any effort to gain the assent of clergy. It was agreed that before proclaiming decrees the bishop must consult those clergy whom he was bound to consult—that is, the cathedral chapter—and that if he failed to consult the chapter the decrees might be held null unless afterwards made valid by Rome. Though he needed to consult the chapter if the decrees were to have force, he had no need to do what a majority of the chapter advised, and disagreement with the chapter did not make decrees invalid.

All this was laid down after Spanish disputes between bishop and chapter during the Counter-Reformation (case of Urgel 1581, Burgos 1627). In 1689 the chapter of Seville cathedral claimed that their consent was needed before the archbishop could summon a valid diocesan synod, and that to make the decrees effective they should subscribe their signatures after the signature of the bishop, and that the assent of a majority of the clergy present at the synod was necessary to make the decrees valid. They lost on all points. The chapter must be consulted but its assent was not needed. The synod was the bishop's synod, in most dioceses he alone signed decrees at the end of the meetings.

Therefore the diocesan synod had no parallel with the meetings of a provincial council—that is, of an archbishop surrounded by the bishops of his province. In provincial council each vote was equal, all bishops subscribed decrees, a majority of bishops could carry resolutions against their president. In a diocesan synod the clergy had no possibility whatever of carrying a resolution which their bishop disapproved, and very little possibility of deterring a bishop from a course upon which his heart was set.

Bishops with very small dioceses saw no point in specially assembling their clergy.

For these reasons the decline of synods hardly troubled ordinary clergy.

In connection with the synod the bishop claimed the contribution from beneficed and some other endowed clergy for his *mensa*. Hence the money was called *cathedraticum*, or *synodaticum*. But this gave rise to argument. The old rules said that the tax must not be more than two solidi, or old Roman gold coins. But since no one knew the current value of 2 *solidi*, dioceses behaved according to custom or statute and were not uniform.

All taxation is likely to give rise to ample argument about its incidence, and the *cathedraticum* generated plenty of cases for the Congregation of the Council at Rome to settle. More important was the barrier which it could erect between a bishop and his poorer clergy. Pope Clement XII (1731) threatened strict penalties against men who delayed to pay. The payment was too important to the *mensa* to be lost.

Once the tax lost direct connection with the meeting of the synod it was not important as a cause of resentment against synods among clergy. Synod faded away, more because clergy cared little than because they resented. The one power which they possessed in synod was to approve the bishop's nomination of examiners at the *concursus*. In theory this enabled them to ensure that the standard of examinations before ordination or appointment to a benefice were not raised to any unusual standard. Since examiners could only control the bishop's choice by excluding candidates as unworthy, this was not an important safeguard. In the many years when no synod met, bishops chose examiners and had their nominations approved by the cathedral chapter, with Rome's consent as the law of the Church provided, but they did not always trouble or remember to ask for that consent.

The bishop's power

If the bishop was a good bishop, and a good man, he was the most powerful man in his diocese; more powerful than any governor, or large landlord, and subject only to the rules of a perhaps distant government and in ecclesiastical matters to Rome.

This power rested ultimately on *virtus*. He represented the unseen world —no more than the mendicant saint, not so much as the saint, but if the people regarded their bishop as a saint, the combination in a single person was formidable. He was more likely to be regarded as the people's man than as the government's man—the only person likely to be able to protect them against the oppression of the landowning grandee, or to persuade government to change a policy which begot disaster for peasants, or to collect food from distant parts in time of famine. When the parents of St. Agatha's in southern Italy went to find work in the hills for certain weeks in the year, they left all their children at a crêche in the bishop's palace. This crêche was sufficiently unusual for it to be recorded. But nothing about the evidence suggests that the people of St. Agatha's found the resource other than natural. Though not in the least one of the working class, the bishop somehow belonged to the working class. The Mediterranean countries produce little evidence from this age of bishops regarded by peasants as an offensive variety of oppressive landlord. In Germany bishops were princes, in France some of them were rich courtiers, in Spain the sees of Toledo and Seville were ways of keeping members of the royal family in comfort, even in Italy the Archbishop of Taranto and the Bishop of Lecce still had criminal jurisdiction, in the Papal States some bishops were also governors. But in Spain and Italy at least the bishop, grandee though he might be and at times unpopular because of puritan or sumptuary restraint on liberty, was still the people's man. In Italy the people were more likely to identify a rich abbey with the oppressor class.

Partly this depended on social opportunity. In Bologna babies found abandoned in the streets and taken to a clinic were found later to die or suffer permanent damage because nurses hired to suckle them were syphilitic. The person who concerned himself with trying either to find healthy wet-nurses or to get hold of cows' milk and goats' milk was the archbishop.

But even apart from social opportunity, *virtus* was a source of popular emotion.

Monsignor Francesco Piccolomini was Bishop of Pienza. His pretensions grew. In March 1764 the governor in Tuscany decided to arrest. The captain sent to make the arrest found the bishop in bed. He refused to get up. He took the crucifix and said that he would suffer all for the love of God, that he would be happy if he were bound or beaten. By the time he was driven into leaving, a crowd had assembled outside, some on their knees and many shouting. They struggled to kiss the prisoner's clothes as he passed, priests gathered and cried for his blessing.[136]

In affairs of the Church a bishop's authority, though high, was limited. A very large fraction of the Church money and priests of his diocese was almost wholly outside his control—the monasteries and nunneries, exempt and dependent on Rome. Within the diocese he was likely to find at least one other collegiate church of canons beside the cathedral chapter, and all these chapters, though seldom exempt like a monastery, had traditional

[136] Venturi, *Sett. rif.* 2.94-5.

rights of independence which made it not easy to interfere when interference was needed. In his dealings with his clergy he was subject to the weakness that they could appeal from his ruling to Rome. In appointments to many parishes he was limited by the rights of patrons.

Always the appeal to Rome stood, a continual threat that a decision would be rescinded. In 1728 the Bishop of Larino (south Italy) decided to give his cathedral a new officer called a chanter. Not all the canons agreed. His opponents contended that a bishop had no power to create a new and unheard-of dignity in a cathedral. Rome said that they were right.[137] A bishop's decrees in diocesan synod, however, had no need of Rome's approval to have force. Rome only entered if someone appealed.

Nevertheless the bishop's power was extensive. Apart from the prestige and history of his office, he had a *mensa* which usually enabled him to help parishes in trouble and so gave him a lever with priests who neglected their work. He had not sole control of ordination because he could only ordain persons whom examiners certified as worthy at the *concursus*. But within that list he had freedom, and he personally chose the examiners. To benefices which had no patron he had the free right of appointment, and these benefices were not few.

That the bishop could fine his clergy was part of canon law. This was still an important part of his power of discipline. He could fine a priest for being non-resident, or disobeying some resolution of a diocesan synod. It was an absolute rule that the proceeds of these fines should go to charity, lest the bishop be suspected of disciplining men for the sake of his pocket. As the eighteenth century wore on these fines, which were once applied with impunity even to laymen in certain ecclesiastical cases, began to appear to conflict with civil rights and were discouraged by Rome even where they were not at once in conflict with lawyers.

Over laymen the bishop had the power that he could still summon to his aid the secular arm. If an adulterer persisted after admonition, the bishop could report him to the governor. The efficacy of such a measure varied according to the friendship or hostility between bishop and governor and the rank or power of the culprit. In France the lawyers with their Parlements had very effective means of restraining bishops from interfering with the liberties of the subject without due process of law. But in other parts of Europe it could be powerful. Even in the Neapolitan region under the government of the anticlerical minister Tanucci, bishops could break up scandalous cases of fornication by appealing to the governor and getting one or other or both the parties sent to prison. This

[137] Benedict XIV, *de synodo*, col. 1318.

censorship on morals most affected the not numerous middle class, because
the high ranks could protect themselves, and the very frequent cases
among the people were not regarded as causes of scandal. If a bishop
attempted to bring a powerful adulterer before the courts he risked loss of
influence with government or even demonstrations against his person or
palace by the grandee's henchmen. Against evil livers a bishop could
secure from government banishment, or seclusion in a monastery, or at
least imprisonment in a State fortress; and if a culprit evaded penalty by
bribing the civil authorities, a bishop was sometimes inclined to regard
the bribe as satisfactory because the painful equivalent of a fine. In many
cases the bishop was the real judge, for if he was popular, police or
magistrate could hardly resist his application. In theory this procedure was
always a request from the spiritual power to the civil power. But bishops
might talk laconically in such phrases as 'I did not put the banishment into
effect.' Governors were not always pleased at these interventions, nor
always thought them wise. The Governor of Arienzo wrote to his bishop
about three offenders: 'I have just signed the order for their exile, but I
hope to God a greater evil will not follow!'[138]

In this way the old Puritan ideals of reformation and Counter-Reformation were often maintained until the end of the century and the coming
of revolution.

The ancient sanctions of a bishop were excommunication and interdict.
Both these continued to be used. But as the century wore on excommunication grew rarer and interdict much rarer.

The interdict as applied to the individual—for example one who failed
to make his communion at Easter—meant (1) exclusion from church
services, which the culprit could no doubt endure, (2) refusal of burial by
the Church—a very formidable penalty since no one had any other
recognized place of burial, and all sorts of fears were suspected for those
whose bodies lay in unconsecrated ground, (3) the placarding of their
name for everyone to read upon the main door of the church. This last was
a grave penalty. For ordinary folk saw it as a kind of outlawry. They
avoided all social intercourse with such a man. In some states he lost civil
rights and thereby became indeed a kind of half-outlaw. But even where
he lost no rights in law, and the penalty was nothing but ecclesiastical, it
usually carried weighty consequences for man's place in society.

Therefore the use of excommunication as a mode of discipline, or even
of collecting debts, did not always demand religious faith in the vast

---

[138] Berthe, 2.110.

majority of the people in the country where the penalty was imposed. It might imply that. But it could only be inferred safely that religious faith was once strong enough to allow legislators to make the kind of law where the excommunicated man lost civil rights. Educated classes knew enough not to be afraid. The Viceroy of Sicily once wrote to his master with a smile, 'A Viceroy of Sicily, unjustly excommunicated by Rome, would at once become the best theologian in Sicily.'[139]

The laying of a general interdict, however, was either an act of madness or evidence of widespread and deep faith among the people. The authorities of the Church deprived not only selected culprits of receiving sacraments, but whole populations of all religious rites. No masses on Sunday; churches closed and locked; no processions through the streets; no viaticum carried to console the dying; no absolution for troubled consciences— it was so terrible a penalty that it could only be contemplated by bishops confident that its imposition must bring culprits to repent.

When therefore interdicts occur, as in parts of Sicily during 1713, they are evidence of the religious hold of the Church over the minds of the common man. The plainest testimony is the belief of government that they could not hold the political allegiance of the Sicilian people unless they forced the churches to reopen.

The Church was not foolish in applying an interdict; that is, it continued to allow rites which the people could not do without, the sacraments of baptism, confirmation, confession, masses at Christmas, Easter, Pentecost, the Assumption and Conception of the Blessed Virgin. It refrained from prohibiting sermons or the Sunday school or the Angelus or marriage (provided the marriage had no ceremony), for to ban marriage promoted fornication.

The interdict in four dioceses of Sicily was precipitated by a trivial incident: taxing by revenue officers on a sale of beans, collected as tithe, by the agent of the Bishop of the Lipari Islands, who claimed that the sale was exempt from tax as the beans were church property. The battle between bishop and tax officers soon went up to the supreme ecclesiastical court of Sicily, the Monarchia Sicula. On the doubtful basis of a bull of 1098 the Sicilian government claimed to exercise all the powers of the Pope in Sicily and acted through this court. The court absolved the tax officers from excommunication by the Bishop of the Lipari Islands. In 1712 Pope Clement XI, who had more courage than prudence, told all the bishops that absolutions by the Monarchia court were invalid. Bishops

---

[139] Scaduto, *Stato e Chiesa nelle due Sicilie*, 1.150 n.84.

who obeyed were expelled from Sicily and interdicts laid upon their dioceses. The interdict was placarded on the church doors of Sicilian villages.

The power of the interdict, even in 1712–13, is shown by the reply of the State. Government could not allow the interdict nor neglect the closed churches. Royal officers appeared in Girgenti, absolved the city, broke open the church doors, caused mass to be celebrated, and proclaimed severe penalties on clergy who observed the interdict. When Pope Clement XI confirmed the interdicts, some 400 Sicilian clergy were refugees in Rome. Nuns who observed the interdict were locked in their convents, with windows walled, and were given poor rations for food. Monks were allowed not to go to services but must let their church stay open. In Girgenti the nuns of the Holy Spirit convent displayed high on their bell-tower a crucifix clothed in a black veil. Some monks of Girgenti prepared for a siege, even (it was alleged) with boiling oil. In Palermo, which was not under the interdict, a procession on St. Agatha's day fell apart when it was found that an interdicted priest walked in the ceremony. By the last months of 1714 parts of Sicily were near the point of open rebellion.

The government was too strong and won. It filled the parishes with clergy who took no notice of the interdict and were glad to have a chance of getting a parish. But nothing was happy. A memorial of 1718 to the new Spanish government of Sicily illustrated one aspect of popular religion and its connection with social life. The memorialists begged for settlement with Rome. Parishes and church administration are in the hands of clergy who accepted the interdict and are of a far lower standard than clergy who went into exile. Innocent people have suffered, consciences are troubled, the secular and religious affairs of Sicily are as bad as they could be. We ask for the settlement of the conflict and leave for exiles to return. We pray that without surrendering the privileges of the kingdom, the land be restored to peace.[140]

In northern Catholic Europe general interdicts were not laid. But in south Italy the weapon still had leverage enough to rock thrones. Nothing showed so dramatically the power in a people's religion. In the heel of Italy Bishop Fabrizio Pignatelli of Lecce was arrested by government and expelled from the diocese. Before he left he placarded an interdict on church doors. Government confiscated his *mensa*, threatened clergy who obeyed,

---

[140] Sentis, 154–5; Scaduto, *Stato e Chiesa nelle due Sicilie*, 1.148–52; *Bull. Rom.* xxi. 590 contains a description of events at Girgenti.

behaved like the Sicilian government. But the interdict on Lecce stood for six years; and when he was given back his *mensa* and returned from Rome, the common people of Lecce received him as a conquering hero.[141]

[141] *Archivio storico napoletano* xxiv (1899), 165–6; Benedikt, 537–8; Saverio La Sorsa, *Storia di Puglia* iv (1955), 194–5. But the Vatican archives show that the accepted accounts of the Lecce interdict are not in all respects correct, and the controversy deserves fuller treatment; see Bishop Pignatelli's few surviving reports in *Relationes ad limina* (Lecce), vol. 2; Nunziatura di Napoli, 142/239, 142/245 and 256 etc; 144/840 and 856; 351/254, 271 ff., 389; etc; S. S. Vescovi, 120/246; *Bull. Rom.* xxi. 463, Clement XI's *motu proprio* confirming the Lecce interdict.

3

MONKS AND NUNS

Numbers

IN the age of the Reformation monasteries and nunneries collapsed with hardly a noise in most Protestant countries. That showed how vulnerable was their way of life, and was taken to mean that they needed reform and supervision. Communities of dedicated prayer or good works might easily be found. But the Counter-Reformation laid a heavy hand on monasteries and a heavier on nunneries. Catholics suppressed some houses because they regarded them as useless, turned others into seminaries or gave their buildings to the Jesuits for colleges, revived still others by the insistent call to purity and prayer, ascetic life and meagre food, strictness of enclosure and severity of punishment. This reform varied in pace or effectiveness according to country, district, or even bishop. Into some monasteries, into a few whole orders, the Counter-Reformation hardly penetrated. They were as vulnerable, and perhaps useless, in 1750 as 300 years before—if not more vulnerable because meanwhile the world changed. But in other monasteries or orders, and by creating new orders, the Counter-Reformation refashioned the morale of the monastic movement and led to a new flowering of the religious life.

Inside the monasteries could be felt the tension which afflicts every impetus towards perfection. The religious life called to a higher way. Nearly all the saints canonized by Popes during the seventeenth and eighteenth centuries were monks or nuns or members of orders. The vow of poverty could mean little but simplicity of manners, the vow of obedience might be happiness in community, the vow of chastity sacrificed the family and may have had within the psyche consequences inaccessible to the historian. But if the religious life did not mean a mode of existence containing some element of self-sacrifice it meant little.

Monasteries and nunneries housed too many men and women for this high notion of vocation to be tenable universally. The number of monks and nuns went on rising. It rose irregularly, houses declined, new houses were founded, old orders stood still or faded, new orders were approved, but until the second half of the eighteenth century the general number increased: more monks, more friars, more nuns, more endowments dedicated to the sacred end, more land lost to taxation by the State, more clergymen exempt from control by bishops.

The numbers would not so have risen unless the ideal commanded the assent of Catholics. But they rose for other reasons besides the quest for virtue. Solitude drew men who wanted nothing but to be left to be alone with their Maker. It drew souls troubled by sense of guilt who looked for grace. It drew mystics who sought the vision of God. But religious houses contained many men and women who had small desire to be alone, were unmystical, felt a negligible sense of guilt. They gave vocation to men and women who wanted to teach the young, or nurse the sick, or become missionaries, or keep hotels, or profess scholarship at a university, or develop a faculty for music. They housed an unknown but probably not small proportion of men whom a later age would class as unemployed, or unemployable, or tramps. Monasteries and nunneries made the medical services and school systems of Catholic countries. They were social insurance and a large part of social welfare. In a country like Spain, or a city like Cologne, their numbers rose to between 1 and 2 per cent of the population. They were bound to contain many persons who had no rare call to heroic virtue. Many French bishops thought that more than half the number of male monks had no vocation to that way of discipline, and lived there for a pension or to avoid starvation. Examples of rising and static numbers are given in Tables 4 and 5.

Tables 4 and 5 do not conform to what historians have written of monasticism declining in the age of Enlightenment. General numbers continued to rise, though not fast, until the third quarter of the eighteenth century. Contemplative orders were static or (in numbers) declining. Active orders give a different picture. Orders which preached (Capuchins, Jesuits) or taught (Jesuits, Piarists, Somaschi, Barnabites) or nursed (Sisters of Charity, Augustinian nuns) needed and used more and more men and women.

These large numbers were evident in odd ways. A traveller from Dresden to Rome (1755) had a young Jesuit in the carriage as far as Augsburg. At Augsburg he could not get a seat because all south-bound carriages were booked by Jesuits going to elect a general. Between Ancona and Loreto he had as companion a Carmelite from Bohemia who entertained the company with his violin.[1]

Numbers in the City of Rome[2] are given in Table 6.

---

[1] Justi, 1.525.   [2] Giuntella, 63 n.1.

4

Order	Numbers	
	1682	*1771–3*
Franciscan Conventuals	about 15,000	about 25,000
	1698	*1747*	*1754*
Capuchins	27,336	32,239	32,821
		1600	*1788*
Carmelites		about 13,500	about 15,000
		1679	*1749*
Jesuits		19,998	22,589
	1700	*1724*	*1733*
Barnabites	726	788	774
	1646	*1706*	*1724*	*1784*
Piarists	500	950	1,680	about 3,000
	1700	*1724*	*1790*
Sisters of Charity	1,000	1,600	4,300

The Somaschi, founded in the Counter-Reformation, reached their maximum in the year 1769.

5

Order	Numbers	
	1514	*1789*
Carthusians	196 houses (the maximum in their history)	126 houses
	1683	*1768*
Cistercians of strict observance (not Trappist)*	60 houses	56 houses

* We may presume that some of those who would naturally have joined this order were drawn to the newer Trappists.

6

City of Rome	*1719*	*1750*	*1789*	*1798*
Male monasteries	100	118	114	127
Nunneries	53	54	52	54

Nunneries were more static than monasteries. This may be a sign that parents felt a little less obligation to send to a nunnery a daughter who could not or did not marry. But the obligation remained strong all the century.

General figures for Spain show the difference between monks and nuns (Tables 7a and 7b).

7a

	Monks and novices	Nuns and novices	Total
1787	52,300	25,813	78,113
1797	53,098	24,471	77,569

7b

	1719	*1770*	*1788–90*
Monks in Rome (percentage of population)	2·6	2·5	*c.* 2
Nuns in Rome (percentage of population)	1·3	1·06	0·8–0·9

But the population in Rome was slowly rising. In some ways it was a class society; noble ladies among noble ladies, bourgeois among bourgeois, peasants among peasants (rare), peasants (much less rare) as lay-brothers serving their betters who were the choir-monks.

Talk of class society among nuns and monks must be qualified by a sense of extreme discrepancies between houses and ways of life. The term *religious life* covered manifold groups of persons of the same sex living together, and was an umbrella over societies which had few other similarities. Exquisite nuns of St. Mary in Venice had hardly anything in common with rough Redemptorist mission-preachers almost starving at Ciorani. The immense incomes of certain old monasteries of France or the Rhineland could be paralleled in Italy and Spain. The Charterhouse at Parma was proverbial among Italians for wealth. The Jesuits at Policoro in Apulia ran a farm of many acres which (about 1760) had a stock of 5,000 sheep, 300 cows and oxen, 400 buffaloes, 400 goats, and 200 horses, all under the care of 300 servants. But Italian houses existed where macaroni was luxury and which gathered fuel by sharing in the right of the commune to carry dead wood from the forest. At Iliceto (central Italy) an impoverished monastery of Redemptorists lived on black bread made of rye mixed with flour and bran, soup of steeped bread or vermicelli or black beans; for fruit they ate chestnuts, peas, crab-apples; they had no money to repair their leaking roof, their windows had oiled paper instead of glass. Conversely an English traveller waxed ecstatic over the quality of mutton cooked in the Carmelite house on Monte Gargano, and in the Celestine house at Taranto (a town which lived off fishing) was surprised to find himself offered fifteen different kinds of shellfish. Even the very austere Redemptorist house at Pagani (August 1756) owed 200 ducats to the butchers and tradesmen and must therefore have eaten meat.

In this way the notion *religious orders* contained groups far sundered in purpose, social composition, wealth or poverty, education, and environment.

Mendicants were usually of lower social origin.

In eastern France an interesting group of aristocratic dames, called the Royal Clares of Pope Urban IV, slowly abandoned the cloister and the nun's habit. They had separate lodgings and their own money and could receive or make bequests. They still took the three vows of chastity, poverty, and obedience. Franciscans tried to make them mend their ways but in vain. They were a comfortable circle of well-bred ladies living round a chapel. Their nunnery resembled a country club more than the world's fantasy of a nunnery.

And in Seville was a Poor Clare nunnery where the rule was kept rigorously, the nuns slept on wooden planks, were not allowed to wear linen next the skin, walked even during winter in coarse sandals with no stockings, and could only converse with their families from behind a thick curtain.[3]

Any portrait of the religious life in that age must begin with a recognition of the extreme varieties of purpose, function, and atmosphere.

Social Needs

The social needs which they met were as diverse as possible.

(1) *Pension*

To be an unmarried mature woman was disreputable, in parts of Europe disgraceful. Many nunneries were homes for middle-class and upper-class women who had no possibility of marriage. In that prolific age a nunnery might take on a whole family. In 1781 the Benedictine nuns at Matera in southern Italy included seven daughters and five sisters of the local baron. Local houses had traditional connections with neighbouring princely families. For generations the Sciara family placed its daughters in the nunnery of St. Mary the Virgin by Palermo.[4]

Such women were born to rule. In Palermo during the last years of the eighteenth century the abbesses or prioresses of nunneries in the environs

---

[3] *D.I.P.* 2.1152; *The Life of Blanco White*, 1.122.
[4] Penco (1968), 128; Pitré, *La vita in Palermo*, 2.174–7.

of Palermo included no fewer than thirteen daughters of Sicilian noblemen.

We must not exaggerate. Baretti calculated (1768) that Tuscany had 310,000 unmarried women and only 9,000 nuns. Most Italian parents, he wrote, were sorry when their daughters decided to become nuns. He underestimated the nuns and in any case had no means to gain reliable statistics. But Baretti also noticed that in Italy, unlike England, an 'old maid' was an object scarcely ever to be seen.[5]

(2) *Dole*

Religious houses gave out alms. All monasteries and many nunneries expected to give and were expected by the public to give relief to the poor, usually in food and clothing but sometimes in money.

The Benedictine house of St. Martin at Palermo was restricted to blue blood and had revenues sufficient to sustain elegant life for its members. Every day those same revenues fed in the courtyard of the monastery between 150 and 200 people on soup, macaroni, bread, and wine.

This was a duty whether or not the house was fat with money. The Redemptorist house at Ciorani in central Italy struggled with such desperate poverty that it could hardly feed its members. Yet they reckoned that only ten or twelve families in Ciorani received no dole from the monastery.

The middle class needed nunneries for their women. Labourers and unemployed needed religious houses because they collected money from the middle class and gave part of it to the poor.

A portion of the alms went to diminish the class structure of the nunneries. To become a nun, as to become a wife, an applicant needed a dowry (of which more later). Religious houses quite often assisted in this way girls from poor homes who felt a vocation to be a nun or whose parents thought that she should be a nun.

(3) *Homes and asylums*

A related function was served in looking after persons who were not well fitted for the world—men who in a modern age would be tramps, or unemployable, or weak in the head. They tested them, and might reject them as unsuited to the way of life or likely to disturb the even tenor of the community. If they received them, they normally received them as monks if they were educated or educatable, as lay brothers if they were not. Throughout Europe (not of course in every community) monasteries

---

[5] Baretti, *An Account*, 2.6–9.

and nunneries housed a proportion of persons who in a world better provided with asylums would have ended their days in a home.

Here is a curious case from Genoa. Maria Fossa Victoria married Francesco Venatio and then found that she was so promiscuous that her husband had to keep rescuing her from the poor house where the police put her when they picked her off the streets. Then, the court record went on soberly, under God she decided to become a nun, and her husband agreed and said that he would have become a monk had he not old parents to look after—and so it was agreed that she should become a nun provided this husband, aged thirty-four, had no objection and provided that he undertook to remain celibate. She was only twenty-five years old, and the record does not say what happened.[6]

Monasteries and nunneries housed other persons besides privileged and rare souls consecrated to God—though some of those also.

(4) *Hospitality*

Houses had a traditional duty to give shelter to wayfarers, in a guesthouse outside the enclosure. In parts of Europe they were the only, or only clean, hotels. In southern Italy where inns were few and nests of lice, monastic hospices served the traveller. The Englishman Henry Swinburne, who toured Italy and Sicily (1778–80) stayed at inns in big towns and monasteries everywhere else, and had more comfort at the monasteries. On cols of the Alps or Pyrenees or Apennines monastic buildings sheltered pilgrim or trader who crossed the passes. On top of the St. Bernard, in one of the highest monasteries of Christendom, a sadly divided group of regular canons still ministered to wayfarers after a continuous history of seven centuries and housed not only kings and merchants and pilgrims but early tourists.

In a jubilee year, when pilgrims sought the shrines of Rome, the Camaldolese hermits near Turin, who kept a visitor's book, counted 11,000 people whom they sheltered and fed. That was an average of nearly thirty beds and thirty meals every night of the year. In ordinary years travellers were far less numerous, but not a night passed without a few.[7]

Such numbers were burdensome and might destroy quietness in the religious life. Monasteries did not profess doubt whether they had a religious duty to receive strangers, but they started to organize their hospitality. In towns where there were two houses of an order, superiors were known to set up a rota. A traveller who knocked at the door of the Dominican house at Messina might be sent off to the other Dominican

[6] *Thesaurus Resolutionum*, 2.163.   [7] *Annales Camald.* 8.521.

house in the town if it was not the turn of the house where he knocked. When Swinburne toured southern Italy, he needed to visit the president of the provincial government at Trani to secure an order to the monasteries of the region for his lodging.[8]

(5) *Economy and society*

In earlier centuries Cistercians and other more remote monks brought tracts of untilled land into cultivation. That could still happen in the wide spaces of eastern Europe, and even among the mountains of Italy, but rarely. When the Cistercians of Buonsallazzo in Tuscany looked useless the duke sent them packing and brought in the reformed Cistercians known as Trappists; who amid their revivals of ancient discipline gave stimulus to better farming of the land. A Jesuit house in Sicily was famous for advanced methods in agriculture. In the plain of Ripolo monks ran prosperous estates, on the Vallombrosa hills monks planted forests, Capuchins at Venice were well known as pharmacists, the Swiss abbey of Einsiedeln was celebrated for its breed of horses. At the lower hermitage of Camaldoli in the Casentino may still be seen the old test-tubes and instruments of their much valued factory of drugs and medicines.

None of this was normal. The purpose of a monastery was not to farm or improve property. A poor house scratched a dismal living from its smallholding. A rich house leased its land and property like other landlords and lived off the rents as unearned income. The Jesuit house in Palermo owned several shops, a little house-property, country estates including an inn and a water-supply, an olive-grove, and the right of pasturage on a mountain.[9]

(6) *Hospitals*

Nearly all the hospitals of Catholic countries were staffed by nuns. Chaplains in hospitals were usually friars, in Italy mostly Capuchin, for this was the greatest age of the Capuchin order. Sometimes the nurses were not the nuns but the nuns' servants; as at Oudenarde where a community of Bernardines was limited by statute and tradition to twelve sisters.[10] The Augustinian nuns at Bruges served a hospital and serve to this day though in a different building. The order founded by Camillus de Lellis, usually regarded as predecessors of the Red Cross and known as the 'Regular clerks who nurse the sick' (*Chierici regolari ministri degli infirmi*) were commonest in Italy and Spain and Portugal. Nineteen Camillans out

[8] Labat, *Voyages* 5.123–4; Swinburne, 1.277.   [9] Renda, 376–7.   [10] *D.I.P.* 1.1386.

of twenty-five died in the plague at Messina (1763).[11] They reached their maximum number in 1782 but time made them more ecclesiastical and moved them partly out of hospitals and into parishes. Pope Benedict XIV made Camillus de Lellis a saint (1746) and so by symbol and repute fostered this nursing order.

(7) *Education*

Catholic schools and colleges were conducted by religious orders. Though the university of Salzburg (founded 1617) was Benedictine, the Jesuits dominated most higher Catholic colleges and universities. In primary education nearly every order had a hand. The Piarists had schools as their vocation and in Italy were called Scolopists from *Scuole Pie*, 'godly schools'. But even houses with a contemplative ideal might find themselves engaged with orphans or small girls. Rosa Venerini (died at Rome 1728) founded a school for girls in her birthplace Viterbo and soon had a group of religious for running this and other girls' schools under the odd-sounding name *Maestre Pie*, 'godly schoolmistresses', and among them an extraordinary colleague Lucia Filippini who became the leader of another group of educators. Then a Carmelite friar, Isidore of the Nativity, saw the need and founded a third order of 'Theresian Carmelites' which had eighteen houses by the time of his death (1769). This was the age when the education of girls from poor homes first became matter of social conscience, and no one but a nun was regarded as perfectly satisfactory for the work. The Sisters of the Child Jesus were founded in 1708 and soon fixed their headquarters at Soissons and about seventy years later had twenty houses, all with the vocation to educate girls. Many little Augustinian communities were in charge of schools for poor boys.

In the then Catholic spirit, teaching anything was not to be separated from the monastic ideal. Any form of education was likely to cause a community. In Augsburg (1704) two ladies formed a nunnery, in type of the third order of St. Francis, which was really a school of cookery. The members bound themselves for a common life of one year, and from the community issued a Cookery-Book for the Holy Roman Empire. This community outlived the Napoleonic wars.[12]

The needs of the age required new and more flexible types of religious community. By the end of the seventeenth century and during the first half of the eighteenth century began that process, which flowered only in the nineteenth century, whereby little groups kept forming for a particu-

[11] Heimbucher, 2.117.   [12] Heimbucher, 2.24.

lar local purpose, usually under the bishop's control, making no effort to attach to an older and famous order, in aim pastoral or devotional.

(8) *Learning*

Most monks did not enter the cloister for the sake of knowledge. They were too occupied with liturgy, too busy in teaching or caring for the sick, too concerned with administering the group or its property, too idle or too ignorant, to read more than missal and breviary. 'Franciscans nowadays', said Bishop Ricci of Pistoia with a mixture of sadness and contempt, 'are mostly uneducated, and at best have got snippets of grammar from some old curate and know no Latin'.[13] Simple and illiterate monks were as remote from the Enlightenment as the peasants from whom they were drawn.

Educated men, even educated monks, looked critically upon monasteries as seats of learning. They eyed monastic libraries with horror when they were treated as store-rooms. Bishops found houses where the books had been sold or transferred, houses where serious study was discouraged or forbidden. At one house in Tuscany the bishop on visitation asked to see the library and, after a long delay while his guide looked for a key, found a tiny room full of old papers, cobwebs dangling against his face. When the bishop asked after the library at another house in Tuscany, a monk said that their only books were a calendar in the sacristy and an almanac in the kitchen. A visitor to Rochefort in Belgium (1744) saw a decayed library which none of the eight resident Cistercians used.[14]

Monks were ignorant because they came in ignorant and nothing in their monastic life diminished their ignorance while it partially kept them from what went on in the world. But some orders, or some houses, or some superiors, or some private monks, did not always think learning fit work for a monk even when that monk was capable of learning. A Camaldolese hermit of St. Saviour's near Turin[15] was a very learned man and had in his cell the manuscripts of numerous books until he was led by his superior to see that all this was vanity and went out and burnt the work of years. This was not unique. It was a historic feeling within the monastic movement. Not all Camaldolese felt it. One contemporary was professor of geometry at Pisa, another made learned contributions to the history of counterpoint in music.

Many of the most learned men were still in monasteries. This was re-

---

[13] De Potter, *Ricci*, 2.6.
[14] De Potter, *Ricci*, 2.3; Canivez, *L'Ordre de Cîteaux en Belgique*, 54.
[15] *Annales Camald.* 8.601–2.

cognized far and wide. Only monasteries gave the leisure and the libraries. The German scholar Winckelmann came to Rome and considered whether to be a monk. He had no vocation whatever to be a monk. He could not see how otherwise to win a living which would enable him to study books and works of art.[16]

In France the Benedictines of the Congregation of Saint-Maur laid the critical base for the study of the early Christian centuries and the early Middle Ages and stand at the foundation of modern historical studies. An Italian Benedictine Cardinal Angelo Quirini (died 1755) became the Vatican librarian and one of the most encyclopedic men in Europe, though his mind was more disorderly than a well-organized encyclopedia. To become a scholar in Italy was to be a monk or a librarian or a nobleman with private money or one of the handful holding endowed chairs at universities.

Educated monks could be among the most educated men in Europe and were no more immune to French or British philosophical ideas than any other well-read person. Yet it was hard to persuade some contemporaries that this was true. A visitor on several occasions to the Carthusian house at Seville saw at first the men of prayer, standing still as statues at their devotions, prostrate in their white mantles, an hour at a time, on the marble pavement. But a young Carthusian took him into his cell and showed him Voltaire's *Pièces fugitives* from the shelf and spoke of it with rapture. The visitor was instantly persuaded that the young monk's heart rebelled against his order. The visitor may have leaped into error. It did not follow that a Carthusian was wretched because he had a volume of Voltaire on his shelves.[17]

The German Benedictines followed France more slowly. In the second half of the eighteenth century they started to publish vast and learned folio volumes, sometimes on local history, sometimes on the history of their house or their order; in the Black Forest the house of St. Blasien sent its young scholars to be trained by the French Benedictines, and its Abbot Gerbert (abbot 1764–93) published nine volumes of *Germania Sacra*. But Germany was slow, slower than either Italy or France. Catholicism in Germany suffered much disadvantage from the refusal to use the German language in education. Latin was used by the monasteries, by the universities, and by learned men; the upper classes spoke, or wrote letters, in French. The Jesuits steadily insisted that the vernacular had little place in education—until after the middle of the century when young radical

[16] Justi, 1.641.   [17] Doblado, 231–3.

Jesuits ran a campaign to use German in education. By then it was late. The Jesuit order was close to destruction.

In this age rich abbeys built or extended libraries. The library of St. Genevieve in Paris was said to be the best in France after the king's, the library of La Cava near Naples was said to be the best in the kingdom not excluding the king's. Cardinals who collected fine libraries often left them by will to monasteries. Cardinal Fabroni left his library to the Oratorians of Pistoia, the Dominican Cardinal Ferrari left his library to the Dominicans of Santa Sabina in Rome. When the Bishop of Chiemsee died leaving 9,000 books and they came up for sale, the Abbot of Ochsenhausen in south-west Germany seized the chance to buy the lot. In the same region the historic Benedictine house at Weingarten had so rare a library that after suppression it became the founding collection of one of the two royal libraries in the kingdom of Württemberg. Cistercians were not known for reading. But the Cistercian abbey of Dunes in Belgium, which started from zero because it was burnt down in the wars of religion, had 8,763 books in the catalogue of 1740 and about 12,000 books half a century later. That was an average rate of acquisition of sixty-five books in a year.[18]

In more remote countries, certain orders had a special part in education and culture. Barnabites taught in the seminaries of many dioceses in eastern Europe. In the former Turkish empire Capuchins made new centres of culture which was odd because elsewhere they had a reputation for being too simple. In Byelorussia and Slovakia the Basilian order of Josaphat monks held Catholics of the eastern rites in their allegiance to Rome. They had printing presses at Vilna and three other cities, founded schools, extended Catholicism along the Carpathian mountains, and were felt by Turks and Russians to be a threat. Their prosperity ended when the partitions of Poland brought three-quarters of the Basilian order under Russian rule.

The Mechitarists served a similar purpose among the Armenians. Peter Manouk (died 1749), with the nickname of Mechitar (Comforter), founded a little Armenian congregation in Constantinople. He was forced to flee for his life, disguised as a merchant, to the Venetian possessions in southern Greece. At Modon in the Peloponnese he began a regular Armenian community which by request of Rome later adopted the Benedictine rule. When (1714) the Turks threatened Modon, he fled with eleven monks to Venice and hired a house near St. Mark's. The Venetian senate gave him the island of San Lazzaro, which since then has been called

[18] Erzberger, 339 ff.; Canivez, *L'Ordre de Cîteaux en Belgique*, 81–2.

San Lazzaro of the Armenians. The island became the centre of Armenian studies, the source of Armenian missions, the place where Armenian books were printed. Twenty-four years after the founder's death one part of the monks, then residing at Trent, began to call themselves Mechitarists.

But the stream of learning grew wider during this century. In the Counter-Reformation the religious orders possessed almost a monopoly of the big works of scholarship. The eighteenth-century monks produced such men; but more common were secular priests and even laymen; like the Ballerini twins of Verona who edited the works of Leo the Great and new documents vital for medieval history and who, though defenders of papal power, boldly criticized the pseudo-Isidorian decretals which many defenders of the Pope were still unhappy about abandoning; or the Assemani uncle and nephew at the Vatican, by origin Maronites from the Lebanon, who placed the study of Syriac in early Christianity on a new footing; or the French historian Tillemont, a secular priest; or Scipione Maffei, a count.

Internal strain in religious orders

The archives of that age are as full as medieval archives of the quarrels of monks—litigation, argument over precedence or property, constitutional rights, resistance to bishops over exemptions or demand for help with parishes. He who reads the acts of the Irish Dominicans will fancy that they did little but battle over that which was less important. What the age did was to organize. A vast amount of constitution-making went on, revision of rules, limiting of a superior's tenure, interpretation of enclosure. That this was necessary is shown by the difficulty suffered by the Dominican nuns who had to work under old statutes now obsolete but could not agree on revision.

One aspect of the making of constitutions was the movement to federate religious houses. Independent houses, or independent groups of houses, were integrated with wider groups. Part of the object was to combine for strength, in resistance to the growing efforts of bishops to control the clergy in their diocese, or growing pressure to undertake pastoral work, or work in school. Part was the desire to protect the poorer by the richer, the weak house by the strong. But a lot of this endeavour resulted in changes on paper, and had small effect on the religious life of the age.

One strain came from the perpetual argument between conservatives and reformers. The world of the eighteenth century, outside the monasteries, enjoyed life where it was middle class. The ethos of a monastery or nunnery, still under rules several centuries old, could feel or look out of date. To maintain rules rigidly was to injure any natural common life, or to repel young novices who came from middle-class homes. Was it right to adapt old rules to new needs like schools or the care of the sick? Should monks become gentler in a gentler climate or were they called to be a protest against too gentle a climate? In that humane age traditional monasteries suffered repeated crises of conscience.

The ideal remained so timeless. In the many-volumed collection of lives of the saints, monks may still be read of who lived in the eighteenth century yet are enshrined in biographies which could have appeared in the same words 700 years before. In Calabria dwelt Angelo of Acri, of humble origin, a self-flagellant, lying long hours on the pavement each Friday, stretched out in the form of a cross; a famous preacher of missions, though with a bad leg injured when a storm threw him out of the pulpit; a man of ecstasies, with the gift of rising into the air, a healer of the sick in plagues—the reverent Latin of the biography (*Acta Sanctorum* October XIII, 661) has the eternal purity of its genre, its affection, and wonder, and at the same time its monotony, and its remoteness from what was beginning to matter. If we pass from Angelo of Acri to the nuns of Venice who were his contemporaries, we seem to traverse not merely the length of a peninsula but half a millennium.

The Italian master Gianantonio Guardi painted a famous picture, now in the Correr museum at Venice, called the *Parlatorio*; that is, the room in which enclosed nuns of the convent of St. Zaccaria met and conversed with relatives and friends through a metal grille. This 'grille' is no confined little space of ironwork but three large windows each about 6 feet square. Inside are clusters of decorative and chattering novices. Outside is an elegantly dressed gentleman with ladies, while two exquisitely dressed boys are kept happy by a Punch-and-Judy show. Baretti said that these vast grilles were exceptional to Venice, that grilles in Italy were generally narrow, and that the largeness of the Venetian grille 'has ruined the reputation of the Venetian nuns'.[19]

These were well-born ladies. Harmless customs of the world could not but be reflected in the cloister. Such nunneries cheerfully allowed concerts within their gates and liberal communication with the city. Habits began to flow more amply, with billowing folds. Three or four feminine orders designed a costume which, if the nuns went to a ball (which they did not), would have drawn all eyes. Black veils and sleeves to the ground could be an ornament; the Dominican nuns of St. Bartholomew at Aix-en-Pro-

[19] Baretti, *An Account*, 2.17.

vence had a frilly cap and tucked sleeves and a pleated skirt; the Augustinian nuns of St. Mary at Venice were famous for their elegance, in waving cloak and draped cap. Occasionally even male canons carried sartorial distinction to unusual lengths. Such fashionable clothes were exceptional, and contrasted with the plain black of Oratorians or the simplicity of Sisters of Charity. The mode of the day was not for the impoverished near-working-class wing of the monastic movement. The vocations of nursing, or of teaching ragamuffins, encouraged no beauty of garb.

The historian of the Belgian Cistercians calls this century 'the frivolous century'.[20] The judgement is intelligible but so sweeping as to be absurd. The religious were humane enough not to be frightened of acts which horrified the Counter-Reformation, like the soloist nun at Milan (p. 88), or concerts of professional music given inside some abbeys. The archives of the Belgian house of Baudeloo contain the receipt for payment to a dancing master (1750) for dancing lessons in preparation for a comedy to be played on Shrove Tuesday.

The mood of the world saw little harm in being open. So we find monasteries where the refectory disappeared and the monks dined at separate tables, cells attractively furnished, good horses ready in the stable, each monk with pocket-money sent by his family, tobacco or coffee or shirts; sensible modifications of old austerities which sometimes went without notice and sometimes were accompanied by faint feelings of guilt that all was not quite right. They would enjoy retirement from the world if they could not hear whispers in plenty to tell them that no one should so enjoy this retirement.

The formality of contemporary life appeared in medallions or badges, even in titles. Since the military knights of the Middle Ages some habits carried badges as part of their uniform. These badges might be and usually were very simple—cross, Sacred Heart, pyx, skull and crossbones. During the eighteenth century they grew commoner. Just as in the age after the restoration of Charles II of England the Anglicans codified titles for clergymen, *Reverend* and *Right Reverend*, the hierarchies of religious orders felt titles appropriate. Among the Barnabites, who were drawn from the upper and upper-middle class, the title *Reverend*, formerly confined to superiors, was extended to all clerics, and superiors became *Right Reverend* while by the end of the century the superior-general became *Most Reverend*.

The result of all this was detailed regulation about dress, hair, games; not only against powdered hair or crimped curls, but down to the cut of

[20] Canivez, *L'Ordre de Cîteaux en Belgique*, 51; cf. 474.

beard or colour of shoes. To decide the length and shape of a Barnabite's beard the cause went up and up till it reached the desk of a pope. The beard was regarded as an ornament and unbecoming among monks. Camaldolese had beards, all missionaries overseas had beards, the full Capuchin beard was their badge and had the sanction of the Pope. The collection of briefs in the Vatican archives show how the trivial details of a monk's costume were carried right up to the Pope for decision. On 5 July 1727, for example, Rome needed to decide whether the sandals worn by discalced Austin friars of Spain and the Indies might be black in colour.[21]

Fighting as ever against 'secularity', the Counter-Reformation drove nuns back into the cloister and sought to ring them in strict seclusion. These imprisoning rules became a burden and a handicap when nuns needed to go out more freely into hospitals or village schools. Battles were fought between bishops insisting on rules and nuns insisting that they must do what they must do. The foundress of the Sisters of the Child Jesus meant to go to Noyon and had to go to Soissons when the Bishop of Noyon refused to bend the discipline of the cloister. In order to escape the rules St. Vincent de Paul refused to allow his Sisters of Charity to be defined as nuns. Early in the eighteenth century Rome began to change the rules by allowing the taking of vows without entry into strict enclosure. This was necessary to the development of modern nunneries. But it hardly happened often, and the strain remained.

Another change, forced by pastoral need, made nunneries less dependent upon males. Hitherto a nunnery must be subject to an Ordinary, who was either the bishop or (much more often) the head of a male house. It was therefore a stage in pastoral freedom when Rome began to authorize active orders of nuns which stood in no dependence upon male orders.

This peeping out into the world was typical of the generation. The spirit of the Counter-Reformation was still powerful. Communities and orders were constantly being troubled or divided between souls who wanted to revive or stand by the puritan heritage, and souls willing to adapt the way of life to the gentler temper of the times. The most celebrated of these appeals to a primitive rule were made by the Trappists with their silence and bodily strictness. Monks like Trappists who demanded rigour had the excellent argument that thus novices began to come in plenty.

In Portugal the 'Jacobeia' was the name of the puritan movement which ran through the religious houses and caused turmoil, and needed a pope's

[21] *A.S.V.* Index Brevium (Benedict XIII) 68/460–1.

intervention, and troubled even the Portuguese government. It was called Jacobeia because some Austin friars in the community at Coimbra formed a group for special devotion and used to meet at the top of a staircase which they called Jacob's ladder.

Where the vocation of the nunnery included enclosure authority did what it could to preserve the rules. In such houses, for example, the sacrament was received through a little window from the convent into the church; and through this window the bishop confirmed nuns, or gave a habit or veil to a novice, or consecrated nuns. The Counter-Reformation insisted that nuns might not freely partake of holy communion at their own wish, that they should receive the sacrament only as the confessor of the community approved, and therefore (by a decision of 1617) the window should have two locks, of which the confessor kept one key and the abbess another. Early in the eighteenth century this rule became troublesome to nuns and even to some abbesses; partly because the authority of confessors was not always so supreme, and partly because nuns felt a growing desire not only for frequent communion but for freedom to receive communion as their souls wished. In a nunnery in Genoa, for example, the nuns got hold of the keys whenever they liked and received communion as often as they liked; until the case became controversial, and went at last to Rome, which after reflection ruled that nuns must not be allowed these keys, that only confessor and abbess might have keys, and therefore that nuns might only receive the sacrament as their confessor approved.[22]

The nun was often placed in the nunnery as a child. She grew up with the idea that the world is a peril and marriage is slavery and a husband is a brute. Her instinct for career and vocation might be fulfilled by her duties in the nunnery, her instinct for a husband might be fulfilled by the spiritual marriage of the soul; but unless the house nursed or taught her, her instinct for motherhood was less naturally sublimated. Among so many nuns these sublimations were likely to be the crown of a minority; and life in nunneries was never so idyllic as not to be marked or marred by over-anxiety, or over-scrupulousness, or jealousy, or accidie, or any of the other children of an enclosed discontent.

It is enough to turn back the pages to the case of Renata Maria, the nun who was a witch (p. 9).

If a nun pined or faded in her enclosure, and the doctors thought her to need a holiday, or even if she thought herself to need a holiday and had a complaisant doctor, she could get leave without much difficulty. Doctors

[22] *Thesaurus Resolutionum*, 3.130.

who cared for nuns' health, and bishops who cared for the rules of enclosure and disliked the sight of nuns in the streets, were known to disagree.

Yet for all these complaisances about the world, the enclosure could still be very sacred. General chapters of orders often used to reinforce the rule that it be strictly observed. Occasionally the observance turned dramatic. A male within (unless bishop, confessor, father superior, or doctor at a time of dire need) shocked. He trampled on the ideals which nurtured the community. When boots pushed at the doors, even nuns were known to run to violence. On 10 January 1782 the Palermo chief of police knew that his cousin was ill in the Scavuzzo nunnery, and asked leave to visit. The abbess refused. He threatened. The abbess was adamant. He brought policemen and smashed down the doors with axes. From behind a hasty barricade the nuns fought desperately with stones and pots of boiling water. The abbess was put into prison. She had a good conscience, for she felt that she was right to yield entry only to force.[23]

The contemplative ideal on one side, human comfort on the other, always pulled at an endowed monastery to adjust its rule, even to desert the ends for which it was founded. A group of women set out to care for prostitutes. They organized house and rule to that end. But in time repulsive strands in the work brought tension into the community; and then those who believed that the nun's best work was prayer could conscientiously lead the nunnery to close its care of prostitutes and be conventional in enclosure. This happened at a house in Palermo. It was far from being a unique case of such a progression. No one should blame the nuns. In that society prostitutes could be properly redeemed only by a body of religious. Yet in certain circumstances, and among certain types of people, the work was not compatible with a corporate life of peace and edification. The founding nuns could do the work, their successors discovered that if they continued they tore themselves apart.

The nun's dowry

The class-world, obvious in the rich abbeys with luxuriant marvellous architecture—Ettal, Fécamp, Melk, Benediktbeuern, Einsiedeln, Engelburg, La Cava, Orval in Belgium, and many another—was even more far-reaching in the demand for a dowry at the admission of a nun.

A new nun should not become a burden to an ill-endowed convent. A

[23] Pitré, *La vita in Palermo*, 2.189–90.

Roman decision during the Counter-Reformation allowed nunneries to ask for dowry, that is, capital endowment to bring annual revenue.

The dowry was regarded as necessary to guarantee the future security of the nun. Bishops liked it because it protected houses from idlers and vagabonds, governments liked it because it restricted the number of religious and simultaneously disliked it because it increased the amount of charitable property exempt from tax. Convents liked it because everyone likes to be given money. Not to give a dowry needed a special dispensation. The dowry must be deposited (at Rome in a *Mons Pietatis* or bank) when the girl became a novice. Experience showed that a promise to pay meant that girls, who knew that their parents had promised to pay but had no money to pay, spent their year as novices not in learning how to be a nun but in worry. If a novice withdrew or was rejected at the end of the year, the dowry was returned.

Dowries gave rise to complex legal problems when the nun's profession was found to be invalid. If she were expelled from the nunnery—a very improbable fate—she had no right to the return of the dowry. But if she could afterwards assert that she entered the nunnery under compulsion, novitiate and profession might be held invalid and then she could regain her dowry which she would need to marry. To assert that father was a tyrant who drove her into the convent against her will was a resource open to a nun who wished to retire and recover her dowry. And some predicaments were more perplexing.

Alexandra Becchelli entered (1709) a nunnery of Poor Clares in the diocese of Spoleto. A few days after her profession a year later she whispered to her brother that she thought herself to be a hermaphrodite and that the male sex was prevailing. The brother told the bishop, who quietly and without alarming the convent got her out to her brother's house and had her examined by doctors; and the examiners reported that in their opinion she was right. The authorities then held that her profession was invalid and that the dowry must in due course be refunded; and probably the other nuns never knew what happened.[24]

Lawyers, and intelligent superiors, worried about dowry. It seemed to declare that a poor girl had no vocation to be a nun unless some charitable grant would pay. The scrupulous argued with themselves over simony, on the unreasonable ground that to require a dowry was to give a religious office in return for a fee. Convents were known which used dowry outrageously to exclude all but the daughters of the very rich—the Visitandine nuns at Paris exacted a dowry of 10,000 *livres* and more. St.

[24] *Thesaurus Resolutionum*, 2.129.

Benedict could not have approved. Still, most dowries were modest sums. Convents were social security and social insurance, and in this light exacted contributions like any modern scheme for pensions. To ask for money as fee for entering a nunnery was simony. To ask for money to help with future keep was lawful if not essential—unless the convent was rich when, if not precisely simony, it had 'the appearance of simony' or 'verged' into the sin of greed.[25]

How necessary was the security was shown by the rare cases where an abbess could no longer clothe and feed her nuns and must send away a group. Rather than commit such personal tragedy abbesses allowed even their walls to be in danger of collapse. The most dilapidated of all religious houses still occupied were impoverished nunneries, cloisters shored up so as not to kill the walkers, infirmary walls crumbling on the patients, windows broken and patched with planks.

New orders

Most new orders were little reforming groups within old orders and made for a special need. Characteristic of the century was pastoral need but prayer was thought of as a kind of pastoral need and a community easily formed round an individual, male or female, with unusual vocation to the life of contemplation. A holy Capuchin of Palermo gathered (1717) a few girls into a little house for purposes of prayer and soon they were an order of contemplative nuns whom the people knew affectionately as the Cappuccinelle, the little Capuchin nuns. They gave their name to a street in Palermo and in 1970 still had twenty-seven nuns.[26]

A new community might gather from above or from below, either from a leader or from a popular demand. With older orders static in numbers and remote houses under pressure to survive, convents stood empty in the countryside and by law could be used only for religious purposes. Bishops were known to ask existing orders to send a colony of monks or friars. Local landowners concerned for their people heard of a group looking for a home and invited. Villagers felt reverence for a passing penitent or hermit or missioner, and begged him to make his home there as a blessing to their community. Village elders or town council were known to take a conscious decision to offer the empty buildings.

Charisma was never far away. A community could spring up spon-

[25] For scruples, cf. Benedict XIV, *de synodo* xiii, cols. 1277–81; Liguori, *Theol. Moral.* 1.403–4.
[26] *D.I.P.* 2.199.

taneously, without anyone designing. Maria Francesca of the Five Wounds of Jesus Christ (1715–91) was a lady who lived in her house and dedicated her life to prayer. She predicted that after her death the house would be used by a convent of nuns. A godly woman came to care for so blest a house and dressed as a nun and the house became a resort for prayer—until Maria Francesca was made a saint and after several decades a chapel was consecrated in her honour and so nuns came to look after the sanctuary.[27]

The monastic ideal of experience was always spilling over into popular religion. Holy women often lived at home, practising the nun's way of life. In southern towns pious middle-class women filled their homes with little altars and rococo statues of saints. Between the professed religious in her ordered community and the unofficial godly woman was no sharp line. The one shaded easily into the other, in ideal, experience, worship, and way of life. The age of Enlightenment made no difference.

Two priests conducting a mission at Sarzana noticed a girl with an unusually devout attitude in prayer. They asked her questions and found that she wanted to be a Capuchin nun. They offered to help. Her father said he could not afford the dowry, it was too expensive; and then she had a vision that God wanted her 'in the world'. When she went to religious services, especially to holy communion, extraordinary physical effects ensued. The bishop judged that she was possessed and had her exorcised. Exorcism changed nothing, manifestations continued, spectators gathered, the bishop was forced to allow her to receive holy communion in private. Round her a little community grew. She served in hospitals at Rome and Genoa and Pisa, with ever-increasing numbers of miraculous cures, and ended her life (1719) teaching young girls in Sarzana and revered by the town as 'our little saint'.[28]

Into the mountain village of Scifelli in the Papal States came a wandering Frenchman, Louis Arnauld. He lived there as a charitable hermit, helping the peasants with alms, but without church or priest. Suddenly he vanished without a word to the village. Five years later he came back at the head of carts with materials to build a church and a priest's house, himself now an ordained priest. He asked the villagers that in return for this bounty they should change the name of their village to St. Cecilia in memory of his French home. The villagers agreed but found it hard not to call their village Scifelli.

In 1773 he gave a meal to some passing Redemptorists, and offered them

[27] D.I.P. 3.1723.   [28] D.B.I. s.v. 'Brondi, Maria Caterina'.

the property and the chapel if they undertook to take care of the village. And so a new, though very poor, community was founded.[29]

The Redemptorists

Alfonso Liguori (1696–1787) came of a noble family in Naples, son to a serving naval officer and a mother of Spanish descent. He was called to the bar and left because when one of his clients, no less than the Duke of Gravina, failed in a suit he rightly saw the judgment to be corrupt. He renounced the courts, was ordained, and quickly discovered a talent for parish missions. On 9 November 1732 at Scala near Amalfi he founded a community of priests to preach missions in villages—this was the origin of the Congregation of the Most Holy Redeemer, known later as the Redemptorists. Nearly all his first brothers left him and the first lasting community was founded at Ciorani three years later. Rome approved them (1749) without much difficulty.

His work was to found a theory of parish mission, especially for the neglected villages; how the preacher should go about his business, how to organize care, how and when to go back a few months later, how to avoid long words, what to emphasize in a gospel. Though he talked much of passion, and cross, and judgement, and self-discipline, the emphasis lay on what men can do to meet God's mercy. In 1750 he published the book *The Glories of Mary*, magnifying her place in the economy of salvation.

The fifties, when he was head of the institute and not yet a bishop, were the years when he became known as a writer and thinker. The practice of making language simple enough for the people spilled over into his style. This theologian was easier to read than any of his predecessors. But when he was attacked for his doctrines, antagonists found that the simplicity was deceptive and that underneath the apparently unintellectual missioner was a scholar equipped at all points.

He successfully refused the archbishopric of Palermo. But in 1762 Pope Clement XIII Rezzonico, who not only regarded Liguori as a saint but feared an alternative choice for the see, ordered him, though already sixty-six years old, to accept the unimportant little diocese of St. Agatha-of-the-Goths. A few years later he became paralysed, but two Popes in succession, still afraid of the King of Naples, refused him leave to resign; until Pope Pius VI (1775) took pity on the old immobile man and allowed him to return to his communities. The last years were sad with schism in the Redemptorist order between those in the kingdom of Naples

[29] Berthe, 2.331–8.

who needed the approval of government and to that end were prepared to sacrifice permanent vows and a measure of exemption from bishops, and those in the Papal States who had no such need and were determined to keep the original rules. The schism meant that the Pope withdrew recognition of the founder as one of the Redemptorists. It was not healed till after Liguori's death. He was beatified (1816), canonized (1839), made doctor of the Church (1871) as the master of moral theology for the modern age.

In 1784, three years before Liguori's death, a wandering German hermit and student, Clement Maria Hofbauer, asked to be a Redemptorist in Rome. Soon sent to the Baltic lands and Poland, he began a series of flourishing Redemptorist houses centred upon Warsaw and thence into several countries north of the Alps.

Hermits

Instant conversion was frequent. The French governor of the castle of Ischia suddenly retired to be a hermit in a cave. The Archbishop of Santa-Severina in Calabria left his little diocese to become the disciple of a visionary, who also drew a noble-born canon of Naples cathedral. A Camaldolese hermit near Ancona wore crosses in front and behind with points pressing into his body, a chain round his waist, never sitting at table. We keep meeting these tremendous changes in a way of life. At Mantua a Camaldolese had the gift of healing with lustral water and relics, even the diseases of cattle.[30] Statistics are unreliable and it may be that the cause is only better evidence. But we have more evidence of new hermits in the eighteenth than in the seventeenth century. A census of 1734 shows 1286 hermits in the single diocese of Pamplona. On the eve of the French Revolution the diocese of Toul had sixty-five hermits in twenty-five hermitages. The diocese of Regensburg had thirty-three hermits in 1769 and ninety-one hermits only twenty-seven years later—but perhaps some in the increase were godly refugees.

The typical hermit was a wanderer who settled by a remote picture or statue or cross or chapel in a wood, or on a mountain, usually near the top. They were almost all male, for a woman was not safe and if she desired solitude would retire to be a recluse in her nunnery; and even among male hermits the number murdered by robbers was not negligible (seventy-nine out of 1,000 in one enquiry). One Italian prefect sent a platoon of

---

[30] Swinburne, 3.23; Mincuzzi, 122; *Annales Camald.* 8.576 and 609.

troops to protect a hermit and hermitage occupied by a robber band with an abbot among its leaders.[31]

A hermit was wise to possess credentials. To distinguish him at first sight from a malefactor hiding in the maquis was not easy. If he had no papers he could be as suspect to passing officers as a pilgrim who had no ticket of confession and communion, especially if he were not in his native land. An aristocrat from Verona became a hermit in Poland. He lost the satchel in which he kept both his prayer-book, places marked with straws, and his certificate. Because he had no papers he was arrested on suspicion and put in prison until he could find someone to produce a testimonial.

In the sources the reader still breathes the air of the old Egyptian solitaries, of St. Peter Damian and the historic tradition of the single life. French troops came over the Alps and built a road near the hermitages of St. Saviour near Turin and cut down the forest. It was very inconvenient, traffic came by the hermitages which no longer had cover from trees, the solitary life was public. When the French retreated over the mountains, the hermits blocked the new road. Then they gravely debated whether to cultivate the ground from which the trees were cleared, or whether they should replant. They replanted.[32]

The average age of hermits was higher than the average age of monks, for all theorists subscribed to the old doctrine of the earliest Egyptian athletes that only mature monks should become hermits, and to the proverb 'Young hermit old devil'. In the hermitages near Rome the average age of new hermits was between forty-three and fifty years. Most of them had lived in monasteries first. But bishops resigned their sees, statesmen office, soldiers a command. Few of them came from the parish ministry. Some were illiterate, but pictures of the eighteenth century often portrayed hermits with books. A smaller percentage than among monks were priests. They won admiration from the pre-romantics.

Organizers sought to bring them under control. In Carthusians and Camaldolese they already had two historic and orderly communities of hermits and sometimes had acquaintance with the Greek ideal of the *lavra* as a community of hermits loose enough for solitude and close enough for succour or discipline. In this age the ancient group of hermits on the island of Majorca were made at last into a community with orderly rules. On Monteluco overlooking Spoleto hermits lived since the earlier Middle Ages. Most were Italians, but quite a number were foreign, especially French. They had a library and a common meditation in church and ad-

[31] *D.I.P.* 3.1209, 1234; *D.H.G.E.* s.v. 'Ermites', 781; *Annales Camald.* 8.519.
[32] *Annales Camald.* 8.519, 596.

mitted women to visit the mountain on three days in the year. As they accepted 100 novices between 1590 and 1700 they were never numerous. Strictly they were two groups, for so they were organized in the eighteenth century. They were famous and attracted famous men—the secretary of the Venetian senate, a singer from the Pope's chapel, the Latin Patriarch of Constantinople (who built them a new church), a papal chamberlain. Strict solitude was driven out by fame, they became a place of retreat for men of the world, even for tourists till the bishop made order that no outsider might stay for more than a fortnight (1756). A flamboyant Polish count got the Pope's leave to go there though his wife still lived—and so the institution declined into quaintness and after the revolution the last surviving hermit, now eighty-six, was solemnly reinstated on the mountain in the vain hope of reviving a vanished world.[33]

On a rocky hill 6 miles out of Cordoba in southern Spain, shortly before 1800, lived twenty hermits, all laymen. Round a central chapel each had his hut with a door so low that it could only be entered stooping, a wooden bed, and a little table with a crucifix, a human skull, and one or two works of devotion. Over each door hung a bell which the hermit could ring in case of sickness or danger. They neither visited each other nor conversed. Every morning a priest climbed the rock to say mass in the chapel. Pulse and herbs for food were distributed to them daily. Apart from prayers and reading, they wove mats and made little crosses of Spanish broom 'which people carry about with them as a preservative against erysipelas', and instruments of penance like scourges or wire bracelets. Usually they were by origin peasants; but one of them was a former colonel of artillery, with the cross of a historic order of knighthood.[34]

The hermit ideal had Catholic critics. An occasional bishop doubted whether such profound solitude was good for the soul, or good for the mental balance, and one French bishop thought that he saw signs of premature old age among hermits. Reforming Catholic governments refused to regard hermits as useful, and prosaic governments, like that of Tuscany under Duke Leopold, ordered them not to exist. But hermits were more useful than urban politicians thought. They were the men who cared for lonely shrines. Of the nineteen hermits in Styria (1782) only six had no little income of a regular kind. The rest rang bells, cleaned a chapel, served mass when the priest came into the forest or mountain, and nearly all drew a tiny stipend from the church.[35]

[33] *D.I.P.* 3.1169 ff.   [34] Doblado, 233–6.
[35] Chevallier, *Loménie*, 1.210; Wolf, 60–2.

From the archives we have a study of the group of hermits in part of Garfagnana, a remote mountainous region north of Lucca. In 1694, 6; 1710, 8; 1718, 7; 1728, 7; 1734–40, 8; 1755, 6; 1776, 8; 1791, 3; 1822, 3. In all the region (both dioceses) the average for the century, until a decline during the last two decades, was about ten.

Most were laymen, in effect sacristans caring for a distant oratory in woods or hills; men of the people, not remote from the people, in some cases chosen by a village to look after a near-by shrine; had no link with a religious order, and were tied to no special school of prayer, and were not likely to use the intellectual language of contemplation; but wore a habit, and so far as they received the impress of a single order, it was that of the Franciscan tertiary. Almost all were local by origin. A few of them on the passes served hospices for travellers. To their picture or statue villagers in need came to pray, and left their votive offerings, which made a pious little clutter in the sanctuary. Some hermits paid for the upkeep of the sanctuary by begging, very few had a tiny endowment. The begging was not resented by the villagers who were glad of their hermit. The votive-offerings making the shrine untidy were a religion of gratitude, the thankfulness of a common people for favours received.[36]

Critics of the monks

From Voltaire downwards articulate critics thought that monks and nuns were too many and ought to be fewer.

Peasants were seldom on their side. In a local strike over tithe, or a dispute over rent, peasants became enemies of their local abbey even to violence. Commonly they were of the opposite opinion. To them the coming of a monastery meant alms for sure, employment perhaps. They would parade at a foundation with cheers and salutes. Their pleasure was not merely material. Believing in the power of holy men they hoped that good monks coming among them would bring a blessing upon crops, health, children, prosperity, and future destiny. Contemplative nuns were as welcome as the most energetic of nursing sisters. They revered men who wore hair-shirts or tied chains round their necks or spoilt the taste of their food with bitter herbs or slept on straw instead of a bed. They wanted, first the *virtus*, and secondly the dole. In more than one instance, when a village knew that *their* monks had decided to leave because they could maintain a house no longer, peasants blocked the tracks with carts and weapons to stop them going. If they heard that the order came from a

---

[36] Giulio Fabbri, in *R.S.C.I.* xxix (1975), 403–37.

distant superior, they were known to beg the local curate to write a letter to that superior beseeching him not to take away his monks. In one such case the arguments which they used were unusual. They would lose, they said, sermons and sacraments and schooling, and the church and the image of the Virgin would not be cared for and would not draw the veneration of the faithful.[37]

The nun's clothing as a novice, or her profession, was like a wedding, with bridal dress and family jewels. As she was escorted to church she moved through a crowd of encouraging onlookers, their hearts touched and excited and moved. Only Protestant tourists were moved in the opposite direction at the thought of this girl having her hair shorn, imprisoned in a cell, abandoning her hope of motherhood. The common people of Italy and Spain felt no such sensation.

Naples was a city with far too many monks for its good, 104 male houses and thirty-four to forty female in 1697. Several of these were swollen with money. Their architectural improvements are still a glory and raise a scruple in the eye of the beholder. The slum people of Naples were as miserable as any urban class in Europe. They loved monks and nuns. The professions, civil servants, doctors, lawyers, academics, economists, merchants, secular clergy—these were the critics of monks in Naples. And orders of monks blamed other orders.

(1) *Parish priests*

Accepting the monastic ideal, parish priests were known to be cool to monks settling in their parish. A new chapel would be opened; perhaps with a new reputation for spiritual power; probably with a measure of popular appeal; certainly competing, even if silently, for the worshipping parishioner; certainly drawing away gifts and money which could help after they opened because the clergy of that place resisted intransigently. The clergy could win despite the people. The lord of Sordevoli in the diocese of Vercelli asked (1746) the Camaldolese to found a hermitage. He promised site, church, bell tower, cells, and an endowment. The monks sent a delegation to enquire. They then agreed to come if he would do all that he said and get permission from government and from Rome and from the Bishop of Vercelli. But then the richer people of the parish objected, the parish priest opposed, and so although the people wanted them because they needed the alms which they would bring, the elders thought it unwise and thanked Count Oliver but refused.[38]

---

[37] *Annal. Camald.* 8.606–7.   [38] *Annal. Camald.* 8.677.

(2) *Bishops*

Bishops might be, but often were not, critics of monks. Monasteries were one of the sources which supplied bishops. Unlike their parish priests they had a constitutional relationship with monks and nuns in their diocese. Where the house was not exempt from a bishop's control, it was part of his pastoral system. Where it was exempt, as more commonly, he still needed or might need it for pastoral and social work. Bishops without enough religious in their diocese were vigorous (if they were otherwise vigorous bishops) in fostering certain types of monk or nun. They wanted them as confessors, educators, heads of seminaries, nurses, missioners, shepherds of unshepherded flocks.

But their critical faculty seldom slept. Exemption was always a rub. A bishop could control most of his monks and nuns only by working through Rome. But he needed control, if he was to arrange effective care of all his parishes, or intelligent training of future priests, or discipline of all his clergy. The constitution and the pastoral need so disagreed, the jurisdictions were so prone to overlap, that from time to time conflict between bishop and exempt monastery was inevitable. To settle these battles was one of the weightiest tasks of the Roman Curia.

A bishop cared as eagerly as any superior for the reputation of monks and nuns. It was he who suffered when a fugitive monk took to crime, or if a monastery among his mountains became a nest of bandits or a nunnery was notorious for furnishing mistresses.

Because monks were numerous; because some men entered monasteries to be kept, or because they were unemployable, or because they would not otherwise eat, or because they wanted leisure for study; because some nuns entered nunneries because their parents drove them, or because they had no other future but disgrace—no one could expect monks and nuns to be all as perfect as St. Benedict or St. Francis would wish. A few such men and women in a religious house need not destroy its morality, or its ideals, or its reputation, or its sense that it was a retreat of contemplative prayer and good works. At times even a prosperous and pious community suffered agony from a little disruptive group, which at least demanded rare skill in abbot or abbess and made discipline hard to administer. Larger houses dealt with these troubles more easily than smaller. Where the community was very small, a handful of rebels could come at last to dominate the house and its ethos and its way of life. Too small communities generated the scandalous cases of monastic crime.

Older houses inherited buildings which once sheltered flourishing com-

munities and now stood almost empty. Land and property were inalienable. A community of three, or two, or even one looked after the site. In
so tiny a society even one 'bad' monk could dominate, prevent order, enforce relaxation, bring in women. In these little groups occurred the
worst incidents. One Cistercian abbot who tried to enforce obedience
found himself threatened in bed with guns, and therefore recruited army
deserters to be a bodyguard and make life uncomfortable for his eight
monks. When this indecorous method failed, he let them do what they
liked because he had nothing else to do. The policy failed to end his trials,
because among other ways of increasing comfort they liked to raid
neighbouring peasants for food and wine.

The Counter-Reformation with its succeeding age was like all reforming movements in reforming only part. The reformers achieved success by
making new and imbuing old orders with a fresh spirit, often in parishes,
schools, hospitals, missions, orphanages. Discreditable houses, which
once made abbeys so easy for Protestants to abolish, still existed in the
Catholic countries of the eighteenth century; not in majority, for most
houses of the older orders were places of ordered comfort, not of crime or
disgrace; but in a sufficient number to make Catholic bishops prefer
fewer monks, and to strengthen Catholic politicians who envied idle endowments. The French had a proverb which ran: 'Whatever shall we do
with that wastrel? Better send him to be a monk.'[39]

More telling than any of the incidents of disgrace was the need to train
confessors how to answer a harlot who came in penitence and asked
whether she ought to give back to monks the money which they paid;
and the moral advisers took the charitable view that to get harlots to confession was hard enough and to make them restore all that they had been
given would drive them to despair; and consoled themselves with the hope
that the money which the monks paid was not the abbey's money but
pocket-money sent by their families.[40]

Saints were secret, villains notorious. Bishops and Popes worried continuously and were among those who wanted to reduce quantity to gain
quality. 'The worst pest among monks', wrote Pope Benedict XIV, 'is
too many monks.'[41]

(3) *Educated laymen*

An enquirer[42] has examined the evidence for *reputation* among religious

---

[39] Chevallier, *Loménie*, 1.65 and 200.
[40] Chiericato, *Synopsis Decisionum* (Venice, 1703), 227-8.
[41] *De synodo* xiii, col.1432.   [42] De Maio, 16 ff, 108-9.

orders in Naples early in the eighteenth century. He felt able to make a catalogue of orders divided into respected and disgraceful:

respected: Capuchins, and some other forms of Franciscan, e.g. Alcantarini
Oratorians
Scolopists (a teaching order)
Missioners of St. Vincent de Paul

disgraceful: Unreformed Franciscans
Canons regular
Dominicans at one house
Benedictines at one house
Mercedarii
Olivetans

Reputations seldom correspond wholly with reality, and are hard to judge from the scraps of information which are now the only evidence. But it can scarcely be accident that in this list the ill repute hangs round the historic medieval traditional orders, the valued men lived in active orders founded by the Counter-Reformation.

The same enquirer judged that nuns were not nearly so unpopular as monks. No one could miss the social need.

Thus educated laymen were troubled by the scandals which also afflicted superiors, bishops, and Popes.

If they were politicians or financiers or theorists of Church and State, they looked with anxious eyes at the acres of land in mortmain, owned by monasteries, growing every year with each new dowry and many new bequests, but inalienable because it was sacred from the moment that it was given to the Church.

Merchants resented competition from trading monasteries which by reason of charitable status were exempt from tax. Townsmen noticed how tax privileges worked, especially when trade fell into slump. Then they began to murmur against tax-free trading in textiles, or brewing, or wine. Wise superiors tried to avoid these frictions which were inherent in the nature of legal exemption.

The monastery prison

The religious house was a private world. During the second half of the century political theory penetrated the growing number of educated minds and led them to doubt whether practices within that private world were compatible with the rights of citizens in the State. This was part of the same mental change which begot criticism of the rights of sanctuary.

Monasteries administered discipline over their erring monks. The new monk joined a private society the rules of which he accepted by a vow of absolute obedience. Therefore the private society exacted penalties for disobedience or misbehaviour or crime. From the Middle Ages such penalties included beating, or low diet, or confinement, or if all failed, expulsion. Since it was out of tune with the medieval mind to think of handing over a criminal monk to the courts of the outside world, monasteries made their private system of justice which was not distinguished from ordinary discipline. A monastery had one or more cells as its prison, and appointed a monk as its gaoler.

The Counter-Reformation lifted standards by making discipline more severe. As reformers raised the moral demand upon monks, they did not shrink from heavy penalties upon those who failed. Like any private system of justice, this private system might be humane, but being subject to no outside control of public opinion easily grew rigorous, arbitrary, and at last tyrannical. St. John of the Cross spent many months in the prison of a Spanish monastery; and the accounts of his experience breed no trust in the penal system. A historian does not console himself by remembering that other penal systems of that age were arbitrary.

This rigour persisted into the eighteenth century, and rare traces may be discerned in the nineteenth. But the new ideas of the early Enlightenment began to affect opinion. Whether or not a monk accepted the rules of a private society, he never lost his rights as a human being. Secular judges had a duty to see justice done even within private societies. Therefore penalties grew less barbarous within monasteries as they grew more humane in the outside world. Among State lawyers opinion hardened that if a monk was alleged to have committed an offence worthy of prison, it was the State's prison with fixed rules in which he should be confined. They were putting their penal systems into better order, and their concern for private societies was part of the general revision of attitudes.

Certain religious orders founded in the Counter-Reformation, like the Somaschi and the Theatines, in any case allowed an appeal to 'the secular arm' in charges where the monastery had no penalty adequate to the offence committed.

From the human point of view this softening of attitudes, as part of the same humanizing which rid the courts at last of torture, had nothing but good. From the monastery's outlook it had loss as well as gain. It allowed a growing number of cases where a monk, condemned by his superior, appealed to an outside court. In France, where the system of Parlements made outside courts effective, these appeals were known to destroy the discipline of old communities and the authority of superiors. A gain lay in the removal of an element destructive of harmony in the society.

Monastic congregations, or even areas, used a special house set aside for delinquents. Much paper mounted in the files on the proper amount of money to be paid by the house which expelled a delinquent to the house where he was to be immured. Several Sicilian orders used the house Gibilmanna as their home for recidivist monks. The house at Polistena served the same purpose in Calabria. The Benedictine congregation of Saint-Maur preferred to get its prisoners away to the sea-girt monastery at Mont-Saint-Michel. That helped other houses but turned a prison-monastery into no monastery. About 1766 the monks of Mont-Saint-Michel consisted of sixteen prisoners, two lunatics, and six monk-gaolers to supervise.[43]

To be secluded in a monastery for a crime could be very pleasant. The earlier objection to monastic prisons was that they protected culprits from the rigour of the law. Even late in the eighteenth century a prisoner in a monastery could in certain circumstances have a good time. Pablo de Olavide was shut up (1778) in a Spanish monastery. Though he disliked the prescribed reading of books of devotion, he loved the services, and the quiet, he had two gardens in which to walk, could receive visitors, and kept his own staff of servants. Even so, he took his chance to escape.[44]

The difficulty was to know what else to do but keep a prison. If a male-factor was held long years in a monastic prison, it caused inconvenience and disturbance in the house and forced monks, whose work ought to be the praise of God, to become gaolers. But if a malefactor were at once expelled, he was discharged upon a world which would suffer by his criminal character; and suffer all the more because he might commit his crimes under the pretext and using the occasion of a monk's habit. Some superiors thought this the only way, and the community could wash its hands of an erring member. To expel a man (and worse, to expel a woman, for it was not an unprotected woman's world) was contrary to everything for which the movement stood, the profession of permanent dedication to a way of life, the obligation of permanent pastoral responsibility by a com-munity. In the 1740s Pope Benedict XIV considered these unpalatable alternatives soberly and reached the conclusion that though superiors ought to shrink from expulsion, there came times when expulsion was necessary.[45]

[43] Pitré, *La vita in Palermo*, 2.139; Chevallier, *Loménie*, 1.195; *D.I.P.* 2.273–5.
[44] Defourneaux, *Olavide*, 376 ff.   [45] *De synodo*, xiii, col. 1438.

As a more enlightened world met old systems, the anachronisms were made plain by cases of special agony. The worst scandal hit Naples.

Pasquale Perez de Bivador, whose name in religion was Father Leopold, said that he was the son of a Piedmontese sailor. At the age of sixteen he became a discalced Augustinian in Naples, that is of an order where the reforming ideals of the Counter-Reformation carried a group of monasteries out of a historic order into what was in effect a new order.

In 1757 Father Leopold was discovered or believed by the other members of his house to be a criminal of the neighbourhood, stealing money from other monasteries, posing to collect money on false pretences, swindling, gambling, and going out after women. They examined witnesses and held him guilty.

The case became a scandal because Father Leopold showed genius as an escaper.

Locked in a room over the refectory, he climbed onto the dome of the choir and claimed sanctuary. Locked in the monastic prison and manacled, he twisted through the window of his cell and lowered himself to the street but broke a leg in the final fall. Locked in a dungeon under the outer wall of the monastery he so desolated the community with shouts of blasphemy across the courtyard, tearing up a breviary, threats of murder, that at last some monks in the house could bear it no longer and without leave engineered his escape. Many miles away he was picked up in lay clothes by the police.

He was destroying the morale of the community. The law of the Church prevented them from turning him loose upon the world. They could not reintegrate him because he was unwilling to be reformed. Some of them were hopeless, seeing no solution till he died—'He doesn't die because scoundrels are immortal but when God wishes it will be a singular grace.' The monks divided, one party holding that it was their duty to bear this cross, the other that no man should be kept under such conditions in a monastery.

On 23 April 1763, after Father Leopold occupied his dungeon for six years, the divided house held a meeting of the chapter which was unedifying and tumultuous. They disputed over the election of new officers. This touched the king. Therefore Marquess Cavalcanti appeared in the monastery to enquire into the dispute—and discovered Father Leopold.

So the affair became public. A professor of law took up Leopold's case, the name of the Augustinians stank in the city as torturers; sightseers wanted to look with horror at the dungeon under the wall where a man was 'buried alive', the king intervened, anticlericals in government used the case as a stick against all forms of ecclesiastical jurisdiction. Hardly anyone believed Father Leopold innocent. The anticlerical prime minister Tanucci used the case to advantage. But even he took the charges of cruelty with salt. For five years later he proposed that Leopold's principal judge among the monks should be the queen's confessor.

The papal nuncio fought a losing battle for the old world. Monks are members of a holy society and rightly exempted from secular courts. Therefore there must be prisons in monasteries. It will be exceedingly inconvenient if superiors cannot proceed against delinquent monks but must hand them over to magistrates. That a monk should appear in a court charged with crime will have a bad effect on the morality of the people. . . .[46]

So the bygone age and the coming age fought over the body of Father Leopold who should never have become a monk while a boy. In a changing mood of public opinion his dungeon endangered the repute of many more monks than the discalced Augustinians of Naples.

A Naples law of 1769 abolished prisons in monasteries, removed penal rights from superiors, and gave the jurisdiction to the archbishop's court. Lombardy abolished monks' prisons the same year. Tuscany a year later, Austria still a year later. The Austrian law allowed a locked cell of punishment which must not differ from the other cells, and be always open to inspection by bishop or magistrate. Remote houses took small notice and hardly knew that it passed. They continued their historic way of life. Since many had on their hands senile or mad monks or nuns, they were accustomed to cells which must be locked.

In the Benedictine nunnery at Göss in Styria lived a Sister Columba, of noble birth, always weak in the head, maintained by a small pension paid regularly by the family. A Salzburg canonist attended (1779) the election of a new abbess and noticed that Sister Columba failed to come to record her vote. He asked after her, was told that she was mad, and visited her in a cell below ground and damp with mildew. Hearing evidence in her favour, and suspecting that she was really in prison because she criticized her superiors and because she claimed that she was forced into a nunnery and said that she had no desire to be a Benedictine, a way of life which she hated, he reported to the Bishop of Seckau who seems to have done nothing. Three years later a commission sent to dissolve the nunnery found

---

[46] Nuncio to secretary of state, *A.S.V.* Nunziatura di Napoli, 272/50–3. The stories of Leopold and his superior are impossible to reconcile. Leopold's petition in *A.S.V.* Nunziatura di Napoli 270/75, memorial to the king of 5 Oct. 1763; superior's story in petition to the king dated 3 Dec. 1703, Nunziatura di Napoli 270/173 ff. For Tanucci, de Maio, 348.

her imbecile, fetched her out, and put her in charge of a private woman in
the town of Graz.[47]

This, and similar cases, caused government to order a thorough search
of all monasteries, and the removal of several mad nuns and a mad Franciscan friar from their cells to public asylums.

Thus these prisons enraged the reformers of the Enlightenment. When
the nuns of San Giorgio fled from falling shot as French troops attacked
Mantua, soldiers ran into the convent to take cover and heard cries; and
down in the cellar found a girl aged about twenty-two chained by her arms
to a chair.[48] The prison made part of that hatred of religious houses which
began to obsess radical minds.

Mortmain

When monks were too many, and confessed by everyone to be too many,
and when monasteries had fat untaxed endowments and modern states
needed more income than ramshackle states, and even a Pope suppressed
the Jesuit order—every Catholic ruler moved against 'useless' monasteries, 'useless' monks.

The *dead hand*, law of mortmain, was in never-ending dispute. All
critics agreed that churches and monasteries of Catholic states were too
abundantly endowed for the welfare of the State. Popes and bishops, always without enough money to do what they wanted, often in debt and
sometimes almost bankrupt, and seeing many clergy and monks near or
below the level of subsistence, denied the claim with vehemence.

No church money or land could ever be diverted to other purposes—
except under the (often large) taxes which Popes allowed governments to
raise. No redundant church, or even redundant vicarage, could be sold for
secular purposes. Church endowments must therefore grow. Pious persons liked to leave something in their wills. Comfortable persons liked to
give an endowment that mass might be said for their soul in perpetuity.
Every nun must bring into her convent the dowry—little in each case, but
over all the thousands of vocations not to be neglected by a state which
saw wealth slowly disappearing into untaxable charities. Nunneries or
monasteries could invest their money in Mounts of Piety the charitable
lending banks, to receive interest. But they were not always happy about
the *usury* of lending money at interest, were conscious that money can fall
in value, and therefore preferred to use dowries or bequests in the purchase
of land or property.

[47] Wolf, 72–6.   [48] Napoleon, *Correspondance* I (1858), 376–7.

Educated laymen saw buildings or land lying idle. A monastery, once great, inherited a palace and many fields. It declined; a handful of men, perhaps even two or three, were all that survived of a numerous community. Yet neither building nor land could be diverted from the sacred purpose. This was what was attacked as idle endowment. Southern educated Catholics were far from admiring Protestants. But their knowledge of the Protestant north led them to suspect that the prosperity of northern Europe might be due in part to the ruthlessness with which Protestant states treated the land and money of their old monasteries.

A monastery, let us suppose, inherited by bequest a farm. As a charity it had a duty to maintain the endowment and if possible to extend its value. It was not entitled to sell the farm and use the proceeds as income or give them away in charity. It must keep the farm and use its rent either as charity or as income to maintain itself. Therefore, if it had capital, it improved the farm by buying near-by fields, and by using near-by common land to pasture flocks and herds; and because it was exempt from regular taxation was stronger than the small proprietors of that place. The cry against mortmain came not only from prime ministers and finance ministers who counted the total acreage exemption from tax. It came from smallholders and farmers under sudden pressure from a bigger landlord, in this case an ecclesiastical corporation. In some villages of Spain every peasant became in this way a hired labourer on church land.

Monasteries had stout defenders. If you take away the money of the monasteries where does it go? To armaments, or palaces, or the pockets of civil servants? Monasteries are the only means of keeping unemployed from starvation. Let comfortable critics who prate of utility go down among the queues at monastery gates and find out how the suppliants would live if they could not stand in that queue. A monastery often employs some fifty or sixty people, singers, woodworkers, decorators, farm-labourers, builders, foresters. Who will find work for these men, and food for their families, if their monastery is suppressed or impoverished? This attack upon monasteries is harsh. For it is also an attack upon the destitute and upon all those least able to defend themselves.

Only comfortable men of middle and upper classes denounce poor relief because it encourages beggars. And when lawyers or politicians assailed monasteries for failing to do what they could in famine or slump, defenders of monastic endowment produced numerous examples of countrymen being saved from starvation. When attackers said that wealth corrupted the Church, which should return to the simplicity of primitive ages, defenders asked why laymen should demand this of others when they had no intention themselves of returning to live like Germans or Lombards during the barbarian invasions.

Catholic opinion hardened against monks and nuns during the four last decades of the century. Censorship kept the attack restrained, but wherever censorship was weak, attacks on monks proliferated. Though the *dead hand* was the ultimate reason, the attacks had other causes. Reforming bishops always assailed the exemptions of religious houses and wanted them to be more useful in parishes. Parish priests suspected convents which rivalled them for esteem and gifts and pastoral care. But after 1760 a new and ominous note crept into the pamphlets.

With the attack on the Jesuits, economists collected statistics, usually erroneous; but however vague, they drew everyone to the extraordinary fraction of land and property which monks possessed. Table 8, for example, gives one such statistic, collected by an enemy of monks in northern Italy.[49]

8

Town	Population	Total income	Number of monks and nuns	Income
Tortona, 1770	40,000 plus	754,582 *lire*	358	247,067
Alessandria	59,086	1,868,472	551	492,653

Therefore it came to be accepted statecraft in all Catholic states, that government must pass laws of mortmain to limit further property—at least land or houses—passing into the dead hand. If they were more radical, they might also attempt to limit the number of novices to diminish the need for dowries; and if still more radical, they might wish to suppress monasteries, especially if housing tiny numbers or 'useless', and take their endowments into the national purse.

9 gives numbers of observant Franciscans[50] in the province of Naples

Date	Priests	Laymen
1778	485	163
1797	235	127

[49] Venturi, *Sett. rif.* 2.205.
[50] De Maio, 349.

Monks in Venice[51]

1766	*c.* 7,700
1778	5,055
1781	4,166
1785	4,692
1790	4,265

Spain was a country relatively untouched by such ideas. Yet even in Spain, where monks had still increased in number, came the sudden turn downward;

Spanish monks and nuns[52] 1787: 78,113; 1797: 77,569.

In Naples Father Genovesi taught as early as 1737 that the prosperity of the State was impossible unless it took church property. The minister Tanucci, who liked individual Jesuits and hated the Society of Jesus, did what he could to diminish other monasteries, but that was little. During the ten years after 1779 the minister Caracciolo closed all the Capuchin novitiates in Sicily, in the effort to lessen the number of friars. A decree from Naples prohibited the clothing of new friars without the king's leave.

France passed a law on mortmain (1749), Tuscany two years later. The flood of laws limiting bequests to church charities and monasteries came in 1761–7; Spain, Portugal, Austria, Bavaria, the Palatinate, Lombardy, Genoa, Modena, Lucca, Parma, Mantua, and finally Venice.

Governments wanted first to close useless or little used houses and take their money, goods, lands and houses; prevent boys and girls from taking vows so early and therefore raise the age at which the young could enter a monastery or a nunnery, though no government presumed it sensible or practicable to follow Bishop Ricci of Pistoia and abolish vows for men and allow vows only to women aged forty; get rid of foreign superiors where an order was organized internationally, and insist at least on a local vicar-general who was the superior's deputy with full powers. They intended to maintain discipline, but on occasion had the opposite effect. Like Tanucci in Naples, they sometimes intended to distribute the lands among peasants, but almost everywhere in Europe the lands of suppressed houses went either to government or to upper-class landowners. Tanucci's strenuous efforts with ex-Jesuit lands in Sicily secured nearly 60 per cent of the endowments for small men. The endeavour made not much eventual difference.

In southern Italy, for example, a terrible earthquake of 1783 killed about

---

[51] Venturi, *Sett. rif.* 2.149–50; Cecchetti, 1.223 ff.   [52] Cf. p. 213.

30,000 people and so devastated Calabria that the plight of starving and homeless survivors could be met only with dictatorial action by the State. With the consent of Pope Pius VI government created a central treasury, the 'Sacred Chest' into which all endowments of nunneries and monasteries and chapels were paid; and suppressed all houses with fewer than twelve members. The intention was pure, and the act long acclaimed by historians. Modern enquiry cast grave doubts upon the issue. The upper and middle classes got the benefit, the Church lost much of its land which helped to protect the peasant from immediate domination by feudal lords, and seeds of a pro-Church anti-feudal revolution were sown.[53]

In 1766, in the wake of Jesuit suppression in Portugal and France, both the governments of France and Venice appointed commissions to reform the monasteries. The French commission finally recommended the dissolution of 386 houses with a total of 10,438 inhabitants, and received evidence from bishops which left them and posterity with no high opinion of the state of French monasteries. The Venice commission reported that the republic had thirty-five orders, 441 houses, and 7,703 monks and nuns; that the revenues came to nearly 1,000,000 ducats a year and these numbers made a heavy burden on the State; that many of the impoverished little houses could maintain no proper common life; that the larger houses should be given a maximum number and be not permitted to accept novices where the number now exceeded this maximum.[54]

Among certain Catholic reformers, found occasionally in France and Venice and Naples, more commonly in south Germany, appeared the idea of utility. Monasteries fulfilled very varied social functions. The contemplation of God in solitude was not an activity easily understood in the age of Enlightenment, and several rulers forcibly swept away all the hermits in their territory. Prayer for other people was still seen in most countries as a social function for which monks and nuns were necessary. But when politicians looked critically at monasteries, they began to apply the idea of utility like any Protestant, and demand usefulness in society which was more definable. Nunneries served a social purpose merely by housing unmarried women. Monasteries should be suppressed unless they fulfilled one of three functions: teaching, or ministering to the sick, or care of parishes. And an occasional Catholic voice could be heard with still more extreme language. The life of a monk is *unnatural*; it is *not appropriate* in the modern world; vows of poverty are *bad for society*; charitable endowments *persuade beggars to stay unemployed*. 'Of course good monks exist.

[53] Placanica, *Cassa Sacra* and *Il patrimonio ecclesiastico*.
[54] Cecchetti. 2.114–15.

but the best monk would be a better man if he were not a monk.'[55] This kind of tone is not to be found commonly.

Austria carried out far the most systematic attempt to reform monasteries. But Austrian reform was part of a new pattern throughout Catholic Europe in the relationship between Church and State.

To abolish a living community was like throwing a lot of men or women out of work suddenly. When it happens, the signs of human tragedy never fail. When an official visitor told the Cistercian nuns at Gutenzell in south Germany that their nunnery was to close, and asked each of them whether she wished to leave, he recorded their replies. They are such as these: 'My only prayer is to end my life in a nunnery'; 'I never have the least desire to leave'; 'Rather a poor nun than to go into the world with a pension of 1,000 florins'; 'The end of the nunnery would be the worst disaster for me. I should be very unhappy'.[56] Men were much readier to find new work and home. They were more easily employable, and less insecure in that world. The existence of numbers of men in monasteries who felt no special vocation to the monks' way of life meant that 'useless' male houses were almost as easy to dissolve by Catholic governments of the eighteenth century as by Protestant governments of the sixteenth century. Provided the pensioner's pension was secure, he was glad of liberty. He lost nothing but rules and a wall by the abolition of his house.

To abolish a monastery might mean resistance from peasants. If the monastery had a function—as in a school, a parish, a hospital—the function was performed inefficiently if the monastery was a case for abolition; but sometimes an inefficient school was better than the alternative which was no school. Where the Pope suppressed an order, a few old people usually managed to continue their lifelong way of prayer and rule, sometimes in the same building. In 1626 Rome suppressed an order which was one offshoot of the Franciscans, the order of Reformed Conventuals, and ordered its members to join one of the three main orders of Franciscans. The order was obeyed, but not without bitterness, and a few houses persisted for half a century till the old people died. The greatest of the papal suppressions before the eighteenth century happened when Innocent X (1652) suppressed several hundred houses with tiny numbers, for example 217 Carmelite houses, 242 Franciscan Conventual houses, mainly in Italy. Even then he allowed a number of the 'suppressed' houses (ultimately) to survive.[57] Therefore no one could be surprised that when Pope Clement

---

[55] *Deutscher Zuschauer* iv.102; cited E. Hegel (1975), 14.   [56] Erzberger, 396.
[57] *D.I.P.* 2.472; 3.49, 102–4.

XIV abolished 22,000 Jesuits, a good many communities survived in at
least a concealed form. The Pope could abolish a uniform, not so easily
could he end a way of life.

To Joseph II of Austria is ascribed a stern letter to his agent in Rome,
Cardinal Herzan.

As I myself hate superstition, I will drive it from the minds of my people; and
therefore I will expel monks and abolish monasteries and put them under the
bishops of their dioceses. . . . To those things we owe the degradations of the
human mind. . . . The principles of monasticism have been directly opposed to
the light of reason. . . . These untrue ideas about religion have spread among
ordinary people, and they know God no more, and trust in their saints.[58]

The text of this letter is so extraordinary as to give rise to doubt about its
authenticity. Most authors accepted it as genuine. But it is not. It is part
of a collection of forged letters. To judge Joseph's reform of the monasteries by such a letter is wrong.

Austria suppressed so many monasteries not because Austrians rejected
the monastic ideal but because they needed money to reform the Church.
Whenever the central Church fund for parishes and education ran short of
money to pay for pastors or found schools, its managers looked for another
abbey to suppress.

Austrian enquiries uncovered fewer scandals than French enquiries. But
wealth and utility were not always companions. Rich houses were
specially vulnerable. Houses and orders which attracted dedicated novices
were seldom houses and orders possessing thousands of acres. The Prae-
monstratensian abbey of Tepl in Bohemia looked to visitors like a country
club of well-to-do and hospitable gentlemen with liveried servants to
attend their needs. The Cistercian house of the Golden Crown in south
Bohemia had an income of 464,141 *gulden* which supported nineteen
monks.[59]

In November 1781 the Emperor Joseph issued a degree appointing commissioners to make lists of the monasteries and their property, and to
abolish those which were contemplative and were not in the work of
teaching or of nursing the sick. The endowments gave pensions to the expelled, and the remainder to the central Church fund to help parishes. The
commissioners were ordered to be gentle; not to deprive monks of the

---

[58] *Briefe des Josephs des Zweiten* (3rd edn Leipzig, 1846), ed. F. Schuselka, no.21 pp.96–9:
for the spurious letters of Joseph II see Derek Beales, 'The False Joseph II' in *Historical Journal*
xviii (1975), 467–96.
[59] Winter, 115–16.

'personal possessions' to which they were used in their cells, and to allow the aged and infirm to remain in their houses.

In the Austrian part of the Empire, more than 400 houses were abolished. The number of monks and nuns fell from 65,000 to 27,000. In 1782 the property which passed to government totalled 10,000,000 *gulden*. Despite waste and cheap bargains, inevitable in so big an operation, the central fund got about 60,000,000 *gulden* by Joseph's death.

Friars were forbidden novices and were not allowed to beg. Hermits were abolished. Joseph did not trust superiors to manage their estates, and though he allowed priors in remaining houses to be supreme in discipline and religious life, secular clergymen or laymen were put in as 'abbots in commendam' to manage the property.

In Vienna Joseph founded four hospitals and a school of surgery and so started the growth of Vienna into a centre of medical research. The buildings of former monasteries were used as schools or factories or shops. One monastery church became a theatre, another a Protestant chapel. Manuscripts and rare books were collected and most ended in the libraries of universities. Some 'obsolete' books of theology were pulped, some works of art were sold abroad.

No resistance to these arrangements came from monks, nuns, or the common people. Most monks if not old passed into curacies or vicarages or schools. Most nuns of dissolved houses preferred to go back to their families with their pension, and not to change house or order. Where nuns agreed to continue in a house with nuns from other nunneries, the union seldom worked. Former ways of life were too diverse, even among nuns from different houses of the same order. Peace was disturbed by difference over rules, ways of worship, choice of confessor.

An incumbent who disliked friars protested when given a friar as his curate.[60] He complained that friars are chief sellers of indulgences and miraculous pictures, promote brotherhoods and vain devotions, are not very loyal to the State and make a poor foundation for religion. Such a protest against ex-monks or ex-friars was very unusual.

10

Monasteries in Austria							
1773	2,163	=	abbeys	238	monasteries	1,334	nunneries 591
dissolved by 1786	738			82		395	261
leaving	1,425					1,095	330

[60] Wolf, 68, 157, 168.

To make about a third of the religious return home, or become parish priests or schoolmasters, left Austria a country where monastic orders were still important in the social order. After the Emperor's death superiors were again trusted to manage their money and the 'abbots in commendam' went.

But the main changes lasted, partly because despite the Emperor's fussiness they were moderate. Monks and nuns were not ill treated except that it is ill treatment to be forced out of home. Whatever losses occurred at auctions by sales too cheap, most of the money went to help the Church, the poor, and the schools. Joseph made a reasonable system of pastoral care before any other Catholic ruler.

More Austrian money went into art and architecture before 1782 than after. This was always the result when many monasteries were ended. But it meant negligible losses in libraries and no loss in learning; perhaps advance in learning, as endowments were taken from the divine praises and given to schools and universities.

4

THE OFFICE OF THE POPE

Authority

The Pope was the successor of St. Peter, and the centre of unity in the Roman Catholic Church. Therefore he had an authority beyond that of all other ministers. Men have only so much authority as other men will allow; and the question of the extent of this spiritual authority, or its limitations, was a delicate discussion carried on by the Latin tongue in Spanish and French and German and Italian lecture-rooms. But everyone agreed that this was the vicar of Christ, and that his authority extended, or could in certain circumstances extend, as far as the authority of the whole Catholic Church.

So much was received by many Catholics before the Reformation. The events of Reformation and Counter-Reformation strengthened this pillar of the constitution. Radicals who denied the Pope's spiritual authority no longer claimed to be within the Roman Catholic Church and therefore need no longer be considered. The defence of Catholicism against Protestants had something of the same effect as, two or three centuries before, the defence of Christendom from Arab or Turk. It made the centre of Catholicism more supreme as the centre. It identified Catholicism more manifestly with Rome; so that when a Protestant used the word *Catholic*, he might henceforth be presumed to mean *Roman Catholic*.

This authority was defined to rest upon Bible and Church. In fact it rested upon the profession of Catholic faith by most ordinary men and women in the Catholic states. The Spanish confessed that the Pope was the head of their Church. Through their long struggle against Muslim invasion they identified their Church with their nationality, so that a Spaniard not a Catholic was no longer a Spaniard. Therefore the Pope had real power inside Spain, not just theoretical power or spiritual power derived from a theological principle or the explanation of a text of the Bible about the keys of St. Peter. In certain matters the Spanish government could hardly act without first making sure that the authorities of the Church agreed with its action. And so, though less obviously, in Portugal, France, Italy, Austria, and the south-German states.

High theorists on behalf of the Pope believed that Popes had not only this spiritual power which extended as far as Catholicism and therefore as far as the human race, but a secular power, given by God for the benefit of the nations; an international authority which, though without an army, had the right and duty of maintaining peace and justice among the striving nations. More moderate but still high theorists of the Pope like Cardinal Bellarmine argued for an 'indirect' power—that the Pope could not simply depose a king as he removed a bishop from office, by the fact of his direct power as God's minister, but that he could nevertheless declare a king to be deposed if it were plainly necessary for the good of men's *souls*. These high claims were necessary, less by reason of the theory on which they rested, as by reason of the past acts of Popes, whether in the Middle Ages or in the Counter-Reformation. It was hard in any other light to justify the act of the Pope in freeing the English people from their allegiance to Queen Elizabeth I on the ground of her manifest heresy; or of sending a legate to strengthen the French Catholics of Paris in resisting their lawful king because he was a Protestant.

But the doctrine of a power, even an indirect power, in secular governments, was never accepted by many Catholics. They saw the Pope as a supreme leader; as Christ's vicar; as the chief shepherd set over all the shepherds who should lead Christ's flock towards the fold. After the treaty of Westphalia in 1648, we hear less discussion of those old claims to an international authority among the nations. Catholic Germany found it necessary to accept Protestant rulers as rightful and legitimate, Catholic Switzerland to accept Protestant cantons, Catholic Netherlands to live side by side with Protestant Holland, the European states-system to accept Protestant England and Scotland. The Pope ceased to be an international authority of the type which a long tradition down to Bellarmine and after expected. By the nature of his supreme spiritual power he still wielded a kind of international authority; first because some governments could hardly act in certain spheres without securing his complaisance or stopping his intervention; and secondly because he had a right, which was more than a vestigial survival from different days, to mediate in conflicts or wars between Catholic states. At least he claimed this right, and quite often tried to exercise it; not wholly in vain. For the most part warring nations went on with their fight and took no notice of peaceable exhortation. But sometimes, as between Catholic peoples or governments, a Pope could still be seen to be a force pushing them towards negotiation instead of guns, and seeking to still the passions of Catholic Christendom. This status was accorded to him especially by the governments of countries under fire from non-Catholics—Poles under threat from Russians or Swedes, Austrians or Hungarians under threat from Turks.

Nevertheless, for various reasons the Pope was now restricted, far more restricted than formerly in the exercise of an international authority.

First, he was not neutral among the nations. Europe was divided between Protestant countries and Catholic countries, and everyone knew on which side the Pope stood. If war raged between England and Spain, or England and France, or France and Prussia, or Poland and Sweden, the Pope was useless as a mediator. The Protestants could not believe in his impartiality, and he could not believe in it himself. Between 1648 and 1915 the ancient role of peace-maker among the powers could not be fulfilled. If fulfilled at all, it must be adapted, to mean peace-maker among Catholic powers. The Pope could not be an 'international court of justice' or of arbitration in the old sense, for in any conflict which could be described as Catholic versus Protestant, he could see Catholic victory as fruitful in Catholic advance.

He was under no temptation to turn the wars of Louis XIV into crusades. But hardly anyone now appealed to him as arbitrator, or proposed Rome as a suitable place for making treaties. For three-quarters of a century, from 1562 to 1648, Europe suffered from the wars of religion; and even though the wars were often over religion only in name, Europe wanted to move away from the terrible memories of conflict between Catholic and Protestant. With these memories the Pope's name and title were entangled. Henceforth when men wanted a 'neutral' city, they did not think of Rome. The Spanish once proposed Rome as the seat for negotiation. The French would have none of it. International treaties were made in Münster, Nymwegen, Utrecht, Ryswick. If men wanted 'neutrality' in Italy, they were more likely to think of Venice than Rome. One proposal for an international parliament suggested that it sit at Regensburg. Another, from a Catholic abbé, suggested that an international court sit at Utrecht.[1] A third, an eminent Catholic, was among the first to cast his eyes upon Switzerland as a neutral territory. He wanted his proposed international court—this time a court for the Catholic powers—to meet in Lucerne. But even he wanted the papal nuncio, who then lived in Lucerne, to be transferred to Freiburg so that he should not exercise undue influence upon the court.

Prelates in the age between the Reformation and the Revolution have no high reputation. Anglican prelates are a case in point. Though they never

[1] Schnürer, 3 ff.

emulated Cardinal Wolsey, we are not somehow surprised that many hotels on the continent of Europe are called after the name of an English eighteenth-century bishop, or that the Bishop of Llandaff in Wales lived away from Wales on the banks of Lake Windermere. It was a mellow world. Anthony Trollope described Barchester cathedral and close as though it were all of 1850; but really Barset was of 1750—a sunlit country-side world without the rumblings of revolution; assured, stable-seeming, comfortable, archaic, well paid, esteemed, kindly, courteous, and doing good by benevolence. That was what most Popes of the eighteenth century were like: humane, comfortable, paternal, considerate. One Pope of that century said to the artist who was painting his portrait, 'I'm the pastor of the people, so make me look gentle.'[2] At times the Counter-Reformation almost seemed to be forgotten—until suddenly men thought of the cuirassed kingdoms of a Borgia or a Farnese, the skilled financial jugglery of a Medici, which vanished never to return. These were good men; not heroic men usually, but open-hearted, friendly, trying to do what little they could to smile upon the world of men to make the human race happy and well-doing and better prepared for eternity. The Popes of the eighteenth century had a pleasant front to the world; like their city, dignified, aesthetic, ceremonious, baroque—with the new façade to Santa Maria Maggiore which the Pope erected in the middle of the century, fine, grand-looking, not paying enough attention to the quieter but nobler heritage of the old church of Santa Maria Maggiore, and disturbing the Pope when he saw that after all his architect was a Philistine; or with the most marvellous staircase in Rome, the Spanish Steps, erected in 1725 to commemorate the Year of Jubilee; or with the gayest of all the fountains of Rome, the Trevi, ordered by the Corsini Pope Clement XII and finished in 1762; or with the familiar Vatican Museum itself, which in its main features was the work of the last Pope of the century, the Pope least able to afford the expense, but making the Vatican that which it is now, and towards which it moved rapidly during the eighteenth century —one of the artistic centres of the world.

In a good-humoured age, then, mostly good-humoured men led the Roman Catholic Church; and made a contrast, an astounding contrast, between the missioner-evangelist lashing himself in the pulpit at some fiery service of conversion, and the cultivated heads to whom he owed his allegiance.

[2] Andrieux, 7.

Election

In early Christian days the Bishop of Rome was elected, like other bishops, by clergy and people of the city and with the consent of neighbouring bishops. But popular elections became impossible unless they were tumults; and so the State intervened, first to ensure a peaceable election, and then to secure a candidate acceptable to the State. As the Roman Empire turned into early medieval Europe, the office grew in prestige and therefore in power. The more powerful the office, the more unacceptable an election by a few clergy or barons in Rome; the more international the office the less appropriate a civic election; the more civil power became attached to the spiritual power, the less possible and the less desirable a local election carried out without reference to governments. Roman Emperor and then Byzantine Emperor and then Holy Roman Emperor started to intervene, and more than one Pope invited such intervention. When Emperors were strong, they appointed Popes. When Emperors were weak, barons in Rome ensured that the new Pope was their man. The election by clergy and people survived in ritual forms.

For 800 years only a Roman was elected. The first bishop from another see was elected in 882. In 1059, as new and stronger Popes began to establish their independence against German Emperors, Pope Nicholas II published the decree *In nomine* which limited the electors to the cardinal bishops of Rome—and other cardinals with clergy and people had the right to accept or reject. This plan did not meet the needs of controversies which followed, and at the Third Lateran Council of 1179 Pope Alexander III created the system which survived the centuries: only cardinals may vote, and a two-thirds majority is needed for election. Nearly a century later, after a failure to reach a two-thirds majority for almost three years (the longest election on record), the Council of Lyons in 1274 introduced the Conclave, following the example of some other elections in Italian cities and the way by which Dominican friars organized their elections. By the Conclave the cardinals must be shut up together and go on meeting till they elect. In 1406, after more difficulty, the ballot was used, probably for the first time. From 1389 only cardinals have been elected, and some have thought that only a cardinal is now eligible, but this is not certain or even probable. As lately as 1691 some votes were cast for men who were not cardinals, but almost certainly the voters had no hope or expectation of success when they so voted.

The number of cardinals was fixed by Sixtus V at seventy after the elders of Moses. This number was not exceeded until 1958–63.

In its near-final form the mode of election was laid down by Pope Gregory XV in a bull of 15 November 1621 (*Aeterni patris filius*). The object of this bull was to prevent Catholic governments interfering in the election; that is, to keep the cardinals free to choose whomsoever they thought fit. The arrival of Spanish power in Italy made Popes, who since the Counter-Reformation had higher standards, more uncomfortable about the ease with which cardinals could be bullied or cajoled. The Conclave was made stricter and more secure, and the cardinals must not elect until they were formally immured. The election by the two-thirds majority should normally be by secret ballot, but 'arrangement' or 'acclamation' were also allowed. The bull finally forbade any cardinal to vote for himself. A bull of the following year, 12 March 1622 (*Decet Romanum Pontificem*), laid down the ceremonies in minute detail.

This arrangement was first altered by Pope Pius X in 1904.

Every Pope elected between 1522 and 1978 was an Italian. Sometimes the majority of Italian cardinals was very large. At the time of the Conclave of 1676 there were sixty-seven cardinals of whom fifty-eight were Italians, the others being three French, three German, two Spanish, and one English; and on this occasion one of the Germans raised bitter complaint at Italian dominance. But a complaint in this form was unique, and most non-Italians accepted that an Italian majority was necessary. The cardinals were the Pope's lieutenants in administering the Church. They needed to be in Rome. Therefore they were likely to be Italian, because they could not control or organize or even understand the civil service in Rome if they were foreign. This Italian majority of cardinals remained until 1946.

In later years Popes allowed the title of cardinal to men who were not part of the Roman Curia, or rather who were only formally part of the Roman Curia by possessing that title: eminent archbishops or bishops who continued in their own country, and came to Rome only to take part in electing a Pope. But they were expected to be few. An Italian majority among cardinals was accepted as a necessary consequence of the heritage that the head of the Catholic Church was also a bishop and ought to reside in Rome. The Council of Trent obliged Popes to make cardinals of all nations whenever possible, 'so far as he has a chance sufficiently to know them and be sure that he can trust them'. The limitation was important. Unless earlier in life he was a nuncio at one of the courts, he could hardly know anyone but Italians.

This Italian dominance of the Curia was the less painful to non-Italians because modern 'nationalism' was still in embryo. Italy was not a unity

even in idea. Rome was still the heir of an international idea as wide as
Christendom. So far as Italian cardinals were Roman, they were as much
international as national. But though a majority of future Popes served for
a time in the Curia at Rome, a majority were not Roman by origin. Of
the eight Popes of the eighteenth century, four came from the Papal
States, but two of these four from the Romagna in the north; two came
from the kingdom of Naples, one was a Florentine and one a Venetian.
Not one of them was born in Rome. The divisions of Italy still ran deep.
When the Venetian Rezzonico was elected Pope (Clement XIII) in 1758,
the Venetian embassy in Rome spent extravagantly on fireworks and
handed out free wine for the three following nights. The election changed
the relation between the Pope and the government of Venice. That he was
Venetian was more important than that he was Italian.

The foreign cardinals, though few, were weighty. They were select;
powerful men in their own countries; representing the wider world of
Catholicism outside Italy. They did not all come to Rome, some not once
during their lives; and some made no effort to travel to Rome even to
elect a new Pope. Cardinal Mazarin could exert more influence on the
election of a Pope from his office in Paris than if he appeared in Rome in
person. The cardinal's hat was a matter of prestige to a Catholic government. Once the Pope started to bestow the hat on distinguished men who
need not work in Rome, the governments of France and Spain and
Austria began to be indignant if at least one of their prelates was not a
cardinal.

These foreign cardinals complicated the smooth functioning of the
Conclave. They needed to come from far, and that took time. Meanwhile
expediency pressed the cardinals already in Rome to make an election as
soon as they could. The Pope was not only a Christian leader, he ruled a
secular state under a constitution best described as benevolent despotism
tempered by hidebound tradition. Still, however tempered, it was government by a single man. Therefore the death of the ruler created, if not a
vacuum, at least a weakness of public power. Everyone knew that the new
Pope to be elected would not follow the same policy as the old, that high
servants of the State would be changed. The Governor of Rome continued
in office and had the duty of suppressing disorder. But everyone knew that
he was not likely to remain in office much longer, and it was a question
whether the police would obey his orders so instantly. Therefore every
death of a Pope carried with it a fear of trouble in the streets—window-
breaking at the least, riots and looting at the worst. When a Pope lay
dying, rich men who lived in Rome barred their doors or carried away

their precious possessions to a safe place. The moment the Pope's death was announced by the tolling of the big bell on the Capitol, the Governor of Rome put armed men on the streets. If an interregnum occurred without the smallest disturbance of public order, it was a matter of news in the services of information. No popular émeute in the eighteenth century compared with one or two of the dramas from the rougher times of the Middle Ages. But the institution had a long memory; and some cardinals will have known how on 7 April 1378 forty armed ruffians headed a rabble that broke into the Conclave and threatened to hew the cardinals to pieces, while the mob broke into the dead Pope's cellar and fed their violence with his wine, and in the Castel Sant' Angelo six cardinals at first dared not cross Rome to crown the new Pope. These were more decorous, and better ordered, times. Nothing in the eighteenth century resembled such horror. But events like the 1378 election were not easy to forget. Even in the eighteenth century, if the Conclave was long and tension began to rise outside, cardinals became anxious and thought that they dared delay no longer. As late as the 1730 election an angry mob besieged the staff of the last Pope in their house, and his chief administrator Cardinal Coscia had to slip out of Rome disguised on a stretcher.

Therefore the cardinals, immured in their Conclave, had strong motives, apart from the discomfort of the rooms and lack of liberty, for reducing the length of the interregnum to the shortest space consistent with a good and valid election. The necessity for a two-thirds majority was thought by some to make a protracted election inevitable; until the speed of nineteenth- and twentieth-century elections showed that it could be done within a day or two. The average length of Conclave during the eighteenth century was only just under three months; the shortest (1721, Innocent XIII) ran to just over five weeks, the longest (1740, Benedict XIV) to just on six months, which was a longer Conclave than any since the days of the Great Schism during the later Middle Ages. The cardinals were divided; they were often intransigent; they seemed sometimes to delight in negotiation—but it is safe to say that left to themselves the Italian cardinals would have drastically reduced that average length of Conclave. The foreign cardinals needed to arrive; and into the Conclave they brought considerations which were foreign in another sense than that of nationality.

In various Conclaves the Italian cardinals discussed whether to elect before the arrival of the foreigners who were so long in coming. But generally they felt this to be and to look like a risky manoeuvre. The resolution to wait for the foreigners could be irritating in its consequences.

In 1769, for example, when the Italians agreed to wait for the foreigners, none of the three Germans came and only two out of the six French; and the French Cardinal de Bernis took five weeks to arrive, while the two of the three Spanish cardinals who could make the journey were blown back by storms and came by land; so that the later of these two Spaniards did not enter the Conclave until two and a half months after the other cardinals were immured. This was particularly vexatious because during the weary weeks of waiting they could do almost nothing. 'I greatly pity the poor old cardinals', wrote the English agent as he watched this appalling Conclave, 'who will be confined so long, and who must twice a day play at choosing a pope, though their only care must be not to choose one by inadvertence.'[3] They could not so get on with their work that they would confront the two Spaniards with a virtual *fait accompli* then they arrived. The cardinals of 1769 were infinitely bored. Their tedium was broken only when the Emperor Joseph II of Austria visited the Conclave on 16 March and addressed the assembled cardinals in courteous terms; the first of Holy Roman Emperors in Rome since the Emperor Charles V came in the age of the Reformation.

The fears of the Italian cardinals, which made them accept these otherwise intolerable postponements, also rose out of the long memories of history. Terrible schisms happened over the elections of a Pope, schisms from which Catholicism suffered damage never afterwards mended; a long while before, but under this system of election by cardinals. The election must be valid, and must be seen to be valid, beyond all possibility of cavil. No modern Henry VII in Spain or France must be given the chance, if he did not afterwards like what a new Pope did, to declare that the electing body was unrepresentative. Everyone who was a cardinal must be allowed to attend. Cardinal Ottoboni appeared at the Conclave of 1721 though he had not yet been ordained. His vote was accepted as valid. Cardinal Coscia fled from the city at the death of the Pope in 1730, for the best of reasons that he behaved criminally and the people were out for his blood. His vote was accepted as valid. Cardinal Alberoni, once Prime Minister of Spain, played the politics of Spanish power in Italy and fell into depths of disgrace with the just dead Pope, so that he was regarded as a kind of outlaw. Because his vote must be valid, the cardinals gave him a safe-conduct to attend the Conclave of 1721, a pass which should expire ten days after the election. Cardinal Alberoni came, admired by vast crowds in the streets of Rome, but the cardinals in the Conclave would not speak to him except on barest business, and he spent his time

[3] Horace Mann to Walpole, 24 Feb. 1769; *Letters of Horace Walpole*, 7.90.

thinking how to safeguard his own future instead of sharing in the election of a Pope. The cardinals were determined to be seen to obey the laws. Whatever Pope came from their Conclave must be an undoubted Pope. Therefore Italian cardinals bored themselves, waiting miserably for foreigners to come.

In the crisis at the end of the century, when General Bonaparte's officers kidnapped the Pope, Pius VI specially decreed that the cardinals need not wait for the statutory ten days (minimum for distant cardinals to arrive) before electing his successor. Though he restored the obligation before he died, the vacillation made no difference at the coming election, which lasted more than three months and saw strenuous activity by non-Italian cardinals.

All Conclaves since the Council of Constance in 1417 were held in Rome, except the Conclave of 1800 after the kidnapping of Pius VI by the French, which was held in Venice to be secure from the French.

No one could wish to prolong a Conclave for any private reason. The little cells were uncomfortable. Within the Vatican between forty-five and sixty-five cardinals were imprisoned, together with two or three servants or chaplains each, certain officers of the Conclave, doctors, chemists, carpenters, altogether between 200 and 300 people. If the foreign cardinals failed to arrive quickly it could be worse than boring, for old men cooped up without exercise, into the heat of the Roman summer.

The foreign cardinals delayed the Conclave not only because they must travel to Rome. They represented the Catholic powers of Europe, whose interests differed from the interests of Italian cardinals. Austria, Spain, France, Bavaria, Portugal, and Poland were agreed on one thing only: they did not want a rigid Pope, a Pope who would press the old claims of a Hildebrand against modern governments, a Pope who would protest against them if they did what they wanted with the Churches in their country. They wished for a friendly Pope. If they could not have a friendly Pope, they preferred a complaisant Pope, even a weak Pope. They were afraid of a strong Pope; of an effective Pope; a young Pope. In 1667 Cardinal Farnese was much respected by many of the cardinals; and had the merit (if it was a merit) of belonging to one of the most powerful families in Europe. But it was agreed that he would be difficult to elect because he was able, and it was believed that Catholic governments would not like to have a Pope so effective in business. But Italian cardinals themselves often shared this opinion, that to have too active a Pope had perils. They were in the position of fellows at an Oxford or Cambridge college who elected their own president, and preferred not to entrust that authority to someone who would deal too drastically with their conservatisms; with the addition that in the cardinals' case they chose a head who, once elected, could exert undefined but vast authority.

For this reason came the proverb, 'He who enters the Conclave a Pope comes out a cardinal.' Before the Conclave men looked about for 'obvious' men, *papabile*. But men were 'obvious' because they did much, and won adherents, and gained the respect of their colleagues. If they did much, they were also men of controversy, men who made enemies. For such men the two-thirds majority was difficult to find. In the late seventeenth and in the eighteenth century the opinion is often found that if you wish to elect a man Pope, you must prevent him from being too prominent beforehand. When Queen Christina, the ex-Queen of Sweden, wanted her candidate elected Pope, she practised an elaborate deception publicly to show the world that she believed him to have no chance of election. Some believed that Cardinal Ganganelli would never have been elected Pope in 1769 if he had not remained quietly in his cell, and taken almost no part in the discussions.

Catholic governments exerted pressure on Conclaves. The extent and nature of this pressure varied from election to election, according to the changing political situation between the powers, according to the possible candidates, and to the number of adherents which they could muster within the college of cardinals. Occasionally they exerted a pressure which felt almost overwhelming. The weight of this pressure, the length to which their agents would go, is a chief sign of the importance within the Catholic world of the Pope's office, even during that eighteenth century when historians have written of the Pope's weakness.

First, the pressure was less than sometimes it seemed to be. The rule of two-thirds majority made it difficult to elect anyone. It thereby safeguarded the liberty of election thus far at least, that no government, nor combination of governments, even when using every device to influence or threaten or cajole, could force the cardinals to elect the candidate whom governments wanted. The pressure was enough to prevent, never enough to elect. Catholic governments were continually forced to be content with an election which, from their point of view, was third best or fourth best or 'worse'. Usually governments disagreed among themselves, and then the cardinals were confronted with pressures that cancelled. But on the rare occasions when governments agreed, and when therefore the pressure felt most heavy, efforts to secure a candidate created a special nature of resistance. This was a free election. At every Conclave were some cardinals resolute to vote against a candidate whom a government wanted, because they were determined to vindicate their freedom. These cardinals made a coherent group, known at first by their critics as the flying squad or *volanti di coscienza* 'the flying men with consciences'. In 1689 the Austrian ambassador called them scornfully 'God's party'.[4] The nickname which at last stuck was *zelanti*, the zealots. Only once during the eighteenth century were the *zelanti* able to elect (not the man whom they wanted first but) the man whom they wanted second, Clement XI Albani, in 1700; and then only because relations between the Catholic powers were so tense, the King of Spain died during the Conclave and armies mobilized for the war of the Spanish Succession. But though the *zelanti* could not achieve, they also could prevent. They stood for incorruptible elections. They were numerous enough to ensure that every Pope elected was personally worthy of the office. The man elected was never the best possible from the *zelanti* point of view, that was not to be expected, and if ever achieved might have damaged the Catholic Church in Europe. But at no Conclave did the cardinals give a two-thirds majority to a candidate solely because a grand alliance of Catholic powers drove them so to cast their votes.

They had however apocalyptic feelings of the risks they ran, the calamities which could ensue if they were forced into a foolish choice to get the elusive majority of two-thirds. 'If we make a mistake this time,' wrote a cardinal in his diary within the Conclave of 1769, 'the Church is in ruins.'[5]

The Counter-Reformation failed in some of its endeavours and certainly could not make all cardinals good men, still less make them holy men. But it stamped the cardinals' college with a certain stamp; and because the college of cardinals was a self-perpetuating body, this inheritance remained. Therefore, though it was not at all impossible for a bad man to become a cardinal, it became impossible for a bad man to become Pope; not enough cardinals would vote for the candidate.

The pressure of governments is easy to exaggerate by reason of the nature of the information about Conclaves. Much of the evidence comes from letters home to their prime ministers by ambassadors in Rome, or by their equivalents, foreign cardinals or agents within the Conclave. These ambassadors or agents had incentives to overestimate the usefulness of their endeavours and to report accordingly. A true judgement must rest upon what was actually achieved and not what an ambassador reported as achieved. In 1667 the French king claimed to have appointed Clement IX as Pope. The evidence shows that the claim was unjustified, the Pope was

[4] Pastor, xxxii.526, 'fazione di Dio'.   [5] Pirelli's Diary, 8 Apr. 1769.

elected after far more complexity and difficulty than the French ambassador liked to describe. Papal historians who studied Conclaves were hostile
to any outside intervention and partially blinded by their archives into
exaggerating the success of the pressure from governments.

Catholic sovereigns were usually successful in keeping out. With the
final result they were content perforce. The imperial agent said sadly after
the Conclave of 1769, 'We wanted a good Pope and could not get one.
We were against a bad Pope. We have made a Pope betwixt and between,
because no one better could be got.'[6] In these sentences the words *good* and
bad had no ethical content. The agent meant only, they had now a Pope
who was not quite satisfactory, but who would not be too harmful, from
the point of view of Austrian policy.

Governments exercised pressure by means of agents in Rome. From the
third quarter of the seventeenth century their ambassadors became more
and more important, as the bearers not only of news but of instructions,
menaces, or blandishments. Spanish and French ambassadors had the
worst records for high-handedness. The Conclave was immured, and
secret. But active ambassadors were known to pass messages in and out,
usually by the hands of 'conclavists', personal assistants to cardinals within
the Conclave; they could fairly easily smuggle papers into the enclosure
by means of a valet or an abbé; we hear of a basket constructed with
secret drawers for this purpose, and at the same Conclave two cardinals
conversed with the Austrian ambassador through a window. In 1724 no
less a man than Kaunitz, special envoy from the Emperor to Rome,
climbed up some wooden steps, knelt on a window sill, forced his head
and arm through a high narrow window, stuck the Emperor's letter on
the point of his sword and stretched out so that the imperial cardinal at the
barber's shop within could reach.[7]

Illicit breaches in rules of the Conclave were specially necessary in the
numerous cases of deadlock. Catholic governments were determined to
prevent 'unacceptable' candidates. Their cardinals would arrive with lists
of acceptable and unacceptable. But in the course of a long Conclave new
names appeared unforeseen, and then there was hurried desire to consult
Paris, or Madrid, or Vienna for an opinion on whether it was safe to agree
to the proposed election. In these circumstances it might be necessary to
prolong negotiations in the Conclave until the courier returned with a
reply. Sometimes such negotiations could not be prolonged. A message
from Mazarin in Paris arrived too late to ban Pamfili (Innocent X) in

[6] Cordara, *Commentarii*, 368; speaker Cardinal Albani; Kratz and Leturia, 24.
[7] Pastor, xxxiv.21, 23, 102–3.

1644, a message from Madrid too late to ban Conti (Innocent XIII) in 1721.

Among the cardinals certain men came to be known as 'crown cardinals', *cardinali delle corone*. The three great powers Austria, Spain, and France expected to have a cardinal charged with their special interests at Rome. We hear occasional talk of a Polish crown cardinal, a Sardinian crown cardinal, a Portuguese, a Venetian. In the eighteenth century the crown cardinal was often known as the 'cardinal-protector' of France etc. These cardinals had the special function of representing the interests of their government. For this service they drew a stipend or honorarium. Catholic governments might also pay pensions to other cardinals whom they regarded as their agents in Rome, and once France paid a pension to the chief of the Pope's civil service, the secretary of state. Such bonds would tie a few Italian cardinals to the interests of the power paying the stipend.

The veto

The Catholic powers had crude bludgeons; talk of refusal to recognize, loose talk of schism, threat of reprisals in their own land, threat of military action (if Austrian or Spanish in Italy, if French in Avignon). These instruments were at times used, for all their roughness and high-handedness. But the regular instrument, which required no illegality or force and was accepted constitutionally, was the veto.

Holy Roman Emperors sometimes acted as though they could exclude candidates whom they disliked. It was a sign of political dependence, and the need for help from Catholic powers, that the claim first became legal right, and was admitted by Popes to be legal right, in the age of the Counter-Reformation. The more necessary Spanish power became to the safety of Popes, the more silently or readily the right of veto was admitted. The Emperor Charles V claimed it, and his son Philip II. The French claimed because the Emperor claimed. The Austrian Emperor claimed because after Charles V he was successor to the Holy Roman Empire. Other powers tried to claim it—Naples for a period, at one time even Portugal. The cardinals did not allow these claims of lesser powers. As the right became finally established towards the end of the seventeenth century, it was restricted to Spain, France, Austria.

The case for admitting it was strong. Catholic governments had sanctions which they could inflict if they failed to get their way. And the Roman Curia thought it obvious that they should not elect a man who offended one of the leading Catholic states. Some papal theorists wrote papers to show that no right of veto existed. Pope Clement XII or his advisers issued a bull (*Apostolatus officium*) limiting its force or doubting its exercise. German canonists were divided into three different opinions, first that only the Holy Roman Empire possessed a veto, second that it was mere corruption, and third that the Church silently accepted it as right. This silent acceptance continued all the eighteenth century. A motive for accepting it lay in the desire to regulate, and remove the worst threats of abuse. Cardinals needed to be sure that no one admitted a claim by French or Spanish king to exclude any candidate whom they disliked. Accordingly they admitted the right of veto, and then tried to limit its force.

For the use of the veto a Catholic power need give no explanation. In 1644 Cardinal Albornoz on behalf of Spain vetoed the excellent Cardinal Sacchetti. He was asked for his reasons. He had the sufficient reason that Sacchetti was on close terms with Cardinal Mazarin and was a favoured candidate of the French. But he simply replied that he was not bound to give any reasons. This was one of the most sensational of vetoes; usually they were more routine. Another dramatic intervention came in 1758 when the French vetoed the excellent Cardinal Cavalchini because he wanted Cardinal Bellarmine to be made a saint and because he stood against the policy of the French government over the Jansenist controversy. This intervention was specially dramatic because the supporters of Cavalchini, though he did not want to be elected, had just collected promises of the necessary two-thirds majority. The French had not wished to pronounce a formal veto. They found themselves forced into it reluctantly as Cavalchini collected more and more votes.

For with experience statesmen saw that the veto was powerful if it were not used, and a failure in policy if it must be used. Though it was accepted in the constitution, and therefore different from a crude threat, its use came to seem clumsy and offensive, and its consequence to be not what the government intended. 'I don't understand the French language; but I tell you, you resist the Holy Spirit', said an indignant Italian when in 1758 they vetoed Cavalchini.[8] The French cardinals and their supporters at once lost influence in the Conclave. The cardinals admitted that the veto was lawful, but hated it when it happened, and gathered support to frustrate the aim of the government that used the weapon.

In the middle of the eighteenth century this came to be well understood. The Austrians instructed their cardinal in 1758 that the veto was a pistol which if it were fired could only shoot a single man, but if it were kept loaded and not fired, could prevent several men. In 1724 the imperialist

---

[8] Petrucelli della Gattina, 4.156.

Cardinal Cienfuegos advised his government that the use of the veto always fostered the growth of a hostile party. Austria sent its representative to the Conclave of 1721 with the instruction that he must use the veto only in extreme necessity.[9] Nevertheless at that Conclave the Austrian cardinal Count Althan vetoed the secretary of state and caused consternation. A memorandum for the court of Vienna in 1730 recommended a very careful use of the veto—'it is a sword which if it is unsheathed will not serve more than two or three times at most, but if you keep it in its sheath can kill as many men as you like.'[10]

Experienced men became skilled at handling the threat. An expert in the Conclave might propose the name of someone whom he did not want, but whom he knew that France or Spain would veto, and thereby weaken the future possibilities of resistance by France or Spain to his second proposal when it came later. Not only Italian cardinals could play this manoeuvre. In a time of European war the French might put forward a name which they knew the Austrians would veto, in order to weaken future Austrian resistance to their real candidate.

If the veto were not used, it was the principal instrument of the powers. An able historian has written that at the crisis-Conclave of 1769 the powers who happened for once to be in agreement, vetoed twenty-three candidates.[11] If understood formally, such a feat was impossible. But the veto when unused kept out many; partly by showing the cardinals that it was no use proceeding with that name and they need waste time no longer; partly because the veto was so offensive that cardinals went far to avoid provoking it; and partly because the placing of the veto against a man's name was like a blackball which his friends preferred to avoid. They were content to know that if necessary the veto would be forthcoming, saw that he had no chance of election, could gain no merit from persisting in his candidature by way of a protest, and turned to other names. In this way the veto excluded many more than those few who were vetoed formally.

Civil servants with realism protested occasionally at the doctrine that the veto should *never* be used, for then it would fall into disuse and if the need for it ever came its validity might be challenged. But others saw the danger that if it were used too frequently, it would force the cardinals to

[9] Pastor xxxiv. 8.
[10] Pastor xxxiv. 309.
[11] Schnürer, 51. Actual vetoes: Sacchetti, Spain 1644 and 1655; none, 1667; d'Elce, France 1669, Brancaccio Spain; none 1676, 1689, 1691, 1700 (but the 1700 election nevertheless helped to develop the full right of veto). 1721, Paolucci Austria. 1724 none. 1730 Imperiali, Spain, Paolucci Austria. 1758 Cavalchini France.

protest liberty and drive through an election against the wishes of the Catholic sovereigns.

To prevent a Pope expected to be hostile was not difficult. The difficulty lay in judging the unknowns. A man who looked innocuous to France might be transformed by elevation to responsibility and power. These things were difficult to predict. All governments received regular reports on the persons and views and behaviour of the cardinals. And still when matters of moment and controversy lay immediately in front, governments wished to minimize the risk attending the election of an unknown.

From time to time, therefore, the question of *capitulation* came on the agenda—that is, was it possible, before agreeing to the election of a cardinal, to ask him whether if elected he would promise to do this or refrain from doing that? Was it possible to make conditions before sanctioning an election, even to exact undertakings? In long past history such undertakings were not unknown, the college of cardinals themselves had on occasion demanded a promise before election.

The system of election helped to safeguard the cardinals from this particular form of pressure.

First, some of the cardinals whom men might want as Pope had no wish to be Pope, and were immune from requests for undertakings. Others were equally immune because they were men of honour and would not compromise themselves for an instant by making a promise to anyone to secure their own election. In 1700 the French demanded a declaration from Cardinal Marescotti as the price of support. Marescotti retorted simply that he came to this Conclave to elect a Pope, not to become a Pope.[12] Exactly a century later the Austrian Cardinal Herzan, who at that moment commanded votes enough to prevent anyone being elected if he disapproved, tried to persuade Cardinal Chiaramonti to promise, if elected, to appoint as secretary of state a certain cardinal friendly to Austria. Chiaramonti replied humorously: 'Anyone who makes undertakings at a Conclave is automatically excommunicated. Surely you don't want an excommunicated man as Pope?'[13]

Where it was possible to work upon a cardinal by persuasion—where for example the declaration which would be asked of him was believed to fit his attitude and would merely prove what was already believed about him —those who wished to secure such a declaration must go delicately about their task. It must not be public. For if it were public, other cardinals

---

[12] Gravina to Pignatelli, 20 Nov. 1700, in G. V. Gravina's correspondence printed by A. Sarubbi (ed.), *Curia romana e regno di Napoli* (Naples, 1972), 53.

[13] Leflon, *Pie VII*, 1.591.

would accuse the proposed pope of simony and react against his election. Opinion in the college of cardinals was strongly against such declarations. In 1724 the French wanted Cardinal Olivieri. Someone, probably an opponent of Olivieri, distributed a memorandum inside the Conclave with a list of numerous concessions to the French government which Olivieri had already undertaken to make if he were elected. Such uproar ensued in the Conclave that the candidature of Olivieri collapsed. A foolish monsignor in Naples once proposed to his prime minister that fierce men should go to the Conclave and make all the cardinals sign undertakings.[14] Far milder versions of such a proposal always had the opposite effect from that intended.

If no direct or formal undertaking was possible, those who wished to satisfy their minds on future policy must be content with more informal means. They could send to the candidate an envoy who would hold him in conversation upon the disputed subject or programme, and then return to report what he said. The border-line between neutral discussion and informal undertaking was impossible to draw.

Thus in 1689 a French government wanted promises from Cardinal Ottoboni before they would allow his election. Ottoboni refused to make any such promise. But the cardinals who were promoting his election felt able on his behalf to give the necessary assurance.

In 1721 the French government demanded a cardinal's hat for Pierre Dubois. Since Dubois was chief minister of the French king, they felt their prestige to be at stake. The previous Pope had been reluctant to satisfy this wish, for Dubois was no model of a Christian clergyman. Cardinal Conti himself gave an assurance (probably but not quite certainly a written assurance, vague in formulation) that he would make Dubois a cardinal. One of his servants in the Conclave reported his intention, and later another gave vague assurances to the imperial cardinals. The election of Conti as Innocent XIII was the first election of the eighteenth century when a clear understanding was given. Dubois was made cardinal six weeks after the election.

The next and weightier case is the undertaking (if any) which Pope Clement XIV gave before his election in 1769. Four of the Catholic powers—France, Spain, Portugal, Naples—were determined to force the new Pope to destroy the Jesuits. Their envoys appeared at the Conclave with an air of ruthlessness. Spain and Portugal kept demanding that no one should be made Pope who had not given a written understanding, or at least made a verbal declaration before witnesses. Though the French

---

[14] Pastor, xxxviii.39; cf. xxxiv.101–2.

wanted the same, they would not countenance the plan. The French ambassador believed that not a single Italian cardinal would have a troubled
conscience about giving a promise. His cardinals knew more about
Italians than he; and were at last supported by the French minister in
Paris, Choiseul, who told his ambassador that his methods were the way
to make the worthiest cardinals refuse to be Pope.[15] The Spaniards said
that they would vote for a likely candidate, Cardinal Stoppani, if he would
promise to suppress the Jesuits. Stoppani was sounded, but would make no
promises; and when the news passed round the Conclave that the powers
wanted Stoppani, all the *zelanti* deserted his cause.

But on 12 May 1769 Cardinal Ganganelli had a long conversation with
one of the assistants in the Conclave and spoke freely against Jesuits. The
next morning the Spaniards began a campaign to promote him as a candidate, on 17 May an assistant to the French Cardinal de Bernis visited
Ganganelli. He again spoke freely about Jesuits and about French policy.
On 18 May the French joined the Spaniards, and the result was now only
a matter of time. Ganganelli gave no outright undertaking to suppress the
Jesuits. But he was willing to say that he thought the new Pope *could*
suppress them and that it was to be hoped that he would satisfy the governments. Ganganelli was elected unanimously on 19 May. It had taken only
a week, after nearly three months of Conclave.

An observer among the cardinals in that terrible Conclave made this
comment in his diary: 'He [Ganganelli] will certainly get from the powers
more than anyone else could have done. . . . No one is more capable of
doing more good in the circumstances of today. No one is more capable
of ruining the see of Rome.'[16]

This observer had neither wanted nor expected Ganganelli. We who
have earlier met Cardinal Ganganelli, as the author of one of the most
humane documents ever to be written about the Jews, are not surprised to
find that at length he was a considerable candidate. But this was not how
he looked at the Conclave. The observer laughed at the name when it was
first mentioned. But in the end he thought him best, whatever the risks,
not best in an ideal situation, but best inside the straitjacket by which
Catholic governments tied the arms of any Pope.

Partisans who hated Ganganelli talked of simony, of buying the see by
a pact. The prime minister in Naples, Tanucci, believed that Ganganelli
promised to suppress the Jesuits. But both Spanish and French cardinals

---

[15] Choiseul to Aubeterre, 2 May 1769; in F. Masson, *Le Cardinal de Bernis depuis son
ministère*, 101.

[16] Pirelli's Diary, 313 (18 May 1769, eve of the election).

afterwards denied that he promised. To deny it was in their interest; but probably it is true. One of the assistants certainly suggested to Ganganelli that he write down his opinion; and certainly he refused to do so, but declared that, provided the suppression of the Jesuits was not contrary to canon law, he considered it possible and profitable. The Spaniards persuaded him to sign a document, but the wording was so general that it could not bind: to the same effect, in his view as a theologian the order might lawfully be dissolved provided that the dissolution were not contrary to canon law and the rules of prudence and justice.

Pope Clement XIV Ganganelli was afterwards clear in his mind that he gave no undertaking; and that however he acted as Pope, he must not be seen to act as though he acted in fulfilment of any such undertaking.[17]

Ganganelli was afterwards charged by hostile historians with double-dealing to become Pope. What the affair shows is the nature of rumour, reported or half-reported conversations, second-hand accounts of what was said, as the struggle went on to predict what an unknown cardinal would do if suddenly he were elected Pope. No man might give an undertaking. But a man immured at too close quarters for three months with forty or fifty other leaders of the Catholic Church, could hardly be debarred for all those days from discussing what ought to be done in the crisis that confronted the Church.

Cardinal Ganganelli was imprudent to let the conclavist fill in his questionnaire.

The third case is of the same type.

When Ganganelli died in 1774, after he abolished Jesuits, everyone knew that the Conclave would be controversial. He was Pope only five years; intended to make a lot of cardinals but never announced their names; and therefore left a college of cardinals in which the cardinals of his pro-Jesuit predecessor had force. The Catholic powers, and some of the cardinals, were determined that whatever else was done no Pope should be elected who would reverse the decision and restore Jesuits. So far as the powers were concerned, Ganganelli was thought to be the wisest pope of the century. When the King of Spain was found earnestly praying that Clement XIV Ganganelli might not die because they would never get another one like him, the atmosphere of the Conclave was likely to be tense. Therefore the crown's party wanted a prior undertaking from any candidate that he would not restore the Jesuits.

The Conclave was difficult and long; until at last it became clear that a

[17] Reports of Cardinal de Bernis in Theiner, *Geschichte des Pontificats Clemens' XIV*, 1.238 ff.

sufficient majority would vote for Braschi, who was to become Pope Pius VI. Then at the last moment Braschi had to be 'cleared' with the governments so that no one lay a veto. Braschi gave no undertaking and was asked for none. Cardinal Giraud reported to the Spanish cardinal what Braschi said; the Spaniard went to talk to Braschi, and then reported to the Spanish ambassador both Giraud's conversation and his own conversation; the imperial ambassador saw that he could only stop the election by using the veto and believed a veto undesirable; and thus Pius VI was elected. The Spanish cardinal gave the Spanish prime minister the impression that those conversations amounted to a statement of intention not to go back on his predecessor.

Clement XI Albani (Pope 1700–21)

None of the Popes of the eighteenth century was a bad man. That does not mean that they were all good Popes. The saintliest of the men was the worst Pope of the century.

They were almost all old. The average age at accession of all the Popes elected during the eighteenth century was almost sixty-four. The average age at accession of the five Popes elected between 1721 and 1758 was just under seventy. The average age in the last year of their pontificate of the same five Popes was just under eighty. This constitution, theoretically absolute, was limited not only by custom but by the age of those who held supreme power.

The old age of the Popes, it has been argued, came from the desire of the Catholic powers who wanted Popes to do little or nothing. Experience does not confirm the theory that old men do little or nothing. 'I've got to get a move on,' said humorous Pope Alexander VIII when he was elected at the age of seventy-nine, 'because the eleventh hour has already struck.'

The cause of seniority lay in the nature of the election. The cardinals were electing a powerful person who was unpredictable, and if they elected a young man and made a mistaken choice, they must live with their mistake for long years. Moreover the criss-cross of interests inside the Conclave—reformers, conservatives, French, Spanish, Austrian, friends of the late Pope, opponents of the late Pope—made the two-thirds majority hard to find; and after weeks of negotiation the party which found itself in a minority was more likely to accept an old man, because they saw a new election within foreseeable time, when conditions might be different.

Because old men vary in their habits and capacity, the system sometimes produced a Pope incapable of business. Clement X Altieri (1670–6), aged seventy-nine at election, could not act, and had no desire to be bothered. He would not attend to business, and his kinsman (the father-in-law of his niece but he took the name Cardinal Altieri) was supreme. The Pope gave audience only to sign papers on request, and the cardinal kept away difficult problems. It became a saying in Rome 'the Pope's job is to bless and consecrate, Cardinal Altieri's job is to rule.' Yet the election was a success, for the government of the Church was managed with skill and love of peace during this pontificate.

In 1700 the cardinals astonished themselves by electing the most power-full cardinal under the previous Pope, and made him one of the youngest Popes, Clement XI Albani. This unusual election was due to the news during the Conclave of the Spanish king's death and therefore a shock of urgency before the looming war of the Spanish Succession.

Cardinal Albani tried to refuse office, and the attempt set off a long debate whether an elected candidate could decline. Cardinal Albani had only fifty-one years, so his desire not to accept the office did not spring from age or infirmity. His protest was more than token. When they could not overcome, they submitted the question to four theologians, whether a man who felt himself to have no capacity for the work could refuse unanimous election. The theologians were not quite agreed but gave the advice that he could not refuse unanimous election for he would resist the will of God.

But once the two-thirds majority was clear, many elections were made unanimous, with the exception that the cardinal elected was forbidden to vote for himself.

Clement XI was wholly suitable; highly educated, vigorous, eloquent, pious, able to keep secrets, experienced in the administration of the Curia, with a fine presence, tall of stature with high forehead and grave face, long endurance in hard work, a sweet clear voice, and a friendly and forth-coming air. Originally a protégé of the Barberini family, he had coped successfully with the last affairs of the abdicated Queen Christina of Sweden, and with the plight of the Jacobites in England. Such a man was more like an experienced civil servant, a lawyer, or a governor of towns, than a divine. He was only ordained priest shortly before the Conclave which elected him Pope, when he was already ten years a cardinal.

He had all the qualities for which men looked. And since under the shock of threatened war he was solitary as a Pope whom the *zelanti* wanted among their first choices, the outcome of his reign was of special interest. More calamities happened to the papacy during this pontificate than under any Pope since the Reformation. In large part they were the calamities of circumstance, and under some Popes they might have been more and worse. But for all his ability and perception, Clement XI contributed by mistakes.

In two spheres the results changed the course of papal history and the working of the Pope's office: in politics, and in the authority of the Pope in doctrine.

Politics

In his office as head of an Italian state the Pope was always the leading power in Italy. His state was not richest nor most highly populated, but he compensated with an international authority which no other Italian prince could rival.

By geography and history Italy was the battle-ground between powers of the north and west, Austria, France, Spain. In the age of the Counter-Reformation the Spanish dominated Italy, and when Clement XI became Pope the Spanish still ruled in Sicily and Naples and Milan and on the coast of Tuscany.

But in 1700 the France of Louis XIV was the great power of Europe. Any Pope was bound to admire the French king; who extended Catholic power against Protestants in the Rhineland and fostered the Catholic cause in Britain and sheltered the exiled Stuart king and showed his piety by expelling most of the Huguenots from France. French stature helped Popes politically. When Spaniards ruled Milan and Naples, Popes were in danger from Spain. The great power of France protected the Pope from an excess of Spanish interference.

A relationship with any powerful Catholic sovereign brought discomforts. The French liked to limit Roman power in the French Church, and preached that General Councils were supreme over Popes. But the link between Rome and Paris was strong. Clement XI was in this sense a 'French' Pope. His past career led him to expect that the best future for the papacy lay in alliance with Louis XIV; not too close nor too evident an alliance, for Popes must be seen to be neutral, but resting on a belief that France could help where Spain with its Italian possessions could endanger.

When the line of Spanish Habsburgs failed, rivals claimed the throne of Spain; a Bourbon Philip of Anjou protected by Louis XIV, and a Habsburg Charles of Austria, younger son of the Holy Roman Emperor. Clement XI at once recognized Philip V as king—and had the excuse that in that moment Philip looked to be in peaceable possession of Spain.

To have a French king in Madrid overset the European balance of power. Though in the European war which followed, Protestant powers stood on the side of Austria, the war was at base a war between Catholic powers and therefore terrible for the Pope, since whichever side he failed to support would hit and hurt the Catholic Church.

The war was even more terrible to the Pope because it was a war for the Spanish possessions in Italy. To the Pope as Italian prince it mattered most who ruled in Naples. Rome got meat from the Abruzzi, oil from Apulia, many revenues for its clergy from south-Italian benefices. A hostile king in Naples could impoverish the Papal States.

Therefore the war meant marching and counter-marching in Italy, with the Pope professedly neutral but too evidently preferring French and Bourbon looters to Austrian and Habsburg looters. Clement XI became a ruler who, outwardly neutral, backed the losing side in a war. The Austrians conquered Naples (1707); and the next year saw actual war between the Pope and the Austrian Emperor over the occupation of northern papal lands in the Romagna. In November 1708 20,000 of the Pope's troops had to surrender at Ferrara. At that moment the Pope feared another sack of Rome, undisciplined Protestant mercenaries of a Catholic Emperor advancing south to take revenge upon a Pope who was an enemy in war. He wondered whether to flee, perhaps to Avignon, perhaps to Malta. On 15 January 1709 he made a humiliating surrender, which included total disarmament, recognition that the Austrian troops had free passage to Naples, and an implicit (later explicit) recognition of the Habsburg claim to the throne of Spain. This put Bourbon Spain into six years of schism from Rome (1709–15). When the Spanish returned to conquer Sardinia and Sicily, Clement XI stood decidedly on the Austrian side.

To observers of the later eighteen century looking back, all this appeared an anachronism; the Pope behaving like a European politician, or a Renaissance prince, raising his army, at war. Popes ceased to try to behave in this way. No Pope again went to war on his own account except against Bonaparte and in the middle of the nineteenth century when the Pope raised an army to fight the Piedmontese. Men realized that the Pope had no army except to keep order, and that his power lay in less tangible force. Looking back, observers thought the change an improvement. President de Brosses came from France to Rome, only thirty years after the surrender at Ferrara, and eyed the fortified passage which the Borgia Pope built in the high Renaissance, to enable him to flee from the Vatican to the Castel Sant' Angelo, as a safeguard against revolution or invasion. De Brosses wondered how best the Pope might now use this corridor—perhaps if it were made wider and straighter it might be occupied to exhibit pictures. For no Pope will need to flee—they are 'respected by their subjects, and honoured by the princes of Europe, since they have wisely confined themselves to exercising legitimate power abroad and govern moderately at home.' De Brosses could not know that only three decades before, during the threat of a sack of Rome, Pope Clement XI ordered that corridor to be got ready and did not see it only as a historical monument.[18]

To the Pope's eyes the war of the Spanish Succession was like a Catholic civil war. He was a more influential person when Catholics allied to fight Protestants than when Austria and France and Spain fought each other. Like a Pope of the Counter-Reformation, Clement XI paid secret money to the Pretender James III to help him wrest back the throne of England; organized a crusading league when the Turks declared war on the Venetian empire, sent a blest sword and hat studded with pearls to Prince Eugene, talked of saving the holy sepulchre from the hands of the infidel, ascribed Eugene's victory over the Turks at Peterwardein to the intercession of the Blessed Virgin, and in commemoration extended the Feast of the Rosary to the world.

Clement XI was able, courageous, devout, with the single fault that under pressure—and he came under as savage pressure as any Pope—he could not make up his mind. He worried to and fro indecisively. Not a worldly man in the wrong meaning of the epithet, he was nevertheless the last of the great Popes in a worldly sense; the last to play a part upon the European stage as much because he was an Italian king as because he was the spiritual leader of an international Church; the last Pope, as one born out of due time, of the political Counter-Reformation. His pontificate proved that the world had changed, and that the historic role was obsolete.

As the Pope's political power diminished, one or two intelligent prophets saw that he might again be useful as a mediator, at least between Catholic nations. De Brosses still had the sense that the Pope was a source of unity in Christendom. Because he lost his power among governments, he could again be weighty by neutrality, by encouragement of peace, by the respect which all nations feel toward his office. De Brosses thought that even Protestants were losing their old hatred and might not refuse his arbitration. Though an intelligent lawyer, de Brosses suffered illusion

---

[18] De Brosses, 2.147–8; F. M. Ottieri, *Istoria della guerre avvenute in Europa* (Rome, 1755), 5.156.

about the willingness of Protestant Europe to forget, and about the Pope's ability (as yet) to rise above the political entanglements of his station.

These events raised a small but not minor point about the Pope's office. In one of his moments of travail and melancholy and self-distrust, Clement XI talked of resigning his office. He said that it was nothing but a crown of thorns.[19] Though a cardinal was held not to be able to refuse the papacy if elected unanimously, few doubted that he could resign. In the late thirteenth century Pope Celestine V solemnly declared that a Pope could resign, and resigned; and the right to resign was solemnly confirmed by his successor whose validity would otherwise be in doubt. The precedent was not encouraging. The option was more theoretical than real. But it was held to exist.

The teaching office

The arguments and disputes which rose from the churches, and came at last to Rome for settlement, were sometimes, though not often, entangled with argument about the truth of Christian doctrine. A disagreement over the way in which priests heard confessions was found to rest on a difference of theological principle. An argument over the best method of missionary work in China was found to derive from contrasting axioms in divinity. The question whether or not a published meditation upon the New Testament was fit to be commended as reading for devout souls could not be settled without a decision which touched truth equally with expediency. In these ways the functions of supreme court and supreme teacher were inseparable.

Such were the most anxious questions. To order a monastery to submit to an archbishop touched only the virtue of obedience. To order men to believe this, or not to believe that, touched consciences. Therefore these questions always arose on disputes with practical consequences. The Church received a body of truth from the Apostles. No one intended to add a jot to that truth. No one was interested in making a definition to satisfy professors of theology in a lecture-room, who would not be satisfied by any definition. The questions at bottom were practical—the nature of pastoral advice to parishioners, the rightness or wrongness of a book which some thought a marvellous help to the people and others thought to corrupt the people, the legitimacy or illegitimacy of innovations in modes of preaching the truth, or of bringing the people to pray.

In directing such questions the Pope had important tools at his disposal. A wise Pope guided a dispute in such a way that he would not be forced at

[19] Pastor, xxxiii.148, conversation with the imperial ambassador.

last to determine some question of theory. He could demand that dispu-
tants hold their tongues and throw away their pens. Several decrees of the
eighteenth century ordered silence. But if the argument touched men's
consciences they burned to speak or write; and then an order to silence
won only respite. Once when Pascal heard of the recommendation to
keep silence he said 'Saints never keep silence.'[20] These successes could
hardly be more than temporary.

Then, the Pope could use personal favour to encourage one set of minds
by preferment and to discourage another set of minds by censure. But
neither preferment nor censure bound his successor. One day another
Pope might be elected who would encourage where he censured and reprove where he favoured, and so begin the argument afresh. Just occasionally it seemed to some Popes that a matter must be settled finally for the
good of the Catholic Church, and that the only way to settle finally was
by formal definition of a doctrine, which sought to commit the Church
in perpetuity.

This last frame of mind led in 1713 to the bull *Unigenitus*.

Unigenitus

The French Oratorian Pasquier Quesnel (1634–1719) composed a meditation, later extended and published as *Moral Reflexions on the New Testament*. The treatment was excellent, quiet, pious, and in such simple
language as to be useful to the growing body of educated laymen and lay-
women whose devotional practice included the devout study of the Bible.
Through the meditations, which were uncontroversial, shone the sense of
divine grace in the work of redeeming souls. But it happened that Quesnel
attached himself to a master famous as the controversial leader of French
Jansenists, Antoine Arnauld, then being assailed in France as teaching
Protestant or quasi-Protestant doctrines in faith and morals. When Arnauld was forced to seek refuge in exile at Brussels, Quesnel joined him,
remained there till Arnauld's death (1694), and was afterwards imprisoned
for a time on the order of the King of Spain. He escaped to Holland and
began to publish a row of controversial books to defend Arnauld, himself, and the *Moral Reflexions*. He and his book were identified as leader
and symbol of the Jansenist movement since Arnauld's death; and since
France was convulsed over the battle between Jesuits and Jansenists,
Quesnel's book ceased to be only a gentle and peaceable devotion and
became the flag of a cause. This made it more famous, and demanded

[20] *D.T.C.* 13.2.1503.

numerous editions. In 1695 the work was approved by de Noailles, Archbishop of Paris. The doctrinal question asked whether Quesnel's teaching
on grace was the classical doctrine of St. Augustine, or whether he had
adopted opinions like those of Calvin.

On 13 July 1708 Pope Clement XI sent a brief condemning the *Moral
Reflexions*. Such an act was a normal act of papal authority. The French
Church was in turmoil, men appealed to Rome, something must be
settled. Rome was persuaded that Quesnel was quasi-Protestant, the *Reflexions* should be kept from the devout reader, the brief determined no
doctrine but disapproved a devotional practice, that of reading a particular book which interpreted the New Testament. But here Rome tampered
with the constitution of France. The Parlement of Paris (not a representative body like the British Parliament but a corporation of lawyers with
the power of registering acts so that they had the force of law) refused
legality to the brief.

The fault, in part, belonged to King Louis XIV. He believed in strengthening his kingdom by achieving religious unity if not uniformity. He had
persecuted and expelled the Protestants, now he would use the Pope to
crush Jansenist religious opposition within the Catholic Church. Finding
that Quesnel's work on the New Testament was the symbol of Jansenism,
he began to demand from the Pope a formal condemnation of all its
errors. His applications to Rome were repeated and insistent.

The Pope was being asked, if not required, to make a declaration of
doctrine which would (it was alleged) unify a disputing Church and thereby unify a state. The king undertook to use his power to make French
bishops conform to the Pope's decision. Pope Clement XI would have
preferred to condemn a book, and be silent on particular doctrines of the
book. But he was pushed; and something in the intellectual atmosphere of
Rome in those years ensured that he was not too reluctant to be pushed.

God gives his grace freely to men; all salvation is of God; it is not of
ourselves but of him; these were beliefs not only of Luther and Calvin,
but of St. Thomas Aquinas and St. Augustine, indeed of the Epistle to the
Romans. But in the Counter-Reformation a powerful school of divinity
wished to go as far as was possible in asserting the need for men to do the
best morally that they can. The one school took the text 'The just shall
live by faith', the other the text 'Faith without works is dead.' In French
divinity of the seventeenth century the schools were identified as 'Jansenist' and 'Jesuit', though the labels were always vague. Quesnel claimed
to be neither a Protestant nor a Jansenist but only a disciple of St. Augustine.

The Roman schools of that moment happened to be dominated by the 'Jesuit' school. The Pope nominated a commission of five cardinals and nine theologians (only one real Jesuit among them) who were required to examine 155 propositions extracted from Quesnel's book and translated into Latin. The commission found it slow work detecting heresy in the book. Father Ledrou, a Belgian member of the Austin friars then teaching in Rome, contended that many of Quesnel's words had a perfectly orthodox sense, and after the twelfth sitting was excluded from the enquiry. When the theologians reported, the texts were referred to the Roman Inquisition, which had twenty-three sittings with the Pope presiding. The archives show the Pope working constantly with his hand at the draft. The fatal bull was due not only to an erring judgement on the part of King Louis XIV and the theological fashion of contemporary Rome. It issued because Pope Clement XI shared that fashion, and intended to guide the Catholic Church towards a particular school of Christian divinity, as far away as possible from the doctrine of the Protestants, and pledged to the encouragement of earnest moral endeavour.

If the bull *Unigenitus* is to be understood rightly it must be placed in the European context of thought. This was the age when Protestants themselves began to leave aside in silence their foundation of justification by faith, and preach the need to do good. The supreme Protestant philosopher of morality, the Anglican Joseph Butler, published his sermons only thirteen years after the bull of Pope Clement XI; the archetypal Protestant preacher of morality, Archbishop Tillotson of Canterbury, died nineteen years before.

Because a doctrinal definition was set in history, it became impossible to disentangle its motives either from the political (as distinct from the intellectual or religious) circumstances which appeared to make it desirable, or from the prevailing principles which happened to rule the theology of the age but which were not necessarily acceptable for all time as the only principles possible for a Catholic.

The bull was signed on 8 September 1713 and published on 10 September 1713. It condemned 101 propositions translated into Latin from Quesnel's *Moral Reflexions*. It arrived at Fontainebleau on 25 September and delighted King Louis XIV. In a letter to the nuncio the Pope expressed the hope that this would establish peace, truth, and unity.

No expectation was ever more falsified by the event.

All the Augustinian doctrines of grace were condemned. No longer would there be place in the Catholic Church for men who thought with

Augustine or Aquinas, let alone with Jansen or Luther, if the bull were received at its face value.

The grace of Jesus Christ is necessary to every good work. . . . Thou command-est in vain, Lord, unless thou grantest to us that which thou commandest. . . . The grace of Christ is the supreme grace without which we can never confess Christ, and with which we never deny him. . . . Grace is the working of the all-powerful hand of God, which nothing can resist or delay. . . . No graces are given except through faith. . . . The reading of Holy Scripture is for everyone. . . . Sunday ought to be kept holy by devotional reading, especially of the Scrip-tures. . . . A fear of unjust excommunication ought not to deter us from doing our duty—

—sentence after sentence where many devout Catholics held with Ques-nel was condemned. They were not all asserted to be heretical. Some of them were only declared to be 'offensive to pious ears' or 'harmful to the Church.' But the bull did not distinguish propositions which were false from those which were only harmful.

A majority of the bishops, clergy, and laity of France accepted the bull. Elsewhere, except in Italy and the Netherlands, it was received (at first) almost without comment. The Catholic world was like the contemporary Protestant world in being deeply concerned over ethics and the theology of moral endeavour, and was hardly disturbed by the condemnation of a tradition of divinity which included Luther and Calvin.

But St. Paul wrote of justification by faith. St. Augustine taught of pre-destination and irresistible grace. The Dominicans guarded the inheritance of St. Thomas Aquinas whose thought descended from St. Augustine. Quesnel was a devout man who refused to accept the name Jansenist. To a numerous body of men, especially in France, the bull was impossible, or only possible to receive by a feat of intellectual gymnastics in the way of interpretation. And round their scruples gathered the French lawyers de-termined that the liberties of French subjects should not be crushed by a Pope from outside France. The bull released the worst controversy of the eighteenth century; dividing France, troubling Catholic authority, dis-tressing consciences, causing schism within universities, discrediting the authority of the French kings, and fostering the power of French unbelief.

Little difference was made by the death of Quesnel in 1719 or the death of Pope Clement XI in 1721. Succeeding Popes could seek to repair the damage but could not withdraw the bull. One of the new Pope's advisers recommended explanation of the text. Pope Benedict XIII was rumoured to have appealed to Pope Clement XI not to publish the bull. Himself a

Dominican he helped the scruples of the Dominican order by declaring in a brief of 6 November 1724 to the Dominicans that the bull did not touch the doctrines of St. Augustine and St. Thomas Aquinas about predestination and efficacious grace. A bull *Pretiosus* of 25 May 1727 further praised the teaching of Aquinas. Thereby the sting of the bull was drawn, for now the error in the propositions must not lie in their obvious meaning but in their context, or in the use to which they were put, or might be put. But the emendation could not settle the dispute. Rome and the French kings ceased to mind what was meant by the words of the bull but must insist that it be accepted. Some minds, headed for a time by Cardinal de Noailles of Paris, and more grimly or prayerfully by Bishops Colbert of Montpellier and Soanen of Senez (Soanen being the solitary French bishop to be suspended from episcopal functions for resistance) would not accept the bull whatever liberties of interpretation they were allowed. In their eyes it was a bad untrue bull which every loyal Catholic should resist. They could rely on many lay supporters, especially among the lawyers, who cared little for points of theology and much for liberties of Frenchmen.

A bull intended to make peace caused war. It could not help the Catholic Church that four bishops should appeal from the Pope to a General Council, and that a devoted and pious pilgrim, after kissing the foot of Clement XI, should hand him the appeal; or that the chapter of Utrecht in Holland elected a bishop in separation from the Pope (27 April 1723) and found a French missionary bishop willing to consecrate, thus beginning the schism later known as Old Catholic; or that when copies of the bull were at last affixed in Paris they needed guards to prevent them being ripped; or that the Benedictine congregation of St. Maur, where historical scholarship flowered as never before, resisted the bull so steadily that the congregation came within a hair's breadth of being dissolved, and never quite recovered its stability; or that Charles Coffin, famous among hymn-writers (*On Jordan's bank the Baptist's cry*; *Holy Spirit, Lord of grace*; etc.), and once rector of the university of Paris, should die (1749) without sacraments because the archbishop vainly demanded that the dying man should first accept *Unigenitus*; or that Coffin's funeral should become a demonstration by the university against the archbishop.

Shortly after the Austrian Emperor forbade the bull *Unigenitus* in his territories Pope Pius VI, then about to leave Vienna, was asked by Hungarian bishops for advice on what they should do. According to the minutes of the meeting, Pius VI replied in these words: 'We must talk of it as a matter of history, not as a matter of dogma (*historice, non dogmatice*).

What sort of a theologian would he be who did not know the bull *Unigenitus*? However, it is not at all necessary to argue about it in public. So you can publish the emperor's decree with the declaration that the emperor aims to prevent disputes on the subject.'[21]

The centenary of the bull in 1813 was celebrated but modestly; by sixteen Jansenists who attended low mass in the cathedral of Notre-Dame, and then went to the house of the lawyer Louis Silvy, afterwards famous as the acquirer and preserver of the ruins of Port-Royal. There someone made a speech in commemoration but what he said is lost.

The historian Ludwig von Pastor argued[22] that the bull was needed and that Clement XI should not be blamed. Controversy existed, and would have continued without *Unigenitus*. The bull brought to light the extent of the evil which it was better to uncover than to hide. 'The real cause of the mischief' was Jansenism and Gallicanism deep within the Church of France.

But this bull took an old controversy of theology and turned it into a new controversy of jurisdiction. The question ceased to be of the theology of grace or of good works. It became a question whether or not a solemn bull must be accepted, whatever it meant. Therefore *Unigenitus* had as one consequence a new debate on the limits or nature of the teaching authority of the Pope within the Catholic Church. At one end professors even in Sicilian seminaries taught that General Councils were supreme over Popes, and used *Unigenitus* to show how Popes could err. At the other end began, in the second quarter of the century, and as a direct consequence of the attacks upon *Unigenitus*, a serious modern discussion of the idea of the Pope's infallibility.

Unigenitus turned the Jansenism of Port-Royal from a French debate about religion into a question of European importance.

The debate on infallibility

Catholic theorists of Church authority, when confuting Wycliffites or Hussites in the later centuries of the Middle Ages, tried to define the nature of the Pope's authority, and rested upon the text of the New Testament that the faith of St. Peter cannot fail. Some who wanted to confute Protestants made use of the conviction that the see of Rome cannot err. Towards the end of the sixteenth century Spanish schoolmen began to use the hitherto unaccustomed word *infallibility* to describe the much older idea. In the later Counter-Reformation Cardinal Bellamine was the standard

---

[21] Gazier, 2.125.   [22] Pastor, xxxiii.313.

authority in treating the teaching office of the Roman see, and did not yet use the word infallibility as a key-word. But by the end of the seventeenth century it began to be the word used to describe a teaching authority which could not err. With the French claim that General Councils were above Popes, theologians needed to consider the nature of infallibility, its part in the teaching of the whole Church against which the gates of hell could not prevail, its limits or extent. They sought to determine what conditions must be fulfilled before the Church knew that the Pope spoke infallibly, and whether this promise of truth extended only to statements of Christian doctrine accepted by Catholic tradition, or reached also to matters which affected such statements. If the Pope condemned doctrines of Quesnel, was he infallible simply in the truth of the doctrines, or was he infallible also when he said that these were the doctrines of Quesnel, i.e. was he unerring about the fact as well as about the truth? When he made a man a saint, was it part of Christian faith that the new saint was a saint?

Everywhere the battle over *Unigenitus* caused a decline in the reputation of the see of Rome as a teacher of doctrinal truth. These debates over infallibility were not widespread in their influence. Either they were weapons in a public quarrel, or they were matters for lectures by Italian and Spanish professors of divinity. Though they had their importance to the later course of the debate during the nineteenth century, they were not yet of high religious importance among many Catholic laymen.

The disagreement was partly national. Few French or German writers defended papal infallibility during the eighteenth century. In the Italian and Spanish schools it was commonly defended. *Unigenitus* brought into the open a hitherto latent argument about the nature of authority and truth. This was to be important a century later. The work of the most widely read Italian defender of the Pope's infallibility, St. Alfonso Liguori, was republished in time to affect the Vatican Council of 1869–70, when papal infallibility was defined as a dogma of Christian faith.

Why Liguori's treatise was important is characteristic of the entire force of papal action in the Church. He put it inside his textbook to guide confessors. Not a theory of the lecture-room, nor a debate between academics, but a necessary way of being sure of those truths which were the foundation of moral decision—this was why Liguori was read where professors were not, and made the link between the idea of infallibility and a people's religion. Germans and French thought it untrue, or unimportant in devotion. Liguori and his successors thought it so central to right devotion that it could not but be true.

Yet, even in the far south of Italy, *Unigenitus* cast its long shadow over the Pope's authority. A cleric of Catania in Sicily said to a German traveller, 'We feel free from the chains which bound us so long. We no longer judge a man by his creed, but by his ability and his heart. We laugh at the infallibility of the Church, and of those who want to order us what to believe.'[23]

The Chinese Rites

In these same years when a Roman decision failed to make peace in France, a less troublesome but very awkward matter came out of China for a decision.

From the second quarter of the seventeenth century Catholic missionaries in China were divided about the attitude to adopt towards Chinese customs connected with the cult of ancestors, and about the words which might be used to translate into Chinese such words as *God*. The Jesuits always sought to go as far as they could in using the religious instincts or aspirations of the non-Christians whom they wished to persuade of the Christian truth. They used Chinese classical literature, and sought whatever was best in the ethics of Confucius. They supposed that the partial truths were memories of God's primitive revelation of himself to mankind. The friars, on the other hand, preached an uncompromising faith which rebutted the 'worship' of ancestors, regarded non-Christian rites as superstitions, and saw in Confucius nothing but a teacher of error. The Jesuits wanted Chinese Christianity not to look like a European import but to be truly Chinese. The Dominicans and Franciscans wanted Christianity to be pure, and untouched by Chinese superstition. Both sides behaved heroically and had their martyrs. Both sides conducted the argument with a growing bitterness. The missionary methods of the Jesuits were far the more successful, for educated Chinese could be brought to see Christianity as the fulfilment of their higher non-Christian aspirations. But the friars suspected that the faith to which Jesuits led their Chinese converts was hardly Christian.

This internal Catholic controversy became notorious in all Europe when in his fifth *Provincial Letter* Pascal assailed the Jesuits for allowing Chinese Christians to practise idolatry.

The Jesuits accepted that their converts might perform the customary rites connected with the worship of ancestors. They denied that these were idolatrous. In their view the rites were social and not religious; or, so far as they were religious, were no more than that reverence for parents and

[23] Tuzet, 485.

grandparents which every Christian should properly fulfil. They had this in their favour, that by reason of their attitude they made strenuous efforts to penetrate Chinese literature and the Chinese mind, which they understood far better than their opponents.

Distance hampered Rome. A Dominican deputy appeared out of the East accusing Jesuits of letting converts hide a crucifix among the flowers when they venerated their ancestors according to Chinese practice. The charge would be laid before the Jesuits who after investigation would report it unfounded—but three years of delay, in travelling and enquiry, might elapse. Rome often had to decide on insufficient evidence, and vary its mind when further evidence arrived.

Settlement became urgent when a French vicar-apostolic of Foukien, Maigrot, who reached China in 1683, pronounced vigorously against the rites with the intention of making Rome reconsider its permissive attitude, and with the result that the university of Paris (1700) condemned the rites publicly. In Rome the commissions of enquiry worked deliberately, struggling to understand a strange and distant culture and the reports of contradictory witnesses. In the same year 1700 the Jesuits persuaded a friendly Chinese emperor in Peking, Kanghi, to state officially that the honours paid to Confucius and to ancestors were purely social and had no religious content.

But by now the affair of the rites was caught into a wider argument. What should have been decided as an internal question of missionary method, became part of the mighty battle in France between Jesuit and Jansenist. A Dominican, de Navarrete, had published at Madrid an extreme indictment of Jesuit methods in China. The book was useful to Frenchmen who needed to indict Jesuit methods in everything. Therefore other pressures began to fall upon Rome. The settlement must be conditioned not only by the facts of China, but by political strife in France, or by the desire of Catholic apologists to free themselves from a handicap in the debate with Protestants. Cardinal de Naoilles of Paris wrote to the Pope that he must act if they were to stop Protestant accusations that Rome tolerated idolatry in China.

In 1704 Clement XI condemned much Jesuit practice in the Chinese rites. In particular he condemned all ritual homage to Confucius, and the forms of veneration before the tablets of ancestors. The cardinals of the Inquisition were determined to avoid not only superstition but anything that looked like superstition. Clement XI worked hard at the evidence, and showed that same willingness to take a very difficult decision which he showed in *Unigenitus*. His attitude was articulate. The missions must not be suspected of superstition. To the argument that thus he risked destroying the missions, he replied that the missionaries could not be hampered by losing a probable source of corruption in their endeavours and a sure occasion of strife among themselves.[24]

Implemented, the decree made revolution in the missions. Clement appointed his legate in China, the Frenchman Charles Tournon, to carry it into practice. In December 1705 the Emperor Kanghi courteously received Tournon in Peking. By March 1706 the Chinese Christians of Peking suspected the legate of wanting to abolish their customs. In December 1706 the emperor turned against all missionaries who would not accept the Chinese rites, and two months afterwards expelled the papal legate to Macao where in 1710 he died, newly made cardinal. Clement confirmed the prohibitions by two more strenuous decrees (1710, 1715). An attempt to carry out in China the decree of 1715 produced numerous apostasies and had small success among Chinese Christians, who continued, unless of low social class, to use the rites. When the decree of 1715 was known the Chinese government ordered (1717) missionaries to be expelled, churches destroyed, and converts forced to abjure. Some missionaries stopped celebrating sacraments because they felt bound by Rome not to administer sacraments to persons whom they knew to be practising the rites. More of them celebrated the sacraments out of pity for their people, and hesitatingly disregarded the authority of Rome. The state of mind among the missionaries was of pathos or despair, as they watched the Church built with infinite labour over a century crumbling before their eyes.

Under threats from the emperor, another papal legate Mezzabarba (1721) allowed concessions to the missionaries, for example that purely civil rites for the dead are permitted, including the laying out of food, lighting of candles, and burning of incense before tablets or before the grave, and the cult of Confucius so far as it is a civil ceremony. The permissions stated that Clement XI's decree was still valid, but effectively cancelled its force. But they were too late to recover the trust of the Chinese authorities, and were instantly controversial in Rome. For the rest of the eighteenth century the missions worked at best on sufferance from the Chinese government, for Christianity was banned officially, and at worst in conditions of martyrdom.

On 11 July 1742 Pope Benedict XIV issued the bull *Ex quo*, confirmed the decree of Clement XI, ordered that for the sake of a pure Christianity

---

[24] De Noailles to Clement XI 1701 in Pastor xxxiii, 414; Clement XI to the king of Portugal, 1716, *Epistolae et Brevia*, 2106–8.

free from superstition no one should seek to evade its force, and condemned the permissions accorded by the legate Mezzabarba. This final
bull left no loophole. A Jesuit in Peking, then the chief Chinese astronomer,
thought that it made no difference. 'By now', he wrote home, 'Christianity in China consists only in a few poor people who are hardly able to
pay for food and lodging, and are very far from capable of paying for
sacrifices to their ancestors, or of building temples in their honour.'[25]

The effectiveness of a Pope's action during the eighteenth century is illustrated dramatically by the contrast between *Unigenitus* and the settlement
of the Chinese rites. In both cases Pope Clement XI issued a bull unacceptable to a strong minority. In the case of *Unigenitus* he attempted to narrow
the limits of doctrine possible for loyal Catholics. The attempt failed because the traditions of thought on which Catholicism rested were too
strong and too broad, its substance needed to be withdrawn, and thereby
left a bull which must be 'accepted' but which restricted no one's freedom
of thought. In China the prohibitions were so effective that they destroyed
a young Church almost totally.

    In both cases 'politics' entered the decision. The Pope condemned the
ideas of Quesnel's book because King Louis XIV was determined to kill
Jansenism. In the affair of the rites the interests of the Chinese Church
must be sacrificed to the interests of the European Church. Politically and
ecclesiastically the Church must at all costs be cleared of a Protestant and
Jansenist imputation that it sanctioned superstition. Even the Jesuit general
came at last to the belief that the Society's name must be freed from this
incubus on their European work. But in another aspect the settlement of
the Chinese rites showed the Roman congregations of enquiry in a light
which elicits admiration. They wished to cleanse the Church, not just
because Protestants accused them of uncleanness. It was the heritage of the
Counter-Reformation. They invited grave loss in worldly terms for the
sake of an ideal of purity in faith and religious practice.

    Both bulls show the confidence of Rome in its own authority. To settle
a theological argument which lasted for centuries, or a missionary argument which lasted a century, demanded in the court of appeal a conviction that it had the right to decide and would be obeyed by loyal Catholics. Clement XI worked for hour after hour at his desk studying the
questions and drafting the decisions. In both cases he received warning
from members of the Curia that what he sought to do could lead to
calamity. But a majority of the Curia cardinals had no more doubt than

[25] *Epistolae anecdotae R.P. Augustini Hallerstein,* cited *D.T.C.* 2.2.2389.

Clement XI that they had the duty and vocation to determine these controversies. When historians write of the weakness of the papacy during the eighteenth century, they overlook the ingrained habit of authority inherited from the Middle Ages.

Both these decisions had the same important side-effect: to lower the European reputation of Jesuits. *Unigenitus* was taken to be approval, the settlement of the rites to be disapproval, of doctrine and methods associated with the Society of Jesus. But the manner both of approval and of disapproval reflected upon Catholic Europe's opinion about Jesuits.

Innocent XIII Conti (Pope 1721–4) and Benedict XIII Orsini (Pope 1724–30)

In 1700 the cardinals elected a young and effective Pope. The next three Conclaves elected men aged sixty-five (within five days of sixty-six), seventy-five, and seventy-eight. The sixty-six-year-old Conti had been obliged to resign the see of Viterbo two years before on grounds of health. He was fat, suffered from gravel, and was not expected to live long. These contrasts with the youth of Clement XI were not mere accident.

Any new Pope gave a chance for a change in policy. Clement XI was never able to recognize the Austrian conquest of the kingdom of Naples, though probably he would have welcomed the chance. His predicament with France and Spain made it unwise. The new Pope had never been committed to France, was not liked by Spain, and was on good terms with the Austrians. Almost at once he recognized Austrian rule in south Italy in return for Austrian recognition of his own right as feudal suzerain. It was his only important political act.

Benedict XIII was a holy and lively old Dominican. What struck observers was not his age but his profession, for he was a friar. Cardinals felt doubt about electing friars. They were thought to be too severe, or to have no knowledge of the world, or to be unwilling for the humane compromises of government. Cardinals in Conclave often respected a monk or friar but had small desire to give him their votes. Yet Benedict XIII was not the only Friar-Pope of the eighteenth century and two of the four Popes after the Napoleonic Revolution were members of religious orders. As late as the Conclave of 1846 cries of 'No friars no foreigners' were heard on the streets of Rome during a Conclave.

Benedict XIII (1649–1730) was the heir of the Duke of Gravina and grandson on his mother's side of a Frangipani who was Duke of Grumo. Despite opposition in the family and visits to the then Pope by his mother and uncle, he renounced his dukedom and became a Dominican at the age of eighteen. In the marriage contract of his younger brother, his mother arranged with the Pope that he be made a cardinal, and he became a cardinal at the uncanonical age of twenty-two. This made no difference to his fervour or to his keeping of the friar's rule. At the age of twenty-five he was reforming the diocese of Siponto, frequent in visitations, synods, missions, and creating a model *Mons Pietatis* as a savings bank which was imitated by other bishops in the kingdom of Naples. On sanctuary and exemption he was rigid; and because this rigidity bred local quarrels, Rome moved him (aged thirty) to the see of Cesena in the north, and then back (aged thirty-seven) to the archbishopric of Benevento, where the archbishop was also the governor. Here he found fights between barons and churchmen, a clergy doing as they liked, about a hundred clergy with concubines, a cathedral chapter of little use, and a limping civil service. In his reign at Benevento he followed the model of the Counter-Reformation and revered St. Charles Borromeo as his guide to the rule of a diocese. Within ten years the clergy had no concubines, peace reigned between barons and churchmen, the property of the *mensa* was inventoried and organized. He brought in several more monasteries and nunneries, invited the Jesuits to hold annual missions, consecrated numerous churches and altars, held two provincial synods and frequent diocesan synods, printed a beautiful folio volume of synodical decrees, founded a *Mons Pietatis* as a lending bank to repair ruined churches and monasteries—and all with an extraordinary fervour like one coming out of a past world which was everyone's ideal and hardly anyone's practice. He experienced mystic ecstasies, was obsessed about relics, protested to Pope and king of Naples against the teaching of atomic physics at the university of Naples. An earthquake brought down the bishop's palace at Benevento and almost killed him, killing the man with whom he was talking; and the escape was widely regarded as miraculous.

In Conclaves he was always a leader of the *zelanti* party, determined to have no truck with the powers. Perhaps he was a saint, perhaps he was too complicated to be a saint, certainly he was the best type of Counter-Reformation bishop. His sternness and ascetic life made him the butt of malice and gossip.

A bishop who was a saint of the Counter-Reformation could still be a superb diocesan bishop, at least on papal territory. But now they elected him Pope. Habsburg fought Bourbon in the Conclave and blocked. The cardinals must seek a neutral. Their candidate must have had no previous political responsibility or he could not be seen as neutral. He must also be old or very old to give a hope of a new election. Cardinal Orsini fitted the criterion. Here was a deeply respected man, successful administrator of a diocese, otherworldly, a man of prayer and not at all of politics, and already seventy-five years old.

The Pope was a bishop. But the office of the Pope was not at all like the office of a bishop. The question was whether the ideal of a godly pastor, as framed in the mid-sixteenth century, and still applicable in a diocese of central Italy, was not an anachronism in a Pope; or, if not an anachronism, whether these were the only qualities which an international institution needed, and whether the qualities now necessary to a Pope between Habsburg and Bourbon were compatible with the qualities which the Cardinal Archbishop of Benevento had eminently.

Benedict XIII was a true friar. His face was stern and ascetic. He refused to be carried into St. Peter's but went on foot. He continued to treat the Dominican general as his superior and kissed his hand. He refused to use the papal apartments in the Vatican and for a time occupied simpler and smaller rooms until he built himself a hermitage with whitewashed walls and without a view. At meals several times a week he waited on thirteen poor men. He personally visited hospitals, accepted invitations to consecrate bishops or churches, heard confessions, sometimes taught the catechism to a class of little children. He was a truly good pastor.

This he saw as the Pope's function—to be pastor to the people of Rome; as Christ's chief minister, to be an example to all the ministers of Christ. He knew that he had no experience of business, and disliked its secularity. For his first six weeks he refused to do business. The secretary of state found access to him difficult, for he was too intent on his prayers or his ministrations. If people urged him for the sake of his health not to attend so many and such long services, he would say that a Pope should die with his cope on his back.

Therefore the papacy was ruled by someone else. The Pope resembled the general of an army who cannot direct the battle because he likes to be down among the troops and to show privates how to fill sandbags. The cardinal who gathered power was neither of the two usual delegates of a Pope, cardinal-nephew, or secretary of state. It was Niccolò Coscia who while a teenager had been picked out at a visitation in the diocese of Benevento, was drawn to take orders, and thenceforward always in the private service of the archbishop. Coscia became a cardinal in June 1725, and in September was given the right of succession to the see of Benevento. Their relations were such that men suspected a bewitching when the two first met.

Pope Benedict XIII trusted Coscia absolutely. He left all business in his hands, and would not listen to those who criticized. Coscia ran the States of the Church with a team, almost a gang, of Beneventan cronies, all of whom made money. The administration of the Church under the saintly Pope was the most corrupt in modern history. It had all the traditional evils of nepotism without any nephews. The story was believed that Prince Borghese gave Coscia 10,000 *scudi* to have his son (aged thirty-three and not eminent) made a cardinal. No taint rubbed off upon the Friar-Pope. He moved simply and quietly through Rome refusing to listen to evil about any man, unaware of the wickedness of the world. The ambassadors' reports show that they felt nothing but contempt, and their attitude to the incapacity of the man at times spilled over into scorn of his office. Cardinal Boncompagni said of him: 'He was like the holy sepulchre in the hands of the Turks.' His successor but one, Pope Benedict XIV, said of him: 'He had not the first idea how to rule.' The failure did not make the cardinals infer that Popes ought not to be saints. It strengthened their feelings that Popes should not be friars. Yet four Conclaves later, driven by their needs and the Catholic powers and the entanglements of that day they found a way out by electing another friar.

And yet, if the corruption and maladministration of the Papal States are passed over, the old man's pontificate was surprisingly successful in spiritual matters. The Roman synod of 1725 (see p. 115) was important in diocesan life for all its ineffective provisions. Because he was a Dominican he stood by the Augustinian tradition in the doctrine of grace. His brief to the Dominicans that the bull *Unigenitus* did not condemn the Augustinian tradition or St. Thomas Aquinas helped to lessen the terrible conflicts with the French Jansenists, though less happily than the Jansenists hoped, because a bull also declared that the teaching of St. Thomas Aquinas must not be confused with that of Jansen or Quesnel who were in error, and because the minutes of the Roman provincial Council recognized *Unigenitus* as a rule of faith. In his agreements with the States Benedict XIII put the needs of the spiritual above historic temporal rights, and was inclined to concede largely, a policy which disturbed many cardinals but which eased the old tensions of Clement XI's day between papacy and Catholic powers.

These concessions were smoothed because agents of the powers poured gifts into the pockets of underlings of the Pope whom he did not know to be corrupt. But they fitted the Pope's attitudes. He was too otherworldly to care much about temporal or historic rights. He was the first modern Pope to give the spiritual a total preference over the temporal.

The one humiliating failure with governments touched a spiritual matter, and thereby showed how in the Pope's office the occupant must find it less easy than might be expected to compromise in the indifferent things of this world while he refused to compromise in things of the spirit.

The Pope in the Middle Ages most celebrated for exercising authority over kings was Hildebrand who became Gregory VII. For he forced the Holy Roman Emperor Henry IV to wait in the snow at the castle of Canossa in order to receive absolution and so avoid deposition. In the beginning of the seventeenth century (1606) Pope Paul V made Gregory VII a saint. Pope Benedict XIII (1728) made the feast of Gregory VII a feast of the whole Catholic Church.

It could hardly be claimed that the canonization of a saint was not purely spiritual; or that the extension of a feast day trespassed upon secular prerogatives; or that the forms of service sanctioned for the day were not solely within the Pope's jurisdiction. One of the lessons at the service of nocturns ran thus: 'Against the ungodly efforts of the Emperor Henry he remained strong and stable, like a wall protecting the house of Israel; and when Henry acted wickedly, he excommunicated him, deprived him of his kingdom and released his subjects from their allegiance.'

This lesson had nothing in it that was not true, if the judgement on morality was made from Rome. The Viceroy of Naples regarded it as dangerous, and so reported to his master the Austrian Emperor. The Catholic government of Sicily and the Protestant government of Holland each forbade the publication under heavy fines. Venice protested to Rome. Six French bishops forbade their dioceses to use the service which the Pope had ordered. Belgium prohibited the use of the lessons. In Paris the police stopped the breviary from being printed. Pope Benedict XIII[26] declared invalid all these decrees of governments against his liturgy.

Some years later (1753) a very different kind of Pope, Benedict XIV, one of the skilful statesmen to occupy the throne of St. Peter, concerned himself with the beatification of Cardinal Bellarmine, who stood in the minds of Europe for the theory of the indirect power of the Pope, for the sake of souls, even in matters that were not directly spiritual. When the French government said that if Bellarmine were made a saint they would never recognize him, Benedict XIV gave way with a good grace, saying that he would not go that way 'so long as the bull is on the rampage'.[27]

---

[26] *Bull. Rom.* 22.860.
[27] Benedict XIV to Tencin (ed. Heeckeren), 19 Sept. 1753, 2. 287–8, 292.

Clement XII Corsini (Pope 1730–40)

Corsini came of a rich and famous family of Florentine bankers, with vast possessions in the kingdom of Naples and much influence both in Tuscany and the south. For a moment he looked like a Renaissance prince, a Medici or Farnese or Borgia from the old world, leading Italy in politics and culture by uniting the Pope's office to the ramified power of a princely family.

The ducal families of old Rome exercised very little pressure upon Popes. The ancient names still appeared in the college of cardinals— Colonna, Medici, Orsini, Corsini, Chigi, Doria; and when a Colonna was put aside at a Conclave his brother-cardinals behaved to him with a particular courtesy not to offend his family. Here were two Popes in succession, one an Orsini and the next a Corsini.

Everywhere in Europe dukes were still important. But now their importance was more social and historic than political. These two Popes were the last two Popes of the kind. All the Popes of the eighteenth century were noble Italians, but Italy extended far the word *nobleman*. Pope Clement XIV Ganganelli was son of a general practitioner near Rimini but his mother came of minor nobility.

Clement XII Corsini was seventy-eight at his election, already sick and going blind. Two years later he was blind and suffered grievously from gout, later still from hernia. His weakness and blindness forced him to leave business to his nephew Cardinal Neri Corsini and his hand was perforce guided to sign papers. In his last years he was always prone. The Curia expected the Pope to die before long, and therefore did as little as possible; Cardinal Corsini was constitutionally timid; and since the Pope foiled expectation by living ten years, and ten years was too long to mark time, the consequence was lack of direction at a time of European war when Italy was again a battlefield. At one point of 1736 the Papal States were hardly under the Pope's rule. Corsini money and influence prevented the war, fought across the wounded recumbent body of the Pope's secular monarchy, from being quite so appalling a disaster.

Benedict XIV Lambertini (Pope 1740–58)

This was the Pope under whom the changing nature of the Pope's office first became clear. He was elected after the longest Conclave of the century, more than six months, not because anyone specially wanted him but because the cardinals were exhausted.

Benedict XIV was at the opposite pole of Popes from Benedict XIII. The two Benedicts shared a common background in a diocesan bishopric, Lambertini being an excellent Bishop of Ancona and then Archbishop of Bologna. His excellence was founded on principles different from the Borromean ideals of Benedict XIII. He had long experience in the Roman administration, and was the expert in a rugged territory, that of applying the decrees of the Council of Trent to modern circumstances. He was truly learned, an able lawyer, a man of imperturbable common sense. As secretary of the Congregation of the Council which was now the most powerful of the curial offices, he learnt the business of adapting old and seemingly rigid rules to situations which they no longer fitted. Hence, unlike Benedict XIII who could not understand compromise, he was by instinct and training an adjuster, a man who understood precisely how lawyers get round nonsensical rulings and make them useful. He was a good man, and devout, and respected mystics. But he did not eschew crude words in his conversation, could shock by his humour about serious subjects, and amid the corruptions of Cardinal Coscia had profited without himself becoming corrupt. He was so unceremonious that behind his back a critic said that he was a clown.[28] He took vain resolutions to cure his own slang or outspokenness. If Benedict XIII was the Pope who ruled by mystical piety, Benedict XIV ruled by earthly common sense and willingness to adapt to hard facts.

As a lawyer who understood Roman administration, and who was engaged in a successful remaking of parish structures, he used the Roman curial offices as his instrument of change. For the first time in papal history the secretary of state became a minister like the secretary of state with whom the modern world is familiar. Benedict XIII had no notion how to choose men, Benedict XIV surrounded himself with wise advisers. In international affairs he approached the sovereigns with gentleness. He was willing in the various Concordats[29] to hand over much of what they demanded, without resistance, shocking old-fashioned cardinals by his yielding, putting religious interests above political. In Church affairs he made possible the lessening of the number of feast days, worked on the reform of the Breviary to be rid of legends, stood up for the rights of Indians, slightly weakened the rigidity of the ban on usury (1745), brought up to date the Index of prohibited books and made the work of that office less inefficient and less capricious, ended the ban on writings to defend the Copernican system of astronomy. Though he was not successful as a politician, no Pope did more to adapt the structures of the Counter-Reformation to an age of looming revolution.

He was fortunate. The peace of Aix-la-Chapelle in 1748 at last ended the near half-century of war which fought over the soil of Italy. The Seven Years War (1756–63) concerned the Pope indirectly; but did not disturb Italy, which during the thirty-eight years after 1748 enjoyed the longest time of peace which the country has yet known.

Benedict XIV was a man of the Curia who developed the Curia. During his rule the authority of the college of cardinals took a further plunge. The more effective the administration, the less needed the ancient cabinet. He consulted the cardinals in the customary way, especially when great public decisions had to be taken. But he was hardly ever impressed with the report of a committee of cardinals, and preferred a more expert mode of government.

With some of his entourage he won the reputation, especially as he grew older, of doing nothing. This mainly meant that for a Pope he gave an unusual amount of time to study, still preparing books or illustrating his own briefs with rare information.

A Concordat was a treaty between a Pope and a state about the government of the Church in that state. It usually meant that the Pope agreed to give the sovereign certain rights which 'normally' belonged to the Church —like the right to nominate bishops or abbots for election—in return for guarantees from the State to recognize traditional claims by the Church, like the exemption of clergy from taxation or secular lawcourts.

Arrangements of this kind went far back into the Middle Ages. The most celebrated of all Concordats was the agreement between Pope Leo X and the French king (1516) which gave the king such extensive rights in selecting the high officers of the Church that it conditioned the separate Catholic development of the Church in France.

The eighteenth and early nineteenth centuries were the supreme age of Concordats, and Benedict XIV the chief Pope among makers of Concordats. Like the governments of France or Prussia or England, Catholic states tried to set up more modern systems of law and administration. They wanted an efficient civil service, an equitable system of taxation, an abolition of local rights which obstructed the justice or the prosperity of the whole state. To achieve these ends they must take more power over the Catholic Church in their territory. If this was to be done without schism or turmoil or popular emotion, it must be done by Concordat, that is,

Popes must be persuaded to agree. How they were to be persuaded depended upon the political influence, military force, unscrupulousness, and stability of the persuader. If the Pope could not be persuaded, he must be cajoled; if not cajoled, his servants must be bribed; if bribery failed he must be bullied, by throwing out his nuncio, seizing ecclesiastical lands, or in last resort by moving an army into the Pope's helpless outlying domains like Avignon, or Benevento, or Comacchio, or Ferrara. If all these failed, then the threat alone remained, to make a schism like Henry VIII of England. This last threat was on occasion feared in Rome. But every informed person knew it to be violent bluff. A Catholic king who turned Protestant might not be long on his throne.

However the Concordat was to be got, it must be got; for without it government could not be improved. And most Concordats were agreed with relative harmony especially, to the alarm of some of his cardinals, under Benedict XIV. They were in the interests of both sides, however long the negotiations over detail.

The advantage lay with the State. For the movement of the century was always in the direction of ending more and more exemptions which the Church claimed—exemptions of clergy from secular courts, rights of sanctuary, tax-free status, monks' prisons, bishops' prisons. The strength of the State was often shown by its ability to wait. If it failed to persuade one pope to agree, it would succeed with the next—or at least with the next after the next. Thus Concordats were a series of concessions step by step, which the Pope allowed because he saw that only in this way could he preserve other freedoms of the Church in that territory. Every agreement fenced the Pope's sphere of action a little more narrowly. Every agreement fixed the surviving rights of Rome a little more firmly in the laws of that land for a time, but only for a time.

The secretary of state

The office of a Pope's private secretary became a public rather than private office early in the sixteenth century. He was called *secretarius intimus*, personal secretary; but under Pius IV (1559–65) Cardinal Charles Borromeo, who was the cardinal-nephew, strengthened the position as subordinate to the cardinal-nephew. He began sometimes to be called *secretarius maior*, chief secretary; and about 1580 we find the description secretary of state, a title established by 1605. He became necessary because of the nuncios. From the capitals the nuncios were expected to send reports once a week. Documents poured into Rome and someone had to read, analyse, and report. This was a case where the Foreign Office did not create the embassies, the embassies created the Foreign Office.

Thus the office grew in weight because this was the man who possessed the information, and without whose aid no advice to the Pope could be well grounded. Because he was in origin the personal and private secretary, he always had direct access to the Pope. The staff started small. About 1570 his office had a staff of five, one of whom was an archivist. But from 1644 the office was marked as established because its holder henceforth was always a cardinal.

In the forty years before 1692 the weight of the office depended on the Pope's wishes and the existence or non-existence of a cardinal-nephew. As business grew, the civil service became less of a group of personal assistants. This was symbolized by the transfer of archives. Since the secretary of state was often the lieutenant of the cardinal-nephew, the papers ended up in the cardinal's family; so that to this day reliable files of historical documents are in the collections known as Barberini or Farnese, Chigi or Borghese, after the names of Roman aristocrats.

To select a cardinal-nephew was to select from a much smaller circle of candidates than the group of men available when the Pope selected a secretary of state. Cardinal-nephews were not usually chosen for efficiency. Though some were efficient, some were idle or incapable. Therefore the secretary of state took more and more business which the nephew could not or would not manage.

Because he lived in the Vatican palace, and inherited functions of the cardinal-nephews, the secretary of state governed the papal palace and all its offices. This shows how in this post were mixed the personal and public characters of government. The old world could not easily distinguish between the private household of a king and his public rule. As they were now framed, the functions of the secretary of state showed traces of that ancient unity.

By 1721 when the Austrian cardinal vetoed the secretary of state because Austria wanted a change of policy, the office grew near its full stature. A sign of this increased weight was the interest of the powers. They now planned to get not only the Pope they wanted but a secretary of state who would help their policy. When—as happened invariably—they could not get the Pope best for their interests, they tried to compensate by getting a secretary of state whom they liked.

The secretary of state was never all-powerful, even under a Pope who had no desire for the business. But now he had both chains of command in his hands. He was ex officio Prime Minister of the Papal States and thereby held the secular strings of that power which was supposed to be despotic and was in fact weak. And controlling the system of nuncios, he had the influence which comes to a man who has expert information on delicate and insoluble problems which came to the Pope as an international person.

Under Clement XII Corsini the secretary of state was less important in government than two or three other cardinals.

Benedict XIV recognized what had happened and governed the Church through the curial offices with the secretary of state at their head. He chose excellent men, Valenti Gonzaga 1740–56, though ill from 1751, Alberico Archinto 1756–8. Valenti Gonzaga was the first secretary of state whose office and function manifestly resembles the office and function of the holders in the nineteenth and twentieth centuries. He opened the Sapienza college to new sciences like physics and chemistry; mapped the Papal State and tried to foster its trade and its ports; was a patron of learned men.

Nevertheless the bureau was still primitive. Most of the staff were paid in kind, some worked long years without pay in hope of a post, they accepted 'gifts' for services and were comfortable. Valenti Gonzaga had a dwarf who followed him devotedly. Within the bureau was still the 'honourable forger' (*falsario*), an office found elsewhere in the *ancien régime*, as at the court of King Louis XIV of France, with the special work of imitating the handwriting of the Pope when he needed to write a personal letter.[30]

This development of the Curia was necessary to effective papal action in the Church and the world. Cardinals so resented what was done that the next Pope, Clement XIII Rezzonico, made them a reconciling speech, which sounded like the words of a constitutional monarch:

I have had enough experience of the task [he had been Pope for fifteen months] to know that its problems are beyond the capacity of mere mortals to solve, let alone myself. I know that I shall have God's help. But I also need your cooperation and counsel. Your wisdom and experience will help me to settle business. You will be useful to the State, help me to good advice, strengthen me if I am weak, and comfort me when I get anxious.[31]

The speech was well intended but could not stop the way in which business ran into the permanent offices. Pope Rezzonico's secretary of state Torrigiani was as powerful as either of the secretaries of Benedict XIV.

Even after the end of Benedict XIV's reign cardinals occasionally complained that Popes were wrong to have instituted the curial offices called

[30] *R.S.C.I.* 1976, 207.   [31] *Bull. Cont.* 1.250.

Congregations because they made for government by secret decision of one or two men instead of government by consensus of cardinals. In 1769 a cardinal complained, not merely that the Congregation of the Council absorbed the power which rightly belonged to the whole consistory of cardinals, but that if the president and secretary of that Congregation agreed, they acted without even holding a meeting of the Congregation which at least contained a few cardinals.[32]

For all its primitive staffing, exiguous membership, and lack of adequate pay or curious modes of payment, the Curia was more centralized in 1769 than thirty years before, and this was in good part due to the most curial of the popes of the eighteenth century.

A further sign is a change in the place of the cardinal-nephew.

The cardinal-nephew

In the age when loyalty was the loyalty of the family or clan, and not of the nation or the State, nearly every ruler used his kin to help him govern; for his sons, and nephews, and even his consort, were those whose loyalty was least in doubt, tied to him by the bonds of interest as well as nature. The 'absolute ruler' of the seventeenth and eighteenth centuries was partly protected from the corruption of these family needs because he was a hereditary ruler and his son or daughter must constitutionally succeed. Secular rulers achieved the supreme act of 'nepotism' as a necessary part of the constitution; confessed by all to be so, desired by all to avert praetorian struggles for power or civil war at the death of a monarch. Even the Holy Roman Empire, in which the Emperor was elected, achieved this happy state from about 1500, since the Habsburg ruler could almost always get his heir elected to succeed him, and thereby turned the Empire into a domain hereditary by custom though not by right. Family pride and loyalty was in it; but stability of the State was in it too, and for the peoples that stability was a boon which they sometimes felt they could hardly over-value; as when England 'restored' King Charles II.

Like the Holy Roman Empire, the papacy was an elective monarchy. Unlike the Emperor, the Pope had the chance of appointing at least some of the men who would elect his successor. But he rarely had the chance to choose a majority of those who would elect his successor. When Pius IX died in 1878, he had chosen all but four of the sixty-four cardinals qualified to elect his successor. But the length of his reign was unique. Fifteen years was a long reign for a normal Pope. He could at best leave only a strong

[32] Pirelli's Diary, 42, 163.

minority of cardinals to influence an election which would not repudiate his policy.

Not that any Pope had the least notion of turning his monarchy into a 'hereditary' state, hereditary from uncle to nephew because he must be celibate. Hereditary descent from uncle to nephew was not unknown to Christianity, as with the patriarchate of the Assyrian Christians. At no point, even in the darkest century of the earlier Middle Ages, did the papal office come anywhere near this kind of institution. The danger lay rather in Roman nobles who wanted to turn the lands of the Church into secular principalities, not in the turning of the office.

To prevent bishops from converting their domains into hereditary estates was one of the motives of reformers of the Middle Ages who insisted on the celibacy of bishops and priests. That danger was averted. And yet it continued to appear in subtler forms. In the absence of loyalty to State or nation, and in the absence of a trained civil service, a Pope needed his family to administer his State. Like every other human institution, this system could go awry.

Moreover high considerations, whether of expediency or moral right, demanded that he look after his family. He was a monarch. The public did not care to see members of the 'royal' family living in squalor, and blamed a Pope who allowed it to occur. If a Pope took his nephew and gave him an important post in the administration, general opinion thought it natural and right, and only blamed the Pope if the young man proved to be corrupt or incompetent. Men did not reproach the Pope if he promoted his nephew from Siena; they blamed the Pope if he left his nephew in poverty at Siena. One of his moral duties was the fulfilment of the command to honour his family; and this moral duty usually coincided with his public duty. Until the middle of the seventeenth century the chief administrator of the Papal State under the Pope was generally, though not quite always, known as the cardinal-nephew. Until 1692 most people accepted that the hierarchy in the Pope's government was not (as later) Pope/secretary of state, but Pope/cardinal-nephew/secretary of state.

The system worked as well as, certainly no worse than, any other mode of administration in a theoretically absolute monarchy. It worked best with a Pope of not too aristocratic and not too plebeian origins. It risked trouble if the cardinals chose as Pope a member of a family powerful in Italy—Borgia, Medici, Farnese, or Barberini. For then the power structure of Italy was such that the member of the family who was Pope became the weightiest link in a chain of political influence across the Italian states. Under such Popes as these the place of the Pope as Italian monarch seemed to outsiders to take precedence of his place as spiritual leader among the nations. The States of the Church never recovered control over the duchy of Parma and Piacenza which in 1545 the Farnese Pope Paul III conferred upon his son Pierluigi; and when the male Farnese line died out in 1731 it passed to a branch of the Bourbon family. The Barberini Pope Urban VIII made one of his nephews prince of Palestrina (1630), who after the Pope's death needed to be chased out by an army. Palaces in Rome, like the Palazzo Farnese and the Palazzo Barberini, to this day bear witness to the wealth and power of papal families.

It could work equally ill—sometimes it could be worse—if the cardinals elected a Pope who sprang from lowly and simple stock. The office of the Pope was in one aspect the most democratic place in Europe. It was the only state where a man, born in a gutter, could rise by ability or by spirituality till he became a sovereign among the sovereigns of Europe. This was one important fact in distinguishing the office as essentially spiritual or ecclesiastical. When it happened it could produce a Pope of striking ability. But it could also produce a Pope who felt himself a stranger in his new environment, a child in the hands of mature politicians and men of the world. A good man whose life was largely passed in a monastery or in the study of canon law, might find himself thrust into a place of apparently despotic authority. Unlike Barberini or Farnese, his family needed help, they had to be fetched from the back streets. Surrounded by men inherited from his predecessor, men perhaps who disliked his election and were determined to resist his policy, caught up in a political web for which he had nothing but distrust or even fear, pressed by the stern messages of foreign princes demanding, he turned with relief to members of his family as the men whom he could trust; and since they came from as simple a background as himself, their ability or experience was rarely adequate to handle the affairs entrusted to them, and their consciousness of sudden access to riches presented temptation.

In the troubled seventeenth century the word *nepotism* became a bad word—the Barberini clan began to make it sound ill. But the Barberini were men of exceptional ability. And suddenly under Pope Innocent X (1644–55) it was a scandal. He tried nephews but found them incompetent, until the real power fell into the hands of an ugly domineering sister-in-law, Olimpia Maidalchini, without whose advice the Pope would do nothing and who was open to grateful presents from the powers. The idea of cardinal-nephew never recovered from this shock to the constitution. It was necessary for the next Pope, Alexander VII Chigi (1655–67) to declare on his election that he would have nothing to do with 'nepotism'.

'As Fabio Chigi,' he said, 'I had a family. As Alexander VII I have none. You won't find my new name anywhere in the baptismal registers of Siena.'[33] Though the idea is older, the word *nepotism* only became meaningful at that time. The *Oxford English Dictionary* marks in 1670 the first appearance of *nepotism* in the English language.

The problem was not easy. Pope Alexander VII's family lived modestly in Siena, and he forbade them to come to Rome. But soon it was represented to the Pope that it was improper and unseemly that he should be Pope while his relatives lived in poverty, indeed that his family had a *right* to be looked after and that he had a moral duty to help them— a majority of cardinals took this view. So the family came to Rome and soon were well endowed. But there was a difference. They were allowed little part in business. The office of secretary of state grew in authority. A majority of the world did not blame Alexander VII for looking to his family. They recognized his moral duty; and so far as administration went, people preferred dealing with a nephew to dealing with bureaucrats. They suspected a smell of the modern 'Curia' when it was only in embryo.

His successor but one again had to have a cardinal-nephew as chief lieutenant; not without comment. Public opinion in Rome was divided. Pope Innocent XI (1676–89) three times at least, planned a bull to denounce nepotism in Popes; but he could not persuade a majority of the cardinals to support the plan, which he therefore withdrew. But when the new Pope, Alexander VIII (1689–91) went back to direct rule by cardinal-nephew, the austere Innocent XII who followed him issued the bull of 1692 (*Romanum decet pontificem*) which is usually taken to mark the end of the system of government by cardinal-nephew and a momentous step in the rise of the secretary of state. The bull abolished various sinecures commonly held for nephews, and limited narrowly the amount of stipend or endowment which the nephew of a Pope might draw while his uncle was in office.

The bull of 1692 did not end the argument. In a theoretically absolute government the alternative to a *nephew* might be a *favourite*, and if confronted by this choice the cardinals knew which they preferred. Only three out of the eight Popes of the eighteenth century did not make their nephew or brother a cardinal, and two of those were the two friars. Clement XIV Ganganelli was asked, after his election in 1769, whether messengers should be sent to tell the family about his election, and replied: 'The moment a man becomes a friar he ceases to recognize that he

---

[33] Sforza Pallavicino, *Della Vita di Alessandro VII* (2 vols. Prato, 1839–40) I.280.

has a family.' Benedict XIII said the same in similar words.[34] But these two Friar-Popes were exceptions which proved a kind of rule. They were the two Popes of the century who took least notice of the college of cardinals. Both ruled, not by nephews but by favourites. When the Dominican Pope Benedict XIII was blind to the briberies of his Cardinal Coscia, some of the cardinals besought him to appoint a cardinal-nephew. They preferred a nephew to a favourite.

The bull *Romanum decet pontificem* of 1692 therefore struck at the system. But it was ended more by the development of the secretary of state's office and the civil service, than by any bull. They could not dispense with a cardinal-nephew until they accepted someone in his place.

The eighteenth-century cardinal-nephews varied much in their weight and power. None of them was any longer the exclusive head of the administration as under some popes before 1692. The cardinal-nephew of Pius VI Braschi hardly took much part but to enjoy his honour. The cardinal-nephew of Clement XII, Neri Corsini, was the head of the administration because his uncle was old and blind, and was quite like a cardinal-nephew of the previous century, controlling appointments and policy. But even he had to reckon with the secretary of state—who, however, was not influential under this Pope. Neri Corsini was the last of the old-fashioned cardinal-nephews. But the Corsini family was so rich, it did not need the traditional sin of nepotists, feathering the private nest.

How eminent the office, or place, of cardinal-nephew remained even in the high eighteenth century is shown by the saying of Cardinal Albani, who was prone to melancholy: 'A Pope's nephew dies twice—the second time like all men, the first time when his uncle dies.'[35]

The survival of the cardinal-nephew had an effect upon papal elections. The old cardinal-nephews were always the natural focus or centre of 'the old Pope's party' at a Conclave. This was the function which survived into the eighteenth century. At the Conclave of 1721 Cardinal Albani, nephew to the dead Pope, assured the imperialist leader that no one could be elected Pope without his consent. In this way the nephew stood for a measure of continuity in policy as the elective system sought to compensate by seeking a Pope who would have different qualities from those of his predecessor. Under Clement XII the cardinal-nephew consciously promoted cardinals to enable him to exercise a veto at the next election. At the Conclave of 1769 the nephew of the late Pope led the party of cardinals which was strong to maintain the tough policy of the late Pope.

[34] Pastor, xxxiv.185; xxxviii.94. [35] De Brosses, 2.177.

But he was an excellent man, and would have been a leader even if he had not been a nephew.

A nephew who was not a cardinal nor even a clergyman could still thrive, and public opinion thought that as the Pope's nephew he ought to thrive. The worst nepotist of the age was the last Pope of the century, Pius VI Braschi, whose nephew Duke Braschi made a fortune at negligible cost and built the Palazzo Braschi where now is housed the Museo di Roma. The money of Duke Braschi became notorious when his uncle the Pope appeared in person at a lawsuit over his right to a private inheritance. But in that age Italian opinion hardly thought it odd. It was a visiting English-woman Hester Piozzi who expressed her astonishment. And the English agent in Florence reported to Horace Walpole in England, how the Pope was held in utter contempt in Rome for his avarice.

The college of cardinals

The cardinals were not more than seventy, after the seventy elders whom Moses chose, and therefore a few less owing to vacancies caused by death. Occasionally the number sank below fifty. In 1686 they were only forty-three, but this was so unusual that the Pope was suspected of keeping numbers down in the hope of shortening the next Conclave.

Between three-quarters and five-sixths of the college was always Italian. Of the 342 cardinals appointed during the eighteenth century seventy-three were not Italian—higher than one-fifth.

Certain offices were always held by cardinals; for example the heads under the Pope of the Inquisition, the Congregation of the Council, the Congregation of Bishops and Regulars, but not invariably the heads of all the departments in the Curia, not even that mighty department which ruled the missions, the Congregation of Propaganda. Nuncios at certain capitals were invariably made cardinal at the expiry of their service abroad—Madrid, Paris, Vienna, Lisbon. Bishops or archbishops in the chief Italian sees might expect to become cardinals, but this was not an absolute rule; the Pope was free; but if he refused the hat to a great Italian archbishop everyone commented on the ill favour into which that prelate had fallen.

The college of cardinals was far from being dependent upon the Pope. Under the prevailing view of the constitution they had no power but that of offering advice. This doctrine did not correspond with truth. A majority of the Pope's advisers had not been chosen by the Pope but by three or four of his predecessors, and those predecessors with different policies and viewpoints. If a Pope reigned many years it was different, Clement XI made seventy cardinals in his twenty-one years, Pius VI made seventy-three cardinals in his twenty-four years. But even a long-reigning Pope could not build a cohort of cardinals to control the election after his death. Under the aged Clement XII death was expected for eight years; and therefore the cardinal-nephew Neri Corsini and his friends built a group of cardinals of the same mind to be influential at the next Conclave; but even when they were reckoned to have achieved seventeen cardinals, they could do no more than stop candidates, and had no chance of controlling the election of the new Pope.

No instance is known of a man successfully refusing to be a cardinal when the Pope wished him to serve. In the late nineteenth century John Henry Newman almost succeeded in declining the hat inadvertently. Plenty of instances are known of desire to refuse, sometimes reiterated. The magnanimous Spaniard Belluga was invited (1720). He wrote to Pope Clement XI a godly letter, saying that he abhorred the very idea; he wanted a retired life; and he had taken a vow not to accept new dignities. Clement XI was perplexed whether the existence of this vow disqualified Belluga from accepting. He consulted the cardinals, and after hearing their opinion wrote to Belluga a charming letter, releasing him from the vow and ordering him to accept in holy obedience. Belluga became a cardinal.[36]

A cardinal could resign his office. Two famous aristocrats, Este and Medici, resigned because family circumstances needed an heir lest the line die. Cardinal Este unexpectedly became Duke of Modena and could not do other than resign (1695). A simple godly bishop resigned because he could not afford the expenses. A Spanish prince resigned because his father forced him on the Pope when he was a boy and when he was an adult he knew it mistaken. When revolution came two cardinals resigned, to the disgust of the Pope who thought them cowards. One of them, Antici, afterwards tried to take part in the Conclave of 1799, saying that only threats and health forced him to resign. The cardinals rejected this plea, addressing him in the letter as Signor.[37] Antici pleaded that Cardinal de Rohan, when arrested and on trial for the affair of the Diamond Necklace alleged to be sold to the Queen of France, was suspended and allowed to remain a cardinal.

But although a cardinal could resign, he could hardly be removed from

[36] Clement XI, *Opera*, 2.2394.
[37] Este, Novaes xi.64–5; Filippucci of Macerata, Novaes, xii.90–1; Medici, Migne, *Dictionnaire des Cardinaux*, col.1232; Antici, Baldassari, *Histoire de l'enlèvement et de la captivité de Pie VI*, French trans. (Paris, 1839), 299 ff.; Leflon, *Pie VII*, 1.550; Gendry, 2.444–6.

office, and thereby had security under a new Pope. Once in the Reformation a Pope deprived a cardinal of his hat because he thought him a Protestant. In 1716 the Pope threatened the French Jansenist Cardinal de Noailles that he would have his cardinal's hat taken away if he did not submit within two months. Noailles failed to submit, and the question dragged on until he offered unsatisfactory submission, and died a cardinal. Cardinal Alberoni, when he fell from high office in Spain, was accused of manifold crimes and put on trial by the Pope. But a judicial commission, after sitting for nearly four years (1720–3) reported that evidence did not justify removal from the office of cardinal. Even Coscia, who was condemned to ten years in prison in Castel Sant' Angelo and a major excommunication, did not cease to be a cardinal, though being locked up he ceased to attend consistories; yet he attended the next Conclave as cardinal. In the French Revolution Loménie de Brienne accepted the civil constitution of the clergy which Pope Pius VI hated, and received a fierce rebuke, whereupon he resigned office as cardinal.[38] Despite all these alarums, no cardinal was deprived. Cardinal Maury, despite his compromises with Napoleon, ended his days in disgrace but still a cardinal.

Paradoxically the college of cardinals declined at the time when the states achieved success in controlling its composition. From the end of the twelfth century the consistory, that is the meeting of all cardinals present in Rome, won an established place in the government of the Church, recognized by lawyers as possessing a decisive share by the side of the Pope; almost to the extent that the Pope could take no important decision without first consulting a consistory of cardinals. This habit of mind among cardinals persisted into the nineteenth century, so that even in 1878 the first letter which Pope Leo XIII wrote to the German Emperor was attacked as unconstitutional because it was not considered in consistory.

The new bureaucracies of the Counter-Reformation quickly took over business from the ramshackle arrangements inherited from the Middle Ages. They were more specialized, more effective, better informed, and usually in closer touch with the Pope. Therefore the college of cardinals slowly lost authority before the selected cardinals who directed the Congregations. That meant, the Pope's direct power increased, and Benedict XIV carried the process a stage further.

When it is said that a Pope at the head of Congregations had more direct power than a Pope as chairman of a meeting of cardinals, he was

[38] Letters in Gendry, 2.140–1.

not like a dictator whose bureaucrats are imagined to jump at his nod. The Congregations took a life of their own, inherited attitudes and developed customs, and knew that they continued while their elderly master was temporary.

Even an eighteenth-century Pope helped himself by appealing to the just rights of the college of cardinals. In 1730–1 Pope Clement XII wanted to vary the terms of the very unfavourable Concordat conceded by his too otherworldly predecessor or his predecessor's too worldly administrator Cardinal Coscia, to the kingdom of Sardinia. The Concordat gave the king rights over the Church which many cardinals criticized with reason. It suited the new Pope to say that the Concordat was never agreed by Rome because the college of cardinals was not consulted and had a right to be heard. But usually Popes went ahead after consulting whomsoever they wished, and they usually wished to ask the advice of those cardinals who had their confidence. Very occasionally the cardinals spoke out as a college. When Clement XI threatened the Holy Roman Emperor with excommunication (not quite the only time in the century when a Pope dared anything so old-fashioned), and the Emperor flung back a ferocious retort, it was put about (and it was true) that the college of cardinals was divided in its opinion of the Pope's wisdom. Accordingly the cardinals sent the Emperor a stalwart letter of protest in support of their Pope. But this act was so unusual that the document which they sent has been suspected of being a forgery.[39]

On those rare occasions when the administration of the Pope collapsed, or was weak, the cardinals revived the old claims, that the college of cardinals had rights in government, even to co-ordinate jurisdiction with the Pope. In 1689 when Alexander VIII was too old or too disinclined for business, they began to revive as a college. In 1725, when the crookedness of Cardinal Coscia was notorious, and the Pope would listen to no protest, some anonymous hand wrote a biting pamphlet with all the legal evidence from the Middle Ages that the Pope was not absolute but a constitutional president among his cardinals.[40] If the Pope was absent from Rome the powers of the cardinals revived.

Regular consistories were held. A consistory contained men with valuable experience in the Roman civil service or overseas; wise Popes treated their cardinals in consistory with all dignity. The cardinals hardly forgave the two friar-Popes, Benedict XIII Orsini and Clement XIV Ganganelli,

[39] Buder, 2.115 ff.; Onno Klopp, *Der Fall des Hauses Stuart* xiii (Vienna, 1887), 95 ff.
[40] Pastor, xxxiv.128.

because they took little notice of consistories. Clement XIV was even said to have insulted a consistory by pulling out a snuff-box when he ought to have pulled out the manuscript of a speech.

This high-handedness with a consistory was not typical. Yet meetings of cardinals grew more formal, more ceremonial, and less effective as transactions of business. The real decisions passed into the curial offices, the Congregations.

The consistory was of three kinds: a solemn ritual, for the giving of the hat to new cardinals, or for canonizing a saint, or for worthily receiving a visiting king; secondly, a 'half-public' consistory, in which the Pope was openly seen to ask and take the advice of the cardinals, but in fact the exercise was purely ritual and a relic of the past; and thirdly, the private consistory, where the Pope announced new cardinals, or new bishops or archbishops, or new dioceses; and this last was the consistory which dealt with the very small area of important business which still came to consistories, far the most important being the conflicts of Church and State where a Pope had no idea what to do and wished to spread the responsibility or really to ask advice. This might be especially important if a Pope wished to act in such a way that he seemed to transgress a stern rule solemnly laid down by one of his predecessors.

For example, Pope Sixtus V accumulated a vast gold reserve, put a million gold *scudi* into the Castel Sant' Angelo, and on 21 April 1586 presented a bull to the cardinals in consistory on the conditions under which gold might be extracted from this reserve. It might only be taken for a crusade; or in case of famine or pestilence; or if the Papal States were invaded—and then only one half might be used. In the following year he put a second million *scudi* into the castle and a third million the year after.

This wonderful piece of housekeeping founded the credit of the papal monarchy as a financial institution. But in various of the terrible crises which afflicted the papacy during the eighteenth century Popes wondered if they could not solve their immediate plight by pillaging part of Pope Sixtus's treasure. Later in the eighteenth century famine forced two Popes to dip their hands into the old chests in the castle. But Clement XI suffered many scruples. In 1708 Rome was threatened with sack. The case appeared plainly to be covered by the bull of Sixtus V. But Clement found that two of his cardinals objected, and his delicate conscience hesitated. However he found that thirty-two cardinals consented, so it was agreed, and he took the money and tried to provide that the treasury be compensated from future revenues.[41]

[41] F. M. Ottieri, *Istoria della guerre avvenute in Europa* (Rome, 1755), 4.105–7.

Here was a case where a conscientious Pope needed the old consistory of cardinals to reassure him in his plan to do what was sensible to do.

It is a general rule that the consistory was largely a relic of the past except in times of extreme crisis, when Popes turned this way and that to every possible instrument.

When the Pope proposed new cardinals, he must do it in consistory, so that the other cardinals had a right to protest if they wished. But though more than one disagreement occurred in consistory, and in the case of Coscia a strong minority protested against his elevation, there was no known instance of a majority of cardinals declaring themselves against a new cardinal proposed by the Pope. The Portuguese government kept pressing a recalcitrant and dubious clergyman Vincenzo Bichi, the nuncio in Lisbon, upon Rome. Three Popes in succession stood up to black-mail by the Portuguese, though the third, Benedict XIII, started to weaken, much to the disapproval of many cardinals. When Bichi still got no hat, the Portuguese cardinal Pereyra used the consistory to protest by melo-dramatic exit. Meanwhile other cardinals signed a memorial against Bichi, and a year later still another memorial; and then this Pope was sus-tained to follow his two predecessors in doing nothing for Bichi. However, the fourth Pope, Clement XII, accepted apologetic excuses from Bichi and for the sake of the Church in Portugal made him a cardinal[42] after which Bichi vanished from history. Cardinals were not pleased at the concession.

Thus, by memoranda, by speeches, even by theatrical behaviour, car-dinals could resist a proposed new cardinal. But the decision was the Pope's.

The number of cardinals present in consistory varied but might be small when the function was ceremonial. At a promotion it could be numerous—the Museo di Roma has a picture of a promotion in the early eighteenth century with thirty-nine cardinals present; and another picture, dated soon after 1700, of the Pope and twenty-six cardinals railed in a little enclosure, with much walking across to consult and converse, and with the public outside the rails. When advice was badly needed and crisis loomed, the meeting could be numerous. At the consistory of 27 June 1716, during the height of tension over the bull *Unigenitus*, thirty-eight cardinals were present—but such numbers were not usual. In 1760 forty-one cardinals attended to approve the investiture of the new King of the Two Sicilies with his feudal rights.

If the college of cardinals had been able to act as the pamphlet of 1725 claimed, to be a co-ordinate part of the Church government, it would have been able to maintain an underlying continuity of policy. In matters

[42] Pastor, xxxiv.181, 403.

of moment continuity was dictated by the needs of the hour, harsh facts which no change of ruler could alter. Nevertheless, in matters of moment a change of policy from one Pope to the next could be startling, as with the conceding of the Sardinian Concordat and then its attempted revision as soon as the next Pope was elected. The cardinals always elected a Pope who should not be too like his predecessor. In trivial matters, as whether or not clergymen might lawfully wear wigs if they wished, the change of policy from one pope to the next could occasionally be absurd. Pope Innocent XI (died 1689) was an austere puritan and banned opera from Rome. His successor Pope Alexander VIII (died 1691), outgoing and cheerful for all his seventy-nine years, loved music and encouraged theatre, and allowed the new theatre of Tor di Nona to be erected expensively. His successor Pope Innocent XII (died 1700) was austere and made himself unpopular by ordering the demolition of the new theatre. Benedict XIII the friar (died 1730) abolished all lotteries. His successor Clement XII (died 1740) reintroduced them to cope with the irremediable deficit.

The title *Eminentissimus*, 'Your Eminence', was one of the titles of the Byzantine emperor and thence passed to the Holy Roman Emperor, from which it afterwards passed to leaders in his court. Apparently at Richelieu's suggestion, Pope Urban VIII in 1630 restricted it to cardinals, who until then were usually entitled 'most illustrious' and 'most reverend', to the three ecclesiastical Electors of the Holy Roman Empire, and to the Grand Master of the Knights of Malta, who bears the title to this day, the only layman so honoured. (*L.T.K.*).

The tourists who began to come to Rome during the eighteenth century looked upon the cardinals in their red and their carriages as interesting giants of the city. The Corsini palace was and is famous for its treasures, which were more easily accessible to visitors in the middle eighteenth century than in the later twentieth century. Cardinal Alessandro Albani assembled the richest collection of classical works of art outside the Vatican. But not all cardinals made a good living, some could not afford the office. The simple and good Bishop Filippucci of Macerata was made a cardinal in 1706 and before the end of the year applied to resign the office. The Pope tried to provide an income. But sometimes he could not, or sometimes only a small income. If he wanted a cardinal but could not find the money, he might reserve the name *in petto* ('in his bosom'). He nominated a cardinal but made nothing public—until he could find the means; if he died before the announcement the decision did not bind his successor. If a man became a cardinal he needed private money to maintain his

station. As soon as he was nominated *in petto*, a stipend could begin to be
built up in readiness, so that he could receive a capital sum when he was
nominated openly. Clement XII, who as a Corsini inherited much money,
is said to have lamented thus: 'The higher I rise the lower I get. As a priest
I was rich. I became a bishop and was comfortably off. I became a cardinal and was poor. Now I am Pope I am ruined.'[43]

Nomination *in petto* was not used only on occasions of difficulty over
pay. It was also used diplomatically; that is, the Pope wished to promote a
national from one of the powers but might offend other powers if he too
quickly announced the name.

Not surprisingly, a few lucky or temptable cardinals accepted pensions
from governments to represent their interests in Rome. After a controversial Conclave the rewards of success could be substantial. For services
at a difficult election Cardinal Pietro Ottoboni (famed for his debts as well
as his extravagance) received a present of 30,000 *livres* from the French
government, and Cardinal Annibale Albani a ring and the promise of a
pension from the Austrian government. (Neither of these cardinals came
from poor families.) Such rewards were normal with French or Spanish
national cardinals. But to few Italian cardinals was this a possible mode of
supplementing income. Cardinal Giudice died in 1743 leaving a vast fortune. He had been the leader of the Austrian party, and received an Austrian stipend for his services. He happened to die almost at the same time
as a learned and simple monk, Cardinal Pieri. It was found that Pieri had
not left enough money to pay the cost of his own funeral. Rome was more
edified by the funeral of Cardinal Pieri than by that of Cardinal Giudice.[44]

In nominating two-thirds or more of the cardinals a Pope was fairly
free to choose men who would serve the Curia effectively. But with the
more international variety of cardinal—the famous archbishop, the prime
minister of a Catholic state—he was more limited. Crown cardinals,
special representatives of Catholic powers, were forced appointments; and
apart from the crown cardinals, the Pope must be careful to achieve public
balance. If he nominated a Frenchman he must simultaneously nominate
a Spaniard or an Austrian (or both) lest he be accused of partiality.

The first governments to have crown cardinals were those of Madrid
and Paris and Vienna. Naturally Portugal and Sardinia and Naples and
Poland soon tried the same claim. The Pope never admitted the claim by
the smaller powers, and yet in 1747, using the device of simultaneous
appointment, Benedict XIV nominated ten cardinals, nine of them on the
recommendation of the governments of Austria, France, Spain, Portugal,

[43] De Brosses, 2.117 ff.   [44] Benedict XIV to Tencin, ed. Morelli, 1.49.

Venice, Sardinia, Poland, and the King of England—this last the Pretender James III. The Popes steadily paid the Stuart family the compliment of treating them as though they were equal to other Catholic sovereigns (until the death of James III, when Clement XIII faced reality and would not do the same for the former Bonnie Prince Charlie, who certainly shed no credit on the Roman Catholic Church). At this same consistory Benedict XIV made a cardinal of the grandson of James III, who after the Battle of Culloden abandoned the hopes of a crown and took orders, and so the Stuart line of Britain ended when the 'Cardinal of York' died in 1807.

In 1756 Benedict XIV repeated this for all the same governments—with the single exception of Venice, which was behaving badly.

On occasions these crown cardinals produced scandals. But normally the system worked satisfactorily, or at least tolerably. The presence of cardinals representing the Catholic powers was desirable as well as necessary. Government nominated a good man and the Pope cheerfully accepted the proposal. If the French government nominated Fleury and the Spanish nominated Fernandez de Cordova, both honourable statesmen and excellent divines, the Pope was pleased to have such men as members of the college. Of the sixty-seven foreign cardinals during the eighteenth century some caused anguish to the Pope because they had more devotion to their sovereign at home than to their sovereign in Rome. It was hard to welcome the French nomination of Pierre Dubois because he became French minister, or the Portuguese Carvalho because he was brother to the anticlerical minister of Portugal Pombal, or the Italian Alberoni because he was the minister of Spain. Pope Clement XI would have given much to reject Alberoni but could not dare. From the Pope's point of view this loftiness of the cardinal's hat in the secular Catholic world of the eighteenth century gave him the advantage of a 'mere title' which he could bargain for real advantages. But if he used the cardinalate in this way he needed to be sure that its reputation was not lowered and that the hat remained a distinction which prime ministers of great powers coveted.

In one such case the Pope, or rather his acting advisers, conceded to a crown an abuse not seen since the days of the Counter-Reformation. King Philip V of Spain demanded (1735)—and behind stood his queen, Elizabeth Farnese, a tough woman never easy to satisfy—that his son, who was nine years old, be made cardinal. The king's motive was money. He wanted the rich revenues of the see of Toledo. Pope Clement XII (or his nephew managing during his blindness) did what he could to accommodate the Spaniards. He suggested that Luis become the administrator of the see of Toledo and archbishop when he reached the proper age. When this would not do he accepted Luis as a cardinal in December 1735. The philosophy of the Curia saw that a title might easily be exchanged for the welfare of the church in Spain, or even in Italy where Spanish troops were rampant in the war. Perhaps, as with the Cardinal of York, they were not blind to the advantage of a royal presence in the college. Public opinion was not so easily satisfied.

The Infante was not an active cardinal. Aged fourteen, he did not appear at the Conclave of 1740. But in the following year, Benedict XIV, pursuing conciliation of Spain to the limit or beyond, allowed the boy to become also the lay administrator of the Archbishopric of Seville. At the age of fifteen this cardinal nominally held the two mighty archbishoprics of Spain. In 1754, at the age of twenty-eight, Luis realized the mistake of it and resigned both sees and the cardinalate.

Such difficulties were relatively few. No Catholic monarch of the eighteenth century dreamed of Napoleon Bonaparte's demand to nominate one-third of all the cardinals. The powers were content if they had one or two cardinals, pleased if they had three. In the nomination of Italian cardinals these difficulties did not press. Naples, or Sardinia, or Venice, might demand; but the Pope was always strong enough to resist bad nominations by Italian states. In this way the Pope controlled the vast majority of nominations.

Thus the standing Italian majority in the college of cardinals was an indispensable condition of the Pope's freedom of action. The Italian nominations interested the world, for they were reliable signs of a Pope's policy (more reliable than his foreign nominations, which were forced) and affected the future of the papacy. The European information services took careful note of the men, and the kind of men, whom a Pope made cardinal.

Even when the crown cardinals are subtracted, the Pope was more limited in his choice of men than appeared at first sight. Because certain posts were expected to carry, or often did carry, the customary right to be a cardinal or probability of becoming a cardinal, what mattered was the selection at a less senior level; and this had been done partly by a previous Pope or secretary of state and partly by the bureaucratic machine. The apparently unrestricted Pope had little elbow-room, in the sense that he chose from a small number of pre-selected prelates. His principal liberty was in the elevation of men from the religious orders, who traditionally supplied most of such learning as adorned the Sacred College; and these choices would not always turn out comfortably for that Pope or the next, as the independence or truculence of the Benedictine Cardinal Angelo Quirini showed. Even in the choice of monks the Pope must exercise a certain balance as between representatives of the historic religious orders.

Twenty-seven cardinals nominated in the eighteenth century were monks or friars or Jesuits. The two Friar-Popes were therefore untypical of the system. Of the twenty-seven the Dominican Pope Benedict XIII appointed nearly a third, among them four Dominicans, a Franciscan, and two Benedictines, one of whom was Angelo Quirini. In the century which saw the abolition of the Jesuits three Jesuits were made cardinal; but they were made by the first Pope of the century before the question pressed; the third of these was Cienfuegos, accepted as cardinal reluctantly (1720) at the Emperor's request, a man afterwards of much service to his masters by his diplomatic skill and to historians by his reports. A fourth was almost made by Pope Clement XIII when the question of Jesuit abolition pressed hard and he needed a Jesuit as an act of defiance.

Educated Italian churchmen were often learned, some the most learned men in Europe. This respect for knowledge was hardly reflected in the election of a learned Pope in Benedict XIV, for his election was an afterthought not intended to promote learning. But occasionally Popes made cardinals just because they wanted expert information. Knowledge of canon law was the first need of the Curia's advisers. Lambertini, who afterwards became Benedict XIV, was made a cardinal because he was an expert canonist, the leading canonist of the day. But learning of other sorts came into the college, as with Tolomei (1712), eminent as an orientalist. When Lambertini became Benedict XIV he sought to include scholars among his cardinals. But the two extraordinary cardinals, who became a famous part of the cultural renaissance of that age, Quirini and Passionei, became cardinals not because of scholarship; Quirini (1726), because he was an eminent Benedictine and the Friar-Pope looked for a Benedictine, Passionei (1738) because he had been nuncio in Vienna and was therefore 'entitled' to the hat. Both were eccentric, difficult and fascinating. It was observed that no other European court could have numbered such colourful oddities in its cabinet.

Occasionally someone was made a cardinal just to reward an otherworldly pastor, or a mission-preacher. Such men disliked the administrative duties which the wearer of the hat was expected to carry.

Like the Popes, many of the Italian cardinals were of high social standing. Among the ranks of cardinals are found the names of Italian history, a very few of the names again and again. Seven men with Colonna in their surname became cardinal during the eighteenth century, and four more with the related name Doria. Middle-class men came into the college by the old route of the Church hierarchy, but they were rather less common than in the Counter-Reformation.

The cardinal's hat was also useful to Popes for internal purposes of government. It was very eminent, but carried little power unless associated with another office like the presidency of a Congregation. Therefore Popes sometimes used the hat as a way of ridding themselves of unsuccessful civil servants, governors, or treasurers. Some Italians were promoted, publicly because they had succeeded, privately because they had failed. A clear illustration of this mode of kicking upstairs is first found in 1729 when the major-domo Cibo was made a cardinal to get him out of the office of major-domo. This new use of the office of cardinal was another sign of the changing balance between cardinals and the curial offices. Cibo was not at all unique. A secretary of state once (1817) gave a visitor a ticket for a consistory at which cardinals were proclaimed. He was frank. 'Look at the louts. We had to let them in, so as to appoint to the posts which they occupied.' The visitor expressed his surprise that they should let into the Sacred College men known to be opposed to the secretary of state. 'It's right, isn't it,' said the cardinal 'that the common weal should prevail? They were made cardinals to get them out of their jobs.'[45]

A consistory for a promotion was an exciting public event in the city of Rome, with crowds waiting in the courtyard to hear, couriers ready to dash with the news. For such a consistory would make new officials, start a new round of changes in office, and be a reliable pointer to present policy.

Nuncios

A different part of the civil service was made up of cardinals who had been nuncios in the Catholic capitals. These were important to the advice which the Pope received in consistory, for they were the men with European experience, and had personal knowledge of the Catholic world outside Rome. Nearly one-fifth (sixty) of all the cardinals nominated during the eighteenth century had distinguished service as nuncios at one, two, or three of the capitals. Only one of the eight Popes of the eighteenth century served as a nuncio (Innocent XIII), but that was a lower average than the previous century. By convention the nuncio was not a cardinal, for the cardinal was expected to serve in Rome. The hat was the natural reward of his foreign service.

The nuncio was at first a legate or envoy sent from Rome for a particu-

[45] Beck, *Wessenberg*, 294.

lar errand and for a limited time. As modern diplomatic intercourse grew the Pope needed ambassadors like other monarchs, because his interest reached into all Christian states. Therefore Popes began to keep permanent ambassadors, with the name *nuncios*, at the chief European courts. The earliest example was created in 1500 at Venice. At first these envoys were often lay diplomats. During the second half of the sixteenth century the standing nunciature became the norm, with the object of supervising Church reforms decreed by the Council of Trent. That the nuncios should be in holy orders became a rule.

In Catholic countries the nuncio was more than a mere ambassador. Like an ambassador he represented Rome to the government, and sent back confidential reports on acts or opinions in the state to which he was accredited. But he was also an agent of the Catholic Church to see that the decrees of Trent were enforced. Therefore he grew larger than any envoy or newsvendor.

Because reform was uncomfortable, and demanded legal changes hard to get, nearly all countries were reluctant or tardy to receive the new decrees of Trent. Nuncios were created in Lucerne and Cologne, not only like ambassadors to persuade government to do what Trent ordered, but to see that the orders were executed. Thus they became a new power in the churches and therefore within the Catholic states. France and Venice were successful in keeping down the nuncio's authority. Sicily held him off by its old privilege known as the *Monarchia Sicula*. Piedmont kept down his jurisdiction except in Sardinia which was Piedmontese from 1720. In Cologne, Vienna, Madrid, Lucerne, Naples, Lisbon the nuncio became as mighty as the mightiest archbishop, a channel of the Pope's authority over clergy and people, with his own tribunal to which men could appeal from the courts of bishops, sometimes with his own prison and band of constables, with a power claimed to be equal or superior to that of bishops in issuing licences or dispensations.

Whenever a Catholic government had a fight with the Pope, it expelled the nuncio. This was like a government expelling the ambassador of an unfriendly power. But it was more. It suspended the court and the authority which were the Pope's legal instruments of power in that country.

According to the lawyers the nuncio could not hear appeals of the first instance. His court was a court of appeal from the bishop's court—not the only court of appeal, for an appellant could appeal to the archbishop, or directly to Rome. The nuncio could dispense from vows and censures and marriage-bars, and allow indulgences. The doubt of the lawyers concerned a bishop's duties: to ordain, visit, consecrate churches, approve confessors.

Normal doctrine held that since a bishop succeeded the Apostles with a God-given duty to these ends, a nuncio could not interfere except in a crisis—when the bishop was ill, or incapable, or a heretic.

Here were sources of strife. In a world where marriage and wills were spiritual matters and within the sphere of church courts, but which touched important issues of public policy, a local court of appeal, under a head not of local origin but sent from Rome, easily raised charges that it interfered where it had no right. The German imperial court often quashed cases in the nuncio's court. Secondly, a bishop and a nuncio might be expected to disagree whether a bishop was incapable or a diocese in crisis.

In the Holy Roman Empire these acts of nuncios became matter for complaint at Diets, and for undertakings by emperors before they were crowned.

The Archbishop of Cologne was also the Bishop of Liège and ruled the diocese of Liège by a vicar-general. Pope Clement XI (5 May 1708) told the Cologne nuncio Bussy to visit the Liège diocese. He said that because of war and other reasons the bishop could not look after his people and the nuncio should visit. The nuncio visited a nunnery, licensed a confessor who had failed the bishop's examination, allowed a nun to leave her convent, appointed a schoolmaster—all against a stream of protests from the bishop, carried at last to the meeting of German princes at Regensburg. The nuncio finally overstepped the bounds when he interfered in a disputed election to the headship of the faculty of law in the exempt university of Cologne, and had to be recalled and replaced with a more yielding successor.

The gentler Popes of mid-century, Benedict XIV and Clement XIV, tried to avoid such irritations. But bishops in Spain or Portugal or Germany or Austria or even parts of Italy looked to the crown to protect them from excess of activity by a nuncio. The rising power of Catholic governments over their Churches was not resented by many of their bishops. This was a weighty part of the Pope's difficulties during the second half of the eighteenth century.

'Thank God,' wrote a Catholic gentleman of 1790 who approved of nuncios in their proper place but who looked back over their history in Germany, 'we live in happier times, when Popes are much more modest; and when princes are more careful about their rights, and prevent the excesses of nuncios by princely decrees (*placets*), and when Popes can do more to restrain their nuncios.'[46]

In 1785 a quarrel flared all over Germany because the Elector of Bavaria

[46] *Geschichte der Nuntiaturen Deutschlands* (1790), 113.

Karl Theodor asked Pope Pius VI to institute a new nuncio at Munich. The elector had large dominions and not a single bishop. Munich lay in the historic diocese of Freising, an independent prince-bishopric. All his subjects went to bishops outside his domains, or to the nuncios in Vienna or Cologne or Lucerne. To get a nuncio in Munich was a way of getting his private archbishop.

Therefore the new nuncio touched the rights of many existing bishops. The Archbishops of Mainz, Trier, Cologne, and Salzburg joined in a protest to the Emperor, and moved not just against the new nuncio at Munich but against all nuncios in Germany. The new nuncio Zoglio issued an indulgence to a church in the diocese of Freising, a marriage-dispensation to a couple in the diocese of Mainz, and even appointed an internuncio as his agent in Düsseldorf. At the Congress of Ems (1786) the archbishops agreed by their representatives that henceforth papal nuncios should exercise no authority within the Holy Roman Empire.[47] They took the quarrel to the Diet of Regensburg two years later. In vain: the Elector of Bavaria wanted a nuncio; no Diet could stop a prince. The interesting argument was whether Protestant princes had a right to vote. Were they excluded from the argument because they were Protestants, or had they rights in everything which touched the welfare of the German Reich?

The Protestants were not naturally against nuncios. They preferred distant Rome to near-by Catholic bishops. The King of Prussia recognized the jurisdiction of the Munich nuncio over his Catholic subjects in Cleve.

The argument—power of bishops, intervention of Rome's agent, conflict of jurisdiction—never stopped till swept away for a time by revolutionary armies.

Once it became common for the nuncio to be created a cardinal afterwards, the powerful governments in Madrid and Vienna and Paris started to demand it as of right. It now concerned their prestige that the retiring nuncio should become a cardinal—another sign of the European eminence of the office.

To avoid awkwardness, therefore, tactful Popes turned ex-nuncios into cardinals in batches, so that no government would be offended. In 1706 Clement XI simultaneously made cardinals out of the ex-nuncios in Poland, Naples (two), Spain, Tuscany, Cologne, and Paris. This joint creation was soon the norm. But smaller powers aped France and Spain

---

[47] The so-called *Ems Punktation* had twenty-two articles. No appeal should lie to the nuncio from the ordinary church tribunals; the faculties of dispensing, in marriage cases etc., were no longer to need the approval of the nuncio of Rome but were inherent in the office of bishop; fees for the *pallium* and *annates* should be abolished.

and the Empire. Portugal behaved truculently until peaceable Pope Benedict XIV said that the nuncio in Portugal would have the right afterwards to become a cardinal. Then he found that he had no peace, for the governments of Sardinia and Venice and Naples and Poland started to demand the right which Portugal won. But the elevation of 1753 made cardinals only out of former nuncios at Vienna, Paris, Lisbon, and Madrid.

As the custom of envoys became established at the European courts, Popes and nuncios began to expect or be accorded precedence in the diplomatic corps by reason of the master whom they served. This precedence was finally accepted by the Vienna Congress of 1815, and was later accepted in the Lateran treaty of 1929 and the German Concordat.

Lesser capitals were treated more freely. The second rank became in the nineteenth century *internuncios* (Brazil 1829, Holland 1832). *Apostolic delegates* had ecclesiastical duties only, and were not in Catholic capitals—the first in Aleppo 1762.

The Congregations

These curial offices were and are commonly known as the dicasteries.

Bulls and briefs issued by the Pope were a very small part of the exercise of Church authority by Rome. Many important decisions never reached the Pope but were settled by the Congregations of the Curia. Two or three of these Congregations were weighty in the making of policy. Therefore the Pope controlled, or sometimes hardly controlled, policy by choosing the men who sat on the Congregations, especially their presidents and secretaries.

In origin the word Curia meant the place where a senate or other official body met. In the Christian Roman Empire it came to have a sense of law-court to determine cases, and thence to describe the bishop and his advisers sitting as judges. Gradually it lost the meaning of court and meant all the bishop's staff. Thus it came during the high Middle Ages to mean all the men who worked in the Pope's service at the Vatican or elsewhere, even at Avignon or wherever the Pope lived. From the Counter-Reformation it was mainly used to describe the Congregations or dicasteries through which the Pope exercised spiritual authority or jurisdiction over the Church.

The meeting of cardinals in consistory was a meeting of amateurs. Business was too complex for more than a handful to understand the details. Popes kept needing small committees to examine a problem and report, so that the consistory of cardinals should not work blind. And in areas of rare anxiety the committee became standing. The first was the

Inquisition (1542). The next was the special committee (1564) to oversee the reforms demanded by the Council of Trent. This was the Congregation of the Council, which by the eighteenth century grew into the most formidable of the Roman dicasteries.

The need or utility was proven. The Congregation of the Index (1571), to ban or license books, was next; then the Congregation of Bishops (1572). But besides these four main Congregations functioned a chaos of committees for every sort of particular question—war with the Turks, the heresy(?) of Archbishop Carranza of Toledo, Germany, 'reform', reform of canon law, reform of ritual, Church and State, the jubilee, a new text of the Bible, money, roads, police, water, France, jurisdiction, Maltese disorder, church music, Portugal, Poland, flooding of the Tiber. When in 1588 Pope Sixtus V made all this into a system, he not so clearly invented a new administration as brought order into an existing anarchy.

Of the fifteen Congregations seven were instruments for governing the Papal States (corn, fleet, taxes, university of Rome, roads and bridges and water, publishing-house, and Consulta, which was the supreme court). Four were the existing four (Inquisition, Council, Index, Bishops). One was the medieval high court (*Segnatura di grazia*) in a new edition. One was the Congregation of Rites to determine ceremonies. Of the two others, one prepared business for the consistories of cardinals and was also the Congregation for building churches; the other was the Congregation of Regulars, to settle disputes between monks and nuns as the Congregation of Bishops settled disputes among bishops.

This new structure proved more effective, drew business because it transacted business more effectively, and became an agent in that centralization which marked the modern from the medieval papacy.

Popes continued to make Congregations, whether for temporary crisis or permanent use. The four chief were the Congregation of Buon Governo (1592) a court of appeal for disputes between towns and citizens, and soon weighty in governing the Papal States; the Congregation *de Propaganda Fide* (1622) to rule the missions overseas; the Congregation on Immunity (1626); and the Congregation on Indulgences and Relics, which was designed to restrict abuses and decide whether relics were authentic.

The system suffered from the illusion of administrators that to solve a problem it is enough to form a committee, or the expedient of administrators that to relieve pressure a question must be thrown into a committee to gain time. Popes founded Congregations which lasted a few years, or left almost no records, or lived in limbo because no one gave them money or secretaries, or had a sphere which turned out to be no sphere because their ground was already occupied by an existing Congregation.

When the seventeenth century turned into the eighteenth the effective Congregations (apart from those governing the Papal States, which lost effectiveness by being too many) were the Inquisition, beginning its decline; the Index, under criticism; the Congregation of the Council, gaining more and more power over the pastoral system of the Church; the Congregation of Bishops and Regulars, which came out of a rapid union of two Congregations (that of bishops and that of monks) who found that they covered much the same sphere of decision, disputes between bishops and monks. This Congregation was very busy as bishops struggled to extend their rights over exempt monasteries. A fifth, the Congregation of Immunity, still had weight in 1725 when Pope Benedict XIII tried to give it more power, but despite the endeavours of succeeding Popes it almost died of strangulation when the Concordats and the fall of the right of sanctuary made immunity more of ritual than of reality.

The Inquisition and Index

The Inquisition was its proper name, though it was usually called the Holy Office. It had precedence of other Congregations. This was symbolized by Popes keeping the chair for themselves, though they usually allowed a cardinal-secretary to preside. By original constitution it had power to act throughout the Church and summon the secular arm to its aid. From the earliest days its business included not only heresy but immorality, meaning not only sexual offences but blasphemy, simony, and magic.

The Spanish Inquisition was a separate institution under the control of the king. The Sicilian Inquisition was founded by Spain and modelled on Spanish methods even after the Spanish were expelled. In the New World Spanish institutions lasted in the Spanish empire, and in Mexico City the Inquisition built a marvellous new palace during the 1730s. Most other states followed the example of France in using their own systems of censoring books or policing thought and either needed no Inquisition or, like Venice, used it, though more mildly than the Spanish, as a state instrument.

Therefore, though the Inquisition in Rome was the senior Congregation, and valued by most Catholics as the watchdog of truth, it had little (physical) power outside the Papal States.

At the beginning of the eighteenth century Italy and Spain conducted an old-fashioned hunt for heretic groups, the Quietist mystics. The Spanish Inquisition even charged Bishop Fernández de Toro of Oviedo with Quietism and sent him to Rome. He was prisoner in the Castel Sant'

Angelo for nearly three years until the Roman consultors found him guilty (27 April 1719). The Pope ordered Bishop Toro never to exercise his priesthood, not to hear confessions, to be deprived of his see, and to be shut up in a Roman monastery to do penance. Bishop Toro came from the castle to the Vatican and recanted publicly, kneeling before the Pope and the cardinals. Nine years later he appealed to Pope Benedict XIII and was released.[48]

This dramatic case was by that date unusual. Trials of heretics were rarer even in Spain, and much rarer in Rome. The absence of documents makes it impossible to follow the working of the Roman tribunal. But it is safe to say that during the eighteenth century it heard many more cases touching immorality than cases touching heresy. It was even given lowly tasks like the issuing of dispensations from fasts.

Until the second half of the century the immorality cases still had repulsive aspects like torture of the accused, not with rack nor thumbscrew but still torture. And these were the cases which gave special revulsion to Protestants. A cleric who found that he had not the gift of continence might flee to a Protestant country and there relate his experiences to an avid public. Archibald Bower was a Scottish priest who was consultor of the Inquisition at Macerata. Suspected of improper conduct with a nun he fled, past placards out for his arrest, over the Swiss border. The books which he published when he reached England were full of lies and eagerly used by pamphleteers against the Church of Rome.

Nevertheless the Roman Inquisition, not burning heretics, still had an important doctrinal work. This lay in control of books.

All governments including the Protestants regarded censorship of books as necessary. Part of the work of the Roman Congregations was simply a routine state censorship in the Papal States; books of magic, astrology, superstition, obscenity, treason, revolutionary theory. But it also touched books of theology and regarded this as its important work in defence of truth.

A book might be condemned in three ways. The Pope could condemn it in a brief or even bull—this was the most solemn condemnation. The Congregation of the Inquisition might condemn a book, and if so there was a presumption that further proceedings might lie and that the author might be summoned. But even this rule was not kept. Thirdly the book might be condemned by the Congregation of the Index, which had the duty of publishing the Index of prohibited books. Thus these two Congregations overlapped in duty. The Inquisition met once or twice a week, the

[48] Gams, 3.2.322–3.

Index only a few times in the year. The two Congregations had several of the same cardinals.

Books were referred to eight consultors, of whom four were always Dominicans. As Dominican headquarters lay at the Minerva in Rome, the Minerva became the meeting-place of the Inquisition. The discussions of the Congregations are unknown. We can judge what happened only from their decisions.

The lists show no pattern or reason about the selection of books banned. A moderately anti-papal Catholic stood on the list while a violently anti-papal Catholic was absent. A moderately anti-Catholic book by a Protestant author stood on the list while a violently anti-Catholic book by the same author was absent. Therefore the Congregations were not initiating bodies. No tribe of sharp-nosed secretaries sat down to comb the literature of Europe in fear or hope of finding matter to deplore. The haphazard catalogue can only be explained if the bans came because individuals sent complaints. A bishop grew anxious for the souls of his people whom he found under the influence of an Italian translation of a Protestant book. He told his diocese not to read it and applied to Rome. The Congregation examined the book and if they thought fit lent their supreme authority to the ban. Their work was like that of a high court, not like that of a posse of policemen.

This also explained why books were not condemned until many years after they were written. If a book published in the earlier seventeenth century were not condemned until the eighteenth century, that at first sight suggests that the Congregation of the eighteenth century was narrower or more rigid than its predecessors in the seventeenth century. To find the age of early Enlightenment more obscurantist than the age of high Counter-Reformation would be surprising. The inference would be wrong. Sometimes the consultors of the Inquisition, not all of whom were as literate as they should have been, were not well informed about such an author. But most often the tardiness arose only because no one had yet complained.

Very early in the eighteenth century their attention was drawn to *Leviathan* by Thomas Hobbes, first published in English more than fifty years before. *Leviathan* is a shocking book even to the later twentieth century. Imagination finds it easy to picture puzzled consultors when first they faced its theories. Their predecessors condemned Hobbes's works in his lifetime but before they could have known *Leviathan*. They now, however belatedly, met the Latin translation. They condemned (1701); two years later they condemned again.

Again, Hugo Grotius of the Netherlands wrote a famous book *On the Truth of Christianity*; and though he professed a Protestant faith many Catholics valued the book; Cardinal Barberini (1628) loved it and always kept it at hand. It was first banned in 1715, many years after its author's death and at a time when by lapse of time his influence began to decline. Forty-two years later the Congregation went on to condemn all the theological works of Grotius.

The habit of condemning the complete works of an author was practised from the earliest days of the Index. It could not be helped. A handful of persons of mediocre learning could not pore over every line of a prolific scribbler and decide where he was innocent. Pope Benedict XIV disliked this habit of too-embracing condemnations and for seventy years after his revision no such umbrella bans were issued. Then they began again.

Part of the work was defence of the history of the Popes. A historical work which assailed the *Annals* of Baronius or rejected a few of its documents as spurious was likely to appear on the Index. Even the Catholic Baluze's *Lives of the Popes at Avignon* (1693), an epoch-making book among historians, was put upon the Index, perhaps because Baluze compared the time at Avignon with the Babylonish Captivity. Yet the Congregations failed to veto some outrageous Protestant propagandist history of which men complained that it damaged Catholics. Archibald Bower, ex-inquisitor at Macerata, went to England and became a member of the Church of England. From 1748 he published a *History of the Popes* in seven volumes, which had many English editions and French and German translations. These volumes never came into the Index. If they had received a Latin or Italian translation they could not have avoided a ban.

The language was no trivial matter. Consultors were not equipped. They had small need to read Spanish or Portuguese since these countries kept their own lists and Inquisition. Under Benedict XIV only one person in the Vatican understood German. The Index usually condemned works written in Latin or Italian, until the French Jansenists and later Voltaire drove them into condemning more and more books written in French. If a book was translated into Latin or Italian, they were more likely to list the translation than the original. The first volume of Edward Gibbon's *Decline and Fall of the Roman Empire* was put upon the Index, but in its Italian raiment.

Here was an organ of the Counter-Reformation which the age of Enlightenment inherited. Roman leaders never questioned whether it should exist. It was generally popular among Catholics even, or especially, in Spain. But it was designed for a different world. It looked like a stage-

coach in an age of lorries; cumbersome, ornamental, slow-moving, dignified, liked by the spectators, but no longer the best way to carry goods.

By the middle of the eighteenth century the Index of prohibited books
must have looked absurd to informed readers if any informed readers
bothered to peruse it with diligence. Books from a forgotten world continued to find a place on the list because no one re-read them or wondered
why they were there or knew what they were about. Titles of books and
names of authors were often printed inaccurately. Authors appeared in
alphabetical order of first name (e.g. Luther among the Ms, Calvin among
the Js) and so could not be found. A book by a famous missioner Paolo
Segneri, which was put upon the Index in a fit of excess and then in wiser
opinion removed, continued to appear on the lists because editors or
printers failed to catch up with the second decision. Though it might be
well that the Congregations condemned the works of Thomas Hobbes,
the reader might be pardoned for not knowing that he was forbidden to
read *Leviathan*, for the author's name was placed (among the Ts because of
his first name) as Gobes—though it was true that under Hobes (*sic*) was a
note directing the reader to Gobes.

The Congregations sent decisions to bishops and nuncios and placarded
them in the city of Rome. No other serious attempt was made to bring the
ban to the notice of the Catholic world except in the not very rare cases,
like the French *Encyclopedia* (condemned 1759) where the book was regarded as so offensive that its ban was enshrined in a bull or brief from the
Pope. Outside Italy copies of the Index were hard to find in any library
but the largest. Not many copies were printed. The printed list was not designed for the world, but to inform authority.

Most Catholics who went into a bookshop had no idea what books
were prohibited. Printers published and bishops cheerfully allowed the re-
printing of a book long ago banned and never removed from the list. An
Irish archbishop (1825) told a committee of the British Parliament that he
wondered whether in all Ireland there were ten people who had ever seen
the Index.[49]

If the shepherd-Church was supposed to warn its far-flung flock of the
wolves that menaced, the list was a very inefficient means to that end. An
ordinary clergyman would have difficulty in discovering whether a suspect author was banned.

In this way the Congregations of the Inquisition and the Index dealt
with local complaints, and decisions often remained local in result. They
affected Italian booksellers, especially in the Papal States and in Naples,

[49] Parliamentary Papers (1825), viii.654.

and librarians who chose books to buy for the shelves of seminaries. Book-sellers kept behind the counter banned books which scholars needed. Auctioneers when they catalogued books for sale were supposed to put asterisks against books which were banned. The decisions hardly affected customs-officers who examined the luggage of travellers crossing a frontier, for no copy of the Index lay for reference in the office. The customs on occasion acted because a decree of government ordered that (for example) the works of Voltaire be not imported. A bookseller in Catania hid Grotius under manuals of devotion when he knew that the censors were about to pay him a visit.[50] Evidently he did not normally bother to conceal.

If a work helped the progress of a subject Catholic authors used and quoted it without warning that it was banned. Pope Benedict XIV, writing the best of all books about the canonization of saints, cited with approval an earlier treatment of the subject without any sign that the book which he commended fell under the ban.

Old rules of the Counter-Reformation needed adapting and were silently adapted. During the Thirty Years War an oration (1633) in praise of the Swedish King Gustavus Adolphus was circulated in the streets of Rome. At that moment of history and in that place it was treason. The discovery perturbed the Curia into passing the sort of general decree to which in the age of religious war Congregations were too prone, that *no one should praise heretics*. At first the rule was not hard to keep. But as the seventeenth century turned into the eighteenth, it looked ungracious. Catholic authors saw that Protestant authors made fundamental contributions to the study of the Bible, the interpretation of the Greek and Hebrew languages, the sifting and dating of early Christian texts. Protestants helped the Catholic Church to understand itself. Scholars who used these books wanted to express gratitude. When Pope Benedict XIV wrote a book on the number of the feasts, he included a preface to apologize for citing so many heretical books without a note of blame, for (he wrote) he was sure that abuse is useless, but he kept the rule of not praising heretics. The sterner Spanish Inquisition, in its later and mellower age, banned epithets given to heretics like 'very good', 'pious', 'very learned', 'very wise', 'prince of scholars', 'glory of our age', etc.; but allowed 'elegant poet', 'distinguished mathematician', 'great Greek scholar'; for these are gifts which God bestows upon men outside the Church. No scholar outside the Church might be given the title of Master or Doctor because heretical universities could not confer valid degrees—so ruled this Spanish Index.[51]

---

[50] Tuzet, 491–2.   [51] Reusch, 2.82.

Protestant authors cared not at all if they were put upon the Index. They sold no fewer copies and saw their titles in a curious but official list for booksellers. Catholic authors were infuriated, and likely to accuse the censors of obscurantism, stupidity, or prejudice.

Galileo and Copernicus were condemned. Their works stood large on the Index. Many educated Catholics believed that the earth went round the sun; at the *seminary* in Padua was one of the leading Copernican institutes in all Europe. The inquisitor at Florence wrote (1734) to the Roman Inquisition that people in Florence planned to erect a monument to Galileo in the church of Santa Croce and asked whether they disapproved. The Roman Inquisition replied that they had no objection but asked to see the wording of the inscription. In 1758 the works of Copernicus disappeared from the Roman Index. The *Dialogues* of Galileo were still prohibited officially until twenty years after the fall of Napoleon.

But living authors were infuriated while dead did not mind. When Muratori was vexed almost at the end of his life, the methods of the dicasteries in lowering the repute of so famous and so godly a Catholic author came under adverse scrutiny. Authors complained that they were condemned without knowing why, even without hearing which passages were alleged to be offensive, and with no opportunity to explain what they meant; that sentences were torn out of their paragraphs and understood in an ill sense though in context they bore a different and Catholic meaning; that consultors fell into heresy-hunting habits of mind, and fancied themselves virtuous if they found words to disapprove; that books were condemned on insufficient evidence, as for example in the verbal report of only one referee; that famous Catholic scholars, whose other books were valued in the churches, ought not to lose face because an unknown and unscholarly referee in the Congregation so decided; that Dominican domination of the censorship made a particular school of divinity the measure of orthodoxy, and regarded opinions, which Catholics were free to deny, as though they were infallible dogmas; and that schools of divinity which differed from the Dominican suffered most from the acts of the Index.

Censors were unimpressed by these grievances. To accuse them of condemning men unheard was absurd, they argued, when texts stank so high of heresy that any Catholic mind saw how the Church would suffer if they were not immediately rejected. To charge them with turning opinion into doctrine was unjust, because many Catholic doctrines had never been defined by the Church and yet might not be opposed by any true Catholic. The prestige or comfort of a single author weighed like a feather compared with what lay in the balance, the eternal salvation of a mass of simple folk. Above all they were a Congregation of the see of Rome, with the sacred duty of safeguarding truth in the Church, and decided in the name of the Pope, to whom every Catholic owed obedience.

Pope Benedict XIV was the Pope who knew what he was about because he had served on both Congregations. His experience taught him that the Congregations debated carefully and sensibly, but that censors to whom they referred books were sometimes incompetent or prejudiced.[52] In *Sollicita ac provida* (1753) he laid down new rules for censors; no one to be condemned unless two referees agreed, the second not to know the name of the first; the consultors, the Congregation, and in weighty cases the Pope must agree. Reports of referees must be in writing and list precisely the passages reproved and why. Authors of repute must be given a chance to explain and defend what is attacked. Examiners are not to engage a book in a conscious quest for error but to seek a right judgement with care and with a profound study of the question, not judging the author without the context, and not treating opinions as though they were infallible dogmas.

His revisers then created (1758) the most accurate Index which had ever appeared, more accurate than most of its successors. The names appeared for the first time in order of surname. This new Index remained at the base of every edition until the Index was abolished in 1966.

An occasional diocesan synod promulgated the sinfulness of reading banned books. That a synod should so utter was a sign that men read illegal books with a measure of impunity. Moralists taught confessors that they should teach the sin as grave. But amid the various handbooks to help confessors it is hard to find the question 'What should be done if the penitent confesses to enjoying a forbidden book?' If the book was merely heretical it hardly interested parishioners. If it was obscene, priests condemned it more because it was obscene than because it was illegal. Yet uncomfortable evidence survives; as of a Spanish youth who was lent a prohibited book written by the famous and approved Muratori, and knew that moral duty should make him confess that he read the book, and fell into an agony of mind.[53]

In this way the two Congregations hampered the progress of thought less than they enraged individual scholars. Any reputable student or teacher easily gained leave to read prohibited books. A specially lamentable class of books (like the French *Encyclopedia*) were placed in the cate-

[52] Benedict XIV to Tencin, 1 Aug. 1753, ed. Heeckeren. 2.281-2.
[53] *Life of Blanco White*, 1.47.

gory of books which even those with licence were not allowed to read. Few people noticed this refinement.

Nevertheless the two Congregations, inefficient as a censorship, were effective in a much more important task.

In doctrine, or in morals, a series of condemnations was more powerful than a ban on a single book. The Inquisition spoke with all the Pope's authority. They made it plain what attitudes should be adopted by loyal Catholics. They embodied papal *policy* on doctrinal truth. If for example they condemned a book by the Jansenist Bishop Colbert of Montpellier, most Catholics had no idea what the book contained, and probably never heard that it was condemned. But if Inquisition and Index condemned a long series of Jansenist books, men understood that Popes stood against Jansenists, the feeling grew that loyal Catholics could hardly be Jansenist. In this way the two Congregations, regarding themselves as watchdogs of Christian truth, could be far more effective on broad issues than in efforts to stop particular books being read. They prevented few men directly from believing or teaching the opinions taught by Jansenists. But they made the name Jansenist disreputable—and thereby dissuaded a lot of people from practising the variety of devotion, severe in the confessional, infrequent at communion, associated with the name Jansenist.

Thus they were the true executants of the Pope's policy, or of the reigning Pope's beliefs, about the nature and definition of Catholic tradition. If the Pope condemned Jesuit compromise in China, they had a lot of work among books which defended Jesuits. When the Pope condemned Molinos as a Quietist mystic, they had a lot of work among devotional books which taught a passive type of mystical resignation. These were moments when zeal generated excess. Consultors, knowing that the Pope disapproved Jansenist moral theory, found it hard not to detect error in otherwise harmless theology written by known Jansenists.

As the century passed, State censorship diminished further the influence of Inquisition or Index. The French allowed the Index no force in France,[54] while the Paris Parlement burnt numerous books. Spain had its own Index, more severe than that of Rome, but not including many books which the Roman Index banned. More than one Spaniard discovered to his dismay that a licence from the Pope to read prohibited books was not accepted as valid in Spain. The Austrian government in the Netherlands (Belgium) would not allow auctioneers at book-sales to mark books as banned. They banned Benedict XIV's new Index because it prohibited books which government allowed.

[54] Two historic courts of the Inquisition survived till 1722 at Toulouse and Carcassonne.

Catholic governments had no wish to deny the principle underlying the work of Inquisition and Index. They wished to do it better. In Austria the Empress Maria Theresa (1753), governments in Portugal (1768), in Bavaria (1769), in Austrian Lombardy (1768), instituted royal commissions to censor. Venice, which long kept the Inquisition on a leash, ruled (1767) that the Inquisition could do nothing without the assent of three senators. In 1739 the Inquisition at Florence arrested a ducal officer for abuse of the clergy and four years later government suspended the Inquisition's authority. When it reopened in 1754, three laymen representing government sat with the inquisitors. In 1782 it was abolished. Austrian Lombardy abolished it in 1775, Sicily in 1782.

Slowly the problems of the Roman Congregations were swallowed up in the far wider difficulty of press censorship in the European states.

Abolition only canonized the disappearance. When Sicily abolished and threw open the prisons, they found three women accused of witchcraft. The last burning of a heretic in Sicily happened fifty years before.

The Spanish Inquisition

The Spanish Inquisition was slower to mellow. In its history the middle of the eighteenth century marks a still unexplained turning-point.

Llorente, who was a former inquisitor, saw many archives of the Spanish Inquisition during the age of revolution, including documents which he or others afterwards destroyed. He calculated the number of executions under each grand inquisitor from beginning to end of the Inquisition. These calculations he founded only in part on counting, and otherwise estimated. Without being reliable as detail they are to be trusted as general pattern.

In the heyday of King Philip II in the later sixteenth century executions ran at about 120 a year. For the first half of the seventeenth century they ran steadily between sixty-four and eighty a year. From 1665 deaths fell dramatically, but in the first third of the eighteenth century they still ran between thirty and fifty a year. Until the death of King Philip V (1746) the court continued in its old ways, torture, *autos-da-fé*, death by burning; among the convicted many relapsed 'Jews', blasphemers, bigamists, sorcerers, promoters of superstition. Even when the critic subtracts persons guilty of gross immorality or crime who were nevertheless condemned for a heresy alleged to cause the immorality or crime, until almost the middle of the eighteenth century the acts of the court stank of unreliable confessions extracted by torture. The most pathetic case was that of the

Carmelite nun Agueda da Luna, regarded by her district and beyond as a true saint, to whom were ascribed miracles and ecstasies. The parents of the future historian Llorente took a sick child to be touched by her, but in vain. For alleged Quietist heresy she was denounced to the local office of the Inquisition at Logroño and there made all manner of confession under tortures from which she died before she ever came to court.

With the accession of Ferdinand VI in 1746 executions suddenly became fewer, and with the accession of Charles III (1759) fewer still. Charles III learnt while in Naples to dislike the court. But the change in legal habits was due less to his personal influence than to the general belief that all was not well with an archaic system and that both Spanish government and Spanish Church ought to consider reform. The character of successive inquisitors-general was known to be humane and compassionate. The courts, confronted by evidence more compelling than evidence which only twenty years before led to execution, adjourned cases and took no further action. Denunciations hardly decreased, courts sat, evidence was taken; but the number of cases which went further was far fewer. Sometimes the courts suspended public proceedings and laid a private penance upon the culprit.

The last execution by a court of the Spanish Inquisition was at Seville on 7 November 1781, of a woman accused of witchcraft, who could have saved herself by an act of penitence. The right to condemn to death was not abolished. But the supreme court of the Inquisition took pains to see that it was not inflicted. And in Spain, as everywhere else in Europe, lawyers had ceased to believe in the utility of torture. Beccaria's book *On Crime and Punishment* received (1774) an early Spanish translation.

The decline in executions and ending of public *autos-da-fé* did not mean that Spain looked upon the Inquisition with the eyes of a London Protestant, as barbaric, obsolete, or crooked. Most men respected it as a necessary and historic system of courts for keeping Spain sane and moral and religious and Spanish.

Censorship of books remained important. All the same, the censors began to waver, as the cases of Copernicus and Galileo showed.

To maintain the movement of the earth as a theoretical hypothesis was permissible provided the author did not declare it to be true. Neither authors nor censors found the line which divides fact from hypothesis easy to draw; and hence irritations, redraftings, prudence, permissions with ambiguous clauses. Some educated Spaniards believed the movement of the earth, and many of the clergy were the most educated. But they could not quite say what they thought. And in these conditions the appeals to the evidence of the senses, and to the authority of Scripture, were still common. 'Reason proves', said Father Murillo, 'neither that the earth moves nor that it does not move. Therefore it is better to keep to what the Bible teaches.'

The Benedictine Feijóo was more outspoken. We cannot attack the doctrine that the sun goes round the earth so long as an Inquisitor rules in Spain, heavy with obsolete lumber, thunderbolt in hand, threatening any book that says one of the innumerable things that Spain does not know already. But by 1774 a learned priest, Father Mutis, taught Copernican doctrine openly at the college of Santa Fe de Bogotá. The Dominicans at the university there denounced him to the inquisitors, who refused to act. By that date the Spanish knew that Copernican doctrine was being taught in Italy, and by eminent churchmen. A Spanish ex-Jesuit, expelled from Spain to Italy, dedicated his time there to the study and exposition of Copernicus and Galileo.[55]

Until the French Revolution started, the inquisitors were fairly lax about the importing of books by the French philosophers.

Two examples from among the late cases illustrate the continuing power and the changing practice of the Spanish Inquisition.

Pablo de Olavide had a controversial career in the colonial administration of Peru. He loved modern books, had a rare library, admired and visited Voltaire. He was a generous and charming man with a universal curiosity and a knowledge of theology. In Spain he was used in reforming education and agriculture, and then given charge of someone else's plan to colonize the Sierra Morena in southern Spain with German immigrants. This became a herculean labour because immigrants arrived long before camps or supplies were ready. Though their hardships would have worsened but for Olavide, he was saddled with a scheme which bred misery.

Slowly inquisitors started to eye Olavide with suspicion.

At his table he would say what he liked to the company—that rocks showed Genesis to be wrong about the age of the earth, that the Bible is not clear on original sin and the Old Testament does not teach the immortality of the soul, that despite the authority of St. Paul he thought marriage a higher life than celibacy; and sometimes, to entertain his visitors, he would go out to his library and fetch a volume of Montesquieu, or Helvetius, or Voltaire, and offer a commentary upon the text for his guests. He encouraged French fashions among the settlers, arranged dances on feast-days, and told women that they could come to church with head uncovered. He wanted the churches in the settlements not to have a

[55] Sarrailh, 491–5.

clutter of altars, nor statues of saints, nor too many masses for the dead; he tried to help Germans feel at home by writing hymns and having them sung during mass; he disliked processions in the streets, and stopped bells being rung in time of storms. Someone heard him talk rashly about 'imbecile' friar preachers. Yet he was a very devout Catholic, never going to bed without prayers and several signs of the cross both on his bed and on the four corners of the room.

Olavide was at risk because he was in charge of a half-failure; because he was backed by unpopular members of an unpopular government; because he talked too freely for his generation. But his worst trials came over the Capuchin superior.

The founders wanted all the new settlements to be in parishes under parish priests and therefore tried to exclude monks and nuns. But since they could not find parish priests who spoke German, they were forced to apply to an international religious order. They asked the Capuchins.

The Capuchins sent Father Romuald Baumann who after 1768 had instituted at Amoltern in south Germany a variety of Christian commune, which was successful enough to make him a good choice to care for new colonies in the Sierra Morena. He began friendly to Olavide. Four years later he regarded Olavide as a calamitous head; and the personal conflict rose to such tension that in March 1776 government ordered the expulsion of Father Romuald from Spain. He left, bequeathing to the Inquisition a long series of denunciations against Olavide, and material for thinking him the most unpleasant Capuchin of the century.

He accused Olavide of denying miracles; of accepting Rousseau's theory of religious education; of saying that religion is better observed in England than in Spain; of believing that the ultimate authority in the Church is neither with Pope nor bishops but with all the faithful; of abusing monks as ignoramuses and misers; of mocking celibacy—and a lot else.

The Inquisition was widely believed to be toothless, a dying piece of machinery surviving out of a brutal world. The case of Olavide caught the imagination of Europe; the case of an intelligent and devout public servant, arrested 14 November 1776 and two years later condemned to eight years seclusion in a monastery.

The court refrained from any public *auto-da-fé*, except for the presence of nearly seventy lords and prelates present by invitation. Olavide abjured humiliatingly, and after two years' comfortable imprisonment got himself transferred to a sanatorium near the French frontier and escaped into France. Here he settled as a legend and heroic exile. When France broke into revolution, he wrote a pious book, *The Triumph of the Gospel*, to show how a false philosopher was converted back to faith by the argument of a good Catholic, and so won readmission to Spain. The book became one of the most widely read books in Spain.[56]

Olavide's case was the most famous case before the Inquisition in all the eighteenth century. It shows the institution changing. The trial needed leave from the king. The case mingled pornography or misgovernment with old-fashioned heresies like writing letters to notorious anti-Catholics. The verdict was held in a private court, but not so secret that the conduct of the court was not visible to impartial minds. No public *auto-da-fé* was exacted. By the standards of only a few decades before, the punishment was light. Nevertheless educated Europe felt it to be an anachronism.

Miguel Solano, priest of Esco in Aragon, was proved to have convinced himself, by reading the Bible and nothing but the Bible, that Church, Pope, bishops, their teachings were in error. He condemned purgatory, tithes, the Pope's dispensing power. The local inquisitors at Saragossa brought theologians to persuade him that he was wrong; in vain. They then condemned him to an *auto-da-fé*. The supreme court in Madrid under the grand inquisitor refused to accept their decision and after trying other expedients to avoid an *auto-da-fé* ordered enquiry into the pastor's sanity. The Esco physician gave sufficient evidence of illness to warrant charitable presumption of enfeebled reason. And while arguments and interviews continued, Solano (1805) died. The local inquisitors refused to let him be buried in consecrated ground but interred the body within the walls of the Saragossa Inquisition. They considered whether they should burn an effigy of the dead man, but were stopped by the supreme court in Madrid.[57]

This mellowing was very plain to tourists. An English clergyman travelled in a coach (1786–7) and found himself sitting between two inquisitors. His host pulled his leg. 'The inquisitors of the present day are become more gentle than their fathers and seldom regale themselves with human flesh; but look sharp, for they have not yet forgot the taste of blood.'[58] 'I am inclined', the Englishman soliloquized in retrospect, 'to think, that in proportion as light has been diffused in Europe, even inquisitors have learnt humanity.' Still, he thought that the jurisdiction by its very nature must be liable to abuse.

The Roman Curia had no sway in the Spanish Inquisition. But its senior

Congregation was its own Inquisition. Neither the Protestant north, nor all the French, distinguished between these two organizations with a common name, common aim, and sharply different practices. No Pope was responsible for Olavide. Yet a case like Olavide, making the name of 'the Inquisition' stink outside Spain, could not do other than subtly affect the international reputation of the Roman Curia.

The Congregation of the Council

This was instituted at the end of the Council of Trent to supervise the execution of its reforming decrees. Its business slowly extended. For many years after its foundation it had small sphere of influence; in the second half of the seventeenth century its power rose, until by 1720 it ruled large areas of the pastoral life of the Church; directly in the Papal States, very clearly in most of the rest of Italy, less in Spain, still less in Catholic Germany, and not in France. From 1591 it was allowed to publish its decrees *in the name of the Pope*. To the parishes at large a decision of this Congregation came with the force of a papal decision, and claimed an obedience due to the Pope. Its special function was the discipline of the clergy; watch over synods; a supervision of the visits to Rome which Trent ordered, and of the reports which bishops were supposed to send regularly from their dioceses.

It extended its sphere successfully, not only because of its duties, but by the long service of two exceptionally able secretaries. In the later seventeenth century it had Fagnani, a canonist of brilliance and long experience. Then Prospero Lambertini (afterwards Pope Benedict XIV) was secretary for seven years (1720–7) and by learning and temperament was suited to make the organ a wise instrument of government. From 1732 they began to publish the proceedings; in separate folios at first, seven years later in systematic volumes; which not only illuminate the social and religious life of the eighteenth century, but breed in the reader a respect for this dicastery and its proceedings.

When Benedict XIV became Pope in 1740 he consciously extended the sphere of the Congregation into areas hitherto allotted to other Congregations; first with the questions of marriage and nullity, and then with the question of religious vows. This made an enormous increase of work for the Congregation of the Council, and was part of the slow process of centralizing the Curia. Its decrees became so weighty in the Church at large that they began to receive commentaries from theologians.

Its difficulties were numerous. Distance meant time, and if a case came from Belgium or Portugal, or even Lecce in southern Italy, appeal to Rome meant long delay before settlement. The Congregation supervised synods, and yet knew that many bishops, perhaps most bishops, feared or disliked synods. They were supposed to supervise the bishops' regular visits to Rome and knew that these visits were exceedingly irregular, except formally by proxy. They were supposed to read pastoral reports from all over the Church; paper poured in, bishops introduced their reports (sometimes) with a whole history of the diocese since apostolic times, few eyes to read, heaps of unread reports mounted, cupboards full, bishops clamoured for decisions that tarried. To remedy this Benedict XIV instituted a new Congregation with the duty of reading bishops' reports; in effect a subcommittee of the Congregation of the Council, and known by an appropriate nickname, 'the little Council', *Concilietto*. This did not help much. The Congregation of the Council tried to exercise an ever-widening jurisdiction with an exiguous and ill-paid staff.

So far as Popes exercised real government over the parochial work of the Church, they acted through this dicastery. The Congregation was wise, and grew indispensable. When near the end of the century revolutionary armies entered Rome and brought the work of the Curia to a standstill, the Vatican tried to keep this Congregation above all in a continued existence of emergency, lest the parish machinery of the Church grind into chaos.

The action of the Pope

The Pope acted frequently and effectively provided that the action was kept within defined or well-understood limits. Rome was the final court in disputes within the Church. In so far flung an organization with rules or conventions centuries old, the law of the Church was often matter for argument in new circumstances. This was the regular routine of the administration of the Church, to make bishops or monks or parish clergy behave sensibly, which probably meant compelling them to give up a cherished or pretended right.

In the Philippine islands, the history of the conversion to Catholicism ensured that religious orders—friars and Jesuits—took charge of most of the parishes. Exempt by old custom and privilege from the jurisdiction of bishops, their parishes refused to accept visitation from the archbishop. If the archbishop conceded their claims, he stood in the absurd predicament that almost all his diocese was removed from his direction. The orders said that if the archbishop insisted on visiting them, they would resign the parishes.

Here was a characteristic case; both sides were right in law, but circumstances produced a ridiculous anomaly. Both sides appealed to Rome. The Pope (1705) told the orders both to stay in their parishes and to submit to the archbishop's visitation.

Such a case was typical of Roman action. A very similar difficulty existed in England. The only legal chapels of the small Catholic minority were either the chapels of the embassies of foreign powers (Sardinia, Bavaria, Spain) where the ambassador chose his chaplain or private chapels on the estates of Catholic noblemen where the squire chose his chaplain. Other parishes were shepherded by members of religious orders, Benedictine or Jesuit, who were exempt from bishops and took orders from their superiors. Therefore the bishops (called in England vicars-apostolic since the reign of the Catholic king James II) had almost no power over their clergy, and hence rose an endless correspondence with the Congregation of Propaganda at Rome, or even with the Pope, while Rome sought, decade after decade, to persuade men locked in constitutional conflict to be reasonable. Rome's rulings might be disobeyed for a time, on grounds of inadequate information, or disputed interpretation. But sooner or later they were obeyed, and less friction brought to the pastoral care of the Church in England.

A decision might or might not be resisted by minorities. But usually contenders accepted the judgement of the supreme court, and even when they continued to fight, carried on the battle in conditions transformed by Rome's bull. Sometimes a ruling snatched peace out of schism or near-schism. The Maronites of the Lebanon were rare among easterners in their loyalty to the Roman see, but like most Christian subjects of the Turkish empire, like most oppressed bodies in any empire, suffered disruption over jurisdiction. When their patriarch died in 1742, two different groups of bishops elected rival patriarchs. Amid devastating scenes in the congregations, the rivals appealed to Rome. Pope Benedict XIV pronounced both elections invalid, and by exercise of the supreme spiritual powers declared that a candidate who was the senior bishop and had first refused the office should be enthroned. Members of the Curia were alarmed at so high-handed an exercise of papal power—to appoint a patriarch, whom none had elected, in an Eastern Church with a Syrian liturgy—and feared that the Pope would be disobeyed. But he had been well advised by his informants on the spot and within two years achieved ecclesiastical peace in the Lebanon.

In this function of supreme court, a high proportion of the time of the Curia was spent in settling matters connected with the religious orders.

Monasteries and nunneries, being (often) exempt from the control of the bishop of their diocese, looked to the Pope as their ultimate superior or adviser. More than half the briefs issued from Rome during some years of the eighteenth century concerned the right, privileges, or behaviour of religious houses.

Let us select at random one volume of the *Bullarium*. This contains the important encyclicals and briefs for the first two years of the pontificate of Clement XIII Rezzonico (1758–60). The volume ranges in subject from Valencia to Posnan, from Paris to Naples. It contains the usual spate of monastic questions—how abbots-general are to be elected, a dispute between the abbot of Monte Cassino and the Bishop of Capua, the conferment of canonries in the cathedral at Gnesen in Poland—and other small ecclesiastical questions like the repair of vicarages at Compostella, or putting a good Italian priest into a new diocese, or an argument among the Lateran canons about conducting services. Universities, like religious orders in being exempt, are also represented—in bulls confirming the statutes of the university of Carpentras, approving the foundation of a Polish university, allowing individual university libraries to retain books listed in the Index of prohibited books, and exempting librarians from the duty to attend choir offices except on high days. A very few concern politics—the bull investing the new King of the Two Sicilies with his kingdom, recognized since the Middle Ages as a fief of the Pope; preserving for the Pretender to the throne of Britain the right to nominate to Catholic sees; stirring the governments of Austria and Poland to intercede with the government of Turkey to help the Franciscans, guardians of the holy places in Jerusalem and under attack from the Greeks; extending areas, like the city of Rome, where no one might carry arms; warning the republic of Genoa against interfering in a bishop's visitation of the parishes in Corsica; asking the help of the Empress of Austria against Lutheran princes threatening the Duke of Hesse-Kassel. Two concern clerical behaviour and the Christian life, the first against priests or religious who engage in trade for the sake of gain, the second supporting a strenuous interpretation of the decree on fasting. Three concern books condemned. Two of them congratulate the theological faculty of the university of Paris, and the grand inquisitor of Spain, for censuring Helvetius's book *De l'Esprit*. The third was famous among all these encyclicals or briefs, the condemnation (3 September 1759) of the French *Encyclopedia* for all its pernicious errors.

Such two years of papal acts were not untypical in their range, variety, and limitation.

The bulls or briefs in the Bullarium for the first four years of Pope Clement XII contain the following: over ninety on monks and nuns; ceremonial privileges of bishops, eight; colleges (statutes, libraries, archives), eight; government of Papal States and Rome (including a remarkable decree on the privileges of bombardiers at the castle), six; indulgences, six; brotherhoods, three; rules of Conclave, two; banning of book, one; seminaries, one; theology, one (ordering *silence* on the dispute over grace); *In Coena Domini*, one; politics, two (duchy of Parma, Saxony); jubilee in the present necessities of the Church, one.

The jubilee

A jubilee was a holy year when special indulgences were granted to pilgrims who visited the holy places of Rome. The first which history records clearly was that proclaimed in the year 1300, with intention that these special ceremonies and prayers should be held every hundred years. But fifty years later the Pope allowed a jubilee, and forty years after that, and then it was ordered every thirty-three years to fit the years of the life of Christ, and then (1423 and 1450) the interval was twenty-seven years, and so from 1475 it became each quarter of a century and was celebrated regularly until 1775 inclusive. The Brotherhood of the Holy Trinity was chiefly responsible for hospitality, and kept a list of numbers of pilgrims whom it sheltered. They showed no steady increase: 1675, 280,496; 1700, 299,697; 1750, 194,832. Originally these jubilees had a part-motive of bringing revenue to Rome. Although the calculation is hazardous, by the eighteenth century the expenses may well have exceeded the revenue. It was an act of religion, and a demonstration that the holy shrines of Rome were still the focus of Catholic devotion. Painters or journalists of the eighteenth century were glad to portray the magnificence and movement of the rite when the holy door was thrown open to symbolize the opening of the gates of mercy. Churches were cleansed and beautified, vigils of prayer kept them open at night, famous missioners like Leonard of Port-Maurice preached in the squares.[59]

Since the later Counter-Reformation Popes were also in the habit of publishing a special jubilee for prayers on their accession; and just occasionally in times of terrible crisis, as by Clement XI in his political agony of 1709.

[59] P. Fedele, ed., *Gli anni santi* (Rome, 1934); H. Thurston, *The Holy Year of Jubilee* (1900). Chracas's *Diario ordinario* is worth attention as it loved to describe these ceremonies.

PART II

Reform and Revolution

5

THE FALL OF THE JESUITS

As king and politician the Pope was weak. His power, so far as not spiritual, lay in the ability to concede or sell to kings rights over the Church in various countries, in appointments, money, tax, exemption, dispensations. These were very important. But they were being eroded by the system of Concordats and the pressure of Catholic sovereigns.

Peace after 1748 was a blessing. No hostile armies trampled the Papal States. The Catholic powers were near harmony. And their harmony was not in all respects a blessing for the Pope.

France and Austria were natural rivals in Italy and remained so until the war of 1914. This helped Popes. A Pope could not long be bullied by France because Austria would protest nor by Austria because France would protest. But in Germany Prussia was rising. For the first time in the modern history of the Holy Roman Empire Austria feared for the leadership of Germany.

Thus the rise of Prussia affected Popes. The Austrians needed French and Spanish help against the threat of Prussia.

After 1750 Popes were confronted with a Bourbon alliance between France and Spain which Austria did not like too firmly to oppose. A Pope could no longer be sure of independence because governments disagreed. He might be faced with a united demand from all Catholic sovereigns.

Never in all the history of the papacy were the ambassadors from Madrid, Paris, Vienna, Naples, and Lisbon so mighty in Rome as during the half-century of peace after 1748. To the Pope they behaved with ceremonious decorum. His secretaries of state, favourites, friends, confidential advisers, chaplains, and cardinals they threatened and bullied where they could not bribe or persuade.

The ghost of Henry VIII walked abroad among the Catholic governments. Cardinals, who had long memories, kept reminding themselves what happened in England when a Pope too pertinaciously resisted a Catholic sovereign. Cordara, who knew much about the cardinals of those years, wrote this: 'By the example of Henry VIII advisers of Popes are nowadays wont to frighten them, so that however villainous a prince they refuse to resist with the courage that befits a priest.'[1]

The critics of the Jesuits

The Jesuits were the leading order at the Counter-Reformation and identified in the mind of Europe with its political and religious success. Protestants therefore regarded them as the most papalist and most unscrupulous of the Pope's followers. From the middle of the seventeenth century, during the time of the Thirty Years War, the word *Jesuit* was used to imply someone oversubtle or underhand.

A single document was very influential and was still being printed and used by propagandists during the eighteenth century (and into the middle of the nineteenth and after): the *Monita Secreta*. This was written in Cracow in 1614 by a Pole Jerome Zahorowski who had lately been expelled from the Society. This document purported to be the secret instructions on how to get money, how Jesuit houses could become rich without losing the repute for poverty, how to procure the friendship of rich widows, how to get the ear of Great Men, etc. The document was very crude ('Never settle in a town not wealthy', 'Princes have always desired a Jesuit confessor when they have been engaged in hateful practices that they might not hear of reproof') but coming just before the Thirty Years War it was serviceable in the passionate political strife over religion, and was undoubtedly couched in the Latin style and appearance of authentic Jesuit rules and constitutions. Leading historians rejected it as a forgery. But it was too useful to vanish: and this lasting utility, in a document which deserved to disappear overnight, is a sign how deep in the European consciousness was already the controversial reputation of the Jesuits. As late as 1760 a terrible satire circulated in Rome, *The Wolves Unmasked* (*I lupi smascherati*) which translated and 'refuted' the *Monita Secreta* and explained how its principles led to Jesuit plots to murder kings.

The Jesuits educated most of the Catholic upper and middle classes; were famous for training future priests; were much in demand as conductors of missions and of the Spiritual Exercises; were most commonly selected as confessors of kings. Protestants feared and loathed the order. Some Catholics began to dislike them almost as fervently.

As educators they controlled so many colleges that they found it hard to fill chairs with worthy professors, they maintained an excellent but old-fashioned classical syllabus, they refused to adapt to those who wanted

---

[1] Cordara, 236.

science and history. They controlled the higher education of the Catholic world. And the leading minds were convinced that this Catholic education was falling backward behind Protestant. In 1746 the Bishop of Augsburg founded a new college with the special object of getting an up-to-date syllabus and taking the seminary out of Jesuit hands.[2] Still, an order which in 1750 had more than 22,500 members had a reputation which continued to attract.

The movement for their destruction was sudden. Probably it could not have happened if the ground were not prepared, first by *Unigenitus* and its aftermath, and then by the vast publicity attending the Pope's condemnation of the Chinese rites.

Paraguay

From early in the history of Latin American missions, the religious orders realized that the Indians could not be protected from settlers unless they were gathered into reservations. The most famous reservations were the Jesuit *Reductions* in Paraguay. Reservations, if remote enough, needed little protection at first from the encroachments of colonists. But early in the eighteenth century European settlers who wanted land began to meet old-established Indian protectorates and to resent their protectors. To the missionary guardians the oncoming settlers looked like pirates and bandits. To the settlers missionaries looked like archaic props of an obsolete world. A strong economic and physical force drove out a weak.

In the past European governments were sometimes powerful enough to lend law and military force to save the protectorates from destruction. As the settlers grew in number, they became impossible to control without an exertion beyond the wish or strength of home governments. No one could any longer protect the Indian protectorates. Being like little kingdoms with an autonomy under the sovereignty of the home government, and possessing frontiers which no man might cross without leave, they became eldorados of legend, distant countries where gold and silver might be had for the asking. Men said that the Jesuits were setting up a kingdom in Paraguay. Colonial administrators recommended that the ordinary government take over the government of the reductions in Paraguay.

Early in that century a French engineer and traveller, Frézier, published *A Voyage to the South Sea*; and to its editions was added an appendix, not by Frézier, called in the English translation of 1717 *Some Account of the Settlement of the Jesuites in the Spanish Indies*. From internal evidence this

[2] Duhr, *Geschichte der Jesuiten*, iv.i.250–1.

description was not first hand. But it described how the Jesuits ruled 300,000 families, that their land was 'the finest part of all that continent,' with temperate air and fertile soil and hard-working Indians, a country fruitful in timber and orchards and 'many simples of great use in pharmacy', producing 'the herb paraguay' used everywhere as tea and worth the best part of a million crowns a year, and above all with gold and silver mines in plenty; and how the rule of this paradise was communist and oppressive, each Indian bringing his produce to a common warehouse and being given his ration of food, each kept apart from any visitors even to being ordered indoors if a European visitor walked down the street. Such a traveller's tale was not unique. By the middle of the century many Portuguese and Spaniards believed that the Jesuit 'kingdoms' guarded wealth to which they had no right and maintained their power by an unjust and undesirable system of society. The Jesuits denied neither that the social system was unusual, nor that they preferred to keep out visitors. They vehemently denied that they produced more wealth than they needed to survive as communities. They were not believed. Their desire to protect the Indians by keeping away Europeans was interpreted as a wish to hide gold. The local bishops disapproved the reductions. For Jesuits were exempt from the visitation of a bishop, and thereby removed many Christians from normal church administration. Twice over they were a kingdom inside a kingdom —both in State and in Church.

In 1750 Spain and Portugal agreed a treaty for a better defined frontier in South America. Spain gave to Portugal the land where seven of the thirty reductions stood. The Indians must be moved to the further side of the River Uruguay, at a tiny compensation of 28,000 *pesos*. The hardships of such an emigration were not understood in Madrid, Lisbon, or Rome. Two Jesuit generals in succession, who had no notion of local circumstances, told their men to obey.

The missionaries voted by 68 to 2 that the emigration was impossible. In June 1752 the emigration began, and proved so full of suffering that the Indians refused to move. Spanish troops tried to make them, and the effort grew into a little war, in which the army occupied the reductions. Madrid and Lisbon both believed that the Jesuit heads of the reductions caused Indian resistance and bloodshed. A religious order was 'at war' with the Portuguese state and Portuguese commerce. Yet the government of Portugal found the same religious order powerful within its borders, as confessors to sovereign and royal family and nobility, and as controlling all higher education in the land. The little Indian war in Paraguay switched the fierce hostility of government against Jesuits within Portugal. It was a classic case, often seen in history (at its worst in Turkish massacres of Armenians) where a group within the state suffered criminal persecution because identified with an enemy outside the state. In such circumstances no one asks whether individual members of the society are guilty or innocent. It is enough that the individual belongs to the hated group.

The moment happened to coincide with another important point of Portuguese history: the effort to modernize an archaic state through a despotic prime minister.

Because of the sugar trade and the gold of Brazil, the crown had money, and freed itself from control by the representatives of the people in the Cortes. The power of cabinet ministers rose steadily. Like all modernizing ministers of the eighteenth century, they must demolish or weaken the two pillars of old society, the nobility and the Catholic Church.

King José I (1750–77) disliked work and entrusted the government to Carvalho, known to the world by his later (1770) title, the Marquis of Pombal. On 1 November 1755 central Lisbon was destroyed by two earthquake shocks within ten minutes and a tidal wave an hour later. Not without reason, Pombal gained the credit of coping with the national crisis, and henceforth as a saviour of his country exercised near-despotic authority. He used his powers to improve the Portuguese economy, develop the textile industry, regulate the trade in port wine, reform the universities and education, and foster art and architecture. Upon the nobility and the Church he trampled ruthlessly; torturing and executing several lords on unproven charges of conspiracy to assassinate the king.

In March 1758 for the first time the Portuguese envoy in Rome spoke to Pope Benedict XIV the radical threat against the Jesuits; 'Either rigorous reform or abolition'. Men—no longer Protestants but Catholics— said that Jesuits fermented revolution; engaged in illicit trade to build up wealth; pursued power with such ardour that soon their missionary kingdoms would be impregnable. In those last few months of his life Benedict's chief adviser in the matter was the Jesuit-hater Cardinal Passionei, who like the secretary of state Cardinal Archinto was afterwards sent a diamond ring for his services to the Portuguese government. Benedict XIV issued a brief appointing the Portuguese Cardinal Saldanha to reform the Portuguese Jesuits.[3] Saldanha was a creature of Pombal.

The Neapolitan minister Tanucci afterwards believed that dying

---

[3] Benedict XIV, *Bullarium*, 12.403 ff.; Pastor, xxxvi.20–1; 295.

Benedict XIV's brief was the ultimate cause of the calamity which fell on the Jesuits. It ordered Cardinal Saldanha to act with moderation, but to find out whether the Jesuits in South America, who were accused of trading illicitly to the disadvantage of a legal monopoly in commerce, disobeyed the canon laws against trade by priests, or whether they only sold their surplus produce like any monastery selling vegetables from its garden. The brief turned the eyes of Europe to Jesuit activity in the markets, to the size of their estates, their management, and their endowments. They were declared now to be under suspicion, not merely from an oppressive minister, but from the Pope. Suddenly the idea was in the air that the Pope might, and could, abolish Jesuits.

After an official enquiry Cardinal Saldanha issued an edict (printed before the enquiry) that the Jesuits were guilty of 'scandalous trading', contrary to canon law and the orders of the Pope. He confiscated the accounts, and banned commerce under penalty of excommunication. Pombal ordered the Cardinal of Lisbon to ban the Jesuits in his jurisdiction from preaching or hearing confessions, and the Cardinal signed the ban, weeping.

In February 1759 Pombal confiscated all Jesuit property in Portugal. That April he expelled them from Portugal or imprisoned them in various forts; on the charges that they started war in South America, were linked with the attempt to murder the king, and engaged in trade against their rule. At first he thought of sending them to the penal settlements in Angola. But on 24 October, without warning, a Ragusan captain landed 133 Jesuits from Portugal at Civita Vecchia in the Papal States. Hundreds more followed in various batches, including those from the Portuguese empire in India and Brazil. The numbers are inaccurate enough, but of the 1,698 Jesuits in the Portuguese branch of the Society, more than a thousand were deposited in the Papal States. The exempted were novices and those willing to abandon the Jesuits rather than face exile. Out of 453 Jesuits in Brazil and Paraguay 170 preferred to leave the Society rather than be sent to Europe. In China and other lands outside Portuguese government the members of the Portuguese division of the Society were untouched.

The expulsion destroyed many missions in Paraguay and Brazil. It also forced a reconstruction of higher education in Portugal, not before time. Pombal imprisoned 124 Jesuits in the fort at the mouth of the Tagus and left forty-five of them there, without a trial, for nineteen years. A famous Jesuit Gabriel Malagrida, once a missionary in Brazil and regarded by the common people as a saint, was condemned by the Inquisition, which Pombal used as a crown court of repression, and executed as a heretic on

12 January 1761. Against this holy eccentric the charges did not bear examination.[4]

The judicial murder of Malagrida shows how far the Pope's writ still ran. He could not protect the Jesuits in Portugal because they were accused of crimes against the State and in Italy he had no way to disprove the charges. He could only ask for accusations which never came, demand that innocent members be not heaped together with guilty, and issue protests. But the Patriarch of Lisbon, and most of the Portuguese bishops, were submissive on Pombal's side and were seldom displeased to be rid of Jesuits. The Bishop of Bahia was removed because he protested too forcibly their innocence. The Pope was powerless to help.

But his law still ran. This was one reason why Pombal never brought the victims to trial. Canon law prevented State courts from trying clergymen, and canon law was accepted in Portugal. Pombal demanded from Rome that the old right enabling clerics guilty of high treason to be tried in a secular court (the so-called Court of Conscience) should be extended to the higher clergy and religious orders and made perpetual. Because Rome granted the exceptional case (2 August 1759) but refused the perpetual right, Pombal rejected the exceptional permission. Therefore he could not put the Jesuits on trial before a secular court but must either concoct charges of heresy before the Inquisition or keep them in prison without trial.

In 1760 Pombal expelled the nuncio and withdrew his ambassador from Rome.

The Pope had only the power of prestige. He could know that many common folk in Portugal disliked the tyranny over Jesuits in Portugal; could stir up a neighbouring power to intervene on behalf of the Catholic Church, and to that end invited King Charles III of Spain and King Louis XV of France and the King of Sardinia; but simultaneously must seek to avoid hard words lest they led towards schism, and the hurt of the Church in Portugal. The only power which could use force was Spain; the Spanish were not likely to support Jesuits; and the British government, over which the Pope had no influence, was resolute to keep Lisbon free from Madrid. The best if not the only hope was time. No government can for ever desire unpopularity with a large number of its subjects, prime ministers are not immortal, and most men like honours. The Pope distributed favours that some men liked, and for the sake of the welfare of the Catholic Church was cheerful about humiliating himself in bestowing

[4] W. Kratz 'Der Prozess Malagrida nach den Originalakten der Inquisition' in *A.H.S.I.* 4 (1935), 1–43.

honours. Some Portuguese were specially open to this pleasant bribery by titles. In those days they were apt to take excessive notice of show. In return Popes were willing. Early in the century (1716) the Archbishop of Lisbon became the patriarch, later the cassocks of his cathedral canons were scarlet, the patriarch used the papal tiara with crossed keys as his arms, the King of Portugal (1748) was granted the title of *Most Faithful*. Pombal's war with Rome stopped all these honours. The breach lasted ten years, while Pombal appointed what bishops he liked. As part of the peace made in 1769–70, the flow of titles began again; and again Rome was not too proud to accept humiliation for the sake of the Church in Portugal. One of the conditions of peace exacted that Pombal's brother Paul Carvalho be made a cardinal. Clement XIV cheerfully bestowed a title for the sake of the peace of the Church. But the Pope was partly saved from humiliation because Paul Carvalho died before news of the honour reached Lisbon.

The attack upon the Jesuits was not intended as an attack upon the papacy and the Church. Many Catholics who now wanted Jesuits changed or abolished had no wish for anything but the welfare of the Church. They might desire to see the power of Roman ecclesiastical administration diminished in their country. Frenchmen especially disliked the bull *Unigenitus* for seeming to identify Rome with a moral divinity suspect and associated with Jesuits. But since the Pope sent a brief to reform the Jesuits in Portugal, apparently hinting at their probable guilt in commercial speculation, and since the same Pope condemned the Jesuits for practices in China, Catholics were aware how members of the Curia disapproved or feared the attitudes or teaching which they attributed to the Society of Jesus. The assault upon the Jesuits was no more a necessary onslaught upon the Pope than Philip the Fair's destruction of the Templars four and a half centuries before.

The Jesuits were neither very centralized, nor very 'ultramontane'. Under pressure from French public opinion, the French Jesuits made a declaration (1757) that they taught the Gallican Articles of 1682, which raised General Councils above Popes. In those years attacking Jesuits was not at all the same as attacking Popes. Antagonists might even suppose themselves to be assailing religious not loyal to the Pope.

While Jesuits were under fire, all kinds of assailants joined. A Venetian accused their schools of being upper class. Priests who hated the emotionalism of parish missions related graphic stories of the superstitions and excesses fostered among their people by Jesuit preachers, told how a village near Vicenza expelled their missioner by threatening to shoot; or how a missioner at Murano in the lagoon of Venice made even the nuns laugh; or how missioners made money by selling crowns and statuettes and trinkets.[5]

The Jesuit 'conspiracy' in Portugal, the trial of Malagrida, the expulsion of the Jesuits, were followed with fascination by the rest of Europe. The Portuguese government made sure that plenty of information was given. It undertook a campaign of pamphlets to justify its conduct. A Venetian publisher of 1760 counted more than seventy Italian books or pamphlets caused by the events in Portugal. In the history of Europe it was a new kind of event. Men eagerly bought books about Paraguay, or the attempted murder, or Pombal, or Jesuit trading. A flood of anti-Jesuit brochures poured through France and Italy. Joseph Baretti passed through Lisbon on his way from London to Italy, and told how 'the eyes of all Europe' looked towards Portugal. He wholly disbelieved Pombal's declarations, was contemptuous of the charge of attempt to murder the king, and could not understand what the Portuguese government gained. Nevertheless he thought Jesuits dangerous, not because they tried to kill kings, but because they were 'indefatigable accumulators of riches'.[6]

In Roman cafés drinkers argued for and against Jesuits, for and against Portugal. Roman wine-merchants were said to tell stories of Jesuit speculations in the trade, the oil-sellers said to grumble that Jesuits dominated their commerce.[7]

These Portuguese events came at a time when some Catholic governments were trying to break the Jesuit near-monopoly of higher education. In Turin and Vienna and Milan was already a campaign that Jesuit education fell behind the times, and that a new system of upper schools and colleges must be devised, that the Jesuit system was archaic and too narrowly classical. Certainly some of the Jesuit schools were hopelessly old-fashioned.[8] Cries that boys must be taught history, or natural sciences, or modern languages, were loud enough to give educated men in Naples, or Palermo, or Florence, or Munich, and certainly in Rome, the doubt that 'modern culture' and higher Catholic education were out of step, and that the cause was backward looking by those who conducted higher education; for in former days they had reformed an entire system of schools and colleges, with such triumph that they put the result into a glass case and refused to doubt its value for all time.

[5] Venturi, *Sett.rif.* 2.102.   [6] Baretti, *A Journey*, 1.180 ff.
[7] Venturi, *Sett.rif.* 2.25–6.
[8] German and Austrian evidence in Merkle, *Die kirchliche Aufklärung*, 49 ff.

The whole affair of the Jesuits in public opinion touched upon attitudes, intangible and difficult to seize, towards the Counter-Reformation. The pastoral system of the Church owed a vast debt to the Counter-Reformation. Bishops and priests still struggled to bring into practice the ideals of the Counter-Reformation, St. Charles Borromeo was the model of a Catholic priest, the methods in mission and devotion, confessional or rosary, music or preaching, had been tested and found excellent. But a world into which Voltaire was born, and Madame de Pompadour reigned, and the eunuch Farinelli was political adviser to a King of Spain because he had so pure a singing voice, and the astronomy of Galileo was not only respectable but taught in leading seminaries for training priests, and devout priests like Mabillon and Muratori and Tillemont founded modern methods of historical study, and the heirs of Malebranche sought to adapt Cartesian philosophy to Catholic ends, and the Oratorian Richard Simon had begun the first Catholic studies in modern Biblical criticism, and Mozart began to write masses in an idiom far distant from the hallowed idiom of the past, a world of Catholic intelligence looked back upon the Counter-Reformation as a narrower world from which it grew and which was restrictive if it sought to keep thought within outmoded channels. The Counter-Reformation was in question. Still the key to the pastoral care of the Church, it appeared the enemy of modern education. Yet education was a part, possibly even the crux, of the pastoral care of the Church.

With the Counter-Reformation Jesuits were identified. Founded in the age of the Counter-Reformation, intended to be the instrument of its policies, large in historical accounts of its course, engaged with the wars of religion, the Society of Jesus was the symbol of the Counter-Reformation. Anyone who wanted the Church to grow out of the Counter-Reformation suspected Jesuits instinctively, and hardly noticed that Jesuits themselves had been helping the Church to grow out of the Counter-Reformation. They were not only too conservative in higher education. They were a flag, a legend.

According to an older conventional view of the Enlightenment, the destruction of the Jesuits was one of its noblest thrusts against obscurantism. History shows that this simple view will not stand. The Society, being in charge of the higher education of Catholic Europe, had minds open to new ideas. Some Jesuits were as obscurantist as anyone blindfold, others were pastors without interest in ideas, as it was said of the Jesuits of Aragon that they preferred doing to writing. But others looked forward, sought to extract what was best from new ideas, and were no minor part of Catholic Enlightenment; from ideas of toleration or penal reform to the latest developments in mathematics or the natural sciences.

The battle against the Jesuits was not quite a battle of moderns versus ancients, or light versus darkness. The cry for battle first came from Portugal, the least enlightened country in western Europe. Even in Italy the first and worst conflict came in a republic far from enlightened, Genoa. This was not quite accidental. Enlightenment was identified with toleration, and the expulsion of Jesuits was one of the most intolerant acts by Catholic states during the eighteenth century. Portugal, or Spain, or Naples did not blush at their laws against Jesuits because they were familiar with the notion that toleration is sin.

The eighteenth century was uneasy with the problem. Its intellectual prophets found monks useless and wanted to stop men becoming monks. Compulsion was necessary, otherwise too many became monks and the State sank towards poverty. Though they preferred to educate men not to be monks, they found it needful to turn monks out of doors because they wanted their houses and their money. Yet simultaneously their intellectual prophets stood for toleration, and therefore for a man's right to be a monk if he chose.

The French Jesuits

Pascal's *Provincial Letters* and then *Unigenitus* made the Society more controversial in France than in any other state. Pope Benedict XIV in his brief of 1758 seemed to assent that they were at least suspect of dubious commercial practice. By coincidence France suddenly witnessed a case of commercial scandal.

Lavalette was a capable Jesuit who reorganized the Jesuit properties in Martinique and Dominica in the West Indies. He turned a miserable unprofitable group of lands into a profit making and prosperous estate; by borrowing money from Paris, buying more land, remitting the surplus produce to Europe, and running the estates efficiently. His reputation grew until he became (1754) head of all the Jesuits in the West Indies. In 1754–5 the French Government—seeing that same conflict between the colonists' trade and the religious order which the Portuguese saw in Paraguay— ordered Lavalette not to engage in trade. Lavalette continued to organize his commerce and to borrow more money. To repay the debt he sent two ships full of sugar and coffee to Bordeaux; but an English fleet, on the verge of war with France, seized the ships and their cargo. Further ships sailed for Holland, and thirteen more fell into English hands. In February 1756 the Paris agents, whom Lavalette employed, went bankrupt, and brought down Lavalette in their fall. He owed more than 3,000,000 *livres*. For a time he tried to save himself by local speculation in West Indian trade.

The French Jesuits debated whether they owed this money and resolved that whatever the legal liability they must pay. But Father Frey, the new Parisian superior, seeing how his French houses would be loaded with debt under an apparently limitless commitment, decided that the West Indian mission was alone responsible and refused to accept liability. The creditors sued the mission; and one firm, after failing in a demand, sued the French Jesuits corporately, to make them responsible. The court held for the creditor, and therefore every other creditor sued the Society. Since the judgement was doubtful law, (for the Jesuit general was not owner in law of property in all the separate houses or provinces), the Paris Jesuits appealed to the Paris Parlement, which (8 May 1761) upheld the lower court, declared the whole Society to be responsible and ordered the debts to be paid within a year. The disgraceful publicity continued when the four other French provinces of Jesuits appealed again to Parlement to exempt them from responsibility as the debts were caused only by the Paris province which controlled Martinique. As they now needed to find 4,500,000 to 5,000,000 *livres*, they faced corporate ruin. The 5,000,000 *livres* increased daily through interest charges.

The Paris Jesuits appealed to the Jesuit general in Rome, Ricci. It was a bad time. Ricci was then maintaining out of his funds more than 1,000 Jesuit refugees from Portugal. The only richly endowed provinces at the moment lay in southern Italy and Sicily. On 23 April 1762 the Paris Parlement solved Ricci's problem by sequestrating all Jesuit properties in France for the non-payment of the debt. A Jesuit visitation in Martinique held that Lavalette traded contrary to canon law and the rules of the Society, kept no proper accounts, squandered resources, neglected pastoral work for his commerce, used crooked agents, and caused the death of negro labourers by excessive punishment. He was sent home in disgrace, left the Society, and died in obscurity.

The Portuguese told the world that the Jesuits engaged in illegal commerce in Paraguay, and were secret in a conspiracy to assassinate their king. Rome suspected these charges to be fabricated. But now French Jesuits were proved to have engaged in financial jugglery of unprecendented scandal. Lavalette delivered the Society of Jesus into the hands of its vocal French enemies. King Louis XV would have liked to protest, Pope Clement XIII was stalwart that the many innocent must not be condemned with the few guilty, the French bishops unlike the Portuguese bishops testified in majority to the good which was done by the Jesuits. The new Paris Provincial, de la Croix, tried to lighten his burden by publicly rejecting the doctrine that tyrannicide was sometimes permissible and the doctrine that the Pope had any indirect authority in the government of a state. But the case of Lavalette made successful defence in France out of the question. Even the general Ricci told the French Jesuits that they had done more damage to the order than could be done by its worst enemies.[9]

For a few months there was talk of drastic reform; by separating the French assistancy from the orders of the general in Rome, by insisting on the teaching of the Gallican articles by French Jesuits, and by removing their exemption from the control of bishops. The French Jesuits published a statement that their general could give no order contrary to the laws of the land, and that they would not use their privileges of exemption in cases where they clashed with the rights of bishops and other Church authorities. They accepted a demand that they should teach the Gallican articles. The general Ricci refused to approve this last declaration. The secretary of state Torrigiani told his nuncio in Paris (4 November 1761) that the Pope could only approve the Jesuits so long as they remained loyal to Rome. For the Jesuits these theoretical and constitutional questions were naturally far less important than their work—the right to keep their schools and colleges.

Ricci now accepted the possibility that the whole Order faced destruction. He wrote to Bernard Routh, an Irish Jesuit teaching at Poitiers, 'If the Society cannot be preserved without a crime on my part, it had better be destroyed. No one ought to commit even trivial sin in the effort to save it. I shall mourn at the ruin, and comfort myself that I am innocent.' But while he maintained an adamantine front to the French, he tried to excuse to the Pope the Jesuits who agreed to teach the Gallican articles in France. Uncompromisingly Ricci rejected constitutional change, like the independence of the French assistancy of the order. 'I will not govern any Order except the one I have inherited from St. Ignatius and his successors.'[10] He reported to Pope Clement XIII, and at this interview may have uttered the famous sentence of this controversy, 'Aut sint ut sunt aut non sint', 'either they must exist as they are or they must not exist.'

Whether or not Ricci spoke these words, they do not show, as they are sometimes understood, that the Pope yet imagined the possibility of a total abolition of the Society. The answer refused a French demand for change in constitution. Some French advisers thought that the refusal ensured the expulsion of Jesuits from France. In Rome they were aware

[9] Pastor, xxxvi. 400–3.   [10] Pastor, xxxvi. 424, 439 n.2.

that other countries would follow the French example in demanding Jesuit independence of Rome, and that the Order would break into national groups without coherence.

During the spring and summer of 1762 various French Parlements ordered the expulsion of Jesuits from France. Their schools were closed, houses occupied, novices sent home. They were allowed to remain in France if they left the Society, took an oath to be loyal to the king, opposed the morality associated with their name, and taught the Gallican articles; and if they so remained and were priests, they were to receive pensions from the confiscated estates. In some areas of Burgundy and south and south-west France local sympathies for Jesuits and their schools delayed until 1763 the execution of these decrees. In a few isolated places, like Besançon or Bar-le-Duc, with strong local support for their schools, they managed to hold out for another three years. Archbishop Beaumont of Paris issued a courageous defence of the Jesuits and was banished to La Trappe.

Pope Clement XIII could refuse concession to the French government. He had no means of protecting Jesuits in France, who in many areas were intensely unpopular. The question of a thunderous bull or brief was anxiously debated in Rome. On 9 June 1762 he addressed such a brief to the bishops in France, denouncing the attack on the Jesuits as persecution. The French refused to allow it to be published. On 3 September 1762 the Pope held a consistory of cardinals and delivered an allocution declaring null all the decrees of Parlements against the Jesuits. As Parlement might burn it if it were printed, he refrained from publishing. On 13 April 1763 he condemned a pastoral letter of Bishop Fitz-James of Soissons who taught that the Gallican articles were of faith. The language of this condemnation was strong. But the nuncio in Paris was carefully instructed not to condemn the Gallican articles, only to condemn the doctrine that they were part of the faith. The thunder sounded, but its explanation always sought not to embarrass to the point of rupture. In autumn 1764 Rome condemned similar doctrines published by the Bishops of Angers and Alais, but was careful not to publish the two briefs. The Pope sent Archbishop Beaumont of Paris a letter of sympathy in his exile and suspension.

Some 2,900 Jesuits now needed help, and as with the Portuguese Jesuits other states would not admit them as refugees. A few dozen crossed the border into the papal territory of Avignon. A few were found posts in the foreign missions, especially in China and Malabar. Ricci allowed many to continue for a time living privately as laymen in France. Benedictine or Carthusian or Sulpician houses received a number of priests, French bishops used several as curates in parishes whenever the taking of the oath to leave the Society was not enforced, the royal confessors were given fat pensions, and refugees were found in Switzerland, Belgium, some German states; fifteen were accepted in Poland; probably the largest number of refugees was given shelter within the Jesuit houses of Spain.

Clement XIII (Pope 1758-69)

Clement XIII Rezzonico was a Venetian nobleman aged sixty-five at election. He was educated by Jesuits and then the university of Padua. After a time in the Curia Clement XII made him cardinal and Benedict XIV consecrated him as Bishop of Padua where he succeeded in combining excellence as a bishop with popularity. Benedict XIV regarded him as the most godly bishop in all Italy, tireless in pastoral work, living in his palace as though it was a monk's cell, and giving away his income to the poor.[11] When he was Pope, the ambassadors did not think him intelligent, but respected his religious life. He was corpulent, hard-working, kind, and outgoing. He had much trust in human nature, and even appointed Casanova a knight of the Lateran and protonotary apostolic because he knew little about his character.

He also distrusted himself. He quickly made his pious nephew Carlo Rezzonico into a cardinal. Observers expected that Cardinal Rezzonico would become the effective head of business, like a cardinal-nephew of tradition. But the cardinal kept himself away from the administration.

The new Pope consciously used consistories of cardinals more than his predecessor. Nevertheless much business lay in the hands of one man; not for the first time, because in Benedict XIII's time it lay in the hands of Cardinal Coscia; but for the first time it lay in the hands of a secretary of state. The Pope appointed one of Benedict XIV's men, Cardinal Torrigiani. If the Pope was not always decisive, this mattered less because Torrigiani was resolute.

Torrigiani was much attached to, and determined to defend, the Jesuits.

The Spanish Jesuits

The campaign against the Society of Jesus was now formidable throughout Catholic Europe. They were expelled from Portugal, men believed, for conspiracy to murder a prince; from France, for embezzlement; their

[11] Benedict XIV to Tencin, ed. Morelli, 1.355.

moral teaching was notorious, their conduct in China a scandal, their hidden wealth legendary. The Spanish government had reason to encourage these opinions. It had the same motive as the Portuguese for breaking Jesuit power in South America, and could see ample use for the endowments which would be freed by abolishing the Society. Portugal and France clamoured that Jesuits be abolished because only by abolition could their own measures be justified. A personal dislike entered the argument and gave the last necessary push towards total abolition. King Charles III of Spain disliked Jesuits and would hear not a word in their defence. He won from the historian Pastor[12] the title *destroyer of the Jesuit Order*.

Charles III (King of Spain 1759–88) had small ability and much diligence, was honest, just, and religious. Earlier as King of Naples he was popular, and had qualities which made for popularity in Spain.

In March 1766 the government attempted to make the kind of law which can only be enforced by dictators who first save their country. It banned within towns the wearing of Spanish capes and hats and ordered everyone to dress like the French, in wig and three-cornered hat. Such folly was only to be explained by a strong feeling in government that Spain was behind the times. The result was mass demonstration in the streets of Madrid, violence and the killing of demonstrators, the fall of the king's ministers, and a threat to the king. The petty tyranny over dress allowed general discontent over the price of food to be harnessed to a cause.

The government had no evidence that Jesuits sparked the riots and the theory is in the first degree implausible. But Jesuits were linked in the public mind, since their expulsion from Portugal, with conspiracy against kings. A month after the riots rumours spread. The minister Campomanes sent the commission of enquiry two reports, the first in June holding the clergy responsible, the second in September pointing directly to Jesuits. On 29 January 1767 the commission of enquiry decided that the Jesuits must be expelled from Spain and their property taken by the State. They usurped a kingdom in Paraguay, spread ideas of revolution in Spain from their pulpits, printed pamphlets on secret presses against government, and turned hat and cloak riots into religious war. No one could reform such a body because it was *utterly depraved*. All its members must be banished.

On 27 February 1767, after advice from his ministers, King Charles III accepted the proposal and decreed banishment of Jesuits and appropriation

[12] Pastor. xxxvii.6.

of Jesuit property—to be executed 'with the greatest humanity'. The decree was made effective on the first three days of April. It was sudden. Less than two months before the king gave licence to forty Jesuits to sail from Cadiz as missionaries to Paraguay and Chile. In July Jesuits calling at Montevideo were ordered back to Europe. Throughout the American colleges the fathers were arrested and expelled, usually without suffering, sometimes with intolerable affliction, especially for the aged of some remote institutes of education. In two mining towns in Mexico popular riots in their favour were suppressed with hangings and exile.

Spanish bishops and monks did not disapprove these measures, and some were warm in praise of government. The nuncio in Spain, Pallavicini, advised Pope Clement XIII not to protest. Someone spread a story that the Jesuits alleged Charles III to be no son of his predecessor but the bastard of adultery between the queen and Cardinal Alberoni. In Catholic Europe the Society of Jesus acquired all the qualities of a scapegoat. In the city of Rome those who wished to swim with the tide were already changing their confessors or excluding Jesuits from their salons. Jesuit guilt was so axiomatic that no one need ask for serious evidence or listen to a word of defence. In mid-April 1767 Pope Clement XIII sent the king a heart-rending appeal to his kindness and sense of justice. He believed that whatever frailties might attach to individual members of the Society, nothing in the rules or constitution made it other than pious, useful, and holy. Pastoral care in Spain will suffer, the missions will suffer worse. It was an imploring letter, not the letter of an old medieval thunderer.

Now the Pope, advised by the secretary of state and by the Jesuit general Ricci, took a decision with grievous consequences in human suffering, and perhaps gave the last nudge to the general destruction. The Pope told the king that he could not admit the expelled Jesuits to the Papal States.

Each Jesuit banished from Spain was given a pension from the endowments of the society. But the Pope was the prince of a modest state already trying to maintain Jesuit refugees from Portugal or France. He feared that if he accepted more Jesuits, he would be unable to support them and would encourage other states to unload their helpless Jesuits in the harbour of Civita Vecchia. Some cardinals were afraid of 20,000 refugees. These Spanish refugees were the responsibility of Spain. King Charles III ordered the captains of ships bearing Jesuits to make for Civita Vecchia and protest if they were refused leave to land their human cargo—so the whole world should see how the Pope refused to care for his own.

On 18 May the Jesuit-bearing ships, repelled from Civita Vecchia, sailed for Corsica by agreement between Spain and the Genoese government. But the commander in Bastia refused to let them land for he was fighting a war against rebels, he had not food for his men, he had no means of feeding or housing refugees. For a month the ships lay in harbour at Bastia while the argument raged. At last leave was given, but for five months many Jesuits lived on board for want of other rooms; and all were short of food, had no way to celebrate mass, had almost no books, and some lived in huts of mixed sexes. Some of them (wrongly) blamed the general Ricci for refusing to let them into the Papal States. Numbers had only one idea, to be exempted from their vows and return to Spain. The superior of the province of Andalusia gave everyone freedom to do as he thought best. The losses by flight were more than compensated by the dumping in Corsica of the Jesuits from the Spanish colonists (2,576 from Spain, 1,812 from the colonies).

In May 1768 Genoa ceded Corsica to France. The French still had to fight the Corsicans in civil war and began to land Jesuits on the mainland in the bay of Liguria. In September 1768 a starving and tattered band of 800 Jesuits made their way down from Liguria to the Papal States, exciting horror and sympathy among the population as they passed. The Spanish and French government started to subsidize this exodus, paying more if a man would leave the society, though the Spanish would allow none, not even ex-Jesuits, to re-enter Spain without special permission. At Rome the Curia co-operated by making it easy for them to leave the Society. Between one-tenth and one-fifth of Spanish Jesuits (according to the province) left the Society. The native-born South American members caused feeling by their desire to do everything possible to get back to South America. Out of a total of 4,388, 719 Jesuits of the Spanish provinces left the Society then or within the next three years.[13] The sterner or more loyal majority regarded them as deserters. That so large a majority refused the blandishments of officials and the prospects of comfort has justly been seen as a sign of the spirit of the order.

Meanwhile Rome, without openly withdrawing its refusal to accept responsibility, organized relief. The Castilians and most Mexicans were cared for in communities at Bologna, the Aragonese and Peruvians at Ferrara, other different Spanish or American groups were collected in appointed parts of the Papal States. The Spanish government threatened to cancel all pensions unless the Jesuit general ceased to call these new homes by their Spanish or American names. The stories of hidden wealth were still widely believed, and houses empty of Jesuits were ransacked.

[13] Pastor, xxxvii.173, 181.

The Spanish ambassador in London (Prince Masserano) was made to enquire at the Bank of England in search of £16,000,000 in sterling said to be deposited there by Jesuits. The Portuguese ambassador in London, more gullible than his Spanish colleague, believed that the Jesuits were buying armaments in England and intended to hire mercenaries for war in Paraguay, and the report sufficiently disquieted the Spanish government to make them ask their ambassador in London to investigate. Lavalette, the former West Indian bankrupt, was alleged to be recruiting in Flanders to sail with an expedition to conquer Paraguay or Chile for England.

Jesuits in Naples

The Spanish dependencies in Italy followed the example of Spain. In Naples the minister Tanucci did what he could to encourage his old pupil the Spanish king and gladly executed the expulsion in Naples and Sicily. He followed the Spanish vestige of justice in providing pensions. His difficulty was, they could not be accused of anything. No assassination, nor riot, nor embezzlement, could be laid to their charge. Tanucci could only accuse them of 'blind obedience to their general', and then of vile moral teaching and their conspiracies in other states which proved them dangerous. The expulsion from Naples had to be postponed because Vesuvius erupted and the people might connect the two events. The decrees in Naples were of 31 October and 3 November 1767, executed 20 November (Sicily 29th). Of the 786 Sicilian Jesuits, only 352 went into exile, and in the next three years, seventy-two more left the Society.

The north-Italian anticlerical Carlantonio Pilati wrote a legend, *The Kingdom of Cumba*. In the fabled land of Cumba the Church was rich, devotions rare, monasteries always more powerful, practice of religion ever advancing. Meanwhile the population fell in numbers, weeds and brambles covered the fields, more and more ground lay untilled. Everyone who wanted work became a friar, or a student of literature, or picked up other people's leavings, or just begged. The lawcourts were corrupt, the schools taught the children subtle logic, unreal conceits, prejudice, and lies. So in time the monks became the government of the State. But the moment they got power they began to quarrel, friars versus Jesuits, every community was rent into furious parties, and said nasty things about each other which happened to be true. A young king with a wise minister (Pilati meant Ferdinand IV of Naples and Tanucci) tried to re-establish order—with the result that the clerics started conspiracy and murder. The king told how he found the treasury so empty, the kingdom in such turmoil, the State's power in such ruin, that he turned them all out into exile.[14]

Portugal, France, Spain, Naples, Sicily—and because Spain and Portugal were the colonial powers, most of the missions in the Americas and the East—had expelled the Society of Jesus. These were all Catholic powers, none Protestant, and nearly all were ruled by Bourbons. These Bourbon states hoped that they made themselves stronger by destroying a semi-independent community in their territories, pleased their colonists, and benefited their budgets (not so abundantly as some of them hoped) by confiscating endowments.

To their internal and international policy it was now a practical necessity that Jesuits be abolished.

Everyone knew that Pope Clement XIII would never abolish. On 7 January 1765 he issued a tremendous bull, *Apostolicum Pascendi*, approving the Jesuits, declaring their vows pleasing to God and their society a nursery of saints. After January 1765 the powers must be patient for the Pope's death, make sure of a successor who disapproved of Jesuits (not a difficult task to find such among archbishops and cardinals), and then see their justice and their prudence vindicated when a Pope himself should destroy so fatal a body.

Clement XIII, or his uncompromising secretary of state Cardinal Torrigiani, gave them excuse to act by force.

Parma

Little Parma in north Italy; once part of the Papal states, then a separate dukedom of the Farnese family but under papal suzerainty; then, when the Farnese family died (1731), a disputed territory seized by the Spanish Bourbons and made a Bourbon state which rejected any Pope as overlord; only a little territory with the twin towns of Parma and Piacenza, a not important station in the structure of Bourbon power across Europe— little Parma became for a moment the centre of this Catholic argument over Church and State.

What was done to control the Church in Paris, or Madrid, or Lisbon, or Vienna, or Munich, or Naples, might be resented by Popes, and might be criticized. Popes sent notes of protest but bore the pain because they had small other resource, and ended by conceding most of what Catholic states wanted. But when Parma so behaved, it was unbearable. For Parma was tiny and weak; it was sacked and ruined by war early in the century;

[14] *Riflessioni di un italiano sopra la Chiesa* (1768), 18 ff.; Venturi, *Sett.rif.* 2.294–5.

it had memories of the Counter-Reformation. Popes still claimed that it was part of papal territory; and because of its papal and Farnese history, its clergy and monks were numerous and powerful.

On 16 January 1768, as the climax of a series of measures to control the Church, the Duke of Parma issued an edict on the relations of Church and State. It banned all appeals by clergy to Rome unless by leave from the duke; forbade clergy from applying to Rome for pensions or offices; made it illegal to confer a benefice on anyone not a citizen of Parma, and every such appointment needed the duke's permission; and declared invalid all bulls and briefs from Rome or anywhere else unless they carried the duke's signature.

Pope Clement XIII replied swiftly. On 30 January 1768 he issued a brief known as the *Monitorium*, proclaiming the Duke of Parma's edict to be null;

an edict full of outrage and calumny, full of wicked doctrine tending to divide the Church, with the aim of separating the faithful from their head, and with the result that it overthrows the authority of the Church, turns sacred order upside down, lessens the rights of the Holy See and puts them under lay control; and reduces to a state of slavery the Church of God which is free.

All the decrees listed are null, and all the officials responsible are excommunicated unless they withdraw.

Thus, for the first time in long years, a Pope claimed to quash a series of laws passed by the government of a state. He claimed this right partly because Parma was 'papal'—'our duchy'—and partly because of the annual bull issued on Maundy Thursday, the bull *In coena Domini* which year by year excommunicated in general terms all who trespassed upon the rights of the Church.

The world was astounded. The friends of Jesuit refugees in north Italy blamed the Pope because his thunder would worsen their plight. Priests in north Italy thought it an act of blindness, the Cardinal-archbishops of Milan and Bologna criticized, the Parlement of Paris banned, the French minister Choiseul said 'The Pope is a fool and his secretary of state is an ass',[15] Tanucci in Naples was full of glee because of the consequences sure to follow and produced a plan to partition the Papal State among its Italian neighbours.

In April 1768 the ambassadors of the Bourbon powers at Rome demanded that the *Monitorium* of Parma be withdrawn. France occupied Avignon and the Venaissin, Naples occupied the papal enclaves of

---

[15] Rousseau, *Règne de Charles III*, 1.250.

Benevento and Pontecorvo. They threatened more occupations to follow.
Voltaire wrote a pamphlet to prove that the Pope ought not to rule a
state.

Europe thought of Clement XIII as reviving an age which they
imagined to have vanished, when Popes excommunicated kings and
released subjects from their obedience. Frederick of Prussia expressed the
feeling: 'The Grand Lama of the Vatican is like a tight-rope walker who
has grown old and in the sickness of old age wants to repeat the triumphs
of his youth, and so falls and breaks his neck'.[16]

It was a turning-point.

The ancient claims to international power over the morality of the
nations were symbolized in the tremendous and historic bull of general
excommunications called *In coena Domini* because it was read each Maundy
Thursday. The version revised in 1759 anathematized Hussites, Wycliffites,
Lutherans, Zwinglians, Calvinists, Huguenots, apostates, and 'all heretics';
all who appealed from Pope to general council, whether they were
individuals or universities; pirates, corsairs, sea-robbers in the Mediterranean 'especially on the coast from Monte Argentaro to Terracina';
those who steal from wrecks; those who impose new taxes without leave
of Rome; all who forge briefs; all who help Saracens or Turks or heretics
with arms or metals or ropes or information; those who hinder the supply
of food to the Roman Curia; those who attack pilgrims, or litigants
coming to Rome; assailants of cardinals, legates, bishops; appellants from
Rome to secular power; secular judges who haul ecclesiastical persons
before their courts; those who publish or use decrees to limit the liberties
of the Church; those who occupy any part of the Papal States, or usurp
ecclesiastical property. The bull ordered that absolution from these
censures be reserved to the Pope. It was to be put on placards at the
Lateran and St. Peter's, and sent to all bishops, and read in their churches
once a year or more often if needed.

Governments long disliked this bull and restricted its use. It was
generally read in cathedrals at times when no one took the slightest notice.
Venice made sure that it was read only in Latin at times when nobody
would be present to hear. It remained a symbol; believed by many to be a
piece of ritual from an old world; smiled at even by Pope Benedict XIV
who once said, 'I like to leave the Vatican lightnings asleep'; and suddenly
shocking when Pope Clement XIII appealed to it to justify the *Monitorium*
against Parma.

[16] D'Alembert to Voltaire, 13 May 1768: Voltaire. *Corr.* lxix.110; Venturi, *Sett.rif.* 2.230.

Therefore the year 1768 was a turning-point. The rhadamanthine bull was read for the last time that Maundy Thursday, the final year of the life of Pope Clement XIII.

On 19 October 1768 Clement XIII refused the demand of the three Bourbon powers, Spain, France, Naples, that he withdraw the *Monitorium* of Parma.

They had a hold on the papacy. They took its historic land, could take more, would refuse to evacuate till they got what they wanted, uttered dire threats of schism and separation, were not without support from churchmen in their countries. To retain his hold, whether over his lands or over the Churches in the Bourbon countries, the Pope must concede. And since he must concede, there was one thing which they wanted even more than the withdrawal of the *Monitorium* or the silencing of the bull *In coena Domini*. They wanted the Jesuits destroyed, and knew that they were strong to insist.

'This', wrote Horace Walpole to Horace Mann in Florence, 'is a crisis for the Court of Rome from which it will be impossible to recover.'[17]

Thus European politics and opinion forced Rome into the straits that it became its own interest to destroy the Jesuits. If the Pope persisted in maintaining the Society, he identified himself before European public opinion as one who encouraged low moral standards, tyrannicide, corrupt methods in foreign missions, obsolete habits in education, and unscrupulous efforts after ecclesiastical power. To support Jesuits was to identify with Jesuits. Early in the first half of the sixteenth century Rome came into crisis and schism because its moral standards failed to satisfy Catholic Europe. In the second half of the eighteenth century it fell into crisis and risked schism because it refused to condemn without trial what two-thirds of the Catholic leaders joined with all Protestants in condemning without trial. The secretary of state Torrigiani once talked of himself as a Jonah whom the Pope should jettison to lighten his ship.[18] Some cardinals in Rome now thought that wisdom demanded the throwing overboard, not merely of the secretary of state, but of the entire Society of Jesus which he defended.

In addition to reasons of public policy the Pope had on his hands some thousands of useless religious who could be made useful again if no longer members of the religious order, and a crowd of refugees who could be made comfortable. When the Jesuits were expelled from Naples, four out of eight cardinals present in the consistory argued for dissolution. This

[17] *Letters of Horace Walpole*, 7.11.   [18] Pastor, xxxvii.292 n.1.

Society had done good, could still do good. But now Catholic governments so hated it that its existence harmed the Church.

> O blessed and triune God
> Grant that for the peace of men
> And for thy true glory
> This society of Jesus may die.

Pope Clement XIII took a contrary view. If, as was confessed, they did
good, and were not allowed to do good in some countries, then they
should do good in other countries. Tanucci, the Prime Minister of Naples,
thought that it was waste of time dealing with so stupid a Pope and they
must place their hopes in his successor.

The fact was, four Catholic governments had publicly committed
themselves to the suppression of the Jesuits. They could not now afford to
fail. If they failed, they raised doubt about the justice of what they had
done, caused unsettlement among their people, lowered their own
prestige throughout Europe, and gave the Pope the biggest boost to his
authority since the Council of Trent. Every plan for modernizing their
states by lessening Church immunities and endowments might be in
jeopardy.

In January 1769 France and Spain and Naples formally applied to Pope
Clement XIII that the Jesuits be suppressed. Clement, who was a dying
man, was reported to Tanucci in Naples as saying that he would cut off
his hands before he signed a brief of suppression. He died on 2 February
1769, the evening before a consistory of cardinals to debate an answer to
the powers.

Horace Walpole wrote from England to his friend in Florence asking
when the cardinals would elect 'the last Pope'.[19]

Clement XIV Ganganelli (Pope 1769–1774)

Chapter 4 showed how the powers were determined that the new Pope
of 1769 should be an opponent of the Jesuits and how they sought at the
Conclave to secure a promise that the Jesuits would be destroyed. The
Franciscan Cardinal Ganganelli was known as a critic, though not a
prominent opponent, of the Jesuits, and as one who disapproved Clement
XIII's *Monitorium* to Parma. Efforts to elicit a guarantee failed, but
sufficient conversations were reported, and after a Conclave, tedious and
tense, of just over three months, Ganganelli was elected (19 May 1769).

---

[19] Pastor, xxxvii.331–6, 356; cf. *Letters of Horace Walpole*, 7.117.

He had been an able student, and was learned. That Clement XIII made him cardinal proved that in 1759 he was not noted for hostility to Jesuits. His earlier document against the legends of ritual murder by Jews proves him to have been a man of character. He was likable, talkative, and unpretentious as befitted a friar, and enjoyed humour and practical jokes. He remained for hours at his desk but he found it difficult to be responsible for even minor decisions, and was confronted with one of the most agonizing decisions which ever faced a Pope. He liked to be liked, shrank from displeasing, and therefore suffered temptation to say pleasant things to both sides and to procrastinate lest decision be unpleasant. He more easily worked through private friends than through official channels. His private secretary the Franciscan Bontempi was more powerful than the secretary of state. The cardinals were neglected and some accused him of trampling on the constitution. Clement XIV took small notice of the outward trappings of convention. He played billiards and bowls, snared birds, and offended by riding out in lay dress.

His private conversation to the Portuguese ambassador was at once sufficient (November 1769) to restore relations between Rome and Portugal. Two months later Clement XIV made Pombal's brother Carvalho into a cardinal. Carvalho had been prominent in the trial and condemnation of the Jesuit Malagrida. The policy of concession began. But Carvalho died before the honour reached Lisbon. Another of Pombal's men, the Archbishop of Evora, was made a cardinal.

In his first Holy Week 1770, the Pope caused the Maundy Thursday bull *In coena Domini*, of general excommunications, not to be read. This was half to withdraw Clement XIII's excommunication of the government in Parma. Each year afterwards he ordered that the tremendous bull be not read; until in his last year (1774) he ordered that it should never henceforth be read.

Two months after the election, the French ambassador Cardinal de Bernis presented on behalf of the three Bourbon powers a renewed petition for the suppression of the Jesuits. The Pope said that he regarded the memoir as premature and a sign that he was not trusted.

A Pope who thought it in the interest of the Church to suppress the Jesuits—whether he took the strenuous view that the Society was bad for the Church or the weaker view that the reputation of the Society was bad for the Church,—was confronted with no small difficulty. He must do it against the wish of a majority of the cardinals and the Curia. He must be seen to act aright. He must not provoke a *coup* in the Papal States. He must not destroy the numerous colleges of Catholic education, and the less numerous missions, which Jesuits still controlled. Above all he must not find that other Catholic powers who had not expelled Jesuits were resolute to maintain them in disobedience to the Pope. Of these Catholic powers— Austria, Bavaria, Poland, Venice, Sardinia/Piedmont—far the most weighty was the Austrian government. The Empress Maria Theresa in Vienna was probably the single person in Europe who might be able to save the Society of Jesus.

Clement XIV was sure that he must destroy the Jesuits. The nearer he approached the decision, the more melancholy his mood, the more anxious his misgivings, the more grievous his insomnia. The Bourbon ambassadors argued that quick decision cut short trouble, and postpone- ment allowed opposition to organize. The Pope believed that only time and delay could reconcile minds to so sweeping a destruction. Whether or not the Pope was timid and fanciful, he was afraid of Jesuits and their power. Three years after he became Pope the Jesuits existed still.

So late as January 1772 the English agent fancied that after all the Pope meant to save the Jesuits, and his subtle tactics could save them yet. 'The cunning Frate near us will in all appearances at last gain his point, and save his janizaries.'[20]

Little by little he withdrew their privileges. He instituted a visitation to the Roman college, as though its teaching were suspect, ejected the Jesuits from its chairs, and closed its hostel for young noblemen which they directed. He refused to lend them a customary escort of Swiss guards for a Corpus Christi procession. He encouraged the process for making a saint out of Palafox, Mexican bishop of the seventeenth century who was a famous critic of Jesuits. He took away from them the Irish college in Rome. He forbade refugee Jesuits in the Papal States to be used as preachers, confessors, or catechists. When the Jesuit general Ricci sought an audience, the Pope refused him entry. When the Pope went out driving and saw Jesuits kneeling to revere as he passed, he turned away his face and would not give a blessing.

At last he even cancelled the pensions which his predecessor paid to the destitute refugee Jesuits from Portugal. Some friends of the Jesuits believed that this Franciscan played a deep and calculated game. On the one hand he postponed the decision from month to month, on the other he fobbed off Spanish pressure by showing his public dislike of Jesuits. They wondered whether his real intention was the saving of the order. What impressed them was the refusal to make the stroke of the pen which not merely destroyed Jesuits but simultaneously recovered Avignon and Benevento.

[20] Mann to Walpole, 25 Jan. 1772; *Letters of Horace Walpole*, 7.372.

One intimate of the Pope told a reliable witness that the Pope hoped indeed to save the order, and that the only way was delay until political circumstances changed. Cordara compared Clement XIV to Pilate, who scourged Christ in the hope of saving him from the mob. Others took a different view. They thought that Clement believed in the necessity to lower Jesuit prestige in Rome and in other parts of the Catholic Church where it was still high. By acts of disfavour or rebuke or neglect he would lead the Romans to think the Spanish right.

At this crisis in their fortunes, the Jesuits were fortunate in their general. Ricci (1703–75) was a Florentine who early entered the Society and became novice-master and later professor at the Roman college. He was a gentle and affectionate man, much loved by his pupils, whose confessions he heard and meditations he directed. One of his pupils said that he was a director of souls without an equal. At the 1755 election of a new Jesuit general the Roman province sent him as one of their delegates, and so he became known to leaders of the other provinces. The new general Centurione made him general secretary of the Society, a post which he accepted with repugnance, pleading that he lived among books and knew nothing of administration.

Centurione died after only two years in office, and in spring 1758 the Roman province again sent Ricci as a delegate to elect the new general. The delegates went to the meeting expecting to elect the assistant of the German province but were disturbed to see how ill he looked. So they turned to the Greek Father Timone, vicar-general, that is the general's deputy who summoned the meeting and was already sixty-seven. But that day at dinner they heard read in the refectory the passage of Rinaldi's *Annals* where the cardinals felt it wrong to elect Cardinal Bessarion as Pope because he was a Greek. They took this as a warning. Various names were then put forward, including Ricci's. When the first ballot was counted, several were surprised to find Ricci's name with most votes, because he was the candidate with no experience whatever of government. This circumstance drew others to his side, and at the second ballot he was elected by 63 votes out of 87, and so became general, the most famous of all Jesuit generals after the founder St. Ignatius Loyola.

Upon the wisdom of this election Jesuits afterwards differed. Ricci was quiet, simple, sincere, peaceable, straightforward, as far as possible from double-dealing; with a temperament wishing rather for retirement than action; reserved, and occasionally timid-seeming.

Cordara, who observed the destruction of the Society with more intelligence and inside knowledge than any other Jesuit, thought that at this terrible crisis in its fortunes, the Society needed a man of action and force, who knew the world, and understood how to influence courts and kings. For Cordara, Ricci was too passive, too soft-mouthed, too resigned in the face of calamity. He loved the man, but he said: 'I grieved that over this innocent head should blow such storms, and felt that he could easily be knocked over by the hurricane'.

Many other Jesuits afterwards thought the opposite. Even at the time of election some said, 'The only way to meet a storm is to run before the wind.' Whatever the general did or did not, could make no difference. The circumstances of the Catholic world and of the Church drove the Society irresistibly to its death. Therefore the best kind of general was a man in all respects opposite to the demon-portrait of the Jesuit in legend. The Jesuits were notorious for understanding the world too well. Their new general had not a remote idea what was meant by intrigue. History or fable recounted how subtly Jesuits schemed and burrowed. No one could imagine Ricci scheming, nor even being subtle. He said his prayers, and let things happen which must happen. If the Society had to die, it would not die because its last general was guilty of the faults for which the world wished it to die.

Seeing his inexperience they gave him Father Timone as an assessor for the Italian province. Father Timone had the two qualities which Ricci lacked, for he had confidence in himself and experience of government. Cordara thought that this was not good for the Society. To have too diffident a general, with too confident a chief assistant, was in Cordara's judgement a recipe for ruin. So, wrote Cordara, 'even the life of our family—God's secret providence guiding—looked towards the destruction of the Order.'[21]

In March 1772 the Spanish replaced their ambassador in Rome. They sent José Moñino, afterwards to be celebrated in the history of Spain as the Count of Floridablanca. Moñino was chosen to force the Pope to delay no longer. He had a reputation for toughness. The Pope saw this powerful incomer as little as possible, pleading skin disease, the need for Turkish baths, his delicate health. But the noose tightened. The Pope for secrecy's sake only used Bontempi as intermediary for Spanish negotiations.

On 23 August 1772 Clement XIV received Moñino and suggested a sensible plan. The Society of Jesus should admit no further novices. Its existing members should be forbidden to preach or hear confessions. The general's supreme power should be so divided among the provincial

21 Cordara, 228–9. For Ricci's election, documents in *A.H.S.I.* 44 (1975), 236–44.

superiors, that the Order became a confederation of national religious societies. This plan for slow death had the merit of avoiding the drama of sudden destruction, and of maintaining the work in education and missions in states where they were allowed to continue. It had the demerit that the Bourbon governments were too committed to total and instant destruction. 'Toothache', Moñino told the Pope, 'can only be cured by extraction.' A fortnight later (6 September 1772) the Pope accepted the necessity to see a draft brief of suppression. Moñino was using a mixture of threats and gold to frighten or cajole the Pope's advisers, or cardinals who might waver. By this double method he won the Pope's close friend and confessor, the Franciscan Father Bontempi, to the cause. In mid-December Clement XIV asked an anti-Jesuit prelate in Rome, Zelada, to work with Moñino on drafting a bull. (*Bull* is right. The original draft was a bull; converted later, intentionally to the form of a brief.) By the end of 1772 they agreed a draft. On 11 February 1773 the Pope sent the draft for comment to King Charles III of Spain. Charles III sent a letter to the Empress Maria Theresa in Vienna.

Maria Theresa, a pious Catholic with some pro-Jesuit and some anti-Jesuit advisers, replied (4 April 1773) that she had always thought well of the Jesuits who did good in Austria. But if the Pope thought that Catholic unity depended on the suppression of the Order, she would not oppose his decision. She reserved the rights of her government to deal with Jesuit property if the Order were suppressed.

Austria's refusal to resist a bull (if the Pope so decided) removed the last political obstacle which faced the Pope and the Spanish. Five new cardinals, among them Zelada, the drafter of the brief, were made in March and April 1773 to strengthen the anti-Jesuits in the college. In Bologna the Pope encouraged Archbishop Malvezzi to a local suppression, using force where necessary to dissolve the community. Early in June Clement at last signed the brief of suppression. It was dated 21 July 1773.

The brief instantly became one of the most celebrated of all papal decrees, as *Dominus ac Redemptor*. It was not published till 16 August, so that copies might have time to reach Versailles, Lisbon, Madrid, and Vienna. A cardinal's commission was almost simultaneously created to supervise the suppression of the Jesuits. Its president was Marefoschi, the fiercest anti-Jesuit among the cardinals. The new cardinal Zelada, drafter of the brief, was a member. The commission remained in very close touch with the Spanish embassy, which saw its confidential papers.

The Jesuit constitution included a special vow of obedience to the Pope. Though their habit of mind nevertheless included freedom to obey God rather than the Pope if they believed the Pope ill informed or badly advised, as with the Chinese missions, to resist a bull of suppression was unthinkable. Till beyond the eleventh hour the general Ricci could not believe that the Pope would commit a judicial act without an enquiry, or destroy so much higher Catholic education and so many missions, because four governments threatened.

Dominus ac Redemptor began by stating that the vocation of the Church is to bring peace to mankind, and that if something, even dear to the Pope, hurts peace it must be sacrificed. It declared the precedents by which Popes abolished religious orders. Then followed a history which represented the Society as causing envy and division since its foundation. It can no longer be useful, the peace of the Church cannot be restored so long as it exists—and 'after mature and informed consideration, and in the fulness of power which we have received from the Apostle, we dissolve, suppress, extinguish and abolish the said Society.'

Novices were to be sent away. Members who had professed simple vows must choose another vocation within a year. Members who had professed solemn vows must either join another order or become a parish priest under a bishop. They were ordered out of their houses, unless this was impossible, when they might stay as secular priests until the house was needed for other charitable purposes.

Through an excited Europe ran the news that Pope Clement XIV abolished the Jesuits. No Pope made so instant and so favourable an impact upon general opinion. The only parallels in the centuries since the Reformation came when Pope Pius IX stepped forward on the side of liberal Italy in 1846 and when Pope John XXIII announced the plan for *aggiornamento*, reconciliation with the twentieth century. It seemed as though Popes put aside their old weapons, anathemas and excommunications and inflexibilities, and sought peace with the world, throwing away claims to order men about, and seeking the influence of a pastor instead of the power of a king. Protestants said that if the sixteenth century had seen Popes like this, the Catholic Church would never have divided. In north Italy a poet praised him in panegyrical language, making the name of Ganganelli a synonym for virtue and declaring him one of the heroes of the centuries.[22] In England the antipapal ex-Catholic historian Edward Gibbon, who came to Rome and heard the barefoot friars sing vespers under Clement XIII Rezzonico, wrote in his *Memoirs* in praise of

---

[22] *Le notti clementine* (Arezzo, 1775), by Giorgi Bertola; still more panegyrical in the French translation (Paris, 1778).

Ganganelli. Years afterwards William Ewart Gladstone more than once listed as models of Catholic faith at its best the three names: Pascal, Bossuet, and Ganganelli. The Marquis Caraccioli edited four volumes of *Interesting Letters* as written by Clement XIV, in which the author appeared as a wise and liberal mind and a simple unpretentious friar. These letters were rapidly produced in French and English and aroused an interest which went still wider when Voltaire denounced them as forgeries; and many historians, at least in part, have agreed with Voltaire. Archbishops sang *Te Deum* in cathedrals. Men talked of the miracles which he wrought, or suggested that he be canonized as a saint, or predicted that history would know him as Clement the Great. Europe warmed to this friendly, kindly Pope who threw away armour and came forward with appeals to peace and charity. In April 1774 French troops evacuated Avignon and restored the papal bearings.

In their private correspondence between the capitals, diplomats wrote more cynically. They observed the glum manner of most of the cardinals in Rome. Not all the common people of Rome were fond of the Pope. Rome said that the Jesuits were the price paid for Avignon and Benevento. Common people of Rome were heard to use against the Pope the proverb, 'Good ends do not justify bad means.' Cordara thought that the Pope was more unlucky than wicked, that he might have been a good Pope if he had lived in a different time, and though it was wrong—'who will say that anyone else could have acted differently?'[23]

Though the ex-Jesuit general Ricci preserved a silence of dignity, and though some ex-Jesuits preached sermons on the rightness of the Pope's act if he found it expedient, some of Ricci's men were outspoken against the Pope. Nuns with the gift of prophecy predicted the restoration of the Order or the imminent death of the Pope.[24]

Ricci held a document from Pope Clement XIII empowering him to alienate precious possessions. Ricci himself made no use of the faculty. But a few less scrupulous ex-Jesuits tried to sell off goods from their houses before they were confiscated, or wrote anonymous pamphlets. These acts brought accusations of disloyalty or theft against the order and therefore against its general. A detective searched through mounds of ordure at the German college in the quest for a suspect brochure. Father Stefanucci, who was growing a little senile, talked too freely of the nuns' prophecies. Ricci was accused of stealing money and precious articles by passing them away into a bank. At first the charge mentioned 50 millions. On 23 September

[23] Cordara, 420–2.
[24] For the prophecies in Valentano, see the papers in *A.S.V.* Fondo Gesuiti, 24 and 30.

1774 Ricci was imprisoned in Coscia's old room at the Castel Sant' Angelo, with his five assistants and seven other ex-Jesuits. They were treated severely, at first with no fires in winter, and were thought to need sixty German mercenaries as guards. Nothing showed so dramatically the fear of a pro-Jesuit *coup* in Rome.

Ricci denied either that they possessed wealth of the sort mentioned, or that he or anyone else with his knowledge sought to abstract any part. Nothing against him was proved; but he died in Castel Sant' Angelo two years later, victim of suspicion and the Spanish government. Pius VI negotiated for his release, under promises, to his birthplace Florence, and the Spanish ambassador reluctantly agreed. But while the Habsburg governments of Tuscany and Vienna were being asked for their approval, Ricci died. Despite the Spaniards, Pius VI ordered that though the funeral must be at the church of St. John of the Florentines, he be quietly buried, as he desired, at the Gesù.

A Jesuit preached Ricci's memorial sermon in the church at Breslau which Jesuits continued for a time to control. This powerful and moving utterance was widely circulated:

Is it expedient that our Company perish for the public good? Let it perish—but why invent crimes to justify its perishing? If Ignatius formed his company to be a rampart against the destructive errors of Luther and Calvin, why would not Ricci sacrifice himself and his men to pacify the troubles of Christendom?

Rise from the darkness of your tomb, Clement, and see the work of your hands. The Lord put you to a rough test when he set you up as the new Abraham, and ordered you to sacrifice an innocent and cherished body. The whole world knows how you felt the greatness of the sacrifice, it saw your tears, it saw your hand raised, Isaac waiting for the angel . . . but this time the knife came down, the victim fell to the foot of the altar of God who knows how to turn, when he pleases, stones into the children of Abraham.

Some Jesuit drafted a pamphlet to doubt whether even a Pope could condemn a lot of people without trial. Is a Pope to be obeyed if he orders injustice?[25] This was not the mind of the Society. They were led by Ricci to kiss the rod.

A Jesuit Father Scarponio started to write a history of the suppression and to print. He reached the French suppression and was forbidden to continue, and what was already printed was made to vanish. Father Scarponio tried to write a life of Ricci. In the royal library at Brussels lies

---

[25] *Se possa dal Papa abolirsi senza processo la Compagnia di Gesù*; discovered by the investigators of Father Stefanucci's papers: Jesuit MSS, Hist. Soc. 225.50–63.

the fragment which he wrote, with a note at the end: 'not continued by its author, who was persecuted by the Curia'.[26]

Cordara wrote in manuscript a brilliant history of the suppression in the form of autobiography. He started writing a year after the brief of suppression, and finished in March 1779. Then he decided that to print was premature, and died with a deliberate resolution not to make it public. For more than a century the precious manuscript was kept from the historians.

In a few countries where Jesuits were much valued came tiny popular demonstrations. In the Catholic cantons of Switzerland, Poland, the Austrian Netherlands (Belgium), little signs of such feeling were evident, like a sudden access of crowds to a Jesuit church. But where strong feeling existed governments were wise and quietly continued the Jesuits as ex-Jesuits with the same duties, and thereby avoided either offending their people's piety or ruining their colleges of higher education.

This continuity of work between Jesuits and ex-Jesuits was common, far commoner than was later described by historians who saw the hurt suffered by missions, schools, or loss of property. In Spain and Portugal especially, and also though less evidently in France, the suppression was damaging to many institutes of higher education; and a calamity to the missions in those many countries where Spain and Portugal were still the colonial powers. But these hurts came from acts of governments, not from the Pope's abolition. Elsewhere Jesuits frequently continued to do the same work as before, though now ex-Jesuits and subject to the authority of the bishop.

In the most favourable circumstances they continued to live in the same buildings and in community. This happened in the Catholic cantons of Switzerland, in England and Scotland and the missions of the English colonies in North America. The difficulty which they faced was the end of power to recruit, and therefore the need to fill vacancies, after death or retirement, with secular priests who had no Jesuit training and might not share Jesuit ideals.

In nearly as favourable circumstances they continued in community, and did the same work, but must sacrifice their buildings. The brief of suppression intended buildings and endowments to be used by bishops for charitable purposes after pensions were paid to ex-Jesuits in need. But in German lands governments insisted on allocating the Jesuit endowments to state purposes; so that the Jesuit house in Vienna became the War

[26] Jesuit MSS 17985. fos. 2–41.

Office, and the houses in Prague and Antwerp became barracks. The Bollandists, famous group of Jesuits engaged on publishing the lives of the Saints, had to move house twice, ending in the ex-Jesuit house in Brussels, until swept away by French revolutionary armies. In this way the old work in school and parish continued, though under voluntary rules, and more insecure because more liable to interference by bishop or government. In rare cases special disabilities were imposed. Because Jesuit morality was suspect, ex-Jesuits in Austria were banned from professorships of theology or ethics or philosophy—but not from other professorships, and an ex-Jesuit was still tutor to the sons of the heir to the throne (his name was Hohenwart, an ex-Jesuit who ended his life as Archbishop of Vienna).

A less favourable state existed where an unfriendly government refused to allow ex-Jesuits to live in communities, but allowed them with due submission to teach or be parish priests. This was sometimes associated with the suspicion that they concealed treasure. Bavaria and the Elector of Mainz treated their Jesuits in this way, which could be harsh to elderly celibates thus ejected from home. An occasional ex-Jesuit house suffered damage from treasure-seekers hoping to find bags of gold concealed in the walls. The government of the Austrian Netherlands was still harder, and came near to following French precedent, for it refused most Jesuits leave to work in colleges or as parish priests.

Poland, where Jesuits were popular, might have been expected to follow the friendliest pattern of government; and 270 ex-Jesuits continued in schools or colleges, and others in parishes. But Poland was in a state of civil war, and had just suffered its first partition. In the anarchic conditions the houses and property of a suppressed religious order were tempting morsels, whether to robbers or to corrupt commissioners sent by government. Ex-Jesuits with pensions could not always receive their money and were destitute. The good Polish system of education was hurt because the end of the chief teaching order happened by accident to coincide with political upheaval.

Libraries were dissipated, old books sold off as junk, some important medical manuscripts disappeared, pictures of Italian or Flemish masters passed to numerous museums like the Vatican museum or the imperial gallery in Vienna. In Rome branches of the Franciscan order took over the churches, Capuchins came to the Gesù; Dominicans became professors at the German college which did not flourish because fewer candidates came from Germany. Many ex-Jesuits continued as schoolmasters both in Rome and other towns of the Papal States. In the Papal States the endowments could not yet serve other purposes, for they were saddled not only with the pensions of Roman ex-Jesuits but with the support of Portuguese and other refugee ex-Jesuits in Italy.

Goethe came over the Alps in 1786 and stopped at Trent. He stood in the ex-Jesuit church contemplating the architecture. An old impoverished priest muttered: 'Well, they have expelled the Jesuits but they ought at least to have paid them what the church cost them to build.' A few moments later Goethe heard him still talking to himself. 'The Emperor didn't do it. The Pope did it.' He did not know that Goethe was there, and turned towards the street, and said 'First the Spaniards, then we, then the French. The blood of Abel cries out against his brother Cain.' He went down the steps of the church, still muttering continuously. Goethe inferred that he was an old man whom the Jesuits supported, who went mad after 'the tremendous fall' of that order, and 'now comes every day to look in this empty shell for its former inhabitants, pray for them a little, and curse their enemies.'[27] No incident so brings home the personal agonies of the dissolution as the accidental meeting of Goethe in the church at Trent.

Not everyone instantly familiarized themselves with what happened. In some places in southern Italy the Jesuits had provided the best accommodation for travellers. Five years after the suppression travellers might be advised to go there for their beds; and when they arrived found no beds, but an empty house full of dirt and cobwebs.[28]

Nothing could replace the Jesuit missions in the Americas and the Far East, within the Spanish or Portuguese empires. Franciscans did what they could in the Americas, Carmelites in parts of southern India, bishops made what arrangements were practicable. But nothing could stop the lovely churches of remote Paraguay falling into romantic ruins.

Some examples:

1. *Missions*

India: There were 220 Jesuits at dissolution. A few held on in south India. At Pondicherry they only changed their name but could not recruit.

Canada: They continued work under different names, sometimes as pastors of parishes, but could not recruit. In all French missions there were 152 fathers at the dissolution. They continued and died out gradually.

East African coast: Of seven Jesuits, all were removed.

Peru university: Jesuit professors were replaced by Franciscans.

Philippines: Father Garcia was expelled with 147 other Jesuits on 1 August 1768.

Delayed by storm, and encouraged by popular demonstrations as they

[27] Goethe, *Italian Journey* (Eng. trans. London, 1972), 40.   [28] Swinburne, *Travels*, 4.52.

crossed Mexico, Father Garcia's group arrived at Cadiz two years later and were sent on to Spezia in north Italy, where they disembarked for Bologna. In smaller groups as secular priests they made their homes in several smaller towns of the northern Papal States, always diminishing as men left or died or found other work. When the brief of suppression was published, Father Garcia was imprisoned and then expelled from Bologna. Two years later he is found at Ferrara. Twenty years later he lived among the Oratorians at Sinigaglia. By revolution in Italy he was drawn back to his native Spain where he became a preacher at his birthplace until banished again. In 1801 he went to Rome and heard that a 'Jesuit' college was opening in Naples, applied to join and was accepted. But Rome preferred him to go back to Sinigaglia to join other ex-Jesuits from the Philippines.[29]

2. *Protestant countries (except Prussia)*

Holland: The thirty-two priests in twenty-one parishes signed a submission and continued as secular priests.

Britain (except Ireland): The 285 Jesuits (140 in Britain, the remainder in the colonies) continued as secular priests, but a number were French, who returned to France.

Switzerland: They continued as secular priests.

3. *Catholic countries*

Bavaria: Jesuits might teach or be parish priests but unlike ex-Jesuits of Austria or Switzerland might not live in community.

Mainz: They were ejected from their houses and at first were not allowed to exercise their priesthood. But slowly many were absorbed into teaching or curacies.

Rome: The chief substitutes for the Jesuits were as follows: Gesù, the Capuchins; S. Ignazio, Franciscan minorites; St. Peter's (office of penitentiary), the Franciscan Conventuals. Works of art were sent to the Vatican museum, but some to cardinals like Corsini or Zelada. In elementary schools many ex-Jesuits were employed as schoolmasters. The German college was transferred to the Dominicans. The Roman college was closed in 1772, then opened as a new university in November 1773, with some ex-Jesuits on the teaching staff.

If a scholar was good enough he easily found employment. Matteo Canonici was a Jesuit expelled from Parma. He was forced to leave behind his collection and a fine library. He moved to Bologna and started to collect

---

[29] Cf. Cushner; and E. J. Burrus, 'A Diary of exiled Philippine Jesuits, 1769-70' in *A.H.S.I.* 20 (1951), 269-99. On the problem of lodging ex-Jesuits, see *A.S.V.* Lettere de Vescovi e prelati, no.302. fos. 704-18.

again, until six years later he lost all a second time when the Society was suppressed. Now he moved to Venice and restarted, and here built a famous collection for the use of scholars. 'I could have sold my library in London', he wrote (1804), 'for a vast sum of money but I keep it for the Jesuits for whom I designed the collection.'[30] In 1798 he moved back to Parma to direct the public library.

The world had the illusion that Jesuits were all very conservative and therefore expected ex-Jesuits to be obscurantist. It was surprised. These had been the educators of Europe and their young men had ideas. Frequently they are to be found in the intellectual argument of that age, sometimes on its radical left. Freed from the closed communities, and from their vows of obedience by a Pope, they began to follow the argument wheresoever it led, and found that it led them far. In Ferrara several ex-Jesuits belonged to the group which advocated radical reforms in Church and State. One ex-Jesuit of Florence, who decided to stay in Florence after the suppression, and was the biographer of Galileo, was so free in mind that less than twenty years later he was one of the most famous assailants of papal absolutism in all Italy.[31]

Thirteen years after the destruction of the Jesuits Mrs Piozzi came from London to visit Rome. She found that Italian public opinion still thought it good that the Jesuits were gone; 'whilst all men must see that the work of education goes on worse in other hands'.[32] The monks who took over, she thought, had less knowledge of the world, and therefore were worse educators, than their vanished predecessors. She failed to realize how many ex-Jesuits vanished only in name.

Still, the vacuum in education was hard to fill. Other religious orders expanded to meet the need. In Benevento the Jesuits were turned out of their magnificent college five years before the dissolution, and left the buildings to be a barracks for the occupying troops from Naples. In 1774 when the troops went reluctantly, the college became a school. But since the Jesuits were no more, no one could run the school, until the canons persuaded the archbishop to invite the Redemptorists to occupy the old Jesuit house—an extension of their work, for early Redemptorists disliked houses in towns, knowing their vocation to peasant villages. A Neapolitan report (1777) advised the suppression of Redemptorists on the ground that they were crypto-Jesuits.[33]

At least ten Jesuit houses in Italy were taken over by bishops at last able to house their seminaries adequately.

[30] Irma Merolle, in *A.H.S.I.* xxvii (1958), 5–58.   [31] *D.B.I.* s.v. 'Luigi Brenna'.
[32] Piozzi, *Observations*, 2.136–7.   [33] Berthe, 2.436; 402–3.

The Jesuit property at Tivoli passed at a nominal price to the nephew of Pope Pius VI, Duke Braschi-Onesti, who founded upon it the fortune which enabled him to build the Palazzo Braschi (now the Museo di Roma) with the grandest staircase in all Rome.

The royal library at Palermo was founded in the Jesuit college and inherited its books.

The Jesuit college at Catania became a technical institute for training (e.g.) watchmakers.

Sicily decided to divide Jesuit lands among the peasants. The upper and middle classes got a goodly proportion, but after difficulty Tanucci succeeded in saving the property from crude sack, and holding something like half, at least temporarily, for peasant proprietors.[34]

We may tabulate the development of the eighteenth-century papacy.

Clement XI ruled, and with integrity, in later years helped by nephews.

Under Benedict XIII a corrupt favourite ruled.

Under Clement XII an upright cardinal-nephew ruled.

Benedict XIV ruled himself, with sobriety and common sense, but using a fairly upright secretary of state.

Clement XIII was ruled by an upright secretary of state.

Clement XIV was ruled by the Spanish ambassador.

This too crude formulation shows what really happened: (1) the final decline of the office of cardinal-nephew; (2) the rise of the secretary of state; (3) the increasing power of Catholic governments over the Pope—and therefore over the churches in their respective lands.

Dominus ac Redemptor was extorted from Clement XIV by the Spaniards using the aid of Naples and the French. The force was a threat to close monasteries, abolish nuncios, strip Rome of its jurisdiction, and invade the States of the Church. The promises to encourage were the security of other religious orders, the reopening of the nunciatures, and the restoration of occupied territory. The brief carried with it gross injustice to a small number of individuals and unhappiness, bearable but still very melancholy, to a much larger number of men whose way of life was destroyed. It stated no approval of what kings did to Jesuits, but seemed to stamp high approval by the Church upon the injustices wrought by the Kings of Portugal, Spain, and Naples. It said no word about the legends of the Jesuits, but could not help confirming Protestants in their opinions about the intrinsic wickedness of the Order. It put the seal on vast damage done to missions overseas and to schools and colleges.

[34] *D.B.I.* s.v. 'Braschi-Onesti'; Tuzet, 336; Renda, *Bernardo Tanucci e i beni dei gesuiti in Sicilia* (1974).

But most of the damage to missions and schools was done before the brief, and in schools was rather less extensive than at first sight appeared. Meanwhile the brief saved Pope and Church from afflictions. It was also the most popular bull or brief ever to come out from a Pope.

The Spanish ambassador in Rome sent Pope Pius VI a memorandum (31 May 1775) to discourage him from any attempt to help ex-Jesuits especially by releasing the few prisoners from gaol. His argument compared the state of the Church at Clement XIV's death (1774) with the state of the Church at Clement XIII's death (1769). Before Clement XIV was elected, Portugal and its overseas empire was almost in schism, Spain had expelled the nuncio and was minded to abolish papal authority, France occupied Avignon and the Venaissin and encouraged Gallican doctrines among the clergy, Naples occupied Benevento and Pontecorvo and was about to occupy more, in Vienna, Milan, Mainz, Trier, Parma, Tuscany, Venice, Genoa, and Lucca antipapal laws were being passed or prepared. And now—'the storms have ceased, the cloud dispersed.' Not to see the good done by Clement XIV, 'a man must be blind.'[35]

In a view longer than any contemporary could take, the argument could be extended. The stranglehold on Catholic education needed breaking if the Church was to educate for the nineteenth century. While Jesuit schools and colleges were better or much better than the restaffing which now must be fixed desperately, Catholic education was sure to profit in the long run from a more varied type of school and a less conservative standard of curriculum. To start afresh in the missions was disastrous. To start afresh in education was painful and lowering but may have been necessary to a longer advance.

Spain, and Naples, and Portugal, too slowly moved into modernity. If they failed to compel the Pope to abolish Jesuits, after public rampage and international excitement, they raised the Pope's prestige at the very moment when the programme of modernization insisted that he be less powerful in their states. The destruction of the Jesuits was seen as a step on the road towards a better constitution in Catholic states.

Nevertheless he who reads the details of the treatment of Ricci in his cell at the Castel Sant' Angelo, the maltreatment of an innocent, holy, and prayerful general, keeps being reminded of the saying then current in the streets of Rome, 'Good ends do not justify bad means.'

Forced or unforced, the brief was the most tremendous use of power in the Church ever achieved by a Pope. To abolish the strongest of religious orders without an enquiry, and with no reason alleged, was a unique act of

[35] *A.S.V.* Fondo Gesuiti, 24.

international supremacy. It could not have been done if St. Ignatius Loyola had not made obedience the supreme virtue of a religious life.

When men asked the unanswerable question, which Pope contributed most to the suppression of the Jesuits, they did not always give the praise or blame to Clement XIV. Observers like Cordara held that Clement XIV could do no other. Observers like Tanucci fancied that the predecessor Clement XIII made it inevitable when, as one born out of time, he so loftily defended the rights of the Roman see in other states. At least one cardinal thought that dying Benedict XIV was guilty by approving the request for Portuguese enquiry and therefore giving the world the impression that the cooked-up Portuguese charges might well be true. And finally, he who reads Jansenist pamphleteering in France during the middle years of the eighteenth century, and sees the fanatical orchestration of abuse against Jesuits, can only explain its bitterness by the war over the bull *Unigenitus*, and suspects that if any single Pope made the destruction possible it was Clement XI as author of that bull.

The English agent Horace Mann held a still cruder explanation, which two centuries later Stalin would also hold. 'The Pope', he wrote shortly after he heard of the brief *Dominus ac Redemptor* 'had no fleet to support his Jesuits.'[36]

Clement XIV had a biographer Caraccioli who represented him as a liberal and a Jansenist. This biography sold widely in Europe and caused the supreme posthumous reputation among Protestants that this was the best of all Popes. He seemed to stand for the due rights of states, for modernity, for quiet and unostentatious pastoral care, for justice to the Jews. Men said that if he had been Pope in the time of Henry VIII England would still be a Catholic country. They said that his pontificate proved how the Counter-Reformation was at an end. Stories circulated of his holiness, even his miracles.

But his acts were too weak to make him the saint of Catholic reformers. He gave those who knew him the impression of a man driven by events and tormented in mind. The Pope who saved the papacy from worse fates was a man neither of stature nor of wide education. To face the world he had little more training than experience in a friary and as an officer of the Inquisition. But he steadily or unsteadily pursued conciliation, and were it not for the criminal injustice to Ricci, and the trust in the bribable Friar Bontempi, his reputation would be as high among some Catholics as it is among Protestants.

[36] *Letters of Horace Walpole*, 7.506.

Between Rome and Milan two Verri brothers debated in letters the importance of that reign. They were not quite sure. The policy was wise, disputes faded, the peace of the Church reappeared. Pietro in Milan believed that by suppressing the Jesuits the Pope had grievously wounded the authority of the Curia. 'Pay off the praetorian guards and the janissaries—dangerous troops for a despot but the bravest—and the Curia has lost its trustworthy garrisons abroad. Bishops will get back power, sovereigns will help. . . . The suppression of the Bellarmine-athletes tends to change the way the Church is governed.' Alessandro in Rome saw Avignon again the Pope's, Benevento restored, the threat of an occupation of Rome disappeared, and that it was right to sing a heartfelt *Te Deum* for what this Pope achieved. But when Clement XIV died, Alessandro summed him up as morose, solitary, impenetrable, sick in heart, mourned by no one for all the skill and prudence with which he directed policy.[37]

The attempt to survive

Prussia

Frederick the Great was a man of the Enlightenment, a Protestant of the left wing. By his annexation of Silesia and western Poland, strongly Protestant Prussia acquired a numerous Catholic people, whose education hung largely upon Jesuit colleges. Though no friend to Jesuits he was determined that his Catholic subjects should not suffer by their dissolution.

He at once ordered that the brief of suppression be not published in any of his Catholic lands. He told the suppressed Jesuits that he intended to prevent them being suppressed.

The Silesian Jesuits were at first inclined to accept the king's protection against the Pope. Father Reinach, King Frederick's friend among the Jesuits, told him that the Pope was not infallible. They had no *official* knowledge that they were suppressed, though anyone could buy the brief in the shops or read it in the newspapers. For a time they could argue that to continue need not offend their special vow of obedience to the Pope because this Pope acted under duress, the brief was not his real opinion, he might allow an exception in Prussia at request of their king, and even if he refused his successor might reverse the brief. Upon these axioms they continued to accept novices—four during 1774—and to write to ex-Jesuits in other non-Catholic lands, including England, inviting them to link with the Prussian Society. They even talked of electing a new general

[37] *Carteggio di Pietro e di Alessandro Verri dal 1766 al 1797* (Milan, 1923), vi.112, 168; vii. 739; Venturi, *Sett.rif.* 2.341–2.

to succeed Ricci. A few of them were outspoken about Pope Clement XIV—one talked of the Ganganelli raving, at Neisse a Jesuit father made the boys play in the theatre a drama of the destruction of the Jesuits by the Pope and their rescue by the king, where parts of the text were so offensive to the Pope that a few of the audience walked out.[38]

The optimism was short-lived. The bishop regarded them as rebels against the Pope and started to appoint other confessors to nunneries and to refuse to ordain their young men. Laymen drifted away from their churches and pulpits and confessionals. On 8 December the Jesuits at Glogau normally heard some hundreds of confessions, in December 1773 they heard about twenty. Nuns began to doubt the validity of their absolutions. Members of other orders started refusing invitations to attend their ceremonies. The people were more papist than the religious order dedicated to Popes.

At the vacancy in the see of Rome in 1774 Frederick ordered his Roman envoy Ciofani (a man of too small a stature to compete with Cardinal de Bernis and the other Bourbon ambassadors) to tell the new Pope that the work of the Society of Jesus was essential to Prussia. He did not mind whether they were called Jesuits or wore the clothes of Jesuits but they must be allowed to do what Jesuits did. Ciofani formally asked the new Pope Pius VI Braschi whether he would not change the name of the Jesuits and let them get on with their good work.

Pius VI was elected Pope because he was willing to make it sufficiently plain that he would not try to resurrect what his predecessor killed. The Prussian request embarrassed him in his relations with the Bourbon governments. Rome could hardly be seen to allow Jesuits in one country while pretending that they were not Jesuits.

In August 1775 the Pope told Ciofani that he accepted the validity of the king's arguments but could not go back on what was decided. He had hoped to be able to use clemency to the suffering individuals of the Society (he was then trying to free Ricci from Castel Sant' Angelo despite ranting Spanish resistance), but in vain. He could not allow the Jesuits to be a community, even in the Papal States. But 'the respect which I have for Berlin', Ciofani reported the Pope to say, 'makes me refrain from condemning the Silesian Jesuits as irregular, and the king is too intelligent not to find some way of achieving his just ends'.[39]

This private conversation was soon known, and caused friction between the new Pope and the Spanish government.

[38] Hoffmann, 33.
[39] Ciofani to Frederick II, 26 Aug. 1775; printed by Hoffmann, appendix no.84.

By the end of 1775 Pope and king reached agreement. The ex-Jesuits might remain in control of their schools and colleges, but must leave their dress and abandon their name. Thus the Prussian resistance only postponed for two and a quarter years a state of affairs which Austrian and some other Catholic lands reached immediately after suppression; with the important difference that the Silesians could train, if not novices, at least their future schoolmasters.

Some ex-Jesuits at first were sad; deserted by Pope, bishop, people, and now their king. Into the college diary at Glatz the superior entered at 21 February 1776 this lamentation: 'This is the worst of all days. On this day the last little lights of our holy father Ignatius were put out, and an order canonized by Popes and then oppressed with a heap of calumnies by the Pope who died lately, is vilely deflowered. What our king could do against the suppression, he did.'

But there was no further resistance. Frederick II met his old friend Father Reinach and saw the new dress of the secular priest, and said 'That's a more becoming costume than the old habit.'[40]

The Prussian government took control of the finances. It reformed the Jesuit curriculum, introduced history, and demanded a university degree before ordination. Thus though the ex-Jesuits came under bishops in pastoral matters they came under the government in education, except in theology and religious education. They were called by the title Priests of the Royal Schools Institute. They enjoyed revenues from the old Jesuit estates, and had the power, not yet held by any other group of ex-Jesuits outside Russia, of training new members.

Odd survivals remained, probably not slips of the pen. So late as 1784 the head of the college at Emmerich near the Dutch border signed himself Wilhelmus Classen S.J.[41]

Russia

Catherine the Great of Russia had a mind of the Enlightenment and was no natural friend of Jesuits. But by the first partition of Poland Russia got many Catholic subjects and good Jesuit schools. And policy entered. In the eyes of the Russian government their protection of Jesuits helped to make new Polish subjects loyal.

The brief of suppression was never published in Russia. Government prevented it being known. The Jesuits knew privately but were not bound to obey till they knew officially. Individual Jesuits were uneasy in con-

---

[40] Hoffmann, 129, 146.   [41] Pastor, xxxix.200.

science and asked to become secular priests. In White Russia and eastern Poland most Jesuits continued undisturbed.

The head of the Jesuit college at Polotsk, Czerniewicz, asked the nuncio Garampi in Warsaw what he was to do if the Russian empress ordered him to continue as a Jesuit and the Pope ordered him not to continue as a Jesuit. The nuncio thought silence the best answer. Though personally he disliked the suppression, he loyally carried out the order of Rome. But he gave those orders a lax interpretation, for one of his orders said that the schools should continue, and the Russian government said, no Jesuits no schools. He advised the Jesuits to intend to be ex-Jesuits as soon as they could, and to dress more like secular priests. But even he suspected the Jesuits of wanting the Russian government to insist on Jesuits, and advised an archbishop to keep a spy in one of the Jesuit colleges.

On 15 October 1775 Czerniewicz appealed to the new Pope Pius VI. He wrote that as the brief of suppression had not been made official in Russia, many of the Jesuits continued their rules, dress, and name. Would the Pope show that he did not disapprove? Though now they had no novices, might they be allowed to enrol ex-Jesuits from other countries?

Cardinal Rezzonico presented the petition to Pius VI who received it kindly but could say nothing. The Russian Jesuits observed gratefully that he did not condemn. Czerniewicz acted like a general of the Society, requiring obedience on the same terms, though his authority as provincial now rested, not upon Rome or his non-existent order, but in theory upon what he could extract from his reluctant bishop and in practice upon the Russian government.

In January 1777 a Cologne newspaper published a genuine letter from the Russian governor of White Russia to Czerniewicz planning to secure Rome's leave for a Jesuit novitiate in Russia. Troubled Rome gave the Bishop of Mohilev full powers over all the regular clergy in his diocese. The bishop (1779) sanctioned Jesuit novices, saying not quite truly that, out of respect for the empress, Pope Clement XIV had not applied the brief of suppression to Russia and that Pius VI had refused to condemn the continued existence of the rule, dress, and name.

The Jesuits were again in being; only in White Russia; to the anger of Bourbon governments and the public embarrassment, though not the private regret, of Pope Pius VI.

Cardinal Pallavicini condemned the action of the bishop as scandalous. Rome made it public that these were ex-Jesuits and not Jesuits in Russia— 'A habit does not make a monk—still less a Jesuit.' But behind the scenes a different voice could be heard. The Pope (August 1780) told the French ambassador Cardinal de Bernis that he regretted how the Empress Catherine was the only ruler with common sense enough to see what advantage she gained from the refugees.

In October 1782 the Jesuits of White Russia met at Polotsk and elected Czerniewicz as vicar-general. Under fierce pressure the Pope sent a private brief to the kings of France and Spain declaring that everything that had happened in Prussia or Russia since the suppression was null and void. But almost simultaneously the Pope gave an audience (3 March 1783) to the Coadjutor-Bishop of Mohilev Benislawski, and heard that the vicar-general was elected by command of the empress. Then the Pope said, 'I don't disapprove' (Je n'en disconviens pas').[42] Nine days later the Pope gave him another audience and turned the negative into a positive—'I approve', said three times.

Fifteen months later Bishop Benislawski (July 1785) made to the Jesuits a formal affidavit of this verbal approval. Cardinal Pallavicini instructed the nuncio in Poland to contradict any such claim. The story ran through the European courts that the Pope sanctioned the existence of the Jesuits in Russia. Rome strenuously denied the alleged sanction. The more scrupulous consciences among the White Russian Jesuits were calmed. They were assured, and were now convinced, that the Pope refused to condemn them and if only he were a free agent would approve publicly. Ex-Jesuits from outside Russia, especially Germans, applied to join the little congregation. The vicar-general was happy to admit them in theory but with only 100,000 Latin Catholics in the area could not use many.

The conduct of Rome towards the Jesuits or ex-Jesuits in Russia proves the political nature of the abolition of Jesuits. The order must be abolished because in Spain, Portugal, France, Naples, and Parma it was a burden too heavy for the Church to carry. But in Russia the attempt to destroy it might ruin Catholicism. Therefore Rome must publicly disapprove what was done, but refuse to utter the direct condemnation which would affront the Empress Catherine, and simultaneously allow private encouragement for the sake of pastoral concern.

A curious sign of the international difficulty appeared in Parma. There lived ex-Jesuits, with pensions paid out of ex-Jesuit endowments, qualified to teach but not used in teaching. The schools of Parma had not enough teachers. The State could find the teachers which it needed, at little cost, by re-employing the ex-Jesuits. The plan was formed. It failed, because Spanish memories were painful and Parma lay under Spanish influence. In

[42] Pastor, xxxix.263, 288–90; the truth of the story is denied, with the then secretary of state, by Gendry, 2.385 ff.

1793 the Duke of Parma asked for the loan of Jesuits from Russia, and a few ex-Jesuits of Parma were granted membership of the Jesuit congregation in White Russia.

Pius VI could not approve, but would not disapprove.

Some ex-Jesuits were absorbed into other orders. They joined the Society of Jesus because they felt a monastic vocation, and when the Society ceased to exist they followed their vocation elsewhere. New orders came into being to meet their needs—the Society of the Heart of Jesus (1794) founded in the Austrian Netherlands, the Society of the Faith of Jesus founded (1798) near Spoleto—all the founding members wore the Jesuit dress—and soon united with the society of the Heart of Jesus. Some members wanted to join the Jesuits of Russia, others refused, until the group split.

The next Pope, Pius VII, elected in 1800, was not committed like his predecessor to not altering the brief of suppression. Nor did he depend upon the Spanish government. Indeed, revolution in France caused him to look with ever more interest at the power of the Russian government. Asked by the new Tsar Paul I for an approval of the Russian Jesuits, Pius VII freely gave it (7 March 1801) by the brief *Catholicae fidei*.

The White Russian Fathers had been accused of disobedience and schism, of being rebels pretending to be monks. After twenty-two years they were justified. They were not ex-Jesuits as the world said, but Jesuits, authentic. It was the first step in cancelling Clement XIV's brief of suppression.

Even into the era of revolution the old stories were still curiously important to the argument. Men like the King of Spain blamed Jesuit political theories for the coming of revolution. Others blamed the destruction of the Jesuits for a weakening of Catholic regimes which led to revolution.

The true argument was less prominent. A teaching order had done a necessary work. It might have done it less well than formerly, it had not met all the wants of the age. But still the work was necessary. For extraneous reasons, connected with the conflicts between colonists and missionaries, this order had to be destroyed. But no adequate provision was made for the work which it did. The need continued to exist, men continued to be available. Gradually it became a prediction that a papacy, forced by politics to destroy the instrument, would think to recreate it once the politics changed.

6

THE CATHOLIC REFORMERS

THE motives which led men to want change were as various as possible. At his simplest the reformer was the old medieval preacher who saw how people who came to church still murdered or fornicated, and wanted the Church to preach better, or discipline more rigorously, so as to raise the moral standards of Christian men. This kind of new Savonarola welcomed warm devotions and new cults and revivalist missions which stirred the hearts of the common people. If he were more sophisticated, he turned his attention to the training of pastors, so that more instructed or more devoted priests might help their congregations to righteousness—this was the reforming drive typical of the Counter-Reformation. If he were eminent and won high office, he found himself perplexed amid the legal niceties of State law and Church law and tried to amend the constitution—inevitably by seeking the aid of the State. For the glaring necessity was to take old endowments which did no good and convert them to parishes or causes which needed money; and such fiddling of rights of property or sacredness of trusts could not happen without the aid of lay ministers willing to risk hostility from vested interests—in short, using State power to trample upon ancient rights. If he were a lay politician, he was frustrated by this need every day; and how far he was prepared to go depended on his prudence or rashness, his ability to persuade lords or bishops, and the readiness of his sovereign to give up a quiet life and face trouble.

Into these traditions of the Counter-Reformation, and cutting across their assumptions, came a new kind of Catholic reformer. He may loosely be defined as one who turned against the excesses (as he saw them) of the Counter-Reformation. Though he stood by the inheritance of the Counter-Reformation, in wanting dedicated priests, celibacy of the clergy, the enforcement of the canons of the Council of Trent, he criticized some features of the Catholic tradition which the Counter-Reformation fostered. Get the people into church and all will be well?—but still they murder and fornicate, we should repel from church when we must. Make excuse for the sins of a suffering people, be gentle when you hear their confessions?—on the contrary, they may need severity, even to a refusal of the absolution which they ask until they show signs of doing better. Stir consciences in church with emotion and revivalist mission and new cults to which they are drawn?—it risks superstition by excess, credulity towards images or pictures or relics or sacred springs. Ordain more priests because priesthood is a higher life for everyone who is called?—but the need of the Catholic Church is part of the call, excess of clergymen lowers the repute of ministry, we want good priests instead of many priests. Let the warmth of a people's devotion flower in procession, pictorial dramas of redemption, dedication to new and powerful saints, more holy-days, a social existence dominated by the feasts and customs of the Church?—but men must earn their bread, the Church wants happiness in this life as it safeguards happiness in the life to come, and it must beware of charities which deter men from working, or so many holy-days that hands too often are idle. These new Reformers wanted to go a small part of the way which Protestants travelled before them—though they would not have listened to the voice if a Protestant spoke.

In Germany, Italy, and Spain these reformers were known loosely as Jansenists.

The Jansenists

South-west of Paris, beyond Versailles in rolling wooded country, is a hollow by a farm where the traveller may still see the church, now a museum, and the graveyard which is all that is left of Port-Royal of the Fields, for the cloister buildings were demolished by government in 1711–13. The visitor may sit upon a wall in the sun and meditate upon a sad age of French history, how good men and good women, following ideals in quietness, were trapped in a world of ecclesiastical strife and international politics which they hardly understood, and helped willy nilly to break the unity of France.

The Jansenists were a French movement, and Port-Royal was their symbol. They were inseparable from the history of France. But over the Alps the name Jansenist became a symbol for a movement of a rather different kind: a group of men, or series of groups, who set out to reform the Catholic Church. The link between these Italian groups and the quiet little field in the woods beyond Versailles is not haphazard. But it was vaguer. Some of the Italians read French books, meditations on Scripture, moral divinity. But they were not in any sense direct disciples of Cornelius Jansen. They cared nothing about predestination, pondered little on grace and justification, had hardly any desire to make communion rarer lest the sacrament lose by familiarity. At times Italians used the word *Jansenist* almost as the English at first used the word *Methodist*, to mean anyone alleged to be unduly strict in his mode of life. A bishop who advocated stiff old rules of fasting, now in charitable disuse, was called by critics a Jansenist. Benedict XIV, before he became Pope, once said that Jansenism in Italy was only a ghost invented by Jesuits. Cardinal Bona defined Jansenists as 'Catholics who do not like Jesuits'. The Augustinian general Vasquez who was violent in his enmity to Jesuits, told his provincials not to be afraid if their critics called them Jansenist—'the name's as empty as a ghost.' A still more extreme Italian made this definition: 'Jansenism was and is nothing else but a Jesuit conspiracy to murder their enemies.'[1]

Though these critics were not Jansenists in a narrow sense, they were encouraged, first, by the Pope's condemnation of Jansenism, and later (even more) by his destruction of the Jesuits. In 1713, by the bull *Unigenitus*, Pope Clement XI condemned the Jansenists of France and their doctrines of grace. This condemnation was cast into such embracing language that it was accused of condemning St. Augustine if not St. Paul. The bull *Unigenitus* therefore weakened the authority of the Pope. Men who cared about Christian doctrine of grace doubted the Pope's wisdom and then sat more loosely to the Pope's authority. Even in Sicily appeared traces of this weakening, which observers ascribed to the consequences of *Unigenitus*. In Tuscany and the north, intellectually so near to France, the signs are everywhere among the little groups of thinking clergy.

Though too wide and varied a movement to make the name Jansenist (in the French sense) quite fitting, many of them looked to France as home of the leaders in Catholic reform. So far as they printed or imported foreign books they were usually the works of French Jansenists (that is, proper Jansenists)—especially Quesnel's meditations on the New Testament, a lovely piece of quiet verse-by-verse interpretation and moral reflexion. Though they were not Jansenists in the French sense, many of them looked upon France as the home of true divinity. Canon Simioli was head of the seminary at Naples. On 13 August 1769 he wrote that in his seminary prayer took a large place, and also the reading of good books, Quesnel's *Pious Thoughts* in an Italian translation, Baillet's *Lives of the Saints*, Bossuet's catechism—and then, he wrote, 'I envy you, Auxerre and Paris and all France, because you have so much light, and books full of light are printed every day. . . . I have all the works of Colbert and know them by heart.'[2] Colbert of Montpellier, great-nephew of the statesman, was a leading and uncompromising Jansenist bishop. French books all, in

[1] Jemolo, 116–17; *Nouvelles ecclésiastiques*, 82.7: Jedin, *Handbuch*, 5.623; Gazier, i.255.
[2] Vaussard, *Jansénisme et gallicanisme*, 35–6.

that seminary at Naples—France the home of the spirit, the source of understanding of Scripture, the way to purer theology.

The Jansenists of Italy were almost unanimous in wanting to lessen the power of the Pope. At first sight this was not an obvious wish, for Popes were educated and in art and civilization Rome was the first or second city of Europe. For the eighteen years while Benedict XIV was Pope, moderate 'Jansenists' could almost claim the Pope as their own. But the predicament thus far resembled that of the age of the Reformation: few reforms were possible without interfering with legal rights. Only the sovereign, be he Emperor or king or city council, could change the law, and every change in church law required the assent of Rome. Therefore every reformer wanted to diminish the number of cases where the assent of Rome was necessary; or, if we put it as the other side saw it, to increase the power of the State, and of the bishops, in the Church.

They rejected the charge that they were touched by Protestant ideas. They believed themselves true and loyal Catholics. They were usually learned in the fathers, often wanted a liturgy which the people could follow, thought the arrangement of parish priests and mass-priests ill adapted, liked to restore a relation between mass and receiving the holy communion at other times than at Easter, wanted sermons to be more integrated into the liturgy, suspected new or newly developed cults like the cult of the Sacred Heart, liked to make monks or at least monasteries fewer to get quality of monks rather than quantity, and thought of diverting more endowments away from cult or masses into pastoral care.

Germany still looked to France as the source of light and culture. Though the Germans adopted Jansenist authors late, and were not much influenced until after the middle of the century, the influence was powerful when it came. Its sources were various. Sometimes it came with immigrants. In Vienna the centre of the Jansenist group, which began to guide the Church policy of the Empire, was a physician from the Netherlands, Gerard van Swieten; one of his colleagues was an Italian who studied the historian Muratori; in Trier and the Rhineland Jansenist ideals passed directly from France or Belgium; the leaders at Würzburg and Salzburg learnt their Jansenist inclination while they studied at Rome. German Jansenists or Jansenizers were mostly in universities, or in the big well-endowed monasteries with excellent libraries and a tradition of learning. More markedly even than in Italy, it was a movement of intellectuals. It had no popular base.

Near the strands of Jansenist thinking, sometimes quite distinct, sometimes interwoven with them, were new advances in knowledge, above all in history. The intervention of printing, the creation of modern libraries, the development of palaeography, the comparative criticism of old manuscripts each in their turn raised a new step upon which the science of history climbed. In the study of early Christian texts Protestants had usually led the way. They were freer, and more willing to jettison texts as spurious even if the texts were hallowed. But by 1700 Catholic scholars dominated the study of Christian history. They had most of the best manuscripts in their libraries. They collected groups of monks who had the sympathy for Catholic origins which Protestants lacked and therefore showed loving care over detail and the sensitive understanding which compassion brings. The Benedictine congregation of St. Maur in France gathered round Mabillon a team of experts who changed Europe's ideas about the early Middle Ages.

Few of these monks were Jansenists in the technical sense. But they were highly educated scholars, scorned narrowness, and so resented the bull *Unigenitus* that the controversy which ensued made them disliked by authority and almost ended their academic usefulness. Mabillon always talked of the Jansenist leaders with respect.

Directly associated with the heirs of Port-Royal was Tillemont, a charming and humble French priest who collected the recently discovered knowledge of Christian origins into a marvellous new synthesis which quickly replaced, everywhere outside rigidly traditional schools of history, the *Annals* of Cardinal Caesar Baronius, that definitive history written to synthesize and expound what the Counter-Reformation understood of early Christian Europe. Tillemont was very Catholic, very devout. But he was not embattled like Baronius, the atmosphere is gentler, this author (the reader feels) wants only truth and does not equate finding truth with demolishing Protestant versions of what happened. Mabillon and Tillemont were living witnesses that in history, as in other spheres, the Catholic Church grew away from the postures which it was forced to strike in the Counter-Reformation.

Muratori (1672–1750)

Educated Catholic Italy stood in the forefront of European historical studies. Italian scholars laid the foundations on which the historical revival of the nineteenth century afterwards built. The instincts of the historian saw the religion of the people with discomfort. The painting of the holy Virgin by St. Luke was beloved by the people, but these new historians wondered whether St. Luke could be the painter. The people found *virtus* in the relics of holy men, but the historical attitude to famous relics became as sceptical as the cynicism of Erasmus in the beginning of the Reformation. Historical minds no longer passed without discomfort over legends which they must read in the breviary.

Muratori was ordained priest in 1695, worked for five years at the Ambrosian library in Milan, and in 1700 at the age of twenty-eight became the duke's librarian at Modena, where he remained till his death fifty years later. From 1723 a series of twenty-five volumes collected the texts of Italian history, many till then unprinted. From 1738 to 1743 he published at Milan *Antiquitates italicae medii aevi*; in the third volume (out of six) he printed for the first time that primitive list of New Testament books soon called the Muratorian canon, and so made his name immortal. From 1744 he published twelve volumes of annals of Italian history to his own day. Long before he died he had a European fame. The first biography appeared nine years before his death.

Though one of the rare few who marked an epoch in the history of historical writing, Muratori found time to write other books. He was a polymath, who wrote about economics and politics. The first historical work he ever published was a propaganda pamphlet about his duke's right to the territory of Comacchio which the Pope (justly) claimed. These political writings were important to his future, because they won the confidence of the Emperor and therefore the Emperor's money to pay for his printing of historical sources, and imperial protection against his critics.

In those days when learned congresses could not exist and periodicals were rare, Muratori undertook a correspondence with the librarians, archivists, and scholars of Europe. His collection of letters still numbers more than 6,000. The archives of history lay largely uncatalogued, and everyone who wanted to see them was suspected of trespass among the secrets of state. He first gained access to closed Italian archives because King George I of England wrote letters on his behalf to the Italian princes. A circle of royal patrons received his dedications and encouraged the sales of his books.

Since he published something on almost every subject under discussion, his life at Modena was more retired than uncontroversial. His views on saints and the cult of St. Mary led to an uncomfortable interview with a Polish traveller who called to tell him that he had lost his once high reputation in Poland and that his book ought to be burnt publicly. The Emperor's agents intervened to shield him from an alleged plan by the Roman censors to prohibit his books on the antiquities of the Este house in Modena. The protection of Vienna was important. The Austrians could not afford to allow censure on a writer whose historical enquiries indicated the Emperor's claim to the Comacchio district of northern Italy.

This was no Jansenist. He accepted the bull *Unigenitus*, and his ideas of reform had not the radicalism found among Jansenists. Yet many reformers learnt from his attitude. Muratori was the finest type of Catholic reformer in the eighteenth century; where the critical intelligence assailed popular superstition at the same time as a pastoral heart longed for the well-being of a people's religion.

About his soul his extensive correspondence is reticent. He was self-controlled, morally scrupulous, and never likely to become effusive. He was brought up by a devout parish priest whom he revered and in whose praise he later wrote a memoir. The priestly ideal was that of the Counter-Reformation, his model for the clergy was still St. Charles Borromeo. He practised and preached a daily meditation and an annual retreat, the Passion was the staple of his religious reflection.

In 1711–13 he passed through a religious crisis. We cannot quite tell why. It was the time of the Comacchio struggle, where he found himself on the side against Rome, and this might have had something to do with the crisis. Since 1713 was the year of *Unigenitus* this also has been put forward to explain what happened, though the only evidence is Muratori's very marked silence on the subject.

He met the Jesuit missioner Paolo Segneri the younger, who was sent to conduct missions in Modena and the surrounding country. At the feet of Segneri he underwent some sort of conversion, and then took the work of Segneri's assistant on further missions near by. He found himself, so to speak, on the wrong side. His intelligent and learned friends distrusted the tumults of missions and mocked Segneri. Muratori the intellectual found himself upon the side of simple faith and conversion. The impression never faded. He later wrote Segneri's life.

As a direct result of these religious experiences he decided that his soul needed parish work. He accepted the incumbency of the church of Pomposa (1716), where he dedicated himself to the pastoral care of his people and to spiritual exercises for the neighbouring clergy. For nearly three years his history came to a standstill. He spent a lot of money on the church, began a choir school, looked after the nuns, and created a new lending bank (*Mons Pietatis*) for the poor.

For reasons of health he resigned the parish in 1733 and continued to live in the vicarage with his successor who was also his nephew and biographer. But he was active in the parish only two or three years. Then history reclaimed his time.

This union of scholarly reputation with pastoral experience and religious affection made his reforming book, when it appeared, of rare weight.

From the fifteenth century some universities demanded the 'blood-vow' on taking office; that is, a candidate swore to defend with his blood the doctrine of the Immaculate Conception of the Blessed Virgin Mary. When the Jesuits won control of higher education they adopted the blood-vow, which in 1649 became obligatory in Austrian universities. Muratori published under the pseudonym Lamindus Pritanius a religious tract, *On the Moderation of Minds in Matters of Religion*, in which he reproved the blood-vow. The tract started a series of pamphlets for and against, among which Muratori wrote a second essay, *On Avoiding Superstition* which directly assailed the blood-vow, and then a third series of letters to defend the second. Even in the year before Muratori's death a student at the university of Innsbruck, on the occasion of his taking the blood-vow, spoke fiercely against Muratori.

Life is too high a good to set it at risk without necessity. If the Church had defined the doctrine of the Immaculate Conception, it might be another matter. But it is not defined. No one can be right to talk of risking life for the sake of an opinion. This was Muratori's argument. He hardly talked of the unreality of the business, so characteristic of fanaticism, when men swore to stake life for a matter where life could never be in danger.

The coming of scholarly Pope Benedict XIV to the papacy (1740) helped Muratori. He knew Benedict earlier as Cardinal Lambertini at Ancona and Bologna, and wrote to a friend of his happiness that God had given a Pope who would encourage scholarship.[3] They corresponded over the dedication of a book, the reform of the breviary, the history of Italy.

When therefore in the evening of his long life Muratori published a powerful essay about religion, he was no obscure librarian at Modena: the most famous historian in Europe; a writer whose work was already used as textbooks in Austrian universities; protégé of an Emperor and adviser of a Pope; notorious in Poland, and among the leaders of popular cults, but otherwise respected universally.

He attacked false miracles, had little poetry in him and small desire to allow beauty in legend, was against the story of St. Veronica wiping the

[3] *Carteggio* 3, nos. 450–1, 453, 513, 518, 600, and especially 664; also 14, nos. 107 ff.; see also Muratori's view of Benedict XIV in *Annali d'Italia* xii (Lucca, 1764), 358, but this is suspect because it was public and the Pope was still alive.

sweat from the suffering Christ, disbelieved the holy house at Loreto and the stigmata of St. Francis and the fables of the Spanish about St. James, thought Cardinal Baronius partisan in his *Annals*, and was specially hostile to claims by prophetic women to private revelations.

His book *On a Well-ordered Devotion* was published in Italian at Venice under the old pseudonym Lamindo Pritanio.[4] This became the classical statement of Catholic reforming ideals in the eighteenth century. Not everyone was able to take all. The English translator omitted several important chapters and altered the numbering so that no reader can see how much was dropped.

Most writers who tell fanatics not to be fanatical sound arid by reaction. Muratori's book was shot through with affection of the soul. Simple men, he saw, treated the worship of God as though it meant reverence before a statue of Christ or before the Host in the eucharist, and allowed it to make small difference to what they did. The heart of Muratori's essay is the inwardness of true devotion; the offering of the self as moral being; the danger of substituting external acts and yet the necessity of external acts, and their rightness when they focus the aspiration of the soul; deep reverence in receiving the holy communion, or meditating upon the life of Christ. It was as though he tried to bring the common man, who lived upon the circumference of faith, to its centre. In parts the essay reads more like a book of prayer than a tract of controversy. But it contains tough language. The desire to make Christian devotion ethical led him suddenly to reprove the 'madness and blindness' of Protestants who say that 'faith alone' can save. Nor was it the book of a theologian. 'Theologians write big works on virtue. They ask questions which are interesting but useless. All theology, whether for learned men or illiterates, comes down to one thing: doing what pleases God.'

Most of the book attacked no one. But in its course Muratori came, by way of a climax, to an assault upon the abuses of his time: in the inability of congregations to follow the mass (two chapters contained an Italian translation of the mass with commentary for the uninstructed); in shocking misbehaviour sometimes seen in church; in the follies and exaggerations of preachers; and above all in the cult of saints by excess of saints' days to prevent the people working, by reading of ridiculous and incredible legends of miracle, by attributing to the power of saints or relics what could only come from God, by devotion to the statue or picture instead

---

[4] *Della regolata divozione dei Cristiani* (Venice, 1747); for the writing, P. Stella in *L. A. Muratori e la cultura contemporanea*, in *Atti del Convegno Internationale di Studi Muratoriani* (Florence, 1975), 1.241 ff.

of the person portrayed by the statue or picture. This was the part of the
book which roused Cardinal Quirini to complain to Rome, and made
English and Spanish translators bowdlerize their editions.

This book of devotion which was also a critical book became a symbol
of the Catholic reforming ideals of the later eighteenth century; obedient to the Pope, not at all Protestant in spirit, reverent towards the Blessed
Virgin and the saints, but fierce against ways of worship and superstitions
common among the people. Cardinal Migazzi of Vienna gave it to the
Emperor's daughter. Grand Duke Leopold had it printed at his own cost
to give to all his clergy.[5]

In the year after Muratori published his book *On a Well-ordered Devo-*
tion, his friendship with Pope Benedict XIV was put to the test. The
Spanish published in 1747 a new edition of their Index of prohibited books,
and included 'an Index of Jansenist books' on which appeared some not
at all Jansenist publications, and even famous Jansenists were misspelt. The
general of the Augustinians was shocked to see upon this illiterate list the
history of the Pelagian controversy by the much respected Cardinal Henry
Noris. He complained to Pope Benedict XIV, who protested (31 July
1748) to the grand inquisitor. He said that good books should not be
banned because they contained errors. 'How much is there in Muratori's
work which is censurable! I have myself found many things in my own
reading, and many of his opponents and accusers have lodged charges
against him. We have not banned his works and will not, because a ban
would do much more harm than good.'

The Pope rashly gave a copy of this letter to the Augustinian general,
who published it in breach of privacy. Thus the rebuke, though intended
to be private, became known to Muratori. On 16 September 1748 Muratori wrote to Pope Benedict XIV that he had been condemned without
anyone knowing why, and begged to know what was censurable so that
he could recant and find grace. Benedict XIV (25 September 1748) replied that the Augustinian general published a private letter, and had been
banned from the palace. Cardinal Quirini got hold of the letter; and as one
who resented Muratori's views on saints' days must have been tempted to
use the Pope's words, but refrained in honour. Benedict XIV told Cardinal
Quirini that he had done well, for his criticism had nothing to do with the
argument over saints' days, but concerned his language about the temporal power of the Popes.

The book *On a Well-ordered Devotion* continued to alarm men who
valued the cult of St. Mary and the saints as Catholic, and suspected Mura-

[5] Reusch, 2.846; Zlabinger, 110–11; Wandruszka, 2.124, 136.

tori of lukewarm devotion. A preacher in Naples attacked the book in sermons, the censor of the Sicilian inquisition Father Plazza published a book of 800 pages to defend the saints, the supreme controversialist of the day Father Zaccaria demanded that the book be taken out of reach of the laity. Cardinal Quirini engaged in a battle of pamphlets against the doctrine that the number of saints' days had increased and ought to be diminished, until Pope Benedict XIV ordered silence on the question. Because of Plazza's book, the Holy Office of the Inquisition formally examined the book. Its verdict was satisfactory; the book deserves no censure—or, if any, the lightest possible. Muratori attacks abuses of popular religion which the Church has never defended.

Father Plazza numbered Muratori among 'Jansenists'. Muratori was not inclined towards the French Jansenists. But his spirit fitted that mood which Italians of his day called Jansenist. Less moderate men who came after him learnt from his attitudes as well as from his history.

As early as 1742 the feeling between historians and conservatives who loved legends of the prayer-books was strong enough to persuade Pope Benedict XIV to promote an enquiry and attempt a reform of the breviary. The numerous papers which he collected still lie among his 'consistorial bulls' (the name is improper) in the Vatican archives, but produced no result. Reformers were few, conservatives many. The reform of the breviary was postponed.

Muratori's local influence was small. His diocesan synod (1739) made him an examiner, but its decrees show no trace of his spirit. An official in Rome even suggested (1744) that he be the new Bishop of Modena but the plan was not sensible. His music school and his spiritual exercises for clergy soon failed. As his successor in the library the duke nominated his enemy Zaccaria. Twenty-four years after his death Pomposa was united to a neighbouring parish, and even his bones were translated. In Poland, and Mainz, and Sicily, men regarded his name as offensive. In a pulpit at Naples Father Pepe hailed his death as the saving of the Church.

But the books survived. Henceforth no one could be a historian without using Muratori. And his treatise *On a Well-Ordered Devotion*, received translation after translation, Latin, German, French, Spanish, Hungarian, Czech, English. Between 1760 and 1795 it had eighteen German editions. It stood for a truly Catholic sense of religious reformation. Make our Lord the centre of faith, not the Blessed Virgin or the saints. Help common people away from superstitions or credulities which corrupt their devotions. Turn the eucharist and the communion into the heart of worship instead of an extra. Enable the people to understand what they do when they worship at mass. And all this should be done in faithfulness to the highest ideals of St. Charles Borromeo and the Council of Trent.

For the first time the new and profound Catholic learning of the early Enlightenment applied itself directly to the religion of the common people.

Many Catholic reformers of the later eighteenth century learnt from Muratori. The Austrian bishops were among the chief. But in works of reformation no one easily retains the spirit of moderation. Something about Muratori was too gentle, too Tridentine, too quiet, too restrained for his successors. However they drew from his source, they preferred the Jansenist model of reform; still religious, but louder, more radical, less respectful of the past, and unlike Muratori in that their books were worded so that no Pope could protect or approve. Before he was dead thirty years, the bitter journal of French Jansenists expressed wonder that anyone should bother to translate into French *On a Well-Ordered Devotion* when France possessed many better books for the purpose.[6]

Pietro Tamburini

Among the north-Italian towns Brescia was the city where the influential group of Italian Jansenists was formed. The most learned cardinal of the century, Quirini, was Bishop of Brescia and, though himself hardly an innovator, gathered about him enquiring minds. The professor of philosophy at the Brescia seminary, Pietro Tamburini, became the leader of Italian Jansenists. Unlike Muratori he was a true Jansenist; professed himself a disciple of Jansen; started his public career by writing books about the doctrine of the grace of God. He was no moderate, but a radical who enjoyed controversy.

The next Bishop of Brescia (1772) made Tamburini leave Brescia cathedral. When he and his colleague Giuseppe Zola were expelled, Brescia went into mourning, and for a week clergy and monks met daily at his house to show support.[7] Cardinal Marefoschi, who was famous for leading the campaign in Rome to destroy the Jesuits, found him a post at the Irish College in Rome. He remained in Rome for six years and made many friends. But as his radicalism made him ever more suspect, he

---

[6] *Nouvelles ecclésiastiques* (1778), 155–6; P. Hersche, 'Il Muratori e il giansenismo austriaco' in *La Fortuna di Muratori*, Atti iii.268.

[7] *Storia di Brezzia*, ed. G. Treccani degli Alfieri (Brescia, 1964), 3.195.

accepted a professorship at the university of Pavia, then under Austrian rule.

At Pavia he began to publish a series of radical writings; on the duty as well as the right of Christian people to read the Bible in translation; on the right to disregard the Index of prohibited books; on the need to return to the fathers of the primitive Church and to test the present Church by their teaching; on the divine right of bishops, who owe the Pope as primate a canonical obedience not an absolute obedience; on the liability of Popes to err, and the lawfulness of appeals to General Councils; on the proper place of laity in the Church, and the need to remember that all authority is not concentrated in clergy; on the corrupt nature of indulgences; on Jansenism as only the development of St. Augustine's teaching; on the Inquisition as contrary to the spirit of primitive Christianity; on the error of the opinion that truth should be maintained by physical force unless (as with atheism) the social order is put at risk.

So far as Italy had a head of a Jansenist party who was truly a Jansenist, it was Pietro Tamburini at Pavia. His followers were not numerous, very few were laymen, and fewer still were famous. But among them were two bishops who became notorious far beyond the Italian peninsula: Ricci of Pistoia and Serrao of Potenza.

Pavia where Tamburini taught was in Lombardy, and Lombardy was part of the Austrian domain, and therefore Pavia university had freedoms denied to bishops further south. Moreover it was a university of international fame, whereas the two 'Jansenist' bishops presided over unimportant little sees and no numerous clergy. Tamburini was a thinker, widely read, whereas neither of the bishops was more than an earnest practical unsubtle pastor. Yet only when the two bishops attempted to embody these ideas in their dioceses did Italian Jansenism assume its European authority.

Giannone

The university of Naples flourished. Its faculty of law contained professors who knew the French legal and ecclesiastical theorists of Louis XIV's reign, and took ideas which are loosely termed Gallican, in contending for the sovereign's power in religion and the limits of Rome's legal power. In 1713 the passionate battle over Clement XI's bull *Unigenitus* stirred up universal interest in the limits of Roman power, especially in countries where some issue between Church and State was acrimonious—and no Catholic country then existed in which no issue was acrimonious. The current battle in southern Italy concerned the Bishop of Lecce in Apulia and his tithes. We have already (p. 208) met that Bishop of Lecce placarding an interdict in his diocese.

In Naples was a young lawyer who had lately graduated from the law faculty and came from a family of Apulia: Pietro Giannone (1676–1748). He had been reading French Gallican theorists. He was briefed by the inhabitants of Lecce who protested against the efforts of the Bishop of Lecce to tithe all their olive trees. His thesis (1715) was a plea *For the owners of olive trees in the fief of St. Peter in Lama against Mgr the Bishop of Lecce, lord of the fief, about the demand for tithes on the olive trees.* Such a plea could not interest the public. But it caught the attention of the lawyers by method, and outspokenness. Giannone went to history. Leaning on Gallican historians, he traced tithe from the Old Testament to the present and used this historical evidence to prove that it was a mere State tax and that no basis existed in the law of God. The statement had touches of anticlerical passion. This was a young man from the south battling for the welfare of smallholding peasants like those whom he knew at home. Late in life the prisoner Giannone looked back upon his career and saw how the tithes on the Lecce olive trees helped to form his mind.

Thirty years before an Anglican clergyman, Gilbert Burnet, visited Naples and printed an account of his journey. Burnet's description of Naples was lively. And as he was a good Protestant the liveliest passages touched the contrast between poor people and rich monasteries, declared that the Jesuits were masters of half of Apulia, that the Church controlled the trade in olives and tin, that this ecclesiastical wealth caused the miseries of southern Italy, and that Naples was 'suffocated' by convents loaded with privileges. This attack by a foreigner was resented by Neapolitans. But upon Giannone and his intellectual peers it left a scar. Caricature though it might be, it was too near a truth which Giannone hated.

In 1723 he dedicated to Charles VI *The Civil History of the Kingdom of Naples.* As history it had many defects. As political programme it was one of the most influential books of the century. From the Gallican theorists— whole pages came out of the Gallican Dupin—and from the Belgian canonist Van Espen, he learnt to trace the present practices of the Church to their origins in primitive times and to make that contrast which in the Reformation was so familiar to Protestants. From Dupin and Van Espen he likewise acquired something of the new attitude of Catholic but anti-Roman writers—confidence of being in the right, outspokenness, sense of moral right against obsolete law.

The chaotic history of southern Italy he explained by a single clue: bad Church gaining power, good State limiting that power. He contrasted primitive monks with the monks of his day and 'we shall not be able to see without astonishment how all their orders have with time been able to multiply in our kingdom, and found numerous and proud monasteries erected on the ruins of the citizens whose property they now possess, even to most of the kingdom.' Privileges of the clergy, temporal power, rights of exemption were late and conceded by kings and can be abolished by kings. Informed persons, wrote Giannone, say that the Church possesses four-fifths of the property of the kingdom, including nearly half the land. Soon they will get all, and be able to buy the whole city of Naples and within a century will be masters of the kingdom. Compared with the successors of the Enlightenment half a century later, Giannone was crude. Uninterested in economics, or agriculture, or administration, he was more an assailant of the Church than a reformer of Church or State.

As soon as the book appeared, the preacher at the Jesuit church denounced the author and was banned for causing a disturbance. The Archbishop of Naples ensured its fame by excommunicating the author. The power of excommunication was shown when Giannone could no longer walk safely in the streets. Urchins shouted popular ditties under his windows, people called him 'devil' as he passed, two lawyers were assaulted because one was thought to be Giannone.[8] Moderate potentates who might have protected him were repelled by the tone of the book. He retreated to the Emperor at Vienna and was given a pension but no employment.

In Vienna he used the leisure to educate himself in the philosophy of the European Enlightenment. He passed into a wider culture, led not by Germans and Austrians but by Frenchmen or Italians, with a freer access to libraries. He discovered the long tradition of antipapal thought in the political theory of the Holy Roman Empire, found the books of famous Protestants like Grotius, Thomas Browne, and later Hobbes, became interested in English deists and in Spinoza. He grew out of the brash young rebel from Naples into a European frame of mind.

But in 1734 politics tumbled about his head. The Spanish reconquered southern Italy, he was hardly acceptable in Vienna. He moved to Venice, where he felt at home, but was soon in trouble with the Inquisition and fled across north Italy, to Modena (where Muratori met him and afterwards needed for his own reputation to deny that they met) then to Milan, where he was ordered to get out within two days, and finally to Geneva whither Protestant friends beckoned with promises of support and a secure home.

[8] Ricuperati, 151 and 310.

The Genevan leaders would have liked a convert. Such a change would not only have destroyed Giannone's influence among Catholic states but would have denied a vague but genuine Catholic feeling within his heart. To make his communion at Easter he crossed the border into Savoy and was tricked into arrest. The last twelve years of his life he spent a prisoner in Savoyard castles, usually treated well, sometimes handled roughly. He wrote an autobiography and several important books to explain his philosophy of the State. On 24 March 1738, weakened by imprisonment and influenced by a Catholic priest whose arguments he could despise but whose holiness he must respect, he signed in Turin prison a recantation.

All over Catholic Europe, in the minds of politicians and intelligent critics, Giannone scattered the idea that the rights of the Church, which they found hampering to government and prosperity, were not of divine right, were not even necessary to the good of the Catholic Church, but were conceded by governments and might freely be abrogated by governments. More than 2,000 pages in folio were soon translated into French, German, and English. The later politicians of Naples said that Giannone made Naples into a new kingdom.

Giannone's fate, though the most tragic, was not untypical of the lot suffered by extreme Italian theorists on Church and State. Despite increasing freedom to publish, especially in Venice, several leading Italian advocates of the power of the State in religion found themselves in exile at Potsdam, or England, or over the border into the Grisons and Switzerland. Italian governments might like these ideas but could not afford to risk trouble caused by too outspoken statements of the programme. Pablo de Olavide in Spain was arrested by the Inquisition (14 November 1776) and vanished for years, at a time when his royal master befriended several of the ideas which he propagated. Governments legislated, and then jettisoned a scapegoat when new laws disturbed their people.

The Enlightenment

The Enlightenment is commonly understood as an anti-Catholic movement. The word was regarded as synonymous with Voltaire, or satirical assaults upon tradition. But it was new learning, and as such affected Catholic colleges, professors, and bishops. It used to be thought that Catholicism was always an enemy of Enlightenment. The progress of history has shown the strength of a Catholic Enlightenment.

Its adherents were usually against Jesuits. They disliked Jesuit monopoly of higher education, and the old-fashioned curriculum of the colleges.

They wanted to be free to use Protestant books of scholarship if they were the best books available. They had interest in the improvements of education in the schools and in rational devotion like the removal of superstitions or legendary readings from the books of prayer. Above all they had a sense of history. Their adherents wished to use the new knowledge and perspective given by historians like Muratori or Mabillon, to introduce history as a course into the colleges, even to found chairs of Church history. They had a continuing interest in French and Italian Jansenists.

The Enlightenment was a European movement more than Catholic, reaching its climax in the third and fourth quarters of the eighteenth century. It deeply affected Catholicism; partly because 'enlightened' Protestants grew even more, if that were possible, anti-Catholic; or grew anti-Catholic on different grounds; not because the Church of Rome had wrong dogmas but because it had dogmas; not because it clung to dubious traditions but because it was obscurantist; not because monks had no warrant in the Bible but because they were contrary to the instincts of man; not because celibate priests were unscriptural but because they were unnatural.

Catholic minds were affected. Fortified by the Pope's destruction of the Jesuits and then by the suppressions of numerous monasteries in France and Austria, Catholics also began to doubt monks. They looked for the happiness of man in this world as well as the next. They were practical men, often, who wanted better farming and prosperous industry; who believed that good ideas would have better chance with less censorship; they retained their prayers and their holy orders, but felt at liberty to be fierce against Popes or Curia or bishops.

During this last quarter of the eighteenth century all German universities and colleges revised their syllabuses and teaching methods. This was forced by the suppression of the Jesuits. The revision was always marked by the spirit of Catholic Enlightenment. Usually they needed to use young men for the task; in the colleges of the Rhineland the new professors were often men in their twenties or early thirties. Since they were consciously amending the tradition which existed, and had no other tradition on which to draw, some of them began for the first time to look with attention at the methods and structure of Protestant universities. During this age several Catholic teachers liked their students to pass a time at the university of Göttingen. We find a Benedictine student being sent with a travel-grant from his prince-bishop all the way to Königsberg to meet and talk with the philosopher Immanuel Kant.[9]

[9] E. Hegel (1975), 25-9.

Febronius

Johann Chrysostomus Nikolaus von Hontheim, a youth of good family
from Trier (1701–90), travelled in Italy, lived several years at Rome, and
rose through a professorship of Roman law at the university of Trier, and
then the headship of the seminary, to become (1748) the Suffragan Bishop
of Trier. Two years later he published a valuable work in three volumes,
the history of the city and see of Trier, with numerous charters and documents hitherto unpublished, and with learned annotations.

In 1763 a pseudonymous book appeared at Frankfurt under the name
Justinus Febronius Jurisconsultus, and with a false printer's mark. Hontheim had a niece Justine, who became a nun and took the name Febronia.
The book was entitled *De statu ecclesiae, On the state of the Church and the
lawful power of the Pope, written to reunite Christians who differ in religion.*

The first words of the book were deceptive and yet contained the seed
of troubled recantation: 'Joined to the see of Peter as the centre of Catholic
unity, from which no one may be separated; moved with profound respect for the Holy See . . . full of sincere veneration for him whom God has
placed in the apostolic see, and to whom I pay due reference and submission as the successor of St. Peter . . .'

He wanted the return of Protestants to the fold. Armies failed to convert. Controversialists failed to convert more than a handful. Let us try
moderation. Protestants will not come while the claims of Rome are high.
History shows that these high claims were not primitive but arose from
forged decretals of the 'eighth' (actually ninth) century known as pseudo-
Isidore. Therefore, he appealed to Pope Clement XIII. Abandon this
claim to excess of power; moderate modern pretensions; return to that
primacy among bishops which was the primacy among early Christians;
trust not the Curia, whose interest is to magnify papal claims. The Church
was never founded to be an absolute monarchy. That the Pope is infallible
is no article of faith. General Councils are the ultimate government of the
Catholic Church and should meet more frequently. That the Pope has his
see at Rome is not of divine right, but is the ordering of St. Peter and
could be changed by the Church. We have to recover freedom in the constitution of the Catholic Church. The Curia must be watched; national
councils must be summoned; princes must act to reform, though with the
advice of bishops; excommunications need not be feared, and national
Churches or princes may rightly resist power when it is exercised without
warrant.

Febronius had a desire to make Germany a better state, in creating the chance of union between Catholics and Protestants, by reviving the idea of a national Church which could help to unify the land. But Febronius moved outward from the State into a wider programme, for which his basis in canon law was too narrow: the Catholic reform of all the Catholic Church.

That a book of such well-known views west of the Rhine caused a European storm is at first sight matter for surprise. But for a moment this author looked almost like a new Luther; here was the first German Catholic who attacked papal power because he wanted to place the Pope in a better Christian constitution and to make it easier for Protestants to reunite with the Church. He claimed to derive his critique from his faithfulness to Catholicism and to the Pope. He was also the first German bishop to use the new and wider knowledge of history and canon law, acquired in the age of Muratori, to judge the existing constitution of the Church.

But the European perturbation was chiefly due to the circumstance that the author was soon suspected of being Hontheim. Protestants throughout Europe rejoiced to find a Catholic bishop saying so much that they said themselves, and simultaneously rejected his plea that they would find it thereby easier to become Catholics. They were amazed and pleased to find a Roman bishop beginning his book with a dedication to Pope Clement XIII Rezzonico, and ending with an explanation how best to resist the Pope if he excommunicated.

On 27 February 1764 Febronius was placed upon the Index of prohibited books. Hontheim continued to expand the work in a series of appendices and supplements, until the single volume turned into five. It was translated into French, German, Spanish, Portuguese. The Index continued to list the editions. Several German bishops condemned the book. In Austria it became almost a textbook of political theory. Three times examined by an Austrian committee, it was three times acquitted of error. Spain and Portugal made it a handbook of Church law. Challenged by the nuncio with the authorship, Hontheim denied. He continued to deny authorship; a lie defensible only on the plea that the book was almost entirely a compilation out of Gallican writers and French Church historians and a book of his friend the Trier professor of canon law George Neller. But the plump little man was not of the stuff of martyrs. He was easily worried and embarrassed, had little of the serene well-being usually found among the higher clergy of the German Church, and cared much for the piety of the Catholic Church and the 'true' place of the Pope. Even to high old age he climbed more than a hundred steps, morning and evening, to say the office in the chapel where he was dean, and on his last bed edified the minister by his holy preparation for death.

The nuncio steadily pursued a work of detection, and at last tracked the canon who helped with the printing at Frankfurt, persuaded him to un-witting indiscretion, and so saw papers which proved Hontheim's author-ship.

Famous Catholic divines of Europe tried their hand at confuting: among them Alfonso Liguori, Zaccaria. Not all the replies helped their authors. Zaccaria who succeeded Muratori as librarian to the Duke of Modena, was banished from Modena for publishing (1767) *Antifebronius* and found his book prohibited in Austria. Pope Clement XIII, in letters to the German bishops, was sure that Hontheim was entirely mistaken in his belief that the lowering of the power of the Pope would correspondingly increase the power of bishops. Even the Archbishop of Trier condemned the book. But his secretary wondered whether the numerous condemna-tions by German bishops did anything but advertise the book, and doubted whether its contents were worthy of such sustained attention.

From time to time other German Catholics begged Rome to do no more. Hontheim himself believed that he owed the success of his book to over-reaction by the Roman Curia.

Professor Isenbiehl of Mainz, lecturing on the Old Testament, told his students that the interpretation of Isaiah 7:14 'a virgin shall conceive' was not right and the text could not refer to the gospel birth. He was removed from his chair. He wrote a book (1777) to defend his opinion and was put first into the bishop's prison and then into a monastery. Pius VI con-demned the book, Isenbiehl cheerfully submitted.

Hontheim had not agreed with Isenbiehl's thesis, but could not see what was wrong with maintaining the opinion. This lost him the confidence of his Elector of Trier, who was disturbed by Isenbiehl. The quarrel between the elector and his suffragan turned towards *Febronius*. For the sake of the peace of the Church the Elector pressed his suffragan to withdraw *Febroni-us*. Hontheim submitted but shrank from the publicity of the act. The elector insisted on public recantation. Hontheim drafted a recantation which Rome amended, and Hontheim made no trouble about accepting all but one of the emendations. He confessed that the Bishop of Rome was by God's appointment successor of St. Peter, and not merely by decision of the Church; and that the decisions of General Councils need the Pope's confirmation. On 1 November 1778 he signed the approved draft of the recantation.

Pope Pius VI caused it to be read in open consistory of cardinals, most solemn and most public because it was read after the mass on Christmas day.

Rumour spread that this was all forced and insincere. On 2 April 1780 Hontheim publicly declared that his recantation was wholly voluntary. But moved by the discontent of his friends he published a *Commentary on the Recantation of Febronius*, dedicated to Pope Pius VI. It satisfied no one, for beneath tortured language it seemed to withdraw little. 'I have re-canted like Fénelon to avoid quarrelling and unpleasantness. But my re-cantation hurts neither the world nor the Christian religion, and will never profit the Curia of Rome. The world has read, examined, accepted my book. My recantation will move intelligent men as little as the various refutations by monks or papal flatterers.'[10]

The old argument, once so hotly fought at the time of the great schism in the papacy, but since the Reformation almost confined to France and Belgium and Venice, about the place of the Pope in the constitution of the Catholic Church, was started again by Febronius. What he began con-tinued as a key issue within German Catholicism until the first Vatican Council of 1870, which tried to kill the debate, and thought that it suc-ceeded, but was later proved wrong.

In the age of Febronius the word *ultramontane* first gained its modern meaning of a person dedicated to the universal power of the Pope. Except in France it only meant 'over the Alps', in 1756 Winckelmann in Rome wrote of 'us Ultramontanes' when he only meant 'us Germans'. Febronius himself used it in Latin in a chapter-heading (i.10) in its modern sense; but his German translator turned it into 'over the Alps'. During the sixties its meaning became secure. In 1768 a French minister, writing of Clement XIII's Parma *Monitorium* which was at the centre of the fight over the Jesuits, called it 'the old excesses of ultramontane pretentions'.[11] A new word had been added to the vocabulary.

The Emperor Joseph II

The Holy Roman Empire was name and prestige and ritual, Diet could no longer decide, supreme court could hardly act. But something about its name, and ritual, and history, still spoke of the place of the Emperor with-in the Catholic Church. He was anointed of God and historic protector of the world-wide Church.

[10] Raab (1973), 42–3.
[11] H. Raab, 'Zur Geschichte und Bedeutung des Schlagwortes *Ultramontan* im 18. und frühen 19. Jahrhundert', in *H.J.* 81 (1962), 159–73.

The Habsburg rulers in Vienna owed their real power to hereditary estates. But the defence of Vienna against the Turks, and the thrusting back of Ottoman power, raised their European power and made them seem specially Catholic, like crusaders who fought for the sake not only of Austria but of Christendom. Inheriting both the tradition reaching to Charlemagne and the reputation of crusade, the rulers in Vienna felt themselves to have more of a place, or duty, or vocation, in protecting and reforming the Catholic Church. All modern Catholic rulers wanted to restrict the independence of the Church. The Habsburgs came to the task with a special sense of mission; that is, they married a 'secular' desire to help their state by making bishops or monks less powerful, to a 'religious' desire to reform the Church by freeing it from past incubus. Therefore the Austrian endeavour at Church reform, however parallel to what went on in France or Piedmont or Spain or Portugal or Bavaria, had a unique feeling. It was the most successful of Catholic reforms during the eighteenth century.

In history it has a special place, for it marked the end of an era. In Reformation and Counter-Reformation princes reformed the Church because without them no reform was possible. In the nineteenth century, with the coming of popular governments, Churches had to reform themselves since no government could do the work for their sake. The Austrian reform of the later eighteenth century, and its ensuing heritage in Bavaria, were the end of the old world. They were the last occasions (except for revolutionary France) when Catholic governments reformed the Catholic Church without asking leave of the hierarchy.

Two political needs drove the oligarchs.

One was to strengthen the State, merely to keep pace with the times and survive. This meant, to weaken the legal weight of the Church in the State. Hence a few politicians had only this interest. They were hostile to the Church, had small interest in Catholic reform, were disciples of Voltaire in wishing to smash the power of the Church. Something like this habit of mind is discernible in the Austrian chancellor, Prince Kaunitz, or the Spanish minister Campomanes. These were not Catholic reformers but nominal Catholics who wanted efficient government and disliked the Church.

This first attitude was less common than the other. Catholicism must be helped by better Catholic government. The interest of the Church, as well as the interest of the State, will be helped if the State exercises its historic mission to cleanse the Church from the corruptions of the centuries. The chief motive of strengthening the Catholic State is to help the people to be more truly Catholic not less; that is, by closing useless or immoral monasteries, ensuring that priests and bishops are well qualified, removing the stumbling-blocks of sanctuary and exemption, destroying the scandals given by superstitious cults among country folk, and pressing for better education both of the clergy and of their people. None of this could be done without the State taking more power and therefore forcing true Catholic reformers to be allies of anti-Catholic reformers.

This discomfort caused a sense of disquiet within the breasts of individuals; not least among them, the Austrian Empress Maria Theresa (who reigned 1740–80).

She was devout, conservative, prayerful, frequent at daily services, regular in confession and communion. She could not bear the idea of toleration. Probably by accident and not intention she acquired a Jansenist physician and a Jansenist confessor.

Decisions by three Popes made Austrian lords look critically at Popes.

In the War of the Spanish Succession (1702 onwards) Clement XI backed the Bourbon and French claims to Spain and was in league with enemies of Austria.

Then, when the direct male Habsburg line died out, and Austrian succession to the Holy Roman Empire was disputed, Pope Benedict XIV recognized (1742) the unanimously elected but doubtful Wittelsbach claimant Charles VII while Maria Theresa struggled for her rights.

Finally, Ferdinand of Parma, excommunicated so tremendously by Pope Clement XIII on 30 January 1768 (see p. 365), was Maria Theresa's future son-in-law.

This treble failure of Rome to support Habsburgs made the very pious royal line feel no undue affection for Popes.

Austria ruled that part of the Netherlands which is now Belgium, by neighbourhood to France and links of language open to French ideas, especially Jansenist; by neighbourhood to Protestant Holland and links of language open to reforming Catholic ideas, especially Jansenist—the Austrian Netherlands became a gateway through which Jansenism entered the Austrian Empire. The symbol of this influence was Gerard van Swieten (1700–72), a Dutch physician and devout Catholic, affected early in life by Jansenist ideals. Called in desperation to the labour of the wife of the governor of the Austrian Netherlands, he failed to save her life. But the manner of this endeavour won respect, and in the next year 1745 the office of personal physician in Vienna to the dead woman's sister, who was the Empress Maria Theresa. She treated him as part of her family, and started to ask his advice on other matters besides health. She began by consulting him about the schooling of her children, got his aid with the medical faculty in the university of Vienna, and ended by allowing this doctor of medicine to help improve the faculty of theology and advise her on reforms in the Catholic Church. A Jansenist physician from Holland began to guide the judgement of a prayerful Catholic sovereign.

Van Swieten discovered a south-Tyrolese lawyer, Karl Anton Martini, to develop the faculty of law in the university; professor of law from 1754 and soon entrusted with the schooling of Maria Theresa's children. Martini's Jansenism was Italian; more moderate and less embattled than was natural to Van Swieten who had known the mighty struggles in the Netherlands over the bull *Unigenitus*. Martini came from the world of Muratori and other scholarly critics found in cities of Italy from Palermo to Venice.

Under Maria Theresa's pious government, the Austrians refused to resist the suppression of the Jesuits. She instituted a commission to supervise the administration of Church property, limited the access of papal bulls, effectively ended sanctuary, made the clergy liable to tax, diminished the number of saints' days, banned all penalties (other than purely spiritual) ordered by Church authorities without State agreement, compelled clergy to announce government edicts from their pulpits, took over the supreme administration of universities and schools, limited the further growth of monasteries, abolished monastic prisons, ordered that no one should take a monastic vow before the age of twenty-four, renewed the laws of mortmain, limited the size of dowry which novices might bring. Under Van Swieten the censorship (1764) allowed Febronius. His recantation was suppressed. Bishops used the book.

Meanwhile she organized missions to convert the Protestants in Carinthia and Upper Austria, and the unconvertible were forced to move to the remote but historic Protestant area of Siebenbürgen in Transylvania.

In some mountainous parts the orders of government were quietly neglected. But her chancellor Kaunitz used Lombardy as the laboratory for all this legislation about the Church; because Lombardy stood immediately under government, whereas elsewhere survivals of the old Austrian federal system remained. The foundations of what history came to know as Josephism were laid as early as 1768 in Milan. And because this Austrian territory was Italian, and lay next to the Papal States, it caused more agony in Rome than anything that happened over the Alps until Maria Theresa was succeeded (1780) by her son Joseph II.

Though godson of Pope Benedict XIV, Joseph II could not quite share his mother's traditional piety. The ten years (1780–90) while he was Emperor witnessed a flood of legislation about the Church. To contemporaries the endeavour looked extraordinary. Pamphlets appeared with lurid titles: *The Reformation in Germany at the end of the Eighteenth Century*, or, *The Emperor Joseph and Luther*. This latter ended with the words 'This is what the blessed Luther achieved, and it was left for Emperor Joseph to complete what Luther started.'[12]

So far as the endeavour was vain, it failed because he was unpersuasive, and an old man in a hurry. But most of it was not vain. It changed the course of Austrian history.

The Austrian Church still had a medieval structure; monasteries reaching back to AD 1000 dominating the social life of mountain valleys in Styria and Carinthia; a parish system out of date if churches should stand where people live; clergy under no bishop because their bishop sat outside Austria, in Salzburg or Passau.

Therefore an obvious need was a system of dioceses and parishes. Decrees of 1782–3 made this possible. The canons of Linz and St. Polten still wear a pectoral cross with Joseph's initials on the back, to remind them when they were founded. New dioceses appeared, Passau and Salzburg were excluded, 255 new pastorates in Lower Austria, in Upper Austria 121, in Styria 180, in Carinthia eighty-three.[13] New parishes were ordered to have a school, and so make a national grid of elementary education. Children were compelled to attend school. New parish priests were endowed with sufficient stipends. Government managed this reconstruction by a Church Affairs Commission.

Without asking leave from the Church the Austrian state created the parish system which in essence lasted until now. A high-handed Emperor made possible the parochial advance of the Church during the nineteenth century. It was sensible, and met no resistance. More than one generation of Austrian clergy blessed the name of Joseph.

This plan of refounding and re-endowment needed a lot of money. This money could be found in only one place, monasteries and nunneries. Maria Theresa's men had already raised the possibility of closing monasteries for good ends; and by abolishing Jesuits and releasing their property Pope Clement XIV, however unwittingly, did everything he could to encourage the scheme. We have seen (p. 250) already, how Joseph took many monastic lands to his central fund for Church reform.

[12] Winter, 100; Padover, 157.
[13] Wodka, 309: for the exceptions (parishes under bishops outside Austria) see Jedin, *Handbuch*, 5.520.

The Emperor ordered student-grants for ordinands in training and against his better judgement allowed a low standard of examination. Too few men came forward. He decreed (1783) that henceforth all clergy should be trained in 'general seminaries'; that is, six larger colleges to replace the smaller diocesan seminaries. These colleges were at Prague, Vienna, Pest, Freiburg im Breisgau, Louvain, and Pavia, with dependent colleges. At first sight this was sensible. Some diocesan seminaries were miserable institutions, bigger colleges would have more money and better professors, and their curriculum was easier to oversee and modernize. The course was fixed at six years, which shortage of priests soon reduced to five; succeeded by a time of testing in a clergy-house under the bishop. Discipline was strict, vacations brief, food austere, physical exercise compulsory. Abbot Rautenstrauch's syllabus included Jansenist authors like Pascal, schoolmen were hardly read, ordinands studied the Bible and the fathers of the early Church, and learnt Greek and Hebrew. The young men must also study natural science, agriculture and how to teach. In the refectory they were to read political, learned and religious journals. They were to be taught the differences between the confessions, and to keep the peace with other denominations.

Some Jansenist professors taught in these seminaries. In Louvain, at least one doubted the necessity for celibacy of the priests, denied that canon law had any force as law without confirmation by the State, and taught that the infallibility of the Pope is an opinion held by few.

The time-table became a burden.

Lectures were often given in the vernacular—German in Vienna, Hungarian in Pest. These general seminaries gave lively encouragement to the languages of the peoples under Austrian rule.

The general seminaries failed to survive Joseph II. They were too radically out of touch with the tradition of seminaries since the Council of Trent. The diocesan seminary might be wretched but it brought the student into touch with the bishop, and bishops were not willing to support general seminaries. And it happened that the students of the general seminary at Louvain sparked off the revolution which finally severed Belgium from Austrian rule.

The Emperor's commission on Church affairs was fussy about detail. It undertook to order lesser matters of parish life, like the number of masses, their length, music, litanies, furniture. The Emperor's idea to rid the realm of superstition was executed in a series of decrees vexatious to the people: no processions unless approved by authority, no pilgrimages likewise, no clothes on statues of Mary, no lights on graves, fewer relics, sacks instead of coffins (this was particularly offensive to the people and had to be rescinded), relics not to be kissed, holy pictures not to be touched, rosaries not to be used, no talk on religion in beerhouses, no kneeling in the streets when the Host passed (but hats to be doffed), no fees for baptisms, marriages, or funerals. His commission tried to reduce the number of side-altars and votive tablets. Nothing made the Emperor more unpopular than these measures, which in no way lessened 'superstition.' The people specially hated the stripping of garments from statues of Our Lady, and the removal of hallowed pictures. When the Madonna at Maria Dorn was about to lose her clothes, the congregation armed and made a garrison. When Joseph II died, these vexatious regulations were tactfully 'postponed'.

Brotherhoods (642 in Austria, 121 in Vienna) were abolished (1783). Their revenues went part to poor relief and part to elementary schools. In name they were amalgamated into a single general brotherhood for charity. This was the same as abolition. A brotherhood was nothing if it was not local, particular, based upon a visible group and a special need, conducted by laymen who knew each other.

Pope Pius VI in Vienna

From the first moment of the reign the Emperor's policy made the Curia anxious. The conflict of jurisdiction which moved the Pope was the determination to extend the government's nomination of bishops to the Italian province of Lombardy. But when this was succeeded by the plan to dissolve so many monasteries, Rome was faced with high-handedness not unfamiliar among Bourbon governments but new in the special protector of the Catholic Church. To the Curia with its long memory the Emperor revived the ancient battle between papacy and Holy Roman Emperor.

As early as 1781 Pius VI alarmed the emperor, astonished the world, and vexed some cardinals who thought him naive, by proposing to visit Vienna. He was the first Pope to go out of Italy for three centuries. No Pope had visited Germany since 1415, the year of the Council of Constance.

On 22 March 1782 Joseph met the Pope at Neunkirchen outside Vienna, and together they drove into the city amid packed streets.

The Pope stayed at the Hofburg in Vienna for a month. It was a time of liturgies, visiting sepulchres, private discussions, and greeting the people. The visit showed how the realm of popular reverence and the realm of

power were divided. In the streets, wherever he went, whenever he
appeared, he met crowds and demonstrations of reverence, he was forced
to come out again and again upon the balcony at the Hofburg. These
plaudits were enough to make the Emperor and his advisers nervous of the
consequences if the Pope excommunicated the Emperor. But in the
reality of the argument, as they met to talk of *Unigenitus*, or marriage dispensations, or general seminaries, or censorship, or monasteries, the Emperor was courteously unyielding and had no need to yield. Privately he
thought much of the talk 'nonsense about theology' which he did not
understand.

On 22 April 1782 the Pope left for Munich. Joseph was very pleased to
see him go, and so be relieved of the crowds besieging the palace, bringing
scapularies and rosaries to be blessed.

At Munich the Pope stayed with the Elector of Bavaria for five days,
visited Augsburg where Protestants joined with Catholics in respect,
crossed the Brenner pass, and spent Whitsuntide in Venice, and sang *Te
Deum* in St. Peter's, Rome, after an absence of nearly four months. The
only practical success of the journey was a lifting of the more rigid
Austrian ban against the discussion of the bull *Unigenitus*. But it had an intangible success, in persuading the Pope that the Emperor, however mistaken, was a good Catholic trying to do his best.

Leopold of Tuscany

In Italy rulers of Naples and Parma and Piedmont and Tuscany followed
the Austrian example, and thereby helped the scattered groups of Italian
Jansenists to propagate their ideas of Catholic reform.

In Tuscany the two movements coincided, with a force which shocked
or astonished Europe.

Leopold was another son of Maria Theresa, and became Grand Duke of
Tuscany in 1765. He was regular in church-going, read his Bible and the
Imitation of Christ daily, was educated and instructed, a follower of the
Enlightenment, tolerant but not lukewarm, disliking Jesuits and determined to keep priests out of prying where they had no business. Not a
theologian, untroubled about doctrine, he supposed clergy to be more use
to their people if they knew a little medicine and law and beekeeping than
if they knew only Latin and divinity. He recommended his daughter to
allow no irreligious talk in her presence, and no theological argument,
'which is not at all suitable for the understanding of women'.[14]

[14] Wandruszka, 2.19.

As soon as he arrived in Tuscany he looked for educated and reforming clergy to promote. A series of bold appointments to sees and cathedrals and chairs gave him allies for a programme of reform. Three archbishops and fifteen bishoprics for about a million people were enough to ensure regular vacancies. But Tuscany was already full of Catholic reformers. During the four decades 1741–81 the Archbishop of Florence was the aristocrat Francesco Incontri, a steady supporter of Catholic reform during the middle years of the century, gentle and mild, protecting Jesuits even while he disapproved their order. To a Tuscan bishop, Ginori of Fiesole, Muratori dedicated the last edition during his lifetime of the book *On a Well-Ordered Devotion*.

Leopold disliked holy beggars. The queue of suppliants at the gate of a bishop's palace, or on the steps outside the west door of a church, was a sign to all the Enlightenment that poor laws needed reform. Since friars begged bread or money for bread, Leopold tried to persuade donors to give their alms to parishes instead of begging brothers, and found that charity refused to conform. He wanted to clear the land of hermits. They were not numerous and lived silent in their cells. The police found 107 in all Tuscany. Government (1776) expelled into the Papal States hermits who were not citizens of Tuscany, forced native Tuscans into employment, and put under supervision ex-hermits too old to work.

Reformers of the Catholic Enlightenment were not liberals in thinking. Nor was the act a politic of prudence. Tuscans were no different from other Italians, they liked simple brothers and solitaries and wished to give them alms. The simultaneous ban on burials inside churches, and removal of graves outside the walls of towns, was equally disturbing to clergy and to peasants. In both cases men lost the grace which came from touching a holy man or holy place or holy object.

Scipione de' Ricci

Leopold found his ecclesiastical guide and agent in the vicar-general of the archdiocese of Florence, Scipione de' Ricci.

Ricci was born in 1741 the son of a Florentine senator. In his youth he was a member of the 'Jansenist' group in Rome which had its centre in Monsignor Bottari at the Vatican library. He was a relative of Ricci the general of the Jesuits. Though against Jesuits he could hardly forgive the Popes for their treatment of Ricci in Castel Sant' Angelo. He was at once Orthodox and reforming, strong against abuses and superstitions, caring for the pastoral work of the churches, a man of courage and energy yet without finesse.

Leopold found in him the perfect instrument for his policy. The part-nership, which lasted more than ten years, was not one-sided. Leopold read much in ecclesiastical literature and had information, but lacked con-fidence in handling Church politics. Ricci was not merely confident but over-confident. Leopold got the advice and action which he wanted. They shared an outlook in religion and liked each other. Leopold could not quickly discern how clumsy Ricci might be, how little he understood what was possible in politics. This rising adviser was soon abused by his enemies as 'the Pope of Tuscany'.

On 24 June 1780, at the duke's nomination, Ricci was consecrated in Rome as Bishop of (the united sees) of Pistoia and Prato. The see had been occupied by reforming bishops for nearly fifty years, and his immediate predecessor was Jansenist enough to be an eager reader of books from Port-Royal.

In the following year died the Archbishop of Florence. By chance Leopold met Antonio Martini, the scholar who translated the Bible into Italian and was ecclesiastical adviser to the King of Sardinia. Leopold felt the impress of this personality and on impulse offered him the archbishop-ric. This appointment caused jubilation among reformers. Martini was known as a defender of State rights, an advocate of a moderate 'Jansen-izing' divinity, and an enemy of the Jesuits.

The alliance between Peter Leopold, a prince who took as his model the behaviour of his brother Joseph II in Vienna, and Ricci a prelate who took as his model the ideals of the French Jansenists, begot the most fascinating and coherent reform movement of the Catholic eighteenth century.

What was done in Tuscany and Pistoia was a pattern of what the reform-ing movement wanted. Ricci was a convinced Jansenist, in no vague sense, he was a disciple of the French Jansenists and in close touch by letter with contemporary leaders of their party. For the first time the movement found a prince who sufficiently shared its aspirations and was prepared to back Jansenist reform by choice of men, by public encouragement, and by legislation.

The centre of religious life must be the parish and its liturgy. This meant, first, getting rid of religious orders or at least of the rivalry of their churches with parish churches; secondly getting rid of all the little private chapels, shrines, oratories, which drew men and women away from their parish churches on Sundays and feast days—in these two ways the parish church would have no competing places of worship for anyone to attend on a Sunday.

Every parish should be made a reasonable size and with a proper number of priests to the parishioners; so that the scandal of far too many priests in one place and far too few priests in another was cured. This meant redrawing parish boundaries everywhere, reducing greatly the crowded little parishes inherited in old cities from the Middle Ages, and creating new parishes in the country; secondly, limiting the excessive number of ordinations, especially of priests with no real pastoral work ahead of them, and of clergy in minor orders who were in no sense pastoral but received such orders only so that the choir or the acolytes in church should seem to be 'clerics'; thirdly, to get closer control over appointment to parishes, partly by amending laws about the rights of patronage and partly by abolishing surviving rights by certain congregations to elect their pastors.

Inside the parish church the service must be made congregational. And here doctrine entered. The liturgy was not an act done by priest for the people, it was 'a common act of priest and people'.[15] Therefore all the liturgy, even the prayer of consecration which was said secretly, should be said in a loud voice, and the congregation was to be encouraged to share. The reformers asked themselves whether logic must not demand liturgy in the vernacular instead of Latin, and plainly believed that in principle this would be right; but knew that in practice neither their people nor the Church at large would tolerate such radical departure from hallowed tradition. Nevertheless the people should be helped to understand by being provided with vernacular translations and by readings of the gospel in the vernacular after the Latin reading. In this was nothing specially Jansenist. Muratori asked no less.

Inside the parish church the congregational nature of worship was destroyed by two features; many little private masses competed for worshippers with the main parish mass; and mass was separated from communion, partly because the people came to mass every Sunday but received communion only once a year, and partly because communion was not given to the people at its proper place within the rite but from the reserved sacrament after the end of the rite.

The reformers failed to say so very loud, but the ending of separate masses must have the consequence of ending fees for masses and altering the many trusts whereby people bequeathed money that private masses might be said for their souls. They were clear that they wished to be rid of

[15] *Actes et decrets du Concile diocesain de Pistoie* (French trans., Paris, 1789), I.351.

private masses and especially of fees for masses; for they found people commonly believing that they need only pay money to a priest to gain benefit (not necessarily spiritual benefit) from the ensuing mass. They recognized that this goal of abolishing fees could not be immediate because they must make other provision to pay the clergy; and this other money could only happen from any or all of the following sources, (1) the hoped-for fewer clergy and therefore more money to go round, (2) monasteries or nunneries which would be suppressed like Jesuits or the Inquisition, (3) endowments from parish brotherhoods. But all these three sources of money they thought to be desirable on other grounds.

Brotherhoods intruded into the tidiness of a pastoral system where each church was ruled by a parish priest and his curates. Some of the money would be needed for the State to make better provision for the poor, but another part might help the clergy and destroy fees for masses.

Inside the parish church the services must be made simpler; that is, the people should find their focus in the worship of the altar more than the sacred picture or venerated statue. Therefore pictures or statues which promoted superstition should be removed; statues which were clothed for special reverence should lose their clothes; legends of obvious untruth should be removed from the readings or the pictures; cults which promoted unhistorical beliefs should be pruned; tables of indulgences should be removed from the doors of churches; and music should be kept from invading the solemn moments of the liturgy and likewise should be pruned.

All this attack on 'superstition' could touch the tenderest nerves of a people's devotion. It became the chief reason for the downfall of the reformers.

Instead of superstition and untrue legends of the saints the people should be taught to read and understand their Bibles.

The parish clergy, thus given new and higher status in relation to canons, monks, or brotherhoods, needed to be not only better paid but better educated. This was not an insoluble problem because Tuscany was a state in which several seminaries flourished; and the reasonable condition of Tuscan training may have helped to make support for the reformers. Leopold and Ricci both wanted a higher college above the seminary, called the Ecclesiastical Academy, to which seminarists might proceed for a type of university work; and both wanted no man to be ordained unless he first proceeded through a seminary. Meanwhile the parish clergy already in office should be given better books. Both the duke and Ricci looked to Italian translations of French Jansenist books—especially

Quesnel's *Moral Reflexions on the New Testament*. These choices of Jansenist books, and provision of Italian translations, and giving of them free to the clergy, were in theory excellent; Quesnel's book was pious and useful. But it happened to be the book which gave rise to the bull *Unigenitus* in 1713 and was therefore one of the most controversial books of the century. To recommend it to the clergy, and to give it free to incumbents, must look like disrespect, if not insult, to the see of Rome. This was the third rock, after the attack upon superstition and the enmity to monastic orders, upon which the reformers' ship was wrecked.

Part of the work was done by order of the State: the making of new parish boundaries in Pistoia (1783) where three colleges of clergy were suppressed and the parishes reduced to ten beside the cathedral; endowments from guilds and brotherhoods were taken to form a central fund called the *ecclesiastical patrimony* for the needs of the Church and relief of the poor, leaving in each parish one brotherhood to accompany the blessed sacrament in procession, bury the dead, visit the sick and prisoners, distribute alms, and perform such other charitable duties as should be requested (1783, in Pistoia and Prato, 1784 in all Tuscany).

Leopold and Ricci realized that they could not get what they wanted only by State acts. Government could alter endowments, make the clergy liable to secular courts, restrict ordinations. But if the order of service in parish churches was to be changed, they needed the help of bishops and clergy. They observed much difference in the speed or lack of speed with which bishops and dioceses responded to pressure from Florence. In Pistoia and Prato the ideal went ahead with élan and acceptability. In Chiusi and Colle the bishops moved nearly as fast. In Fiesole nothing happened that they wanted. Various dioceses moved at different rates or were not seen to move or were suspected of moving backwards.

Therefore they needed to place a plan of reform before the clergy, gathered in their diocesan conferences, which bishops should be driven to summon (for we saw how reluctant everyone became to summon a diocesan synod, how rare their appearance, pp. 198 ff); the clergy should debate the plans, their views should be reported to Florence, and then the duke should summon a national synod which should decree reforming resolutions for all Tuscany.

Such was the plan. It started promisingly and ended in total failure.

The Diocesan Synod of Pistoia

By a circular of 2 August 1785 Duke Leopold required all bishops to hold a diocesan synod. Six months later (26 January 1786) he presented the agenda to be discussed at these synods. This agenda was known as the Fifty-Seven Points. When Parisian Jansenists read these Fifty-Seven Points they compared Duke Peter Leopold to the great Christian monarchs of history, Charlemagne, Theodosius the Great, Stephen of Hungary, Alfred the Great.

The Fifty-Seven Points, though an agenda for debate by synods, was drafted in such a way as to lead synods towards certain conclusions. They were asked to consider how to purge the breviary of false legends; how to encourage the reading of the Bible; to examine whether it would be useful to have the liturgy in the vernacular instead of Latin; whether popular elections to parishes should be stopped; whether useless oaths should be abolished; how the bishop's authority was to recover its proper rights from the interference of the Roman Curia, especially in the giving of dispensations; how to get the teaching of St. Augustine on grace into seminaries and universities and monasteries; how to cure the excess of ordinands and their low quality; whether an annual retreat should be made compulsory for the clergy; how to get drapings off statues; whether all monks and nuns should be under the bishop; how feasts should be diminished in number; and how it is right to read certain books, like Muratori's *Of a Well-Ordered Devotion*, Quesnel's *Moral Reflexions on the New Testament*, and the *Moral Theology* by the leading Italian Jansenist Pietro Tamburini of Pavia.

The tone of these Fifty-Seven Points, however pleasing to Jansenists in Paris, began to alarm the Tuscan bishops. It sounded more radical than most of them wanted or thought prudent and possible.

Bishop Ricci, who probably drafted or helped to draft the Fifty-Seven Points, summoned his synod to meet at Pistoia in September 1786, the first diocesan synod in that diocese for sixty-five years. He invited Pietro Tamburini from Pavia to be the theological guide or *promoter* of the synod.

This most famous of all diocesan synods opened at the church of St. Leopold in Pistoia on 18 September 1786; 246 clergy attended. It maintained the usual forms of a diocesan synod. Ricci sat in cope and mitre at the west end under the organ pipes, in front of him a table, and in front of the table a lectern with an open Bible; to his right, high in the wall, was the pulpit whence the decrees and propositions were read. To each side were as usual the disciplined ranks of clergy by seniority, in cassock and surplice and biretta; at a table in the central aisle sat Professor Tamburini, on each side of him two secretaries.

Some of the resolutions were like those of the many diocesan synods with which we are familiar; the behaviour or dress of the clergy, the ideals of pastoral life, the agenda of clerical conferences, the certificates of midwives, the keeping of registers, the age of confirmation, the securing of reverence in services, the closing of shops in times of service. All this was normality.

But the tone of the minutes of the synod shouts the difference from the routine of Italian diocesan synods. This was due not only to the radical tone of the resolutions, but even more to the attitudes of the participants.

First, Bishop Ricci really believed in consultation. Afterwards, when men could not understand how nearly 240 clergy could vote for such resolutions, they spread tales that the clergy were tyrannized by the bishop, the canard was even told that he locked up anyone likely to oppose, and so was able to keep opponents down to tiny numbers between four and eight, several of them members of religious orders.

Other bishops summoned clergy to hear their decrees. Ricci started by telling the clergy: 'It is you as well as I who rule in the Church and must share in the reform. . . . I have no desire to dominate, nor to make you swear blindly to the decrees of the bishop. . . . The kingdom of Jesus Christ is not a despotism or a monarchy.'[16] So far from the majority of the clergy doing just what the bishop wanted, or being overawed by the national prestige of Professor Tamburini, there is evidence that they went further than either Ricci or Tamburini thought prudent. Certain resolutions appeared in a more provocative form than Ricci and Tamburini wanted.[17] Both Ricci and Tamburini were radicals, Tamburini probably more radical than Ricci, and certainly based on far firmer radical principles. Ricci was like a fatherly but limited archdeacon, Tamburini owned one of the most thoughtful minds in all Italy, but both men had more knowledge of the world and of what was possible than the most radical among their men.

Not all the clergy, but a majority of the clergy were prepared to back Ricci because the diocese had already fifty years of bishops friendly to Jansenizing reform. They plainly felt him to be a good and even holy father in God, partly because he really wished to consult, partly because they believed in his policy, partly because he had done much already to raise their stipends and elevate the pastoral ministry against its rivals, and partly because he so evidently possessed the backing of his sovereign. They

[16] *Actes de Pistoie* 1.20 ff.   [17] Evidence in Mantese, *Tamburini*, 91.

had a sensation of enthusiasm, as though they were on the verge of a great act not only for the diocese of Pistoia but for the Church at large. They had the sensation that they could lead the Church to be free of childish superstitions, to be rid of the formalities of casuistry in confession, and to bring back the use of the Scripture. They voted by enormous majorities for what the managers proposed.

The world afterwards mocked the folly of a handful of clergy in an unimportant diocese believing themselves capable of starting a reform of the Catholic Church.

The third reason for the difference between the Pistoia minutes and the minutes of other synods lay in the drafter. They were so ably written, with a sense of theological perspective, at times too difficult for some of the clergy, but usually with clarity and at times with a potent fascination, that they were plainly drafted by Tamburini. Indeed there is evidence that Tamburini arrived in Pistoia from Pavia with drafts already in his pocket.[18]

The meeting began by accepting the Council of Trent, professing the creed of Pope Pius IV, praising St. Charles Borromeo, and adhering to the centre of unity in Rome. This was not a revolutionary start. The synod had no intention of being Protestant.

Its resolutions may be divided thus:

(1) Against modern errors

    (a) Against the abuse of indulgences, on which the synod more or less agreed with Luther.

    (b) Against the adoration of the humanity of Jesus, that meant against the cult of the Sacred Heart. The Synod declared that the cult of the Blessed Virgin should be in accord with the mind of the Church.

    (c) Against the practice of parish missions, 'the irregular apparatus of these new practices called Exercises or Missions', such sudden excitements 'seldom or never produce real conversion'. Behind this dislike of the mission was the ordinary distrust of the parish pastor, who represented normality, for the incoming religious who represented abnormality. But in the mind of Tamburini and the more instructed can be discerned a still deeper motive. The formality of absolution, easily bestowed in confession with a bare collect as a penance, was a symbol of the attitude that men's hearts could be changed overnight as it were by miracle; and the quest for sudden conversion in mission they held to be based upon a mistaken view of the nature of sanctification and

[18] Mantese, 87 n.31.

the steady or unsteady growth of the soul. The Synod thought of quick absolution for the gravest offences as 'the most fertile cause of evil in the Church'; and in this view it was characteristically Jansenist after the French pattern.

(d) Against the stations of the cross; not as condemning stations, but popular belief that to perform a fixed number of stations brought special blessing.

(e) Against statues in which the people place a special or superstitious faith. The Synod suggested that Biblical scenes painted on the walls would be more helpful to true religion.

(f) Against oaths. The Synod asked government to abolish oaths in law courts and elsewhere and substitute affirmations. But this was what government had suggested to the synod in one of its Fifty-Seven Points.

(g) Against any legal obligation to be contracted by engagements to marry, for the synod saw how the Italian customs of the engagement promoted a sleeping together before marriage.

(h) Against the wide extension of the prohibited decrees of affinity for marriage. In mountain villages everyone was related to everyone else, and the present restrictions led either to fornication or to an endemic quest for dispensations.

(2) Aim to make worship more congregational

(a) The priest to say mass audibly.

(b) The congregation to be encouraged to share. The Synod held the suggestion made in the Fifty-Seven Points, that mass might be in Italian, not to be right at the present time, but they asked that the people be given translations of the liturgy.

(c) Each church to have only one altar.

(d) No flowers nor relics to be placed on the altar. Authentic relics may be placed underneath the altar.

(e) The people to be exhorted to receive communion whenever they go to mass, and priests to give them communion at the proper place in the mass and not afterwards.

(f) Everyone who can read to be encouraged to read the Bible. It is not necessary for salvation but only those who are incapable can be excused.

(g) To understand the Bible, the people to be encouraged to read Italian translations of certain French books, including Quesnel's *Moral Reflexions on the New Testament*.

(h) Fees for masses to be abolished as soon as they can be.

(i) Feasts to be diminished in number.

(j) A new and reformed breviary to be planned with the legends deleted and more Biblical readings.

(3) Reform of monks and nuns

(a) All monasteries and nunneries to be under the bishop. Exemption to end.

(b) No monastic chapels to be open on Sundays or feast days.

(c) All religious orders to be united into one order, based upon the Benedictine Rule and guided by the practice of Port-Royal.

(d) No city to have more than one monastery, preferably situated outside the walls for the sake of quiet.

(e) The old division between choir monks and lay brothers to end.

(f) Only one or two monks to be ordained, enough to serve the chapel.

(g) Permanent vows for men to be abolished. Monks to vow for one year at a time, nuns not allowed to take permanent vows before the age of forty or forty-five.

(h) Nunneries perhaps are best located within the city.

All these last provisions about monks and nuns meant revolution and not reform. It is curious now to see the mixture of plans which never had a chance, like the union of all monastic orders, with plans which for decades looked revolutionary but which during the 1960s and 1970s became normal in the pastoral ideals of the Roman Catholic Church.

The constitution of the Church

Infallibility rests only with the whole body of the Catholic Church and therefore its mouthpiece is the General Council and not the Pope. The Synod accepted the four Gallican articles of 1682 and even incorporated them verbatim into its resolutions.

The meeting at Pistoia ended with a sense of solemnity, Ricci at one point in tears. He at once announced that he would govern the diocese in accordance with their resolutions, and appointed a bishop's council of eight priests to meet each month. A fortnight later he sent out to his clergy free copies of that 'golden book' Quesnel's *Moral Reflexions*. But when he asked the duke's leave to publish the decrees of the Synod, he was told that this should be delayed until after the forthcoming national council. That winter of 1786-7 many (but not all) of his parish clergy started altering and simplifying their services after the mind of the Synod. Tamburini returned to Pavia with a ducal honorarium, but was robbed of most of the money when he stopped at an inn in Mantua.

Meanwhile rumour was busy. The little handful of opponents in the synod started to talk, protest, write. Pamphlets began to fly, with smell of heresy. The charge that Ricci was a heretic mounted, until simple people in the diocese heard the ill rumour and began to wonder and suspect. In that atmosphere Leopold's dearest plan for a national synod looked doubtful. The Pistoia synod asked the duke to summon the national synod, but privately even Ricci was not yet sure that it was wise. Leopold hesitated sufficiently to invite all the bishops of Tuscany to a preliminary consultation at the Palazzo Pitti in Florence, 23 April to 3 June 1787.

The meeting of bishops at Florence agreed several things that the duke and Ricci wanted. It asked that the national synod be summoned. It agreed to the reform of oaths, that they needed a new breviary, that oratories should be shut or in total dependence on the parish, and that sermons in monasteries should be held behind closed doors. But whenever any very controversial point came under discussion, the bishops were not agreed and therefore agreed to leave it to the discretion of each bishop acting in his own diocese, which was not at all what Leopold wanted in his quest for uniformity of reform throughout the land. And whenever one particular subject appeared on the agenda, all the Tuscan bishops but three or four shrank back—the place of Rome in the Church. They refused to claim that the bishops ought to have the rights of dispensation hitherto reserved for Rome; or that a bishop's oath to Rome be abolished; or that Quesnel's book, which Rome condemned, should be prescribed reading. They wished to make no demands disrespectful to the Holy See.

But, as the bishops debated in the Palazzo Pitti in Florence, there happened a calamity which changed the entire prospect. This was the riot in Prato (20–1 May) over the Madonna's girdle. This riot shocked the duke, the bishops, and Ricci. It frightened a lot of would-be reformers.

Ricci's crusade against superstition began to find its reward.

The riot at Prato

A fourteenth-century Dominican Andrea Franchi lay within a tomb at the old Dominican church of Pistoia, and was venerated by the people as a saint. Restoring and replanning the church, Ricci wanted wide space and moved the tomb to the church of St. Leopold, saying that nothing authentic was known about Franchi and that the body was not certainly Franchi's body. When a dilapidated but revered picture of the Virgin at Chianti was whitewashed in course of a restoration, and a new picture was placed on the high altar, a parish priest led a demonstration of his people to the former place of the old picture, disregarding the new. When the bishop issued revised prayer-books or litanies for the edification of his people, torn copies of the new books were thrown ostentatiously and repeatedly into the town gutters. The climax of this conflict came in May 1787 when the rumour ran through the town of Prato that the bishop intended to demolish the altar sacred to the girdle of the Virgin. In the evening a crowd assembled with sticks and hatchets, climbed the tower, rang the bells for several hours, tore out of the choir the bishop's throne and coat of arms and burnt them in the market square, illuminated the church all night to exhibit the girdle for veneration, sacked the bishop's palace, fetched parish priests from their beds, carried statues from a store to the cathedral, invaded the seminary, and threatened the professors with death. The tale spread, and in the morning the peasants of the countryside poured into the town to make the round of the churches. Order was not restored until troops arrived to barricade the streets, close the shops and bars, and make numerous arrests.[19]

Ricci offered to resign his see, and had his resignation refused. But every bishop was now aware of the force in the religious conservatism of the people. Even Duke Leopold, for all his abuse of bishops and his continued backing of Ricci, silently changed direction, seeing that the waters were deeper than he expected.

He continued his policy but by decree. He could not have a national synod. The bishops, to whom he was extremely rude at the end of their meeting in the Palazzo Pitti, were useless. He went ahead by ducal power. He allowed the decrees of Pistoia to be published (2 October 1788); asked Ricci to send him a plan for national reform which he could apply to all Tuscany; abolished the Roman Nuncio in Florence (20 September 1788); ordered (2 October 1788) that no Tuscan monastery should have a foreign superior, that monks could appeal to the civil courts against their superiors, and that any Tuscan who entered a monastery abroad thereby lost his civic rights as a Tuscan.

But he never found it convenient to act on Ricci's national plan for reform and put it quietly in the archives. In 1789 Belgium rose against his brother the Holy Roman Emperor Joseph II, with the religious policy of Joseph as one among the motives of revolt. In 1790 Joseph II died, and Leopold succeeded to his throne in Vienna and left Tuscany. Riots broke out again, in Leghorn and Pistoia. Leopold advised his successor that Ricci was a liability, and that his resignation should be accepted with the provision of a good pension.

[19] De Potter, 2.198–202; Bolton, 119; *Nouvelles ecclésiastiques* 87.197–200.

After his resignation, Ricci retired to Florence and a quiet life, and later wrote his memoirs. Those memoirs are the chief document for the prosecution. If they give a just picture of their author, he was a small-minded man, full of resentments, with the illusion that a diocesan synod could reform the Catholic Church. Those modes of reform headed directly towards schism in the church of Tuscany, and towards the shaking of the duke's throne. Ricci was no passionate moral reformer. Though at one point of his later unpopularity he fancied himself a new Savonarola, no one could have been less like that sternest of preachers. Ricci was no confessor with a willingness for martyrdom. But from the influence of Port-Royal or of Pietro Tamburini he saw change needed in the Catholic Church of his day and found a prince willing to order the Church about, and had the courage and unwisdom to make the attempt.

Two members of the same Florentine family stood at opposite poles of Italian Catholicism in the later eighteenth century. Ricci the Jesuit general stood for the supreme act of self-negation even before an unjust Pope. Ricci the bishop stood for reform of the Church by State power without asking leave of the Pope. But the fate of the second Ricci was made possible, personally and publicly, by the fate of the first Ricci. The destruction of the Jesuits, by encouraging every Catholic government in Europe to go further in dealing with religious orders and reallotting Church revenues, helped to make possible what happened in Tuscany.

Toleration

In no state of Europe before the Revolution, whether the state was Catholic or Protestant, were members of a religious minority treated as equal in rights with members of a dominant majority. The only place where this happened was Transylvania, for the four confessions Roman Catholic, Lutheran, Calvinist, Unitarian, because these denominations won privileges under Turkish rule and Turks could not or would not distinguish between Christianities.

The question at first was whether a minority might settle or remain though under legal disadvantages; as the Jews were secure in many cities of Europe and yet were not regarded as citizens. Germany was familiar with the elaborate mosaic in which Protestant communities lived side by side with Catholic communities. They hardly mixed, but whichever was dominant in the area was forced by imperial law to tolerate. In areas like the Palatinate a mixed population had rights to share the same church for services at different times.

When Louis XIV expelled the French Protestants in 1685, the world was still such that intelligent observers thought the expulsion to be useful in promoting public order. This expulsion was larger, and probably more disastrous for the country, than any expulsion in the eighteenth century. It had no backing from Pope Innocent XI, who disapproved its methods while he celebrated a *Te Deum*.

Piedmont was forced to do with the Waldensians of the Alpine valleys (1694) what France did to the Huguenots. But the Waldensians were willing to fight, and easily won international backing, and little Piedmont had to rescind the expulsions.

Prince-bishop Firmian of Salzburg ordered the worst expulsion of the eighteenth century. The Protestants of the mountains felt themselves threatened and in some valleys began to baptize or marry or bury in the open, which in strict imperial law was illegal, and to arm. Firmian decided that they menaced his state, borrowed soldiers from the Emperor, and (31 October 1731) ordered the expulsion of all Protestants, 20,000 to 30,000 souls. The scandal was international. Most of the refugees emigrated to Prussia, some helped to people Pennsylvania.[20]

In Spain, Portugal, and Italy outside Piedmont almost no dissenters lived.

Travellers and tourists were more common, and their habits bothered a few Italian bishops. Venice needed German merchants, its university of Padua had German students whom it failed always to treat with equity. Leghorn had a chapel for German and Protestant merchants. International trade and travel confronted Italy with the need to allow Protestant visitors a chapel, and why not Protestant residents?

Instructed Italians had also a sensation that northern countries advanced into prosperity and that part of the secret of advance lay in accepting diversity in the State. Intelligent Italians saw that censorship hampered the spread of ideas and wanted to liberalize, though not usually to abolish, censorship. If they demanded liberty for Voltaire and the French Encyclopedia, they would not be intolerant of Protestant divines; and one of the wishes of Catholic reformers was freedom to use Protestant books if they were good and useful books.

Prussian conquest of Catholic Silesia, and extension of Prussian power in the Catholic Rhineland, and the partitions of Catholic Poland between Prussia and Russia and Austria, gave new force to Catholic ideas of toleration. Behaviour like that of Bishop Firmian of Salzburg might not benefit Catholicism for it justified Prussian maltreatment of Silesians, Rhine-

[20] H. Widmann, *Deutsche Landesgeschichte: Salzburg*, 3.384 ff.

landers, or Poles, and English maltreatment of Irish. In theory they could claim toleration for Catholics who lived under Protestants or Russian Orthodox or Turks, and still deny liberty of worship to anyone who dissented from Catholicism in a Catholic state. Stiff minds continued to propound this theory into the nineteenth century. But whatever the theory, in practice the attitude was possible only to persons who knew little about Protestants or about Catholics in non-Catholic states. Catholic statesmen saw that to demand toleration in Prussia or England was to concede toleration in Austria or Bavaria.

All forms of repression threw up cases of injustice. Some French priests were pleased with the missionary results of the *dragonnades*, where soldiers worked with missionaries to convert Huguenots. Other French priests lamented the hollow and unedifying nature of what happened in these 'conversions'. The Catholic Church was familiar with, and accepted, the custom that every adult Catholic must receive holy communion at Easter. Few men minded a measure of compulsion applied to Catholics. When the same compulsion was applied to nominal Catholics whom everyone knew to be secret Protestants, a sense of sacrilege and repulsion touched minds. Whether or not the attack on the Camisards of south-east France was such a case of injustice, the Calas case (1762) in south-west France became a scandal throughout Europe because Voltaire paraded the injustice of a local community. Slowly throughout the century the man under penalty not for antisocial behaviour but for his conscience began to win more and more sympathy; or (as it would be better described) more and more people began to refuse to identify conscientious religious dissent by otherwise good men as antisocial behaviour of such gravity as to warrant repression.

The arguments for intolerance were strong. The public presence of men of other faiths weakens faith and the practice of the community, which is the bond of society. It slowly leads to indifference, which all Christians agree to be an evil. In villages and small towns it causes social scandal and division, disturbs souls, and can lead to disorder if not to riot.

The Empress Maria Theresa wrote letters to her son Joseph II (1775–7). He argued that men must have liberty to believe and could only be enlightened by the Spirit of God, and were merely troubled by human laws on creeds. His mother became anxious about the state of his soul. Toleration is carelessness about truth and will end by destroying religion. Joseph (20 July 1777) wrote her a remarkable letter:[21]

[21] *Maria Theresia und Joseph II: ihre Correspondenz*, ed. A. von Arneth (Vienna, 1867), 151–2.

The sole cause of our disagreement is the definition of the word *toleration*. May God preserve me from thinking that it does not matter whether our citizens remain Catholic or change to be Protestant. . . . I would give all that I possess if thereby all the Protestants of your states became Catholics! By the word *toleration*, I mean that I, in all temporal matters, would employ anyone without taking notice of his religion, would allow him to own property and follow a profession, and be a full citizen, so long as he was suitable and could help the State and its economy.

The Emperor Joseph II's patent of toleration (1781) was the weightiest single act of relief.

When Joseph succeeded to sole power, an edict of toleration was forced upon his government by the unrest of the Protestant peasants of Bohemia and Moravia, and the failure of traditional use of force. The freedom of worship so granted was only to Lutherans, Calvinists, and Eastern Orthodox, not to deists or unbelievers, and only permitted the exercise of private worship; no bells, no public porch on the street, no spire nor tower. Non-Catholics must continue to pay usual fees to the Catholic priest for baptism, marriage or burial. But among so many Catholic peoples, the edict of toleration was the best of the Emperor's efforts to harry his state into the modern world. The censorship, still banning books against religion (no German translation of Voltaire but allowing the French original) was centralized in Vienna and made far more liberal, so that Protestant books began to circulate freely. No one (of the permitted faiths) lost civil rights by reason of his faith.

Catholic bishops found it not easy to administer. Clergy needed now to abstain from controversial preaching lest their people be excited to harm a minority, and uncontroversial preaching is duller. Priests were used to confiscating erroneous books from their flocks, or compelling unwilling families to bring a non-Catholic corpse for burial, and had to be discouraged. Police must protect Protestant services from interruption. Special delicacy was needed about the interment of Protestant bodies in Catholic churchyards. The Emperor was unwise enough to order that no Catholic might become a Protestant until he had engaged in Catholic religious exercises for six weeks. The philosophy of these exercises rested on the axiom that a Catholic would be likely to become Protestant only because of bad education or corrupt information. During the six weeks no Protestant pastor or schoolmaster might have access to the would-be convert, who could not attend non-Catholic worship.

A visitor to some parts of Transylvania will find that many older

Eastern Orthodox churches go back to the reign of Joseph II, and were the consequence of his policy of toleration.

An edict of January 1782 gave toleration to Jews in Lower Austria. The edict of toleration with its supplementary decrees was not generous. They could not own land, were limited in numbers, could not have public synagogues in Vienna, and could not open shops outside the Jewish 'quarter'. They must still pay a special tax. For all business transactions they must use the language of the country and not their own language. They must take German names. Nevertheless they must send their children to school, could build their own schools, engage in crafts, commerce, banking and industry, and need wear no special dress. They could go to universities. They could even have Christian servants, and appear in the streets on Sundays, and wear a sword.

Similar edicts followed for the other parts of the Empire. Galicia, where Jews were numerous, received its edict almost at the end of the reign, an edict without limit on numbers.

All Jews were made liable for service in the army, being allowed a variant form of the oath of loyalty. Pious Jews could not accept this compulsion. A conscripted Jew must eat food in barracks and march on the sabbath. The Jews hated and feared military service. The mountains of Galicia were full of young men who hid. By flight from recruiting officers, emigration, turmoil and protests, the Jews persuaded Joseph's successor (1792) to allow a heavy payment in return for exemption.[22]

The reaction after the death of Joseph II withdrew a little of the toleration. But the edict was another landmark in the history of Europe.

Pope and Catholic Emperor went opposite ways; the Pope to keep Christians pure and therefore raise the walls which hid the Jews, the Emperor to make Christendom more just and therefore knock down the higher walls and let the Jews be seen. Priests do not invariably possess a more enlightened conscience than their sovereigns. The layman had a lowlier motive beside justice, namely, money for his State. The Pope sought to benefit the souls of Christians, the Emperor sought to benefit their bodies. Still, Joseph II cared not only about 'assimilation', or racial harmony in his state, but also for justice; and, if it be allowed that Pius VI also cared about justice, the Emperor cannot be denied a more sensitive understanding of the needs of justice in contemporary society.

The Austrian patent was a model for the French Act of Toleration, 1787. It had wide influence in Catholic Germany. To make ideas of tolerance

[22] Dubnov, 4.667 ff.; Padover, 181–2; Mahler, 229 ff., 274 ff.

consistent was exceedingly hard for the new mentality of that age. From safety on the Swiss border the Italian radical Carlantonio Pilati (*Di una riforma*, 1768) issued passionate appeals to Italians to tolerate different religions, and assailed the Inquisition for driving all the best minds out of Italy; but in the same breath demanded that government put spies among monks to find excuses for closing monasteries, and abolish friars gradually but totally by forbidding novices. Those who revered Clement XIV Ganganelli as the greatest because most liberal of Popes found it hard not to praise him for intolerance towards the Jesuits.

When Joseph II issued his patent of toleration, the Austrian-ruled land of Breisgau in south-west Germany went into uproar, said that their people were all Catholics except for one hairdresser, and begged to be excluded from the edict.[23] In Belgium violent protests weakened the Austrian regime.

Politically the Catholic Church must surrender the sword. No other course was open. But like the claim of the Jews the Catholic claim to truth was absolute. In religion, as distinct from politics, few enough people believed in toleration which they identified with contempt for truth and therefore with sin. Popes and clergy tolerated because they were forced by the needs of the hour to tolerate, not because they believed in toleration as virtue. Revolution, singing a hymn to absolute equality before the law, came upon them while they still regarded the frame of society as too brittle unless its citizens, or nearly all its citizens, or at least its full citizens, professed a common religion.

The attack upon celibacy

Catholic attack upon the celibacy of the priest had not been heard since the earlier days of the Reformation.

The origins of the onslaught were French, in Voltaire and Diderot and the *Encyclopedia* article on celibacy. It started in earnest when a French priest, Pierre Desforges, published (1758) *The Advantages of Marriage*, a confused and repetitive book, but containing in its two volumes a mass of historical ammunition for an attack upon celibacy. At first it had little European importance; but in the year 1768, at the time when Italy moved against Pope Clement XIII for the *Monitorium* of Parma, Desforges' book was given an Italian translation, published at Florence. The question became urgent for a practical reason. Thousands of Jesuits were thrown out of their houses. If a monk was ejected from his monastery through no

---

[23] Geier, 208.

fault of his own, and told to go and make his living in the world as schoolmaster or librarian, was he to be held for ever bound to the unmarried life for a vow which he took, perhaps, in his late teens? The argument, once the staple of controversy between Catholics and Protestants, started to be an argument between Catholics.

Pope Clement XIV charged the famous controversialist of the day, the Jesuit and then ex-Jesuit Zaccaria, once Muratori's successor as librarian at Modena, to defend celibacy. Zaccaria produced a fat work with the characteristic title *A Polemical History of Holy Celibacy* (Italian 1774, German translation 1781). He gave as his reasons for writing the need to reply to anonymous Italian pamphlets and an Italian translation of Desforges. Zaccaria's book was learned and able and retained for a hundred years the repute of being the best defence of the celibacy of the priesthood. He admitted that one apostle at least had a wife but there was no evidence that they lived together with wives after they became apostles and the evidence is to the contrary since they left everything to become disciples. No one who reads the New Testament can deny that the unmarried state is higher in the sense that the single person can more easily consecrate himself to God and give his undivided time to his people. The Catholic people is deeply attached to single priests. And if men say that no one should be compelled to adhere to a vow of which they could not foresee the consequences, nobody compels people to take holy orders; or, if families sometimes compel, that is not the Church's fault.

Zaccaria, strong maintainer of the Pope's prerogative, admitted that the Pope could abrogate the law in theory, because it is an apostolic order and the Pope has power equal to the apostles. But if he did, he would put the steadfastness of past popes in doubt, lower the glory of those who suffered for their chastity, hurt the spiritual work of the clergy. No sufficient reason can be seen for so vast and dangerous a change in the discipline of the Church.

Zaccaria was a splitter of hairs and forced bits of the history to dance to his fingers as he pulled them hither and thither. But it was a masterly defence. Every Catholic who wanted now to argue for a married priesthood had to face this collection of embattled information.

With the coming of Joseph II Austria started to fill with rumour that the Emperor would abolish the law of celibacy. The reason was obvious, for he forced men and women out of monasteries and nunneries and were they to be held to the single life? These rumours unleashed a wave of pamphleteering on both sides.

The arguments of the Austrian assailants of celibacy were these: It is not in Scripture. It was not a continuous practice in the Catholic Church. Even if Christ treated the unmarried state as higher, that does not mean that it is right to insist on it for everyone. Experience shows that marriage brings into many men a more balanced attitude to life. Enough immorality exists among the clergy to make the law of celibacy doubtful because it is so often and so inevitably broken. The sexual drive is irresistible and excommunications and anathemas are powerless against its force. The law brings danger to the man dedicated to the single life in his youth; danger to the man who must sit in the confessional; danger to the man who cannot do without a housekeeper; danger, not to his morals but to his person, by the shrivelling of affections and the separation from normal life among the laity. If the Church can do something so extraordinary as to abolish Jesuits, it would be no more extraordinary to abolish the celibacy of priests.

In all this argument Lorenz Hübner, priest and journalist at Salzburg, took a prominent part. But all south Germany and Austria threw up pamphleteers of the same type; among them Benedikt Werkmeister, then novice-master at the Benedictine abbey at Neresheim.

You say [wrote Werkmeister] that no one is forced to take orders. But prebends beckon! A love of souls beckons! Does the Church want only frigid men or evil livers? Does not the best of men, if driven by his work to live among women and children, have an innocent wish to take his woman to his heart and kiss her, though he never thought about it when he was ordained and promised the opposite? I believe that other things being equal it is the man who is the natural father who will make the best spiritual father. . . . I say to you without circumlocution, a sentence as clear as any proposition in Euclid, give them their wives today instead of tomorrow! Give them wives, so that they can do honourably what they now do with scandal! If seventeen or eighteen general councils and a hundred local councils met and cried one thing, *Holy Celibacy*, it would be no use. They cry against nature. If all the stars in the sky joined in that chorus, it would still be no use. . . .[24]

By the end of the reign of Joseph II ominous revolutionary voices began to be heard. One Josephist suggested that since sacramental marriage was impossible for priests, they should be permitted unsacramental marriage. A vehemently antipapal ex-Jesuit of Vienna raised the moral question of the confessional, what is to be said to a priest who confesses that he is secretly married: is he to put away his wife? and reached the startling new conclusion that he was not, that the marriage was valid in the eyes of God and he should be encouraged to remain a secretly married man in the hope that one day authority would recognize his marriage as lawful.[25]

[24] Werkmeister in Picard, 174 ff.   [25] Picard, 174 ff.

In Josephist Austria of the 1780s a few such secret marriages of priests appear to have been celebrated.

The argument caused anxiety at Rome. A fragment of a speech by Cardinal Pallavicini, secretary of state to Pius VI, has survived, 'If priests can marry, the papal hierarchy falls, the Pope loses respect and supremacy, married clergy will be tied by their wives and children and be dependent on the State . . .'[26]

The reform of the liturgy

When German hymns became popular, the question of mass in language understood by the people began to be discussed. Latin was the only international language, and a wish to turn the service into German or Italian met the obstacle that Germans and Italians were divided by different dialects. The movement for a vernacular liturgy became urgent in south Germany, for Latin was a language more 'natural' to Italians or Spaniards than to Germans. To persuade, would-be reformers needed still to argue that German was 'now' a refined language, capable of bearing the prayers of a people.

Conservatives had the argument of hallowed association. Ordinary people preferred not to understand the words of the most sacred portions of the mass, thinking that they were being turned into Lutherans if they heard German prayers, and there is evidence that when they heard one of the rare German liturgies they understood as little of the German as the Latin and were more ashamed because now they were supposed to understand. The advocates of change argued that no curtain should fall between priest and people; that the vernacular was the custom of the primitive Church; and that to understand a service is to avoid the danger among peasants of a superstitious use of formulas as incantations.

Educated men grew more articulate and critical in their attitudes to what went on in church on Sunday. Formerly they accepted what the Church decided, or hoped to do little more than guide or regulate an excess of popular fervour. In Spain and Portugal and Southern Italy, even in most of France and Austria, the attitude of uncomplaining or happy acceptance remained dominant.

But in parts of Germany and Switzerland Catholics lived near or among Protestants. And in that age Protestants experienced a wave of criticism of what they did in church on Sunday, new awareness, discussion of the purpose of worship and its forms, intelligent analysis of liturgy. Is the language of prayers drafted for God's sake or to make effect upon the

[26] Carové, 2.637.

minds or souls of those who pray? Prayer said aloud must intend to affect the congregation—at least to lead them in reverence, perhaps to persuade them into moral attitudes. This debate appeared among priests in Catholic Germany. Though touched by Protestant argument, it would have arisen without the Protestants; for it had the same cause, the developing education of middle-class laymen, a widening gulf between literate and illiterate, larger towns with the first signs that in towns men need to be *attracted* into church on Sundays. A south-German priest looked across at his Protestant neighbours and envied their power to make what he understood to be such striking improvement in ways of worship.[27]

For a time Catholic pastors felt free to experiment. Pope Clement XIV Ganganelli seemed to call all the Church to pull itself up to date, and to cast off or amend whatever inheritance from past ages hurt the present work or worship of Christian people. And scholars, chiefly French, published the folio series of ancient liturgies which changed the study of the history of Christian worship, and showed how old forms of prayer were modified to the need of new generations.

Those who were bold to print that they wanted change, were only a handful: a court-chaplain, a vicar-general, a Bavarian pastor; but even an occasional congregation with its pastor changed habits. The prince-bishops of Germany were not all of a mind to discourage such experiments. These ideas were found in places as far apart as Vienna, Constance, Stuttgart, Munich, Mainz. And many Roman Catholic chapels in England held the service of benediction in the English language without asking leave of anyone.

The innovators saw that ways of worship cannot be changed speedily. Old forms are hallowed, and may not be destroyed but must be purified, adapted, made intelligible. They inherited a series of prayers which had little structure, and observed an attitude which expected mechanical repetition of those prayers. To put soul into dead rites and meaningless ceremonies was their aim. They wanted order, clarity of structure, services dedicated to a single theme. They wanted to explain worship, so that ordinary men and women understood what they did. The danger lay in turning liturgy from the vessel of a sacrificial heart into moral exhortation.

Songs in German, prayers in Latin—this was not the chief reason why a few reformers wanted mass in German. All the arguments for simplicity and understanding and moral instruction pointed to mass in the language of the common people. This plan had the special barrier that the battle

[27] Werkmeister: see Ehrensperger, 93 n.246.

between Reformation and Counter-Reformation linked German prayers with Protestant ideals. Thinking men who cast off such prejudice still preferred Latin words, hallowed by long usage, to new flat prosaic-sounding German. They felt it to strip liturgy of its grandeur with its mystery. One of the noblest of Catholic reformers, Johann Michael Sailer, believed that language mattered little because aspirations of the heart were always too deep to be expressed in language. 'God', it was said humorously, 'understands Latin quite as well as he understands German.'[28] Others thought that to translate the mass into German risked that destruction of worship which turned its direction away from God and towards man.

Those who wanted a German mass offered arguments. Already laymen followed mass in private German translation. A congregation should be a union of priest and people. If words are to have heart they must be understood. They kept quoting the text of 1 Corinthians 14: 19: 'in the church I had rather speak five words with my understanding, that by my voice I might teach others also, than ten thousand words in an unknown tongue.' Occasionally they used the argument that thus they might recover non-Catholics. Given liturgy in their language, Protestants would at last understand the mass.

The first mass in the German language was written in 1786 by the Benedictine Benedikt Maria Werkmeister for the Catholic chapel at the palace in Stuttgart. The prayer of consecration remained in Latin. Werkmeister intended this liturgy for a private chapel to be the model which other Catholic states of Germany should copy.

A number of those who wanted mass in German were content with priestly services in Latin, for priests (usually) knew Latin. But others wanted priests to say their office less mechanically and believed that the use of German would help. Most nunneries contained simple or near-illiterate nuns, certainly nuns whose Latin grammar could not pass examination. Chaplains to such nunneries desired offices which a less instructed community might use intelligently. A *breviary* was needed, for the use of clergy and devout laity, in the German language.

The type of *concursus* examination shows the subtly different colouring of ideas in this unsettled age. Here are examination questions in the spirit of Benedikt Werkmeister in south-west Germany in the years 1808–9:[29]

Is the primacy of the Pope a divine law or a human creation?
Does the practice of the early Church encourage the use of prayer in the language of the people?

---

[28] Ehrensperger, 176.   [29] Hagen, *Aufklärung*, 118–19.

Does the gospel favour vows?
What are the abuses connected at the present time with brotherhoods?
A Protestant labourer arrives in a Catholic village, sickens, and dies. What is the duty of the priest (a) while he is ill, and (b) after his death?
A woman says she is possessed by a demon. What is the priest to do?

This last question could have been asked by the Italian trainers of confessors. But the other questions could not have been asked, quite in that form, in the Church of the old world. They have too evidently begun to expect a certain kind of answer, or are designed to make the candidate think critically.

The diocese of Augsburg asked the discalced Carmelite Johann Anton Dereser, professor of oriental languages at Bonn university, to give them a vernacular breviary. Dereser wrote it for clergy and nuns 'and any good Christians'. The Elector of Cologne approved it; the Suffragan Bishop of Augsburg also, though with many emendations by Johann Michael Sailer without author's leave; the Prince-bishop of Würzburg, Erthal, used it himself and recommended it to his chapter, the Vicar-general of Constance, Wessenberg, encouraged its use in his diocese. The Archbishop of Trier, Clement Wenceslaus moved against it and its favourers. But it had a sixth edition 1809–10, an eighth and last 1819–21.

The German breviary omitted much that was traditional, in the way of hymns, responsories, antiphons. Instead of ordering all the psalter to be said within a week, Dereser chose eighty psalms and wrote 'We have chosen only those which are specially edifying to the Christian'—a witness to the spirit of the Enlightenment. The historical psalms were regarded as useless, the war-songs and songs of revenge were eliminated, for this was not an age of allegory. Dereser chose the psalms of trust, praise, penitence, and suffering.

The readings dropped lessons from the Old Testament and the Fathers and drew all from the New Testament. The prayers tended to prosiness. 'Give us our daily bread' became 'Give us our daily bread and the satisfaction of our essential needs.'

For all its defects, Dereser tried to make a breviary based upon Scripture and understood by the people. The devotion and taste of reforming Catholicism in that age, from Cologne to Vienna, regarded it as an excellent work of reformed prayer. But only for a time. All these pastoral efforts were overtaken too soon by the collapse of the old political world and the ensuing reaction.

By the time that revolution came, the Catholic reformers had achieved (1) a strong state-guided movement, mainly in Habsburg or other allied and neighbouring territories Bavaria, Lombardy, Tuscany, Belgium, but also in Spain, Naples, France, Portugal, and the Italian states, to limit monks, restrict the power of Rome, control brotherhoods, improve the training of clergy, diminish popular superstition, foster parish life and make worship a little more congregational; (2) among a more extreme group, a movement for vernacular liturgy, more ethical hymnody, and a few bold or shocking voices calling for the celibacy of the priest to be made optional.

This movement was intelligent, not non-Catholic, repudiating the charge that it was Protestant; and in certain areas of Europe it had a profound if long unseen effect upon the pastoral development of the nineteenth century. Its weakness was the absence of the people's assent. It depended largely on small groups of professors and abbés who used oligarchs in government with power to compel a people to do what they had no wish to do. And they were approaching very near to a time when the oligarchs were swept off the face of Europe.

Thus the eighteenth century witnessed five different types of reforming movement within Catholicism which were never separate:

(1) The direct ideal of the Counter-Reformation still active in parish life, in parts of Italy and Spain only now becoming dominant and successful in parish life, and which threw up a traditional and yet subtly new kind of leader, like Alfonso Liguori or Leonard of Port-Maurice.

(2) Jansenist, or at least 'Jansenist' reform, a truly religious reform, wanting more of the Bible and better education and less dubious casuistry and good history and far better parochial life; of which the climax and downfall was Ricci's synod of Pistoia.

(3) Reform as seen by the men of the Enlightenment, who were often half-Jansenist, but whose first interest was the practical reform of law, penal codes, economic conditions, and across whose path lay old privileges of the Church, like the right of sanctuary or exemptions from secular courts or from tax, and the too extensive properties of the Church not all of which were used to the advantage of the people; and who especially wanted a national system of elementary education under State control.

(4) Reform conducted by the eighteenth-century State in its own interest, to centralize authority and create an effective government, and which must therefore diminish the powers of the Pope or the exemptions of the clergy; and which in France and Germany latched on to the old Gallican and episcopalian tradition as in Febronius.

(5) 'Reform' advocated by once-Catholic but now anti-Catholic

propagandists, like Carlantonio Pilati on the borders of north Italy or Gaetano Filangieri in Naples, almost always associated with a touch of freemasonry and often wanting to abolish monks, have married clergy, destroy the Papal States, and move towards a more universal religion which one day would harmonize with a reformed Protestantism; and therefore, unlike the other four modes of reform, which together made the strongest Catholic forces of the century, a plan for reform which had no serious influence on the stream of events as Europe was borne along towards revolution.

7

REVOLUTION

Revolution in France

The French constitutional reformers of 1789 had no intention of assailing the Church. As late as June 1793, in the midst of the terror, government still paid the clergy in office, that is such clergy as accepted its policy and laws, and that same month the feast of Corpus Christi was celebrated with public processions at which passers-by knelt in the streets.

Yet the overthrow of the Church in the French Revolution was one of the momentous events of modern history. Its land and buildings were taken by the State, constitution knocked about, monasteries made illegal, many priests expelled, no small number guillotined. The astonishing fate which befell the rich, powerful, and prosperous Church of Louis XIV had consequences which still work within Christendom. France contained more Catholics than any other state. It housed the headquarters of historic religious orders, Cluny, Cîteaux, Premontré, the Grande Chartreuse, La Trappe. Its theologians and Church historians were respected throughout Europe and America.

In the quest for a new French constitution many clergy voted for the abolition of feudal privileges and of tithes. Nearly bankrupt France could hardly save itself without taking the lands of the Church. To the proposal that the State should take the endowments, pay the clergy, maintain church buildings, and use the remainder for the good of the nation, many clergy were reluctant to consent. That they should become employees or stipendiaries of the State denied axioms, centuries old, about the constitution of the Church and the freedom of its officers. The Assembly carried the law of nationalization (2 November 1789) because it feared bankruptcy. It inserted one undertaking to pay parish priests a minimum wage (1,200 *livres*) substantially higher than many then received, and another undertaking to administer the relief of the poor.

This act was not anti-Christian. It was like the act of the kingdom of Naples, six years before, which took with the Pope's leave church endowments of southern Italy in face of a people's desperate plight after the earthquake.

The sale of lands started next month and continued over ten years and saved the treasury of France. Middle-class and prosperous peasants profited, poorer peasants lost because they were deprived of common rights. Some good Catholics hesitated or refused to take part in these auctions. Lands given to God were in their eyes inalienable, men who acquired them for secular use would not be blest. But others, even pious, cheerfully bid at auction and got property, and when they were later told that they committed sacrilege or blasphemy began to resent the clergy if not the Church.

To take endowments was to ruin monasteries. As radical power grew in the Assembly, opinion was widespread that monks' vows were deplorable because they limited freedom. An act (13 February 1790) banned vows and abolished all orders which had solemn vows and neither taught in school nor cared for the sick. If a religious came out to ordinary life he or she received a pension. Those who wished to stay could be grouped in surviving houses. Most nuns wanted to stay, many monks left. The continuance was temporary. The remaining houses and orders were abolished in August 1792.

Final breach between Church and Revolution came over the civil constitution of the clergy (12 July 1790). At this time most of the leaders of the French state were more Gallican than anti-Christian. The State elevated parish cures as the sole form of church life, and abolished chapters and colleges. It reduced the bishoprics from 135 to eighty-five, and aligned their dioceses with civil boundaries. Every town parish was to contain some 6,000 people, therefore many parishes vanished. The electoral body of the department chose the bishop, the electoral body of the district chose its priest. Stipends were fixed, rules of residence strict, no bishop might ask the Pope to confirm his election. Bishops must work as chairmen of a council of priests from the diocese.

This was Josephist work in a new form. State power was needed to reform the Church, reform meant promoting parish churches, abolishing useless monks and sinecure canonries, and enforcing residence and good conduct. Kings used to nominate bishops, their successors the people should choose. That meant a bishop was to be elected by the electoral assembly of that department. The feudal lord used to nominate the parish priest, his successor the people should now choose. That meant, the curé was chosen by the electoral assembly of the district. The reformers said that they changed no doctrine. 'We only alter geography.'

Thirty bishops out of thirty-five in the National Assembly protested against the plan to reform the Church without asking the Church. But the bishops who had not already fled abroad were divided on the constitution. Some thought the plan bad, others thought that indeed it would help to reform the Church.

King Louis XVI asked the French ambassador in Rome, Cardinal de Bernis, to get the agreement of Pope Pius VI.

To agree was impossible. Agreement was an invitation to other states to seize Church property and abolish monks. Agreement would expose the Pope to onslaught from all the other Catholic powers. It would provoke schism in France, make the plight of King Louis more agonizing, and cause torment of soul to some good parish priests. It would provoke the French occupation of Avignon, where the inhabitants asked to be annexed. Pius VI therefore referred the question to a commission of cardinals, which examined the matter without haste. Historians have blamed the resulting silence of eight months. The Pope had no other sensible course.

Meanwhile events in France moved. Sees must be filled, livings fell vacant. With ever-stiffening rigidity the National Assembly insisted that the choices be made according to the civil constitution of the clergy, and when it met resistance decreed (November–December 1790) an oath whereby any holder of a Church office must swear allegiance to the State and accept the civil constitution. So the Assembly plunged France into schism between oath-takers and oath-refusers, 'refractory priests'. The law of history that persecution always divides a Church was thus fulfilled.

To almost universal surprise more than half the clergy refused the oath; far more than half in the north and the west and Alsace, far less in Paris and the south-east. Who should order the ringing of the church bells, celebrate at the altar, minister at death? Funerals caused a few grievous little riots; the installation of new constitutional instead of ejected refractory caused wild tumult in a few churches, once even to hiding in the tabernacle above the altar a cat which leapt out when the new curate opened the door; crowds of women and children kept crowing like cocks (because of St. Peter's denial) at a new constitutional incumbent, or threw stones at the windows of his vicarage, or dug up his garden, or left ordure on his door- step. Many parishioners, however, could not understand the quarrel. They wanted a curate to baptize, teach, minister communion, hear confessions, and bury the dead; and did not mind whether he swore or refused to swear.

On 24 February 1791, in one of his last acts as a bishop, Talleyrand consecrated two new bishops for the Constitutional Church, and in the next two months Gobel of Paris consecrated more. This forced the Pope out of silence.

On 10 March 1791 Pius VI condemned the civil constitution of the clergy; on 13 April 1791 he declared these new consecrations sacrilegious, and threatened all swearing priests with suspension.

That summer of 1791 many priests recanted the oath which they had taken. Talleyrand pleaded in the Assembly for toleration of refractory priests as part of general toleration, and won the day. But the Assembly could not control the provinces. Refractories were identified with counter-revolution. Local mobs or patriotic leaders interrupted their services or closed halls which they rented.

Schism in France was caused by the rigidity characteristic of a revolutionary government. But it touched questions of high importance for the Church. If the Pope had certain rights in a national Church, and the State was needed to reform the Church, what were the respective rights of Pope or State to interfere in that Church?

In the new legislative Assembly of 1 October 1791 the driving leaders were the Girondins, *petit-bourgeois* young men, deist, anticlerical or anti-Christian, identifying Churches with oppression and counter-revolution and superstition. In April 1792 France declared war on Austria, which claimed to stand for Christianity and justice. Pope Pius VI made the crass error of sending as envoy to the Austrian Emperor the Abbé Maury, an emigrant priest famous for opposition as a member of the Assembly. The Pope thereby announced that the Church was the political ally of powers warring against France. Every priest in France was now suspect as a traitor. The last monasteries were closed, clerical dress was banned. A fortnight after the king was deposed, all refractory priests were ordered out of the country (26 August 1792). A few days after the order of deportation 223 priests, including an archbishop and two bishops, were murdered in the September massacres at the Paris prisons. In all some 30,000 clergy fled abroad. On 23 April 1793 the Convention ordered the immediate deportation to Guiana of any priest who had not taken the oath, and the immediate execution of any deported priest found again on French territory.

So far as the refractory Church of France existed, it went underground. Many constitutionals continued to serve their parishes. But their consciences faced ever new obstacles, the need to approve legal divorce, the demand that priests should marry, and many of them were loyal to the king and disliked the republic. Between summer 1793 and summer 1794 the constitutionals also were driven underground. A wave of de-Christianization rolled across the land. Most churches were closed, some looted, a few pulled down. The feasts of the Church were replaced by feasts of humanity. The calendar was changed to be rid of Sundays. Of the eighty-five constitutional bishops, twenty-three abandoned their religion and nine of them married. And yet Henri Grégoire, constitutional Bishop of Loir-et-Cher, sat on the benches of the Assembly defending Christian liberty with courage.

The Revolution soon needed to deprive its enemies, Prussia, Britain, Austria, of the advantage in propaganda that they championed religion against atheism; and sane government saw that the people of France wanted churches and the country could never be loyal till churches were conceded. The government of the Directory remained ruthlessly anti-clerical. But by autumn 1794 the worst of the anti-Christian Terror, like the worst of the political Terror, of which indeed it was part, was over. Both Catholic sides, refractory and constitutional, began to publish a periodical. The royalist *coup d'état* which failed in autumn 1797 made the Directory so revive the persecuting laws of the Terror that the plight of priests in many areas was still grievous. But the oppression was not so murderous as that of 1793-4, when Prussian troops besieged Verdun and France felt desperate with a Catholic fifth column within the borders.

Revolution in Italy

A historian of France gave an enchanting portrait of what it felt like in a cathedral city, when Barchester was overrun by revolutionaries.[1] He told us what happened to the monks and nuns, and how the canons of the cathedral took their different ways, and which clergymen were murdered and which curates fled into the bush and joined the resistance. Part of the fascination of this portrait was composed of light and shade; of the contrast between the comfortable mellow world of a stable country town, dominated physically and socially by cathedral and close, and the sudden terror of months when every churchman might be suspect of disloyalty or treachery to a regime fighting for its existence and contemptuous of human life.

In Italy the contrasts were not so extreme. By the time the Revolution reached Lombardy and the northern plains, it put aside the worst excesses of terror and tyranny which marred its struggles in Paris. Relations between Paris and Rome were bad, could hardly have been worse. The French revolutionary government annexed Avignon, for many centuries the possession, and once the home, of the Popes. A French envoy in the streets of Rome, Hugou de Bassville, was so beaten by an angry crowd that he died (13 January 1793). French shops in Rome were destroyed, a

[1] John McManners, *French Ecclesiastical Society under the Ancien Régime* (Manchester, 1960)

French hospital invaded. The treatment of French Catholics by revolutionaries could not make the Curia friendly to the French Revolution. But mercifully for Italy and the Pope, the revolutionary government was too busy in Paris and in Brittany and on the Rhine to spare thought or troops for papal iniquity and left Italy almost untouched till 1796. By 1796 the Directory governed France, and the French left behind the time when the guillotine was too busy.

The records of the little town of Imola, in the north near Bologna, show how the inhabitants first learnt that the French were coming.[2] On 9 March 1796 they observed a column of troops in strange uniform marching from the south. When the soldiers entered the town, the people were excited to discover that these were British troops. They believed that for several centuries they had not seen British soldiers in their country. They also observed with astonishment that, unlike other columns passing through, they paid for everything that they took from the shops. This was how the citizens of Imola first discovered that General Bonaparte was crossing the Alps to expel the Austrians from Italy.

The battle was fought at Lodi on 10 May 1796, and six days later Bonaparte entered Milan in triumph. A detachment pushed south-east into the Papal States, occupying Bologna, where soldiers lit their pipes from candles on the altar, and then Ferrara and Imola. Austrian Milan and papal Bologna each welcomed the French with jubilee as deliverers. In February 1797 the Austrian fortress of Mantua fell and the Austrians were almost out of Italy.

French power shattered the authority of the existing Italian governments. The people of Modena moved first. They rose in revolt, drove out the duke, proclaimed a republic (4 October 1796). Bologna threw out the remains of the papal government, and created a Parliament which met in the church of St. Petronio, to the singing of *Veni Creator*. In December the new group of 'republics', including Milan, was encouraged by Bonaparte, and decided to unite in a 'Cispadane republic', which hoped that it would become the nucleus of an Italian republic, with a quiver as its symbol.

Bonaparte was still under thirty years old, a Corsican and therefore with Italian attitudes which were not typical of the French. He believed that to be strong in Italy he must befriend religion. He found himself commanding an army with a province at his feet and a weak government in Paris at his back. He was endowed with the talents not only of a commander but of a ruler. He at once became a proconsul in all but name, arranging the politics of Italy. He needed friendly governments in the

---

[2] Leflon, *Pie VII*, 1.289.

Italian states if his troops were to be secure. Because his orders, and his wishes, made him pay and feed his troops from Italy and send Italian loot to Paris, French rule must be hated by the people. But he sincerely believed in his mission as bringer of liberty to Italy, liberty from feudal rulers and oppressive hierarchs, ordering his soldiers that they were to 'humble these arrogant kings.'[3] 'People of Italy, the French army comes to break your chains; the French people is the friend of all peoples; come before us with confidence; property, religion, customs will be respected . . .'

This union between cynical plundering and real idealism had a double effect. Old-fashioned churchmen disbelieved every word that came from this foreign oppressor. They found liberty to be a word for robbery, equality an introduction of street anarchy.

In the baptismal register of St. Cassian at Imola is a manuscript note. It reads thus:[4]

28 July 1798. By order of the Cisalpine Commissioners, who have created in Milan a republic alleged to be democratic, they have moved the Poor Clares of St. Stephen to the Capuchin nunnery, and the Augustinian nuns called the Madeleines to the Dominican nunnery. They have suppressed St. Charles, and all the brotherhoods, abolished bequests, imprisoned eleven of the cathedral canons in the castle. So democracy, that Liberty and Equality of the Republicans and the French, robbed our Italy.

Nevertheless, Italian states also had revolutionaries. Under a French regime they came out into the open, published what they wanted, demonstrated in the streets, paid off old scores. Lombards saw no reason why they should not exchange Austrian rulers for French rulers till they saw that the French took hostages and robbed. Some academics liked the new freedom from censorship. General Bonaparte wrote from Milan to the eminent astronomer Oriani a letter which breathes the sense of enlightened learning breaking in upon the darkness of priestcraft—

All men of genius, everyone distinguished in the republic of letters, is French, whatever his nationality. Men of learning in Milan have not enjoyed proper respect. They hid themselves in their laboratory and thought themselves lucky if kings and priests let them alone. All is changed today. Thought in Italy is free. Inquisition, intolerance, despots, are vanished. I invite scholars to meet and make proposals, what must be done to give science and the arts a new flowering.[5]

Bonaparte knew enough of the power of the clergy in Italy to want them on his side. When he found priests leading peasant bands to attack his soldiers, like the parish priest of a village by Lodi, he had them shot

[3] Napoleon, *Corr.* 1.187-8. [4] Leflon, *Pie VII*, 1.489. [5] Napoleon, *Corr.* 1.322.

without compunction. When Pavia revolted in a people's storm, and he heard that priests and monks, 'dagger and crucifix in hand' incited the 'rebels', he forced the Archbishop of Milan to go into Pavia with a demand for surrender, and when this proved vain allowed his men to sack the town, shot all the municipal government, and sent 200 hostages to France. 'I don't doubt that this will teach a lesson to the people of Italy.' In the country round Tortona he ordered the destruction of all the church bells which summoned the peasants to arms, organized a man-hunt for a Franciscan who led a peasant band in the hills of Garfagnana north of Lucca, destroyed the house of the Duke of Modena's confessor because he was believed to have incited the Garfagnana rebels, and ordered on the rubble a pyramid inscribed 'Punishment of a raving priest who abused his ministry and preached revolt and murder.'[6]

Continually conscious that his small forces could not long hold a country unless its inhabitants accepted the government, and seeing everywhere what he called the power of 'fanaticism' in stirring peasants to resist, he set out on the unpromising attempt to persuade Catholic Italy that the French invaders stood at their side.

This became more important when the French army occupied the Legations, for their rulers were cardinals, but many of their people disliked the rule of cardinals. A party in Bologna resented recent interference of Rome with local rights, and welcomed the idea that the former Legation should now be a republic under French protection. Bonaparte imprisoned the cardinal-legates of Bologna and Ferrara, but hardly needed to change the rest of the administration. He reported to his government in Paris that even in the Romagna 'Fanatical preachers preach rebellion. A few days ago they organized what they called "The Catholic Army of the Pope", and established their headquarters at Lugo in the Legation of Ferrara.' The reason for this mad tumult was the arrival of news that the new commissioners, who were Ferrarese, intended to remove the statue of St. Hilary, protector of the town. Church bells rang the tocsin, a procession carried St. Hilary to the Carmelite monastery, a band of men forced the citadel to get rifles, they put back the Pope's arms and sent a messenger to ask the Pope's blessing. So Lugo, like Pavia, paid the penalty in a sack and the killing of several hundred peasants.

I hear [wrote Bonaparte to the senate of Bologna] that ex-Jesuits, priests, and religious, disturb public order. Let them know that while the French Republic protects religion and its ministers, it is inexorable against those who forget their

---

[6] Napoleon, *Corr.* 1.322, 340, 343; 2.149, 230.

station and interfere in public affairs. Warn superiors of monasteries that, the first complaint I hear against a monk, I shall hold the whole monastery responsible, expel the monks and give their property to the poor.[7]

This claim to protect religion did not resemble what his nominal masters still did in France, but was from the first a necessary part of his effort to persuade Italians of French goodwill. After holding hostage Cardinal Mattei, the Pope's legate in Ferrara, Bonaparte sent him back to his diocese with praise of his character, a warning that 'every priest who mixes in politics does not deserve the respect due to his character', and a promise of protection for religion and its ministers. He admired what he heard of Cardinal Mattei, but still found his existence disturbing. 'At Ferrara a cardinal-prince with an income of 150,000 *livres* gives it all to the poor and is always in church. I have sent him to Rome on a pretext of negotiation, but really to be rid of his embarrassing presence.'[8]

Protection of religion was a doctrine which issued in kind words. 'It is my ambition', he told the French agent in Rome, 'to be the saviour and not the destroyer of the Holy See.'[9] He liked what he saw of the bishops, and told recalcitrant clergy to behave like their superiors. General Rusca was told not only to shoot peasant leaders in Garfagnana but to summon magistrates and superiors of monasteries and parish priests and tell them this:

As long as ministers of religion hold true principles—men like Cardinal Mattei, and the Archbishop of Bologna, and the Bishop of Modena, and the Bishop of Pavia, men who in wisdom and pure life recall the primitive Church—I will respect them, their property and their customs, as they contribute to public order and the common weal; but if their holy ministry is turned by men of ill-will into an instrument of discord and civil war, I will have no regard for them, will destroy their convents, and will personally punish the curates of villages that behave badly. . . .

He did whatever he could to stop looters or rabble from hurting churches or priests. If French officers visited Rome they were ordered to be moral in their behaviour. 'My special care', he asked Cardinal Mattei to tell the Pope, 'will be to prevent anyone altering the religion of our fathers'. When he invaded the Papal States at the beginning of February 1797 he forced a passage across the river against a crowd of peasant troops encouraged by preachers, crucifix in hand, and was sorry that the laws of war prevented him sacking Faenza 'for the crimes of a few priests'; but instead

[7] Napoleon, *Corr.* 1.477, 542; Leflon, *Pie VII*, 1.299 ff.
[8] Napoleon, *Corr.* 2.13, 68.   [9] Napoleon to Cacault, *Corr.* 2.78–9.

of plundering the town he summoned all the monks and clergy in Faenza and made them a speech: 'I reminded them of the principles of the Gospel . . . They appeared to me to have good principles.'

This desire to conciliate Church leaders became a habit. When Joubert invaded the Tyrol, he was given an illuminating order: 'Cajole the priests. Try to get support from among monks—though you must carefully distinguish the theologians and other learned men among them.'[10]

This Corsican had touching faith in the power of priests to keep order. When there was trouble in the mountains above Mantua, he ordered the Bishop of Vicenza to send missionaries to preach quiet and obedience under pain of hell-fire, and remembered to make careful provision for their travelling expenses.

He was no theorist. But soon he was aware how the ideals of the French Revolution, in liberty, equality, fraternity, might be presented as ideals of the Christian Church. He told the Bishop of Como that equality was the morality of the gospel. A letter of propaganda to the Archbishop of Genoa had the same message, when the army had a mountain revolt near Genoa on its hands, and Bonaparte received the Archbishop's pastoral letter of 5 September 1797.

I thought I was listening to one of the Twelve. . . . How respectable is religion when it has ministers like you! True apostle of the gospel. . . .When the Church has a head like you, why has it such miserable subalterns? . . . The priest preaches revolt, murder, blood. . . . He has sold the poor like Judas Iscariot. . . . The political code of the gospel is the sovereignty of the people, liberty. . . . Prelates like Fénelon, or the Archbishop of Milan, or the Archbishop of Ravenna, make religion beloved because they practise what they preach.[11]

This doctrine, that equality is the moral code of the gospel, commanded a measure of success. The ideal of democracy was so new, or shocking, to all traditional minds of the *ancien régime* that scrupulous consciences easily felt strain about their loyalty to a popular government, especially when the ideal of democracy came marching under the tricolour of foreign plunderers. Yet Genoese clergy were among the first to gather round the tree of liberty. Many Italian clergy were cheerful in accepting republican principles. Bishops held the Church to be uncommitted to any political order, and went on with their work in co-operation with a new government. Many preachers in the north told their people how equality and fraternity were true principles of Christianity. A few priests went

[10] Napoleon, *Corr.* 2.230, 264–5, 300–1, 349, 390; 3.199.
[11] Napoleon, *Corr.* 3.24, 199, 284, 422.

further and baptized republican ideals with a religious fervour. Monks now freed from their vows and happy for good reasons to regain their freedom, some better educated clergy, joined the republican ranks and occasionally, even at this date, were known as 'Catholic democrats'. Jansenist reformers who had not been able to persuade the *ancien régime* to their way of church reform, looked for a new opportunity in a people's revolution. The most important of these radical Jansenists was the priest Eustachio Degola in Genoa, a friend of Scipione de' Ricci and a brilliant journalist. A few priests said already that democracy is a better Christian constitution than monarchy because it demands and furthers the brotherhood of man.

Some bishops were not so much republican as opportunist. Bishop Gazzola of Cervia flattered General Bonaparte odiously in his pastoral letter—'the unconquerable hero who wants to respect the altar, give freedom to Catholic worship, and maintain our holy religion', and identified the liberty of the republic with the liberty of the children of God, and told his flock that 'God calls you to love democracy.' Bishop Belloni of Carpi said: 'May this republic be blessed a thousandfold, to which we owe such noble doctrine, such gentle law, such justice!' The uncompromising Cardinal Mattei of Ferrara, as he witnessed these utterances which he despised, is known to have prayed this hardly Christian prayer—'Please God, get rid of these bishops who have betrayed their consciences out of fear or sycophancy.'

Cardinal Chiaramonti was Bishop of Imola, on the great Roman road from Ancona to Bologna. His sermon at Christmas 1797 is said by historians to have been sensational in its effect. The only witness who recorded, entered a very short statement in his journal: '25 December, cold day, light fall of snow. The cardinal came to chapel for mass. He preached a long sermon'.[12] So the sermon was not sensational in delivery, but became sensational when the French printed it and circulated it all over north Italy at the expense of government.

In that sermon, preached no doubt with agents in the congregation, the cardinal recalled that government is ordained of God and Christians owe obedience. Does this apply only to some forms of government, as Bossuet declared monarchy to be the government which God orders? 'Our democracy', said the Cardinal, 'is not in the least in opposition to the precepts of the gospel. On the contrary, it demands the virtue which may only be won through Christ . . . The goodness of man, found in its fulness only by the teaching of the gospel, is the immovable foundation of our

---

[12] Leflon, *Pie VII*, 1.440-3.

democracy.' Christian virtue makes men good democrats. Christianity teaches justice, which includes equality before the law. Equality is not an idea of philosophers but of Christ when he told men to sacrifice themselves for their neighbours. 'Bring me a man who burns with love for God, and he will find the doctrine of equality before God in his heart.' Before the end the cardinal quoted even Jean-Jacques Rousseau as an authority; and finally, 'Do not believe that the Catholic religion is against democracy.' Obedience to this government will become a new source of merit.

General Bonaparte, though on hearsay evidence, is said to have remarked, 'The Citizen-Cardinal of Imola preaches like a Jacobin.'

The Church was not against liberty. Its principles fostered liberty. It was not against democracy, as some argued, because it was not tied to any political order; or it was in favour of democracy, as others (though fewer) argued, because it was in favour of liberty which democracy bestowed. These ideas were at first attractive to many. Their magnetism diminished as men saw how French-inspired democracy worked.

General Bonaparte sold French ideals to Italy while he looted Italy for the benefit of France. Tax levies, confiscations, sequestrations, pictures, sculptures, statues, jewels; and since the Church was the wealthiest corporation in Italy, to loot Italy was to rob the Church. This might mean only a more extended suppression of monastic houses, with which Italy was already familiar; cutting down of monastic woods, expulsion of foreign monks, closure of 'useless' houses. It might also mean the seizure of valuables, from jewelry which decked venerated statues to silver patens or chalices in parish use—and then forcing churches or monasteries to deliver what they concealed.

Of these acts of loot, the most shocking in Italian opinion was the seizure of the treasure at the shrine of Loreto near Ancona. The holy House, believed to be the home of Nazareth flown to Loreto by angels, and with a great three-aisled church of the fifteenth century, was one of the most frequented shrines of pilgrimage in the Catholic world. We have seen Benedict Joseph Labre lying there in meditation, before the altar in the little house, and the little crowned wooden statue of the holy Virgin, hardly more than a metre in height, with a sceptre and a crowned Child, and a picture of the Crucified said to be painted by St. Luke.

The offerings of pilgrims through centuries made a treasure. This treasure failed to please all pilgrims. St. Francis de Sales, coming to say his prayers at the shrine on his way from Rome to Savoy (1599), could not resist the thought that it would be best if part at least of the treasure were sold to enable good to be done—partly because St. Mary would like her gifts to be used to help humanity, and partly (he thought) because so rich a store could one day provoke the greed of a powerful raider. Popes tried to make it less helpless. Their military architects surrounded it with walls and bastions.

Pope Pius VI saw that the French were coming, and acted. He put the treasure on carts, and had it carried over rough roads to Terracina south of Rome, with the idea (if necessary) of sending it onward to Sicily. When General Bonaparte arrived at Loreto, he found only one-seventh of the store remaining. He reported the capture in a laconic postscript to his government (10 February 1797): 'We are masters of our Lady of Loreto.' He took what treasure remained, and the corn. Five days later he wrote: 'I am also sending you the Madonna, with all the relics. The chest will be addressed directly to you, for you to use as you think fit. The Madonna is made of wood.' The government in Paris was puzzled how to use a wooden statue of the Madonna. For a time it lay in store. Then the minister of the interior sent it to the Bibliothèque Nationale at Paris, with a covering letter asking them to place it 'among the bizarre monuments of superstition and so help to complete the history of religious impostures.' The department of medals at the great library acknowledged the receipt of 'this celebrated monument of ignorance and most absurd superstition'.[13]

Disciples of Ricci, Jansenist reformers, might distrust the cult of relics and want reform of shrines; educated priests who learnt history might distrust unhistorical cults; but common people were offended. Such acts confirmed the worst rumours that crossed the mountains from Paris.

Another reason why Bonaparte found it hard to marry the Catholic Church to democracy lay in the need to found Italian democracies. So long as the French army ruled directly, he could fulfil his promise to protect churches except so far as he needed money. But for security, as well as for his sense of mission, he needed to create satellite republics. One by one, French satellite republics sprang into life all over Italy, fostered secretly or openly by French commanders, but spontaneous in local enthusiasm; first the Legations in a Cispadane republic, then the Legations with Lombardy in a Cisalpine republic (1797), then a Ligurian republic for Genoa (1797), a Roman republic for the Papal States without the legations (1798), a Helvetic republic for Switzerland (1798), and finally a Parthenopean republic for the kingdom of Naples (1799) (without Sicily, which was defended against French influence by Nelson and the British fleet).

Bonaparte needed these republics. But he could not allow them to be

[13] U. Chevalier, 372, 435-6.

so free as he wished. The Cispadane republic was founded in autumn 1796 with his blessing. But when in April 1797 it held elections, he disliked what he saw.

I've just received news of the Cispadane republic. The choice of representatives has been very bad. The priests have influenced all the elections. Cardinals and bishops hurried from Rome to guide the people in how to vote. . . . The Cispadane republic, like Lombardy, needs a provisional government for three or four years while an effort is made to lessen the influence of priests; otherwise, you will have done nothing by giving them their liberty.[14]

Part of the motive for uniting Lombardy with the Cispadane republic into the larger Cisalpine republic was the supposition that so the influence of priests would more easily be controlled. Still, when the new government was inaugurated on 9 July 1797 they had a solemn mass before 30,000 spectators and a blessing of the green, white, and red flag which here appeared almost for the first time and is still the flag of Italy. The French could not set up free republics. They must choose members of a government who believed in French ideals.

Italians who sympathized with the French conqueror were not uncommon, but often were more extreme in their opinions about Church and State, or even about God, than their creator wished. In this way several of the satellite republics became more revolutionary about Church affairs than Bonaparte liked. Many of them were Jacobins who saw churches, monasteries, Popes, cardinals, bishops as the enemy, and therefore converted churchmen into enemies. In the first hectic days of revolutionary Milan the statue of St. Ambrose was thrown down and dragged through the streets, some of the churches were turned into Jacobin clubs, violent anticlerical literature poured from the press, men talked loudly of turning the still-unfinished cathedral into public offices. La Scala theatre nervously put on a scandalous ballet of the Pope; in which Pope Pius VI appeared on the stage about to go to war with the French, but when he hears of the fall of Padua flings off his triple crown and dances comically on the stage in a cap of liberty; bringing the house down by his admiration for his own legs, for the Pope's personal vanity was enshrined in the gossip of Italy. This scene was played to tumultuous applause.

The release of such anticlerical passion did as much as the laws of the new satellite republics or the looting of the French conquerors to alienate the conservative part of Catholic Italy from the ideals of the Revolution. One change was almost too sudden: freedom for anti-Catholic writers

[14] Napoleon, *Corr.* 3.15, 30.

to publish what they liked. Jacobin pamphleteers declared that men ought to feel horror at the Pope's name because the Pope was part of past tyrannies; or that all religious processions should be prohibited because they partake of the nature of political demonstrations; or that legacies or gifts to churches should be banned by law; or that schools or colleges which teach a particular Christian doctrine should be closed; or that marriage should be invariably a civil contract; or that every republic must rigorously forbid celibacy of the clergy; or even that all clergy should be abolished. Pamphleteers of Jacobin Italy were often wild and therefore possessed small influence. But that they could publish at all was new and shocking to many of the Italian people.[15]

The most 'Catholic' of the new republican constitutions was that of the Ligurian republic in Genoa (2 December 1797). But the 'separation' between Church and State in the Cisalpine republic became the norm. Civil marriage was made compulsory but proved hard to enforce. The worst frictions came over oaths of loyalty, popular elections of clergy, and the banning of processions.

The republican government in Milan wanted declarations of loyalty to the constitution and knew that announcements from parish pulpits would do more among the people than their own propaganda. They therefore pressed, even ordered, the two citizen-cardinals, Mattei of Ferrara and Chiaramonti of Imola, to follow the example of the Bishop of Pavia and declare for the republic. Cardinal Mattei consulted Rome and got the answer he wanted, that he might do no such thing. Other prelates evaded the issue by agreeing to do what government wanted and then making their pronouncements in cloudy language which was too vague to be effective.

More awkward for the clergy, as time passed, were the rules demanding popular election of parish priests, for the elections, though held in church, were to be organized by town councils, and presided over by an official of the town council. The choice was to be approved by the minister of the interior in Milan. The candidate needed certificates from the chief of police and the town council. The bishop was allowed the power of conferring or withholding a *certificate of suitability*, but government tried to reduce this right to formality, and refused to accept that it contained a right of veto.

Bishops attempted with hardly a protest to work the system. They were eager that parishes should not fall vacant. When a parish fell vacant bishops avoided popular election by appointing curates-in-charge. The

[15] See a fascinating selection of such documents in *Giacobini italiani*, ed. Delio Cantimori (Bari, 1956).

government partly closed this loop hole by ordering that the minister of police should nominate curates-in-charge. But some bishops at least preferred the police-chiefs' curates to the risks of parish election at a time when politics were inflamed.

By a mixture of diplomacy and fabian delay, bishops succeeded in reducing popular elections to rare events.

On 8 May 1798 the Cisalpine republic, desperate for money, nationalized all the property of the Church and ordered the dissolution of monasteries. It exempted parish endowments from confiscation and provided pensions for religious of suppressed houses and for canons of suppressed colleges or chapters. Hence all the collegiate foundations and chapters now lost their funds, and the bishops lost their *mensa*. The state 'provisionally compensated' the bishops with 10,000 Milanese pounds. But when the Cardinal of Imola travelled to Venice for the new Conclave, he had to borrow his fare to pay the gondolier on the Grand Canal.[16]

By none of these acts were the people much disturbed. *Their* services in churches continued in much the same way.

But the government ordered that its officers should not take part in religious services in uniform or as representatives of government. It banned public processions. That seemed a necessary part of equality, but came from a foolish logic. Processions were part, not only of Italian religion, but of Italian way of life. The banning of the procession of the Madonna at Imola in April 1798 had the same effect upon the people as Ricci's banning of reverence to an image because it was superstitious. A crowd invaded the cathedral, seized the statue, carried it out, were joined by clergy, a procession was improvised, the bishop followed the statue in a carriage. Government gave way, and allowed the military to take part in processions for the sake of public order and provided they were kept to the immediate neighbourhood of the Church. Then the Directory in Milan forbade public funerals. The order arrived at Imola just when they were burying a child—and no order whatever could stop Italians paying tribute to a child and giving comfort to the bereaved.

In Imola cathedral the canons appeared wearing violet copes, their ceremonial garb. Their chapter was suppressed by law, but nothing stopped them saying their offices in the cathedral, and they continued services with scrupulous regularity.[17] They used to appear in cottas. Now they added coloured copes. These vestments were nationalized as part of cathedral property. They made the mistake of appealing from the local republicans to the French general occupying Bologna, who agreed that

[16] Leflon, *Pie VII*, 1.468–77, 531.   [17] Leflon, *Pie VII*, 1.489 ff.

they might keep the vestments. The republicans were offended, and arrested the canons. Three did anything the republicans wanted and were regarded by the others as traitors. The other eleven spent sixty-two days in the fortress, and were then put on trial, and were acquitted partly because the French general agreed and partly because no law stopped them wearing vestments. The canons returned to their cathedral triumphant, and resumed their services, having gloriously vindicated their freedom to wear copes. But out of prudence they henceforth stored away the copes in the vestry and wore cottas.

From the mature and conservative canons of a cathedral chapter was a far cry to the hotheads of the seminary. Ideals of revolution gained them more easily. At Milan the young men planted a tree of liberty in the seminary quadrangle. They planted with the approval of their dean, who used the occasion to bless the tree and make a patriotic and religious speech.

But no group of young men could be unanimous. All over northern Italy seminaries divided over the rightness of the oath. At Imola the quarrels in the seminary got into the newspapers. Professors who refused to swear were ejected. In their place appeared radical professors—the Conventual Franciscan Alberghetti as professor of philosophy. He happened also to be tribune of the Jacobin club. His behaviour mingled sacred with secular. At the seminary he appeared as a Franciscan, and taught philosophy with sobriety. At the Jacobin club he appeared some-times in his habit, but sometimes in a white shirt with a red and black silk damask scarf. At meetings of the town council he wore a blue suit with white shirt and black cravat. An officer of the civil guard noted that his speeches in the Jacobin club were the best of sermons. When a friend rebuked him for appearing like a layman, he said, 'I wear these clothes when I go to the theatre.' At his convent he said mass very early every morning—that the convent was open is odd; perhaps it owed him pro-tection. He was afterwards accused of having sung opprobrious or republican hymns under the windows of the bishop's palace. Charged later with spending nights with patriots instead of his conventuals, he gave an answer the more crushing because it surprises—'There were no patriots in Imola, how could I spend the night with them?'

Whether or not Father Alberghetti sang opprobrious hymns under the windows of the bishop's palace, the bishop saved him from being shot when Austrian soldiers at last marched into Imola.

The Roman republic and the Pope

In this way Bonaparte's plan to reconcile the Catholic Church with democracy was made null, for the time, because Italian democrats acted more sternly against the Church than Bonaparte himself thought wise. The breach became impossible to heal when the Pope himself was caught up in the tumults over the making of a republic in Rome.

By occupying the Legations and starting a Cispadane republic, Bonaparte occupied papal territory. He was under orders to punish the murder of Bassville in Rome four years before, and perhaps to end the papacy for all time, so that Pius VI should be the last Pope. The Austrian threat to his army in the north made him stop his advancing army at Tolentino, where he extorted a treaty from the defenceless Pope. Bonaparte preferred a treaty because he needed money and could extract more money from a Pope afraid than a Pope overthrown.

Under the treaty of Tolentino (19 February 1797) Pope Pius VI agreed— the agreement became very important in later argument—to renounce his claims to Avignon, Bologna, and the Legations, to pay 30 million in *livres tournois de France* (partly in jewelry), to give the French republic 100 precious works of art to be selected by French commissioners, to close his ports to warships fighting against France, to send an envoy to Paris to disavow the murder of Bassville and compensate his family and to free all political prisoners. On his side Bonaparte agreed only to evacuate papal territory (except Avignon and the Legations)—while keeping a garrison at Ancona until the end of the war—and to do no harm to the Catholic religion in the Legations.

No previous Pope had been forced to such concessions. Cardinal Mattei reported to Pius VI, 'Rome is saved, and religion also.' Bonaparte reported to his government, evidently forestalling criticism that he allowed the Pope to escape destruction, 'The old machine will fall to bits of itself.' He meant that the Papal State, deprived of its only prosperous province in the Legations, must fall.

Some Romans felt as the most offensive act in the treaty the loss of ancient heirlooms—'these doctrinaire cannibals running around, catalogues at the ready, in museums and galleries and libraries'.[18]

The treaty did not satisfy Bonaparte's demands. He sent his brother Joseph to be French ambassador in Rome, and several letters after him to say that he must threaten the Pope.

On 28 December 1797 there was a fracas in Rome between a little crowd

18 Napoleon, *Corr.* 2.342; Giuntella, 200.

of republican revolutionaries and papal troops. A bullet killed the young French general Duphot, who was staying as guest of Joseph Bonaparte. The next day Joseph Bonaparte fled to Florence. The accidental death brought decision. Bonaparte ordered (11 January) General Berthier, in command of the north-Italian army, to march on Rome.

On 16 January 1798 news reached Rome that the French army was on the march. Naturally the first fear was for the sack of the city. Three cardinals fled to Naples (Albani, York, Busca). Pope Pius VI ordered relics to be carried round the city solemnly and displayed for veneration in various churches. They were followed by prayerful crowds, and accompanied by the bells of the churches.

On 10 February 1798 the French entered Rome and occupied Castel Sant' Angelo. They took over various convents, Aracoeli, Gesù, Trinità dei Monti, and others to lodge their battalions (the monks or nuns had to find lodging in near-by convents), but announced that they were going to preserve the Church and give liberty to Rome. The troops behaved with discipline. An artillery officer who behaved irreverently in St. Peter's was punished. Once they knew that the army would not sack the city, the Romans did not mind. They looked on, not with hostility but with indifferent curiosity. No one tried to stir them to 'incidents' against the occupying force, except in one sermon by a Capuchin preacher whom the French denounced but could not find.

The little band of Roman republicans took their chance. General Berthier had a secret instruction to make a republic without letting it appear that the French made the republic. On 15 February 1798, five days after the French arrived, republican leaders held a meeting in the pasture which we know as the Roman Forum, climbed the Capitol, celebrated a political ritual round the equestrian statue of Marcus Aurelius, erected a tree of liberty, and banners: 'Religion and Liberty', 'Sovereignty of the People', 'Liberty and Equality', 'Equality and the Rule of Law'. A clergyman kissed the trunk of the tree of liberty, Duke Braschi the Pope's nephew laid a garland at its feet, someone handed out tricolours. The People were solemnly proclaimed Sovereign of Rome. On the document there signed, in the presence of a crowd, large indeed but without the knowledge of most of Rome, was founded the legal basis of the Roman republic. The meeting sent a deputation to General Berthier, asking for his protection. He came to the Capitol, and declared to the crowd, in the name of France, that he recognized the provisional government as the government of all the Papal States, and would secure its independence. To the Directory he sent a message: 'Rome is free.'

It was not so free that he could allow the new government to pass laws or edicts without his leave; nor so free that he could risk the ex-ruler of Rome being left in peace and honour. To Berthier's regret and embarrassment, Pope Pius VI refused advice to flee from Rome. Berthier saw that this new republican government, without roots in popular support or feeling, and with no command over anyone's affection, would be impossible if the Pope remained. To drive the Pope from Rome by force was a policy of danger in the realm of international propaganda. Berthier toyed for a moment with the idea of so maltreating the Pope that he would decide to leave. He dismissed the papal bodyguard and the Swiss, and put French sentries to stop the Pope leaving his three private rooms and to stop anyone coming to see him without a French permit. But Berthier soon saw that he must expel the Pope from Rome.

Without waiting for the new republican government, he issued important edicts modernizing old laws. A decree abolished all rights of sanctuary in churches, and the special extra-territorial privileges of ambassadors (privileges which Popes had long disliked). The French tore down, as relics of barbarism, the old scaffolds which still stood in the forum and in three squares as a warning to criminals.

On 20 February 1798 Pope Pius VI was ordered into a carriage, and sent off to house-arrest in the Augustinian convent at Siena. At towns on the way crowds, both devout and curious, turned out to see him pass. In Rome no one lodged a protest. Not a voice was raised to suggest that people loved Pius VI in his role as a political sovereign. He disappeared as easily as any constitutional monarch turned by force off his throne.

The cardinals and the monsignori were contemptuous of this 'rabble' which the French set up as a puppet government. They saw how little the common people respected its oratory. They resented that the non-Christian funeral of General Duphot should be celebrated in St. Peter's Square with guns and drums and trumpets and patriotic crowns and speeches about ancient virtues. On 25 February 1798 the slums of the city, the Trastevere, rose against the French in that revolt known as the Roman Vespers. The cause was the news that part of the French army of occupation was in mutiny at the Pantheon against the new commander Masséna, who had taken over from Berthier, and had an ill reputation with the army. It was a revolt of half-drunken men from the Sunday wine-shops, with resentments against ill behaviour of French soldiers in the streets, toasts of 'death to the republicans' in the bars, and with an anti-semitic slant, for the French gave Jews equal rights and abolished the ghetto. It was one of those spontaneous upsurges of popular passion without political leadership and with no aim. The crowd carried at their head a crucifix and a statue of Our Lady. They killed any French they met, threw some into the Tiber, slaughtered Jews whom they met and anyone identifiable as a republican or a 'patriot'. The French battalions had only to move to end the pointless uprising. By the evening it was all over, except at Castel Gandolfo and in the Alban hills, where the news sparked off killing of French and their Italian officials. When a troop advanced under General Murat, the main party took refuge in the Pope's palace at Castel Gandolfo. Murat battered down the gates with cannon, and to a man the defenders were slaughtered. For days afterwards groups of men were shot publicly at various squares in Rome, beginning with twenty-two in the Piazza del Popolo.

None of the shot men were middle-class leaders. The cardinals in the Vatican thought it a terrible mistake. It seemed to show them how the common people had no use for the occupying power and its puppet regime.

But they underestimated the republican government. The ideals which the French Revolution made powerful in Europe were powerful among the Italian middle class. The Papal State was ramshackle. A ramshackle state is pleasant for those not poor to live in, but inspires no ideals. The French held up ideals before men's eyes. To have equality before the law; to end the privileges which, in their ecclesiastical guise, were still dregs of feudalism; to take power at last to administer the finances with a plan for the good of the people; to break down the barriers put round the ghetto at night, and other disgraces of an ancient society—these could not but command the assent and elicit the hopes of intelligent and educated Romans who put their faith in French promises of true liberty. Words like justice, freedom, even democracy, had power. The antics of the orators on the Capitol, with their rhetoric about Brutus or Rienzi, were unimportant compared with this feeling among cultured and sensible men. A minority of the educated clergy—no doubt a handful, but several of high intelligence and integrity—supported the republic. Some of them merely climbed upon a bandwagon, saw a chance of money or career or self-advertisement. But others sincerely believed that the ideals of the republic were also the ideals of a Christian man in the modern world. From the pulpit of San Lorenzo in Lucina friars preached sermons that this new order was not contrary 'to our Roman Catholic religion, or to the discipleship of the gospel, or the doctrines of the Catholic Church'. The government took the trouble to print the sermons and distribute copies round the city.

Naturally the Jews supported the republic.

Rome without the Pope

The old government of Rome consisted of the Pope, but of more than the Pope. The college of cardinals was not a Pope but it often acted in the Pope's absence, and occasionally in his presence. The republic was quickly aware that its security demanded the exile of cardinals as well as Pope. Several more cardinals disappeared without being pushed. But still thirteen cardinals stayed in Rome. At dawn on 8 March six of them were arrested and imprisoned in the ex-convent of the Convertites on the Corso; where they were followed by numerous monsignori and lesser officials of the Vatican civil service, especially the former governors of provinces in the Papal State. Two other cardinals were left because mortally ill; three others were expelled from the city. Two, Cardinal Antici and Cardinal Altieri, saved themselves from arrest by resigning their place as cardinals. On 7 March Antici sent a letter to the Pope, and simultaneously sent copies to the French ambassador and the republican consuls. This act shocked not only the Pope. In his prison at the Convertite house Cardinal Doria said 'We are the apostles and that one is Judas.'[19] Cardinal Altieri followed the example a few days later. But he was old and ill, and not blamed for cowardice and treachery like Antici. A French officer tried to persuade Cardinal Antonelli to do the same. Antonelli simply said that a soldier did not run away from his post on the day of the battle. One cardinal, Vincenti di Rieti, bought his way out of prison by paying a ransom, and was exiled from the Roman state. On 11 March the prisoners were transferred by night to the Dominican house at Civita Vecchia. Twelve days later the Directory in Paris ordered the release of all, with exile from the Roman state.

Not only had the Pope been driven from Rome, but his Curia; the entire administration not only of the Papal States but of the Catholic Church throughout the world. Two bishops in partibus were left in Rome, with delegated powers to do whatever could be done; one for the Church at large, one for the city and diocese of Rome. The secretary of the Congregation of the Council continued for a time to give rulings as though the Congregation still functioned.

The Roman republic, as in the days of medieval tribunes of the people, revived historic memories of that ancient republic which conquered the Mediterranean world. It had consuls and a senate, tribunes and aediles. Orators talked of their descent from Camillus or Scipio or Brutus.

[19] Cretoni, 102.

The plight of the Roman republic, as a government, could not have been more hopeless. They inherited the empty exchequer of Pope Pius VI. Their city was no longer the goal of pilgrims or of tourists who would spend, Peter's Pence ceased to flow across the frontiers. To kidnap the Pope was to dry up the main source of Roman revenue. They must raise money from their subjects, maintain several thousand French soldiers at their cost, and give enough loot to allow the French commissioners to satisfy Paris. The task was impossible. The chief resource was wealth tax, sale of valuable objects, and confiscation of property. Unscrupulous modes of taxation had to be worked by rogues, who channelled part of the proceeds into their pockets. The paper scudo became worthless in a few weeks. The French compelled them to substitute the assignat, which followed the example of the scudo. This was not the fault of the republic, but of its guardians the French and of the papal bankruptcy which they inherited.

The republican government of Rome did nothing to make itself popular by changing place-names. Piazza di Spagna became 'The Piazza of Liberty', Piazza Venezia became 'The Piazza of Equality', Castel Sant' Angelo later became 'The Castle of Genius.' The statue of St. Michael above its keep was painted tricolour. Everyone was ordered to use the new French calendar which most Romans did not understand. The recorder of ceremonies at St. Peter's kept the old dates but added the new in brackets. Bishop Ranuzzi of Ancona, at the request of the civil authority, exhorted all the priests of his diocese to use the new dates, on private letters as well as public, and to explain to the people how the new civil calendar did not touch the ecclesiastical year. It was safer to head letters with the correct mottoes. Letters went out from the Vatican headed LIBERTY–EQUALITY, or LIBERTY–RELIGION–EQUALITY. The government removed the papal arms from all buildings. It abolished all titles of dignity and ordered everyone to be nothing but citizen; so that the members of the chapter of St. Peter's started to call themselves 'Citizen Canon', and 'Citizen Dean'.

All this irritated, but trivially. What destroyed the credit of the republic —apart from its total dependence upon occupying guns—was the inflation.

Foremost among capital goods easiest to plunder, whether by French or by republicans, were churches and monasteries with their precious furniture and works of art. Government in Paris and government in Rome were both committed to destroying or diminishing Christianity. Though the Roman republicans protected schools, hospitals, orphanages (even though religious), they began from May 1798 to move more oppressively against the Church. They banned monastic vows (10–11 May); expelled foreign clergy (14 May); suppressed twenty feasts (24 May) and abolished the legal obligation to be present at mass. A rumour spread through the city that they planned to murder every priest below the age of sixty. A Polish battalion in the occupying force gave offence by evident piety, and broke into the locked Polish church to force a mass to be said, crying 'Long live the Pope!' and (as the official complaint stated) 'other similar words, seditious in the new-born state of the Roman republic'. A law of 28 June 1798 ordered no bishop's *mensa* to be larger than 2,500 *scudi*, and in the country 2,000 *scudi*, surpluses to become State property but they should supplement *mensas* in poor dioceses. A weightier law of the same day abolished brotherhoods throughout the republic, and allotted their revenues to existing hospitals or charities for the poor. As the government had no time to make new offices of distribution, the poor lost where they expected to gain.

Brotherhoods were the core of popular religious life, of insurance, pension, devotion, and local loyalty. To diminish bishops' pay meant nothing to common people. To destroy brotherhoods was to invite resistance.

The French were not backward in pillaging goods in kind which might help to maintain the banks—for example on 4 June 1798 at 9 p.m. they removed four wagon-loads of silver from St. Peter's and a group of clergy had to appeal (successfully) for a small number of objects to enable them to celebrate the liturgy.

Of all the outward acts, removal of chalices from churches was that most offensive to the common people. They had seen it before, for special needs; but not on the scale now practised. The statue and the picture might still be holy. And if ruthless appropriation refused to spare, the people felt the crime to be more like murder than theft. Normally therefore the commissioners tried (at first) to avoid taking objects of special veneration. But at Orvieto a little riot had to be suppressed when the Virgin's silver crown was taken. Anything valuable went; censers, reliquaries, lamps, silver ornaments on statues, candlesticks and candelabra, 650 lb. of silver was removed from the Chiesa Nuova. The commissioners left what in their opinion sufficed for the maintenance of services. When the silver was collected, it was the turn of church bells—even the great bell on the Capitol which for 200 years tolled the death of Popes.

The government appointed a Commission on the Church. They placed at its head della Valle, an ex-priest whom the Inquisition formerly imprisoned for two years on account of radical ideas about the Church. On

13 April 1798 della Valle ordered the Vatican to fill no parishes in Rome because this right belonged to the civil power. He evidently sought the chance to reform or 'democratize' the Church from without. Criticized for the letter, he replied that the primitive Christian Church elected its ministers. He was forced to withdraw. The government was too sensible for so direct a clash.

Nevertheless, they sought to weaken the hold of religion in the hearts of the common people. They held ritualistic meetings of patriots, splendid military spectacles on days and at times when men and women were used to go to church; suppressed the chairs of theology at the two universities; banned processions in the street; and forbade the distribution of tickets to the faithful for their Easter communions. The clergy began to notice, not only the occasional acts of sacrilege which in the circumstances were to be expected, but a decline in the number of communicants. On 10 May 1798 a decree ordered every monastery or convent to refuse novices and any novices already accepted must leave within ten days. In June a law ordered religious houses to provide pensions for any monks or nuns who wished to leave (200 *piastres* if over forty years, 300 if over fifty years), pensions for nuns calculated according to the value of their dowry, 50 per cent for those under forty, 60 per cent if under sixty, 100 per cent if over sixty. As monasteries and convents were closed daily, and those that remained could scarcely buy enough food, religious were under strong temptation to accept these terms, and were freely granted lay status by a monsignor in the Curia, di Pietro, who had no precise power but was looked to in the imprisonment or exile of Pope and cardinals. The number of monks and nuns who took advantage of the arrangement was especially high outside Rome.

Among dissolved monasteries the most famous was Trinità dei Monti.

In July the government closed the College of Propaganda, in September the Roman Seminary. In January and February 1799 decrees ordered that no one but 'citizen-bishops' or parochial clergy might preach.

On 7 February 1799 the republic 'taking into consideration the pro-digious number of clergy and the heavy burden on the exchequer' closely restricted ordinations to the priesthood. It also gave municipalities power to exclude, on political grounds, a candidate presented by a bishop. Municipalities were ordered to report regularly on the conduct of bishops and clergy.

The curious state of affairs was evident when in May 1799 the republican police chief summoned all the parish clergy of Rome to a meeting, and asked their help in pacifying the people on the continual want of enough to eat; and a week or two later the French General Garnier made them an appeal to the same end.

On 27 June 1799 government banned the wearing by secular clergy of ecclesiastical habits in the streets. Four days later a codicil exempted funerals and the passage of the viaticum to the sick.

The liturgies of Rome, bereft of Pope and cardinals, continued though with maimed solemnity. On 2 June 1798 Monsignor Passari held ordination at the Lateran; five days afterwards they celebrated Corpus Christi with a numerous procession banned from St. Peter's Square and perforce circumambulating inside the basilica; a fortnight later reverent crowds escorted the presumed bodies of St. Bartholomew the apostle and St. Paulinus of Nola from the church of St. Bartholomew which government had secularized (whether to make a barracks, or a theatre, or a warehouse, was undecided) to the church of Aracoeli on Capitol hill; while a canon took reverent care that a miraculous fresco of the Virgin in St. Bartholomew's should be protected from its new environment. A little congregation at a weekday service in St. Peter's was curiously watched but not disturbed by republicans dressed in tight flesh-coloured blouses.

The question which troubled consciences most was that of the oath. Article 267 of the constitution of the Roman republic compelled every official to take an oath 'to hate monarchy, and anarchy, and to be faithful to the Republic and the Constitution'. For several months no one enforced this rigidly. But as the fate of the republic worsened, and its defenders grew ferocious, consciences were troubled. None of the oath was difficult except the fatal clause to hate monarchy. For the Pope was also a monarch in exile, and good Catholics found it impossible to hate his kingship. A long argument developed between the few Catholics who had no use for the temporal power of popes and were willing to take the oath, and the many Catholics to whom the oath was repugnant. On behalf of the easier course casuists argued that the oath only demanded an 'external assent' on behalf of good order in the present republic, and not an interior assent to hate monarchy at all times and in all places, and that inside himself a man might love kings and still swear.

The argument was so tense that the Church leaders in Rome decided to smuggle out a ruling from the Pope, now in house arrest at Florence after earth tremors in Siena. Pius VI asked advice of theologians among his suite; and in September 1798 said that to take the oath was 'absolutely illegal'. It was perfectly legal to take an oath not to conspire to re-establish monarchy or to overthrow the republic, and to declare one's attachment to the republic, 'in whatever was not contrary to the Catholic faith'.

The professors of the university of the Sapienza, and of the ex-Jesuit Roman College (nearly all of them), were those who made least difficulty about taking the oath. When the Pope declared their conduct scandalous, they retracted the oath.

The number of bishops and priests who swore the oath in Italy was not so high in proportion as in France, but they were not under such heavy or dangerous pressure. And the proportion who swore was not a handful. In the diocese of Brescia 484 priests were suspended when the Austrians recovered the land;[20] and since the days of Cardinal Quirini and Tamburini Brescia was a place where Jansenists were strong. When the Austrians reoccupied Piedmont, 448 clergymen were penalized as *Jacobins*, which was only 3 per cent or nearly of the clergy, but to be a Jacobin was in the eyes of the reaction worse than swearing an oath.

Sanfedists

The 'reaction' of 1799 took astonishing forms, in a series of peasant wars. Under French occupation peasant bands descended from the Apennine and murdered straggling French soldiers or Italian Jacobins. Often these bands believed themselves to defend Catholic faith against infidels. When the French troops were expelled, tottering satellite republican governments lay at the mercy of peasant armies. These pitchfork armies were savage. Wounded French soldiers from Egypt, mostly blind, were driven by storm on to the coast of Italy and instead of rescue met massacre from the inhabitants.

In several parts of Europe little peasants' wars flared; the Vendée in western France (from 1793) the most famous and one of the bloodiest, but also in Belgium, over most parts of Italy, later in Spain and the Alps. These were wars of brutality, snipers behind hedges or walls, swift retreat to mountain or maquis, murder of stragglers, pitchforks and guns taken from the enemy except where (as in Belgium and southern Italy) British or Russian ships supplied weapons; and on the other side burning of villages, taking of hostages, no quarter given, driving off sheep and horses and cattle, polluting churches, taking of corn or wine without payment, regular troops controlling towns and main roads, peasant armies making the countryside unsafe. Many priests stood against the peasants, being against violence and guerilla murder. But all over Europe peasants pushed

[20] Jedin, *Handbuch*, 6.51 n.50.

curates into command. The archpriest of Cottanello near Rieti became one of the terrifying guerrilla leaders of north central Italy, and used both the text of Psalm 144: 'Blessed is the Lord who teacheth my hands war and my fingers to fight', and the words of the Lord: 'Let him that hath not, sell his coat and buy a sword'; at one moment strong enough to threaten the overthrow of the State, at another fleeing in disguise to the Abruzzi mountains. French commanders did all they could to enlist bishops and priests to their aid, persuading them to preach the Christian virtues of peace and obedience.

In north Italy several guerrilla bands operated under the Catholic flag. A peasant leader named Branda formed a group which he called The Christian Army, and had two Capuchin friars as his aides-de-camp, and a bodyguard of priests armed with pitchforks, mattocks, pistols, and a crucifix. He went round pillaging the houses of rich Jacobins, and locked sixty-nine republican priests in the dungeons under terrible conditions. His monks said that he saw visions and was God's emissary, but the Austrians suppressed him and his band.

The provinces of the former Papal State were troubled even while the Roman republic was still in power. French soldiers were less obvious, Jacobins fewer and so more prudent, liturgies and churches less disturbed. Towns and villages continued to celebrate their local feasts with all their customs and pomp. Terracina was astonished to see all its canons arrested in choir and copes at worship on Easter Day. The people of Alatri ran to resist when commissioners tried to take the statue of their patron St. Sixtus and were pacified when told that they could instead give its value in money. At Orvieto a truculent Roman Jacobin was seen or believed to behave irreverently to relics, was savaged by the crowd, and murdered in the piazza. In Umbria at Città di Castello a little French garrison was massacred and bloodily avenged. Prefects in the country round Terracina, afraid of violence, required curates to speak of obedience to law from their pulpits; and some of those curates led their flocks into the fight, crucifix in hand. The Terracina men took a cross from their Passionist monastery, called it their 'tree of liberty', and fought under its banner. They had always been near subsistence and in the social troubles of that age were starving. Religion was no unmixed motive. But they waylaid French stragglers or Jacobin sympathizers. At Alatri they embroidered our Lady of Victory upon their flags. A priest in Alatri (July 1798) issued a call to holy war—'My fellow-citizens, if you do not assemble with all possible force to maintain the Catholic faith, we are lost. Remember that in past ages God gave victory to men who fought for their religion. . . .

Fear nothing. As warriors of true faith, God will reward you, whether in this world or the next . . .'[21]

At dawn on 6 May 1799 columns of peasants climbed up the streets of Arezzo to the cathedral. In the square before the town hall the French commander was reviewing Italian troops. The peasants mocked the soldiers. Then through the surging crowd came a cart drawn by a pair of high-spirited horses, driven by an aged coachman. At the side of the coachman was an old peasant woman waving the imperial eagle of the Austrian Empire. The guards at the town hall could hardly believe what they saw. The old woman threatened them with gestures, they stayed silent. The cart moved on, creating turmoil among the people. The coachman and the old woman clambered out and vanished. Suddenly rumour spread through the town that it was the holy Virgin, come in disguise, with San Donato as her coachman. The bells of the cathedral tower started to ring the tocsin; and from the vineyards and hills and forests peasants poured into the town, destroyed the tree of liberty and erected a cross, and threw out the French garrison. This little revolution was no accident. An unknown mind planned cart, Austrian flag, tocsin, and rumour. Bishop Albergotti of Arezzo was famous for his devotion to the Madonna, had written four volumes in her praise and a fifth on her sorrows. Arezzo was her country.

The bands of Arezzo marched upon Florence, the armed men each wearing the badge of the Madonna hung on his tunic or in the cockade of his hat. When they seized Florence they found supporters of the French, among whom they numbered Bishop Scipione de' Ricci, once of Pistoia, living in retirement. Jansenizers were suspected of being likely to sympathize with the enemy. The Arezzo bands threw Ricci into prison.

When the Roman republic raised armies it was careful to attach a chaplain to each battalion. Clergymen need not be unfrocked to be ardent republicans. A Capuchin, fanatical in his Jacobin opinion, led a force of 350 Roman 'legionaries' against the port of Civita Vecchia when it revolted against the republic; another Capuchin commanded the guerrillas in the mountains of Fasta to overthrow the republic. Republican commanders disguised couriers as higher clergy in the hope that they would more easily carry dispatches through the countryside. The little town of Acquaviva near Tronto held out six weeks against the rebels, partly because it was guided by a republican priest and poet within the valley whom the people saw as their apostle. The Bishop of Perugia told his clergy and people (December 1798) that true peace could only be

[21] Dufourcq, 207, 269–72.

found by faith in God and obedience to the government in power. At Viterbo in the same month, when a crowd was hammering with axes at a house where republicans sought refuge, the ancient Cardinal-Bishop Muzio came out upon his balcony and brought the mob to its knees and so to sense, tranquillity, and escape from French revenge.[22] Cardinal Zurlo of Naples blessed all the republicans of the Neapolitan territory, and denounced his fellow-Cardinal Ruffo for leading a crusade against the Parthenopean republic, and said that the new government was in no way an enemy of Christ's gospel or the Catholic faith.

Cardinal Ruffo took refuge with the king at Palermo, and volunteered to lead a crusade. The satellite Parthenopean republic was proclaimed at Naples on 23 January 1799. Two days later the king made Ruffo his vicar-general on the Italian mainland. Though no one gave him money or weapons, he landed (7 February 1799) at the tip of Calabria with only eight companions, and a banner with the royal arms on one side and a cross upon the other, inscribed 'In hoc signo vinces.'[23] Within a month he commanded a crusading force of 17,000—bandits, ecclesiastics, mercenaries, looters, devotees, and assassins, but mostly peasants. It was called the Christian Army of the Holy Faith, and by its enemies the *Sanfedisti*, men of the Holy Faith army.

Cardinal Ruffo was the last prince of the Church to be excellently fitted as a leader of guerrillas. He understood men, camped with them, ate their food, shared their danger, demanded elementary discipline in so disordered a body, but could not prevent murder and massacre, so that holy war in southern Italy became as bloody as any medieval crusade, not least because the retreating French and republicans killed any of Ruffo's supporters as criminal rebels. By the end of April the cardinal had subdued all Calabria and most of Puglia, in June he besieged Naples from the land while Nelson and the British fleet attacked from the sea, and the Parthenopean republic collapsed amid terrible murders on 19 June 1799.

Among the calamities of this war was the death of the Jansenist leader in southern Italy. Giovanni Andrea Serrao was Bishop of Potenza in Calabria from 1782. As he was a friend of Ricci, it took more than a year and several threats from Naples before Pope Pius VI accepted the nomination. He found a cathedral in disrepair, a seminary closed for the last eleven years. He raised the money for a rebuilding of the cathedral, reopened the

---

[22] Dufourcq, 373 ff., 394, 520 ff.

[23] 'Under the sign (of the cross) you shall win': the words said to have been seen by the Roman Emperor Constantine before the battle of the Milvian Bridge (312): Eusebius, *Vita Constantini*, 1.27–32.

seminary, of which the products were suspect for their ideas of liberty. He was as strong a reformer as Ricci, and with many of the same ideas. He held a diocesan synod which is unknown because the acts were afterwards destroyed by government; but evidently its conclusions resembled those of Ricci's Synod of Pistoia. He may have been more radical than Ricci, for he wanted clergy to be allowed to marry. Under the Parthenopean republic he led his people solemnly into the cathedral and urged them to obey the new government; and at the end of his address the people cried 'Long live the French government. Long live liberty!' and rushed out into the piazza to plant a tree of liberty. Bishop Serrao then accepted the office of civil commissioner of Potenza. When Ruffo's bands drew near to Potenza, many peasants and some priests regarded Bishop Serrao as 'the enemy of the Pope, the king, and God'. Warned to escape, he said that he trusted his fellow-citizens. When the professors and students at the seminary wanted to make a bodyguard, he forbade them to arm. Very early on 24 February 1799 soldiers of the Potenza guard smashed the tree of liberty, and raided the bishop's palace. They came upon Serrao still in bed, and killed him with two shots of a pistol. Bleeding to death, he uttered the words 'Long live the faith of Jesus Christ! Long live the Republic!' The guards broke into the seminary next door, and murdered the rector as his students fled. After sacking palace and seminary they cut off the heads of bishop and rector and carried them in triumph round the city on pikes.

In Salerno counter-revolutionaries found old and infirm Archbishop Sambiase of Conza who came into the town to consult doctors. They seized him among other suspects as a hostage, and put him on board their prison, which was an English ship lying in the bay. As French troops approached the royalist leader decided to shoot his hostages. In the mass shooting the archbishop fell without being hit, and the gunmen had no time to check that all were dead. The French had him escorted to his house, where he died a few days later.[24]

By no means all the martyrs were on the side of the Holy Faith army. One priest, a Dominican Father Tedeschi, witnessed the atrocities against the bodies and then the corpses of Jacobins, and appeared exalted at the bishop's palace at Castellaneta near Taranto to urge the bishop to follow the good example, and with him composed a list of intended victims. After killings on St. Mark's day, he preached in the piazza a 'holy hate' every evening for three months until the crowd stopped listening; but the source which relates these proceedings is no impartial witness. Father

[24] For Serrao, see Cigno's biography; for Conza, Cestaro, 31–2.

Tedeschi later in life was elected Archbishop of Brindisi; where he was loved by some, but loathed by men with long memories.[25]

These guerrilla wars of peasants often had religion as their flag. How far they really fought for their Church, or for their local church, or for a sacred object within their church, is now impossible to determine. As in the 'wars of religion' during the age of the Reformation, the defence of a way of worship was one, and seldom the most important, motive for taking up arms. They would never take their weapons because French or republicans closed a neighbouring monastery, or abolished a college of canons, or impoverished their bishop. They were more disturbed at destruction of their brotherhood, much more disturbed if a popular feast were silenced, or a miracle-working picture removed. If young men were conscripted, it was always a cause of flight to the mountains; and once in the mountains they wanted to fight for ideals, however misty, and with the knowledge of *virtus* in holy men might try to make a respected friar into their commander that so their campaign would be blest.

Peasant War in Belgium 1798–9

The French conquered and then misgoverned Belgium. Food, justice, local patriotism, desire for traditional liberties, provided enough reasons for secret movements of resistance, easily supplied with weapons from Germany or Holland or the British fleet. The leaders were aristocrats, army officers, a canon of Louvain, an abbot of Gembloux.

House by house, government closed monasteries and removed endowments. But till September 1797 the normal worship of churches continued, troubled only by the question whether the priest could make the required declaration of submission to law.

The republican reaction in Paris of September 1797 opened a more persecuting era in Belgium as in France. The law of 5 September authorized the deporting of priests who endangered public order, and imposed on every priest an oath to hate monarchy and anarchy and be faithful to the republic and the constitution. If a priest took the oath, he was despised and perhaps rabbled by his people. If he refused the oath, he saw his church shut, services banned, people deprived of sacraments, and perhaps ended in prison or exile.

To help the clergy, various civil authorities said that the oath had only a negative meaning to do nothing to overthrow the French government. On 19 September 1797 Cardinal Franckenberg, who had been forced into

[25] N. Vacca, in *Archivio storico pugliese* 23 (1970), 150–2.

a quiet retirement at Malines, was required to take the oath and refused. He said he could not vow hate against any man, nor against an institution so long established by God. He willingly submitted to the laws of the republic. This refusal by the cardinal had vast influence over the Belgian clergy.

In October 1797 began deportation of priests for refusing the oath. Cardinal Franckenberg was put into the common prison at Brussels and then across the Prussian frontier. The dean of Tongres, the rector of Louvain university and others were seized so that they could be sent to the penal settlement in Guiana.

II

	Total priests	swore
Malines diocese	1,556	177
Dyle department	1,723	170
Lower Meuse	1,413	252
Brussels	400	93
Louvain	220	52[26]

Several vicars-general declared the oath lawful in their dioceses. In a few areas, especially towards Germany, a majority of priests took the oath. By November 1797 the churches of Belgium, like the churches in France, were divided in schism. Non-jurors taught that jurors were excommunicate, their lay followers (as in France) assaulted or smeared priests who swore. Before 1801 seventy priests in the diocese of Malines, eleven in the diocese of Bruges, retracted their oaths. Government aided the non-jurors by maltreating some of the jurors. Engaged in closing churches, it soon showed that to take the oath was no guarantee of inviolability for a priest's flock or sacraments.

Laws of September 1797 banned all exterior signs that a building was a church or that someone outside a church was a clergyman or monk or nun. In October government banned the ringing of bells. In November a draconian decree ordered that every priest who changed his address without notifying the civil authority was to be treated as an émigré, that is, liable to execution without trial if found on Belgian territory. On 25 November 1797 the Directory suppressed the remaining religious orders, that is, those engaged in teaching or nursing. Pious frauds kept the hospitals going in several towns because nuns dressed in lay clothes and went on with their work.

[26] Verhaegen, 3.210.

In parishes where priests were deported, the faithful often met for service, to have prayers and sing hymns—these services without sacrament were known as 'white masses'. Usually a cleric in minor orders sang the service, sometimes a layman. These practices led to the closure of the church, with seals on its doors. This could not always be achieved except by force. At Anvers on 27 September 1797 French agents were trying to stop citizens clearing 'nationalised' properties from a side-aisle of the cathedral so that the government could not take them as loot. A working man hit their leader on the head with a hammer and wounded him mortally. Although 1,500 people knew the killer no one would give evidence to the French.

Congregations continued to meet, in churchyards, streets, fields, sometimes with sentries posted to give warning of soldiers coming. When the sentries failed, the encounter led to blows or shots. Countrymen felt the silence and removal of church bells. Many church bells were removed and hidden so that the French could not take them for a foundry. The game of hide-and-seek for bells was called the *Klöppel-Krieg*. Another source of blows was the procession. Government abolished processions and pilgrimages, people continued to process and to visit sanctuaries. One exhausted commissioner begged his superiors to destroy the church, nothing else could stop the people going.

Some commissions behaved with tact, some without. On Christmas Day 1797 in the midst of Brussels a priest, who had taken the oath, said mass at St. Mary of the Succour for a crowd so immense that it could not get into church but packed the near-by streets. A commissioner chose this moment to bring workmen and remove the monogram of St. Mary from the façade of the church.

Few people minded the closure of monasteries. As in France the imposition of the oath divided clergy and therefore parishes. Schism created the ground for political resistance. Between September 1797 and the outbreak of a peasant war in October 1798, a violent incident occurred on average more than once a week, over closing of churches (especially on Christmas Day), processions, pilgrimages, demolition of country shrines or wayside chapels, attempts to stop feasts or dances on Sundays. But, as in the Vendée, Belgian peasants rose when (September 1798) they were conscripted for military service. In the last two weeks of October 1798 civil war broke out all over Belgium.

When the resistance mastered a town they threw down the tree of liberty, destroyed conscription lists at the municipality, reopened the church if it was closed, sounded the tocsin on the church bells (if they still hung), brought back the priest if he was in hiding, and sang the *Te Deum* and a mass. The French garrisons easily held, and court-martials exacted ugly revenge. Peasant forces besieged Louvain and threatened Brussels, but despite the parsimonious aid of English sea-captains, had no chance of victory at last. French soldiers poured into Belgium, and this peasant war unleashed the worst oppression of that age.

Because government in Paris treated Belgium as a part of France, and saw priests as heads of resistance and responsible for wayside murder, the suppression of the Belgian Catholics was the most complete in Europe since the wars of religion in the sixteenth century, only paralleled during that age in parts of contemporary France. Monasteries were shut, partly sold, partly demolished. Two cathedrals and many parish churches were shut and then sold or demolished. No external sign of Christian worship was permitted, no bells could be rung, doors must not be open, no public symbols nor distinctive costume; a majority of priests still in the country had refused the oath and were therefore liable to grave penalty if caught. The curé of St. Nicholas in Brussels lived in his own parish through the troubles of 1798-9 but was a connoisseur of hiding and, according to the parish registers, changed clothes up to four times a day. The curé of Sichem entered in his register this proud claim: 'In spite of the terror I baptized all the children between 1797 and 1802'.[27]

About 9,400 people were given orders of deportation. Only 865 priests suffered—thirty-five to Guiana, 774 in various camps or prisons of France or Belgium, especially the islands of Ré and Oléron by La Rochelle, about forty including Cardinal Franckenberg, who continued to ordain priests for Belgium from his refuge at Emmerich, were put across the Rhine. Others went underground disguised as foresters or farm labourers or factory workers, and were not betrayed. Cayenne received only a few because an English warship rescued (10 August 1798) a load of prisoners at sea and the Directory ceased to attempt the crossing of the Atlantic. It was as well, for more than half the total number of priests (French and Belgian) deported to Guiana, perished there or at sea, and of the Belgians thirty out of thirty-five.

Inside churches were tokens of sackings, statues with heads off, broken furniture, gaps where furniture should be. In the nave of Anvers cathedral (1799) debris of altars and statues and paving and bones from desecrated graves cluttered the floor in piles several feet high. Though designated for demolition it was saved by the Anvers prefect. When churches were put up for auction their congregations sought to buy, and usually succeeded.

[27] Verhaegen, 3.216-68.

They tried to do the same for works of art. In several towns the authorities made arrangements with the congregations before treasures came to auction so that they would be preserved. But then they could not for the time be used in worship, and were kept either in a home or in a locked church. One curé buried a beautiful grille in his garden; famous relics like the holy Blood of Bruges were cherished in private houses. Where the furnishings reached auction they went very cheap. The altar in Anvers cathedral, famous for its carved woodwork, went for only 8 francs, a 1501 pulpit for 30 francs. At Louvain the municipal authorities, hearing that the people meant to buy back six 'miraculous' statues from St. Peter's church, secretly carted them away during the night and spread the story that they were stolen by the parishioners.

Some of the empty churches were handed over to the theophilanthropists, the cult designed by some of the Directors in Paris to replace Catholicism as a liturgy for public ceremony; with a vague deism and offerings of flowers and a strongly Christian moral code. They had temples in ex-churches at Liège, Tongres, Brussels, Malines. The cult had no popular appeal; where it worked it was hardly more than a small Jacobin club, and such of the people as knew about it regarded it as play-acting.

Belgian Catholics later looked back upon these days with the same memory of inspiration as English Catholics looked back upon the hidden priests of the reign of Elizabeth I. They were days which identified Catholicism with national freedom, and so made possible the contribution of Belgians during the nineteenth century to the idea of a Liberal Catholicism.

Peasant war in Switzerland

The Helvetic republic (1798), one of the latest of the French satellite republics, was created after a little war against the forest cantons.

The regime demanded an oath of loyalty to the new constitution. Most Swiss took the oath with sullen reluctance but without riot. In various villages disturbances occurred, in Appenzell and Schwyz riot and threat of war, in Nidwalden actual war. In Schwyz parish priests and Capuchins told the people that the oath could be taken with a clear conscience and did not hurt religion; but the people did not believe them and began to arm and riot, until persuaded to refrain under threat of French invasion. In Nidwalden on the south side of Lake Lucerne passionate preachers called the people to arms. The bishop's commissioner at Lucerne vainly proclaimed the oath lawful as an act civil and not religious. But the men of Nidwalden were roused, and would allow no-one to defend a taking of the oath. An attempt by an official to arrest three priests demanded by the republic as leaders of resistance led to a little war. On 29 August 1798 the men of Nidwalden agreed to resist, swore to defend the Catholic faith and their old freedoms, and picked a general. A Capuchin preacher Paul Styger so roused them that they expected miracles to their aid, and they had reason to hope for help from other cantons and from Austria. Women armed to fight at the side of the men, wharves and jetties were made useless for landing, the 'army' consisted of 2,000 ill-armed men with eight cannon. General Schauenburg came with more than 12,000 men, accompanied by looting bands. The French suffered unexpectedly big losses in several attempts to land, and this news not only heartened Nidwalden but stirred neighbouring districts to arm. Two hundred and twelve Schwyzers broke through to join them, thirty marksmen came over the mountains from Uri. If the French had not smashed the rebellion on 9 September all the mountain country would have risen. The conquerors, who lost many more men than they expected, murdered and robbed as they came. The resistance of the men of Nidwalden was the most heroic and useless fight by Catholic peasants in all Europe, a stalwart defence aided only by the difficulty of the country and local knowledge of the mountains against overwhelming odds and armaments. When the mayor of Stans tried with a white flag to surrender the town, the French officer with whom he parleyed was shot down from the Swiss side, the French shot the mayor and took revenge in the town, not only with the usual rapes and grisly cruelties, but shooting the priest at the altar and massacring his crowded congregation of old men, women and children. Nidwalden lost one in every twenty-two of its population, many houses, a church, and eight chapels. General Schauenburg, once he got his troops in hand, did all he could to bring the people home and see that they had food. On 7 October the wretched survivors of Nidwalden took the oath.

The Revolution did to the Roman Catholic Church what the Reformation failed to do. It appeared to have destroyed its structure if not its being. The most numerous of former Catholic states was officially anti-Catholic, its parish life miserable, its priests rent in bitterness. In Italy and Switzerland and Belgium and the old Catholic Rhineland French military power transformed the country religiously as well as politically. The central government of the Church was dispersed and did not direct, so that bishops and priests of necessity decided as they thought best. Nuncios still wrote each other letters as though they had a policy, but these were words not realities, and they did not know how to pay their expenses. Poland was divided between three powers, two of whom were enemies of the Pope. Only in Austria and Bavaria, Spain and Portugal the old Josephist world of Catholic reform continued, hampered all the time by the sense of crisis and need for State money which European anarchy brought even to neutral states. Protestant historians of that moment were almost persuaded that the Roman Catholic Church had reached its end; or at least, if that were impossible among the peoples, that no Pope could ever again have the power of his predecessors, and perhaps that there would never again be a Pope.

The Directory which sanctioned the kidnapping of Pope Pius VI called him 'the last Pope'. On 29 August 1799 Pius VI died in helpless and hapless exile at Valence. At that moment many believed that they watched the crumbling of a historic Christian institution.

Personally, Pius VI was the least satisfactory Pope of the eighteenth century. He had vanity and worldliness mingled with weakness. He displayed very ordinary virtues, and could not be compared with the powerful character of Clement XI, the old-fashioned sanctity of Benedict XIII, the earthy good sense of Benedict XIV, the sweet nature and anxious courage of Clement XIII. His office was respected more than his person. But he was kidnapped and died in exile. In ancient Christianity everything was forgiven to a man who died a martyr. For the first time in many centuries this aura began to surround not so much Pius VI as the office which he occupied.

By an extraordinary overturning of the accepted order of ideas the Pope, who was and knew himself to be one of the pillars of the *ancien régime*, and who was identified by Jacobins with despotism, now began to represent the idea of justice against foreign invaders and military tyrannies pretending to bring liberty. A simplified view of what was happening began already to make the Catholic mentality of the nineteenth century.

The Conclave of Venice

Since 1797 Venice was part of Austria. Several cardinals fled there for Austrian protection against the French.

The oldest cardinal, Albani, had been made responsible by Pius VI for summoning the Conclave. Albani asked protection of the Austrian, Emperor Francis II, who made available the monastery on the island of San Giorgio and agreed to pay expenses. The Conclave opened on 1 December 1799. Only forty-six cardinals existed. Thirty-five (thirty Italians) took part.

The old division at Conclaves between imperial and French cardinals appeared in a new form. As they met under Austrian protection, some wanted to please Vienna; and in pleasing Vienna they were able to argue devotion, tradition, the maintenance of Catholic inheritance from the past. The *ancien régime* stood for Catholic power over the consciences of men, and therefore for the moral good of mankind. French Revolution stood for atheism and cults of reason and tyranny against churches. Let us make a new Pope from a cardinal who is famous for resisting the republic, perhaps Cardinal Mattei of Ferrara.

The other side, suspect to the conservatives as *politicians*, thought it disastrous to select a Pope because he rejected the French Revolution. Hence came deadlock for three months, while every argument of prudence demanded speedy election. At last, almost in despair, they gave the two-thirds majority to Cardinal Chiaramonti, the Bishop of Imola, though at the age of fifty-eight he was thought dangerously young, and some could not forgive the Christmas sermon of 1797 in which he baptized democracy. He took the name of Pius VII in honour of Pius VI. The Austrians disliked the outcome, refused to let him be crowned in St. Mark's at Venice, and said that they would pay not a penny to the cost of the coronation. The new Pope must be crowned in the monastic chapel on the island of San Giorgio. By refusing St. Mark's for the coronation, the Austrians registered the nadir of papal power. The French envoy to Naples, who later was the first French official to be received by the new Pope, was not warm in praise. 'The new Pope', he wrote to Paris, is all that 'is mediocre.' He wrote to Talleyrand that Pius was 'a simple, good and very peaceable man, without a mind, with a touching appearance, but without the least presence; preserving the air of the convent amid the grandeur.'[28]

The new Pope chose as his secretary of state a man who was to be one of the creators of the papacy in the nineteenth century. Ercole Consalvi was secretary at the Conclave of Venice and won Chiaramonti's trust by his management. He had an enormous power of work, needing only four hours of sleep. With a Pope inclined to hesitancy, and a master of diplomacy as secretary of state, the institution was not likely to meet the troubled times with too flinty a face. Both men were conservatives but not blind conservatives; that is, they had small desire to go back to everything that existed before the Revolution, and wanted to use the chance of change to amend while they restored the essence of the old. They had at first almost no machinery and very little power, a Curia to reassemble, a bankrupt Papal State, and a revolutionary general in Italy. They began to issue

[28] Driault, 177–8.

bulls, but the bulls expressed more hope than real change; as when a *motu proprio* of 1802 'reformed' agriculture by calling it the first and greatest of human arts but made small practical difference to how men farmed or sold their corn.

By the battle of Marengo (14 June 1800) Bonaparte threw the Austrians again out of north Italy. For a moment it looked as though the Catholic Church in Italy would revert to the conditions of 1798 or worse.

But this was a different Bonaparte, no longer the servant of a Directory but nearing mastery of France. He saw that the chief hold of the Austrians over the loyalty of Italians was the claim to defend the Church against irreligious France. He decided to remove this source of disaffection. He summoned the priests of Milan to a meeting and made them a speech which, if reported correctly, was extraordinary in the mouth of a revolutionary general:

I am sure that the Roman Catholic religion is the only religion that can make a stable community happy, and establish the foundations of good government. I undertake to defend it always, with whatever means I have. I look upon you all as dear friends. If anyone abuses this religion, which I profess as you do, I will treat him as an enemy of the State and public order and punish him severely, if necessary with death. I intend that the Roman Catholic religion shall be practised publicly and in its fullness. . . .

Modern philosophers tried to persuade France that Catholicism is the implacable enemy of democracy and republican government, and hence the cruel persecution which the French republic directed against religion and its ministers. . . . I also am a philosopher, and know that in society as it is no man can be virtuous or just if he knows not whence he came or where he will go. Reason alone fastens us to earth; without religion we walk always in the dark; the Catholic religion is the only one to give man unfailing light on his origin and his latter end. No society without morality, no morality without religion; therefore only religion can give lasting foundations to a state. A society without religion is like a ship without a compass. . . . France has had her eyes opened through suffering, and has seen the Catholic religion to be the single anchor amid storm. . . .[29]

Whether he said all these words is uncertain. They appeared in a pamphlet at Genoa, the version was accused of being interpolated, French police looked for a forger. But the speech suited an important bit of Napoleon's mind, and his political objective of that moment. He never denied what he was reported to have said. On 18 June 1800 he appeared at a *Te Deum* in Milan cathedral, was ceremoniously received by priests at

[29] Napoleon, *Corr.* 6.338–9.

the portals (for the archbishop had fled[30]) and escorted to a stall in choir on a dais formerly laid out for conquerors and kings. Though shocked by the dilapidated state of the cathedral, still unfinished after centuries, he was proud that the rite was magnificent and the music composed by 'the best musicians in Italy'. This 'respect for the altar', he reported, would impress Italians. One of them said 'If you behave like this, we are all republicans, and ready to defend the cause of a people whose morals, language and customs are most like to ours.'

The Milanese have never forgotten that it was none of their more native sovereigns or archbishops who finished Milan cathedral after so many centuries of effort, but Napoleon.

He was a Corsican easy among peasants. His father was a disciple of Voltaire and had a touch of contempt for popular religion. But Napoleon rebelled against father's opinions, and for all his 'absence' of religious feeling was never in doubt about the power of religious experience and rites over the minds of ordinary people. His mother had faith, and he always thought of himself as her child, especially because he admired her courage and practical nature. At school he studied Rousseau, and later came to respect Robespierre with his doctrine of the supreme being and hostility to orthodox Christianity. He felt himself above the little differences of sect or even faith. When he was afraid that his better treatment of the Pope would make men suspect him of Catholicism, he wrote 'People may call me a papist if they like. I am nothing. I was a Mussulman in Egypt, I will be a Catholic here, for the welfare of my people. I do not believe in any religion, but when it comes to speaking of God' and he pointed at the sky, 'who made all that?'[31] He was not a man who by nature felt mystery in the universe, and after he rose to power was too arrogant to capture humility of mind. One of his courtiers, Madame de Rémusat, said that he paid too much attention to this world to have time to spare for the next.[32] Nowhere does he give any sense of profundity. When he seemed to be the child of a Corsican mother, or in his old age on St. Helena reminisced about the necessity for religion, he sounded at times as though he had a naturally religious soul. When he was in power he was a child of the Enlightenment and the Revolution, hard in the doctrine that religion is useful to government and necessary to the State because it brings public and private morality; but always thinking and feeling upon the surface.

[30] Pingaud, 1.198.
[31] A. C. Thibaudeau, *Bonaparte and the Consulate* (French, 1827), Eng. trans. (1908),155.
[32] Madame de Rémusat, *Memoirs*, Eng. trans. (1880), 2.129.

He had a sense of his own destiny which at moments was akin to a religious doctrine of vocation. But this feeling seldom afflicted when he was triumphant, his success was his own, the vocation became fate when it was failure for which he could not be responsible.

He once said that he could not have achieved what he achieved had he been a religious man, and here the self-perception was both right and rare. 'I am not a man like other men', he said. 'The laws of morality and decorum could not be intended to apply to me.'[33] In the last exile on St. Helena he loved to have the Bible read aloud, sometimes the campaigns of kings and judges in the Old Testament, but often St. Paul. Occasionally in anti-religious mood, as in his dying years of misery, his mind swayed from notion to notion, he decided that Islam was better than Christianity, or that Christ never existed, and would profess astonishment that his old foe Pope Pius VII really believed. He disliked the papacy, and hierarchies, and to that extent thought Protestants to have virtue, and wondered whether he would not have done better to make France Protestant.

But this was not his usual nor his real opinion. European by instinct and Italian by descent, he was a natural rebel against Catholicism but no natural Protestant. And his memories of peasant religion in his childhood prevented him wanting a cooler or more austere religion. He once said that he preferred the Church of Rome to the Church of England because in the Roman Church the people do not understand the prayers, and prayer is a place where clarity is not wisdom.[34] One of his courtiers remembered that when he was Emperor and heard the news of some great danger or deliverance, he often made the sign of the cross involuntarily.[35] He said that he did not like to die without a confessor, and men who tried to make him argue about religion he might ward off with the declaration that in these matters he believed whatever his parish priests believed.

This profession of lack of interest bore small relation to reality. His discussions of religion were marred by superficiality not by boredom. The cast of mind and the nature of military education prevented the argument being satisfactory, not inattention or belief that the subject was trivial. When Napoleon fell from power and Louis XVIII at last reached his capital and kingdom, the new king was surprised to discover that Napoleon's library contained so large a section on theology, and doubtless more astonished to be informed that these books were the Emperor's favourite reading. Talleyrand told this to an Englishman, who thereupon asked

---

[33] Madame de Rémusat, *Memoirs*, 1.91.
[34] Gourgaud, *Journal inédit de Sainte-Hélène* (Paris, 1889), 1.441.
[35] J. Holland Rose, *Napoleonic Studies* (1906), 88.

whether Talleyrand thought that Napoleon was a believer. 'I am inclined
to think that he was a believer,' said Talleyrand. 'But he had a taste for
this sort of subject.'[36] Even though Talleyrand was an ex-bishop of the
Catholic Church his standards of what constituted a believer were lower
than those of other men. Still, so far as Napoleon possessed religion, it lay
nearer to his heart than to his head. He once said that Christianity could
not have lasted through the centuries without the crucifixion and the
crown of thorns, and the utterance fits the memory of a child among
Corsican peasants.

The French Concordat

To negotiate with a French revolutionary leader, even when he offered
to restore Catholicism, was not easy for Pope Pius VII. The Pope's most
ardent supporters were French royalists who must be (and were) shocked
at such conversations. Bishops who refused the Revolution and were
ejected from their sees were regarded as confessors of the faith, so that a
Pope who was readier than they to compromise looked like a betrayer of
martyrs.

The talks lasted from November 1800 until July, partly in Paris and
partly in Rome, Bonaparte accusing the hesitations of Rome as dilatory,
and threatening that if he did not get his way he would set up a national
Gallican Church without Rome and send a French army to occupy the
Papal States.

Despite the threats and even an ultimatum, the Cardinals' Congregation
refused to surrender unconditionally to the terms which Napoleon
wanted, but sent Cardinal Consalvi to Paris with powers to conclude.
When Consalvi appeared before a Napoleon girt by ceremonial on 22
June 1800, he was told to sign within five days or a national religion would
be established. Those who disliked these proceedings saw Consalvi's
journey as the humbling of the papacy. Until the last minute Napoleon
used a mixture of menace with courtesy, now confessing his attachment to
the Catholic faith and now commending the model of King Henry VIII.
After threats, and a situation described by Consalvi as 'terrible'[37], the
Concordat was at last signed about midnight on 15 July 1801.

The Concordat confessed the Roman Catholic religion to be (not the
religion of the State as the Pope wanted but) the religion of the majority
of French citizens. In return the Pope confessed the benefits flowing to the
Church from the acts of the first consul in restoring the Church and

[36] Earl of Rosebery, *Napoleon: the Last Phase* (1928), 193.
[37] Boulay, *Documents*, 3.232.

adhering to the Catholic faith. The Catholic religion was free and public, in accordance with police rules for the maintenance of order; government and Pope agreed on new boundaries of dioceses: the Pope may require existing bishops to resign their sees; within three months the first consul will nominate the new bishops and archbishops, to be consecrated according to the old forms; the new bishops and the lower clergy to swear oaths of allegiance to the State; in all churches the prayer for the government will be used; the bishops appoint the pastors who need to be confirmed by government; the alienated ex-Church property will be left to its present owners; government assures the clergy of a suitable stipend; if a successor of the first consul is not Catholic, the system of appointment of bishops and clergy is to be made anew.

The Concordat was not at all what Rome liked. Rome was accustomed to State appointments of clergy, but not to governments paying stipends to clergy as though they were civil servants. It had to accept the removal from office of bishops who for years suffered in its cause—some royalists and stout Catholics never forgave the Pope or Cardinal Consalvi for accepting this sacrifice. It had to recognize that 'stolen property' was irrecoverable (it insisted on saying that it would not trouble the new possessors and refused to declare the alienation valid in law).

In return it gained a revival of Catholic worship in France. It won also a recognition of extraordinary import—the Pope, without courts or trials or process of law and by mere decree, deposed old bishops and approved new. Never in all the history of France had a Gallican Church recognized such power in a Pope. Neither the Pope nor Consalvi wished or intended this consequence. Consalvi called it 'the massacre of a hundred bishops'.[38] One of his intelligent colleagues in Rome saw instantly what a knock Bonaparte gave to old Gallican ideas. A Pope was forced by a half-Catholic French government, for its social and political purposes, to act in the Catholic Church like a despot.

What both sides intended, and partly achieved, was nothing less than reconciliation between the Catholic Church and the Revolution. The Revolution killed priests, polluted churches, kidnapped the Pope, occupied the Pope's territories. Many clergy in France identified themselves with the cause of the Bourbon king and of the *ancien régime* and implacable resistance to revolution. After the earlier nineties the two Popes had been careful not to identify Catholicism with the German or Austrian armies which tried and failed to overthrow the Revolution. Pius VII was elected Pope, partly because as bishop he felt able to work with the Revolution.

[38] Boulay, *Documents*, 3.570.

But no Pope could baptize the Revolution unconditionally. Those tense negotiations show what his advisers believed impossible to accept.

The two sides negotiated about different things. The Pope was a religious man ignorant of politics. Bonaparte was an able politician for whom religion was an instrument of policy. The one could not get Catholic restoration without the complaisance of a revolutionary general, the other could not reunite France except by using a Pope whom he despised.

Bonaparte was determined that the State should control the Church, and that all religions in the State should be equal. As he would never abandon these two foundations, the papal negotiators had to find formulas which would save whatever could be saved and concede the rest under tolerable phrases. They swallowed one bitter medicine with wisdom. They made no mention of the political safeguarding of the Papal States. The question of those ancient lands of the Pope, Avignon and the Venaissin, which the French Revolution occupied, was not raised—the papacy had entered a new world, for no Pope of the eighteenth century could have negotiated with a French government without mentioning Avignon. Yet even this was less important than the silence on the Legations. These northern territories of the Papal States were necessary to its existence as a state, for they contained the only prosperous or semi-industrial cities outside Rome. By the treaty of Tolentino in 1797 Pope Pius VI could not but yield their sovereignty. Yet the new Pope's secretary of state, arguing with the government which at that moment controlled the future of the Legations, refused to mention them in the argument. They kept their discussion to the religious interests of France and avoided the political power of the Pope—even though the political power of the Pope might indirectly affect the religious interests of the Pope. It is another sign that the papacy was moving out of an old world towards a new.

A gap was appearing between the religious or international role of the Pope as head of a Church and the political role of the Pope as an Italian sovereign. Protestants and others had long complained that the two roles were incompatible. The silence of Cardinal Consalvi in Paris was the first confession by the new papacy that religion and politics were sometimes incompatible and religion was the first duty. For the first time 'the temporal power' became a conscious difficulty within the papacy. The Curia remained conscious of the difficulty for a century and a quarter.

When Consalvi reached Rome, some cardinals hated the article which subjected the freedom of worship to 'police regulations for the maintenance of order' (no. 1) and the article (no. 13) that conceded Church property as irrecoverable. Consalvi at first feared that the agreement might not be ratified. A consistory of cardinals carried the two clauses only by bare majority. In Rome the Concordat was not celebrated until September 1801, in Paris not until Easter day 1802.

The Paris ratification included the 'police regulations' accepted unconditionally in clause 1 of the Concordat. These 'police regulations', known as the Organic articles, restored the control of the Church by the State on which Bonaparte insisted and which his negotiators were not able to write into the Concordat. They restored the *placet*, the right of government to prevent the publication of all bulls or briefs coming from Rome; banned nuncios or other representatives of Rome from exercising authority in the Church of France; made an appeal to the Council of the State the last resort in a legal conflict within the Church (*appel comme d'abus*); prevented bishops from establishing seminaries or chapters without the leave of government; required teachers at the seminaries to sign the Gallican articles of 1682, which made General Councils the masters of Popes; ordered a single liturgy and catechism for all France; banned feast days not on Sundays. Never had 'police regulations' extended so far. In one or two clauses they contradicted the letter of the Concordat, in more clauses they contradicted its spirit. But they hardly went much further than the habits of Louis XIV when he governed the Gallican Church. The Pope protested against the Organic Articles but made no effort to go back on the Concordat.

The gains for Catholicism in France could already be seen to be enormous. Pius VII continued to do what Bonaparte wanted. In January 1803, at Bonaparte's request, he made the four archbishops of Paris, Lyons, Tours, and Rouen into cardinals, Lyons being Bonaparte's uncle Fesch.

The constitutional bishops did not easily submit to the agreement, the anti-constitutional bishops still less easily. For a few months Rome had the danger that all its sacrifices had not settled the schism in Catholic France. In the end only two (anti-constitutional) bishops refused to submit and founded a sect of Catholics who could not accept the Concordat. Their people came to be called 'the little Church' and lasted into the twentieth century. In Flanders a bishopless group of constitutionals remained separate.

The Italian Concordat

Bonaparte was determined to make no second mistake about maltreating the religion of the Italian people. He summoned to Lyons (December 1801) a 'Consulta' of the revived Cisalpine republic. This Consulta had as leader Count Melzi, a half-Spanish Voltairian of integrity and moderation who disliked Jacobins and democrats.

Negotiations about an Italian Concordat took most of 1802 and three-quarters of 1803 because of anticlerical laws already in force, and were not ended without another ultimatum.

The Italian Concordat declared the Roman Catholic religion to be the religion of the State. Government's right to choose bishops was extended throughout, that is, the Pope lost his right to choose bishops in the Legations and Venezia. The Pope would institute these bishops canonically. Bishops and clergy must take an oath of allegiance to government but retained freedom to communicate with Rome. Bishops might ordain as many priests as were necessary for the religious needs of their people, direct seminaries, choose the beneficed clergy unless benefices had lay patrons. All sees were to be endowed. All clergy (unlike those in France) were exempt from service as soldiers. Charities hitherto administered by clergy came under mixed committees. Owners of nationalized property were 'not to be troubled', that is, persons who bought monastic or Church property were (not recognized to have a right, which no Pope could allow, but) henceforth secure in their possessions.

The Italian Concordat was much more favourable to the Church than was the French. It gave endowments for cathedrals and seminaries, and allowed the return of Church property not yet allotted to other possessors. It also allowed the clergy to retain jurisdiction in marriage.

But as in France the government in Milan supplemented the Concordat by regulations; announced by Melzi in a speech of 24 January 1804. These regulations reintroduced the old controls of Joseph II and more, on *placet, appel comme d'abus*, the introduction of a cabinet minister for religious affairs (this was specially odious to the Pope), assent of government required before anyone could become a monk, no monasteries or convents except those which educated or nursed.

Since Pope Pius VII regarded these Italian articles as contradicting clauses of the Concordat which he had signed, he felt himself free not fully to observe the treaty. He kept the agreement that present owners of former Church property should not be disturbed in possession; but he said that they could rightly keep them only if they received absolution from the Pope and gave alms as their confessor might direct. Thus he maintained the position, the ground belonged to the Catholic Church, he recognized its new owners as occupying on behalf of the Church.

These disagreements meant that the Italian Concordat was not fully applied to northern Italy until a decree of Napoleon (22 May 1805); by which time the Italian republic had been renamed the kingdom of Italy.

The Italian Concordat, which applied only across north Italy from Novara to Venice and Ferrara, baptized the new harmony between Pope and Revolution. Though in Germany his world tumbled, and though Italian Catholic foundations still shook, a reluctant Pope accepted agreement; and thus pious consciences could henceforth accept the Revolution, the Revolution could respect Catholic consciences as loyal. Only in the Legations trouble continued, from priests who would not allow that they were no longer subjects of the Papal States.

The coronation of Napoleon

In May 1804 the French senate declared Bonaparte to be hereditary Emperor of the French as Napoleon I. But for several months already the Pope privately thought of Napoleon as Emperor. As early as January 1803 he addressed a letter to Napoleon's wife Josephine de Beauharnais, asking her to influence her husband towards the Catholic faith, and giving her the title of Empress. On 2 August 1804 Pius VII congratulated Napoleon on his election.

Napoleon united occasional or inarticulate religiosity with a sense of history. He looked back at Charlemagne, and imagined himself recreating a holy empire under French sovereignty. Common sense told him that victorious generals do not become hereditary rulers unless their new place is somehow consecrated. He needed crowning. The Pope should do for him what a Pope once did for Charlemagne. From Paris Cardinal Caprara besought the Pope to come to Paris for the purpose, and portrayed the advantage to a Pope so necessary to crown a new Emperor, and simultaneously reported Napoleon's threats if he refused. In Rome Napoleon's uncle Cardinal Fesch, new French ambassador in Rome, worked to the same end. Among diplomats Pius VII was already gaining the nickname of *imperial chaplain.*

From the first moment Cardinal Consalvi saw that the Pope could not refuse. He made as much out of the negotiations as he could, and cast in the way as many difficulties as he dared; partly to make the Austrian and other Catholic kings less discontented, and partly to get as many concessions as possible for the Church.

Not all his cardinals were enthusiasts. At a consistory five cardinals opposed the plan because the 'election' as Emperor was illegal and coronation would sanctify laws against the Catholic Church. Fifteen cardinals wanted to make conditions before the Pope went to Paris. Pius

VII agreed to go, provided he were invited, provided that the Emperor would talk over reform, observe the rites of the Church, and not receive French bishops who held out against the Concordat.

The Church must gain from acceptance. The Church must lose from refusal. Cardinal Consalvi saw it clearly and convinced the Pope. The bestowing of titles in return for more freedom for national churches had always been a useful and not even cynical instrument of public policy.

But to crown a revolutionary Emperor, whose conquests might be transitory, whose status might prove illegitimate, and whose morals were sullied (on 21 March 1804 the Duc d'Enghien was executed, and many regarded the execution as murder) was never a happy undertaking. To all northern Europe from London to Moscow the Pope agreed to crown a tyrant only because he had power.

The Pope crossed Italy and France, greeted as he passed by reverent and sometimes kneeling crowds. On 2 December 1804 he presided at the rites in the cathedral of Notre-Dame at Paris. Napoleon promised to protect the Churches. The Pope anointed Emperor and Empress, and blessed sword and orb and sceptre. In the old rite he should have put the crown on the Emperor's head, but by mutual consent beforehand, Napoleon took the crown from the altar and crowned himself and his wife while the Pope blessed them both and prayed; and then cannon and cheering, banquets and illuminations, receptions and formalities. The Pope remained in Paris for four months. Napoleon gave him a tiara loaded with jewelry but few legal concessions for the church; a promise to restore the church of St. Genevieve which the Revolution turned into the Pantheon, stricter rules against work on Sunday, endowment for the Lateran Palace and the Irish college and the Sisters of Charity. The Pope wanted indissoluble marriage, Napoleon insisted on divorce. The Pope wanted Catholicism to be the religion of the State and Napoleon knew the political unwisdom of the demand. Cardinal Antonelli and some other cardinals had the illusion that the Pope rendered so vast a service to the Emperor that he was able to make extraordinary claims on the French government.

High legitimists in Europe regarded the coronation as a shameful act, a degradation of the Papacy. Even Cardinal Consalvi, writing his memoirs only eight years later, wrote 'I will not mention the Pope's humiliations while he stayed so miserably in Paris. My memory and pen refuse to put down such stories.'[39]

That Napoleon's predecessors the Directory should have asked the Pope for anything was unthinkable. That the Pope should be *needed* to sanction

[39] *Mémoires du Cardinal Consalvi* (1864), 2.404.

this transfer of revolutionary power was an astounding recognition of his utility as a symbol of conscience and duty, because he represented the Catholic ideal which still, in spite of all that had happened, was the faith of most of the French people; and from the viewpoint of French power in Italy, to have the Italian sovereign blessed with such *éclat* by the chief and historic Italian political power showed that the heir of the Revolution needed the Pope like any Spanish Bourbon or Austrian Habsburg of the *ancien régime*.

Hesitantly the Pope asked for his lost provinces: Legations, Avignon, Venaissin. Napoleon sent a courteous reply but did not specify. He suggested that the Pope might care again to take up residence at Avignon or in Paris; and Pius VII said that if he were held in France he would resign his office and become again the 'miserable monk Chiaramonti'.

In Rome men rumoured that he would not be allowed to return. He left Paris on 4 April 1805, crossed France and Italy through respectful and curious crowds, at Florence received the humiliating submission of the Jansenist Scipione de' Ricci, ex-Bishop of Pistoia, and on 14 May 1805 entered Rome. At a consistory he recounted to the cardinals 'all the good' that came from his journey. The Pope gained substantial advantages in endowment and atmosphere for the Churches of France and Italy, and averted unknown but not small damage to those Churches, at the cost of appearing before other rulers of the world as a chaplain willing to bless a despot. But before the Catholic common people his prestige rose higher.

Twelve days after he entered Rome, Cardinal Caprara (26 May 1805) crowned Napoleon in Milan; or rather, Napoleon put the iron crown on his own head with the supposedly historic words, 'God has given it to me, woe to him who dares deny!'[40]

The end of the Holy Roman Empire

For a thousand years the idea of the holy empire stood for the yearnings of peoples for Christian peace and order in Europe. The rise of national states restricted its image until, before the end of the Middle Ages, it was confessed to be, what in reality it was, the Empire of the German nation. But only the head of Germany carried the title of Emperor. Since Charles V in the sixteenth century no German Emperor was crowned by the Pope. But despite the Reformation and a Germany divided into Catholic and Protestant, the German Emperor retained a special relationships with the Pope, a special task of protecting the Catholic faith in German lands. For

[40] Napoleon, *Corr.* 10.448.

centuries the title was hereditary in the ruler of Austria. But still each Emperor must be duly elected by the electors.

Three of the electors were archbishops—Mainz, Trier, Cologne—each ruling not only a large diocese but a state within the empire. From the end of the Thirty Years War the Empire was sometimes despised by men like Voltaire, on the ground that it was but a pale shadowy ritual surviving from a once great past. Some modern histories of the Empire finished with the coming of the Reformation, as though afterwards nothing was worth writing. But although the Emperor could do little, and what he did he could do more because of his private Austrian base than because he possessed imperial power; although the Diet gave up attempts to legislate effectively; although the supreme imperial court (*Reichskammergericht*) stopped working because decisions became too difficult to make or if made impossible to enforce—the Empire retained sufficient prestige as an instrument of legal right to preserve in existence many little states which were helpless militarily. Pre-eminent among these states were the ecclesiastical principalities; not only the three great electorates of the Rhineland, but bishoprics, abbeys, collegiate churches throughout Germany. Bishops and abbots were an important part of the constitution of the Holy Roman Empire, less by their pastoral acts than by their 'sovereign' status within the Empire. Smaller Protestant states were not eager to overthrow these Catholic bishoprics or abbeys. To important but lesser states like Hanover, the overthrow of prince-bishoprics would mean the overthrow of an imperial constitution which also protected lesser states like Hanover.

Before France had its revolution, the constitution creaked with internal tension.

The Peace of Westphalia (1648) after the Thirty Years War tried to create equality between Catholic and Protestant and so end the age when men went to war over religion. As the treaty worked, the Catholic powers remained just in the majority—and slowly increased their weight within the constitution. This began to be in glaring contrast with the religious views of the German people, a majority of whom were Protestants.

The symbol of the tension between real Protestant power and constitutional Catholic power was Prussia. Throughout the eighteenth century, though unsteadily, Prussia rose until by the end it became a rival to Austria for the leadership of Germany. For the first time since the Reformation a single German Protestant state was mighty enough to stand, even if necessary without allies, against the great Catholic power in Germany. Not only were the majority of Germans Protestant. The structure of power between the states of the Holy Roman Empire was altered through the rise of Prussia. Yet the constitution of the Empire maintained the constitutional supremacy of the Catholic party.

The Catholic Church in the Empire, looking mellow and rich and permanent, was weakening. It was tied to a system of government which many Germans, not only Protestant Germans, began to regard as archaic and out of keeping with modern needs.

The treaty of Westphalia, which guaranteed German peace, stood in absurd contrast with the ideals of the Counter-Reformation. The see of Osnabrück had a Catholic bishop and a Protestant bishop alternately—nothing could be more incongruous, nothing more wicked in the eyes of the strict, nothing more reasonable in the endeavour to maintain religious equality within the Empire.

To live under a bishop's crook, so the proverb ran, was pleasant. The taxes were usually lower, discipline laxer, music and art encouraged. They were not very 'reformed' seen from the high viewpoint. Their cathedral cities resembled Barchester more than Calvin's Geneva. They had the quiet hierarchy and the ordered maturity of an old feudal world. But this feudal world was a large part of the difficulty. The states of Germany began to learn how to weaken or destroy the feudal customs which hampered their freedom to act.

In a state where the bishop was sovereign, his ruling work must take precedence of his pastoral work because men must eat before they pray. This made no problem during the Middle Ages and Counter-Reformation because prayer and prosperity were believed not to be different things; because in origin the bishop was but the local agent of a Holy Roman Empire; and because a feudal government made the sovereign only one of the various groups of the state and conceived his work as protection but hardly as economic guidance. The coming of modernity into the German states turned bishops from old feudal suzerains into real sovereigns. New theories of the State, practised in Prussia, expected State interference for the prosperity of the people. And the ideas of Enlightenment weakened the expectation that good harvests were connected with the moral place of a people before its Maker. The prince-bishops became a survival. Hardly any reason was left why the bishop should also be a prince; except the very important reason that this was the constitution of the Holy Roman Empire, and no one knew what might happen to Germany if that constitution were destroyed.

'Secularization' meant the taking of the land of a clergyman—bishop or abbot or collegiate church—absorbing it into the state of a secular prince within the empire, and leaving the bishop only his religious functions to administer not a state but a diocese. Protestant states made themselves into strong states by this method during the Reformation. That mode of gaining power was stopped by the Thirty Years war and the treaty of Westphalia.

The rise of Prussia renewed the idea of secularization. Whenever Protestants were powerful in Germany, someone would think about getting rid of another prince-bishop. But the first idea of secularization in its new and ominous form was put forward within a Catholic state.

Like any Protestant state, a Catholic state could not modernize without absorbing prince-bishoprics. It needed to open its roads, get rid of enclaves belonging to other states, win wider powers for civil service and for police. Across the lands of the Catholic states lay prince-bishoprics and independent abbeys, athwart every endeavour to create effective administration, more athwart than in any Protestant state, which absorbed most of its prince-bishoprics during the Reformation. The Catholic state of the later eighteenth century had a more crying need to eat bishops than any Protestant, for the obvious reason that Protestants ate their bishops 250 years before.

Bavaria had once been the leader of Counter-Reformation in Germany. In this way the Duke of Bavaria eventually achieved an oversight of the churches not unlike that which Lutheran princes achieved in their lands. In 1742–3 it was proposed that Bavaria be made a monarchy and that simultaneously six prince-bishoprics should be secularized and incorporated in its land—two of them the historic sees of Salzburg and Augsburg. The project fell but left behind anxiety among bishops. Henceforth some such plan was from time to time discussed as part of a solution to the constitutional difficulties of the Holy Roman Empire. The most interesting part of the subsequent controversy between bishops and the Bavarian government was the refusal by Rome to support the bishops. Rome preferred a pious Bavarian ruler, using a papal nuncio, to maintaining the old rights of aristocratic bishops.

These German prince-bishops therefore, though the constitutional mainstay of the Catholic religion in Germany, were natural rivals of the Pope and enemies of his claim to interfere in their dioceses. When revolution came they had at first no strong defender in the surviving international authority of the see of Rome. Pacca, the papal nuncio in Cologne who fought his archbishop over dispensing rights and the validity of marriages celebrated without papal leave, said cheerfully, 'Now is the axe laid to the root of the German Church.'[41] Pacca had no desire to

[41] Aretin, 1.422.

overthrow Catholicism in Germany, he strenuously endeavoured to maintain it in all its fullness. But the fight between bishops and nuncios showed how the old German constitution disagreed not only with modern Catholic states within the Empire but with the ideals of Rome for German Catholicism.

The French Revolution destroyed all this, not so much because it was revolutionary as because its people's armies made the Rhineland defenceless by Germans. By 1797 the revolutionary government occupied all Germany up to the river Rhine and revived talk about 'the natural frontiers of France'. Of the three archbishop-electors, the city of Cologne and most of its principality with its elector's palace at Bonn lay on the left bank of the river, the city of Trier and almost all its principality, with its elector's palace at Koblenz, and a lesser part of the principality of Mainz including the see-city but not most of the diocese. On the left bank the Prince-bishop of Liège had twenty-six towns. The sees of Worms, Speyer, and Strassburg all lay upon that bank. The free imperial abbey of Prüm, and other little monastic principalities, stood under French government. A patriotic procession at Bonn ceremoniously hewed to pieces the doors of the ghetto, till then closed nightly. At first Germans believed that this was a brief occupation by foreign hooligans. They were soon disillusioned and must come to terms.

French armies forcibly secularized most of the territories of the weightiest prince-bishoprics of the Empire. A goddess of Reason paraded in Bonn.

Two motives led German governments to carry further the demolition of ecclesiastical states. They felt under siege. Hard pressed by the French they sought power more urgently, new subjects and new territories. From 1795 onwards Prussian statesmen kept wondering how to get more power by grasping more bishoprics. From a short time afterwards intelligent politicians of lesser states saw that probably they could not stop the plan. On 22 April 1798 Hanover asked Saxony to join them in protesting against a plan to secularize bishoprics, and received the reply, 'We cannot prevent it if the bigger states agree.'[42] Terrible negotiations with the French at Rastadt during 1798 forced them to see that they must concede to survive. They must hand over part of the Holy Roman Empire to save the rest.

The French argument proposed to compensate German princes for losing land by giving them the land of other prince-bishoprics on the

---

[42] Aretin, 1.433.

right bank of the Rhine. This principle was accepted by both sides at the Peace of Lunéville (1801).

Some had the idea of moving the electors to new sees and so saving the Catholic constitution of the Empire. Perhaps the Archbishop of Cologne, who was also Bishop of Münster; might move to Münster; Trier, whose archbishop was also Bishop of Augsburg, might move his see city and his electoral rank to Augsburg; Mainz, which had much land on the right bank, might move a few miles eastwards to Aschaffenburg. These desperate plans to save the empire had no chance because the Empire was already breaking. It was an atmosphere of *sauve qui peut*. Prussia and Austria began in 1801 to occupy parts of bishoprics without waiting for anyone's leave. Even the new Pope Pius VII cheerfully accepted the French annexations by sanctioning new sees on the left bank. At the Diet of Regensburng which accepted the Peace of Lunéville (7 March 1801) the Elector of Cologne said how grievous it was to be separated from such loyal subjects but when they considered the welfare of the Empire and its people they must agree. The Bishop of Speyer said the bishops of the left bank were sacrificing their all for the Empire and ought to be compensated or the Catholic religion would suffer hurt.

The arrangement was left to an 'imperial committee' (*Reichsdeputation*). Prussia insisted that no bishop sit on this committee. 'It would be illogical to have the spiritual estates agreeing to their own dissolution.'[43]

A Prussian force moved into Hildesheim and Münster. At this news an Austrian force moved into Salzburg, Passau and the independent abbey of Berchtesgaden. Everything was still unsettled, with consequent danger of fighting until 25 February 1803 when the Reich committee passed the necessary resolution (*Reichsdeputationshauptschluss*). Hardly anyone protested—the Emperor only protested that the Grand Duke of Tuscany was inadequately compensated.

The constitution of the Holy Roman Empire was broken. The German monasteries lost their place in the imperial system. 'Compensation' fell before 'appropriation'. The ancient Church of the German nation vanished in its outward forms. This disappearance was the condition under which developed a new German Catholicism of the nineteenth century.

The prince-bishops disappeared not because they were corrupt. When fate struck them, their lands were prosperous, their government acceptable, their characters honourable. They disappeared because they outlived their day. A Germany constituted like the Holy Roman Empire was too ramshackle, or too gentlemanly, or too divided, to stand up to revolution-

[43] Heigel, 2.391.

ary France. Against Napoleon Germany needed Prussian and Austrian power.

In February 1803, when all was settled, a brief from Rome arrived in Vienna, threatening with excommunication Catholics who took part in secularization. The Emperor Francis was indignant. 'It would have been better', he said, 'if the Curia made efforts for the freedom of Catholic worship and tried to get the lands into the hand of Catholic princes than to groan about the loss of temporal power and property. It is very sad, but the Catholic clergy have only come into the conditions under which they work in every other country of Europe.' On 27 April 1803 he ratified the act. 'All is lost,' was the comment in the Roman Curia. 'The looters are Catholics as well as Protestants.'[44]

The bishoprics fell without resistance. A Bavarian regiment from Munich held a parade with trumpets and drums in the near-by see-city of Freising, removed the bishop's arms from the city hall, and held solemn *Te Deum* in the parish church. The Prince-bishop of Augsburg, humiliated as were few others by the conditions under which he lost his principality, went on living in his palace with court ceremonial. In Eichstätt, the Bavarian commissioner who came to rob the bishop of his principality, reported that the bishop behaved 'like a father handing over the inheritance to a son'.[45] The prince-bishop was anxious that the new authority should honour his commitments to charitable institutions. The citizens saw the bishop's arms taken down but hardly minded for they were relieved not to be put under Protestant Prussia. Formal protests were made by bishops, abbots, and Rome. But the ecclesiastical states were defenceless, and the people did not care. After a few years no one wanted to go back to the old system. When Napoleon fell the Congress of Vienna hardly considered the restoration of the German prince-bishoprics. For political reasons it restored only one prince-bishopric of the ancient Holy Roman Empire— the Papal States in central and northern Italy, an act which left one of the most unstable areas in an otherwise successful peace treaty. But even before the peace treaty, the bishoprics faded into the historic past of vanished Germany.

To general experience that common people did not mind, came important exceptions: Catholics now under Protestant rule; Catholics lately under ecclesiastical rule and now under Catholic but Josephist rule; and a Rhineland under French conquest.

[44] Schmidlin, 1.211; Leflon, *Le Crise révolutionnaire*, 233 from *A.S.V.*

[45] Bauerreiss, 7.438. Eichstätt was first given to the Grand Duke of Tuscany as compensation for his losses in Italy. It became Bavarian only in 1806.

At the Peace of Augsburg (1555) and the Peace of Westphalia (1648) Germany solved its religious problem by putting Catholics and Protestants into different states. This solution was not fully maintained throughout the eighteenth century. Prussia under Frederick the Great occupied Catholic Silesia and proved that a Protestant government could tolerate Catholic subjects. War put Catholic rulers into a Protestant Palatinate and careful legal arrangements enabled the two faiths to live in peace. But Germany had never before tried the mixture of denominations which now it must attempt to make harmonious. Vast numbers of Catholics, formerly the subjects of prince-bishops, passed under the rule of Protestant sovereigns. They were nervous. Though the prince-bishopric of Paderborn was worse governed than any other state of Germany, its inhabitants resented the coming of Prussian bureaucrats. Münster in Westphalia was sullen at Prussian occupation, peasants in the Suabian hills felt it wrong when they found themselves under a Protestant King of Württemberg.

Germany had to try toleration on a scale never before practised. The states issued edicts of toleration. Protestant princes did all they could to reconcile their new Catholic subjects. In many ways Catholic churchmen did better in the Protestant states than in a Josephist state like Bavaria because the Protestant sovereign felt the need of doing more to retain their loyalty.

These edicts of toleration helped Catholics, especially in Prussia. They somewhat displeased Rome; for though Catholics now had the right of building churches in Protestant areas, Protestants had the right to build churches in solidly Catholic areas. 'Toleration', or rather the mixture of population which forced it, could only mean a deepening of antipathy and gulf between Catholic and Protestant. It meant a return to public argument, to controversial sermons, to fight for public opinion. Nor was toleration the same as equality. Prussia, however fair in law to its Catholics, treated them as second-class citizens throughout the nineteenth century.

The old world refused to disappear overnight. Benedict Werner, the last abbot of Weltenberg, argued strenuously against the lifting of the ban on Protestant immigrants into Bavaria—'We need their example as little as their doctrine.' 'What difficulties are entangled with the education of their children . . .'[46]

Catholic peasants under Catholic Josephist rulers suffered more, and here came the only physical clashes to arise out of the fall of prince-bishoprics. Protestant rulers did not care if Catholic peasants were superstitious, they assumed that credulity and magic were natural to Catholics.

[46] Bauerreiss, 7.461.

Strong reforming Catholics were determined to resist the evil and found
among the peasants in their new lands the same cults connected with
pilgrimage, statues, pictures, or relics which they were already trying
vainly to eradicate in their own lands. Therefore peasants, lately ruled
quietly by honourable and friendly if Barset-like bishops, found themselves deprived of monasteries, losing sacred pictures, stopped from
beloved pilgrimage. Bavaria under the minister Montgelas was offensively
bureaucratic and mean-minded in dealing with the credulity of countrymen. At a Munich gate pilgrims rioted and fought the police when they
returned to the city after a pilgrimage to the monastery at Andechs, which
authority had banned. The most shocking thing, not only to peasants,
were orders to open venerated graves to remove relics.

Such evidence as exists points rather to an increase of superstitious cults
during those years.[47] Perhaps this was a social phenomenon like the rapid
rise in illegitimate births during the same years, due to the unsettled
conditions in an age of war and perhaps in a certain mental disorientation
at a time when monasteries were dissolved and peasants changed landlords.
But peasant social and economic life hardly altered. The possessors
gained from the sales of monastic lands, not the peasants.

On the left bank of the Rhine the old Rhenish churches followed the
fortunes of the French church. We know what happened to the monasteries and nunneries in Cologne. Two of the houses became government
offices, at least fourteen became factories or warehouses, two were turned
into barracks. Four churches were demolished. Because many churches
stood empty it was easy for parishes to acquire more convenient or
splendid buildings for worship. The bishop (under French rule at Aachen)
reformed the entire parish structure into new parishes, using seven old
parish churches, six old collegiate churches, and five chapels of suppressed
monasteries. The people were not allowed to go on pilgrimage (pilgrimages began again in a small way in 1811), preachers were stopped from
holding missions ('local clergy are good enough, we don't need outside
preachers'),[48] no outward sign of worship might appear on the streets.
The French Concordat permitted four feast-days, but many workers in
Cologne continued to keep the old feasts. The money from the twenty-
three suppressed brotherhoods was used for church fabrics. The people did
not seem to mind the law of civil marriage, church marriage lost little in
importance.

All this changed the atmosphere of the city. Formerly it was known as
holy Cologne, its soil hallowed by the relics of the three wise men, a city

[47] Phayer, 115 ff.   [48] Klersch. 3.233 ff., 243.

filled with churches and monasteries and brotherhoods, its streets familiar with processions and pilgrimages. Its atmosphere almost disappeared. The French forced the city to take a long step on the road towards a town of modern industry.

The worst damage fell upon culture. The prince-bishops maintained a lot of little courts; with choir, musicians, librarians, painters, architects. The repairers of baroque and rococo churches lost employment. The monastery of Niederaltaich in Bavaria employed 200 people before its suppression, some of whom at least would need to move house if they were to find employment.[49] The monastery of Aldersbach in Bavaria employed a man to repair the walls, glazier, secretary, smith, cobbler, valet, weaver, hat-maker, laundress, ironer, two bakers, miller, a huntsman, fisherman, bird-trapper, two cooks and two head-gardeners, brewer, cooper and assistants at the brewery, male-nurse, bath attendant, servant to guests, shepherd, herdsman, swineherd, poultryman, potter, porter, tailor, butcher, waterman, carter, ostler, greengrocer; many of whom certainly had families, and except for the farm-workers were now unemployed.

Secularization left one prince-bishop—Dalberg, formerly Bishop of Constance and then Archbishop of Mainz and a friend of Napoleon. The Emperor must still be crowned, therefore a German primate must exist to crown. Since the German Diet met at Regensburg, Dalberg was moved from Mainz to Regensburg and became the Primate of all Germany, with a territory of his own round Regensburg and Aschaffenburg.

The Holy Roman Empire had no future. It now consisted of certain outside states with German provinces (Austria, England, Denmark, Sweden), more interested in national welfare than in Germany; of former German powers now swollen with bishoprics or abbeys and therefore able to pursue an independent policy apart from the empire (Prussia, Bavaria, Württemberg); and small states which still needed, but in new circumstances could not get, imperial protection. During the last 150 years the Holy Roman Empire had as its chief *raison d'être* the balancing between divided religions and therefore maintaining German peace. Secularization overthrew the balance, and with it the reason for empire to exist.

On 10 August 1804 the fall of the Empire was marked when the Emperor formally declared the imperial title now to be hereditary in Austria. The reason for this unconstitutional and unilateral step lay in reaction to Napoleon. Hitherto Europe knew only one Emperor of the West, the Holy Roman Emperor, in theory the protecting sword of Christendom

[49] Phayer, 123.

and after the Reformation the protecting sword of Catholicism. But on 18 May 1804 Bonaparte was solemnly declared Emperor of the French. A historic word *emperor* was devalued to mean king of an important nation. Hence the Holy Roman Emperor made himself Emperor in Austria. The Austrians argued that the election was now ritual act and no one lost if the title were declared hereditary. But it marked the withdrawal of Austria from German responsibility into the Austrian lands.

In 1806 Dalberg saw one way of saving the Holy Roman Empire—by offering the crown to Napoleon. This desperate remedy he pursued by desperate means.

Napoleon hesitated over the idea for a month or two. Then he decided against, and compelled the German states to form the Confederation of the Rhine. The Holy Roman Empire existed no more. Dalberg, last holder, (31 July 1806) resigned the office of Arch-chancellor of the Empire. By an ultimatum Napoleon forced the Austrian Emperor to resign, before 10 August, the imperial title of the Holy Roman Empire.

On 6 August 1806, from the balcony of the church of the Nine Choirs of Angels in Vienna, the imperial herald made amid fanfares the last proclamation of a Holy Roman Emperor—that Francis II, by God's grace elected Roman Emperor gave notice to his people that he had decided to lay down his imperial crown and declare the end of the Holy Roman Empire. It was the end of centuries of Christian history.

Perhaps the end of so historic a state, wrapt with the ideas of Europe and Christendom, was less important than the secularizations which made it inevitable. Perhaps its death stripped Germany of illusions and forced Germans to live in the real world. These names and titles, however historic, have intangible consequences in men's minds which no historian can define. Like the papacy, the Holy Roman Empire was a form of continuity between modern Europe and the ancient Roman Empire out of which it grew. Some mysterious weakening of the Roman tradition happened at the revolution, for all Napoleon's reading of Plutarch and talk of himself as the new Charlemagne. Europe's notion of a league of nations rested hitherto upon a Catholic sovereign, the reason for whose existence was the protection of Christendom. If it succeeded in constructing any new form of league of nations, that source of international authority would not be so integrated to the ideals of Christendom. And what happened was a new stage in the old confrontation between Reformation and Counter-Reformation. Always hitherto the supreme ruler of Germany had been a Catholic. Within a few decades of secularization he was to be a Protestant.

The monasteries in Württemberg

The secularization of monasteries is best illustrated from the hitherto Protestant state of Württemberg.

The new powers took possession with solemnity, a parade of troops, a ceremony at the city hall, with speeches about the new head of state, and a *Te Deum* in the cathedral or abbey. If it was a monastery, a commissioner appeared, summoned the community, read them his patent, released officials from their old oath of allegiance, took an inventory of furniture that nothing be alienated, (at some houses took away the furniture, at others only the silver and valuables), told the monks what was decided about their future, and (if the house was to be dissolved at once) explained the provision of pensions.

Unwanted valuables were sold at auction. Protestant churches needed more chalices and bought silver, sometimes a crucifix. No one wanted vestments, which fetched such low prices at dealers in old clothes and embroidery, that two decades later the department of antiquities tried to repurchase what they could find in the stores. Pictures went to State museums and gave excellence to the Stuttgart collection. Several monasteries had libraries of rare quality, which now made the foundation of the scholarly state libraries in Stuttgart.

The size of house made a difference.

A tiny house was easier than a big flourishing community. At Ellwangen the commissioners found four old ex-Jesuits still living in the former Jesuit house, and turned them out to make a barracks. The Carmelite house at Heilbronn had three priests and only two others. But the Benedictines of Zwiefalten had forty-three priests and eight lay brothers, the Cistercians at Schönthal thirty-five priests and two lay brothers. In these larger houses the expense of pensions and the finding of employment made difficulty for government, which failed to fulfil the Reich agreement on minimum pensions and worked eagerly, not to say avariciously, to reduce pensioners by pressing them into new work. From 1803 curates found it harder to be appointed to parishes because the posts were filled with ex-monks.

The suppressed dean of Ellwangen later became Bishop of Augsburg, several of his men became canons of Augsburg, government erected at Ellwangen (1812) a seminary and a Catholic university with five chairs of divinity. Five years later the Catholic theological faculty moved to Tübingen where it is to this day. When the elector visited Ellwangen in July 1803 the clergy gave him an ovation.

Nuns could seldom find suitable work and their communities were on average larger. They were usually allowed to continue in their nunnery.

Government set up a Church committee to oversee these proceedings. Its leader from 1807 was Benedikt Werkmeister the ex-Benedictine. Werkmeister represented a radical type of Catholic reformer in the Enlightenment: keep out interference from Rome, reduce superstition among peasants, limit pilgrimages and saints' days and relics, achieve a high or at least less low level of education among priests, and where possible turn the liturgy from Latin into German.

These ideals were not disliked by some of the ex-monks, and nuns made little fuss when told to say their office in German. But the convents were now ageing groups of women without novices, naturally conservative, and obedient to, but irritated by, orders to innovate in their chapel. The ex-Capuchin friars of Ellwangen helped in pastoral work and sermons and hearing confessions, and were loved by the people, and suspect to Werkmeister as promoters of superstition. But their little Capuchin community, swollen for a time by refugees from other Capuchin houses, was allowed to last till 1829.

Occasionally the sources show personal tragedy. The flourishing Benedictine house at Zwiefalten had numerous priests, a group of students in higher education, and a high school. Abbot Gregory was given a fat pension and free apartments in a castle. But he was deeply hurt, and could not quite believe in the end of his abbey. In his castle he was lonely and got leave for another monk to share his life. He lived simply and used his pension to support other ex-monks or the poor. The thirteen years of retirement before death came were sad. Of his monks, ten became parish priests, others became chaplains to nunneries, others schoolmasters. The abbey church was closed till 1812, when it was reopened as the parish church for Zwiefalten. Its huge and famous organ, of which the biggest pipe was 32 feet high, was taken for the royal church in Stuttgart. In the end the monastery buildings were used as a lunatic asylum.

Nuns stayed together longer. Usually they were allowed part of their convent buildings, the less valuable furniture, a vegetable garden, some cows for milk and butter, and one of the ex-monks as a confessor. At Heiligkreuzthal they were allowed to keep two horses and 'the yellow cart'. Any nun who wished could go, but few nuns left their communities. Enclosure vanished, families could freely visit, they often accepted German liturgies. Their trials were various but not unendurable. Some were impoverished on inadequate pensions. If abbess or prioress or confessor died, the choice of a new one in an ageing society gave cause for much anxiety. Worst was the lowering of morale because they could not receive novices, and as they became a group of old ladies watching each other grow ill or senile.

At Rottenmünster (Cistercian) the last survivor was not forced out of the convent till 1850, when the convent garden became for a time the place of execution of condemned criminals. At Heiligkreuzthal (Cistercian) the four survivors, always more uncomfortable, asked in 1843 to abandon their common life. The Franciscan nuns of Margrethausen were more quickly dissolved, for after only a few years they felt the house full of noise, men wandered round inside as they liked, the nuns' sense of unity and discipline vanished, they could not bear their parish priest and so (1811) asked to leave, and at once put off their habits.

By contrast the Franciscan nuns of St. Ludwig kept themselves happy by starting a school, where they taught the girls knitting and drawing and needlework. The last survivor died in 1860 at the age of ninety-five.

Where government commandeered buildings and offered to move the survivors to another convent, the nuns sometimes preferred to remain in their village and move into lodgings and lay clothes in small groups. A community of nuns at Gmünd maintained their common existence in lodgings.

Where popular affection fastened upon a holy object—the body of a saint in a convent tomb, the wonder-working picture of St. Mary at Rottweil—these were treated reverently and moved to a neighbouring parish church. The famous picture of the Virgin in the Capuchin lady chapel at Mergentheim stood above the high altar and is venerated there to this day; though the monastery was soon empty. But at the Benedictine house of Weingarten a precious reliquary of the holy Blood vanished quietly during the dissolution.

In one place dissolution caused riot and death. When the Grand Master of the Teutonic Order secularized his estates in the Reformation to found Prussia, the headquarters of the Teutonic Order moved to Mergentheim in south-west Germany. Here lived a president and his cabinet and an excess of officials administering the still numerous estates of the order. Many of these lands lay on the left bank of the Rhine and were therefore lost to the French. In the course of war part was allotted (1805) to Austria and the rest (1809) to Württemberg. The people began to resist the new conscription by violence. When a preacher prayed for the King of Württemberg, he was shouted down and none of the sermon could be heard. Officers of the Teutonic Order stopped the worst excesses, but Mergentheim endured a sack and some executions.

Men would not fight because they were changed from the rule of a bishop or abbot to the rule of a king. They resigned themselves to higher taxation, or the loss of some privileged trading. If they fought at all they fought because an ecclesiastical ruler did not conscript and the French taught kings how to conscript.[50]

But Protestant sovereigns were kinder than Catholics. They acquired, sometimes for the first time, a state mixed in religion, and must be seen to behave justly to their non-Protestant subjects. They had good political reasons for fair dealing. Catholic sovereigns could behave more high-handedly to Catholics because no one could suspect them of acting thus by reason of their heresy. Bavaria occupied the bishopric of Freising and the bishop died within a year. Bavaria kept the see vacant for eighteen years. The fall of these great German prince-bishoprics had a special aspect which was not ecclesiastical. It was part of the downfall of aristocrats all over Europe.

The people of the ex-bishopric suffered a little. A capital became a provincial town. They lost their little court, the attractions of a court, the ceremonial occasions, the distinguished visitors; they lost employment for the same reason, and the number in need of poor relief rose. But from another point of view Freising had no special claim but history to its endowments, and these were better used if spread more thinly across Bavaria. And Catholic rulers had precedent. Austria and Bavaria already had Josephist machinery at work. Accustomed to dissolving monasteries, they need create small new management to do what they must.

Napoleon and Italy

Napoleon was called King of Italy. But Italy extended only so far south as Ancona, where the Pope (just) ruled his territories, and beyond the Pope King Ferdinand the Bourbon ruled in Naples and Sicily. But the King of Italy saw himself as King of Italy, and regarded Pope and King of Naples as his vassals. A medallion was issued with the Latin inscription, *Napoleon rex totius Italiae*.

The argument between real power and legal power in Italy ended the precarious harmony between Pope and Emperor.

The behaviour of the Italian government in north Italy, and the way it carried out or failed to carry out the terms of the Concordat, was the first source of strife. Then Napoleon asked the Pope to declare null the marriage

[50] For the dissolutions in Württemberg, see Erzberger; for those in Bavaria, see Scheglmann.

of his brother Jerome to an American Protestant, but the Pope found no ground of nullity and stuck to his opinion (Napoleon, not Jerome, was against the marriage, which had a child born in London). Jerome's marriage was then annulled by a Paris court.

Then the Pope allowed Rome to be a refuge for the left-wing Lucien Bonaparte who fled from his brother. The hunt for four men wearing tricolour scarves who murdered two sellers of cucumbers on the Piazza Navona in Rome led to a war of words and notes between the French ambassador Cardinal Fesch and the secretary of state Cardinal Consalvi until Consalvi could hardly be stopped from resigning.

But the worst friction was the European war. Napoleon thought the Papal States to be part of the French empire, the Pope thought that the Pope was neutral. Napoleon needed to control the ports of Europe. The battle of Austerlitz (2 December 1805) laid Europe at the feet of Napoleon.

To the existence of the papacy as an institution neutrality between warring Catholic powers had not always been necessary. High medieval Popes organized campaigns against Emperors, armies of Renaissance Popes weighed in the balance of power as the French struggled for Italy, in the early eighteenth century Pope Clement XI had an army fighting the Austrians at Ferrara, in the winter of 1796–7 a papal army vainly fought Bonaparte. But this possibility of military action became remote because useless in the new structure of power, more remote because it conflicted with high priestly ideals of the Counter-Reformation. As Europe became a battlefield between mighty forces the Pope could not take sides.

Austria and France were both full of Catholics. Even if Austria were right in claiming that the French were aggressors, the Pope could only hurt Catholics in France by being seen to side with the Austrians. To be neutral in a conflict between Catholic powers became necessary to sane policy in Rome. For this very reason Cardinal Chiaramonti was elected Pope in 1800 so that he might not look like a Pope in the pocket of the Austrians.

This necessity of neutrality applied more widely than in conflict between Catholic powers. France was (mostly) Catholic, England was Protestant and Russia schismatic. Temporary advantage might come to the papacy as a worldly institution by backing a Catholic Emperor against non-Catholic enemies.

But the Emperor of the French was not Catholic enough for this purpose. Even if he were, no Pope in all history could want one power to dictate to Europe. He needed the English though they were heretics and the Russians though they were schismatics. And the Counter-Reformation

raised priestly ideals which applied also to Popes; and then the free critical
air of the age of Enlightenment doubted whether Popes might morally be
soldiers. Too many people in the world, too many priests in the Catholic
Church, too many cardinals in Rome, were repelled by the idea of martial
stirs issuing from the lips of the vicar of the Prince of Peace.

The option of calling for a crusade almost ceased to be open to Popes.

Pope Pius VII (21 March 1806) told Napoleon that to exclude Russians
and Englishmen from the Papal States made him a belligerent, contradicted his mission of peace, destroyed his links with Catholics of every
country, and could not be reconciled with his independence as Pope:

Your Majesty is immensely great, but you are elected, crowned, recognized as
Emperor of the French and not as Emperor of Rome. No Emperor of Rome
exists. No Emperor of Rome can exist without destroying the absolute power of
the Pope in Rome. There is only one Emperor of the Romans; but this title all
Europe including your Majesty recognize as belonging to the Emperor of
Germany . . . and this is only a title of honour and does not lessen the real and
apparent independence of the Holy See.

Despite these courageous words the British ambassador must leave
Rome; through the city spread rumours that soon the Pope would be
forced to Avignon and the Papal State would become French; Consalvi
was driven to resign from being secretary of state; the Pope talked of
retiring to a monastery to die, or to the catacombs. He at last (1807)
allowed his ports to be closed against English ships, there was talk of
turning the Emperor of the French into 'the Emperor of the West' with a
coronation in Rome, and many of the Curia welcomed the idea as a way
of getting better terms for the Church. French demands went on mounting,
that the Pope should adhere to the military alliance against England, and
allow Gallican liberties to the French Church, and abolish monks in Italy,
and extend the Italian Concordat to Venice, and make far more French
cardinals, and agree a Concordat for Germany, and renounce his ancient
claims to Naples.[51] Pope Pius VII only reserved his rights on two matters,
on going to war at the side of Napoleon, and on making cardinals. He
agreed to all else, yielding with misery.

The numerous and extraordinary concessions failed to prevent the
French army occupying most of the Papal States in November 1807. The
Pope reached sticking point. On 9 January 1808 the French foreign minister Champagny sent an ultimatum; unless the Pope accepts the military
alliance against England, and makes a third of the cardinals French, and

---

[51] Schmidlin, 1.89–90.

recognizes Joseph Bonaparte as King of Naples, the Emperor will abolish the Papal States. The Pope (28 January 1808) refused either to join the alliance or to make so many French cardinals. General Miollis occupied Rome five days later (2 February).

Pius VII was in a state of religious exaltation. He told the French that he regarded himself as a prisoner and refused to leave the Quirinal. He ceased to care for the political or diplomatic interests of the Church, compared Napoleon to the Roman persecutor Diocletian and expected schism. In the streets of Rome an alleged saying of the Pope was passed: 'My predecessor lived like a lion when in prosperity but died like a lamb. I have lived like a lamb, but know how to defend myself and die like a lion.'[52]

The French drove most of the cardinals out of Rome, including three pro-secretaries of state in succession, enlisted the Swiss guards into the French army, and disarmed the sentries at the Quirinal. Cardinal Pacca, the third of the pro-secretaries, was being ordered out of Rome when the Pope arrived almost beside himself, told him to disobey, and drew him aside into his private apartments, where the pair kept themselves like close prisoners.

They thought of escape. Two British warships in succession lay off Ostia in case the Pope should wish to flee, and one secret messenger was caught by the French and shot.

The Pope ordered bishops and clergy not to obey, the French expelled or imprisoned or fined clergy who disobeyed. The French determined to celebrate the carnival, the Pope declared a carnival inappropriate to sad times, and the crowds failed to appear on the streets.

The fight of wills could have only one end. On 17 May 1809 Napoleon annexed the Papal State to the French empire, offered the Pope an increase of income, and declared Rome an 'imperial free city'. On 10 June the papal flag ceased to fly on Castel Sant' Angelo and the tricolour flew in its place. Napoleon wrote to Murat in Naples, 'If the Pope preaches rebellion, against the spirit of the gospel, arrest him.'

Cardinal Pacca went to the Pope and asked him whether he would publish the bull of excommunication drafted some time before by two cardinals. Pius VII hesitated and then agreed. The bull *Quam memorandam* imposed the greater excommunication on all who took part in the occupation of the Papal States. It mentioned no name but included all 'however high in rank'. Without mentioning Napoleon's name, it compared him to King Ahab taking Naboth's vineyard. It was nailed in

---

[52] Driault, 519.

broad daylight to the door of St. Peter's, Santa Maria Maggiore, and the Lateran, but was quickly torn down and had small consequence even in Rome.

Early in the morning of 6 July the French burst into the Quirinal palace and disarmed the Swiss, who had orders not to resist. Baron Radet asked whether he would abdicate his monarchy of the Papal States. The Pope said gently that he could not. Radet pressed him until he stood up with dignity and said 'I cannot, must not, will not. I promised God to hold the States of the Church. I will never break my oath. I would rather die. I would rather give the last drop of my blood.' Radet said that he must put him under arrest. Pius VII asked whether this was the return for all the services he had rendered to the Emperor and to France. Radet allowed half an hour to pack. He suffered no one but Cardinal Pacca as companion. A closed carriage took them both unobserved to the Piazza del Popolo where post-horses were harnessed for the Florence road.

Some informed neutrals thought that the French had no alternative. Napoleon was surprised at the arrest, had not intended his vague general order to be so interpreted, but did not blame his officers. Their decision made his Italian work easier, apparently.

By Florence, Pisa, Genoa, Alessandria, Turin, and over the Mont-Cenis to Grenoble the Pope went at last to Valence. There the people and incoming pilgrims illuminated the streets and hung garlands and sang hymns in front of his lodging. On 17 August 1808 he reached Savona exhausted. He remained there three years under house arrest.

He lived in the bishop's palace, and the Emperor ordered comfort. Napoleon offered a large annual income to maintain him in splendour but he would not accept. He refused to go out, or accept invitations from French officers, or hear public mass. But he accepted gifts of food from the countryside and money from friends, and managed to get out at least some letters.

The French thus kidnapped two Popes in succession. It looked as though history was repeated. But the fate of Pius VII had different consequences. Pius VI was eighty years old when mishandled, already a half-broken man, had not been a good Pope, and ruled an institution not respected among European cabinets, the last episode of the eighteenth-century papacy. Pius VII was sixty-six when he was taken and had yet much life. Though not a clever man, nor a subtle politician, he was a quiet man of prayer, more of the stuff of martyrs. It had been said that Napoleon could probably have broken high Popes of the Middle Ages, a Gregory VII or a Boniface VIII. Pius VII was too humble or too unpretentious a character to make a thunderous duel of sovereign authorities in which he must fall. And during the previous decade Napoleon, for his own purposes, raised the prestige of the office. Imperial power in France rested first upon the magic of a great military commander but second upon the gratitude of the French people for a saviour from anarchy, a revolutionary ruler who yet reconciled himself with their Catholic tradition. Catholicism was more important, both to the French and to the enemies of the French, than in the days when Pope Pius VI was prisoner. From his palace-prison, Pius VII exercised an invisible influence which Pius VI never possessed. This was not chiefly due to the differences in the two characters. The environment of European opinion had changed. Napoleon held a captive a little more dangerous than the captive seized by the Directory, and more dangerous by reason of Napoleon's own acts.

The Pope of 1870 was to be much more powerful, both inside and outside the Catholic Church, than the Pope of 1770. The powers of 1770 could force a Pope to destroy the Jesuits. By 1870 no conceivable combination of powers could drive the Pope to such an act.

This change in the papacy as an institution had many causes. But what Napoleon did had weight. Though just pious enough and crudely historical enough to respect the place of Catholicism in society and therefore the papacy, he half-despised the Pope as chaplain and tool in his political machinery. For private policy he raised the Pope so that men saw how Popes were still needed to make Emperors, and then turned the same Pope into a confessor who survived the mirage of martyrdom.

At Savona the Pope lived simply and quietly, praying, reading, taking incessant pinches of snuff, doing his own washing and mending. A British frigate cruised nearby with the hopeless idea of rescuing the Pope by a sudden landing.

Imperial Rome and its Te Deums 1809–14

In Rome the French government expelled the cardinals, confiscated the archives, took away the fisherman's ring, abolished the Inquisition again and sold its furniture, closed many of the monasteries, drove out the large minority of clergy who refused an oath of loyalty to the Emperor (fifteen bishops and 900 priests swore, nine bishops and 500 priests refused, so that a majority was not persuaded of the sacredness of the temporal power). Most of the non-swearing priests were shipped to camps in Corsica or sent to fortresses in north Italy. French law was introduced, Jews were given equal rights, toleration was proclaimed, catacombs and Roman forum were excavated, gardens laid out on the Pincio, streets given better lights, dogs muzzled, nights safer, sanctuaries abolished, dilapidations of St. Peter's repaired. The people of Rome hardly noticed these signs of good government in their dislike of foreign conquerors, distrust of a currency out of control, and above all loathing of conscription for their sons.

Te Deum in a cathedral was the sign of political acceptance. Every regime which conquered a city wanted this solemn thanksgiving sung for its victory. Every new ruler found priests willing to lead praises and bless the change of government. Some clergymen had principles, or a habit, of blessing whatever government had real power, and were willing to sing successive *Te Deums*, sometimes within two or three years, for regimes who were enemies and at war. Choirs held themselves employed by anyone who paid, and sang praises for (say) the King of Naples one year, a republic next year, the King of Naples the year after, and French conquerors five years later.

Below the surface of easy political change were found torments of conscience.

The *Te Deums* in St. Peter's at Rome show how the political command, 'Celebrate!' caused agony of mind.

As Rome was part of the French empire it must celebrate the imperial feasts. 15 August was Napoleon's birthday, and he invented a dubious saint Napoleon for his 'name-day'. The day both of his coronation and of the battle of Austerlitz was 2 December. The feast of 15 August 1809, the first after the removal of the Pope, became a trial of strength. Only one church in all Rome sang *Te Deum* that day, the French church of St. Louis, and even there troops had to fetch and force choir and organist.

Then government imposed the oath of allegiance. That many clergy refused to swear pleased financiers who could thus reduce the number of parishes. Clergy that remained were more complaisant. After several heads were arrested their leader became the timid Monsignor Atanasio who did whatever the French wanted. Still, government wished no trouble. For two years (1809, 1810) St. Peter's stayed shut on the two feast-days.

Napoleon now thought of himself as the new Charlemagne and Rome as the second city of a revived European empire. His son by Marie Louise of Austria should be entitled King of Rome. Paris was not satisfied with Roman silence. For the mother's pregnancy, for the birth of the child, for his baptism, praises were ordered in Roman churches, that is, with 15 August and 2 December, five *Te Deums* required in a single year (1811). Napoleon himself, when he heard that Marie Louise attended a *Te Deum*, told her that she did well but that these things should not be too frequent, they are imposing only if they are rare.[53] This doctrine did not correspond to matters as they looked when seen by clergymen in Rome.

The chapters of St. Peter's, the Lateran, and Santa Maria Maggiore refused to sing. Police interviewed choirmen together and separately. Out of seventy-four choirmen at St. Peter's only fourteen would sing. Saying that the Pope was his king, the master of the music Zingarelli resigned, and was followed by one of the *castrati*. Choirmaster and *castrato* went to prison. Though the choir was very short of voices the baptismal feast of June was celebrated with a magnificent *Te Deum* in presence of the French general and his staff. Zingarelli was sent as prisoner to Paris where he fared very comfortably because Napoleon loved his music.

On 15 August 1812, another *Te Deum*, still with a small choir and empty nave. On 2 December 1812, not knowing that the Grand Army was retreating from Moscow, they had another *Te Deum*, with people filling a quarter of the nave, though in the provinces five canons and fifteen priests were sent to prison for their refusal. As the empire weakened *Te Deums* multiplied. At the news of every victory Monsignor Atanasio attended to sing praises (30 May 1813, 13 June 1813); on 28 February 1813 he was fetched from his sick bed to sing in St. Peter's the *Te Deum* for the new 'Concordat of Fontainebleau' between Pope and Emperor. Pasquino put up on his statue the text

> Te Deum Laudamus
> We have no hope in Bonaparte
> And no faith in him.

On 2 December 1813, *Te Deum* in St. Peter's, nave empty, Murat's troops from Naples lay about the city, one of the Emperor's favourite marshals was guilty of treason, and his army refused this feast day to enter St. Peter's to sing *Te Deum*.

When Pius VII re-entered Rome, the harmonies of the choir at St. Peter's were not easily retuned, between choirmen who suffered and choirmen who stayed comfortable. Four choirmen were ejected. The Pope told the rest to live in peace.[54]

Zingarelli never came back to his place in Rome. He had found in Naples a place, or rather two places, which suited.

---

[53] Méneval, *Souvenirs* (Eng. trans.), 3.116.
[54] Kantner, 73 ff.; Madelin, 584–5; Grove, *Dictionary of Music* s.v. 'Zingarelli.'

Italian churches in the age of Napoleon

Every town, every village had experience that was unique. The records of routine, visitations, synods, reports to Rome, are less frequent, partly because they demanded time and money and local order, partly because communications with Rome were interrupted or infrequent. Where records exist they show a church administration amazingly unperturbed by its apocalyptic surroundings. Bishops used old questionnaires laid out in the old way, priests filled in forms in the old way, parishioners praised or complained in the old way. While outside was turmoil, the documents of church administration hardly recognize that anything has happened or is happening. They breathe the unchanging air of a society independent of kings who rise and fall.

In 1804, safely back under Austrian rule, the new Patriarch of Venice Cardinal Flangini, whose reputation at Rome was middling, wrote a pastoral letter to his diocese on the day of his consecration. He said that a frightful calamity had devastated the country of Venezia; that some of the worst citizens seized the government and trampled on every law of God and man, and flooded the city with books cram-full of blasphemy and error; that every fool and gossip laid down the law on religion and philosophy and politics, and miserably misled the people by holding out a vain dream of happiness, called by the triumphant names of liberty and equality. Now things were better; but he thought that the consequence remained in licence and depravity, the more dangerous because it worked underground. He urged his clergy to the main duty of putting to rights the ideas of the people on 'true equality', 'true liberty' and not setting God's things under man's judgement, and on the need to obey the laws of the universal Church, and on the difference between the true wisdom of the gospel and that charlatanry which impious books boast of as the child of a false philosophy. He summoned monks to write books against modern error and to regard the education of the young as a high vocation; reminding them how early monasteries preserved culture during the age of barbarian invasions.

The new patriarch, it is clear, was shocked by what he expected to find. But when he started his visitation, the findings hardly differed much from the experience of his predecessors, a largely devout people among a band of (in majority) honest hard-working priests.

The first big change was economic. The cost of living in Venice doubled in the five years after 1796, the income of clergy stayed the same, the income of parishioners could give hardly more in nominal terms and much less in real terms. Priests, parishes, parishioners were all poorer. An unbeneficed priest was said to earn less than a porter or a gondolier. The patriarch noticed the effects in a variety of ways: the devices or tricks which some priests used to earn a living, the small number of cases where a priest or sacristan 'borrowed' or misappropriated articles belonging to his church, masses where devotion was disturbed by the intrusive rattle of collecting bags, and the confessor who paid excess of attention to the richer members of the flock.

The second big change was psychological. The Church had a sensation that it passed through crucifixion. A priest Father Piva wrote for Venezia a little history of the times, using the language in which the gospels describe the Passion; of parish priests forced into the Piazza of San Marco to help erect a tree of liberty; of a forced oath to preach the precious fruit of freedom; of nine priests imprisoned on San Giorgio charged with seducing their parishioners by teaching this liberty to be a dream and this equality a joke; of high new taxes, and confiscation of chalices; of divided monasteries; of peasant parishes in clamorous revolt against a Jacobin pastor.

The visitation did not record priests who left; Father Valeriani who married and became a professor of mathematics; or Father Zalivani who took his parishioners to do homage to the Jacobin government and later found himself in trouble with the Austrians as 'a dangerous revolutionary'; Father Collalto, once a professor at the university of Padua, then a colleague in the Jacobin government, deported when the Austrians took the city. The famous preacher Father Zanutti who was accused of being an aristocrat, said that he had always been a Jacobin, and used his pulpit to preach hot for democracy; and by the time of the visitation repented of this weakness; and when death came and his funeral sermon must be preached, the orator made no mention of this flirting with democracy. The visitation records the presence of several priests known to be unwavering enemies of the republican regime, including a future Patriarch of Venice; and of the Corsican father Carega who claimed to be a relative of Bonaparte, and who was expelled by Austrian police for saying in his sacristy that all governments are the same, they spend money on soldiers and pay nothing to poor priests.

What the visitation mainly records of the troubles is the loss of objects: buildings damaged by 'the French invasion', libraries scattered in the effort to stop confiscation, two oratories sacked in the Palazzo Foscarini and still unusable six years later, stealing or levy of chalices, vestments, furniture; schools or brotherhoods which lost money.

. . . . .

Laymen still gave money to make sure that special sermons would be preached; or organized the repair of a church, more costly now; or raised fees to secure a specially early celebration of mass; or paid an annual stipend to a doctor or a surgeon so that he could give medical service free to the poor. The visitation shows no sign of the historic controversies. A parish priest was accused of instituting a sisterhood of the Sacred Heart; but he was accused not because his accusers were Jansenist reformers but because he was alleged to have organized it for his profit. The last patriarch had ordered a Jansenizing textbook of doctrine for use in training clergy and the book was still in use. The numbers of clergy were still large, still almost double the number which in the age of the Counter-Reformation served the same size of city.[55]

Sometimes they had bishops, sometimes not. Vicenza had a good old bishop till he died in 1810. It got its next bishop more than five years later. The see of Venice was vacant 1804–7, 1808–16. From 1811 to 1814 it had a patriarch nominated by Napoleon but he hardly came near the diocese. The changes were made by the secular power with which bishops agreed reluctantly or willingly or temporizingly.

As north Italy became stable under French indirect rule, Church affairs came into reasonable order. Brotherhoods were suppressed, monasteries and nunneries abolished, collegiate churches turned into normal parish churches where they were not destroyed altogether; but provided that the clergy kept away from politics or were in favour of Napoleon's politics, the pastoral system of bishop (or very often his deputy in a vacancy) and priest and parish prospered again modestly. They suffered from lack of money, whether to repair churches, fill canonries, conduct seminaries. Ordinations were very few, most seminaries closed. Some parishes were united and the redundant churches closed; so that in Venice Father Guglielmo Wambel went round collecting bodies of saints and manuscripts from suppressed monasteries or redundant churches, and made such a sanctuary for them at St. Thomas's church that the next bishop gave him the title, *Restorer of holy relics*.[56]

The Italian kingdom under the French was bound by the Concordat to exempt ordinands from conscription. Many seminaries were closed because they lost their buildings or staff could not be found. But conscription had an interesting effect upon the future of seminaries. For all the efforts of Popes and bishops, many ordinands were till then ordained without first attending a seminary. Under conscription the only sure way

[55] *La visita pastorale di Flangini*, especially xlviii ff., lvi ff.
[56] *La visita pastorale di Pyrker*, 86–7.

to prove exempt status was to attend a seminary. It became easier for bishops to force men to attend one of these colleges. At a time when ordinations fell, the number of ordinands in surviving seminaries rose. St. Cyprian, the official seminary for the diocese of Venice, then sited on the island of Murano, had forty-one members in 1812–13, which was more numerous than at any time for more than a century.[57]

The Napoleonic regimes were able mostly to disregard Rome. But they were troubled because they could not easily fill sees, for which Rome's assent was constitutionally necessary; and therefore many dioceses lay vacant for years at a stretch, and ran under a vicar-capitular elected by the chapter if the chapter still functioned. Consequently work limped which only a bishop could propel. Far fewer children were confirmed because far fewer confirmations were held. The worst side of this was the decline of general oversight which bishops could give, rebuke or encouragement, alms to help the needy, study for the newly ordained, efforts to restart or continue the seminary, moral preparation for confessors. In many dioceses the meetings to discuss moral cases vanished or were maintained with the scantiest attendance; partly because they depended on pressure from the bishop; and partly because, in an age of vacant canonries and ill-endowed chapters and dispersed libraries and hard-pressed students, bishops or their deputies found it difficult to find candidates able to fill satisfactorily the two academic canonries of theology and moral divinity on which the further education of clergy in service had leaned so heavily. On bishops also hung the rational working of the *concursus*. The filling of vacant parishes grew less systematic except where the State took a hand; but then the State was not slow to take a hand.

Subsequent enquiry in time of peace proved that though the *concursus* continued to be held where possible, it could hardly be relied on to tell the truth. In certain vacant dioceses no one bothered to keep a list of clergy or confessors, no one knew who had the right to hear confessions. Against delinquent clergy the process of enquiry became disorderly. The examination of ordinands was conducted by individual priests who did not like to fail candidates; and if a congregation laid information against its future priest, no one took any notice. A vicar-capitular, coming to inspect the diocesan siminary in the diocese of Bojano in Molise (south Italy) found persons who were already ordained deacon but knew no Latin grammar. When he withdrew their letters of recommendation they burst into tears and said that they had paid large sums of money to be ordained.[58]

---

[57] *La visita pastorale di Pyrker*, xxxvii ff.
[58] Vicar-capitular's report printed Cestaro, 39 n.35.

Because priests were less supervised, the mass-priest did more as he thought fit. He needed more freedom because endowments for masses lost value, until he could no longer live on the small but steady revenue. Since the number of priests diminished, despite the addition of many ex-monks as assistant curates, the old burden of endowed masses would have become impossible if the terms of all charities were carried out to the letter. Less observed by superiors who would see that a charity was fulfilled, priests did more what they liked, amalgamating, omitting, even drawing the pay of the charity without doing any of its work. This freedom, however temporary, made a permanent difference to the nature of the obligation to endowed masses and so affected the axioms of priestly life.

The kingdom of Naples made a special and interesting case. The French took over the kingdom early in 1806, driving out the Bourbons to Sicily; and Napoleon proclaimed his brother Joseph king and afterwards when Joseph was needed to become Napoleonic King of Spain, made his marshal and brother-in-law Joachim Murat king (1808). Joseph Bonaparte was always a moderate, more moderate than his imperial brother preferred, and in his policy towards his state and its Church moved with a measure of deliberation, even in so universal a policy as the dissolution of the monasteries. His successor King Joachim Napoleon, as he liked to call himself, treated the Church of south Italy more highhandedly, but with the intention of doing it good despite its own wishes.

As the sees were empty, the ministry of ecclesiastical affairs in Naples bullied chapters with fair ease. If canons were obstinate and elected an unacceptable prelate, the ministry found reason to overrule the election as invalid; and if canons were still obstinate, it organized the installation of its own man with full ceremonial and military honours.

King Murat's government intervened ruthlessly. He wanted more restructuring of the Church than anyone in north Italy thought possible or prudent. He united parishes, instituted civil registers of birth and death, used parish priests to organize the conscription, make propaganda against illiteracy and even conduct boys and girls to school, augmented mensas and restored some cathedral property and tried to reopen seminaries.

The breach with Rome meant that new bishops could not be got. Bishops died, their neighbours did not wish to extend their already extended cares, all the bench of bishops grew older, the conditions of revolution made it no easier to reside in remote country, the discipline of the clergy grew more relaxed. Out of the 131 sees in the kingdom of Naples seventy-three were vacant by 1811, and nearly 100 by 1815. Of the bishops still in office, thirteen were over the age of seventy-five, fourteen were openly against the Napoleonic government, vicar-generals appointed as substitutes were despised by clergy and people. Of the twenty-four sees in Calabria in 1812, only nine had bishops; but of these nine, three were absent in Naples without leave, one in Naples with leave, one was not wanted in the diocese because he was a supporter of the Bourbons, one was exiled in Sicily as a supporter of the Bourbons; that left three bishops active for the twenty-four dioceses, and the most active of the three was the Bishop of Nicotera who was aged sixty-nine.

The Bishop of Marsico Nuovo was invited by government to do his duty and reside in his see. He replied:

I have no beds, no linen, no furniture. I have been robbed of everything. Last August the brigands sacked every room in the bishop's palace and burnt it, and then my cathedral and my seminary. There is nothing but a heap of ash. I don't deny that the king has allotted me as a home the suppressed monastery of the Conventual Franciscans; but the building is in ruin, and needs expensive repairs. It has no door, nor windows, and if something is not done soon it will collapse. How can I live there without first repairing? And how can I repair when I cannot pay for my daily bread? At Naples I live free, in my brother's house. In addition, Calabria is troubled. The city of Marsico Nuovo lies among mountains the most unsettled and dangerous of the region. If the brigands burnt cathedral seminary and palace while I was away, what would they do to me if they found me there or met me on the road?

In his letter he did not mention that less than four years before the neighbouring Greek bishop had his throat cut.[59]

If the bishop of a remote country see in south Italy was away in exile, or the see vacant, and the palace empty, and if the local colonel did not quarter his troops in its rooms, the people, or thieves, quietly stripped the house of its contents. We know more than one case where the new bishop after the Restoration came to his diocese to find not a stick of furniture in the bishop's palace. And indispensable documents, like the title-deeds to land or property from which income fed the bishop's *mensa*, were thrown away or burnt. This kind of loss happened elsewhere than in bishop's palaces, in vicarages, canonries, even diocesan registries.

The worst church problems of south Italy were the confiscations of the *luoghi pii laicali*, the funds which provided for the expense of buildings and worship. These funds were now administered as secular charity. But part of this transfer also meant the laicizing of charity, that is, the centre of public benevolence now lay more in the town hall than in the church.

The men were conscripted. This gave the parish churches a different

[59] M. Miele, in *R.S.C.I.* 29 (1975), 473–4.

feel from the days when powerful brotherhoods dominated aspects of pastoral life. Congregations were more female.

Feudalism was abolished and therefore the bishop's old rights vanished. Tithes, though still in part legal, became impossible to collect because tenants refused to pay and no one wished to prosecute them in the courts.

But below the level of vacant sees, the parish system often continued in reasonably good shape. The State ordered reforms which were obvious but which the *ancien régime* could not carry through because it lacked so high a hand.

For many centuries the cathedral of Venice was the church at the eastern tip of the island, San Pietro in Castello. This was absurd, for San Marco was far the most important church in the city of Venice; but San Marco was only the chapel of the now extinct doge. Napoleon's viceroy in north Italy, Eugène de Beauharnais, simply issued an order (1807) moving the cathedral from San Pietro to San Marco; thus bringing San Marco into the diocese and merging the canons of two chapters. The act was politics; it seemed to say, doges have vanished, never to return. In the vacancy of the see the vicar-capitular was ordered to take instant possession. Rome was not asked.

For several years scrupulous clergymen felt unease at this transfer. But if what the State did was sensible, it lasted even if it was the act of revolution.

An old canon or proverb said, 'Sede vacante nihil innovetur', 'While there is no bishop nothing is to be changed.' In all institutions this rule is broken regularly; the Church was no exception.

The State found a diocese of Torcello in the lagoon near Venice with the loveliest of cathedrals but only eleven parishes and thirty churches and most of the clergy living in Venice. It 'persuaded' the chapter of Torcello to hand the diocese to be administered by the Patriarch of Venice. It had far less respect for historic anomalies. It found a diocese of Caorle, with only three parishes, 1,200 people all poor, and a bishop who lived at Venice and only came into his diocese for feasts. The State made things rational by translating the bishop to the see of Chioggia and leaving the see of Caorle vacant, never again to be filled.

The State reduced the excessive numbers of city parishes. The seventy-nine parishes of Venice, for a population of 130,000, were reduced in two stages to thirty parishes, with useless churches declared redundant and then sold or demolished, and other churches made subsidiary churches in a larger parish. Such changes were forced by the abolition of monasteries, for great monastic churches which people loved could not simply be closed but must be converted into parish churches. Some thought this a monstrous devastation, others thought it wise and necessary, and evidently the second opinion was better founded, for many changes survived.

Concerned for the church buildings, a dilapidation caused as much by revolution as by the *ancien régime*, the State in north Italy took an older institution from Austrian Lombardy and extended its use: the *fabbricieri*, officers of the fabric, a committee of two or three who resembled English churchwardens, and administered the funds to maintain buildings and furnish worship. In certain provinces a clergyman might be one of these officers, elsewhere they were laymen. They also survived the revolution.

The *fabbricieri* grew in power and so to be new rivals of the priest. They argued with priests over the right use of money, the choice of sacristan, the cost of furnishing or candles. In one parish where they had unusual authority because the priest was paralysed they quietly chose his successor when he died without asking anyone's leave and saw the appointment cancelled. They were the counter to the clericalizing process which was an indirect and unexpected consequence of the revolution, concealed for the moment by the new access of State power in religion and by the constant interferences of governments in revolutionary states.

The revolution abolished most brotherhoods which were independent corporations of laymen, and so excluded members of the congregation from responsibility. It abolished feudalism, and most of the rights of patronage which feudal lords possessed, and thereby excluded the upper classes from their ancient pressure upon the clergy. In the diocese it continued the process by which the State gained ever more control over the choice of bishops.

The State was taking over slowly the welfare work of the Church, charity, hospitals, education, money-lending at low interest. This process still had a very long way to go. Meanwhile it was leaving the priest to be master inside the church.

In the same way, though the *concursus* was more corrupt, the State filled parishes responsibly. The right of patronage that belonged to former monasteries passed into its hands. It exercised a veto on the choice of parish priests. It had a political attitude, for it wanted reliable men; but also wanted respected men.

If the officers of the State had been Jacobins of the type of Marat or Robespierre this could not have worked. They were not. The leading advisers of the crown in the church affairs of Lombardy and the Legations were not anti-Christian nor anticlerical sansculottes but Italian reformers of the Jansenist tradition, trained in a world of Josephist reform. Giovanni

Bovara started his career in canon law at the university of Pavia and a colleague of professor Tamburini. Under the Empress Maria Theresa he was a member of the *giunta economale* in Milan, the governing committee which reformed Austrian Lombardy, and there held the special responsibility for Church affairs. When Bonaparte created the Italian republic Bovara became the minister of cults and ruled the issue of edicts on Church matters. When Napoleon became King of Italy Bovara filled the same office. Next to him stood Modesto Farina, another canonist from Pavia whose career was much the same, adviser to the Austrians in Italy, then an official of the north-Italian kingdom, finally Bishop of Padua. These were both reformers of the Josephist tradition in their pastoral outlook and their belief in the chance afforded by State control.

The Revolution looked like a clean break with the past. But when the dust subsided, the policy towards the Churches was found to be no break but a continuation of the Josephist and partly the Jansenist ideas of reform, though more extreme because the military State had more power to change what it liked, and because the tumults of the immediate past left an anarchy which needed tidying.

Devotions continued among the people as though Europe experienced neither Enlightenment nor revolutionary war.

In 1801–2 an ex-Jesuit from Bergamo, Luigi Mozzi, led a series of popular missions in the diocese of Treviso. Through the parishes he spread devotion to the stations of the cross, which till then had not reached that region. He was famous for hostility to 'Jansenists' and for devotion to St. Mary. Nearly every parish of that land adopted the stations with solemnity once a month, and an occasional parish reported that its use was 'almost incessant'.[60]

To the rule that brotherhoods were suppressed, an exception was allowed: the Santissimo, the brotherhood of eucharistic devotion. Members attended mass in their insignia at least once a year, often once a month. The brotherhood remained numerous, sometimes 300 or 400 members, though in other parishes even this collapsed and vanished. But it lost its endowments, which were often large, and henceforth existed on modest subscriptions from members. No longer a powerful corporation of laymen out of control of the parish priest, it was turned into a parish organization which helped the parish priest. Its members still chose the objects to which they gave the money which they collected at mass. But they must meet with a policeman present, and not after dark.

[60] *La visita pastorale di Grasser*, 112, 123.

On 31 August 1807 the minister for ecclesiastical affairs for the kingdom of Italy wrote to the viceroy a letter which showed his opinion that the Church would not lose by the measure: 'Abolished and forbidden are the brotherhoods and undisciplined lay societies which under the name of religion introduce frivolity, bigotry and faction. The only brotherhood permitted is that of the Most Holy Sacrament, one in each parish, dependent on the parish priest.'[61]

Priests grew older, and fewer. Often no bishop existed to see after their plight or discipline. Ancient clergymen struggled on in work which they could no longer encompass. Men talked of pensions, or homes for the infirm or the aged. This talk hardly achieved anything.

But in one area apart from jubilation of canons, the Church now grew accustomed to a system of pensions and therefore the possibility of retirement: the ex-monks. An ex-monk drew a pension from the endowments of his former monastery. These pensions were normally mean, that is, they were hardly enough to maintain life. And if the ex-monk took work as curate or schoolmaster, governments were apt to stop his pension on the ground that now he needed no pension. But sometimes an ex-monk kept his pension through a long life of subsequent service to churches or to education; and then he had the chance to retire when he felt infirm because he still had his once-monastic income.[62] Because Father Bonaventura was forced to stop being a Franciscan at the age of twenty-eight he could retire from his parish at the age of sixty-two.

In south Italy King Murat planned a system of pensions. But part of the plan was pay of the clergy by the State, as in France, and in Naples it never worked.

The parish of St. Mary Elizabeth on the Venice Lido was special and sad. The assistant curate Father Pappafava came in 1762 and was made parish priest nine years later and stayed for more than thirty years. The inhabitants were 150, plus for ten months of the year eighty vine-dressers from Friuli. The bishop of 1781 was content with what he saw. By 1805, after turmoil in Venice, everything was dreary, the priest was aged sixty-nine and partly paralysed but had no assistant, catechism suffered, parents took children to the tavern instead of Sunday school. He got a little help for the sick and dying, and priests from Venice for festivals. Sermons were preached only in Lent. He had no mass for the people 'because my situation is most miserable; but I pray for them all'. Only two or three failed to make their Easter duties, but the people, he thought, were addicted to the bottle and to swearing. 'I recommend that something be done for the bad condition of

[61] *La visita pastorale di Pyrker*, xxi ff.   [62] Such a case in Scheglmann, 2.23–4.

this parish, and for my infirmity and lack of help.' Two Armenian priests used to come to help. They came no longer, for he had nothing to give by way of alms.

The visitor of 1805 hardly satisfied the poor old man. He ordered that several ornaments in church be better maintained, and the books properly kept; told the parishioners to respond to their priests' faithfulness and come on Sundays; praised him because under such conditions of health and solitude he kept on ministering the sacraments and because despite the people's unfaithfulness he went on trying to get children and adults to catechism, and told him that he must preach regularly and celebrate a people's mass on Sundays. But the visitor did not, because he could not, get him a pension to retire, or a regular curate.[63]

Most ex-monks found employment as assistant priests, schoolmasters, librarians. Many nuns though far fewer became women helpers in parishes, some still keeping their nun's rule so far as that was possible for a parish worker. But the care of nuns who were too old, or sick, or unfit for the world was a concern for all the Napoleonic states. If they were members of nursing orders or teaching orders they had little difficulty, but continued their old work in a new guise. But where they were members of contemplative orders and felt no vocation to be deaconesses, and could not find a fellow ex-nun to live in a tiny community in the old and godly way, their lot was as dreary as that of any middle-aged woman thrown out of a home with nowhere to go. Therefore governments allowed ex-nunneries to collect ex-nuns who wished to continue a common life.

Here is an example from southern Italy, not tragic but still sad. The town of Campagna had three nunneries, each with nine or ten members; two houses Benedictine, one Franciscan. King Murat's government (November 1810) ordered all nunneries with under twelve nuns to close. Therefore one house of the three was allotted to all nuns who wished to remain. Because the squire's family had an interest in the Franciscans, that house was chosen to survive. Therefore several Benedictine nuns had to live away from their accustomed place, deprived of their own endowments, with dowries lost, forced to share much diminished Franciscan endowments mostly not paid by default of debtors, and urged to keep a strange rule which they neither liked nor understood. The result was misery. 'It was an error', wrote the bishop later 'to unite in a single nunnery nuns of such widely different rules.'[64]

---

[63] *La visita pastorale di Flangini*, 94–5, 268–9.
[64] Lupoli to Ministry of Cults, Naples, 9 Nov. 1821; printed Cestaro. 168 ff.

Napoleon and Spain

French conquest came late to Spain. Spanish troubles did not start in earnest until 1808. After a vain war against the Revolution, the Spanish King Charles IV and his favourite Godoy pursued a policy of subservience to the French. Napoleon had a satellite state without the need to compel. But management by intrigues at court was no substitute for government at a European crisis. The battle of Trafalgar (1805) destroyed the Spanish fleet with the French, and as the reputation of government fell, it became unreliable to Napoleon. A riot at Aranjuez (March 1808), famous because the mob failed to find Godoy hidden under a carpet, overthrew the king in favour of his son Ferdinand VII. Napoleon already had armies in Spain directed at Portugal, took power, and moved his brother Joseph from Naples to be the new French King of Spain.

Wherever Napoleon created satellite states, he confronted Catholics with a double crisis of conscience, touching both patriotism and religion. This crisis afflicted Spaniards with worse anguish than any other of the subject peoples of Europe. The revolutionary persecution of the Church in France had permanent effects in French life and politics and in the European history of Catholicism. The Spanish war of independence against the French touched the people's soul as transformingly. An over-ambitious French general sowed the seeds of terrible division and suffering in Spain. French officers kept private soldiers under strict discipline. The passions roused by an occupying army were not at first due to brigand acts except in rare cases. Such atrocities could not but occur, and as guerrilla warfare grew savage, became by malign nemesis more common. A Franciscan in Castile discovered how his father was shot after refusing to take the oath to King Joseph, took to the hills and became one of the cruellest of guerrilla leaders. A French column passing through the village of Villoviado in the province of Burgos, could not find mules and forced the inhabitants to carry baggage to Lerma. They seized the parish priest, Father Merino, and loaded on him their band, big drum, bugle, cymbals. The priest took to the hills, first as a lone sniper, soon as a guerrilla leader who made all the roads round Burgos unsafe for French detachments and killed prisoners if the French killed rebels.

For this rising against the French was the first rising of a whole people. In the Vendée and Belgium and Calabria and the Abruzzi and the forest cantons of Switzerland peasants rose against the conqueror in social war. But in Spain came a sanfedist war with a new passion. The Spanish were the first to identify social war with patriotic war, the resentment of a conquered nation. The French were not only the oppressors who made their army live off the country, they were overthrowers of shrines and monasteries, assailants of Catholic faith. Napoleon ordered the dissolution of all but a third of the monasteries in 1808, in the following year King Joseph dissolved all monasteries and nunneries, for he needed the money for his new but bankrupt kingdom. Because parish priests or friars were leaders of the common people they were often found at the head of the resistance. Because resistance was most easily roused when the invader demolished a shrine or pillaged a church, the clergy sometimes accepted the lead of a local revolt, sometimes preached or orated so as to rouse rebellion. Centuries before, Spanish unity was forged in crusade against Moslem rulers. That epoch of crusading identified Spanish nationality with Catholicism as nowhere else in Europe, not even in Ireland or Poland.

'The real power in Spain', said the Duke of Wellington, 'is the clergy. They kept the people right against the French.'[65]

In Italy Sanfedist peasants were apt to bless their own arms by turning a friar or priest or (in the most famous case) a cardinal into the commander. In Spain bishops were prominent. Bishop Delgado of Badajoz became for a time president of the supreme junta in Estremadura, one of the numerous local governments which sprang up to resist the invader. That junta ordered all clergy in arms to wear a red cross in cloth on the left side of their tunic. In the Badajoz country bands of guerrillas carried the banners of a crusade. Bishop Martínez Jiménez of Astorga was out on visitation when the invaders came but returned hastily to his see and was made head of the junta for armament and defence until his diocese was overrun; later he suffered deportation from the French. Bishop Menéndez of Santander collected a miserably armed band of 700 men and was made regent of Cantabria but was defeated and fled to England and Portugal. The junta of Asturias made a canon of Oviedo cathedral its minister of justice. Despite many examples to the contrary, feeling hesitated over clergy bearing arms in battle. Many priests therefore helped with the manufacture of arms and ammunition. The cleverest spy behind the French lines besieging Cadiz was a priest.

By cast of mind, Napoleon underestimated the task of conquering Spain, partly because he despised Spanish and Portuguese Catholicism though he knew little about either. 'Believe me', he said to a Spanish canon who was tutor to the deposed King Ferdinand, 'countries where monks are many are easy to conquer.'[66]

Napoleon called the Spanish rising 'an insurrection of monks'. Church-

[65] Carr, *Spain*, 45 (Spanish edn. 57).   [66] Gams, iii.2.428.

men were not so frequently leaders of provincial juntas as these examples might suggest. But the connection between popular war and clerical leadership was sufficiently plain to make atrocities against clergy more common. Warring against a brave guerrilla leader in the pinewoods of the Albarracín mountains. A French officer sacked and destroyed the sanctuary and hospice of Our Lady of Tremedal. Several other magnets of pilgrimage went up in flames amid savage fighting among the hills, even the shrine of Our Lady of Vega, patroness of Salamanca. A guerrilla band took refuge in the Benedictine monastery of Valvanera where was an ancient statue of the Virgin, believed to have come down from heaven and discovered in the hollow of an oak tree, at the foot of which sprang henceforth a stream of healing water, a shrine which was centre for the harvest of Rioja wine in all that region, with a feast where the first-fruits of the grapes were offered before the statue. The punitive force burnt all that shrine and monastery.

The aged Bishop of Coria, who was in his eighties and ill, rose from his bed of sickness, offered his services to the junta of Badajoz, and issued two pastoral letters which rang with Spanish patriotism, urging the young to take up arms and obey their chiefs. A French band from Ciudad Rodrigo surprised him in his refuge at Hoyos, dragged him out of bed, and murdered him with a couple of bullets. He was the only bishop so to suffer.[67]

Bishop Texeiro of Pamplona was a Benedictine of simple life with a narrow background and a career of active unpretentious and generous care for his parishes and clergy. In February 1808 the French army walked into Pamplona. He behaved with perfect courtesy to officers and men. Summoned to Bayonne he refused to go but sent a representative. Required to exhort all his people to obey King Joseph Bonaparte of Spain and expound the new king's virtues, he declined. The governments in Madrid and Navarre tried to insist. He said that he sent out no unnecessary pastoral letters. The diocese was heavily burdened with forced levies on churches and parishes, and by the continual passage of troops. When he retired a few miles from Pamplona, the French turned his palace into a hospital. He went still further away, and could no longer supervise his troubled parishes. They took all his tithes and left him destitute. He kept protesting, said to collectors of money that he had nothing left, expostulated against the decree allowing monks and friars to leave their monasteries, and against the abolition of the Inquisition, and against the use of Church money for secular ends. Invited by the governor to sing *Te Deum*

[67] *D.H.E.E.* s.v. 'Santuarios' and 'Coria'.

for victories over the rebels he refused to go. The general ordered him to come to Madrid with representatives of chapters and monasteries and swear allegiance. He said that chapters and monks were not his affair, and that he was too old and ill. Warned that this was dangerous he fled, 'so as not to prostitute himself', he said, 'by obeying the orders of the most abominable of tyrants'. He left faculties for deputies to act in his place, and took refuge with the Bishop of Lerida. When the Spanish troops retreated, both bishops fled, eventually to Majorca.[68]

As in Italy, pastoral authority fell into confusion. Bishops vanished or died and could not be replaced. By 1813 a majority of Spanish dioceses had no bishop. The rule that in a bishop's absence the chapter should act became very important. King Joseph tried to put six bishops into sees, three of which were vacant because he expelled the occupants, but clergy and people were hardly willing to accept King Joseph's bishops as real.

Only a majority of the bishops were in exile because the French could not tolerate their resistance. One was in exile because he was a friend of the French and the Spanish resistance could not tolerate him, and others went into exile because they could not bear the politics of the Spanish government of the resistance.

The *afrancesados*

A satellite state, as we have seen it in Italy or Switzerland, attempted to win the affections of its people by good government, by holding up ideals of liberty and equality, by sweeping away the petty tyrannies of the *ancien régime* with its archaic structure, by demolishing feudalism and the exemptions of clergy and the excess of Church wealth, by introducing an efficient system of courts of justice, and a code of law which would be enforced. The new King Joseph of Spain tried to govern humanely when in Naples and now tried to govern humanely in Spain. The *ancien régime* was not so popular with intelligent men that these ideals could fail to command widespread assent and bring leading members of the conquered peoples, like Melzi in north Italy, to collaborate with the French as the way to better government and a more just society. Such men had the first motive of collaborators, that the conqueror's force was overwhelming and resistance could lead to untold suffering. At the time the Spanish resistance called them simply by the name *traitors*. History gave them the name *afrancesados*, the Frenchified; and the name is justified because some of them were men of high intelligence and patriotism who believed that a

[68] *Hispania Sacra*, 19 (1966), 7 ff.

Frenchified Spain, in the reigning circumstances of power, was a better and happier Spain than any other which they could imagine.

The *afrancesados* remained a small but not contemptible minority. A few of them were worthless, for example the Benedictine of Asturias who told the French where guerrillas hid dumps of treasure and asked for a canonry as reward, or the priest of Palencia who said that he was tired of being a priest and asked the French to make him a police officer. 'I would like to shed my clerical garb if this were possible. I would prefer anything to the choir and the breviaries.' Monks who mistook their vocation were not displeased when the French abolished monks. But other *afrancesados* had higher and sometimes patriotic reasons for taking the French side. Even intelligent opponents of the French were occasionally sorry to see them in retreat. A canon of Zamora told a passing Frenchman that though he suffered from the occupation he was sorry that they were going. 'A restoration awaits us and I fear it.'

The most interesting of the *afrancesado* clergy was Juan Antonio Llorente (1756–1823). A canon of Calahorra, the French Revolution found him Secretary General of the Inquisition in Madrid, as a result of which the reforming grand inquisitor gave him important materials for a history of the Inquisition. In the events of 1808 he accepted King Joseph Bonaparte and entered Madrid in his train. As one of the few Spanish churchmen to be serviceable, he was now heaped with honours and responsible work, especially the dissolution of the monasteries and the administration of confiscated goods, as well as the custody of the archives of the Inquisition. He used the time to gather materials for his history. Naturally he must retreat with the French and spent ten years in exile until the Spanish government gave him a reprieve. In 1817–18 he published at Paris in four volumes his *Critical History of the Spanish Inquisition*, which scandalized many Spaniards and finally gave the Spanish Inquisition the blasted reputation which it kept. The *History* was instantly put upon the Index of prohibited books. The account was not impartial history. But it was the only account hitherto by anyone who had access to authentic documents and therefore held the field as indispensable. In the perspective of Church history, and the reputation of Spanish Catholicism for bigotry and fanaticism, Llorente's book was the most weighty single outcome of the little *afrancesado* movement among Churchmen.

The Cortes at Cadiz

Meanwhile the gulf between the Spanish guerrillas and their own supreme government began to widen into a chasm in Spanish opinion over Church as well as State.

The various juntas in the provinces accepted, though with difficulty, a supreme Junta for all Spain, and then a parliamentary assembly, called by the revived name of Cortes, at Cadiz. King Ferdinand for whom they fought was a prisoner in France. In Cadiz gathered some of the best men in Spain.

Spanish guerrillas in the mountains fought for king and Church, usually without knowing anything about the king. The members of the Cortes knew a lot. A majority of them saw the chance to reform the *ancien régime*. This desire for a constitutional monarchy, and for liberal legislation, was hopelessly out of touch with the mood prevailing among the fighting bands of the mountains. But it became very important in the future history of Spain.

At first they governed only the city of Cadiz where they met. They were encouraged to legislate because they ruled so tiny a kingdom that their laws could be effective. They had two political pressures pushing them towards liberal acts. The French, who occupied most of Spain, claimed that they brought justice, equality, liberty. The Cadiz government could not be seen to be more oppressive. Spaniards also must stand for justice and equality. Moreover their only ally was the British government, upon whom they depended for food and arms. The British had no desire to be seen to prop up either tyranny or revolution and used their influence to support those in the Cortes who wanted moderate liberal laws. But many members of the Cortes, clerical or lay, did not need these pressures of French or British to act liberally. They were themselves resolute to use the chance of reform.

They had one driving motive for not acting too conservatively towards the Catholic Church. King Joseph Bonaparte could not survive as government without taking the wealth of the Church. The Cadiz Cortes was far poorer. Without Church money it could not carry on war.

The Cortes at Cadiz was as determined as Joseph Bonaparte that Catholicism was the religion of Spain and that any Spanish government must undertake to uphold that faith. But the Cortes declared national sovereignty to reside in the representative assembly instead of the king; sanctioned freedom of the press while reserving religious publications to the censorship of the Church; agreed the Constitution of 1812, which became a model for some advanced liberal parties of the nineteenth century; clashed finally with the Church, or at least with most of the bishops and much public opinion, by abolishing the Inquisition; abolished the Voto de Santiago, a general tax which supported the archbishop, chapter and hospital of the old goal of European pilgrimage, Santiago de Compostella; and restricted the number of damaged or destroyed monasteries which could be re-established. It banned houses of fewer than twelve members, allowed only one community of an order in any town, and forbade new foundations or novices until a future settlement.[69] The liberal majority of the Cadiz Cortes was thus in line with the Catholic reforming movement of the eighteenth century which was still assailed as 'Jansenist'.

Of these decrees the abolition of the Inquisition was the most unpopular in the Spanish Church. The Bishop of Santander, that former commander now in refuge in the north-west, threatened to excommunicate anyone who read the decree. Even the chapter of Cadiz refused to read the decree and four of its members were expelled the city. The Archbishop of Santiago disappeared from his see to avoid obeying the Cortes. The Spanish Inquisition, which after Llorente was to stink in European memory, was a symbol to devout Spaniards of the purity of their Catholicism, a protection against French ideas that led to revolution and the killing or ousting of kings. Even that Irish Protestant the Duke of Wellington, commanding the British army in Spain, doubted the wisdom of destroying the Inquisition.[70]

The Cortes of Cadiz was not in the least an irreligious body, though afterwards it was accused of irreligion. It heard mass daily, had several clergymen among its principal speakers and drafters, was determined to have Catholicism as the only religion of Spain, identified its faith with its patriotic duty, and upon the façade of its new meeting-hall erected the three statues of Religion, Fatherland, and Liberty.

Chief among the prelates who took part in the Cortes and accepted the liberal constitution was the Archbishop of Toledo. He was the son of that Cardinal of Bourbon who was made cardinal as a boy and the administrator of both the sees of Toledo and Seville. Despite his father's marriage, which the court disapproved, he rose rapidly, especially because his elder sister married the prime minister and favourite Godoy. Though not quite so young in his preferments he followed his father's career, becoming in 1799–1800, at the age of twenty-two and twenty-three, administrator of the sees of Seville and Toledo and a cardinal. A quiet and affable man, he at first exchanged friendly letters with King Joseph Bonaparte; but as war came, he threw in his lot with the Spanish rebels, supported them with munificent sums of money, and was made president of the Council of the Regency. During the Cortes he took a moderate and conciliatory place

[69] Lovett, 2.480   [70] Wellington, *Dispatches* (1838), 10.474.

between the parties, forcing the papal nuncio Gravina into exile, approving the liberal constitution, and being content, during the imprisonment of the Pope, to act on his own authority in dispensing. When King Ferdinand came into his own Cardinal Bourbon resigned the see of Seville and found himself confined at Toledo. He was one of the last appearances of the old Spanish grandee world, instinctively liberal, not specially devoted to the Pope, liking the State to be strong in the Church, and not disturbing his course of action by religious zeal.

But the Cortes was not representative of real Spain. Wellington once compared its acts to an artist painting a picture, who worked away at his art without any need to conform to the real world. The more land was freed from the French, the more conservative the complexion of the Cortes. The armies of the mountains cared nothing about constitutions or liberty of the press. They fought for the banners of Church and king, for an unknown exiled Ferdinand, for their shrines and fields. As the conservative forces grew in strength, the liberals at Cadiz became wilder and more grasping of their fading power. They felt the force of the bishops and clergy against them, and in this vanishing phase took those measures which gave them later repute as anticlerical. But their existence and activity were made possible by the king's exile. They could not survive more than a few weeks when on 22 March 1814 Ferdinand crossed the Pyrenees frontier and was again the lawful King of Spain.

Circumstances identified the peasant reaction, visible all across Europe against the French, with the return of a Bourbon monarch who was not in the least sacred but acquired a halo of sanctity as focus and symbol of all for which Spaniards fought and suffered. In Spain at least, Catholicism must enter the nineteenth century identified with the political right, and in an extreme form.

8

RESTORATION

IN 1814 Napoleon was overthrown and exiled to Elba, the Pope returned to Rome, Catholic kings returned to Paris and Madrid and Naples and Turin, exiled bishops or priests poured back into their homelands. For a hundred days of 1815 Napoleon returned to France and the French king fled again from Paris and the Pope fled again, this time to Genoa.

The decline of Catholic political power

In the air was the feeling of Restoration, of a return to a due order and right which existed before the Revolution. But the Catholic Church of 1815 could not resemble the Catholic Church of twenty years before.

Napoleon was overthrown by the armies of Prussia, Russia, Austria, and Britain. Of these victor powers only one was Catholic.

The first change in the place of the Catholic Church was the failure to make good the political losses of the revolutionary years. The balance of power shifted.

Before the Revolution the great powers of Europe were Britain, France, Austria, and Spain with its vast overseas empire in the Americas: three Catholic powers and one Protestant. In addition Poland was a Catholic country, the southern Netherlands (Belgium) was ruled by Catholic Austria, much of the Rhineland was ruled by Catholic archbishops, and Portugal had another vast overseas empire.

Now the great powers were Britain, Austria, Prussia, and Russia; one Catholic power to three non-Catholic. France lay defeated and weak; Spain lost its empire and was a power no longer; Prussia, already formidable in the eighteenth century, gained vastly by its new lands in west Germany; Russia, already formidable in the eighteenth century, entered Europe; Britain won a new empire. Poland ceased to exist, and a majority of Poles lived under non-Catholic rulers; the southern Netherlands (Belgium) was placed under the Protestant king of Holland; the Rhineland archbishops lost their secular princedoms and were nothing but archbishops. And across the ocean a new power, the United States, Protestant in feeling and in its leaders, ceased to be negligible.

Nobody won the wars of religion in the seventeenth century. Those wars left Europe divided, about equally, between Protestant forces and Catholic forces, each too strong to be destroyed by the other. Without meaning to end the Counter-Reformation, Napoleon overthrew the settlement inherited from the wars of religion and left a new Europe in which Protestants were politically far stronger than Catholics. Popes were less weighty to the cabinets because decisions taken in Berlin or Moscow now did more among the nations than decisions taken in Madrid.

Metternich

The statesmen and kings who handled religious restoration most intelligently were Catholics with a touch of that detached scepticism or criticism learnt in the Catholic Enlightenment of the eighteenth century—Metternich, Cardinal Consalvi, King Louis XVIII of France who did all he could to restrain ultras. Where a political leader believed passionately in the union of throne and altar, and threw himself into religion as a political as well as a religious act, it was a sure recipe for calamity. King Ferdinand VII of Spain was one, King Charles X who (1824) succeeded Louis XVIII on the throne of France, was another. When Charles was crowned at Rheims cathedral, post-revolutionary France was astonished and not edified to hear that all the medieval rites were revived, anointings, prostrations like an ordinand. It looked like, and was, an anachronism, a conscious return to the age of St. Louis, a medievalism which only raised contempt among the French bourgeois.

Europe turned the Austrian chancellor Metternich into a symbol of that age. He was not one of those dangerous romantics who fancied that they could conjure a vanished past. He was impresario at Vienna when the successful peace of 1814–15 was drafted; then helped to design the Holy Alliance (Austria, Russia, Prussia) which agreed on an international authority to suppress revolution and prevent anarchy, but which both Britain and the Pope refused to join formally; presided over the maintenance of the Vienna settlement in divided Italy, helping to suppress revolutions in Naples and the Papal States.

The kings reconstructed Europe to assure peace and prevent more revolutionary war. Catholic leaders wanted to use the occasion to seek to construct, rather than reconstruct, a more Christian society.

Inevitably their idea of a Christian society took nearly all its content from the political right. They reacted against revolution, therefore against every Catholic who co-operated with revolution. New bishops (so few bishops survived that most bishops were new) were chosen from men who resisted revolution. This principle excluded most middle-aged clergymen. A bishop must be either so old that he had been driven out by revolution, or so young that he had not had to face compromise with revolution. Only old men or young men could be elected. To be against democracy was almost compulsory, to be against constitutional government was fashionable. That Pope Pius VII himself, when Cardinal Chiaramonti, preached harmony between Christianity and liberty, was concealed. The central idea of reconstruction was that of order; a just society, made just by a Catholic ruler with power, advised by popes and bishops whose advice needed to be taken because their privileges within the State were restored. Nothing was worse than social disorder.

Metternich was a rational upper-class Catholic of the eighteenth century. He went to mass regularly, especially later in life, fulfilled his religious duties precisely, read his Bible in Luther's translation, and for a man of his calling was well read in theology. But he had no enthusiasm, despised devout Catholics in the religious revival as obscurantist, shared none of that spirit which later came to be known as political romanticism, regretted new high-flown theorists of papal power, disliked Catholics who wished to marry their faith to liberalism but hated political-Catholic extremists, regarded all mystics as fanatics, and shared not at all in the theory *Of the Necessity of a Theological Foundation for the Idea of the State*. This last was the title of a book of 1820 by the Austrian philosopher Adam Müller, who was a leading theorist of 'political romanticism' and taught that the external unity of society rested upon the inner unity of faith.

Nevertheless Metternich also believed the Catholic Church to be the cement of society. Protestantism he identified with anarchy, Catholicism with order. Though he distrusted Jesuits, he ruefully admired their founder and his organization as the key to stability; order, discipline, obedience. Slowly Metternich came to take a religious view of his vocation, to be protector of order in Europe, an 'apostle' to conserve the better traditions of the past, at times even an instrument of God for these purposes. Society was a pyramid from Emperor to peasant, the Church was a pyramid from Pope to simple worshipper. Catholic religion was the surest defence of a state against anarchy.

In his outlook was a contradiction which he never quite succeeded in reconciling. As a man of the eighteenth century he inherited the Josephist tradition. The general seminaries had disappeared, but government still maintained controls over Church affairs and communications with Rome.

Metternich was no man to abandon these controls which he thought to be necessary to good government. Yet he lived and ruled in a Catholic age where more men resented these controls, and associated them with Jansenism, and suspected Jansenism of contributing to the weakness of the Church in the Revolution. Metternich wanted Catholicism as the bond of the State, and much of the Catholicism round him was no longer Josephist in its ideas. From about 1830 he slowly turned away from the Josephist tradition. But he never abandoned it, and all his life the contradiction remained.

This political calculator wished to avoid extremism of every sort. Therefore he needed despots who behaved more moderately than the despots in Naples or Madrid were capable of behaving. He wanted the cardinals to elect moderate Popes—not liberal Popes, which he fancied an impossibility, but Popes who exercised supreme power with discretion. The veto at papal elections still existed and was used. But like his predecessors Metternich hated to use it, and therefore could not stop Popes being elected who had more zeal than he liked.

He was at last a dilettante, who saw his only duty as the need to protect the past, and had nothing creative in his soul. He had much common sense, but no passion, little energy, and no imagination. The Roman Catholic world after the Revolution was full of passion, which he could not understand. He was complacent, and never realized how he outlived both the Europe of his past and the Church which he needed.

The age of the Concordats

The word *Restoration* bore only a very partial truth in the Roman Catholic Church.

First, no Holy Roman Empire remembered the heritage of Catholic Christendom. No Holy Roman Empire protected prince-bishops and abbeys in Germany. The secularization of 1803 was never undone. Physically and politically the Catholic Church of Germany was far weaker. Germany could now be seen to be in majority a powerful Protestant country. Pope Pius VII and other Catholic leaders wanted the prince-bishops to live again, but had no eagerness in this desire, and saw that to remake them was impossible.

Secondly, the old privileges which the Church possessed and which Josephists and Jansenists tried to whittle away, were now gone. Few tried to revive the rights of sanctuary. Exemptions where they remained were much less important. Church lands and property retained or recovered charitable status, but were liable to large levies for national purposes.

Jansenism was dead, or looked as though it was dead. But Josephism was not. In Austria the State continued to exercise the controls on which Joseph II had insisted. And the Revolution had made it easier for other states to acquire further control. By stopping the work of the Roman Curia governments stepped into its place. When the Roman Curia was revived, it found itself negotiating with every Catholic government in the effort to get back a minimum of its old rights. The first decades after 1815 saw not the reversal of the State controls sought by the eighteenth century but their expansion.

It was called the *Age of Concordats*; agreements between Rome and a government, including the redesigning of dioceses, the admission that the Church had endowments and freedom, the contrary admission that the State had controls; Concordat with Austria attempted but failing, Concordat with France attempted and agreed but at last failing, Concordat with Bavaria 1817, Concordat with Naples 1818, Concordat with Hanover attempted but failing, Concordat (though not so called) with Prussia in 1821. Though this is called the Age of the Concordats, few Concordats were actually agreed; the reorganization mostly went on by piecemeal agreements.

Whether the agreements were enshrined in a general Concordat or a series of smaller measures, they marked a general increase of State control.

Let us take the 1818 Concordat with Naples.

All the immunities were abolished—sanctuary, benefit of clergy, clergymen were not even exempted from conscription. Divorce and Church offences were left under Church courts but heresy(!), polygamy, sacrilege came into secular courts. Bishops' prisons were abolished but bishops might still send delinquent clergy to monasteries. The Church recognized that land alienated during the Revolution was alienated for ever, and that ex-monks who drew pensions and had no desire to return to monasteries should be left in peace with their pensions.

The State agreed to restore all property that had not been alienated and entrusted the resulting fund to a commission part ecclesiastical and part State. It was agreed (conservatively but foolishly) that every diocese should have a seminary. The laws on mortmain were abolished—the State hardly needed them since far less land belonged to the Church. Anyone who had a certificate from his provincial government might be ordained—the State hardly needed to control numbers of ordinations because they were now fewer. Article 28 allowed the crown to nominate *all* bishops. The chapters (where restored) were appointed by Pope or bishop but on the recommendation or sanction of government. Bishops appointed parish priests.[1]

Steadily the states' rights to choose bishops was further recognized. In 1829 Pope Pius VIII, considering the Duke of Modena's work to improve endowments, allowed him henceforth to choose bishops and canons.[2] The plea was precisely the same as in proprietary churches of the early Middle Ages. Endowments vanished in the Revolution. In return for getting some of them back, governments asked for the right of appointment.

They did more than ask to appoint bishops. They kept insisting. Austria acquired the old prince-bishopric of Salzburg. The Emperor insisted that he choose the archbishop, and the bishop in the Tyrol. Rome argued for two years but gave way. The Emperor insisted that he appoint the bishops to the Austrian possessions in north Italy. Rome argued longer and louder, but ended by giving way. In consequence nearly all the bishops of north Italy now had German as their native tongue.

The Bavarian Concordat makes another example. This was quickly (24 October 1817) agreed with Rome. It conceded to Rome many important rights, the freedom of bishops to communicate with Rome, the security of endowments, the reopening and re-endowment of certain monasteries, a seminary in each diocese, wide rights in education, and strong rights for bishops in censoring books. Protestant Germany regarded this Concordat as a calamity, a return to 'medieval' privileges for the Church. Catholic enthusiasts saw it as a triumph. Certainly it was a sign of friendlier attitudes towards Rome during the age of Restoration.

But the government of Bavaria gained compensations. It won from Rome an archbishopric at the capital Munich, to which the historic see of Freising was transferred; the right to nominate to bishoprics and prebends —a weighty compensation because this royal right had no justification from the past; and the recognition that the lands alienated in the secularization were alienated for ever.

Rome silently accepted the toleration accorded to the now large Protestant population in Bavaria.

Rome under Pius VII and Cardinal Consalvi was right to concede. It was a paradox. State power in religion was suspect if not disreputable; for it was thought to be part of that structure of *ancien régime* which led towards revolution. Catholic clergymen, or many of them, distrusted State power more in 1816 than in 1789. Yet the age of Restoration saw State power in continuous growth.

The reason was simple. A revived Pope saw all about him a devastated

---

[1] Maturi, *Il Concordato del 1818*, 137–58.   [2] *Bull. Cont.* 18, no. 36.

Church—empty sees, obsolete dioceses, closed monasteries, lost endowments, maimed chapters, few seminaries. The Church could only be rebuilt with the aid and consent of friendly governments. These governments, however friendly, exacted large payments for their services.

Whether the government was Catholic or Protestant hardly mattered. Many cardinals doubted whether a Concordat with a Protestant sovereign could ever be right. In return for his services the Protestant Prussian king claimed to choose Catholic bishops. Rome refused, and then (1821) allowed him a veto on the choice by chapters. Unpalatable necessity forced him if the devastated churches were to recover. Protestant king or no, two-fifths of his subjects, Poles and Rhinelanders, were now Catholics.

Suddenly the Prussian ambassador in Rome was weightier. From 1815 he was the historian Niebuhr, a learned, fair-minded, and tolerant Protestant, who fancied the papacy to be dying but respected Pius VII; and who (1819) was allowed to hold regular Protestant worship at the Prussian embassy—the first Protestant service to be permitted within the Papal States, unthinkable thirty years earlier.

Catholics growing more hostile to State interference in the Church, states gaining of necessity more rights to interfere—this contrast was a seed of the ultramontane movement of the nineteenth century.

Spain and the reaction

Girondins and Jacobins in Paris, and later the Directory, gave the world the conviction that revolution went hand in hand with irreligion and so religion was part of a right social order.

Experience of revolution made for extremism. The children of revolution were not by temperament moderates.

To see Catholic reaction in an extreme form it is necessary to look to Spain.

King Ferdinand VII was a worthless man with no idea how to rule. He returned to head the most undiscriminating political reaction in all Europe. His agents hunted down not only Spanish allies of the French invader, which was to be expected after such savage fighting, but Spaniards who had stood at the core of resistance to the French, and whose crime consisted in their service to the liberal majority in the Cortes of Cadiz during the war. In Majorca's rejoicings at the Restoration, festivities which lasted for months, Father Ferrer went through the streets in a cart on which he mounted a brazier and a dustbin, and at the head of a mob raided the bookshelves in the houses of liberals.[3] The mood was like that of liberated France in 1944, as it murdered or shaved the heads of those accused of co-operating with Germans.

The new-found hopes of Catholic leaders rested upon sentiments deeper than a temporary reaction of politics. The Revolution showed that the Church was too strong to be overthrown because it had the backing of the masses. The memory of the Sanfedists was alive, and remained potent all the nineteenth century. This feeling slowly altered the links between churchmen and society. Under the *ancien régime* the work of Pope and cardinals consisted in getting comfortable with the crowned heads of Europe. That work continued unceasingly. But now it had a new outlook; which came from the doubt whether getting on with the mass of the faithful was more important than negotiating with princes, and whether the princes were now so necessary to fruitful work by the Church. Already we see the first signs that a Pope might think it possible to appeal to the people against their masters; which was an attitude not to be reconciled in the long run with the doctrines of altar-and-throne. In the short run it encouraged Catholic leaders to be more reactionary because their peasants resented not only the devastations but the middle-class governments of the revolutionary years, and longed for king and Church. 'Black Spain' triumphed as a political reaction in 1814–15 on a popular wave of emotion which Italy would have called Sanfedism. King Ferdinand VII, though less attractive and less competent and more vindictive than Cardinal Ruffo the Sanfedist generalissimo, resembled Ruffo in being seen by peasants as a commander for the army of the true faith.

A majority of churchmen—how large a majority is not certain—supported Ferdinand, who believed that he needed and used the Church to keep his people in proper subjection. Rafael de Vélez, guardian-general of the Capuchins in Andalusia, was made Bishop of Ceuta, and published at Madrid (1818) *The Apology for Altar and Throne*. This book made vocal all the perfervid mood of Catholic politics on the right wing, and stands close to the origins of that reactionary tradition of Spanish politics which was powerful for the next century and a half.

Ferdinand revived the Inquisition. The liberal Cortes of Cadiz abolished the Inquisition, its deeds were null, the court must be restored. Moreover the Spanish people, contrary to a common opinion, had in majority liked to have an Inquisition as the protector of their faith and safety. During the last years before the Revolution its power grew almost nominal. Therefore, just as Rome restored Jesuits not because it needed Jesuits for practical

[3] Herrero, 396–7.

purposes but for the sake of undoing the past, Ferdinand restored the Inquisition to symbolize the repudiation of the immediate past, especially of the Cortes of Cadiz. So far as the revival had a conscious purpose, it was less doctrinal and more political than the old court. The menace now was believed to be the political radical, not the Jansenist, though an author like Vélez used the word Jansenist as though it meant revolutionary.

The *concursus* in the diocese of Toledo, held in the archbishop's palace in the autumn of 1825, shows a change. The outer appearance was much the same as thirty years before, the form of examination, the kind of examiner, the sort of question set. The parishes to be filled were more numerous. The number of applicants was fewer, about half the number which appeared at a big *concursus* of the same archdiocese in the middle of the eighteenth century. But the most interesting feature of the records lies in the references. These are like the past in containing recommendations about the work in the previous parish, or praise of excellent character, or occasionally a warning that the applicant's life had been scandalous. What was added, in most cases, was the political record, 'a warm defender of Altar and Throne', or 'passionate for the sovereignty of His Majesty'. Sometimes it stood on the record that they helped refugees to escape. Others had an opposite past association in some way with the liberal government, even to serving in its militia. The documents of this *concursus* show that the Church of Spain was less unanimous than historians fancied. Nearly two-thirds of the clergy were regarded as reliable, about one-third were associated at least a little with the opposition to the king's government. When Altar and Throne were said to be united, that did not mean that all who ministered at the altar were likely to prop up the throne. Yet the *concursus* also shows, by the nature of the references of the candidates, that a clergyman was much more likely to be preferred if his politics were reliable.[4]

The secret articles of Verona (1822)

In 1820 an army *coup* drove out Ferdinand's ministry, forced a constitution, abolished the Inquisition. The powers of the Holy Alliance met in the Congress of Verona (1822) and decided that French armies should overthrow the army commanders with their constitution and put Ferdinand back in absolute power. This Congress is usually taken to mark the high point of political reaction after the fall of Napoleon.

To the public agreement made at Verona, secret articles were alleged

[4] A. Martínez de Velasco Farinós, 'Estudio del Clero Toledano a través del concurso parroquial de 1825', in *Hispania Sacra*, 25 (1972), 453 ff.

to be added. According to this allegation, the four Powers (Russia, Prussia, Austria, France) bound themselves to suppress representative governments in Europe, and liberty of the press as its instrument. Then the third secret article ran:

Convinced that the principles of religion contribute most powerfully to maintain nations in that state of passive obedience which they owe to their princes, they declare they intend to sustain such measures as the clergy may adopt for the strengthening of their interests, intimately associated as they are with the authority of princes. They offer their common thanks to the Pope for all that he has already done for them, and solicit his continual co-operation with their views for keeping the nations in due obedience.

No one who has followed this history so far will find these secret articles credible.

They were later alleged to be taken from a document of the French government found during or after the French revolution of 1848. They appeared in books of documents edited by American and other historians, even in a standard volume published in 1973, and were held to account for American determination that Europe should never re-establish Spanish or Portuguese empires in the new republics of South and Central America. Chateaubriand, who was supposed to have signed the secret articles on behalf of the French Government, was asked about them during the 1840s and said that they were a clumsy parody.[5] Historians or politicians who wanted to believe the articles genuine could assume that it was Chateaubriand's interest to deny.

The secret articles were a fabrication, probably by an English observer of Spain. English liberals watched with horror as French armies moved to suppress the Spanish constitution during the spring of 1823. On 11 June 1823 an anonymous correspondent communicated to the *Morning Chronicle* the text of secret articles signed at Verona. At first officials refused to take it seriously.

Nevertheless the forged articles of Verona show the extraordinary change in atmosphere caused by revolution and then reaction. Pope Pius VII was still on his throne, Cardinal Consalvi his secretary of state. The Pope was a gentle pragmatist, no reactionary; the secretary of state very conservative, but sensible.

That these secret articles should be forged in the service of Spanish liberals was important. Spain did more than any other country to associate

---

[5] T. R. Schellenberg, *Journal of Modern History*, 7 (1935), 280–91; cf. Colletta, *Kingdom of Naples*, 2.462.

Catholic leadership with the extreme right. In Spain the clergy and monks stood dominantly for the king and his absolute rule. To the Spanish king Rome committed itself more openly than to any other sovereign.

The forger wished to have his forgery accepted, and not as a skit. Yet he was rash. He dared to make a Protestant King of Prussia and an Orthodox Tsar of Russia thank the Pope for his services in keeping people in order; and to put into the draft of four hard-headed representatives the sentence, 'the principles of religion contribute most powerfully to maintain nations in that state of passive obedience which they owe to their princes.' Nevertheless, he partly succeeded in having his forgery accepted. Men will believe in documents if the documents conform to their later expectation of what happened at the time.

The forger had his unlooked for success persuading Protestant historians who assumed that Pope, Holy Alliance, Metternich, even Chateaubriand, were all identified with extreme reaction. But he also persuaded some historians in Catholic countries that the secret articles of Verona were genuine and credible. For they were not so far away from the theorists of a new and more extreme Catholicism derived from the mentality of émigrés who fled the revolution. Bonald reflected soon after the battle of Waterloo: 'Formerly we thought religion something a man needs. Now the time has come to see it as something society needs.'[6]

A contrast between Spain and Italy will help an understanding of the predicament of Catholicism in the earlier nineteenth century.

French occupation flooded Italy and Spain, two deeply Catholic countries, with the ideals of equality, toleration, freedom of religion, representative government. When the French were ejected, they left behind a country divided between those who identified these ideals with justice and modernity, and those who associated them with illegality or foreign conquest—and with every shade of opinion between. But in Italy the ideals began to be associated with national freedom against Austrians, an association which made the power in the Italian Risorgimento. Most Italian Catholics stood against Austria. Therefore the Italian Risorgimento, despite the anti-Catholicism of its most articulate mouthpiece Mazzini and of its most brilliant *condottiere* Garibaldi, was never in itself anti-Catholic. Italy divided over the Pope's temporal sovereignty, not over the Pope's religion.

No Austrian threat united the Spanish. Their ideals were associated with national freedom against the French who taught them those ideals. But

[6] Bonald, *Pensées diverses*, in *Oeuvres* (1818), 6.294.

after 1815 no outside force united Spain as Metternich brought together so many Italians. The country was poorer and simpler. Therefore liberals who wanted new laws must be more violent in the face of peasant conservatism, and conservatives were more violent in representing liberals. The country divided, as never in Italy, with the Church more than half identified with the side of absolute government and resistance to liberal modernity.

Then, by a calamity of Spanish history, the king's succession was disputed and a civil war (1833) ensued. The civil war was nothing to do with Catholic faith, it had to happen, given the constitutional circumstances. But because the chief social gulf in the Spanish people lay between conservative peasants and liberal middle class, the civil war adopted the social and religious outlooks as rival slogans, and further stamped into the Spanish mind the identity of religion with political conservatism. And since the Carlists lost the civil war, the Church was identified by many liberals, not only with conservatism but with disloyalty to a lawful liberal regime.

Revolution in Spanish America

Meanwhile King Ferdinand had revolution on his hands in the empire overseas.

The Spanish American republics were in revolt. But by the end of 1815 it looked as though the rebellions failed; all countries submitted except La Plata (Argentina), which negotiated for peace. The Pope and his secretary of state Cardinal Consalvi believed that these American revolutions were an appendix to the European Revolution, and that their collapse must follow the fall of Napoleon. At the request of the Spanish ambassador in Rome Vargas, Cardinal Consalvi quickly drafted the brief, *Etsilongissimo*, which called upon the American bishops to exhort their subjects to submit to the most pious and Catholic King Ferdinand VII of Spain, and encouraged them as the Pope wrote, 'to eradicate the damnable weeds of sedition'.[7]

The atmosphere of the age of Restoration thus led the Pope and Consalvi to act with unwise haste. By misjudgement they backed the losing side in war. Nothing in doctrine or the political traditions of the Roman see insisted that the Pope should always support a Catholic king against his peoples when they rebelled. This very Pope abandoned the 'legitimate' successors of Louis XVI of France to crown Napoleon. Catholic doctrine declared that men must obey their rulers; that for tyranny rulers ceased to claim allegiance and might be overthrown; that a revolutionary govern-

[7] Tet in P. Leturia, *Relaciones*, 2.107.

ment which became acceptable to the people also became a government which the Church recognized. All these conditions were fulfilled in time with the Spanish American republics and the papacy soon accepted what had happened. As early as five years after this encyclical Pius VII and Consalvi quietly amended their attitude in the face of reality. But in January 1816, only three months after Napoleon was dumped upon the island of St. Helena a prisoner for life, Consalvi was deceived, not seeing the weakness of Spain devastated by war and civil strife, nor the interest of the United States in democratic republics further south, nor the interests of the British in South American trade. *Etsi longissimo* was not the summit of papal reaction in the age of Metternich. It was a misjudgement about the facts by an intelligent secretary of state.

Pope Leo XII came to the tiara just when Ferdinand VII was restored by the French in 1823, and was by instinct more uncompromising than his predecessor Pius VII and his secretary of state. Cardinal Consalvi left him the opinion that they had given Spain long enough to re-establish control of the former Spanish colonies, and that Madrid must soon recognize independence and allow Rome to make friendly links with the rebels.

Pope Leo seems to have thought absolute government the true Christian theory of the State, and had a horror (excusable after earlier experiences in France and Germany) of popular revolutionary governments. Yet he started by a friendly letter to Bishop Lasso of Mérida, who supported the rebel regime; and in the cathedral at Bogota this letter was read and celebrated with peals of bells. General Bolívar told Lasso (letter of 10 November 1824) that the Pope's letter showed the spirit of St. Peter and of Jesus Christ. Two months before Bolívar so praised the Pope, Leo sent out an encyclical (24 September 1824) to the American bishops which was also for a time alleged to be forged. It condemned the acts of rebel governments against the Church, warned against secret societies, and asked them to praise the piety of Ferdinand VII and to put forward to their flocks the example of the Spaniards in Europe. This encyclical had the same ill effects as the bull of 1816.

By the end of that year 1824 Bolívar finally destroyed all chance of Spanish restoration in South America. Henceforth Rome steadily moved towards recognition. In 1827 Leo began the process of filling South American bishoprics, beginning with the archbishopric of Bogotá, and cheerfully endured the discontent of Madrid. Events were too strong; or the needs of Catholic people always in the end took precedence of the principle of legitimism, even at a moment when legitimism was thought to be of moral obligation for a Catholic; or, as in the eighteenth century, the threat of grave schism was enough to force Rome to weaken its principle—for Bolívar at one time worked under the influence of a Jansenist Monsignor de Pradt, who wanted to take no notice whatever of the authority of Rome and go forward into an independent Church with a local patriarch.

Reaction in Italy

The whole Church suffered from a grievous shock to its assurance. In the years of terror in France and Belgium it endured persecution as never since the England of the sixteenth century or the Japan of the early seventeenth century, but worse in psychology because the persecuting power was the government of a Catholic people, and because the consequences were European.

To recreate government—papal rule—diocesan order—secure parishes —disciplined clergy—monks again—nuns again—brotherhoods again— seminaries revived—was a task which could hardly be undertaken in a mood of quiet planning. Men had been guillotined and shot, two Popes kidnapped, religion polluted in peasant war. Memories were not serene. They felt passionately. Emotion entered the idea of reconstruction and affected its course.

This emotion transformed what would otherwise have been a yearning for the good old days. Marvellous architecture built by rich monks half a century before now stood empty or ruined. Those stones were a sermon. The old world, which they remembered as normality, invited revolution.

The old world left survivals, stranded, absurd as they seemed to the new. In Taranto sat the most charming archbishop of the Christian centuries, Giuseppe Capecelatro (1744–1836), antiquarian, patrician, numismatist, an amiable, entertaining, learned, handsome, and idle prelate. In opinion a Jansenist but too dilettante to be strong in opinion, he disliked monks, private revelations, the Inquisition, emotional lower-class religion, private masses. He wanted to reduce saints' days and to strengthen parish churches. In all Roman Catholicism he was the only archbishop to prefer a married to a celibate clergy. He believed nevertheless that no one could be saved who was not baptized, and that the foetus of a mother dying in pregnancy should be extracted for baptism. He thought that the Pope should be primate in honour but govern as the president of a council of bishops, that all religions should be tolerated, and that enclosed nunneries should be abolished. All his later years, which were many, he spent in a charming house at Naples among a collection of works of art, and presided over a salon of European celebrity where visitors felt at their ease. Everyone admired him and was enchanted by his conversation and visited his elegant apartments to see a monument of the past. Through revolution and counter-revolution and two Bonapartist kingdoms and Bourbon restoration in south Italy he survived, preaching loyalty to whatever government was in power, wearing tricolour cockade or Bourbon cockade, willing to preside at a *Te Deum*, but not escaping without a year's comfortable imprisonment in Naples, and finally (1817) preferring resignation to a return to his diocese. He was now the ex-Archbishop of Taranto but so famous that no one could remember that he had a successor. He observed men, and liked them, and had small wish to change them, and in extreme old age cheerfully submitted by request to Rome, and died at the age of ninety-two with a smile on his lips.[8]

This was nothing like what was intended by the notion of a return to the Catholic past.

Reactionaries in an extreme sense were not plentiful. But the mood of the age brought some of them into posts of authority. There they believed that religion supported authority, authority's interest lay in using religion.

The Napoleonic Code of Laws included an excellent system of courts of justice. The rejection of the code by several states because it was Napoleon's did nothing to improve society, and affected the Church adversely. Tuscany quietly abolished the (very modest) laws giving women a measure of equality with men in rights of property. Rome put the Jews back into the ghetto (but they had hardly left their old home) and Pope Leo XII (20 November 1826) enforced that law which the French abolished, even preventing them from owning real property. Divorce made the thorniest of all these legal questions. The Church could not tolerate a law of divorce in any state which it regarded as Catholic.

The State needed the Church, this was the axiom of that day. The Church knew that it was needed by the State, and said loudly that it was needed by the State. Of course it had always known that it was needed by the State but never before said it so loudly. Therefore in the age of Restoration the balance of power between Church and State shifted somewhat towards the side of the Church, even where determined governments maintained or revived Josephist laws, and even though Popes must go on conceding more and more rights in appointments to states. Piedmont was not the only state to revive laws which a later generation criticised as 'pure clericalism' because they gave back privileges and prescribed severe penalties for offences against the Church.

---

[8] *D.B.I.* s.v. 'Capecelatro'; Croce, *Uomini*, 2.

At first sight men might be forgiven for supposing that all was as it was before. In Genoa friars were everywhere in the streets again, mendicants could beg, Loreto had its crowd of pilgrims with their satchels. When Goethe visited the Rhineland, just freed from the French, and saw the Catholic people of Bingen celebrating the festival of St. Rochus, he marvelled that revolutionary rule had left the religious instinct in all its old force. A procession in Milan for Corpus Christi (1820) was as magnificent to the eye as any in the past, viceroy, regiments, archbishop and all clergy, flags of Austrian empire and St. Ambrose and St Charles Borromeo, passing amid streets just as crammed with spectators; and in the cathedral a crowd of labouring men and women packed tight and manifestly devout. In the streets the spectators were not all so devout, they were as likely to jeer as to genuflect, and one observer wondered whether these jeers were a heritage of revolution and a sign of some deep change in the outlook of the people.[9] But it was hardly different from Roman urchins mocking at the flagellants as a hundred years before they passed so sombrely. Forms were easy to revive.

But something indefinable and yet of vast import had certainly happened. The Revolution showed how frail is faith; or, if true faith has roots too deep to shake, then how insecure is the social structure of a Church in a divided country; and how much that passes for religion is conformity. That was an experience unforgettable in the consciousness of Europe, Protestant or Catholic. It made the ultimate differences between the work of Churches in the old world and the work of the Churches in modern times.

Capece Minutolo, Prince of Canosa, was near to being atheist as a young man. Under the impact of revolution he swung over (1794) into Catholicism, partly as a faith but more as a necessity for social stability. The Catholicism which he needed for society was the mainstay of monarchy and the feudal privileges of aristocracy, and included an infallible Pope as the organ of Christian authority. In the Parthenopean republic he was condemned to death for royalist conspiracy but rescued by the arrival in Naples of Cardinal Ruffo's bands. The royalists then imprisoned him for defending the rights of aristocrats against the king. When Joseph Bonaparte became King of Naples, Canosa engaged in a conspiracy for which friends were executed and a price was put on his head. At the Restoration he was sent as ambassador from Palermo to Madrid and there watched

---

[9] Lady Morgan, *Italy* (1821), 1.76–7; Goethe, *Sämtliche Werke* (Stuttgart edn.), 29.187 ff. The chapel of St. Rochus had been ruined in the war and used as a bivouac, and was just rebuilt.

with joy the reaction of King Ferdinand VII and the restoration of the Jesuits and the Inquisition. In 1816, in the full tide of political reaction, he became minister of police at Naples and secretly enlisted right-wing bands of conspirators to slay conspirators of the left or anyone suspect of sympathy with revolution. He was exiled to Tuscany where under an assumed name he published an apologia for his proceedings as minister of police, that in a revolutionary age we need 'a vigorous and extremely active despotism', and a Church which is indispensable to keeping the people obedient. 'If you will not believe the Pope or in Jesus Christ for the sake of winning salvation in the world to come, then believe him, as we believe him, for the sake of winning salvation in this world.' The Naples revolution of 1820 seemed to justify him, and he was recalled again to be minister of police; and for four months (April to July 1821) he directed illegal repression, arrests without charge, flogging of suspects, re-enlistment of a private army. The ambassadors of the powers, who were all-powerful, forced him again into exile. In 1825 he finished a book which he had started long before, *On the utility of the Roman Catholic Christian religion for the tranquillity of peoples and the security of thrones*. The revolution of 1831 again seemed to justify him, and allowed him to raise a private army in the Romagna (1834–6) until the Austrians forced its disbandment. He died in miserable poverty two years later, and left his name as a symbol for Italian nationalists of everything which they hated in the link between the Church and the political right.[10]

These attitudes were not confined to laymen.

Bonaventura Gazzola was Bishop of Cervia when Bonaparte invaded north Italy and wrote one of those too effusive pastoral letters of welcome. But he greeted the returning Austrians even more enthusiastically, and was known as an opponent of the Italian Concordat. At the Restoration Pope Pius VII translated him to be Bishop of Montefiascone and Pope Leo XII made him cardinal. His letters after the Restoration show another man of the right whose attitudes were stamped by experiences of revolution in north Italy. Once he had an open mind. Now he saw masonic conspiracy everywhere, even in influence on the secretary of state Cardinal Consalvi, thought that Pius VII was weak and unfit to govern, had a horror at the least hint of compromise, and disliked planning or administrative change, with the attitude 'God will provide.' The words (he said) which he wanted to hear from Pope Pius VII were these: 'All things will return to what they were in 1796.'[11]

[10] *D.B.I.* s.v. 'Capece Minutolo'; Maturi, *Canosa* (1944); Croce, *Uomini*, 2.225 ff.
[11] V. E. Giuntella, *R. stor. Risorg.* 43 (1956), 413 ff.

Laymen and clerics who identified the Catholic cause with absolute monarchy are very hard to find before the revolution. They were not nearly so common in the Restoration as is sometimes supposed, but when they appeared they were influential even if controversial, because they fitted a dominant mood of the age.

Archbishop Fortunato Pinto of Salerno suggested in every provincial capital a professorship, *On the truth of the Apostolic Roman religion as the one true faith*, and wanted young men, who aimed at an academic career, compelled to attend the lectures provided and to pass an examination.[12] The bishops grew further away from the middle class, further from some of their own priests. Governments controlled their choice more universally than before the Revolution, and saw to it that safe and high conservatives were chosen. Bishops became even less representative of their clergy.

The restored Pope

The Curia began again to act. The Congregations reassembled, the Roman Inquisition began to hear cases (but only from the Papal States), the Index began again to supervise books, the Congregation of the Council to administer dioceses and parishes. It was not quite the same. The Congregation of Avignon, for example, never reappeared because Avignon was no longer the Pope's territory. And two constitutional changes affected the working of the Curia, so that the machine was more centralized in 1820 than in 1789.

First, the secretary of state Cardinal Consalvi reorganized his dicastery, making it much more like the bureaucracy of any civil power and using more experts. The new secretariat was more efficient and therefore more powerful. By this reform the papacy took another step in the decline of the historic consistories of cardinals. The process did not make Consalvi popular among cardinals. But he only moved further on the way which seventy years before Pope Benedict XIV planned.

Secondly, Pope Pius VII created (1801) a new Congregation, by its intention and title a body to advise in emergency (the emergency being the French Revolution) the Congregation for Extraordinary Affairs of the Church. Until the revolution Popes met emergencies by summoning, and afterwards discharging, special committees. This emergency was so grave that, even under Pius VI during the nineties, the special committee on the affairs of France became a standing committee, never discharged. Pius VII recognized the need and in 1814 reactivated the Congregation with wider

[12] Cestaro, 103.

powers. It had eight cardinals, a secretary with vote, and five consultors.

The emergency of the Reformation created the Congregation of the Council to supervise the enforcement of the reforms of Trent. The emergency of the Revolution created the Congregation of Extraordinary Affairs to supervise reconstruction after the demolitions of Napoleon's wars. Since these functions overlapped, the Congregation of the Council lost a measure of authority, and never again wielded such power as in the eighteenth century.

To the Congregation of Extraordinary Affairs the Pope entrusted advice upon the relations between the see of Rome and the civil powers; the drafting of the agreements (Concordats) 'to cancel the effects of revolution'; *ordinary affairs* in Latin America, in the former Portuguese empire in the east, in Russia and all countries with which Rome had no formal relations. Therefore it left no room for the old consistory of cardinals. This Congregation of eight cardinals began to act like a cabinet, and so continued until the reordering of the Curia in 1908.

In the Curia the intellectual world changed. Canon Settele wrote a book on the movement of the earth. Someone complained to the Inquisition, which (1820) sent the book out to three referees for their opinion. One of these referees was the Dominican Filippo Anfossi, master of the Sacred Palace for Pius VII. Anfossi was celebrated as a writer against Jansenists and Gallicans, and especially for more than one book arguing the rigid opinion that any Catholic who acquired church property alienated during the Revolution committed sacrilege and was morally bound to make restitution. In his old age he was easily shocked. Canon Settele's book disturbed him.

I am surprised [he wrote in his opinion] to see that he makes the interpretation of Scripture depend not on the help of the Holy Spirit but the system of philosophers and astronomers, and on the ideas of Newton and Kepler. . . . [The Copernican system] is a very grave error, pernicious doctrine . . . formally heretical or at least erroneous in faith. . . . The Holy See is that happy land which always says the same and never changes its view of the true understanding of scripture and the Fathers.[13]

Here spoke, not the old world which was more open-minded, but the conservative mind closed by experience of revolutionary years. The other two referees gave approval to the book, which passed the census against the will of the master of the Sacred Palace. Henceforth Galileo and Copernicus were freely taught throughout the Roman Catholic Church.

[13] Colapietra, *La Chiesa*, 60–1, 112.

Even in the Collegio Romano of 1822 the ordinands were being taught to study Locke and Condillac.

The Pope's reputation in 1815 stood far higher than in 1789. He was among the 'victors' of long wars. He was a confessor for the faith.

Pius VII, once as a cardinal the preacher of the Christmas sermon of 1797 and then the Pope who accepted Napoleon by crowning him Emperor, did not die until 1823, aged eighty-one. He left a Church weaker by far in every external respect than the Church of 1789. But when he came to the tiara men talked of the end of the papacy, the last Pope. At his death no one could talk in such terms. Though weaker externally, the institution was seen to be rooted in the popular mind of southern Europe and Poland and Belgium and Ireland, even among many of the people of France. The Pope of 1789 was indispensable to kings because he was the instrument by which they got control over Churches. The Pope of 1823 was seen to be indispensable to kings who wished to stay on their thrones because religion was believed to be the bond of society.

For the last six years of his life, from his restoration until his death, he lived in a quiet and prayerful retreat, and left government to his secretary of state, Cardinal Consalvi, who was hardly an ecclesiastic except in name, conservative, skilled in diplomacy, prudent and no ultra, a hard-working minister who ruled the Church almost as though he was Pope. Against every onslaught Pius VII defended and trusted him, and the trust was not misplaced. Consalvi failed because the problems were insoluble, not because he lacked wisdom.

The Papal States

The fatal inheritance was the northern part of the Papal States.

Because Pope Pius VII was restored in two stages, once by a falling Napoleon and again by the Congress of Vienna, he received his dominions in two stages: in 1814 Rome and the country round and Umbria, and in 1815 the Marches and the Legations. While Cardinal Consalvi walked the corridors in Vienna, Cardinal Pacca and Monsignor Rivarola established the old laws and customs in Rome. Some of these old laws and customs looked quaint when they possessed a prescription of historical continuity, but when restored after the French abolished them, they offended the public opinion of Europe.

In 1814–16 Rome and Latium and Umbria had the most retarded government in Europe; consciously retarded, because its makers supposed that they could rebuild the interesting but rickety structure which stood more or less erect before it was tumbled by the armies of the Revolution.

To gain the Marches and Legations, Consalvi promised modern government. These weightier provinces returned to the Pope with the Napoleonic laws still in force 'so far as they were not contrary to canon law', and under an efficient bureaucratically French type of civil service. The Pope, given his domains in two slices, found himself with two different forms of government.

He also found himself faced with two attitudes among the people. For nearly twenty years the Legations in the north, for eight years the Marches on the Adriatic coast, had lay republican governments with French laws. There the attitude of the people was more truculent than in Rome, where hardly anyone thought French rule better than papal rule. 'The young people', wrote Cardinal Consalvi to Cardinal Pacca (12 June 1815), 'have never known the Pope's government and have a very low opinion of what it is like. They resent being ruled by priests. The old may think differently but do not count. Most of the people's minds are not on our side.'[14]

Afterwards, men blamed Cardinal Consalvi who as secretary of state was responsible for the government and who, according to the point of view, was too radical or conservative. He received two incompatible governments. Being in origin a man of the Enlightenment, and by nature endowed with prudence, he would have liked to amalgamate the ancient and the modern with emphasis on the modern. His fiercest opponents accused him of being a Jacobin, and Cardinal Mattei had his henchmen tear up his edicts. Consalvi talked of conserving the best in historic traditions while they adapted government to the needs of the age. But the opponents were so fierce and so entrenched, that he could only get part of his way. The ancient shouldered its way into the modern, and the system, though less complicated as machinery than the system of the eighteenth century, still looked at times like muddle.

A single government for all the Papal States was established by a *motu proprio* of 6 July 1816. At base it was far more like the French system than the old Roman system; a *delegate* for each of seventeen *delegations* with many of the functions of the French prefect, advised by local consultative bodies of which the members were selected by the secretary of state. The ancient world pushed its way into the structure by insisting that all the delegates be clergymen (in the Legations, as of old, cardinals). Much of the rest of the civil service was opened to laymen but, though not ordained, these laymen wore cassocks. This ban on laymen in the highest posts does not seem to have accorded with Consalvi's wishes. Probably it did not

[14] Leflon, *La Crise révolutionnaire*, 310.

easily agree with the spirit of the assurances which he offered to the statesmen in Vienna. But it was realistic. For he received the bitterer criticism from those who thought it improper that lower ranks of the civil service should be opened to laymen.

Thus Consalvi's model was neither the *ancien régime* nor Rousseau but Napoleon.

A French type of bureaucracy headed by clergymen was a different kind of government from the clerical government of the old Papal States. In the *ancien régime* local rights were strong; feudal privileges, baronial exemptions, municipal customs. Government was weak because it could not ride roughshod over rights centuries old. The French swept away all these diversities while they ruled Italy, not before time. Despite the wishes of Cardinal Pacca and Monsignor Rivarola, they could not be revived. Therefore the modern version of the government was either weaker or stronger according to the circumstances. It could do more: organize taxes more justly, shorten delays in courts of justice, arrange tolls and customs so that they did not destroy trade, mend the roads, and improve the water supply. Being centralized, it had the possibility of becoming a police state at a time of crisis. But this last possibility was to show the danger. In bad times the citizens of the old Papal States blamed the squire, or the municipality, or the hand of God. In bad times the citizens of the new Papal States saw a government which they could blame. To make the government modern, Consalvi also created the possibility that in famine or tumult government would find itself face to face with the people.

The clergymen who now governed were more offensive than the clergymen who used to govern; first because they governed with more effectiveness and therefore more intrusively, and secondly because their assistants could now be laymen. As the prince-bishopric of Italy looked odder because the prince-bishoprics of Germany and Austria were secularized, so clerical government looked odder because it was exclusively clerical only at the top.

Meanwhile the children of Napoleon's Cisalpine republic, and the children of Napoleon's kingdom of Italy, and the heirs of Murat in Naples, aimed to make it look both odd and offensive. Pope Pius VII said anxiously to Artaud, 'Nowadays governing the people is difficult.'[15]

This attempt to marry old with new failed because the old was too strong.

The cardinals never forgot their historic past in the government of the Church and saw Consalvi's type of monarchy as unconstitutional. The

---

[15] Artaud, *Pie VII*, 2.484.

European post-war slump made all government difficult. This prudent
secretary of state made himself more unpopular with his colleagues than
any Pope's minister since Cardinal Coscia a century before, for he was
more powerful than any minister since Coscia; and Coscia was corrupt,
while Consalvi was honourable.

His inability to get all that he wanted was illustrated dramatically by his
words to a south-German visitor. Wessenberg (1817) visited the church of
the Anima in Rome and was almost overpowered by the stink of de-
composing bodies buried under the floor. He later saw the secretary of
state (Consalvi) and expressed surprise that so many corpses should now be
buried in churches though the French government had forbidden the
practice. 'I wanted', said Consalvi 'to leave it as it was. But all the monasteries and congregations were against me, it means so much to them in
burial fees, and I had to give way.'[16]

The Carbonari

Metternich was obsessed about the dangers of secret societies.

The first masonic lodge was founded in 1717 at a London tavern. It
drew upon old customs and rituals of earlier masons' guilds, and being
founded in the time when deism flourished among English Protestants, had
a deist slant, with a picture of God as builder or architect of the universe,
but was not irreligious or even anti-Christian. Masons usually came from
the upper class. English merchants or diplomats or connoisseurs helped to
create masonic societies in all the capitals of the west. In Naples or Madrid
or Lisbon or Brussels the groups began to take on an anticlerical air. They
were meetings of educated and aristocratic laymen who so discussed the
issues of the day, that rumours about their freedom of speech reached
authority. Moreover, as early as 1738 (*In eminenti*) Pope Clement XII (or
rather his advisers, for by that date he was incapable) condemned freemasonry and refused to allow Catholics to be members on pain of excommunication. This condemnation, repeated by Benedict XIV, made
freemasons in Catholic countries more secret, and disreputable, but at
first no less aristocratic. In Holland and Germany, Vienna and Belgium,
we find priests as members, in Germany even the future Archbishop
Dalberg of Mainz. They had little spirit of rebellion.

But with the coming of revolution this began to change. At the
Strongoli palace in Naples an initiation ceremony of a new group had
speeches that Jacobin revolution was the culmination of freemasonry, and

[16] Beck, *Wessenberg*, 295.

the orator urged members to throw off tyranny in Naples. They lit two candles in front of a portrait of Voltaire on the mantlepiece, with a red cap and tricolour attached, and sang the *Marseillaise* in chorus.

In the kingdom of Naples from 1802 was found the name Carbonari (charcoal-burners). These were a secret society, or several secret societies, influenced by freemasonry, but less upper-class, not only with bourgeois but with artisans and even peasants among the members, initiated with a pseudo-religious ceremony, and with tough political overtones and an anticlerical aim. At the initiation Jesus was declared to be 'the great Carbonaro'. In the age of reaction, where the failure of revolution made many in upper-class and middle-class Europe believe that despotism was a necessity for law and order, the Carbonari (or other groups like them) grew to be bands of conspirators, hunted by government, bound by secret oaths, plotting the overthrow of kings and dukes. Some of them adopted the quasi-religious heritage of masonry, others were only clubs to conspire. 'The Sublime Masters of Perfection' had (1819–20) a 'church' at Parma and meetings in Bologna, Cesena, and Reggio. There were Adelfi, Guelfi, Latinisti, White Pilgrims, Seven Sleepers, Faithful Hermits. But also there were groups with secular names which preached tyrannicide, Disciples of Brutus, True Patriots, French Reformers, Disciples of Scaevola. One group forged a papal bull to prove that the Pope approved. Pius VII renewed the condemnation of his predecessors. No Catholic could belong.

But Catholics belonged. In the futile little plots and coups which kept breaking out all over Italy, and less frequently but more ominously in Spain, policemen found themselves hunting priests among the leaders. On the one side Church authorities, especially in the higher ranks, accepted the axiom of that age that public order and civilization were very frail and secured by the strongest government; and therefore south-Italian bishops made reports to police authorities about the state of opinion in their dioceses, and one priest at least informed about a looming plot of which he was believed to have learned in pastoral confidence. On the other side tribunals repressing conspirators seldom failed to find an ecclesiastic among the culprits. General Richard Church, British soldier of fortune who governed the territory of Otranto for the King of Naples, sent a report to government (13 November 1818) that the priests of the province 'are the most dangerous enemies of the sovereign and State'.[17] The secret report of a sub-inspector at Vallo in southern Italy (1828) estimated that they had twenty priests for a population of 3,000 and that of these twenty, fifteen were Carbonari. In Naples the conspirators sometimes met in a café but

[17] B. Pellegrino in *R. stor. Risorg.* 63 (1976), 14 n.32.

sometimes in a canon's house or the sacristy of a church. A misguided band of conspirators on the Cilento collected a posse of only 130 men, with whom they hoped to raise rebellion in all the kingdom of Naples, and began (1828) by seizing a fort and then going into church to sing a solemn *Te Deum*. Though the bull of Pope Pius VII achieved something, because numbers of priests appeared asking for absolution for their former membership of secret societies, other priests took more notice of the cry for justice (as they heard it) than of the Pope. In the new diocese of Nicosia (1820), 107 ecclesiastics were Carbonari, in the old diocese of Patti in Sicily twenty-four ecclesiastics, in the diocese of Syracuse a majority, in the diocese of Catania 124 ecclesiastics, including a Dominican who went round the monasteries collecting money to help war against Austria, in Messina the Carbonari had their headquarters in a convent. In Modena the only person executed after the conspiracy of 1820 was a young priest Giuseppe Andreoli, because he caused several undergraduates to join. It was alleged that the duke simultaneously reprieved a condemned parricide to show that no crime was worse than that of a priest conspiring against his country.[18]

In Campagna three of the canons were among the leaders of the Carbonari (1819) and held weekly meetings by night in the sacristy of the cathedral. Such incautious regularity, and such lights at night, could not go unobserved. The police told them that they should meet somewhere else, so they chose the refectory of the suppressed convent of Observant Franciscans.[19]

In the revolution of 1830, Father Luigi Menichini rode into Naples, armour over cassock, covered in Carbonari symbols, at the head of 7,000 untidy carbonari, some clergy and friars among the regiments, which applauded themselves shouting 'Long live the Carbonari!' In the San Martino museum in Naples is a picture of this triumphal entry. This priest, who suddenly found himself head of an army and a political leader, easily lost his head. They sent him to Sicily, partly to be rid of him and partly to guide the Sicilian revolution. But he guided so badly that they had to recall him; and then the Austrians marched in, Menichini fled to Spain, then to England, and last to America where, 'little loved and less esteemed', he became a Protestant, wrote a history of the Naples revolution, and died teaching Italian in Philadelphia.

In certain areas bishops' and police reports show a statistical relationship between priests enrolled in the Carbonari and priests under suspicion or

---

[18] Spellanzon, 2.79–81, 109 ff., 124, 130–2.   [19] Cestaro, 59.

charge for other forms of clerical misconduct.[20] But this was certainly not the reason why most Carbonari priests joined the movement.

The motives which led priests to join secret societies were as various as the motives of other mortals. An unclear account of motives has survived from a Verona friar, a Franciscan Recollect, superior of a house soon to be suppressed by the Revolution. Italy, he said (it was 1807), can never find peace until it is strong and united. It cannot become strong by federating, we must have a centre of government. 'I hate every sort of revolution because of the unforeseeable ills which it begets. In this sect I see only a way of spreading the benefits and wisdom of Christianity.'

A Carbonari oath from north Italy was taken kneeling, right hand above head, left hand with fist clenched on the heart, and ran thus:

I, free citizen of Ausonia [Italy] . . . in the presence of God the grand master of the universe and of my elected superior and good cousin, swear so to use all my life that the principles of liberty, equality, and hatred of tyranny may conquer; for these are the souls of all private and public acts of good Carbonari. I promise to spread a love of equality in all hearts whom I might be able to influence. I promise that if we fail to establish the kingdom of free men, I shall nevertheless fight on until death. . . .

This was followed by a fearful oath that if he were a traitor he might be crucified like Christ.

Their origins, and political notions, were therefore as closely linked to the Revolution as their ritual was linked to freemasonry. One leading north-Italian group which articulated its plan for united 'Ausonia' had an idea of the Church which followed the pattern of the French constitutional Church, with provincial assemblies electing bishops and rectors of seminaries, clergy paid by the State, Church buildings maintained by the State, Christianity declared to be 'the religion of the majority' but a Christianity remodelled after a primitive pattern, a 'patriarch' elected by a council of bishops. The present Pope will be invited to accept this office and will receive for his life-time a compensation in money for the loss of his lands to the republic of Ausonia. If at his death the *cardinals* tried to elect a new Pope he and they would be expelled from Ausonia. No friar was to take final vows before the age of forty-five, nor nuns (except childless widows) before the age of forty.

Outside Italy [wrote an observer in Rome (12 July 1819)] scepticism and love of liberty sometimes go together. On the contrary, the Carbonari show a sincere faith in the religion of Jesus as we find it in the gospels, and stripped of the

---

[20] Colletta, *Kingdom of Naples*, 2.348; Cestaro, 90.

foreign elements which have been mixed in by theologians during eighteen centuries. Thus they are reformers of religion as well as the State. Among their numbers are many of the lower clergy . . . and even a few dignitaries.[21]

In the kingdom of Naples and elsewhere in Italy authority met a new problem. Determined to maintain the sacred privileges of priesthood, they were also resolute to execute revolutionary priests. Therefore a priest convicted as a revolutionary must be unfrocked. Government never failed to find a bishop who would unfrock, but could not always persuade the right bishop. When Andreoli was to be executed at Modena, the Bishop of Reggio pleaded for pardon, the Bishop of Carpi went to the condemned cell to unfrock. When Canon de Luca for whom police beat the woods in vain, came out of his hiding-place and gave himself up to save the town of Celle from being burnt to the ground, three bishops in succession refused to unfrock, until at last the Archbishop of Salerno consented 'as a duty to the king', and so the canon or ex-canon, and his nephew, also a priest or ex-priest, died together in the square at Salerno. The Patriarch of Venice Pyrker related in his autobiography how he had the duty of unfrocking a Carbonaro priest. He described not only the unpleasant ritual but his feelings of emotion and repugnance. He did not doubt that to unfrock the man was right.[22]

These difficulties are another sign of a new world. Formerly a priest might have escaped the death penalty even for murder, partly by reason of benefit of clergy because men scrupled to kill the Lord's anointed, and if he was to be executed, bishops hardly hesitated to unfrock. Governments of the Restoration, following in the steps of Josephists and Jansenists and (though they must not say so) the French, were resolute to be rid of benefit of clergy except as ritual form; and felt too insecure to treat rebel priests with any vestiges of respect for their office. Bishops scrupled whether a priest whose sincere political opinions led him to join some secret group of revolutionaries, could rightly be made equal to murderer or traitor.

In Soriano (southern Italy) a Dominican novice told (1826) a strange story. Two friars forced him to accept the rules of St. Theobald, the hermit of the eleventh century who was patron of charcoal-burners and therefore of Carbonari. They said St. Theobald's rules were the very laws of God. The novice went to his prior who ordered him to obey, and said that he must appear before all the community to swear, on crucifix and dagger, allegiance to the Carbonari. By night the novice fled to the bishop

---

[21] Saint-Edme, *Constitution et organisation des Carbonari* (Paris, 1821), 4 ff., 110 ff., 192 ff.
[22] Spellanzon, 2.81–2, 136; *La visita pastorale di Pyrker*, 201–2.

—who told him to obey his prior and sent him back to the monastery. At last he got the news to the police who thought him mad.[23]

The stories of this novice were such as could only arise where liberal or revolutionary ideas were expected to infect priests and monks.

In the hills of the kingdom of Naples, in the Abruzzi range and across unpatrollable mountain frontiers into the Papal States was the happiest home of the brigands. Revolution left behind outlaws, refugees, young men who fled from conscription. Between 1799 and 1866 the mountains were never empty of brigands. In January 1821 a band kidnapped all the professors and students of the Terracina seminary for high ransom. The people of the countryside helped the brigands; who in their eyes stood for 'justice' against tax-collectors, feudal lords, policemen, government. A lot of them were still Sanfedist in mentality—that is, even though they murdered, they wore scapulas of the Madonna round their necks, fasted on Wednesdays, and met in the evenings to pray their rosaries.

One south-Italian band (1817) had forty-three brigands of whom only two were priests. The composition of the band is known because they held up the mail-coach on the Auletta road and found 2,000 ducats aboard. Brigands who killed royalists or Austrians were not easy to distinguish in religion from brigands who killed liberals and democrats. This applied in both Spain and Italy.

In these incongruities brigands hardly differed from more educated men. One observer in Naples found it strange to see Prince Canosa in his home plotting deeds of iniquity, beneath the images of the Saviour and the saints, while his rooms were filled not only with informers and assassins but with confessors and friars noted for their sanctity.[24]

The most famous of religious Carbonari shed a brilliant light upon the inward intellectual tensions of that age.

Silvio Pellico

Silvio Pellico (1789–1854), of a modest and devout Piedmont family, won fame at Milan in the year of the battle of Waterloo with a poetic tragedy *Francesca da Rimini*. As a young leader in the revival of Italian literature he was caught up in the nationalist movement in Lombardy and finally, now a sceptic in religion, enlisted in the Carbonari. He learnt religion to be a gag for the common people, and believed in tyrannicide. These Lombard Carbonari differed from the conspirators further south, in being more

---

[23] Spellanzon, 2.124–5; Acton, *The Last Bourbons*, 26–7.
[24] Cestaro, 34 n.24; 58; Colletta, *Kingdom of Naples*, 2.280.

educated, more aristocratic, and more idealistic. Their organ, which Pellico helped to edit, was the *Conciliatore*, a liberal newspaper which (1819) the Austrians suppressed.

Then during 1820 revolutions in Spain and Naples made conspiracy look easy. Pellico worked naïvely and imprudently to enlist others in the Carbonari. He was arrested, tried at Venice, and sentenced to imprisonment of fifteen years at Spielberg, a gloomy fortress in Moravia to which the Austrians consigned all the leading Carbonari who failed to flee abroad. After ten years he was released under amnesty, sick in body, left leg dragging from years of a fetter, and returned to his family near Turin.

In prison, he refound the faith of his childhood. His mother and parish priest encouraged him to write down his experience. The result (1832) was *Le mie prigione* (*My Years in Prison*) which at once became a book of European importance.

It was a religious book; an account of the way a man under suffering stumbled his way back to faith; enchantingly written, with an apparent simplicity, full of charitable interest in the gaolers or their children; the meditations of a man who truly and not ritually forgave his oppressors; devoid of bitterness; plainly not aimed at hurting Austria; a book of prayer and resignation, of the dungeon as a hermit's cell; and unlike most books of devotion in gripping the ordinary reader, by the drama of the situation, the brooding sense of a dark fortress, the secret messages between prisoners, the deaths or illnesses of convicts, humour and kindness lightening the darkness.

Only in appearance is it simple. The book is a work of art, by a sophisticated author, who used his sophistication to create the air of simplicity. It could not have been written by an insincere man. But how it was artistry appeared when, after its success in all the countries of Europe, other French or Italian ex-prisoners from the fortress tried their hand at reminiscence. The only interest possessed by these other books lay in contrast with Pellico's *Le mie prigione*.

The book was extraordinary because its author idealized his world. The repulsive character in the castle at Spielberg was the confessor Stephan Pavlowich, a Dalmatian with secret instructions to use his priestly office to gain information about other conspirators. All the prisoners regarded him as a spy or a Judas, and were relieved when (1828) he was rewarded with the see of Cattaro. Not a word of blame for Pavlowich is found in Pellico's book. *Le mie prigione* made the gaolers more humane, the conditions of life less intolerable, the Austrian government more reasonable, his resignation easier, his faith more instantly comforting, his judges less fierce, the gaoler's daughters sweeter, than the reality.

The reasons of this idealizing were practical and religious. Several friends were still in Spielberg. Onslaught upon the Austrians could only injure men still wearing chains. Even more strongly, religion made him wish to eschew the petty revenge which was all that he could take with his pen.

The reception of this noble book illustrates the predicament of the Catholic world after the Revolution. Angry liberals attacked it as a good book for friars and bigots. Strong Catholics attacked it as a pestilential book to be kept away from the young, with its poisonous idea of a marriage between Catholicism and liberalism.

The book was aimed not to assail the Austrians. It therefore hurt the Austrian government, and helped the cause of the Risorgimento in Italy, more than any book which was bitter against Austria. No idealization could conceal the martyrdom of political prisoners. Metternich said there was not a word of truth in the story. Pellico failed even to mention that the prisoners committed a crime; showed no sign of penitence for what he had done; represented himself and all his fellow-conspirators as martyrs. Metternich badgered King Charles Albert in Turin to suppress the book; but Charles Albert liked it, and issued the order only to content Metternich, and let the publisher go on selling. Metternich pressed the Congregation of the Index to suppress the book. But the Congregation reported that the book had nothing to condemn, and refused. Metternich talked glumly of the book to Veuillot (1850), saying that Pellico had converted a book of prayer into a book of calumny. And Veuillot replied that the book had done its work, and the result was more terrible for Austria than the loss of a battle.

Pellico's book pointed to the Catholic predicament which had not existed in this form before the revolution. Was marriage between Catholicism and liberalism possible? A devoutly Catholic book discredited a Catholic government which was the mainstay of the order established in Italy after the Revolution. To expel the Austrians must mean change in Italy, change hardly to be distinguished from revolution. Such a change was certain to transform the politics of the papal monarchy and therefore the international base of the Catholic Church. And all this was fostered by a book of devotion, written by a Catholic convert, which the Congregation of the Index could not and would not condemn.

Pope Leo XII

In 1823 Annibale della Genga (aged sixty-three) was elected Pope and took the name Leo XII, after a Conclave of only twenty-six days.

The 'alternating' system of Roman Conclaves began. The nineteenth century saw no exception to the rule that if the Pope befriended liberals his successor was a man of the right, and vice versa: except in the one case of Pius IX (1846) where a Pope elected to befriend liberals was turned by experience into a man of the right. Pius VII and Consalvi had reconciling minds; Leo XII was ultra-conservative; Pius VIII was a friend of Consalvi; Gregory XVI (1831) was an ultra; Pius IX (1846) was hailed as a liberal Pope and then lost his liberalism; Leo XIII (1878) was elected as a reconciler.

This alternating sequence was a mark of a change in Conclaves, connected with the consequences of the Revolution. It showed that the elective system followed its own internal laws; in other words, that the governments of Catholic powers interfered far less than in the eighteenth century, and were able to interfere far less, in selecting a Pope whom they preferred. The French government after its recent experiences was less confident about dealing with Popes. The Austrians were still confident till 1848, but Metternich was too Catholic and too subtle to be heavy-handed about intruding in Rome. The Spanish government was too concerned with its own troubles, and was hardly any longer one of the powers. For the first time for more than a century, cardinals elected with a measure of freedom.

This had three main consequences. First, conclaves began to be shorter, since the number of people who needed to agree the choice was reduced as ambassadors or crown cardinals acted less interferingly. When Pius IX was elected after two days in 1846 and Leo XIII after only three ballots in 1878, it was thought almost miraculous. But it was a sign not of non-intervention by governments (for governments intervened) but of less, or weaker, intervention, and of confidence among cardinals. Secondly, a majority of cardinals were for several decades *zelanti*, pious men who wanted the good of the Church and were determined to exclude governments. During all the eighteenth century these *zelanti* were not able to elect their first choice because one government or another refused to allow the election. These refusals had the bad effect of excluding many good men from the office of Pope. But they had a good effect, by exercising a moderating influence upon the cardinals, and preventing the election of extremists or fanatics. The intervention of governments was the traditional way in which Catholic laity had a say in the choice of Pope. As this intervention declined, the election became more clerical. Its motives became purer. But the choice carried with it the danger that an extremist might more easily be elected.

Until 1939 it was an axiom that the secretary of state could not be elected Pope, for he was too identified with the policy of the dead Pope which now needed changing. In 1823 this axiom was as true as possible.

Cardinal Consalvi was responsible for an attempt to baptize the Napoleonic system; was accused of sacrificing the pre-revolutionary rights of noblemen and cardinals; of being a dictator who kept other cardinals away from his government, and ruled solitary. If the conclave of 1823 had an agreement, it was the unpopularity of Consalvi. Several governments would have liked him elected, because they could expect a flexible policy to continue. But no candidate was more unpopular among the electors.

In law, the veto still existed. The governments of Austria, France, and Spain still asserted the right to veto a candidate—and sometimes exercised that right. In their eyes the worst fault of a candidate was rigidity. They worked systems of Church government under agreements or concordats which demanded compromise on the part of the Curia.

In the eighteenth century the enclosure of the Conclave was never kept securely. Secret messages passed in and out illicitly. In 1823 the Austrian Crown Cardinal Albani certainly passed out messages to the Austrian ambassador Apponyi. The man whom he wanted to exclude was Cardinal Severoli, the first choice of the *zelanti*. It looked very like the conditions of the eighteenth century. But it was not. Italian cardinals, who might be expected to be moderates, were too 'Italian' (and therefore suspicious of Austrian dominance) to support anything that Metternich wanted. The French government of Louis XVIII disliked cardinals who had befriended Napoleon, and therefore preferred *zelanti*. Provided that they did not get a Pope who would be a marionette on Austrian strings, the French were content. The atmosphere is shown by a letter of Chateaubriand, now French foreign minister: 'We want a man of the Italian party [i.e. anti-Austrian] who is a *zelante* but moderate. All we ask is that whoever is chosen does not make trouble in our Church affairs. We need nothing out of him in politics.'[25] 'We need nothing out of him in politics'—an impossible utterance for the eighteenth century and a sign of a different world. But not so very different, for Chateaubriand could not keep to his own principles.

[25] Artaud, *Léon XII*, 1.70.

Failing all else, the Austrians via Cardinal Albani vetoed (21 September 1823) the *zelanti*'s candidate Cardinal Severoli. It was a shocking moment, with fierce words passing. And it did not stop the *zelanti*. A week later they elected their second choice, Cardinal Annibale della Genga. The veto, though it still existed, grew weaker.

The cardinals, still resentful of Consalvi's monarchy, forced the new Pope at once to appoint a congregation of Cardinals to govern. As soon as he was fully on the saddle, he rid himself of this Congregation. The days of the old cardinals' system were past, never to return.

Leo XII made an extreme contrast with Consalvi. He was priestly where Consalvi seemed a layman dressed like a clergyman; he was anxious and fussy where Consalvi was strong-willed and dedicated; perhaps Leo had the sharper intelligence, but in a less energetic body, so weak as at times to be languid; Leo knew something of mystical prayer which Consalvi could not understand. Leo was elected to swing against everything for which Consalvi stood. His difficulty was to prevent the swing happening as some of his advisers hoped and intended. He was expected to have little time. At the Holy House of Loreto has been found a prayer to give Pope Leo 'at least a year of life' so that he can see his ideas to relieve his subjects put into practice.[26]

Leo XII was the Pope of the Restoration; that is, elected in the high age of the Holy Alliance, when governments of Europe were determined against revolution. In foreign affairs, especially with France, he was intelligent. In Rome he had little idea how to rule. He had small previous experience of government, and in power had small perception of what was possible.

As Vicar of Rome shortly before his election, he issued an edict of imprisonment (ten days for minors, month for adults) for anyone playing games in the streets on Sundays or feast days; ordered 300 Jews to hear sermons every Saturday, no proxies allowed; condemned elaborate dresses of nuns, even at their profession. As Pope he forbade encores and ovations in theatres. In 1824 he issued the decree which made him hated among the Romans. All alcoholic drinks were not to be sold in bars but at grilles. This rule, though it found parallels in various democracies of the twentieth century, caused drunkenness in the streets and made the people glad when he died.

He banned laymen from wearing priests' hat, habit, or collar notwithstanding any custom to the contrary; prohibited close-fitting dresses for

[26] Colapietra, *La Chiesa*, 162, 176.

women—in the decree Cardinal Zurla asserted that the immodesty of women has been one of the chief causes of so many of the ills which have fallen upon Christianity. The Jews were ordered back into the ghetto, of which the size was extended to prevent overcrowding. The law which forbade them to own real property was revived. One measure for which all the books blamed Leo XII has been proved to be no matter for blame. It was said that he condemned vaccination. That was not what happened. The government of Cardinal Consalvi had issued (June 1822) stringent orders to ensure that the people were vaccinated. Any application for poor relief must be accompanied by a certificate of vaccination. Except in Ferrara and Ancona the people were almost unanimous in failing to come forward. The priests at Forlì and Rimini refused to give out notices from the altar, or sound the church bells to summon to the clinic. Curates started refusing to report births. The medical profession doubted these compulsions. Consalvi persisted; a commission discussed whether to refuse admission to hospitals or orphanages or seminaries without a certificate of vaccination. By the time that Leo XII was elected Pope, government had obviously failed. What the new Pope did was to bow to necessity and make vaccination optional.[27]

The Pope was also accused of abolishing street lighting so that passengers might be lit only by the lamps before the shrines of saints. This also is legend.

Though he was unspoilt by power or ceremony, ascetic, uncompromising, and more remote from the world than suited a Pope of the Restoration, no one supposed that he was foolish. When he concerned himself with Church affairs, he conducted them excellently. He had been nuncio in Germany and understood the wider Church. Towards the governments of Germany or France, Spain or Austria, he pursued a steady and prudent policy, not always successful but hardly less moderate than the policy of Consalvi. In care for the pageants of liturgy in Rome, for the restoration of churches, for the celebrations in 1825 of the Jubilee year, for the growth of the religious orders, and for all Catholic interests as they were religious interests, he proved himself an eminent Pope. But the Pope was also king; and as king he died one of the two hated Pope-kings of the nineteenth century.

Eighteenth-century modes of keeping order were applied incongruously to nineteenth-century disorder. Cardinal Rivarola, tall, dry, red-faced, squinting, and intelligent, who achieved excellent results against brigands round Rome, was sent to the north with exceptional powers. At Ravenna

[27] Colapietra, *La Chiesa*, 117–18.

he closed inns, banned cards and games of chance, forced all citizens walking after dark to be accompanied by a lantern, put on the stairs of the bishop's palace a chest into which informers might drop their papers, imprisoned without trial or only tried in long months, made it illegal to speak against the regime in cafés. In Faenza he arranged twelve marriages between the two murdering factions (in Faenza the people called the Carbonari dogs and the Sanfedists cats) and to this end gave dowries. In Holy Year 1825 companies of friars toured the cities and towns of the Romagna preaching penitence and denouncing sectaries in the piazzas. The *mission* of the eighteenth century had now a political aim as well as a religious. Someone fired at Cardinal Rivarola in his carriage but hit the chaplain who sat beside. Rivarola behaved imperturbably. A writer[28] sympathetic to Pope Leo XII has said of Cardinal Rivarola's regime that it was not tyranny but the grotesque caricature of tyranny: 'a governor governing with the methods of Rossini's Don Bartolo.' Rivarola was sure that the high rate of rape which the people of Ravenna accepted as inevitable, was due to the French occupation.

The predicament of the Papal States was shown by a report of October 1824 from Cardinal Sanseverino on Forlì. This cardinal was no exaggerator. The secretary-general of the Legation, he said, openly favours liberals. His (the cardinal's) first secretary has a mistress and is bribable but cannot be got rid of because he is indispensable. The archivist belongs to a secret society and is fanatical for the Constitution. His assistant is a carbonaro under suspicion. The head of police is incompetent and without energy. Two loyal officers have been shot at. Two civil magistrates are excellent, seven others are Carbonari or at least liberals. The postmaster-general is an old Jacobin and follower of Murat who pries into confidential letters and has sons who are the scandal of the country.

But the cardinal who shattered these attempts at the impossible was Pallotta against the brigands in the south. He issued a decree (15 May 1824) abolishing the courts in favour of his absolute discretion, ordering the shooting of captured brigands within twenty-four hours, and heavy fines on villages where brigands were found. The edict was so shocking that a month later the Pope accepted Pallotta's resignation.

On Christmas Eve that year the brigands paid money to have a solemn mass sung in the church at Sonnino.

The Congress of Vienna restored the Papal States, partly because it could see nothing else to do with Italy, partly because Russia and Britain wanted

[28] Colapietra, *La Chiesa*, 191.

to limit the power of Austria. Only ten years later it was found that they had burdened the Pope with lands and peoples which he could no longer govern. After six more years of turmoil the Papal States again became the home of foreign garrisons, because only foreign garrisons could secure the continued existence of the Papal States. This fateful predicament—the vocation to rule historic lands inalienable; the inability to rule effectively; the presence of Austrian or French soldiers and all that that implied for political independence—conditioned the papacy of the nineteenth century. The Congress of Vienna saddled the Popes and therefore the Roman Catholic Church with a state of life which must affect its attitudes towards democratic or even constitutional governments.

Thus the Revolution and its aftermath developed even the office of the Pope.

It made his government centralized like other governments, though weaker than other governments. At first sight this only applied to the monarchy in the Papal States and not to the international government of the Church. For instead of lessening the power of states over their Churches, it increased their control over choice of men, use of endowments, absence of immunities. At first sight the Pope was less international now than thirty years before because the French went their way with their Church, the Austrians went their way with their Church, and even Protestant Prussians went their way with their Catholic Churches. In legal terms this lessening of the Pope's power was not an illusion.

But underneath the legal forms, a new spirit can already here and there be detected. Just because states took more power, clergy and people began to look to a court of appeal outside the State. The Revolution ended feudalism, and so ended most local rights and exemptions. Like every other group, the Churches were face to face, not with complicated governments of an *ancien régime*, where power lay among various estates of which the clergy was one, but with centralizing governments which inherited the mantle of Napoleon. Instead of looking for help to an archaic constitution, like that of the Holy Roman Empire, or an archaic office like the Archbishop-Elector of Mainz, or a mass of archaic exemptions embodied in canon law, they began to look over the mountains or seas to a distant Pope as the supreme spiritual court in the Catholic Church. Loss of State power by the Pope began to be compensated not by law but by feeling. To the constitution and feeling of the Italian churches the Pope had always been central. To the Churches of the dispersion under Protestant or Orthodox or Turkish rulers the Pope had always been central —Irish, Poles, Uniats of the East. But now Catholic governments at times felt to their Catholic subjects less unlike the governments of Britain or Prussia or Russia, and Catholics not of the dispersion began to find some of the feelings evident in the breasts of Poles or Irish. In addition many more Catholics were now ruled by non-Catholic governments, in the Rhineland, Poland, Belgium. Whether or not that made the Catholic Church weaker, it must make the Pope stronger as a resort of appeal from subjects who had no other resort.

These events gave Popes the sensation, hardly felt since the Counter-Reformation, that they led a mighty revival of religion. They were not mistaken. All over Europe men restored churches, rebuilt chapels, re-opened monasteries, organized schools. The Roman Catholic Church came out of the Napoleonic age feeling that it passed from darkness to light. Persecution was past, reconstruction prospered. With this new prosperity the Pope's reputation rose. Though he might be hated among Popes, the repute of his office was higher. As never in the eighteenth century, Catholics associated the idea of religious revival with the Pope's guidance and leadership.

Sometimes the leadership came from behind; that is, the Pope was faced with the unpalatable need to accept what the revolution did and stamp the change with his approval; either because it was irreversible, or because it was sensible.

For example: we saw the French Viceroy of north Italy high-handedly ordering that the cathedral in Venice be changed, so that San Marco became the cathedral. When the first patriarch of the Restoration secured from Rome his confirmation, Rome characteristically said in the bull that the cathedral was San Pietro in Castello and took no notice of San Marco. The new patriarch Milesi prudently took ceremonious possession of both cathedrals. Five years later a solemn bull[29] ordered the transfer to San Marco. Rome pretended not to know that San Marco had already served as a cathedral for fifteen years. It weighed the considerations judiciously and imperturbably, noticed that the old cathedral close of San Pietro was in 'other hands', and so on various good grounds pastoral and historical decided that the cathedral ought to be transferred to San Marco.

Thus a Pope, in this case Pius VII, accepted what the Revolution did. But he would not accept it because the revolution did it and then no one complained. It had to be shown even now to be sensible. Rome decided to do without blushing what someone else did fifteen years before.

---

[29] *Bull. Cont.* 15, 452–5; *La visita pastorale di Pyrker*, xxxiv–v.

The shadow of the Jansenists

Jansenism died, or seemed to die. Rightly or wrongly it was associated with liberal reform, and that was dead. Some had recanted, some disreputable, none in powerful positions.

Great names from a Jansenist past lived on as shadows. The Synod of Pistoia was condemned by Pius VI in the bull *Auctorem fidei* of 1794, the last of the great anti-Jansenist bulls in the tradition of *Unigenitus*. Scipione de' Ricci submitted to Pope Pius VII in Florence (1805), was resented by his old colleagues, and lived a sad and solitary life writing his Memoirs which vainly endeavoured to retract more than half the retractation. He fancied himself a confessor for the faith in exile, a survivor of Port-Royal. At Pavia Tamburini, though he remained near-Jacobin in his opinions, was restored to be professor of law at the university of Pavia and even after his retirement lived on as director till his death (1827) at the age of ninety; but in the faculty of law he no longer influenced the Churches. In Genoa Degola resented Ricci's recantation, and remained faithful to Port-Royal as a goal of pilgrimage, and privately encouraged the reading of books by the Jansenist fathers. He spent all his last years till his death (1826) in a studious retreat, respected but no longer a public influence. In France Grégoire started again to publish liberal books and in 1819 dared to be elected a deputy to the National Assembly but was forced to retire by an explosion of opinion and lived on in retirement, refusing invitations and pressure to retract. Occasionally were found once-promising priests now on a shelf; like the rector of the diocesan seminary at Treviso who was put out because he co-operated with the French and eleven years after the battle of Waterloo was still, for all his ability, assistant curate in a little parish of 688 souls.[30]

Santa Maria Zobenigo in Venice (1821) had eighteen priests on its staff and two of them interest. Father Fracasso abandoned the ecclesiastical state 'during the time of troubles'. But he was back now, not only an assistant in a parish but valued for his learning and a consultant theologian to the Bishop of Vicenza. The other was Giuseppe Maria Pujati, once the colleague of Scipione de' Ricci and Tamburini, and the leader of Jansenism in Venice; now, though getting towards his ninetieth year, still able to minister in services,[31] no longer representing anything or anyone that counted in this new world, a ghost from a vanished Jansenist past which yet subtly, and underneath, and unseen, worked among the pastoral ideals of Churchmen in the present.

[30] *La visita pastorale di Grasser*, 102.   [31] *La visita pastorale di Pyrker*, 76.

The only place where Jansenism seemed to be alive was in the books of those who confuted its ideas. Vélez's *The Apology for Altar and Throne* (1818) contains a violent passage against Ricci's Synod of Pistoia, which had had no influence in Europe for two decades. Controversialists lived in the mental world of their youths and trampled upon imaginary serpents of the past while they might have been looking out for the real serpents round the next corner.

But, underneath, the pastoral and devotional ideals of Jansenism were not dead. They were no longer seen in public. But children learnt from their mothers who had learnt from Jansenist pastors. Among the leaders of the nineteenth century may be found several with a Jansenist or half-Jansenist upbringing. The great novelist Manzoni, in whose attitudes the Jansenist strand is evident, owed an indirect debt to Degola. Mazzini, reacting against Christianity into deism, learnt from a Jansenist mother the stern sense of vocation which made him one of the two most religious leaders of the Italian Risorgimento. The other was the Tuscan Ricasoli, the 'iron baron' who succeeded Cavour as prime minister of a united Italy. The iron quality derived from a strictness and austerity learnt in the Jansenist environment of his youth. Raffaele Lambruschini, nephew of two powerful cardinals of the Curia during the Napoleonic wars, was the secret vicar-general of the Orvieto diocese while his uncle the bishop was exiled; he was then discovered and taken to Corsica. After the Restoration he began to work in the Curia. Soon he found that the new Curia was no place for one of Jansenizing opinions and left for his Tuscan retreat. There he founded schools, orphanages, journals, pioneered a periodical for Italian education, encouraged better farming; still a priest, at first doubtful whether the Pope was necessary to the Church, always against the Pope's monarchy in the Papal States, but convinced in the end that a Papacy was part of God's vocation for the Church; a priest of the old Enlightenment, wealthy enough to resist the pressures of the conservative world, adapting his principles to a new society and in old age a political leader of the Risorgimento; convinced to the last that liberty rested upon religious foundations.

Other bishops or priests who sided with revolution, or at least co-operated, were sometimes shelved and sometimes continued in post, though an embarrassment both to Rome and their people.

The Bishop of Faenza was bishop under the kingdom of Italy and continued as a bishop, though not well regarded by Rome, till his death in 1826. But he was ancient, and Faenza was a town of bitter liberals, and Rome was not pleased. Not all such bishops were left. Bishop Bratti of

Forlì was nominated by Napoleon and collided with Pope Pius VII. Under Leo XII he was 'invited' to leave the diocese, and went into a Tuscan exile. On the staff of the seminary at Treviso was a liberal priest, Father Giuseppe Gobbato, tolerated as an eccentric; but his eccentricity had an Italian quality, for many years later he was chosen by local leaders of the Risorgimento to preach the sermon in the cathedral to commemorate their martyrs, and so became the canon with a public occasion to praise the name of Garibaldi.

Father Scipione Bonifacio[32] published various works in favour of the revolutionary government of 1797. These were not mere excitement of the moment, or climbing upon the chariot of passing prosperity. They contained a coherent vision of a free Christian society, with the rights of man in harmony with Christian ideals, and with a critique of Mirabeau and Rousseau. Then, when Venetian democracy failed (or was betrayed by Bonaparte at the Peace of Campo Formio) he recanted his previous writings, and under the Austrians showed how impossible to make the Catholic Church democratic. Nor was this the change of a Vicar of Bray. A democrat may lose his faith in democracy when he finds its cause betrayed by its leaders.

How the tension between the old world and the new could affect a bishop was shown by the career of Nicola Caputo. When revolution broke out in Naples (1799) he was a lawyer aged twenty-five, his mother a disciple of Alfonso Liguori. He supported the Revolution, which caused in him a spiritual crisis and decision to seek holy orders. Priest in 1800 and canon of Naples cathedral in 1805, he became a celebrated preacher. In 1818, despite the political record, he was made Bishop of Lecce; and when the Revolution broke out in Naples two years later he preached a glorious sermon at the Lecce *Te Deum*, joined the demonstration in the piazza and was made a member of the committee to choose members of Parliament. He was in the minority. Most leading ecclesiastics of southern Italy stood against the new constitution, as is proved in a report of the Naples ministry of justice (November 1820).

Then the Revolution fell, reaction came. King Ferdinand reported to Rome (10 July 1821) that 'only nine bishops' favoured revolution, among them Bishop Caputo of Lecce. Nevertheless he was not ejected. He probably gave a promise never again to engage in politics. He did what he could to prevent clergy being troubled by the police, and the seminary from being attacked for including 'liberal' books in its courses. He had a

[32] Colapietra, *La Chiesa*, 288; *La visita pastorale di Grasser*, xxx; *La visita pastorale di Flangini*, lxiv-lxv.

crisis on his hands over the cathedral chapter, which had lost many endowments during the revolutionary years, and could only fill eight out of twenty-seven canonries; and another crisis in the seminary, because of the low quality of both staff and pupils. He slowly raised the number of ordinands with training in theology. He held a diocesan synod but despite argument of twelve years and appeals to Rome, could not get leave from government to publish its decrees. He could not tax parishes to help cathedral or seminary because the parishes could not afford to be taxed. When revolution came in 1848, he was silent, and took no part; that year the liberals thought him weak and incapable; the Naples nuncio enquired of the Roman Inquisition (1855–6) for documents about Bishop Caputo and was told that none could be found; and he died aged eighty-eight two years after the unification of Italy in 1860.[33]

In revolutionary years men must choose their side. And then, the world where even a future Pope was liberal, died; and liberal clergymen were not respectable, certainly not to be preferred; and they could only continue their work, softly and unobtrusively, out of favour with the leaders of Church and State.

The end of the campaign against celibacy

Thirty-five years before, men argued about clerical celibacy in Austria, Bavaria, the Rhineland, even in Tuscany, as though sensible men could hope that in the not distant future the rule might be abrogated.

The Revolution changed all this. Following the rights of man the French reformers soon allowed clerical marriage and the possibility that a man might become again a layman if he wished despite his vow of priesthood. As the republicans grew in hate to the Churches, they began demanding clerical marriage, threatening unmarried priests, exempting married priests from deportation. Some of the French constitutional priests who married certainly married in order to avoid deportation or even for the higher motive of staying with their people. Some 3,500 priests in all married during those revolutionary years.

Henceforth the marriage of clergy was associated in many good Catholic minds with the vilest acts of tyrannical government. In 1786 an Austrian could claim with confidence that his plea did not prevent him from being a faithful and loyal Catholic. That confidence was harder after 1800. His critics were more likely to regard him as an apostate.

[33] B. Pellegrino, 'Nicola Caputa (1774–1862) tra Religione e Politica' in *R. stor. Risorg.* 63 (1976), 8 ff.

Napoleon's Concordat provided for the end of married clergy in France and the laicizing of priests, by grace of the Pope, with valid marriage and legitimate children. Ex-Bishop Talleyrand was treated uniquely. He received laicization on condition of giving alms to the poor of his old diocese of Autun.

With the Restoration the argument revived, but only in south Germany. Benedikt Werkmeister was powerful for a time among the new regimes in south Germany. Since Catholic opinion generally had swung decisively against any idea of abrogating the law of celibacy the only chance lay in persuading states to act despite Rome and despite most of their people.

But the difference in the world was shown by the new arguments which were brought. We are *short of priests*, we cannot get the people looked after properly so long as we exclude married men from the priesthood. This was the first time when this plea, so characteristic of the twentieth century, was heard. It contrasted marvellously with the argument of some conservatives just before the Revolution, when they said that as priests were far too many it was a mistake to abrogate celibacy because it would increase their number.

One big mind raised the debate to a new level. J. B. Hirscher, professor at the new Catholic faculty at the Protestant university of Tübingen, printed in the Tübingen journal for 1820 an unsigned review.[34] What concerned him was the entire relationship between moral sensitivity and the married life. It is doubtful morally to compel a man to be married in the hope that thereby he will turn his mind to higher things. The family brings with it the suffering inseparable from private affections, and is the school of compassion; therefore it is wrong to deprive priests, unless they feel the vocation to the single life, of the chance of sharing in these passions and compassions. The article was far the most profound plea to appear on the side of those who wanted change. It came too late to make any difference.

In Silesia and Baden, where the population was mixed in religion, the movement against celibacy was still vocal. In 1828 the two young Theiner brothers at the university of Breslau (one was later to become the celebrated Vatican archivist) published with polemical intent the best history of clerical celibacy written until that moment, a book still useful. That same year twenty-three Catholic laymen headed by professors at the university of Freiburg im Breisgau, petitioned the lower house of the Baden Parliament, the grand-duke, and the archbishop, that celibacy be abolished for Catholic priests. Even two of the Catholic professors of

---

[34] *Theologische Quartalschrift*, 2.637–70.

divinity at Freiburg were strong against celibacy in their public lectures. In 1831 the petition was revived and joined by fifty ordinands. The archbishop (Boll) refused to ordain any of them till they retracted. He forced one of the Catholic professors out of his chair and both he and his colleague soon became Protestants and married. In Württemberg a certain little 'women's movement' was evident, women protesting against the lowering of their sex because of the rule of celibacy. A Württemberg society of some 200 members was formed, and unrest ensued in the parishes. Forty parishes appealed to the king, 'rather no priest than a married priest.'[35]

Here is the career of a German priest whose way was disturbed by revolution. Johann Anton Dereser (whom we have met as a reformer of vernacular liturgy, p. 442) lived 1757–1827, and therefore was at the height of his powers during the revolutionary years. He became a discalced Carmelite and when the French Revolution broke out was teaching oriental languages at the new university founded by the Elector of Cologne in Bonn. He accepted that the Bible was inerrant in faith and morals but that its history must be investigated scientifically. He believed that we must interpret the texts for ourselves, and need not rely on the opinions of the Fathers. He demanded that Catholic dogmatic must be based on a scientific study of the Bible and historical in its approach. These opinions soon made him suspect for heresy and a New Testament study was put upon the Index of prohibited books. In 1790 Pope Pius VI demanded that the elector (Max Franz) proceed against Dereser and other Bonn professors. The elector refused, but in the next year Dereser resigned, and some members of Bonn university thought that they lost their best man.

This record meant that he could never afterwards come to full fruition as a scholar. The world changed rapidly, and had small use for a monk of his opinions. He found a teaching post at Strasbourg under a bishop who accepted the new French civil constitution of the clergy, and himself took the oath to the civil constitution. This did not protect him from arrest and death sentence under Jacobin rule. The fall of Robespierre saved him from execution, and at Würzburg he was absolved for taking the oath. In 1799 he became professor of oriental languages at Heidelberg, and soon afterwards left the Carmelites and lived as a secular priest. In 1806 he taught at the university of Freiburg im Breisgau, in 1810 was city pastor at Karlsruhe but was expelled after fourteen months because of a funeral sermon at the death of the grand duke. Then Wessenberg found him a home at Lucerne as professor, but the fall of Napoleon in 1814 meant that

[35] Leinweber, 72.

many with a doubtful past lost their employemnt, and he was accused of heresy. Nevertheless he found his last haven as professor of dogmatic theology in Breslau.[36] Meanwhile he translated several of the books of the Bible into German, a translation much used among Catholics in the second quarter of the nineteenth century.

The structure of the Church

Bishoprics

Of the 131 sees in the kingdom of Naples, eighty-eight were vacant in 1818. In Germany only five sees were occupied (1814). In Latin America almost all sees had either no bishops or bishops who could not act.

The Revolution abolished some dioceses, usually in fact rather than theory, by failing to fill a vacant see. The men of the Restoration were therefore confronted with certain sees which existed in theory and were obviously good to revive, and other sees which existed in theory and which it would be insane to revive. Sometimes, as in south-west Germany, nothing would serve but an entire reconstruction of dioceses and sees; and then the revival must be matter for argument between Rome and governments, and incorporated in a Concordat. At the other extreme the kingdom of Italy had quietly 'suppressed' the diocese of Caorle with its three parishes and of Torcello with its eleven parishes. To revive was absurd. In 1818 Rome formally suppressed.

History provided a special problem in southern Italy. Near to Greece, the land adopted from a very early epoch the Greek systems of many bishops and many dioceses, every town with its bishop. Therefore the mainland in the kingdom of the Two Sicilies had more bishops per head of population than anywhere else in the world.

In 1800 mainland southern Italy had 131 dioceses; Spain had fifty-four; Sicily had nine; Germany had twenty. The Napoleonic governments in southern Italy solved the difficulty by refusing to fill sees and at the Restoration only forty-three of the 131 dioceses had bishops. The Sorrento peninsula alone had nine bishoprics. It was not only the Greek example. Barons preferred bishops of their private region.

The age of reconstruction reduced these sees in the kingdom of Naples by fifty; in six stages between 1818 and 1834. Reason, or attention to the number of bishops elsewhere in Europe, suggested that they could comfortably lose another twenty or thirty. But for a very conservative government to abolish so many bishoprics was itself extraordinary and

[36] L. Koch, in *Archiv für Liturgiewissenschaft*, 17–18 (1975–6), 80 ff.

only fought through in the teeth of resistance, from squires who still preferred their own bishops, canons afraid for their chapter if the diocese vanished, antiquarians in love with a historic office, townsmen, men of civic pride fearing loss of prestige for their town, provincial governments arguing that the presence of a bishop helped them to be a local centre. Difficult and time-consuming though the process was, it was done. Fifty bishoprics disappeared. The nine sees of the Sorrento peninsula became two. Money was the overriding reason.

The *mensa* of the bishop contained far less money where it had not disappeared. Many *mensae* lost much of their income when feudal tithes were abolished. The *mensa* of the little diocese was even more precarious, because the administration had been less efficient, title-deeds more easily lost, intruders more brazen. At first bishops of small sees in the south found it hard to repair their houses and live honourably, let alone help the poor or subsidise the seminary. The Concordat of 1818 between Rome and Naples laid it down that a bishop must have not less than 3,000 ducats a year net; but this was far easier to agree than to achieve. A long hunt ensued for documents that went missing during the Napoleonic years. The first bishops of the Restoration found the recovery of property for the *mensa* to be their most arduous and time-occupying duty, they passed from official to official according to the district, wrote letter after letter and lamented that answers dallied and the file grew fat. 'I've made number-less efforts,' wrote a bishop sadly; 'I've toured the officials of three provinces where the property is and those in charge of it. I've written and rewritten numberless letters, and I have been at my wits' end to know what else I can do to get possession or even to discover what I own.'[37]

That bishop's archive was found to be the only surviving item in the ransacked bishop's palace; the rooms were naked even of a crucifix; but someone must have hunted through all the papers, damaged as they were by time and water, looking ignorantly for he knew not what, because they were heaped together higgledy-piggledy, and it took a few years of sorting before they were again usable as a system of filing.

At first sight little changed in the bishop's duties.

Pastoral letters of Italian bishops might have been written fifty years before. Visitations felt the same and their reports read alike; diocesan synods were urged from Rome but seldom held, missioners preached; in the summer of 1822 crowds of both sexes came to the chapel of St. Foca near Melendugno in southern Italy because they suffered from a plague of insect bites and went away healed; the number of endowed masses fell

[37] Lupoli of Conza to Ministry of Cults, 14 Nov. 1818; printed Cestaro, 52 n.8.

because endowments were lost but were still high, country priests were still countrymen and needed lifting amid the morals of countrymen; an old administrative system inherited from the Council of Trent and Spanish rule in Italy continued to hamper freedom of action; the diocese of Lecce still had seventy-one churches and 215 chapels for twenty-six inhabited places;[38] the ideal of priesthood was still that of the Counter-Reformation, the model saint was still St. Charles Borromeo; chapters were still divided though they had far fewer canons because they had lost so many endowments; seminaries were still in crisis, or worse crisis because bishops found it hard to reach a tolerable level of students or of teaching staff. In short, at first sight men still lived in the world of the eighteenth century, as though Bonaparte never crossed Rhine or Pyrenees or Alps.

The bishop's cure was subtly different.

Too much had happened to too many people.

Monks and nuns in their thousands were driven out of their convents and perforce made new homes and new careers. Many of them liked these new homes or new careers. Under the rules they were bound to return to their monasteries or nunneries if these were reopened. The idea had only to be put forward to look absurd. Priests had been driven out of parishes or countries and perforce made new careers. Many of these new careers could not be ecclesiastical. A man who left his priesthood under compulsion and twenty years later had no desire to return, could hardly be compelled, whatever the laws of the Church decreed.

Father Napoletani was a parish priest and confessor. In the Parthenopean republic in Naples he took the side of revolution, and in the reaction of 1799 was driven into exile. He enlisted as a soldier in the French army and steadily rose in rank. Sent to service in his native land he became colonel and then general under King Joachim Murat. During this time he married twice and begot numerous children. When King Ferdinand was restored in 1815 he could not possibly return to the priesthood, nor could a runaway priest serve as a soldier. So he applied to Rome, received absolution and lay status, and continued to serve as a general in the army.[39]

A diocese (if in southern Italy, a diocese larger than before) was no longer dominated by monks. The bishop was more evidently the pastoral leader of most of the clergy. He had less frequent need to argue with abbots, or besiege Rome to decide between himself and a monastery. Those arguments and appeals continued. They took less of a bishop's endeavour.

---

[38] B. Pellegrino, *R. stor. Risorg.* 63 (1976), 20, from Bishop Caputo's pastoral visit.
[39] Colletta, *Kingdom of Naples*, 2.354.

He was free (in most places) of the prison, and the office of a judge. If he still sent away delinquent clergy it was more like sending them away to a retreat than to shackles, to a home than to gaol. Good bishops had always appeared as pastors rather than policemen. The Revolution made it easier for any bishop not to look like a policeman. Where he was not so free of the prison, as in the kingdom of the Two Sicilies, he was sometimes perplexed.

During the occupation [wrote a puzzled bishop to the Congregation of the Council] certain priests of this diocese, at a time when there was no bishop, sank so low as to put sons into the world, to the scandal of the faithful. I ordered that they be shut up in a monastery as in a prison for three years. They are still there. Now I do not know what to do. While the children are alive, scandal remains. So long as there is scandal, how can I order that the punishment ends? But here the half-witted fathers and unhappy children clash against each other in my mind. The fathers talk of human weakness, the sons talk of hunger. The fathers ask for forgiveness, the sons for justice. What ought I to do? I am in trouble of mind. In my soul the fire of charity and the hatred of sin are locked in battle. I do not know what to do.[40]

The bishop lost his feudal rights and therefore part of the secular authority which made him a magnate in the state and the secular equal of the provincial governor. But he gained more than he lost. For generations he had fought barons and squires, whether to preserve the property of the Church, or to protect peasants, or to be rid of some criminal priest whom they shielded. Now barons and squires had no such power; and if they tried to steal the glebe or trample upon the curate, the bishop could claim the help of central government. With feudalism disappeared the old rights of patrons. The Restoration allowed patronage a little revival. But patrons were never again what once they were. The bishop had more say than before in the posting of more priests.

In the first few years bishops on confirmation tours administered the sacrament to huge numbers of candidates, some advanced in years, for many districts had had no bishop to confirm for thirty years.

Lists of confessors had names which arrived without anyone knowing how, with certificates of passing an examination which had hardly asked other than very formal questions. Several Italian bishops of the Restoration forced confessors to re-subject themselves to examination, and were disquieted with the results. Of thirty-seven confessors examined by the new Archbishop of Conza, he renewed the faculties of only ten.[41]

Because priests were few, bishops complained that they dare not disci-

[40] Lupoli's *Relazione* (1825); printed in Cestaro, appendix, 143.   [41] Cestaro, 60-1.

pline the priests in service, and had to put up with lay clothes, non-residence, and gabbled masses. Doubtless the standards varied as greatly as before the Revolution. Turin in 1821 reported a high standard among the diocesan clergy.[42]

The Revolution played about with holy days. The ability to transfer saints' days to another day had not been overlooked as an advantage by peasant populations. Local communities moved their saint away from the day in the calendar to the day which suited their market, or their harvest, or their traditional people's ceremony—that is, they started to choose the date for its secular interest; and bishops spent time and too much energy, in securing that the saint was once again celebrated on his proper day.

Visitations after the Restoration have a somewhat different tone. They are shorter, accept brief information and more summary inventories. They are shorter because many dioceses were united and the bishop must go further and quicker and had less time for the paper. They were also shorter because clergy and parishes could even less afford the cost of entertaining and feeding the visitors. Perhaps the bishop's entry to a parish was a little more elaborate, even more ceremonious, with louder fireworks, more flowery arches of triumph, a more clanking escort; but the bishop's entry during the eighteenth century could be very ceremonious. Because they were shorter they could be less searching, and less informative. The reader may learn less of the people's superstition, and sit aridly among lists of church furniture. The bishop probably understood less fully than his predecessor. But he had more people to try to understand.

In many dioceses the repair of churches was more anxious to the bishop's eye. Whether incumbent or patron, congregation or community was responsible, everyone found it harder to mend roof and walls and windows during the troubled years, because materials were expensive and labour scarce and money insecure. In Lombardy and Venezia congregations had the *fabbricieri*, their officers to supervise repair. In south Italy the funds for repair were called *luoghi pii laicali* were taken by government during the Napoleonic years and used for general welfare under a committee of local laymen. If the Church had been repaired not by the community but by the patron, this too was lost because patronage was abolished with all other feudal rights. The 'general welfare' for which the *luoghi* were to be used could include the repair of the church and the expenses of its worship. But in the slump of 1816–17 villagers were starving and their communes had few monies to pay for altar cloths. In at least one place the village gave only money which failed to suffice for

[42] *R.S.C.I.*, (1976), 50–1.

the oil in the lamps, and paid for nothing else. Villages could not afford incense even on high feasts, or candles to escort the sacrament. The Bishop of Campagna used the word *horror* of his feelings when he witnessed 'the indecency and ruin of the worship of God.' His worst agony came when he was forced to take the reserved sacrament out of a church because it had no lamp burning, no wax, no incense; the floor was wet, priests were reluctant to say mass, people had nowhere to kneel. Simultaneously he had news of a fall of lead from the roof at Quaglietta church, and heard that at Buccino those who knelt to pray before the monuments above were threatened with death because they were held only by rotting cords and strands. The bishop tried to comfort himself: 'I have no peace of mind, I pour out my grief before the Lord.' One of the worst things was the behaviour of some new lay administrators of charity in backward parts, who instead of giving money to the priest to buy candles, bought candles themselves and thought it their duty personally to place the candles on, or later remove them from, the altar—not without irreverent clambering about a sanctuary. Bishops made representations that the income of the former *luoghi* be administered by clergymen. In time (1820) the government of Naples made bishops vice-presidents of the committee that administered charitable funds.[43]

This was the beginning in southern Italy, of consciousness of spheres of life, one that of the Church and the other that of the world.

It was also a big social shift. Once the poor man begged his loaf and soup at the door of a monastery. But now the doors of many monasteries were shut for ever. Charitable funds were once administered by the parish priest, now by a lay committee. Formerly the clergy were registrars and had an oversight of engagements as well as marriages. Their oversight still existed, because society expected it to exist, not because the law, with its civil marriage, provided. Once he was buried in the church cemetery or in the church; from 1817 the kingdom of Naples began to provide public cemeteries, and no one could be buried in church.

The Bishop of Campagna, when he visited his cathedral in 1820, was disturbed to find that the windows had no glass. At Calitri he found the parish church with large holes in the walls, gaping clefts in the floor, and the chancel arch out of true and threatening to fall.[44]

How rapid was recovery is hard to determine, because it is not agreed in what recovery consisted. Old-fashioned parishes wanted everything back as it stood before 1789, and however prosperous parochial life now,

[43] Lupoli's letters 1818, 1821, 1823; in Cestaro, 170–1, 177–8, 203–4.
[44] Cestaro, 84–5.

older men remembered a day when they had five brotherhoods instead of one, and easier endowments, and less ill-paid clergy, and more chalices, and more populous pilgrimages. In changing times natural regrets for past time bred their habitual illusions of a more golden age. The Bishop of Treviso knew that before the wars his cathedral had thirty-eight choral prebends and now only twenty. He imagined twenty to be inadequate and applied to government for more endowment. Government refused, and suggested that instead he appoint honorary canons. But the bishop thought honorary canons would cheapen the rank of canon and declined.

In 1826 the little parish of Coste in Venezia reported to its bishop that the parish church was badly off for sacred vessels and furnishings 'because so much silver and other valuables were stolen' during the invasion; but their standards were of the eighteenth century, for the inventory shows a provision which a modern church might think ample, and perhaps it was relevant that the learned incumbent had seventy-two years and served most of his ministry in more prosperous days, and still liked to grumble that he was turning into a sheep among ploughboys and preferred to be away from his parish for longer weeks than his bishop approved.

Nevertheless, not all was imagination. In 1801 French troops sacked the sacristy and relic chests of Pezzan di Campagna. Twenty-six and a half years later the sacristy still looked as though it had been sacked.[45]

Trying to get government to release more ex-Church money to now impoverished churches, a bishop could use the argument from utility: 'In this way [by a better provided worship] the people are made religious and in consequence socially responsible and obedient to law. Take away the foundation and all is disorder.'[46]

Seminaries

Where the buildings of a former monastery stood idle and empty, unconverted to other uses (as happened more often in country than town), seminaries if reopened moved into better buildings than ever before. This was not the common case. Many bishops had the old problem of a seminary where the students, or two-thirds of them, lived in lodgings round the town and could have no common life. And seminaries were hard to revive because priests were in short supply. Bishops dare not decree too strict rules about attendance in a seminary because they needed more priests quickly. This got worse before it got better. The seminary at Ferrara had 114 students in 1814, twenty-five students fifteen years later.[47]

---

[45] *La visita pastorale di Grasser*, 25, 83–5, 129.
[46] Lupoli to Minister of Cults, 1820; Cestaro, 78.   [47] R.S.C.I. (1976), 51.

The end of any need to prove that a man was an ordinand, if he were to be exempt from conscription into the army, may have affected numbers. But this was not the real cause. To restore to young men the habit of coming forward for ordination was no light task. In the diocese of Treviso during the years after the Restoration an average of twenty-two priests died each year, an average of six priests took orders.

Numbers of clergy in the city of Rome are not typical. Nevertheless a comparison (see Table 12) illustrates the age of reconstruction.[48]

12

In Rome	1814	1823
bishops	0	27
priests	1,214	1,395
monks	0	1,565
nuns	0	1,370
seminarists	465	460
poor in hospital	262	1,438
'heretics'		234

But in north Italy at Lodi priests in the diocese, secular and regular,[49] were as follows: in 1772, 1,168; in 1782, 1,070; in 1792, 887; in 1799, 713; in 1816, 565.

After the Restoration things could not right themselves at once, if to right matters was (though it was not) to go back to the same percentage of priests to people as in 1772. The diocese of Lodi had 265 people to each priest in 1816, 414 people to each priest forty-six years later.

The number of priests in diocese of Modena[50] were, in 1797, 1,407; in 1815, 896; in 1832, 791. Part of the decline in numbers rested upon a growing determination of bishops, or sometimes of Josephist governments, to keep standards higher.

In certain states the Josephist hand lay heavy upon the reopened seminaries. According to the Council of Trent, the seminary was the bishop's nursery of priests. All good bishops took a fatherly interest, some bishops joined in the common life where it existed, and even attended the examinations. But in Lombardy and Venezia of the Restoration, government interfered, intruded, fussed. Bureaucrats plagued the staff of the

[48] Colapietra, *Le Chiesa*, 247. It is hard to think that the zero for bishops, monks, and nuns can be correct.
[49] Toscani, in *R.S.C.I.* 28 (1974), 142–90.
[50] G. Verucci, in *R.S.C.I.* 30 (1976), 25–72.

seminary over admissions, expulsions, textbooks, lists, data, and every sort of exhortation. A seminary was supposed to teach agriculture and a small amount of science; but it quickly became also the only secondary school of the city. All the ordinands came from poor homes and had their fees paid. They were not enthusiastic about their studies. If an ordinand came from a middle-class home, he was probably sent away to Padua. Government liked Febronian textbooks of canon law, but neither interfered with solidly orthodox books on doctrine nor pushed the teaching staff towards Jansenist ideas. The staff was ill paid, diet meagre, library poor.

Bishops asked government for books from the libraries of suppressed monasteries at Padua, but lots of those books had come under the auctioneer's hammer. The biographer of the director of the seminary at Treviso raged over the miserable stipend, especially because dancers and mimes and singers earned rivers of gold to mislead the young while the director had a pittance for leading them aright.[51]

Brotherhoods

The largest change in parish life was marked by the near-disappearance of brotherhoods. These lost their money and disappeared. One brotherhood remained almost universally, that of the Most Holy Sacrament (*Santissimo*). Sometimes (San Canciano in Venice) the *Santissimo* tried to help the parish priest to revive other brotherhoods. In 1817 the Austrian government went back on part of the laws of Joseph II by allowing the revival of brotherhoods. But very few were successful in the old way, they were now small groups of the godly who prayed for the dead and cared for the cemetery chapel, or kept special devotion to the rosary, or fostered prayers among a particular group like the Slavs in north-east Italy. The revived brotherhoods of Genoa sent a petition (1826) to Rome that their property be restored. In parts of Spain, especially Andalusia, the decline of brotherhoods was less evident. But except in rare pockets of parish life they never again dominated the religious life of the laity. Country priests became kings of their congregations. Laymen lost a place when that main form of religious life in the old world faded. Perhaps, (some have thought) they also lost interest, the parish church never succeeded in harvesting loyalties like an old brotherhood.

Nevertheless, local loyalties could still be strong. The village of Falzé in Venezia, whose saint was St. Jerome, protested to the bishop against the near-by village of Trevignano, whose saint was Theonistus,

[51] *La visita pastorale di Grasser* xxxi.

because hung over the main door of the church at Trevignano appeared 'an insolent picture' showing St. Jerome at the feet of St. Theonistus.[52] Jerome was a far more famous saint. But Theonistus was the martyr-patron of Treviso.

The Napoleonic wars made movement of civilians difficult, and there-fore knocked pilgrimage, already declining under discouragement by reforming governments. Catholic assailants of pilgrimage grew more outspoken, defenders more lukewarm or softvoiced. By the end of the Napoleonic wars it was widely agreed that a pilgrimage was not an event of the Church but an event of the individual, part not of corporate worship but of private devotion. The habit was broken. Peninsular war made travel to Compostella the riskiest of adventures. It stopped, and after the wars was never renewed in more than a trickle from anywhere outside Spain. Napoleon's armies and Catholic Reformers between them left a vacuum in a people's devotion, not to be filled again, and then in a different way, until the coming of the railway and new shrines like Lourdes.

The jubilee of 1825

In 1825 Pope Leo XII celebrated the only jubilee of the nineteenth century. He was warned against it, because of European opinion and the insecurity of roads in the Papal States. He insisted. The first signs disquieted. The hotel for pilgrims had 5,000 beds and on 2 January 1825 had only 100 pilgrims. But in all May (the highest month) the pilgrims were 41,888, and the total for the year was 94,157, and enabled Rome to claim success. The numbers did not compare with those of the eighteenth century. And the pilgrims who came were dominantly Italian: nearly half the total from the Two Sicilies, (44,973); nearly a quarter from the Papal States (19,857); handfuls from Austria, France, Spain, Poland, Ireland.[53] Europe outside Italy took no notice of this jubilee. It was a resounding proof of the decline of pilgrimage over long distances.

Collegiate churches

In the confiscations of property cathedral chapters and colleges of canons suffered. Many chapters of southern Italy could now sustain only a few canons. The French arrangements provided State pay for parish clergy but no endowments for chapters, and the functions of French chapters remained largely decorative. The clergy were more parochial, the gulf

---

[52] *La visita pastorale di Grasser*, 72.   [53] Colapietra, *La Chiesa*, 252 ff.

between priest and bishop grew wider because chapters no longer made
so strong a middle rank between the country clergyman and his diocesan.
Revolutionary governments disliked collegiate churches. They thought
them liable to foster abuse and idleness, to promote disharmony because no
one could decide, and to use unnecessary endowments when the church
could more easily be directed by a parish priest with assistant curates. Since
those governments needed the money, this last consideration was final.
The Italian kingdom in the north, King Joachim Murat in the south, got
rid of collegiate churches, excepting the chapters of cathedrals in a diocese.

When the time of restoration came, the old canons expected to get back
their rights. And they could not often succeed. The abolition of so many
collegiate churches was not only a way of stealing money from the Church,
it was a genuine reform of Church structure. They made an untidy lump
in a diocesan and parochial ministry. Neither bishops nor governments of
the Restoration were eager to see canons back in their colleges.

This was not a little problem. It can be illustrated from the very different
areas of Vicenza in northern Italy and the receptive churches in southern
Italy.

Vicenza on the edge of the northern hills was not a diocese with many
collegiate churches. But it had a historic college at the church of St. Mary-
on-the-hill in the parish of Bassano. The Italian kingdom (1810) took the
endowments of the college, abolished its structure and left it under a parish
priest. The canons, all natives of Bassano, now applied to be given back
their prebends. But the State had no money to recreate prebends, and with
the vicar-capitular's support (for the see was in a nine-year interregnum)
gave back the prebends as honorary canonries, with due ceremonial in
church, but without pay or vote in chapter. The canons at once began to
behave as though the church was again a college, and started to try to run
the parish church without leave of the parish priest—who asked the
authorities of Church and State what he ought to do. When the parish
priest had his directing power upheld, the canons ceased to appear, or even
to help him in festivals, until some of the laity could not even communicate in their parish church but must go to one of the other churches.[54]
It took six years for harmony to reappear in the parish.

Here was a contretemps illuminating for the age of reconstruction. Men
expected, and sometimes were told, that acts of revolutionary regimes
were null and void, and they therefore expected to come back into their
own. But the money which was once their own had evaporated, being
directed to other ends; and meanwhile governors and bishops preferred

[54] *La visita pastorale di Peruzzi*, 532.

the direct chain of command, bishop–priest–assistant, to these awkward semi-independent chapters which were not the chapters of cathedrals. In such circumstances critics of old colleges easily misrepresented or represented them as comfortable homes for the idle sons of middle-class citizens of the town.

We hear, though seldom, that this destruction was a pity because priests work better in colleges, where they find mutual criticism and mutual encouragement.

Some canons reassumed their colleges and were not challenged. Towards the middle of the nineteenth century can still be found colleges which perhaps had no legal right to exist but which continued to distribute the income in a collegiate way. The canons came into their own at the Restoration, no one challenged, the habit was accepted.

As the Josephists of the north killed the collegiate churches of Venezia, King Murat in south Italy found the 'receptive churches' (1087 out of 3,000 parishes on the mainland) and started to turn them into normal parishes. The Restoration must respect old rights, and disliked everything that Murat did. But it had no desire that receptive churches should continue unreformed. In 1819 the government of Naples subjected the appointment of the parish priest to *concursus*—that is, the bishop as well as the corporation now chose their pastor; and the bishop henceforth could demand to oversee the parish, require residence of the priests (if they drew any part of the income) and see that they attended choir.[55] This new interference caused discontent among the clergy.

The receptive churches had preserved many generations of south-Italian clergy, and south-Italian families, in security and at times in comfort. Numbers of the priests of these churches were now found among the carbonari because they disliked the bishop as an agent of a new and meddling central government. Despite this attempt at drastic reform, receptive churches continued important in the parochial life of south Italy.

Colleges had made the one place where after long service pensions could be had. Then the dissolution of so many monasteries and nunneries familiarized the Catholic world with the idea of elderly ecclesiastics living in retirement on a pension. In parts of the French empire there had been talk, and even action, to get a system of pensions and retirement for old clergy. This idea was much alive in the years of reconstruction. The impetus was not the French suggestion but the need, evident to everyone trying to get a better pastoral system. In Venice tourists were scandalized to see ancient shabby unshaven clergymen, down-and-out, toes coming

[55] Cestaro, 68–9.

out of their boots, tramps in cassocks, hanging about the streets or canals or bars. The need shrieked the louder because the Revolution dislocated the pattern of ordinations and the average age of the clergy was higher.

In the thirty parishes of Venice City (1821) were serving among the 700 clergy a fair number whose ages are unknown. But the majority whose ages are known included one priest of ninety years, sixteen priests in their eighties (one labelled as 'sick', another as in a home, but among the other fourteen were two heads of parishes) and thirty-three in their seventies. The numerous ex-monks were normally secure because they received a pension from their former monastery. Patriarch Pyrker started a home for elderly clergy in part of a former monastery which a merchant had bought for a factory. To persuade elderly clergy to retire thither was so hard that Pyrker's successor got leave from government to house a few of them within the seminary.[56]

The Revolution reduced the number of parishes to confiscate or reallot endowment. The Restoration accepted the reductions as sensible. In 1824 Pope Leo XII even reduced the eighty-one parishes of Rome to forty-four, made from thirty-five of the old plus nine new parishes including Santa Maria Maggiore.

In the reconstruction of parish life the missioner still played a part. In a devastated series of parishes, where the normal system of pastoral care could not quickly be rebuilt, bishops invited missioners to fill the gap. Travelling Redemptorists again spoke to peasant crowds as in the eighteenth century, and often with terrifying effect. It was not quite the same. They were even more unpopular with the middle class and probably with parish priests; and among the *carbonaro*-minded clergy they were accused of being part of the political reaction. This charge was not quite fanciful, in the atmosphere of those years. More than one Italian government, seeing a rebellious countryside, sent missioners among them to restore order. King Ferdinand I of the Two Sicilies was one who believed in them as men who would summon the people to this obedience. He witnessed a Redemptorist mission in Caserta, and said, 'These good fathers get the people into better order than the generals achieve with my troops.'

During a Redemptorist mission in Campagna (1819), a letter from the Carbonari leaders at Salerno to their lieutenants in Campagna was dropped on the road by the postman. The finder gave it to the missioners, who took it to the archbishop, who gave it to the police. The Carbonari were enraged at the missioners, and accused them of wanting to stir

[56] *La visita pastorale di Pyrker*, cviii, 209.

revolution by their use of scourges, litanies, crown of thorns, penitential processions.[57]

In all these ways the parish church and the parish priest were much more important after the Revolution. His force in the *ancien régime* was weakened by

1. semi-independent brotherhoods in his congregations,
2. shrines and chapels of the countryside near by,
3. the frequent presence of collegiate churches.
4. the still more frequent presence of monastery chapels, and the prestige of (many) monks among the people.

All this was changed. Brotherhoods were weak where they existed and part of the parish structure. The old shrines of the countryside, often looked after by a hermit, and magnets for pilgrims or Sunday worshippers, lay in ruins, the hermits were almost forgotten, chapels took men away less often from the parish churches.

Church order was more logical, more intelligible, less cluttered, less cumbersome, more clerical, far less diversified, than Church order before the Revolution. The priest was less often a mass-priest, more often a pastor. He had to do more teaching, indeed more work, because he had fewer priests to help, and far fewer monks.

The revival of the monks

The whole Catholic Church was transformed by the destruction of the monks.

In 1815 almost no monks existed in western Europe, except in Spain where King Joseph Bonaparte had not been ruthless and a number of houses continued, and many houses quickly revived. In Austria–Hungary and in Russian Poland many monasteries continued throughout the age of revolution but in conditions which seldom promoted a high quality of community. In countries where monasteries were only suppressed for a short time—Italy, Spain, Portugal, Catholic Switzerland—remnants of a monastery often remained together, or in friendly touch, near their old house, and without much difficulty reoccupied the buildings.

But in 1815 many ex-monks who could have returned to that way of life failed to return. They had married, or found new vocations in parish life, or in teaching, or in all manner of secular employment. They sent to Rome very numerous pleas to be released from vows. The monks who

[57] Cestaro, 14, 70.

returned to monasteries were a small minority of those who could have returned.

This circumstance must not be thought blameworthy. After the suppressions of their homes many ex-monks found satisfying work as curates or schoolmasters. Of all the parishes in Venice in the year 1821, only eight parishes had no ex-religious as a member of their staffs. The clergy in Venice in 1804 numbered about 1,000, and seventeen years later only 700—but of these 700 more than 150 were ex-monks. They preferred to continue with their new-found vocation and not to return to their old way of life. In certain cases the distinction between the old way and the new was blurred. The parish church of SS Giovanni and Paolo in Venice had only in the revolution become a parish church, it was formerly the friary chapel of the Dominicans. But in 1821, six or seven years after he could have returned to the Dominican order had he wished, the parish priest was an ex-Dominican; and of his twenty-three assistants nineteen were ex-Dominicans. They were in effect a group of religious, no longer living the common life in the old way, not able to keep all their old rule, but intent on a common pastoral endeavour in their old church and buildings. They used indulgences customary among the Dominicans, and had an altar of St. Thomas Aquinas. That this was not the choice of an easier way was proved by the comments of the visiting patriarch who praised them highly for their pastoral zeal and activity. Two of them were blamed for dressing wretchedly; and—this was the danger of a formerly united group continuing as a group in new circumstances—the bishop ordered them when celebrating the liturgy always to use the Roman rite and not the rite of the Dominican order.[58]

A similar group of ex-Carmelites were the large majority of assistant priests at the ex-Carmelite chapel of Santa Maria del Carmelo.

At St. Andrew's church in Treviso (1827) fourteen nuns were attached to the parish, coming from several suppressed nunneries; four Camaldolese, five Benedictines, two Ursulines, two Capuchins (one from a suppressed house in Venice) and a Dominican. Of these fourteen nuns, seven lived a common life. Thus the line between the old way and the new was shadowy.

An Ursuline nun of Treviso, whose house was suppressed by the Republic of Venice in 1777, was still working as a nun in a little village near Treviso fifty years later; not solitary, for as time passed she acquired a lay-sister, a Benedictine from a later suppression.[59] She had found her way,

[58] *La visita pastorale di Pyrker,* cxxv; 22–4; 105–6.
[59] *La visita pastorale di Grasser,* 53, 137.

and saw no reason to return to a community. Governments made no effort to persuade ex-monks or ex-nuns to return. Usually their old houses had fallen to other uses. But bishops of the Restoration on their visitations were known to ask whether these ex-nuns had no need to return to convents and yet might go on drawing pensions. Someone high in Rome raised (1824) the question whether they ought to reassemble the eighty-four secularized ex-nuns living in the city.[60] The Naples Concordat of 1818 agreed that ex-monks or ex-nuns had no need to return to convents and yet might continue to draw pensions.

Some monks fled to Protestant countries—Benedictines from France to England—and since they fled to keep their way of life, survivors returned.

The most romantic and extraordinary of these monk-refugees was the charismatic Trappist Father Lestrange. In 1790 he took his Trappists out of France to Valsainte in Switzerland, and there continued to attract novices. He made new foundations, especially at Westmalle in Belgium. Then the French occupied Switzerland and Belgium. He took his Trappists to Russia, and from Russia to the United States. Thence the Trappists were strong enough to reopen not only Westmalle but La Trappe itself at the Restoration.

Carthusians were among the worst sufferers. Famous Italian houses, like Pavia and San Martino in Naples, were closed during the Josephist age. France had sixty-eight Carthusian houses which all vanished in 1790, Germany had eighteen which all vanished after the secularization of 1803. The Praemonstratensians were hit even harder. They continued on the Great St. Bernard, in Hungary and in Russian Poland. They never returned to what they were before the Revolution.

The Dominicans had eighty houses instead of 500. The Franciscan Conventuals never recovered from the blows of revolution. In 1773 they had 25,000 members, in 1850 despite revival they had not reached 1,500. The Carmelites made a slow recovery but never came anywhere near the prestige and numbers of fifty years before. The Benedictines had lost more than 1,000 abbeys and priories.[61]

Five years after the Restoration an English visitor went into the historic Charterhouse at Pavia, suppressed not by the Revolution but by Joseph II. It was beautiful; quiet and peaceful, with wild flowers growing among the paving-stones, and a fig-tree in fruit, and a caretaker, with wife and child,

[60] Colapietra, *La Chiesa*, 233.

[61] R. Aubert, 'La restauration monastique dans l'Europe occidentale du XIXᵉ siècle' in *Revue bénédictine*, 83 (1973), 10 ff.; Jedin, *Handbuch*, 6.252–3.

using the garden to grow food. In the prior's rooms she found a store of grain.[62]

13

Diocese[63]		Religious Houses	
		male	female
Turin	1780	93	22
	1821	14	6
Bergamo	1796	24	34
	1825	1	3
Vicenza	1796	13	14
	1835	5	nil
Florence	1742	c. 50	60 plus
	1850	27	21
Arezzo	1766	36	25
	1783	30	22
	1806	28	20
	1822	15	10

In all the grand duchy of Tuscany in 1808 there were 6,332 monks and 10,382 nuns; in 1835, 2,461 monks and 3,939 nuns.

In southern Italy Lecce before the Revolution had 14,000 people and thirty-one monasteries and nunneries. When a new bishop arrived after the Restoration, he found five male houses in all the diocese. He continually lamented—for diocesan and parochial reasons—this shortage of monks.

Elsewhere in south Italy, where Joseph Bonaparte allowed some houses to continue:

14

Diocese		Religious Houses	
		male	female
Naples	1797	c. 80	c. 41
	1820	14	11
Avellino	1795	20	1
	1826	4	1
Melfi	1795	11	3
	1826	4	3
Cosenza	1795	49	8
	1821	17	2

[62] Lady Morgan, *Italy* (1820), 1.193–6.
[63] Statistics in *R.S.C.I.* (1976), 28 ff.; cf. *R. stor. Risorg.* 63 (1976), 21–2; Cestaro, 145–7, 155; Jedin, *Handbuch*, 6.250–1.

Not all bishops were like the Bishop of Lecce in lamenting this decline of numbers. Bishop Vincenzo Ferrari of Melfi was so indignant with the ignorance and corruption of monks that he wished to be rid of them all. Some bishops quietly accepted what happened, and made no strenuous efforts to revive. Still other bishops worked hard to recover old monasteries, and sent mournful letters to Rome lamenting that they failed because the endowments were alienated. The Archbishop of Conza tried to reopen monasteries only in parishes where the priests were too old or incompetent or unavailable, and opposed the reopening of the house of Franciscan Observants at Campagna because when they existed they were no use to the people and caused such talk by ill behaviour that most of the people were glad when they were closed and would dislike to see the house reopen.

Tuscany refused to release more than part of the former monastic endowments. In the Papal States all shut monasteries were reopened— provided that numbers were sufficient to maintain common life. The proviso was big. Between provinces long occupied by the French and provinces, briefly occupied, a difference is observable:

15

			Monasteries	Nunneries
Long-occupied dioceses:	Ferrara	1780	33	19
		1829	4	5
	Cesena	1803	20	6
		1824	6	2
Less long-occupied dioceses:	Alatri	1780	3	2
		1824	3	2
	Gubbio	1787	16	14
		1835	12	7

Old monks did not always make the best re-founders of monasteries. The comfortable ways of the eighteenth century were not expected in this new and more emotional world. When bishops revived houses, they found difficulty in getting common life because so frequently they had no or narrow buildings. Rome even proposed (1824) that houses should not continue with less than twelve members, that nunneries without sufficient endowments should be ordered not to receive novices, that those in an order who wished for stricter observance should be gathered in a single house. The plan was not executed but shows the plight of the religious life in the early years of reconstruction. The idea of grouping orders, to help weaker orders, returned from time to time. In 1824 Rome talked of amalgamating Scolopi with Somaschi, and Theatines with Barnabites. Several governments were discontented with the indiscipline or anarchy among revived monasteries. The Pope had to send (1825) a plenipotentiary visitor to Piedmont to reform and reorganize. Much of the work consisted in the reallocation of the fraction of endowment which could be recovered, among the various claimants like monasteries, nunneries, chapters, colleges, charities. It was a legal and pastoral tangle.

The Revival of the Jesuits

They found it easier to renew orders engaged in pastoral work, especially teaching and nursing. Pope Pius VII refounded the Jesuits in 1814 and, despite the reserves of Metternich, saw their numbers grow rapidly, too rapidly for good government, though they never again came anywhere near the numbers when they were suppressed.

In 1773 there were about 22,000 Jesuits; in 1815 about 800 (Russia *c.* 300, Sicily 199, England 84, USA 86, France 47); in 1820 about 2,000 (banned from Russia in 1820—Spain 436, Papal States 400, France 198).

Among the new members was Charles Emmanuel, the abdicated (1802) King of Sardinia and Piedmont. One of those who returned was Prince Raczynski, Archbishop of Gnesen in Poland. He was a young Jesuit before suppression, new dioceses were made for what was once Poland and (1818) he got leave to renounce his see and rejoin the society.

The early years of the Jesuits after refounding illustrated the problem of reconstruction. The classical tension inside a monastery or order before the Revolution, between men who demanded faithfulness to the founder and his ideal, and men who demanded adaptation to the needs of the society in which now they were placed, reappeared at once among the refounded Jesuits, in a tense form. By will of Ignatius, government was no democracy. Naturally the Jesuits at once in command were those who were Jesuits before 1773. They were ancient, ill, incompetent, with ideas about vocation in a different world, and rapidly dying. Young men came in with that excess of zeal so often found in the age of reconstruction, determined to recreate the see of Rome and the work of the order in a way which would be effective in new circumstances. The Society suffered the same awkwardness as the Church at large. Young Jesuits versus old Jesuits grew into a battle which shook the community on its newly revived foundation. The trouble was made no easier because the all-powerful Secretary-Cardinal Consalvi, who had no hand in the revival, disliked them because their reputation made more difficult his diplomatic aim to get the Papacy again accepted among the powers of Europe. And a key-point of controversy lay in the constitutional friction between the order's new government in Rome and the Russian-Polish Jesuits who saw themselves, with reason, as continuity in the Society. Another part lay in the vow of poverty, and how to operate it when for many revolutionary years 'Jesuits' perforce controlled their own purses. Still another lay in the intentions of Pope Pius VII. He must have Jesuits again because their disappearance was somehow connected with the errors of the old world, with Jansenism and even with the coming of revolution. But he wanted Jesuits more as symbol than reality. He made no move to give them back their old exemptions and privileges or to reinstate them in their old work.

Younger men among the Roman Jesuits were determined upon a revision of statutes. And the statutes were not all observed in the revived houses. Many Spanish and Italian Jesuits were quickly promoted to the solemn vow without passing through the old discipline.

When (1820) they needed to elect a new general they were found to be on the verge of schism. The constitutional question which produced the split was a simple one, whether the electors needed to wait for the arrival of representatives from the Polish Jesuits, who had just been expelled from Russia. Some cardinals, especially Cardinal della Genga the future Pope Leo XII, believed that they could not trust them to conduct the election under the old statutes. Nineteen Jesuits appealed to Consalvi (25 September, 1820) that the constitutions of the Society be preserved unchanged. Consalvi let them go ahead to elect. They elected a conservative after a stormy scene and started to expel young hotheads.

Leo XII (1826) whose attitude was feared by the Society because of his intervention as cardinal in this election, proved himself an unexpected friend. He gave the Jesuits back their old exemptions, and put them again in charge of the Roman College.

They were still a symbol; carrying with them the burden of ancient battles and heaped fables; a flag which Protestants feared, and against which the heirs of Jansenists and Gallicans still fought. A lot of people were alive for whom Clement XIV Ganganelli was the greatest of Popes. At times the reader of Catholic anti-Jesuit pamphlets in the twenties and thirties of the nineteenth century wonders whether Pius VII and his cardinals were right to revive the name. But the fact was, an injustice had been done for the sake of expediency; and even if expediency might suggest that no one should remedy the injustice which by now was partly forgotten, the age of reconstruction was not a time when this mood attracted.

The revival of other orders

In Lombardy the Austrians encouraged orders which taught school or cared for orphans or ran hospitals, and Naples and Tuscany did likewise. The 'pastoral' order of monks or nuns was easier to reconstruct than the contemplative or Benedictine type of order; and sometimes the old contemplative order or Benedictine house could only be revived if it took work which was alien to the tradition of the order, in parishes or schools or hospitals. This was why, as early as 1815, even France had already 14,226 nuns. But it was not the only reason for the revival of nunneries. The old social reason could still be heard. When the Bishop of Campagna in south Italy came to his diocese, he was disturbed to find only one house of nuns, a sorely divided community, into which the survivors of nunneries had been collected. He wrote thus to government: 'It is beyond measure burdensome, and intolerable to a town of 7,000 inhabitants, that they have only this single refuge for their daughters.'[64]

The pastoral needs began to break or modify the cloister of nuns. In 1817 Pope Pius VII allowed the Spanish to use *enclosed* nuns to teach in schools.[65]

The monastic endowments of southern Italy had been nationalized, and part alienated. The part which had not been alienated was inadequate to endow all the houses which bishops or communes or orders now wanted to reopen. There was also a problem of conscience; quieting the minds of those now in possession of ex-monastic alienated property. Because the money was insufficient, and controlled by the State, government here also gave precedence to 'useful' orders, that is, teaching and nursing and missionizing.

Slowly the old orders collected themselves. The Grande Chartreuse was reopened in 1816, Monte Cassino as a not strict Benedictine centre five years later.

By way of example, we have a report (1823) from a Lateran canon on the way in which the order was recreated. He said that already they had fourteen houses (sixty Italian houses in 1537). Those in the Papal States (not the Legations) had endowments almost as before the Revolution, though the houses at Orvieto and Urbino had suffered partial loss of income and could only support six canons each. In the kingdom of Naples they had two restored, Naples which dated from 1453 and Bitonto, not with

[64] Cestaro, 168–9.   [65] Jedin, *Handbuch*, 6.158.

all the previous endowment but with ample to exist, and in Bitonto one of the fairest buildings in all southern Italy. In the Legations Fano and Bologna were restarted, each with a little endowment; Bologna would soon flourish because of its pastoral care in the city, Fano needed grants from other houses to survive. In Lucca (site of the original mother house in the eleventh century) and Genoa the restored houses had but a small income but would manage, at Genoa because they cared for a sanctuary with many offerings, at Lucca because they had charge of a big parish. They hoped next to refound in Ferrara. They had altogether thirteen novices. They now jettisoned their scapular. But in the very year that this report was written they united with another historic order of Italian canons of St. Mary in Reno, which had about forty houses before the revolution but had not now the strength to revive; such of its survivors as wished to practise again the regular life were absorbed into the Lateran canons. In this way 100 houses of canons before the Revolution became less than twenty houses in the Restoration.[66]

Monks, especially Italian monks, still adorned the world of scholarship. But the famous were usually older men. The leisure and in good part the great libraries of an old monastic world were gone for the time. Monks were more pastoral, helped in more parishes, taught more small boys, cared for more sick—and they were fewer. The opinion can be found that what the Revolution did to monks led to fewer eminent scholars in monasteries; which meant also, fewer eminent scholars among the clergy. Even in Rome, the schools of divinity were nearer the fringes of knowledge in 1750 than they were three-quarters of a century later.

New religious groups

The nineteenth century witnessed a godly revival of the monastic life. But this revival was due not so much to the regrowth of historic orders as the flowering of new orders, or groups, adapted to the new age. Deprived of the assistance of monks or mass priests, the pastor gathered devout women to be his fellow-workers, they adopted a common life and then a rule, sought the bishop's leave, and finally spread beyond parish or diocese and the name of the group was heard in Rome. Already in the years of reconstruction began the foundation of a bewildering variety of little orders, often diocesan, sometimes parochial, rarely exempt; and with pastoral aims, the work of the parish, the care of the old, the teaching of

[66] *La visita pastorale di Peruzzi*, xxiii–xxiv. The order had fifty-three houses in 1973 (*D.I.P.* 2.107).

illiterate girls. In this way they altered the complexion of the religious life
within Catholicism; making its totality less of a series of independent and
powerful corporations, and more of a kaleidoscopic diversity of groups
brimming with individual vitality. They hampered the revival of the
older and historic orders because they fulfilled the vocation of self-
sacrifice in another direction. Some twenty old (but minor) orders finally
disappeared.

Also, they were lower in social origins. The rich houses to provide
pensions for aristocratic ladies vanished when national treasuries took their
money. But women were still in surplus, new primary schools or nursing
offered occasion, many new nuns raised their station when they entered
the nunnery. Aristocrats might still be found. The system of dowry
continued. But the world of the religious orders was no longer so middle
class.

Giuseppe Benaglio (1767–1836) was just such a priest-founder of the
epoch of reconstruction. As Bonaparte invaded Italy, Benaglio was a canon
of Bergamo cathedral. When the convents were suppressed, he created a
little teaching 'order' of women, called Daughters of the Sacred Heart of
Jesus; and then an evening school for lads in the empty buildings of the
old seminary. When the diocesan seminary returned to life he became a
professor and then its head, very papalist, fighting tenaciously against
every trace of old Jansenism. He wanted to found a religious order of men,
called the Institute of the Sacred Heart, to 'fight Jansenism and preach
missions', and had even acquired premises when the bishop refused his
leave.

At first sight nothing much had changed; a priest with the ascetic ideals
of the Counter-Reformation, revering Borromeo and Ignatius Loyola,
continuing like priests of the eighteenth century to struggle for good
education and extend it to girls, eager for traditional modes of mission.
But the atmosphere subtly altered. The Revolution made this priest a more
vehement man of the Pope, a more passionate enemy of Jansenists, a more
stout defender of Church freedoms from State interference. The name of
his new religious order was not tactful. To call it Daughters of the Sacred
Heart could not commend it to the older priests and bishops of northern
Italy who were disciples of Muratori. The name must offend some whose
support or complaisance might have helped. That the bishop at last refused
leave for a male order, and that the women's order was at one moment in
danger of suppression, will not surprise. Into the devotional attitudes of
the Counter-Reformation the Revolution brought new pugnacity, a
willingness to flaunt, a readiness to provoke opponents for the sake of

winning disciples more committed. Above all, this admirer of St. Ignatius did not put his women or men into historic orders, like Jesuits, or even the more modern Redemptorists who in the age of the Restoration began extraordinary expansion north of the Alps. He preferred a new order, a new name, more local, for local needs, pastoral in its design, more parochial and more diocesan for all its papalism. The reason was at first necessity—he founded in an age when he could not have Jesuits whom a Pope suppressed, and could not have a historic order which the Italian republic suppressed. But as he passed the year of the battle of Waterloo this reason vanished—and still he preferred the new order, new name, new pattern.[67]

So the Catholic Church looked different in 1815, and especially because its monks and nuns were now few instead of many. The parish church became more central in pastoral care because the monastic chapel was no longer central. And priests were few instead of many. Instead of far too many priests in a diocese, bishops struggled to find men to fill indispensable work.

virtus

To say whether the outlook towards *virtus* changed, and so affected popular religious attitudes, enters a realm where tests are hard to apply. We can only record events and contemporary opinion.

If God, or St. Mary, or the saints, had not defended their own against Bonaparte, yet Bonaparte prospered for a time, perhaps the saints were not quite so aweful in keeping away depredators. But a devastation could occur such as was rare before the wars. A gang of robbers (1822) got into the country church of Ospedaletto (Treviso) and systematically stripped it of valuables.[68] Such evidence is doubtful; for in the middle eighteenth century hermits were specially at risk of murder.

In southern Italy and parts of Spain government was rigorous in exacting the fulfilment of Easter duties. The certificate of attendance must be shown to the authorities. At first sight this merely revived the habitual practice of the eighteenth century after disuse during the age of revolution. In Spain and Italy during the eighteenth century whole parishes accepted tickets as a matter of form, without the slightest protest or sense of the incongruous, and with handfuls of shirkers quietly evading and little pursued. But what now happened in the Restoration, though it looked the same, was altogether different. In the old days the ticket showed that you did your duty by God, which was also to do your duty by the community,

[67] For Benaglio, *D.I.P.* 1.1194.   [68] *La visita pastorale di Grasser*, 136.

since prosperity depended upon God. Now the ticket showed, or also showed, that you were less likely to be a conspirator against the State. The police were interested to know whether the ticket existed. You were doing your duty by your king, which was also your duty to God, because every good Christian must obey his sovereign. This dramatic change of attitude in Naples was connected, however mysteriously, with the fall of the Bastille.

In north Italy the system never recovered from the blow which it received from revolutionary armies. While Venezia was occupied by the French, tickets for confession and communion at Easter were often discarded, because they were voluntary and failure to acquire them led to no awkwardness. With the return of Venezia to the Austrians some parishes reintroduced tickets.

In small villages all or almost all parishioners were again found communicating at Easter. In Padernello village the parish priest described himself as following the 'old custom' of tickets, not a way in which men describe an unchallenged practice. In Saletto nearby the parish priest said that he 'greatly regretted' that five failed to come to communion at Easter. At Istrana near Treviso the parish priest not only reported with satisfaction that all his people received the sacrament at Easter but said that he was sure of this completeness because his curate distributed and collected the tickets. Father Milani became parish priest of Sala di Campagna at the age of thirty-nine, in the beginning of the reign of Joseph II. He went on and on, and was still there, among his 350 souls, at the age of eighty-five; when he was able still to record that all communicants received the sacrament at Easter and that the only tavern in the village closed at times of service.

But in towns and larger villages tickets never won their old efficacy. Something 'voluntary'—in a civic as distinct from a religious sense—hung about communion at Easter; parishes did not wish, or could not, bring back tickets. The incumbent of Montebelluna in the diocese of Treviso reported (1826) that parishioners were generally faithful about attending mass but he could not tell how many were absent from their Easter duties because tickets were 'not yet' introduced.

Even in villages prudence, as well as social custom or religious conviction, might make conformity wise. The parish priest of the village of Venegazzù in north Italy reported to his bishop very favourably of the way in which his parishioners received the sacrament at Easter. Only three or four persons failed to receive; and they 'are of ill repute and under surveillance by the political authority'. No doubt Austrian policemen had grounds for suspecting three or four for reasons nothing to do with their failure to communicate. But in a very small world the absence cried for explanation.

Under the occupation taverns had not needed to observe the law of the Church that they be not open at time of service. Except in big towns they almost always observed the old rule and in the Restoration old ways continued. But not quite always. The pastor of Maser (diocese of Treviso) where, under Austrian rule, the law of the Church was also again the law of the State, reported to his bishop (1826) that his village (900 souls) had two public houses of which 'one keeps the rule of Church and King, and the other makes me sad.'[69]

Pastors agreed that conscription made an extraordinary difference to their work among youth. For the first time it took peasant boys out of their village (unless they first fled to the maquis) and put them into a new world of new axioms. Bishops were known to diagnose conscription as the chief source of the difference for the worse which they found among their young men. One bishop described his boys as 'wrested from the Church's bosom and herded into barracks'.[70] The Sunday school in its various forms declined during the revolutionary years; boys lounged about the streets during time of service and no one had the necessary authority or prestige to drive them into the church porch. In northern Italy they had an official catechism, that of Napoleon, for Josephists and Jansenists disliked the papistical nature of Robert Bellarmine's catechism, till the eighties regarded as the customary catechism for north Italy.

They were at once rid of Napoleon's catechism. But that meant, the official catechism was an old text with archaic and in places misleading language. The age of Restoration was not a time for trying to amend texts which the revolution abolished. A Venetian priest was consulted (1827), whether it would be good to revise the old catechism. He said, it would be better to change nothing. There are imprecisions of theology but we put up with them 'not only out of respect to famous men who approved them, but much more that we may not give a motive for priests to raise doubts and new questions'.[71] Such an attitude can commonly be found among the churches of the age of Restoration. It was their form of anti-revolutionary conservatism.

Schoolboys resented the rules. Their predecessors had not been made to go to communion, they were rebellious. Of the pupils in the royal colleges

[69] *La visita pastorale di Grasser*, 69, 81, 105, 126–8, 132, 146.
[70] Cestaro, 32.
[71] *La visita pastorale di Pyrker*, xxxiii n.103.

of rhetoric and philosophy at Paris it was found that only 7 to 8 per cent made their communion at Easter. A church parade at Marseilles (1823) was turned by the boys into a parody, with mocking hoots at the worshippers. The age of violence left an age of student demonstrations, who would have demonstrated against anyone but happened to find restored Jesuits or other religious as their masters. In a school at Rouen the boys were, as of old, compelled to make their confession. Once boys accepted the rule as a natural part of the world. In the age of Restoration the rule caused so furious a mutiny of boys that everyone had to be expelled and the school closed till a new agreement could be reached. In the streets of Venice boys who ought to be in Sunday school lounged about the streets, following in the habits which their elders learnt during the revolutionary years; but now, when they misbehaved, the guard was called out to round up the truants.

Even when nothing so dramatic happened, the pastors found it harder to get the young back to Sunday school. In the visitations of the age of reconstruction appeared frequent comments on 'poor' or 'miserable' or 'thin' or 'diminished' attendance at catechism or 'Christian doctrine'; and sometimes the parish priest, answering his bishop's question, ascribed these smaller numbers to the stormy years through which they had passed. This was not a general rule. Visitations also show that by 1820–5 a majority of parishes again had Sunday schools which flourished. And no doubt, at times, a parish priest whose catechism was ill attended through his own fault, excused himself by blaming recent revolution. The parish priest of the Carmini in Venice reported that in a few years his catechism for girls had grown from thirty or forty attendants to 170 or 180; and this without any suggestion that girls went more zealously than boys, because in a different building he had 200 boys.[72] Many of the Venetian Sunday schools were attended by approximately 10 per cent of the parish. Therefore they flourished again as before the revolution, and the principal difference consisted in the fewer adults who now came.

The Sunday school was not the only meeting which was hard work to revive. The meetings of clergy to discuss cases of conscience lapsed in the revolutionary years, and in bishopless interregna. The bishops of the Restoration set about reviving attendance and found the work hard. The complaints at failure were louder, in some areas meetings were almost deserted, the Patriarch of Venice threatened to take away the licence of confessors who would not come. When the Bishop of Campagna ordered

[72] Dansette, 204–5; Enid Starkie, *Flaubert*, 14–16; *La visita pastorale di Pyrker*, xxxii, 106.

that the meetings should restart, unknown hands tore down the notice placarded in the cathedral sacristy.[73] Still, meetings restarted.

The endowed mass was again a difficulty, hard to carry. When zealous reforming bishops came back into the dioceses after 1815, one of their first enquiries asked whether endowments were being applied according to the intentions of donors and testators; and the question had force because so many endowments were lost. Since during the Napoleonic years the burden was lighter, because priests perforce made it lighter surreptitiously, the re-inforcement of the rules by revived authority made the old burden seem even harder. Complaints about excessive number of masses rose again in stridency.

Archbishop Lupoli of Conza (south of Naples) wrote to Pope Pius VII (2 January 1819): 'Holy Father, it is my humble duty to tell you that the clergy of my diocese cannot possibly bear the burden of endowed masses . . .'[74]

Taste had changed.

Bishops and parish priests were more intolerant of statues in clothes or pictures hung with pseudo-jewelry or side-chapels which looked like junk shops.

Old-fashioned musical ears still loved the sound of the *castrati*. But that form of choir suffered in the revolution a blow from which it never recovered, though it lived on for three-quarters of a century. Musical or moral taste, or a mixture of both, had changed. When the new Hungarian patriarch came to Venice, he found an old *castrato* in the choir of the cathedral (it had just become the cathedral instead of the doge's chapel) of San Marco. He felt horror, and promptly reconstructed the choir and its recruitment.[75]

The secular arm was less easy to invoke. Bishops in certain parts of Europe could still nominate a monastery—or rather, now, the empty buildings of an ex-monastery—as a 'retreat' for their delinquent clergy. But either the clergy were less delinquent or other forms of dealing with clerical crime were preferred. The Hungarian Patriarch of Venice, Pyrker, started a 'house of retreat' for delinquent clergy in the ex-Camaldolese monastery on the island of San Clemente. It never housed more than two or three priests and soon closed.

Doctors no longer abandoned the sick if they had not confessed. An unusual bishop might urge the revival of the old rule but was not heard.

---

[73] *La visita pastorale di Pyrker*, ciii–civ; Cestaro, 221.   [74] Cestaro, 204.
[75] *La visita pastorale di Pyrker*, 214.

Parish priests, who met concubines in their parishes, were no longer sure that it always helped to thunder out the time-honoured penalties of canon law. Where statistics are published as in southern Bavaria, the number of bastards can be seen rising, but it looks as though the increase was not derived from decline in religious belief by the progenitors.

The differences in parish life

An enquirer into peasant life imagined a visitor staying in the vicarage of a Bavarian country pastor in 1780 and again forty years later. What difference would he notice? In the enquirer's view the people were no longer content with the imaginary world of childlike faith in religious means of harvesting good crops or healing sick cows. They still had naïve faith. They begot more illegitimate children. They dreamed a little less of heaven and more of earth, a little less of marrying a princess to live happily ever after and a little more of luxury goods. They submitted less axiomatically to their landlords and superiors. Although clergy were fewer, peasants respected the clergy a little less as clergy (leaving out of account respect due to personal quality) because the clergy were now subject like themselves to civil courts and superiors.[76]

Such differences are, however, hard to prove from the existing evidence. All that is certain is that the lowest class was just as superstitious and got more bastards, the lower-middle class grew less superstitious with widespread education, and the clergy were more subject to interference from civil servants.

Other old rules were not quite so easy to keep. In the countryside shops stayed shut on Sundays, taverns closed at service times, people needing to work still sought leave from their parish pastor. But when the exceptions occurred, they stood out sharply in the social landscape. It did not matter that the parishes along the river Piave were perturbed by the number of Sunday fishermen, for this was no new trouble. Towns were different. Noventa on the left bank of the river, a town of 5,050 souls, had bakeries which helped to supply bread to the city of Venice; there on Sundays the ovens worked away in full view of the public; the parish priest was shocked and appealed to the bishop, who was shocked and appealed to the governor; who in his turn was not shocked, and refused to stop the bakers. The theatre in Treviso, across from the cathedral, horrified the clergy by staying open even at times of service.

The parish priest of a village on a main road in north Italy (Cornuda

[76] Phayer, *Religion und das gewöhnliche Volk* (1970).

near Treviso) allowed that his parishioners kept the precepts of the Church most faithfully; with one exception—because they saw so much traffic on holy days, they could not be stopped from getting out their own carts 'especially after time of service'.[77]

An occasional moral change was established by the habits of the Napoleonic era and never afterwards challenged seriously. The most remarkable change was the attitude to rates of interest. In the Napoleonic empire no one could challenge rates of interest. In the Restoration no one seriously wanted to return to the former and stricter rules. The interpretation of Count Maffei three-quarters of a century earlier won a silent victory.

Father Jeremiah O'Callaghan wrote a book called *Usury* (1824). His pastoral experience led him to think the Church to be failing in its duty. Parishioners were oppressed by borrowing at rates of interest, and the Church had ceased to protect them. His attacks upon usurers became more and more outspoken. His bishop (of Cloyne and Ross) finally suspended him, from which he appealed first to his archbishop, and then to Rome (August 1822). He was encouraged because in July 1822 the restored Roman Inquisition held that a woman of Lyons, who arranged to get interest on a loan, could be absolved without restoring the money. But on O'Callaghan the Inquisition would take no stand, except to send him Benedict XIV's ambiguous bull *Vix pervenit* and recommend him to obey his bishop. The bishop argued that the custom was so deep-rooted and widely accepted that any attempt to declare it immoral must fail and make a priest despised. Seminaries continued to teach their ordinands that usury was wrong. But in the parishes and the confessionals it ceased to be a question. Catholic laity accepted it as useful and harmless, and were too strong for the more conservative of their priests. It was the same power of the laity as was shown over the right or wrong of birth control more than a century later.[78]

But most of the old moral problems remained. The visitation of Treviso in 1825 shows that babies were still so commonly abandoned that the bishop must spend many hours over orphanages and adoption; that both sexes smuggled without a sense of sin. The number of couples living unmarried in towns had increased but not in the country. This rise in concubines was at times attributed 'to the unhappy influence of the recent revolutions'. The canons of Treviso cathedral remarked of the inhabitants of the city, 'There are not a few disorders of incontinence, drunkenness, indifference to religion, small numbers coming to Sunday School. . . .

[77] *La visita pastorale di Grasser*, 95, 166.   [78] Nelson, 124 ff.

These disorders became obvious after the French invasion. Till then the city was a model of good behaviour.'[79]

The language used was occasionally odd by the standards of the eighteenth century. In the large village of Volpago the churchwardens (*fabbricieri*) appealed to the bishop to make the assistant curate, who did nothing, celebrate a mass on Sundays because they had only one mass to go to; and in their appeal they used a hyperbole that we have not met before: 'if not', they said, 'the faith will very quickly disappear.'[80] Their grand-fathers had seen almost as apocalyptic visions when some detail went awry in the parish, but had not imagined the possibility that faith could be destroyed. The churchwardens of 1825 had seen it happen.

Diocesan synods could use new language of this sort. 'We live in an age' said a south-Italian synod of 1827 '. . . when the faithful are deceived by empty fallacies and pulled out of the Church's bosom.'[81] The synod evidently attributed the main cause to books which circulated among their people. But most of the language of such a synod was more ancient. This synod still needed to denounce pacts with the devil, magic arts, men who boast that they can change shape or pacify storms or cork devils inside a phial or abuse sacraments for purposes of incantation.

Cardinal Severoli was Bishop of Viterbo. He was the most old-fashioned member of the reconstructing episcopate. He wanted everything as it was in the days of his youth. He told parish priests to note down all the faults of their parishioners in a secret book; ordered doctors to persuade the sick to confess and to abandon them after three days if they had not confessed; threatened those who failed in their Easter duties with public exposure, including posting of the names on the church door; banned all meetings during Lent, even private. Severoli was the reaction in the most literal sense. Such a bishop was very rare, because sensible men saw that it was useless to command what would not be obeyed.

[79] *La visita pastorale di Grasser*, 19.   [80] *La visita pastorale di Grasser*, 109 n.7.
[81] Cestaro, 120.

CONCLUSION

THE papacy had suffered. The martyrdom began under Clement XIII about 1759, and continued through the pontificates of his three successors, of whom the first was wrongly supposed to be poisoned and the next two were carried prisoner to France. Bourbon kings bullied Clement XIII, Clement XIV, and Pius VI; a Corsican conqueror bullied Pius VI and Pius VII; but it was almost more agonizing to be bullied as a Pope in Rome than as a Pope in exile; and exile brought international sympathy while agony in Rome brought none. The martyrdom continued until Pius VII returned to Rome as one of the 'victors' in the long wars.

This martyr-status was a condition of what happened in the nineteenth century. The status consisted of more than two Popes in exile. That exile stood as a symbol of European suffering, murders, executions, shooting of hostages, pollution of churches, the horror of guerrilla war. The Pope was a known confessor who represented thousands of martyrs unknown and forgotten.

His office was elevated, not in political power, for there he lost rights steadily; but in the feeling of ordinary faithful worshippers.

His office was also elevated ecclesiastically, by the fall of his possible peers. In the old world the bishop who towered nearest to the Pope in worldly prestige was the Archbishop of Mainz; next to him, the Arch-bishops of Cologne and Trier and Salzburg. Now the Bishop of Mainz was less important than the Archbishops of Paris or Toledo or Vienna. The French bishops were stipendiaries of the State; the Spanish bishops were troubled by division and civil war; the Archbishop of Vienna lived under a Josephist government. The Pope of the old world stood above his fellow bishops, but not always far above. In the new world he stood head and shoulders above everyone.

The Revolution hurt Catholic episcopalianism even more than it hurt Popes.

Europe wanted peace, and order. Part of stability was respect for historic institutions. This feeling benefited the papacy; but only in one direction.

In another direction it pushed Catholicism towards that association with
the political right which was not typical of its past. The Popes knew that
they stood for order, and that they were valued because they stood for
order. As the twin forces of nationalism and liberalism began to over-
whelm Europe, the papacy was seen less as a force for order than as a small
additional dam against changes which could not for ever be resisted. This
dam was the weaker because the Congress of Vienna saddled the Popes
with the least stable state to issue from the peace-treaties. It was the old
Papal State revived, but in circumstances which made it either the hand-
maid of Metternich and Austrian reaction, or the sick man of western
Europe. Popes must stand against Italian unity in a generation when
Napoleon had turned Italian unity from a literary dream into a distant
but conceivable ideal.

This link with order, and stance against 'liberalism', was the curse which
the Revolution bequeathed to the Popes. The world at last accepted
toleration. Metternich still allowed the expulsion of Protestants from the
Tyrol, German Protestant states and Great Britain still treated their
Roman Catholics as second-class citizens. But France could never go far
back upon its equality for religions before the law, and in Germany the
populations of the rearranged states were now so mixed in religion that
the clause which once saved Germany, 'cujus regio ejus religio', was seen
to be obsolete and impossible. Into the treaties was built a provision for
fair treatment in religion for the citizens of the German states.

But Popes held an office which taught truth. Their experience of freedom of the press was unhappy. Freedom to publish was freedom to publish
error or immorality. They stood wholly upon the side of the numerous
governments which wished to control presses and censor books in the
interests of truth and morality. A teaching office which *felt* toleration to be
wicked was supreme governor of a Church where most of the members
knew toleration as a necessity of life, German states, France, Holland and
Belgium, some of the Latin American republics.

A break in history has the gain, among its many losses, that an institution
can discard burdens from the past. The right of sanctuary, or benefit of
clergy, had become heavy loads for a Church to carry. Now it had no
need to carry them, except in modest ceremony. The bull *Unigenitus* had
sorely tried the Church of the eighteenth century. It still lay in the books
of canon law. But no one now paid attention, and that was easy, because it
had turned only into a bugle of assault upon the Jansenists, and men fancied
that the Jansenist battalions had fled. The best education of the past had
been Jesuit, and Jesuit near-monopoly became one of the most irritating

brakes upon the progress of the mind. Jesuits were revived, but never again with a near-monopoly. Everywhere the Church was impoverished; and the aristocratic comfort of the German chapters had made a main part of Catholic power in Germany; yet afterwards few could regret that the Revolution destroyed the medley of historic Barchesters.

Revolutions do much. Afterwards they are seen not to have done quite so much as the revolutionaries thought.

When observers mark the difference between the Catholicism of 1820 and the Catholicism of forty years before, they are apt to be blind to what would have happened without revolution. The Revolution shattered western monasticism; but already the number of monks was falling, and with increasing speed. The Revolution confiscated a mass of Church endowments, a confiscation to be in main part irreversible by Restoration, and the effects on Church life were permanent. But already states had begun to order endowments, control, confiscate, reapply, change the destination, especially to create a system of education or help with the relief of the poor. The Revolution turned the parish church into the centre of the life of the Church, perforce, by leaving almost nothing else. But already the Jansenists and their fellows had begun to move towards the same end. The revolutionary wars forced Germany and Italy to tolerate Protestants, and though the world of the Restoration was not by instinct tolerant, this was a landmark in the history of liberty. But Austria and France already led the way in showing how a government might be at once Catholic and tolerant of Protestants.

History needs to escape the illusion that the Enlightenment was always and everywhere anti-Christian and still more anti-Catholic. The Enlightenment in Catholic countries was for the most part a movement of reform by Catholic men. They made mistakes by obstinacy, or tactlessness, or exaggeration, or extremism, as in any earnest movement of reform. But they aimed at the good of the Catholic Church, and through it at the good of humanity. In one form, though in an unusual form, they represented that deep inward thrust ever present within Catholicism, the *ecclesia semper reformanda*, the self-criticism because a Church should ever be judged against the highest of ideals.

The Revolution and the Restoration threw all the reformers into discredit. For a time history thought that their endeavours led only into a cul-de-sac, their work was vain, nothing remained, their fate was typified by Ricci recanting, Tamburini without influence in the wrong faculty at Pavia, Pujati too ancient a curate in a Venice parish, Lambruschini leaving the Curia because he could not bear its spirit in the post-revolutionary mood of that age. Port-Royal was a ruin, later to be a garden with a little museum.

The names of Enlightenment, or of Jansenism, were disreputable and faded into terms of large but vague abuse. But what they stood for was in some part fostered by the Revolution and adapted by the Restoration. They wanted a stronger parish and congregational life, and the nineteenth century developed the parish in a manner unthinkable under the old regime. They wanted a better education of priests; and though the wars ended with priests more ignorant and fewer, this was one of the successful drives of the nineteenth century. They wanted better work in schools, whether weekday or Sunday, and this also the nineteenth century fostered, the more easily since it had only to take part in a general European move- ment. They worked for a more congregational liturgy; and for all the reaction against the vernacular in Germany or against the attempted revision of psalters and breviaries, the Church of the nineteenth century continued to lift the parish mass always more into the centre of the people's worship.

They did not stand for a *liberal* Catholicism. The reformers of the eighteenth century were never specially liberal even though several of their heirs, like Bishop Serrao of Potenza, were murdered for their readiness to accept a satellite French regime. Nor did they stand for a *reasonable* Catholicism; the word is a little more fitting, because part of their strength was the new historical learning of men like Muratori, carrying with it a new critique of legend, a raised dislike of superstition, and at last a more subtle understanding of the nature of doctrinal development.

In men like Johann Michael Sailer, professor at Landshut and later Bishop of Regensburg, we see the link between the old world and the new at its best; men cultivated and intelligent, heirs of the Catholic Enlighten- ment, critics of superstitions and stupidities and obscurantism; distrusted by the neo-conservatives, ultra-conservatives, for their frankness and originality of mind or expression; lovers of the early Christians, and of simplicity, and of the Bible; yet at the same time deep within the renewal of a quest for the authentic and innermost meaning of Catholicism, as structure and as doctrine and as moral system; the forms had been knocked about and found to be brittle forms, far more brittle than anyone had expected; the Church must go back, penetrate behind the forms, and refresh itself with its own possession of truth. In such men can be seen simultaneously the disciples of the best in the Catholic Enlightenment of the eighteenth century and the creators of much that was best in the Catholic nineteenth century.

The epithet then is neither *liberal* Catholicism, which had not yet had its day, nor *rational* Catholicism which suggests a very one-sided attitude to the sources of Catholic doctrine, but rather a *pastoral* Catholicism; understanding the Church less as the ruler of the peoples than as their servant; caring for the affections of ordinary men and women more than for the favour of governments; imbued with a readiness to adapt privileged position for the sake of men's souls, and for the knowledge of the truth in the common man.

BIBLIOGRAPHY

THIS makes no attempt at a complete bibliography. Excellent annotated bibliographies exist in the *Handbuch* (ed. Jedin and others, see below) and the Italian edition of Fliche and Martin. This bibliography lists the works or articles which I cited or found helpful in writing this book. The works of general reference (pp. 614–15) will give further guidance. The place of publication is London unless otherwise stated.

GENERAL

The standard working tool is the bibliography in each number of *R.H.E.* H. Hurter, *Nomenclator*, vol. 4 (1910), is still an admirably useful guide to all Catholic writers of the eighteenth century, even the obscure. *Bibliografia dell'età del Risorgimento in onore di Alberto M. Ghisalberti*, 4 vols. (Florence ,1971–7) has a full bibliography on Church and State in eighteenth-century Italy. See also the encyclopedias, under Abbreviations, p. xx; and the *Enciclopedia Cattolica*, the *New Catholic Encyclopaedia*, and *Religion in Geschichte und Gegenwart*.

General Works

The background to the history of the Church is found in certain general histories of particular countries: A. R. M. Carr, *Spain 1808–1939* (Oxford, 1966); the Spanish edition (Barcelona, 1969) is revised. F. Valsecchi, *L'Italia nel Settecento (1714–1788)* (Milan, 1971). N. Valeri, *Storia d'Italia*, 2nd edn. vols. 2–3 (Turin, 1965). S. Woolf, *A History of Italy 1700–1860* (1979). E. Rota, *Le origine del Risorgimento (1710–1800)*, corr. edn., 2 vols. (Milan, 1948). B. Croce, *Uomini e cose della vecchia Italia*, 2 vols. (Bari, 1927).

For Germany: M. Spindler (ed.), *Handbuch der bayerischen Geschichte*, 6 vols. (Munich, 1967–75); cf. K. O. von Aretin, *Bayerns Weg sum souveränen Staat (1714–1818)* (Munich, 1976). K. O. von Aretin, *Heiliges Römisches Reich 1776–1806*, 2 vols (Wiesbaden, 1967). K. T. Heigel, *Deutsche Geschichte vom Tode Friedrichs des Grossen bis zur Auflösung des alten Reiches* (Stuttgart, 1899).

For Salzburg: H. Widmann, *Deutsche Landesgeschichte: Salzburg*, 3 vols.(Gotha, 1907–14).

For Switzerland: J. Dierauer, *Geschichte der Schweizer Eidgenossenschaft*, 5 vols. (Gotha, 1919–22).

For Portugal: H. V. Livermore, *A New History of Portugal*, 2nd edn. (Cambridge, 1976).

For Poland: *The Cambridge History of Poland*, 2 vols. (Cambridge, 1941–50).

GENERAL HISTORIES OF THE CHURCH

H. Jedin and others (edd.), *Handbuch der Kirchengeschichte* (vol. 5, *1648–1789*; vol.

6. i, *1789*–) (Freiburg im Breisgau, 1963–). A. Fliche and V. Martin (edd.), *Histoire de l'Église* (Paris, 1936–). The original French editions of the relevant volumes were E. Préclin and E. Jarry, *Les Luttes politiques et doctrinales aux XVIIᵉ et XVIIᵉ siecles*, 2 vols. (Paris, 1955–6); and J. Leflon, *La Crise révolutionnaire 1789–1846* (Paris, 1949). But from revised French editions was taken an Italian translation which is extensively and ably supplemented and is now the most effective edition—especially vol. XIX i, ed. L. Mezzadri (Turin, 1974), which gave the original book a new social depth together with remarkable bibliographical guides; and in the Italian translation of Leflon, a chapter by Nasalli on the religious life of Italy 1800–50.

Older books, still useful for materials, are Josef Hergenröther, *Handbuch der allgemeine Kirchengeschichte*, vol. 4, new edn. (Freiburg, 1917). M. Picot, *Mémoires pour servir a l'histoire ecclésiastique pendant la dix-huitieme siecle*, 3rd edn. 4 vols. (Paris, 1853–7).

Good general surveys by single authors are: L. A. Veit, *Die Kirche im Zeitalter des Individualismus* (Freiburg, 1933). E. E. Y. Hales, *Revolution and Papacy, 1769–1846* (1960). Very readable are the two English translations of H. Daniel-Rops, *The Church in the Eighteenth Century* (French, Paris, 1960; English, 1964), and *The Church in an Age of Revolution* (French, Paris, 1960, English, London, 1965). One of the best of all individual treatments is G. Schnürer, *Katholische Kirche und Kultur im 18. Jahrhundert* (Paderborn, 1941). For a series of modern essays, W. J. Callaghan and D. Higgs (edd.), *Church and Society in Catholic Europe in the Eighteenth Century* (Cambridge, 1979).

HISTORIES OF NATIONAL CHURCHES

F. de Almeida, *Historia da Igreja em Portugal*, new edn. (Porto, 1967–); cf. B. J. Wenzel, *Portugal und der heilige Stuhl* (Lisbon, 1958). P. B. Gams, *Die Kirchengeschichte von Spanien*, 3 vols. (Regensburg, 1862–79, repr. Graz, 1956). V. Lafuente, *Historia de la Iglesia en España*, vol. vi (Madrid, 1875). P. Brachin and L. J. Rogier, *Histoire du Catholicisme hollandais depuis le XVIᵉ siecle* (Paris, 1974). T. Schwegler, *Geschichte der katholischen Kirche in der Schweiz*, 2nd edn. (Stans, 1943). K. Völker, *Kirchengeschichte Polens* (Berlin, 1930); cf. *D.T.C.* s.v. 'Pologne'. E. de Moreau, *Histoire de l'Église en Belgique*, 6 vols. (Brussels, 1947–52); cf. *D.H.G.E.* s.v. 'Belgique'. J. Bossy, *The English Catholic Community 1570–1850* (1975). J.Wodka, *Kirche in Österreich*, Vienna, 1959.

WORKS OF REFERENCE

For the most important see under Abbreviations; also *Acta Sanctorum* (Antwerp, 1643 ff.). G. Moroni, *Dizionario di erudizione storica-ecclesiastica*, 103 vols. in 53 (Venice, 1840–61). *Acta historica-ecclesiastica nostri temporis* (Weimar, 1736–90). These annals of the time carry much rare information, especially on Germany.

DOCUMENTS

Invaluable guide to sources in Vatican archives in L. Pásztor, *Archivio Segreto*

Vaticano (Vatican, 1970). *Codicis Iuris Canonici Fontes*, ed. P. Gasparri *et al.*, 9 vols. (Rome, 1923–39). H. Denzinger, *Enchiridion Symbolorum, Definitionum et Declarationum de rebus fidei et morum*, 33rd edn. (Barcinone, 1965). *Bullarium diplomatum et privilegiorum sanctorum Romanorum pontificum* (Turin, 1857–72). *Bullarii Romani Continuatio* (Rome, 1835–46). *Benedicti Papae XIV Bullarium*, new edn., 13 vols. (Malines, 1826–7). J. D. Mansi, *Sacrorum conciliorum nova et amplissima collectio*, 31 vols. (Florence–Venice, 1757–98), continued and reprinted, 60 vols. (Paris, 1899–1927). Guide to local Italian archives, in G. Mazzatinti, *Gli archivi della storia d'Italia*, 9 vols. (Rocca S. Casciano, 1899–). *Decreta authentica Congregationis Indulgentiis Sacrisque Reliquiis praeposita ab anno 1668–1882* (Regensburg, 1883). *Decreta authentica Sacrae Congregationis Sacrorum Rituum*, 7 vols. (Rome, 1898–1947). S. Pallotini, *Collectio omnium conclusionum et resolutionum quae in causis propositis apud Sacram Congregationem Cardinalium Sancti Concilii Tridentini interpretum prodierunt* (1564–1860), 18 vols. (Rome, 1868–95). But better for historical purposes are the fuller records of the Congregation of the Council in *Thesaurus resolutionum Sacrae Congregationis Concilii*, 167 vols. (Rome, 1718–1908). *S. Rotae Romanae Decisiones nuperrimae*, 12 vols. (Rome, 1751–92). For a guide to this mass of legal material, see Plöchl, or Feine (p. 617); or H. F. Schulte, *Geschichte der Quellen und Literatur des canonischen Rechts von Gratian bis auf die Gegenwart*, 3 vols. (Stuttgart, 1880).

CHAPTER I : THE RELIGION OF THE PEOPLE

In Italy: P. Lambertini (= Benedict XIV), *Raccolta di alcune notificazione, editti e istruzione pubblicate dall' eminentissimo. . . . Cardinale Prospero Lambertini*, 5 vols. (Bologna, 1733–40), useful for parish and diocesan life. M. Vaussard, *Daily life in Eighteenth Century Italy*, Eng. trans. (London, 1962). R. de Maio, *Società e vita religiosa a Napoli nell' età moderna, 1656–1799* (Naples, 1971). G. de Rosa, *Vescovi, populo e magia nel Sud* (Naples, 1971). Cf. Ernesto de Martino, *Sud e Magia* (Milan, 1959). G. de Rosa, 'Sainteté, clergé et peuple dans le Mezzogiorno italien au milieu du XVIIIᵉ siècle' in *Revue d'histoire de la spiritualité*, 52 (1976), 245–64, and *Chiesa e religione popolare nel Mezzogiorno* (Rome, 1978). G. Pitré, *Palermo nel Settecento* (Milan, 1916), and *Usi e costumi, credenzi e pregiudizi del popolo siciliano*, 4 vols. (Palermo, 1889). M. Rosa, *Religione e società nel Mezzogiorno* (Bari, 1976), 4, 275–334. See also diocesan synods, p. 621.

In Germany: W. G. Soldan, *Geschichte der Hexenprocesse*, new edn., by H. Heppe, 2 vols. (Stuttgart, 1880). For witchcraft: H. Bächtold-Stäubli, *Handwörterbuch des deutschen Aberglaubens*, 10 vols. (Berlin, 1927–), an encyclopedia of superstitions among the common people of Germany. J. Caro Baroja, *The World of the Witches* (Eng. trans. 1964). L. A. Veit and L. Lenhart, *Kirche und Volksfrömmigkeit im Zeitalten des Barock* (Freiburg im Breisgau, 1956). B. Goy, *Aufklärung und Volksfrömmigkeit in den Bistümern Würzburg und Bamberg* (Würzburg, 1969). Josef Klersch, *Volkstum und Volksleben in Köln*, 3 vols. (Cologne,

1965–8). F. M. Phayer, *Religion und das gewöhnliche Volk in Bayern in der Zeit von 1750 bis 1850* (Munich, 1970).

On the Jews: A. Berliner, *Geschichte der Juden in Rom* (Frankfurt, 1893). S. M. Dubnov, *History of the Jews*, Eng. trans. by M. Spiegel, 5 vols. (New Brunswick 1967–73). A. Milano, *Storia degli Ebrei in Italia* (Turin, 1965). H. V. and P. Rieger, *Geschichte der Juden in Rom*, vol. 2 (Berlin, 1895). Cecil Roth, *The History of the Jews in Italy* (Philadelphia, 1946). R. Mahler, *A History of Modern Jewry, 1780–1815* (1971). This is also useful for the eighteenth-century background. Cecil Roth (ed.), *The Ritual Murder Libel and the Jew: the Report by Cardinal Lorenzo Ganganelli (Pope Clement XIV)* (1935).

Travellers' descriptions: So many were on the grand tour that the material is vast. I give a selection of what is valuable. For guides to further matter, see for the Germans L. Schudt, *Italienreisen im 17. und 18. Jahrhundert* (Vienna, 1959); for the French in Sicily (and others) Hélène Tuzet, *La Sicile au XVIIIᵉ siècle vue par les voyageurs étrangers* (Strasbourg, 1955); and for the English at the end of the period, C. P. Brand, 'A bibliography of travel books describing Italy published in England 1800–1850', in *Italian Studies*, xi (1956), 108–17.

J. Baretti, *A Journey from London to Genoa* (1770), and *An Account of the manners and customs of Italy*, 2 vols. (1768). J. H. Bartels, *Briefe über Kalabrien und Sizilien*, 3 vols. (Göttingen, 1787–92). P. Brydone, *A Tour through Sicily and Malta*, new edn., 2 vols. (1790). C. de Brosses, *Lettres familières sur l'Italie*, 2 vols. (Paris, 1931); cf. G. de Socio, *Le Président Charles de Brosses et l'Italie* (Rome, 1923). Leucadio Doblado (= J. Blanco White) *Letters from Spain* (1822); cf. *The Life of the Reverend J. Blanco White*, ed. J. H. Thom, 3 vols. (1845). C. M. Dupaty, *Lettres sur l'Italie en 1785* (Paris, 1795). Dupaty was a superficial observer but was interested in the Church. J. B. Labat, *Voyages en Espagne et en Italie*, 8 vols. (Paris, 1730), a specially valuable journal. Labat was a Dominican and understood what he described. There is an abridgment in J. B. Labat, *La Comédie ecclésiastique* (Paris, 1927). E. Martène and V. Durand, *Voyage littéraire de deux religieux bénédictins* (Paris, 1717–20). F. Münter, *Nachrichten von Neapel und Sicilien* (Copenhagen, 1790). Hester Piozzi, *Observations in a Journey through Italy* (1789). H. Swinburne, *Travels in the two Sicilies*, 2nd edn. 4 vols. (1789). J. Townsend, *A Journey through Spain in the years 1786–7*, 3 vols. (1792). J. Villanueva, *Viage literario a las Iglesias de Espana*, 22 vols. (1803–52). Other famous diarists touring—e.g. Boswell, Casanova, Gibbon, Goethe, Dr Burney (see p. 619) are not negligible.

On the evidence from canon law: The best guide to this mass of material is W. M. Plöchl, *Geschichte des Kirchenrechts*, vols. 3–5 (Vienna–Munich, 1959–69). All the volumes have a view of the literature. See also H. E. Feine, *Kirchliche Rechtsgeschichte*, I: *Die katholische Kirche*, 4th edn. (Cologne, 1964). *Dictionnaire de droit canonique*, ed. R. Naz (Paris, 1935 ff.). Among the contemporary sources, see especially Benedict XIV, *Opera Omnia*, 6 vols. (Venice, 1767). I. Devoti, *Institutionum canonicarum libri IV* (Rome, 1785). L. Ferraris, *Promptabibliotheca canonica*, ed. by Migne, 8 vols. (Paris, 1860–3). B. Z. Van Espen, *Jus ecclesiasticum universum*, first edn. 1700; in *Opera omnia* (Cologne, 1777–8).

On St. Mary: Walter Delius, *Geschichte der Marienverehrung* (Munich–Basel, 1963). H. C. Graef, *Mary*, 2 vols. (1963–5).

On the Sacred Heart: Good guide in *D.T.C.*, s.v. 'Coeur Sacré'.

On flagellants: E. G. Förstemann, *Die christlichen Geisslergesellschaften* (Halle, 1828). *Realenc* s.v. 'Geisselung'.

On the parish mission: M. de Meulemeister, 'La "vita devota" des missions napoletaines au XVIIIe siecle', in *Revue d'ascétique et de mystique* 25 (1959), 457–64.

Inside the church: R. Berliner, *Die Weihnachtskrippe* (Munich, 1955), full of valuable evidence on the Christmas crib. J. Braun, *Der Christliche Altar*, 2 vols. (Munich, 1924); *Das Christliche Altargerät* (Munich, 1932, repr. Hildersheim, 1973); and *Die liturgische Gewandung* (Freiburg im Breisgau, 1907). H. Thurston, *The Stations of the Cross* (1906).

On sanctuary: L. Mascambrone, *Degli asili de' christiani* (Rome, 1731). 'Pompeo Neri', *Discorso sopra l'asilo ecclesiastico* (Florence–Venice, 1763). J. Gröll, *Die Elemente des kirchlichen Freiungsrechtes* (Stuttgart, 1911). R. G. Bindschedler, *Kirchliches Asylrecht (immunitas ecclesiastica localis) und Freistätten in der Schweiz* (Stuttgart, 1906).

On Bible-reading: S. L. Greenslade (ed.), *The Cambridge History of the Bible*, vol. 3 (Cambridge, 1963). T. H. Darlow and H. F. Moule (eds.), *Historical Catalogue of the Printed Editions of Holy Scripture in the Library of the British and Foreign Bible Society*, 4 vols. (1903). *L.T.K.* s.v. 'Bibelübersetzungen'. *Realenc.* s.v. 'Bibelverbot'. See also Reusch, p. 624.

On pilgrimage: G. Schreiber, *Wallfahrt und Volkstum in Geschichte und Leben* (Düsseldorf, 1934). For Loreto: U. Chevalier, *Notre-Dame de Lorette* (Paris, 1906).

On indulgences: G. Benrath, s.v. 'Ablass' in *T.R.E.* H. C. Lea, *Auricular Confession and Indulgences*, vol. 3 (London, 1896). Ferraris (p. 617), s.v. 'Indulgentia'.

For art and architecture: F. Haskell, *Patrons and Painters: a study in the relations between Italian art and society in the age of the baroque* (1963). Klaus Brantz, *Jubelndes Rokoko* (Munich, 1963). A. E. Brinckmann, *Baukunst des 17 und 18 Jahrhunderts in den romanischen Ländern*, 4th edn., 2 vols. (Berlin, 1919–22). G. Kubler and M. Soria, *Art and Architecture in Spain and Portugal and their American dominions 1500–1800* (Pelican History of Art, 1959). C. Justi, *Winckelmann*, 4th edn. (Leipzig, 1943), important also for life in papal Rome. N. Powell, *From Baroque to Rococo* (1959). A. Blunt, *Neapolitan Baroque and Rococo Architecture* (1975). Sacheverell Sitwell, *Southern Baroque Art: a study of painting architecture and music in Italy and Spain of the 17th and 18th centuries* (1924, repr. 1971). R. Wittkower, *Art and Architecture in Italy 1600–1750*, 3rd edn. (1973, repr. 1978).

For music: Charles Burney, *Music, Men and Manners in France and Italy* (1770), ed. H. E. Poole (1974) [= Burney's *Journal*], and *The Present State of Music in*

France and Italy (1773), ed. P. A. Scholes, *An Eighteenth Century Musical Tour in France and Italy*, 2 vols. (1959); cf. P. A. Scholes, *The Great Dr. Burney*, 2 vols. (1948). F. Häbock, *Die Kastraten und ihre Gesangbuch* (Stuttgart, 1927); cf. Angus Heriot, *The Castrati in Opera* (1956). J. A. Fuller-Maitland, *The Age of Bach and Handel* (Oxford History of Music, vol. 4), 2nd edn. (Oxford, 1939). André Pons, *Droit ecclésiastique et musique sacrée*, 3 vols. (Paris, 1960). E. A. Wienandt, *Choral Music of the Church* (New York, 1963). J. L. J. Combarieu, *Histoire de la musique* (Paris, 1950–). *Grove's Dictionary of Music and Musicians*, 5th edn., ed. E. Blom, 10 vols. (1975). Biographies: e.g. R. Hughes, *Haydn* (rev. edn., 1974). M. J. E. Brown, *Schubert* (1958); P. M. Young, *Schubert* (1970). P. M. Young, *Mozart* (1965); Eric Bloom, *Mozart*, 3rd edn. (1974). *L.T.K.* s.v. 'Kirchenmusik', with bibliography. K. G. Fellerer (ed.), *Geschichte der katholischen Kirchenmusik*, 2 vols. (Kassel, 1972).

CHAPTER 2: THE CLERGY

On preaching: For Italy, A. Prandi, *Religiosità e cultura nel '1700 italiano* (Bologna, 1966). See also the Life of Casini (p. 624), Leonard of Port-Maurice (p. 622), and missions (p. 618). For France, A. Bernard, *Le Sermon au XVIIIe siècle* (Paris, 1901). For Germany, J. N. Brischar, *Die katholische Kanzelredner Deutschlands*, 5 vols. (Schaffhausen, 1867–71). Karl Gastgeber, *Gotteswort durch Menschenwort* (Vienna, 1964). J. Kehrein, *Geschichte der katholischen Beredsamkeit der Deutschen*, 2 vols. (Regensburg, 1843). G. Lohmeier, *Bayerische Barockprediger* (Munich, 1961) (extracts). For Spain, B. Gaudeau, *Les prêcheurs burlesques en Espagne au XVIIIe siècle* (Paris, 1891). J. F. de Isla, *The History of the famous preacher Friar Gerund de Campazas*, Eng. trans., 2 vols. (1772), Spanish edn., 3 vols. (1960). In general, E. C. Dargan, *A History of Preaching*, 2 vols. (New York, 1905–12).

For parish life generally: A. Playout-Chassis, *La Vie religieuse dans le diocèse de Boulogne au XVIIIe siècle (1725–1790)* (Arras, 1976). B. Plongeron, *La Vie quotidienne du clergé français au XVIIIe siècle* (Paris, 1974). T. Tackett, *Priest and Parish in Eighteenth-Century France* (Princeton, 1977).

On seminaries: *Seminaria ecclesiae catholicae* (Vatican City, 1963), a fundamental book of reference with otherwise inaccessible information. A. Theiner, *Il seminario ecclesiastico* (Rome, 1834). For Italian seminaries, L. Cecconi, *Instituzione dei seminarii vescovili* (Rome, 1766). Giovanni di Giovanni, *La storia de' seminarii chiericali* (Rome, 1747). See also Serena, p. 924. For Spanish seminaries, F. Martin Hernandez, 'Los seminarios españoles en la epoca de los primeros Borbones (1700–1808)' in *Hispania Sacra* 12 (1959), 357–420. For French seminaries, A. Degert, *Histoire des séminaires francais jusqu'à la Révolution*, 2 vols. (Paris, 1912).

On celibacy: Augustinus de Roskovány, *Coelibatus et breviarium*, 17 vols. (Pest, 1861–90): contains an indispensable bibliographical guide with valuable notes. Early historical treatments, sometimes polemical but often useful in F. W.

Carové, *Uber das Cölibatsgesetz des römisch-katholischen Klerus*, 2 vols. (Frankfurt, 1832). J. A. and A. Theiner, *Die Einführung der erzwungenen Ehelosigkeit bei den christlichen Geistlichen und ihre Folgen*, 3 vols. (first edn. 1828; Altenburg, 1845). H. C. Lea, *History of Sacerdotal Celibacy in the Christian Church*, 3rd edn., 2 vols. (1907). (The fourth edn. 1932 omitted the notes.) Modern treatment in Georg Denzler, *Das Papsttum und der Amtszölibat*, 2 vols. (Stuttgart, 1973–6). For the discussions in the Age of the Enlightenment, P. Picard, *Zölibatdiskussion im katholischen Deutschland der Aufklärungszeit* (Düsseldorf, 1975). W. Leinweber, *Der Streit um den Zölibat im 19. Jahrhundert* (Münster, 1978).

For the *concursus*: Benedict XIV, *Bullarium* (1826, 2, 5 ff., with historical introduction) and *de synodo dioecesana* (see p. 621). *D.D.C.* s.v. 'Concours', with bibliography. *Thesaurus resolutionum* (see p. 616) frequently, especially 4, 383 ff. (Caserta); 9, 134 ff. (Capua). F. A. Reclusi, *Tractatus de concursibus*, 2 parts (Rome, 1724). L. Higueruela de Pino, 'Los concursos a parroquias en la diócesis de Toledo durante el pontificato del Cardenal Borbón', in *Hispania Sacra* 27 (1974), 240 ff.

For the confessional: On the decisions at meetings of clergy to debate moral cases, *Decisioni di casi di coscienza e di dottrina canonica fatte nel diocesi di Bologna*, 4th edn. (Venice, 1797). Giovanni Chiericato, *Decisiones sacramentales, theologicae, canonicae et legales* (Venice, 1727, new edn., 3 vols. Ancona, 1757). This included among its parts *Decisiones miscellaneae* (= vol. 3, bk 7; also separately, 2nd edn. 1703) and *Erotemata ecclesiastica* (= vol. 3, bk 9).

For the theologians of moral cases, especially Alfonso Liguori, *Theologia Moralis*, 9 vols. (Paris, 1839). A. Reiffenstuel, *Theologia Moralis*, Venice 1752 (original, Munich, 1692).

For the controversy over Probabilism, guide in *D.T.C.* s.v. 'Probabilisme'. Ignaz von Döllinger and H. Reusch, *Geschichte der Moralstreitigkeiten in den römisch-katholischen Kirche*, 2 vols. (Nördlingen, 1889).

On usury: B. Nelson, *The Idea of Usury*, 2nd edn. (Chicago, 1969). J. T. Noonan, *The Scholastic Analysis of Usury* (Harvard, 1937).

For the *Monte di Pietà*: B. Pullan, *Rich and Poor in Renaissance Venice* (Oxford, 1971). Giuseppe Coniglio, *Enciclopedia Cattolica* VIII s.v. 'Monte di Pietà'.

On the morality of sex: J. T. Noonan, *Contraception* (Cambridge, Mass., 1966). The German edition is amended, *Empfängnisverhütung* (Mainz, 1969). J. T. Noonan, *The Morality of Abortion* (Cambridge, Mass., 1970). C. B. Paris, *Marriage in XVIIth Century Catholicism* (Montreal, 1975).

On nullity of marriage: J. T. Noonan, *Power to Dissolve* (Cambridge, Mass., 1972).

On repair of churches: P. Peckius, *De reparandis ecclesiis* (Münster, 1620), and much used as a reference book later. F. A. Reclusi, *Tractatus de re parochiali*, 2 vols. (Rome, 1773).

On diocesan synods: The numerous diocesan synods in Italy almost always printed their minutes and resolutions which form an important body of evidence on church life. A catalogue by Silvino da Nadro of what is printed is in *Studi e Testi* no. 207 (Rome, 1960). Benedict XIV, *de synodo dioecesana*, is fundamental. S. Palese 'Sinodi diocesani e visite pastorale delle diocesi di Alessano e Ugento dal Concilio di Trento al Concordato del 1818' in *Archivio storia pugliese*, 27 (1974), 453–500.

For the duty of residence, see the canonists; and E. Papa 'L'obbligo della residenza nell' episcopato napoletano del secolo XVIII' in *Gregorianum* 42 (1961), 738 ff.

For the law of interdicts: Alban Haas, *Das Interdikt* (Amsterdam, 1963, repr. of 1929).

On chapters: Apart from the canonists (Ferraris, p. 617, Benedict XIV, above, Plöchl, p. 617, etc.), J. J. Scarfantonio, *Animadversiones ad lucubrationes canonicales Francisci Ceccoperii*, 2 vols. (Lucca, 1723). In Germany, *Disquisitio canonico-publica de capitulorum . . . origine* (Amsterdam, 1758). H. E. Feine, *Die Besetzung der Reichsbistümer vom Westfalischen Frieden bis zur Säkularisation, 1648–1803* (Stuttgart, 1921).

On a bishop's visitation: *D.D.C.* s.v. 'Visite canonique'. G. Crispini, *Trattato della visita pastorale* (Rome, 1695) and later editions. Gaudentio de Janua, *De Visitatione cujuscumque praelati ecclesiastici* (Rome, 1748). F. Maria d'Aste, *Metodo della santa visita apostolica* (Otranto, 1706).

Biographies of bishops: E. H. Burton, *The Life and Times of Bishop Challoner*, 2 vols. (1909). E. Regnault, *Christophe de Beaumont, Archevêque de Paris*, 2 vols. (Paris, 1882). *D.B.I.*, *D.H.E.E.*, *D.H.G.E.*, *passim*.

CHAPTER 3 : MONKS AND NUNS

Monks: For general reference, *D.I.P.* M. Heimbucher, *Die Orden und Kongregationen der katholischen Kirche*, new edn., 2 vols. (Paderborn, 1907–8). P. Helyot, *Histoire des ordres monastiques*, 8 vols. (Paris, 1714–19). G. Penco, *Storia della monachesimo in Italia nell' epoca moderna* (Rome, 1968). *Collectanea Ordinis Cisterciensium Reformatorum*, Westmalle, 1965–. *Statuta Capitulorum generalium Ordinis Cisterciensis (1116–1786)*, ed. J. M. Canivez, 8 vols. (Louvain, 1933–41). *Annales Camaldulenses*, vol. 8 (Venice, 1764). J. M. Canivez, *L' Ordre de Citeaux en Belgique des origines au XXᵉ siècle* (Forges-les-Chimay, 1926). O. Premoli, *Storia dei barnabiti (1700–1825)* (Rome, 1925).

For reforming movements in Portugal (Jacobeans etc.): E. Apollis 'Mystiques portugais du XVIIIᵉ siècle: Jacobéens et Sigillistes' in *Annales* 19 (1964), 38–54 (and references there cited).

For the reform movement of the friars in Ireland: H. Fenning 'The undoing of the friars of Ireland' in *Recueil de Travaux d'Histoire et de Philologie*, 6th series, fasc. i (Louvain, 1972), 154–87; cf. also H. Fenning in *Archivium Fratrum Praedicatorum* 45 (1975), 399 ff.; and W. P. Burke, *Irish Priests in the Penal Times* (Waterford, 1914).

For the life and work of the Jesuits: Documents: See *Epistolae Praepositorum*

Generalium ad patres et fratres S.J., vol. 2 (Ghent, 1847). *A.H.S.I.* is a valuable periodical. Of the various histories of the different provinces, that for Germany is specially useful for the eighteenth century—B. Duhr, *Geschichte der Jesuiten in den Ländern deutscher Zunge*, vol. 4 (Munich–Regensburg, 1928). On the Reductions—P. Caraman, *The Lost Paradise: an account of the Jesuits in Paraguay, 1607–1768* (London, 1975). See also the histories s.v. suppression, p. 625.

On hermits: In Italy, *D.I.P.* s.v. 'Eremiti'. In France, J. Sainsaulieu, *Les Ermites français* (Paris, 1974). In Spain, *D.H.E.E.* s.v. 'Eremitismo', with bibliography. *España eremitica* (Pamplona, 1970).

Biographies of monks: A. Berthe, *St. Alfonso de'Liguori*, Eng. trans., 2 vols. (Dublin, 1905); cf. G. Cacciatore, *S. Alfonso de'Liguori e il Giansenismo* (Florence, 1944). The original life by A. M. Tannoia was translated under the auspices of F. W. Faber, 5 vols. (London, 1848–9). See also J. Favre, *A Great Mystic of the Eighteenth Century: Mary Celeste Crostarosa*, Eng. trans. (1935). D. Sandelli, *De Danielis Concinae Vita et Scriptis Commentarius* (Brescia, 1767). G. Tabacco, *La vita di San Bononio di Rotberto 1671–1742* (Turin, 1954). E. Dudel, *Klemens Hofbauer, ein Zeitbild* (Bonn, 1970); cf. English *Life* by John Carr (1939). On Labre: A. de la Gorce, *Saint Benedict Joseph Labre* (Eng. trans. 1952), Canonization Process, 3 vols. (Rome, 1830–6). On Leonard of Port-Maurice: His *The Little Way of Paradise* had an Eng. trans. (London, 1870), Canonization Process (Rome, 1838–9). D. Devas, *Life of St. Leonard of Port Maurice, O.F.M.* (*1676–1751*), (1920). On Paul of the Cross: E. Zoffoli, *S. Paolo della Croce*, 3 vols. (1963–8). M. Bialas, *Das geistliche Tagebuch des heiligen Paul vom Kreuz* (Aschaffenburg, 1976). Father Edmund, *Hunter of Souls* (Dublin, 1946). On Feijóo: I. L. McLelland, *Benito Jerónimo Feijóo* (New York, 1969).

CHAPTER 4: THE OFFICE OF THE POPE

The Popes: F. X. Seppelt, *Geschichte der Päpste von den Anfangen bis zur Mitte des 20. Jahrunderts*, vol. 5, 2nd edn. by G. Schwaiger (Munich, 1959). Ludwig von Pastor, *History of the Popes*, Eng. trans., 40 vols. (1938–53). Leopold von Ranke, *The History of the Popes during the last four centuries*, Eng. trans., 3 vols. (1913). The German edition of 1941 is revised. Both Pastor and Ranke ended in 1800. To continue Pastor, and by intention with the same methods, followed J. Schmidlin, *Papstgeschichte der neuesten Zeit*, 4 vols. (Munich, 1933–9). F. Nielsen, *The History of the Papacy in the Nineteenth Century*, Eng. trans., 2 vols. (1906). Despite the title vol. 1 has much of the eighteenth century. V. E. Giuntella, *Roma nel Settecento* (Bologna, 1971).

For the Roman jubilee: H. Thurston, *The Holy Year of Jubilee* (London, 1900); cf. P. Fedele (ed.), *Gli anni santi* (Rome, 1934).

Papal election and the veto: A. Eisler, *Das Veto der katholischen Staaten bei der Papstwahl* (Vienna, 1907). L. Wahrmund, *Das Ausschliessungsrecht (ius exclusivae) bei den Papstwahlen* (Vienna, 1888). F. Petrucelli della Gattina, *Histoire diplomatique des Conclaves* (Paris, 1864–6). G. de Novaes, *Elementi della storia de'sommi pontefici* (Rome, 1822). Pastor, *passim*; Plöchl; *D.D.C.* s.v. 'Conclave'; *L.T.K.* s.v. 'Ausschliessungsrecht'.

Biographies of Popes: Nearly contemporary biographies, up to Benedict XIV, in a splendid volume, M. Guarnacci, *Vitae Romanorum Pontificum* (Rome, 1751).

Clement XI: *Opera Omnia*, Rome 1729 (Part III: *Epistolae et Brevia*). C. G. Buder, *Leben und Thaten des klugen und berühmten Pabsts Clementis des Eilfften*, 3 vols. (Frankfurt, 1720). F. de Lafitau, *La Vie de Clément XI*, 2 vols. (Padua, 1752). F. Pometti, 'Studi sul pontificato di Clemente XI' in *Arch. della Società Romana di Storia Patria* 21 (1898), 279–453; 22 (1899), 109–50. A. le Roy, *La France et Rome de 1700 à 1715* (Paris, 1892). A. Sarubbi, *Curia Romana e regno di Napoli* (Naples, 1972). These are letters to F. Pignatelli, 1690–1712 from an agent in Rome.

Benedict XIII: *Opera*, 3 vols. (Ravenna, 1728). G. B. Vignato, *Storia di Benedetto XIII*, 6 vols. (Milan, 1952–). *D.B.I.* s.v. 'Benedetto XIII', excellent article.

Clement XII: A. Fabroni, *De Vita et rebus gestis Clementis XII* (Rome, 1760).

Benedict XIV: *Opera omnia. Bullarium*, see p. 616. Apart from *de synodo dioecesana* and the *Bullarium* the most important and lasting was *de canonizatione*. Part of this was translated by F. W. Faber under the title *Heroic Virtue*, 3 vols. (London, 1850). For Benedict XIV while Bishop of Ancona, W. Angelini 'Il card. P. Lambertini ed Ancona 1727–1731' in *R. stor. Risorg.* 56 (1969), 27–43. For Benedict XIV while Archbishop of Bologna, P. Lambertini, *Raccolta* etc., see p. 616. For the indiscreet letters to Tencin, in French edn. E. de Heeckeren, 2 vols. (Paris, 1912); critical text, ed. E. Morelli (Rome, 1955–). *D.B.I.* s.v. 'Benedetto XIV', excellent article. R. Haynes, *Philosopher King: The Humanist Pope Benedict XIV* (1970).

For Clement XIII: *D.H.G.E.* s.v., by Roger Mols.

Clement XIV: *Lettres intéressantes*, 2 vols. (Paris, 1777), Eng. trans., 3 vols. in 4 (1777); but parts, or perhaps all, are not from Clement XIV. A. Theiner, *Geschichte des Pontificats Clemens' XIV*, 2 vols. (Leipzig, 1853). G. X. Ravignan, *Clément XIII et Clément XIV* (Paris, 1854). A. Reumont, *Ganganelli* (Berlin, 1847). Pastor's portrait (*History of the Popes*, Eng. trans., vol. 38) is the best now existing. It was amended by W. Kratz and P. Leturia, *Intorno al 'Clemente XIV' del Barone von Pastor* (Rome, 1935). H. Raab announced a forthcoming study.

Pius VI: J. Gendry, *Pie VI*, 2 vols. (Paris, 1906). J. Leflon, *Pie VII*, vol. 1 (Paris, 1958), which is important for the Church under Pius VI. *D.B.I.* s.v. 'Braschi-Onesti'. J. F. Bourgoing, *Historical and Philosophical Memoirs of Pius VI*, Eng. trans., 2 vols. (1799).

Pius VII: J. Leflon, as under Pius VI, and 'Le Cardinal Chiaramonti, éveque d'Imola et la Republique Cisalpine' in *R. stor. Risorg.* 43 (1956), 427 ff. E. Pistolesi, *Pius VII*, 4 vols. (1829–30). A. F. Artaud de Montor, *Histoire du pape Pius VII*, 2nd edn. (Paris, 1837). E. E. Y. Hales, *Napoleon and the Pope: the Story of Napoleon and Pius VII* (1962); cf. A. Latreille, p. 629.

Leo XII: Fundamental now are R. Colapietra, *La formazione diplomatica di Leone XII* (Rome, 1966), and *La Chiesa tra Lamennais e Metternich: il Pontificato di Leone XII* (Rome, 1963): fine study. A. F. Artaud de Montor, *Histoire du pape Leon XII*, 2 vols. (Paris, 1843). N. Wiseman, *Recollections of the Last Four Popes*, new edn. (1859). Historically speaking this is more important than the title suggests.

For the office of cardinal: Hieronymus Platus, *De cardinalis dignitate et officio*, 6th edn. (1826). C. Weber, *Kardinäle und Prälaten in den letzten Jahrzehnten des Kirchenstaats*, 2 vols. (Stuttgart, 1978). Though about the middle nineteenth century, this has repercussions for the period before the Revolution. See also Plöchl, 3, 151 ff.

Biographies of cardinals: For reference, J. P. Migne (ed.), *Dictionnaire des Cardinaux* (Paris, 1857). P. Castagnoli, *Il cardinale Giulio Alberoni*, 3 vols. (Piacenza, 1929–32). S. Harcourt-Smith, *Alberoni* (1943). F. Masson, *Le Cardinal de Bernis depuis son ministère, 1756–1794* (Paris, 1884). P. Carlini, *Francesco Maria Casini (1648–1719)* (Rome, 1969), useful also for the religious life, and the nature of contemporary preaching. S. Serena, *S. Gregorio Barbarigo e la vita spirituale e culturale nel suo seminario di Padova* (Padua, 1963). J. A. Helfert, *Fabrizio Ruffo* (Vienna, 1882). B. W. Kelly, *Life of Henry Benedict Stuart, Cardinal Duke of York* (1899). Brian Fothergill, *The Cardinal King* (1958). For Angelo Quirini see his *Epistolae*, ed. N. Coleti (Venice, 1756). Cardinal Pirelli's diary of the 1769 Conclave is printed by L. Berra in *Archivio della Società romana di storia patria*, 85–6 (1962–3), 25–319. P. Chevallier, *Loménie de Brienne*, Paris, 1959–60.

Curia: See Moroni, p. 615. N. del Re, *La Curia Romana*, 3rd edn. (Rome, 1970), standard work. F. Grimaldi, *Les Congrégations romaines* (Siena, 1890), too lively to be quite comfortable, but it has much insight. V. Martin, *Les Congrégations romaines* (Paris, 1930).

For the Congregation of the Council: *D.D.C.* s.v. 'Concile (Congrégation de)'. R. Parayre, *La S. Congrégation du Concile* (Paris, 1897). *La Sacra Congregazione del Concilio (1564–1964): studi e recerche* (Rome, 1964).

For Index and Inquisition: J. Hilgers, *Der Index der verbotenen Bücher* (Freiburg im Breisgau, 1904). F. H. Reusch, *Der Index der verbotenen Bücher*, 2 vols. (Bonn, 1883–5). Both Hilgers and Reusch are needed. L. Amabile, *Il santo officio della inquisizione in Napoli*, 2 vols. (Castello, 1892). H. C. Lea, *A History of the Inquisition of Spain*, vol. 4 (New York, 1907), and *The Inquisition in the Spanish Dependencies* (New York, 1908). J. Llorente, *Histoire critique de l'Inquisition de l'Espagne*, 2nd edn., 4 vols. (Paris, 1818). G. Pitré, *Del sant' officio a Palermo e di un carcere d'esso* (Rome, 1940).

For foreign service: R. A. Graham, *Vatican Diplomacy* (Princeton, 1959). On the nuncios, a magnificent collection in P. Maserus, *De legatis et nuntiis*, 2 vols. (Rome, 1709). See Plöchl, p. 617; Mercati, p. 626; *L.T.K.* s.v. 'Gesandtschaftswesen', with bibliography. *Geschichte der Nunziaturen Deutschlands* (Nuremberg, 1790).

On the Papal State: M. Andrieux, *La Vie quotidienne dans la Rome pontificale* (Paris, 1962); Eng. trans. (1968). M. Brosch, *Geschichte des Kirchenstaates*, 2 vols. (Gotha, 1880–2), the standard narrative. L. dal Pane, *Lo Stato pontificio e il movimento riformatore del Settecento* (Milan, 1959), the start of modern study. Thomas Denham, *The Temporal Government of the Pope's State* (London, 1788). For fair-minded treatment of the nephew-system, see M. Laurain-Portemer, 'Absolutisme et népotisme: la surintendance de l'Etat ecclésiastique' in *Bibliothèque de l'École des Chartes*, 131 (1973), 487–568.

CHAPTER 5: THE FALL OF THE JESUITS

For a general popular history, Christopher Hollis, *The History of the Jesuits* (1968). For a more detailed account, T. J. Campbell, *The Jesuits 1534–1921* (1921). No adequate history of the suppression exists. The excellent separate historians of the various provinces were told to stop about 1750 so that there could be an all-embracing history of the suppression. This history was never written. The best of the general histories is Pastor's volume on Pope Clement XIV, written with the aid of two assistants. But though Pastor had the admirable merit of drawing attention to the sources and archives, even he was not quite able to put the suppression in a general perspective. For other general histories see p. 622.

A. Carayon, *Documents inédits concernant la Compagnie de Jésus*, vol. XIV (Poitiers, 1869). This includes a biography of the general Ricci and useful letters from French ambassadors and others. G. C. Cordara, *Commentarii de suppressione S.J.*, ed. G. Albertotti (Padua, 1925). Cordara wrote (1774–9) an autobiography, *De suis et suorum rebus*. This was edited by G. Albertotti and A. Faggiotti (Turin, 1933). The latter part Cordara refashioned into *de suppressione*. The account is brilliantly written and of the first importance. P. Dudon, 'De la suppression de la Compagnie de Jésus', in *Revue des questions historiques*, 132 (1938), 75–107. The letters of Horace Mann, who was the English agent in Florence, to Horace Walpole in England make a fairly informed commentary on rumours out of Rome, often fascinating: cf. *The Letters of Horace Walpole*, ed. W. S. Lewis (Yale edn., 1937–). Alfred Weld, *The Suppression of the Society of Jesus* (1877). Dale van Kley, *The Jansenists and the Expulsion of the Jesuits from France* (Yale, 1975). See Masson above, p. 624. For Prussia, F. Hoffmann, *Friedrich II von Preussen und die Aufhebung der Gesellschaft Jesu* (Rome, 1969).

On Jesuit property after suppression: F. Renda, *Bernardo Tanucci e i beni dei gesuiti in Sicilia* (Rome, 1974). For refugees, see, e.g., N. S. Cushner (ed.), *Philippine Jesuits in Exile: the Journals of Francesco Puig, S.J. 1768–1770* (Rome, 1964).

CHAPTER 6: THE CATHOLIC REFORMERS

Church and State: For the jurisdictionalists, see Van Espen, p. 618; cf. studies of Van Espen by G. Leclerc (Zurich, 1964) and M. Nuttinck (Louvain, 1969). On

Giannone and the *Storia civile*, studies by B. Vigezzi (Milan, 1961) and G. Ricuperati (*L'esperienza civile e religiosa di P. Giannone*, Milan, 1970). For the Concordats, see Mercati, *Raccolta di Concordati*, Rome 1954.

For Church and State in Italy: A. C. Jemolo, *Stato e Chiesa negli scrittori politici italiani del Seicento e del Settecento*, 2nd edn. (Pompeii, 1972). F. J. Sentis, *Die Monarchia Sicula* (Freiburg im Breisgau, 1869). F. Scaduto, *Stato e Chiesa nelle due Sicilie*, 2 vols. (repr. Palermo, 1969). G. Falzone, *La Sicilia tra il Settecento e l'Ottocento*, vol. 1 (Palermo, 1965). G. Nuzzo, *La Monarchia nella due Sicilie tra Ancien Régime e Rivoluzione* (Naples, 1972). G. Falzone, *La politica di Carlo di Borbone in Sicilia 1734–59* (Bologna, 1977). H. Benedikt, *Das Königreich Neapel unter Carl VI* (Vienna–Leipzig, 1927), still valuable from its use of Austrian archives. *D.B.I.* s.v.v. 'Capra', 'Carracciolo, Domenico'. R. Mincuzzi, *Bernardo Tanucci (1759–76)* (Bari, 1967). H. M. Acton, *The Bourbons of Naples 1734–1825* (1956). F. Scaduto, *Stato e Chiesa sotto Leopoldo 1, Granduca di Toscana 1765–90* (repr. Leghorn, 1975). For Tuscany see also Ricci, p. 628. B. Cecchetti, *La Reppublica di Venezia e la Corte di Roma*, 2 vols. (Venice, 1890). For the State hand on the endowments in the south of Italy, and the real extent of the endowments and the efficaciousness or otherwise of reform, see A. Placanica, *Cassa Sacra e beni della Chiesa nella Calabria del Settecento* (Naples, 1970). A. Placanica, *Il patrimonio ecclesiastico calabrese* (Chiaravalle, 1972).

Febronius: Best portrait by H. Raab, in 'Nikolaus von Hontheim' in *Rheinische Lebensbilder* V (Bonn, 1973). *D.T.C.* s.v. 'Febronius'. Among the older studies, O. Mejer, *Febronius* (Tübingen, 1880).

For Church and State in Switzerland: The fundamental (Gallican) book of the age was J. A. F. Balthasar, *De Helvetiorum juribus circa sacra* (Lucerne, 1768); for Balthasar see *Neue Deutsche Biographie* s.v.; and a monograph by B. Laube (Basel, 1956). See Schwegler, p. 615.

For Church and State in Austria see Joseph II, p. 628. In Prussia, M.Lehmann, *Preussen und die katholische Kirche*, 5 vols. (Leipzig, 1878). F. Hanus, *Church and State in Silesia under Frederick II* (Washington, 1944).

On Muratori: Letters in *Carteggio* (Florence, 1975–). Life (still) by his affectionate nephew Soli-Muratori (Naples, 1758). The Congresses of Muratorian studies print their proceedings (*Atti*), the Modena 1972 Congress had valuable articles which were printed in *Atti* (Florence, 1975). A. Dupront, *Muratori et al société Européenne des pré-lumières* (Florence, 1976). M. Rosa, *Riformatori e ribelli nel '700 religioso italiano* (Bari, 1969). For Muratori's relation with Austria: E. Zlabinger, *L. A. Muratori und Österreich* (Innsbruck, 1970). For Muratori on reduction of feasts: L. Brandolini, 'La partecipazione di L. A. Muratori alla controversia del sec. XVIII sulla diminuzione delle feste infrasettimanali', in *Ephemerides liturgicae* 88 (1974), 310 ff. Aldo Andreoli, *Nel mondo di L. A. Muratori* (Bologna, 1972), important for Muratori's religious development. See also Venturi, p. 627.

The Enlightenment in Italy: Documents in *Illuministi italiani*, 7 vols., so far various editors (Milan, 1958–): extracts from the leading authors, with valuable introductions to each. F. Venturi, *Settecento Riformatore* (Turin, 1969–), and *Italy and the Enlightenment* (1972), Eng. trans. of various essays. G. Compagnino, *Gli illuministi italiani* (Rome, 1974). G. Racioppi, *Antonio Genovesi* (Naples, 1871).

The Enlightenment in Germany: Background in M. Braubach, *Aufklärung und Revolution* (Bonn, 1960). Valuable general study in E. Hegel, *Die katholische Kirche Deutschlands unter dem Einfluss der Aufklärung des 18 Jahrhunderts* (Münster, 1975). (For the distance which history has travelled, contrast H. Brück, *Die rationalistischen Bestrebungen im katholischen Deutschland, bes. in der drei rheinischen Erzbistümern in der zweiten Hälfte des 18 Jahrhunderts* (Mainz, 1865), which was for three-quarters of a century the accepted treatment.) E. Hegel, *Geschichte der katholischen theologischen Fakultät Münster 1773–1964*, 2 vols. (Münster, 1966–71). K. Maier, 'Auswirkung der Aufklärung in den schwäbischen Klöstern' in *Z.K.G.* 86 (1975), 329–55. S. Merkle, *Die kirchliche Aufklärung im katholischen Deutschland* (Bonn, 1910), and *Die katholische Beurteilung des Aufklärungszeitalters* (Berlin, 1910). See also Goy, p. 616; Ehrensperger below.

For the argument on celibacy, see Picard, p. 620.

For Werkmeister, see A. Hagen, *Die kirchliche Aufklärung in der Diozese Rottenburg* (Stuttgart, 1953).

For German episcopalianism: F. Vigener, *Bischofsamt und Papstgewalt*, 2nd edn. (Göttingen, 1964) (1st edn., 1913). *D.H.G.E.* s.v. 'Allemagne' (P. Richard). T. C. W. Blanning, *Reform and Revolution in Mainz 1743–1803* (Cambridge, 1974). M. Braubach, *Kurköln* (Münster, 1949). R. von Dülmen, 'Antijesuitismus und katholische Aufklärung in Deutschland' in *H.J.* 89 (1969), 52–80. E. Schotte 'Zur Geschichte des Emser Kongresses' in *H.J.* 35 (1914), 86–109, 319–48, 781–820. Joseph von Beck, *I. H. von Wessenberg* (Freiburg im Breisgau, 1863).

For the coming of Church history: Eugen Saeger, *Die Vertretung der Kirchengeschichte in Freiburg im Breisgau* (Freiburg im Breisgau, 1952).

For reform of liturgy in Germany: A. Ehrensperger, *Die Theorie des Gottesdienstes in der späten deutschen Aufklärung 1770–1815* (Zurich, 1971). S. Bäumer, *Histoire du breviaire*, 2 vols. (Paris, 1905). M. Probst, *Gottesdienst in Geist und Wahrheit: die liturgischen Ansichten und Bestrebungen J. M. Sailers 1751–1832* (Regensburg, 1976). E. Hegel, 'Stadtkolnischer Pfarrgottesdienst zwischen Barock und Aufklärung' in *Zur Geschichte und Kunst im Erzbistum Köln* (Festschrift fur Wilhelm Neuss), edd. R. Haass and J. Hoster (Düsseldorf, 1960), 204–32. L. Swidler, *Aufklärung Catholicism, 1780–1850* (Ann Arbor, 1978).

Jansenism: General narrative in A. Gazier, *Histoire générale du mouvement janséniste*, 2 vols. (Paris, 1922). E. Préclin, *Les Jansénistes du XVIIIᵉ siècle* (Paris, 1929). The central Jansenist journal of the eighteenth century was *Nouvelles Ecclésiastiques* (Paris–Utrecht, 1728–90), but it was often a bitter and deplorably edited journal. In Belgium, *D.H.G.E.*, s.v. 'Belgique'. In Italy, A. C. Jemolo, *Il Giansenismo in Italia prima della Rivoluzione* (Bari, 1928). M. Vaussard, *Jan-*

sénisme et gallicanisme aux origines du Risorgimento (Paris, 1959). In south Italy, G. Cigno, *Giovanni Andrea Serrao e il giansenismo nell' Italia meridionale (secolo XVIII)* (Palermo, 1938). See also Cacciatore, p. 622. In Rome, E. Dammig, *Il movimento giansenista a Roma* (Vatican City, 1945). In the north of Italy, A. Vecchi, *Correnti religiosi nel Sei-Settecento veneto* (Venice, 1962). G. Mantese, *Pietro Tamburini e il giansenismo bresciano* (Brescia, 1942). For Degola in Genoa, *D.H.G.E.*, s.v. 'Degola'. F. Codignola, *Carteggi di giansenisti liguri*, 3 vols. (Florence 1941–4). In Tuscany, A. Wandruszka, *Leopold II*, 2 vols. (Vienna, 1963–6). L. J. A. De Potter, *Vie de Scipione de' Ricci*, 3 vols. (Brussels, 1826). The English version by T. Roscoe, 2nd edn., 2 vols. (London, 1829) is less satisfactory. C. A. Bolton, *Church Reform in Eighteenth Century Italy* (The Hague, 1969). N. Rodolico, *Gli amici e il tempi di Scipione dei Ricci* (Florence, 1920). M. Vaussard edited Ricci's correspondence with Grégoire (Florence, 1963). E. Codignola, *Il giansenismo toscano nel carteggio di F. de Vecchi*, 2 vols. (Florence, 1944). E. Codignola, *Illuministi, giansenisti e giacobini nell' Italia del Settecento* (Florence, 1947). In Austria, see under Joseph II, below. In Germany, W. Deinhardt. *Der Jansenismus in deutschen Landen* (Munich, 1929). D. Hildebrand, *Das kulturelle Leben Bayerns im letzten Viertel des 18. Jahrhunderts* (Munich, 1971).

Jansenism and the Enlightenment in Spain: For background, F. Rousseau, *Régne de Charles III d'Espagne (1759–1788)*, 2 vols. (Paris, 1907). Desdevizes de Dezert, *L'Espagne de l'ancien régime*, 3 vols. (Paris, 1897–1904), 2nd edn. (1928) still valuable. J. Sarrailh, *L'Espagne éclairée de la seconde moitié du XVIIIe siècle* (Paris, 1954). R. Heer, *The Eighteenth Century Revolution in Spain* (Princeton, 1958), so far the best book in the English language on our problem. M. Defourneaux, *Pablo de Olavide ou l'afrancesado (1725–1803)* (Paris, 1959). J. Saugnieux, *Un Prélat éclairée: Don Antonio Tavira y Almazan (1737–1807)* (Toulouse, 1970). C. C. Noel, 'Opposition to enlightened reform in Spain' in *Societas*, 3, 1 (1973), 21 ff. L. Gil Fernández, *Campomanes, un helenista en poder* (Madrid, 1976). On Spanish Jansenism, *D.H.E.E.* s.v. 'Jansenismo'. E. Apollos, *Les Jansénistes espagnoles* (Paris, 1966). M. Menendez y Pelayo, *Historia de los heterodoxos españoles*, rev. edn. (Madrid, 1956).

Joseph II: *Neue Deutsche Biographie* s.v. with bibliography. T. C. W. Blanning, *Joseph II and Enlightened Despotism* (1970). S. K. Padover, *The Revolutionary Emperor: Joseph II of Austria*, 2nd edn. (1967). A. von Arneth, *Maria Theresia*, 10 vols. (Vienna, 1863 ff.).

For Jansenist ideas: E. Lesky and A. Wandruszka (ed.), *Gerard von Swieten und seine Zeit* (Vienna, 1973). P. Hersche, *Der Spätjansenismus in Österreich* (Vienna, 1977), breaks new ground.

For the Church policy: E. Winter, *Der Josefinismus* (Berlin, 1962). F. Maass (ed.), *Der Josephinismus: Quellen zu seiner Geschichte in Österreich, 1760–90*, 5 vols. (Vienna, 1951–7). F. Geier, *Die Durchführung der kirchlichen Reformen Joseph II in vorderösterreichischen Breisgau* (Stuttgart, 1905). J. R. Kusej, *Joseph II and die äussere Kirchenverfassung Innerösterreichs* (Stuttgart, 1908). A. Wolf, *Die*

Aufhebung der Klöster in Innerösterreich 1782–90 (Vienna, 1972, repr. of 1871). K. Walf, *Das bischöfliche Amt in der Sicht Josephinischer Kirchenrechtler* (Vienna, 1975). On toleration no adequate general treatment exists, after the age of the Reformation. F. Ruffini, *Religious Liberty*, Eng. trans. (1912). A. Vermeersch, *Tolerance*, Eng. trans. (1913).

CHAPTER 7: THE REVOLUTION

Church and State in the French Revolution: John McManners, *The French Revolution and the Church* (1969) with its bibliography. A. Latreille, *L'Église catholique et la Révolution française*, 2 vols. (Paris, 1946–50).

Revolutionary Italy: Delio Cantimori and R. de Felice (ed.), *Giacobini italiani* (Bari, 1956). R. de Felice, *Note e ricerche sugli illuminati e di misticismo revoluzionario, 1789–1800* (Rome, 1960). A. Heriot, *The French in Italy 1796–99* (1957). A. Dufourcq, *Le Régime jacobin en Italie* (Paris, 1900). A. Cretoni, *Roma giacobina, Storia della Repubblica Romana del 1798–99* (Rome, 1971). L. M. Kantner, 'Die französischen Besatzungen in Rom 1798–1800 und 1807–14 im Blickwinkel des Zeremonialdiaristen von San Pietro', in *Römische Historische Mitteilungen*, xv (1973), 67–92. A. Pingaud, *Bonaparte, Président de la République italienne* (Paris, 1914). See also Leflon, *Pie VII* (p. 623).

For Napoleon's religion: J. Holland Rose, *Napoleonic Studies*, 2nd edn. (1906). M. Lührs, *Napoleons Stellung zur Religion und Kirche* (Berlin, 1939, repr. Vaduz, 1965). V. Bindel, *Histoire religieuse de Napoléon*, 2 vols. (Paris, 1940).

Concordats: Alfred Boulay de la Meurthe, *Documents sur la négotiation du Concordat et sur les autres rapports de la France avec le Saint-Siège en 1800 et 1801*, 6 vols (Paris, 1897–1905). A. Latreille, *Napoléon et le Saint-Siège 1801–08* (Paris, 1930). I. Rinieri, *La diplomazia pontificia nel secolo XIX*, 4 vols (Rome, 1902–4). See also Schmidlin, p. 622; Dansette, p. 630; Hales, p. 623.

Napoleon in Italy: J. E. Driault, *Napoléon en Italie (1800–1812)* (Paris, 1906). L. Madelin, *La Rome de Napoléon* (Paris, 1906). M. Roberti, *Milano capitale napoleonico*, 3 vols. (Milan, 1946–7). The *Historical Memorials of Cardinal Pacca* have an English translation, 2 vols. (1850). *Venice under France and Austria*, 2 vols. (1824). For a visitation in North Italy during the age, *La visita pastorale di L. Flangini nelle diocesi di Venezia, 1803*, ed. B. Bertoli and S. Tramontin (Rome, 1969). In the south: R. M. Johnston, *The Napoleonic Empire in Southern Italy and the Rise of the Secret Societies*, 2 vols. (1904).

On religious suppressions: J. Rambaud, 'L'Église de Naples sous la domination napoléonienne', *R.H.E.* 9 (1909), 294–312.

On Belgium: *D.H.G.E.* s.v. 'Belgique; Moreau, p. 615. A. Theiner, *Der Kardinal J. H. von Frankenberg* (Freiburg im Breisgau, 1850). J. P. Verhaagen, *La Belgique sous la domination française 1792–1814*, 4 vols. (Brussels, 1922–).

Secularization in Germany: See Aretin, p. 614; Heigel, p. 614. A. M. Scheglmann, *Geschichte der Säkularisation in rechtsrheinischen Bayern*, 3 vols. in 4 (Regensburg, 1903–8). R. Bauerreiss, *Kirchengeschichte Bayerns*, St. Ottilien–

Augsburg, 1949–). M. Erzberger, *Die Säkularisation in Württemberg von 1803–1810* (Stuttgart, 1902). J. A. Bornewasser, *Kirche und Staat in Fulda 1802–6* (Fulda, 1956). Justus Hashagen, 'Die rheinische Kirche unter französischer Herrschaft' in *Studium Lipsiense: Ehrengabe Karl Lamprecht* (Berlin, 1909). Rudolph Morsey, 'Wirtschaftliche und soziale Auswirkungen der Säkularisation in Deutschland' in *Dauer und Wandel der Geschichte: Aspekte europäischer Vergangenheit: Festgabe für Kurt von Raumer* (Münster, 1966). P. Wende, *Die geistliche Staaten und ihre Auflösung im Urteil der zeitgenössischen Publizistik* (Lübeck, 1966).

Spain: The old history of Lafuente, *Historia Eclesiastica de España*, vol. vi, was partisan and is obsolete. P. B. Gams, *Die Kirchengeschichte von Spanien*, iii.2 (Regensburg, 1879), was tired when he reached this point of his famous history and gave nothing but a sketchy miscellany. The general histories are helpful, e.g. A. R. M. Carr, *Spain 1808–1939* (Oxford, 1966); G. H. Lovett, *Napoleon and the Birth of Modern Spain*, 2 vols. (New York, 1965). The best account of the debates of the Cortes of Cadiz is still H. Baumgarten, *Geschichte Spaniens vom Ausbruch der französischen Revolution bis auf unsere Tage*, i (Leipzig, 1865). For biographies and studies of dioceses see the articles in *D.H.E.E.* with useful bibliographies. For the conflict between the Cortes of Cadiz and the Bishop of Orense, see F. Lopez-Aydillo, *El obispo de Orense en la Regencia del año 1810* (Madrid, 1918). For the *afrancesados*, Miguel Artola Gallego, *Los Afrancesados* (Madrid, 1953). F. Marti Gilabert, *La Iglesia en Espana durante la Revolution francese*, Pamplona, 1971, breaks new ground but does not go beyond 1801. The abolition of the Inquisition by the Cadiz Cortes is printed in *Actas de las Cortès de Cadiz* (Antologia) (Madrid, 1964), ii, 1027 ff. Sketch only in E. Allison Peers, *The Church in Spain 1737–1939* (1938). Recent work in J. M. Cuenca Toribio, *Estudios sobre la Iglesia española del XIX* (Madrid, 1973).

CHAPTER 8: RESTORATION

On Metternich: H. Srbik, *Metternich*, 3 vols. (Munich, 1925–64).

In France: Adrien Dansette, *Histoire religieuse de la France contemporaine*, rev. edn. (Paris, 1965), with bibliography.

In Italy: for Consalvi, A. Roveri (ed.), *La Missione Consalvi e il Congresso di Vienna*, 2 vols. (Rome, 1970–1), prints the documents. A. Roveri, *La Santa Sede tra Rivoluzione francese e Restaurazione: il Cardinal Consalvi 1813–15* (Florence, 1974). Severoli's dispatches to Consalvi were printed by M. Petrocchi in *La Restaurazione, il Cardinal Consalvi e la riforma di 1816* (Florence, 1941). M. Petrocchi, *La Restaurazione romana* (Florence, 1943).

For the administration of the Papal States, see Colapietra, *La Chiesa . . .*, p. 624. G. Pignatelli, *Aspetti della propaganda cattolica a Roma da Pio VI a Leone XII* (Rome, 1974). See also N. Wiseman, p. 624.

For south Italy: H. M. Acton, The Bourbons of Naples (p. 626), and *The Last Bourbons of Naples (1825–1861)* (1961). P. Colletta, *History of the Kingdom of*

Naples, Eng. trans., 2 vols. (Edinburgh, 1858). W. Maturi, *Il principe di Canosa* (Florence, 1944), and *Il Concordato del 1818 tra la Santa Sede e le due Sicilie* (Florence, 1929).

The Secret Societies: R. M. Johnston, p. 629. E. E. Y. Hales, *Mazzini and the secret societies* (1956). A. Luzio, *La massoneria e il Risorgimento*, 2 vols. (Bologna, 1925). B. Saint-Edme, *Constitution et organisation des Carbonari* (Paris, 1821). B. Allason, *La vita di Silvio Pellico* (Verona, 1933). C. Spellanzon, *Storia del Risorgimento e dell' Unità d'Italia*, 8 vols. (Milan, 1933–65), the standard narrative with excellent illustrations.

The conditions of Church life are well illustrated by the records published by *Thesaurus Ecclesiarum Italiae Recentioris Aevi*: A. Cestaro, *Le diocesi di Conza e di Campagna nell' età della Restaurazione* (Rome, 1971). *La visita pastorale di Giuseppe Maria Peruzzi nella diocesi di Vicenza (1819–25)*, ed. G. Mantese and E. Reato (Rome, 1972). *La visita pastorale di G. L. Pyrker nella diocesi di Venezia (1821)*, ed. B. Bertoli and S. Tramontin (Rome, 1971). This also contains Pyrker's autobiography. *La visita pastorale di Giuseppe Gasser nella diocesi di Treviso, 1826–1827*, ed. L. Pesce (Rome, 1969). For Gazzola see V. E. Giuntella, 'Profilo di uno zelante' in *R. stor. Risorg.* 43 (1956), 413–18.

The Restoration in Germany: F. Schnabel, *Deutsche Geschichte im Neunzehnten Jahrhundert*, vol. 4: *Die religiösen Kräfte* (Freiburg im Breisgau, 1937). G. Goyau, *L'Allemagne religieuse, Le Catholicisme*, 4 vols. (6th edn. 1909–23). Schnabel's is the deeper treatment. For Görres see *H.J.* 96 (1976).

The Restoration in Spain: M. Artola Gallego, *La España de Fernando VII* (Madrid, 1968). J. Herrero, *Los origenes del pensamiento reaccionario español* (Madrid, 1971), breaks new ground. P. Leturia, *Relaciones entre la Santa Sede e Hispano-américa 1493–1835*, 3 vols. revised (Rome, 1959–60) (Analecta Gregoriana, 101–3). See also A. R. M. Carr, p. 614; Cuenca, p. 630.

INDEX